The Complete Reference to NetWare 5

The Complete Reference to NetWare 5

Bill Payne and Tom Sheldon

Osborne/**McGraw-Hill**

Berkeley   New York   St. Louis   San Francisco
Auckland   Bogotá   Hamburg   London   Madrid
Mexico City   Milan   Montreal   New Delhi   Panama City
Paris   São Paulo   Singapore   Sydney
Tokyo   Toronto

Osborne/**McGraw-Hill**
2600 Tenth Street
Berkeley, California 94710
U.S.A.

For information on translations or book distributors outside the U.S.A., or to arrange
bulk purchase discounts for sales promotions, premiums, or fund-raisers, please
contact Osborne/**McGraw-Hill** at the above address.

The Complete Reference to NetWare 5

1234567890 AGM AGM 90198765432109

ISBN 0-07-211882-2

Publisher
  Brandon A. Nordin

**Associate Publisher and
Editor-in-Chief**
  Scott Rogers

Acquisitions Editor
  Gareth Hancock

Project Editor
  Emily Rader

Editorial Assistant
  Tara Davis

Technical Editor
  Marold Lohrenz

Copy Editor
  Luann Rouff

Proofreader
  Karen Mead

Indexer
  David Heiret

Computer Designers
  Roberta Steele
  Jani Beckwith
  Ann Sellers

Illustrators
  Beth Young
  Robert Hansen

Series Design
  Peter Hancik

About the Authors

Bill Payne, CNI, MCNE, CIP, MCT, MCSE, is an internetworking expert who holds multiple patents in the semiconductor industry.

Tom Sheldon, CNE, is a network consultant and best-selling author of more than 30 computer books, including *The Encyclopedia of Networking, Electronic Edition*.

Contents at a Glance

Contents

Part I

Overview of NetWare and Networking Technologies

Part II

Understanding Network Technology

Part III

NetWare Planning and Installation

11 Novell Directory Services Planning 229

12 NetWare 5 Hierarchy and Security 247

Part IV

Managing Novell Directory Services

Part V

The NetWare File System

Acknowledgments

First and foremost, I would like to thank my wife Patsy and my children, Ryan, Bill, Maria, and Danny, for putting up with me during the writing of this book. More time than I had anticipated has been required to complete this undertaking. I would also like to thank Dr. Eric Schmidt, Ed McGarr, Brad Dew, and Marcy Shanti of Novell for their help.

I extend a warm thank you to all of the people at Osborne/McGraw-Hill who corrected my grammar and translated my feeble sketches into legible figures. This book could not have been done without the help provided by Gareth Hancock as he guided me through the triage of submissions, technical edits, and deadlines to get this book out and on the shelves. Stephane Thomas, Tara Davis, Emily Rader, and Luann Rouff were instrumental in getting this book from basic manuscripts to production.

Marold Lohrenz did an excellent job as the technical editor. He kept me honest and corrected my mistakes. A special thanks to Mark Pierce, coauthor of *Osborne's NetWare 5 Administration Answers! Tech Support*, for his sharing of technical information in the dark early days of the NetWare 5 product introduction.

Last, but not least, a special thanks to Tom Sheldon, who spent countless hours writing the previous edition of this book. He provided an excellent base to work from for the NetWare 5 edition.

Introduction

Welcome to *The Complete Reference to NetWare 5*. This is a completely updated version of the previous edition, *NetWare 4.1: The Complete Reference*. It contains updated material and all new material to help you keep up with the changes in NetWare 5 as well as changes in the networking industry. Since the first writing of this book, more organizations are building wide area networks and enterprise networks. The use of the World Wide Web and the TCP/IP protocols has exploded. At the same time, NetWare has matured and become an operating system for worldwide use. In particular, NetWare 5 and its Novell Directory Services provide you with tools for managing global networks.

As your networks have grown in size and complexity, so have the contents of this book. You'll find more information about planning, building, and managing large networks that are global in scope. You'll also find coverage of internetworking and the protocols that support it, such as TCP/IP (Transmission Control Protocol/Internet Protocol), Novell's NLSP (NetWare Link Services Protocol), and many new services.

Many organizations have been waiting for Novell to improve and enhance the features of NetWare 4.11, and Novell has done just that with NetWare 5. It is the first version of NetWare that can be called a true enterprise network operating system. It is the first operating system that functions in a "pure" TCP/IP environment. Many of the kinks in Novell Directory Services, formerly called NetWare Directory Services, and internetworking have been resolved. Now is the time to upgrade to NetWare 5. The operating system includes enhanced migration tools that make the transition from previous versions of NetWare a snap. In addition, NetWare 5 is reasonably priced, and its improved management features (primarily Novell Directory Services) can reduce administrative costs. An entire network, including user account maintenance, server configuration, and other management tasks can be handled from a central location.

This book is a "how to" guide and an everyday reference that you can use to plan, implement, and manage a NetWare 5 server and network. It supplements NetWare's online documentation and help system. Indeed, this book is much more portable than the online information and provides a structured approach to learning and using NetWare 5. It also provides valuable information for expanding NetWare services, adding new server hardware, and linking with other computer systems and networks (locally or globally). The book is divided into six parts and one appendix. Each part is described next.

Part I, "Overview of NetWare and Networking Technologies"

This section provides a general overview of networks and networking technology. Then it discusses Novell and its networking strategy. You'll also learn about NetWare 5 features, updates, and optional products that enhance NetWare 5.

Part II, "Understanding Network Technology"

This section describes network communication techniques, protocols, and connection methods. It explains local area networks and cabling, internetworks, wide area networks, and advanced internetworking techniques using NLSP and TCP/IP.

Part III, "NetWare Planning and Installation"

This section provides detailed information on planning and implementing Novell Directory Services. It also describes the NetWare security system, the hierarchy of administrators and users, and network access rights. Next, you learn how to plan, evaluate, purchase, and install servers and network equipment. The NetWare 5 installation process is outlined, along with post-installation activities for network administrators.

Part IV, "Managing Novell Directory Services"

This section provides detailed information about how to manage Novell Directory Services. It also describes how to manage objects such as printers, communication devices, and user accounts, and how to administrate network access rights and security. In addition, you'll learn about management tools for monitoring and maintaining NDS.

Part V, "The NetWare File System"

This section explains how to manage the file system in a NetWare server and provides detailed information on NetWare utilities and commands for the file system. You'll also learn about implementing shared CD-ROM drives and managing compression.

Part VI, "Managing the NetWare Environment"

This section describes a number of important NetWare management utilities, features, and functions, including Novell Distributed Print Services (NDPS), Novell Storage Services (NSS), login scripts, backup, accounting and auditing, DNS/DHCP, Z.E.N.works, and Oracle8.

Of course, there is never enough room to cover every topic, but you'll find a wealth of information on these pages. Where necessary, references are made to Novell online documentation or other Novell publications. I hope you enjoy this book and get a lot out of it.

Bill Payne

Stay in Touch!

Catch us on the Web at www.kramerkent.com for updates and other information related to various other Novell products. If you have an e-mail address, please include it so we can send you any and all updates electronically. That way, we'll save on printing and mailing costs and you'll get more information in a searchable file. Our e-mail address is postmaster@kramerkent.com.

The Complete Reference

NetWare 5

Part I

Overview of NetWare and Networking Technologies

The
Complete
Reference

NetWare 5

Chapter 1

Overview of Networking

When IBM announced the Personal Computer in 1981, *personal* was an appropriate adjective to use in the name. It appealed to people who wanted their own computer to run their own applications and manage their own personal files instead of using minicomputers and mainframes that were strictly controlled by an information systems department. Soon, personal computer users started connecting their systems together to share files and resources such as printers. These were the first personal computer networks. About 1985, a funny thing happened. Networks started getting so big and complicated that control soon returned to IS (information systems) departments that could provide management, control, and future planning.

In the mid 1990s, a new technology appeared called the Internet and the World Wide Web. Use of the Internet exploded for both individuals and companies with the advent of browser-based software. Companies were no longer limited to interconnections within themselves. Now, they could access a global network at a fairly low cost.

Most large networks today require management and administration at several levels. Trained and certified people are required to keep things running, monitor the system, and implement security policies. Networks today require communication experts who are familiar with Internet protocols, Web servers, and telephone, microwave, and sometimes even satellite communication systems.

We wrote this book to help you administrate and manage a Novell NetWare 5 network and also to help you understand the basics of networking, internetworking, and interoperability. *Internetworking* involves connecting multiple networks together over local or wide areas and *interoperability* involves connecting many different types of computers and operating systems together into a system that lets users seamlessly access available resources.

Networks Defined

A computer network is a data communication system that links multiple computers and peripherals such as printers, mass storage systems, CD-ROM libraries, modems, fax machines, and many other devices. Network software lets network users exchange electronic mail, work in groups on projects, share licensed applications, and access common resources. Network administrators manage all of these resources and establish security policies that determine user access and restrictions.

The simplest network of all is a switchbox and cable, which lets several people share the same printer. In this arrangement, only one person can send print jobs to the printer at a time. Inexpensive serial or parallel port connectors provide another way to build a network but provide limited communication and file transfer capabilities. To build a truly useful multiuser network, you need network interface cards (NICs) and cabling systems, as pictured in Figure 1-1.

A business network must handle the communication loads of multiple users at a respectable rate. Ethernet, Fast Ethernet, Token Ring, and other networks are capable of

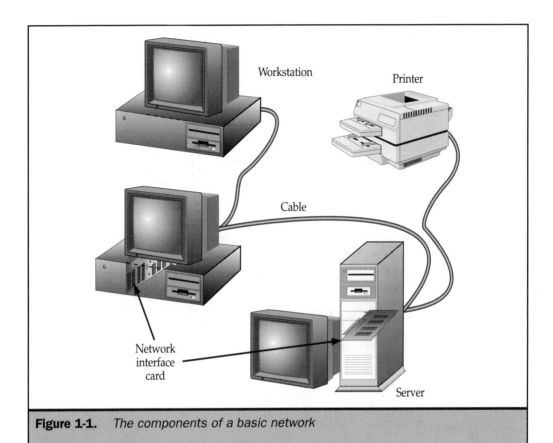

Figure 1-1.   *The components of a basic network*

giving each user a share of the network "bandwidth" so that accessing of files and other network activities are relatively instantaneous, even when other people are accessing the network. Of course, the response time of a network depends on the transmission rate of the network and the number of people accessing the network.

Why Establish a Computer Network?

The answer to why you would want to establish a computer network may seem obvious, but the many reasons for doing so help shed some light on what a network is and what it can do for your organization. Novell NetWare network operating systems are designed to support the following capabilities:

PROGRAM AND FILE SHARING   Yes and no, a network-aware version is one that can run on a network. Many older programs were not able to be run as a shared application.

Network-aware versions of many popular software packages are available at considerable cost savings when compared to buying individually licensed copies. The program and its data files are stored on the file server and are accessed by many network users. When programs are licensed, you need to purchase licenses only for the number of people who will use the application at any one time (when a person stops using the program, the license "token" is made available for another user).

NETWORK RESOURCE SHARING   Network resources include printers, plotters, and storage devices. It is easier to cost-justify the purchase of high-end printers or mass storage devices when large numbers of people can access them at the same time over the network.

DATABASE SHARING   Networks are ideal platforms for database applications and information sharing. Multiple users can access database files at the same time when record-locking features are implemented. Record-locking ensures that no two users change the same record at the same time or overwrite changes being made concurrently by another person.

ECONOMICAL EXPANSION OF THE PC BASE   Networks provide an economical means to expand the number of computers in an organization. You can install inexpensive computers or diskless workstations for network users who access resources on high-powered servers or share sophisticated printers and other peripherals.

WORKGROUP CAPABILITIES   Network-specific software called *groupware* is designed to support methods whereby groups of people interact within an organization, whether sharing electronic mail or working on specific projects. With groupware, people no longer need to be organized into physical groups (i.e., departments). You can form groups of people from geographically dispersed areas; for example, people in sales groups dispersed around the country who share common files. It's also easier to address messages and electronic mail to groups of users.

CENTRALIZED MANAGEMENT   Networks can help organizations consolidate network management. What were once department-based servers can be located in one place, where hardware upgrades, software backups, system maintenance, and system security are much easier to handle. Department managers don't lose control of their servers under this arrangement. Instead, maintenance is handled by a central "information system" department while department managers retain supervisory control of the server. This lets them manage access policies for the people they manage or for people outside their department to whom they want to allow access to the server.

SECURITY   A network operating system must implement sophisticated security methods, beginning with the login process. Only authorized people with previously created accounts can access the systems, and accounts can be tailored in a number of ways using passwords, forcing periodic changes to those passwords, and restricting access during specific time frames or only on specified systems. NetWare utilizes encryption techniques to remove any chance that user passwords can be detected when "crossing the wire."

INTERCONNECTIVITY   Modern networks are now viewed as platforms on which you can attach any type of computer, transparent to the operating system, potentially giving every user on the network access to that system. The NetWare 5 operating system is based on the internationally standardized TCP/IP protocol. It does not encapsulate a vendor-specific protocol into a TCP/IP packet such as earlier versions of NetWare or Microsoft NT. It can support older internetworking protocols such as IPX in the server, and you can route these protocols in NetWare 5 servers. NetWare 5 allows you to construct internetworks using your existing stand-alone departmental networks. Operating natively using the TCP/IP protocol means that NetWare 5 can interoperate with almost every other server or client operating system, including UNIX systems, Windows NT servers and workstations, Windows 95 and 98 clients, printers or, in short, any resource that is assigned an IP address. You'll learn about interconnecting networks in Chapter 7.

ENHANCEMENT OF THE CORPORATE STRUCTURE   Networks can change the structure of an organization and the way it is managed. Users who work in a specific department and for a specific manager no longer need to be in the same physical area. Their offices can be located in areas where their expertise is most needed. The network ties them to their department managers and peers. This arrangement is especially useful for project-oriented tasks in which individuals from different departments, such as research, production, and marketing, need to work closely with one another.

WORLD WIDE WEB ACCESS   With browser-based technologies, companies can communicate more effectively within their own organizations and expand into new markets. Web servers allow a company to post many of its traditional documents, such as policy and procedure manuals, in user-accessible Web pages. Sales and marketing departments can expand into areas that were not attainable in prior years. The company's products and services can be offered to a global community twenty-four hours a day, seven days a week. Orders for products or services can be taken without the intervention of a support person to answer the telephone. Interactive Web pages allow users to tailor information from multiple databases into usable information through the use of various scripting languages such as Java and PERL.

Types of Network Operating Systems

Once you've connected all these components together, you install an appropriate network operating system that enables users to share files and resources. There are two basic types of network operating systems:

- **Peer-to-peer**   A peer-to-peer network operating system runs on individual users' computers. Network users can freely share resources on their computer or access shared resources on other computers. In this arrangement, users control the resources available on the network, although an administrator may provide some management and security controls. Microsoft Windows 95 and 98 can be configured as peer-to-peer operating systems. The disadvantage of this type of network is no centralized security or control. If a user inadvertently turns his or her machine off, the resources are no longer available to the rest of the network. This type of network works fine for ten or fewer workstations.

- **Dedicated server**   Novell NetWare 5 is a dedicated-server operating system. In this arrangement, the operating system runs on a dedicated computer and is used for network tasks such as file sharing, communication, and administration. Information is centralized on the server and managed by an administrator who sets various user access policies, security, data protection, and other requirements.

Both types of operating systems can coexist on and use the same network. For example, a company may implement Windows 98 as the standard desktop operating system so people can share information on their own computers with others. At the same time, dedicated NetWare servers can provide a central place for company-wide information that has more stringent security requirements.

Another important aspect of dedicated servers is their ability to run special multiuser applications in which many users access resources or information at a central location. Examples of dedicated server applications include database "engines," communication services, Web services, and electronic mail. Because the services are centralized, it's easier for managers to implement security, manage the system, and service hardware components. In contrast, peer-to-peer networks are difficult to manage because data and resources are spread out over a wide range of user computers.

In any network, there is a "client-server" relationship in which one system accesses the services of another. Some characteristics of the client-server relationship are outlined below:

- You are a *client* if you use the services of another computer.
- Any computer that provides services to clients is a *server*.
- In a peer-to-peer network, any computer can be either a client or a server.

■ A dedicated server is usually just a server, although it might occasionally act as a client to obtain information from another server.

■ Users who access NetWare servers operate in a client-server relationship.

A client computer that accesses services on a network is often referred to as a node or a workstation. I use the term client *here in most cases.*

Distributed Processing

It's interesting to compare client-server networks with centralized processing systems like IBM mainframes and DEC minicomputers, as pictured in Figure 1-2. In a network environment, client computers access resources on servers and run programs in their own memory and with their own processors. A minicomputer or mainframe system centralizes its processing. User terminals attached to it only send the user's commands and display the results from the central processor. They have no processor or memory of their own.

It's important to keep in mind that the client-server relationship doesn't fully define a network. As an example, the Microsoft NT Server operating system functions as both a client and a server on the same physical machine. In much the same way, the new NetWare 5 operating system supports client applications written in Java, which can be run as applets on the server. Another important aspect of networks is *distributed processing,* in which processors in all the computers attached to the network can be used to perform a specific task. For example, client software in a workstation handles the tasks of formatting and building requests for information from a server. This reduces the load on the server. Distributed processing adds other benefits as well. It is possible to split up an intensive computing task and send parts of it to different computers on the network for processing. The task completes much faster than if performed on a single machine.

Distributed computing environments as pictured on the right in Figure 1-2 encompass distributed processing and distributed database design. In such an environment, similar data is stored on many servers at diverse locations but is updated and kept in sync through appropriate local or wide area links. There are several advantages to distributed environments:

■ The distributed computing model assumes that an organization has many types of data, which are collected at autonomous sites, and assumes that many people in the organization need to access it, not just people at the site where the data is stored.

■ The cost of wide area communication links is motivation enough to decentralize data. If users access data at a remote site often, it makes sense to bring part of the data to the user sites as long as the data is updated with the main site as appropriate.

■ Data that is redundantly distributed to many sites is protected from local disasters.

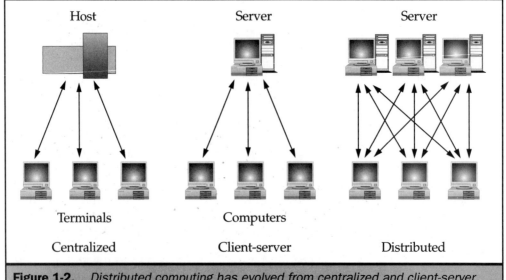

Figure 1-2. *Distributed computing has evolved from centralized and client-server computing*

Novell NetWare 5 supports the creation of distributed computing environments through its directory services and data replication capabilities. Directory services let users quickly locate people, information, and resources at other locations. Data replication copies selected information to other systems and maintains updates such that each copy is informed of changes to any of the other copies. Directory services are discussed in Chapter 10.

As the bandwidth (data-carrying capacity) of communication links improves and use of the Internet to establish Virtual Private Networks evolves, distributed processing is becoming more practical, especially for organizations that maintain offices in many geographic locations.

Traditional host systems (IBM mainframes) have not become obsolete with all this new technology. These systems hold "legacy" data that most organizations are not ready to part with or bring down to the server environment. Data warehousing strategies like that pictured in Figure 1-3 are the answer. Specific information on the host system is transferred to "staging systems" where users in local or remote workgroups can access it. The staging system helps reduce the load on the host while making specific information available to workgroups. At the same time, network connections allow some users to access the host directly if necessary.

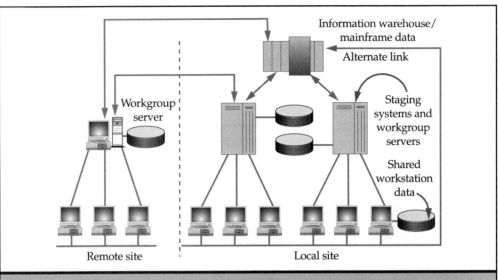

Figure 1-3.   _Access methods in a distributed computing environment_

Think of networks as plug-in platforms that provide a company-wide information pipeline with links to a diversity of resources at many locations. Applications on such a network can even replace traditional business practices. Consider the following:

- Electronic mail is now a common replacement for the phone.

- Computer-to-computer conferencing can replace person-to-person meetings.

- Video transmissions over the network can replace on-site training seminars.

- Web-based information libraries, in-house bulletin boards, and information sharing can replace traditional research methods.

Types of Networks

Local area network (LAN) technology developed in the 1980s, primarily at the department level. Managers saw a need to connect the computers in their departments and let users share resources. Early in this development, most managers would not have considered connecting their departmental LANs with LANs in other departments. Security was a primary concern, but other factors included incompatibility of equipment and communication methods, a fear of loss of control at the department level, and a potential loss in performance as more users gained access to servers.

Eventually, upper management mandated company-wide networks that would provide electronic mail exchange and access to resources by many people in the organization. Security features that allowed managers to restrict user access to files and resources were added to network operating systems. Special devices like bridges and routers allowed managers to join networks or create internetworks while still maintaining some of the advantages of departmental LANs. Figure 1-4 illustrates a local area network and an internetwork joined by routers. Bridges and routers are discussed later in this chapter under "Essential Network Operating System Services."

The term *internetwork* is used in a loose way when discussing connected networks. In the NetWare 5 environment, you create a network segment by installing a network interface card in a server, attaching a cable to it, and attaching workstations to the cable. All the workstations on that segment "hear" broadcasts produced by both the server and other workstations on the same cable.

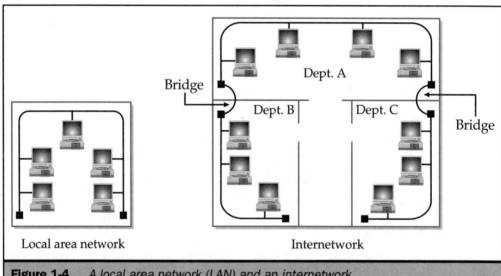

Figure 1-4. *A local area network (LAN) and an internetwork*

> **Tip** *Networks can be compared to radio or TV stations that broadcast over cables. If you're connected to the cable, you can receive the information. However, some stations might be out of your range or blocked, so you can receive only local information.*

If you install another network interface card in a server, then the cable and all the workstations attached to it form another network with its own network address. However, NetWare will transfer, or route, "packets" of data from one network that are addressed to a workstation attached to the other network.

As networks grow, you'll hear networking people refer to them with a variety of terms, especially if communication systems such as phone lines or microwave and satellite links provide the interconnection. Here's the terminology you can use to refer to different types of networks:

- **Network segment** A network segment is typically defined by hardware or a specific logical network address. For example, in the Novell NetWare 5 environment, a network segment includes all the workstations attached to a network interface card in a server. Each segment has its own network address. If you build a network with Ethernet NICs, all the computers attached to a segment receive the same signal broadcasts. Networks are discussed in Chapter 6.

- **Local area network (LAN)** A LAN loosely refers to one network segment or multiple network segments that are connected with bridges. The entire network may have the same logical network address. LANs are also discussed in Chapter 6.

- **Internetwork** An internetwork is a collection of network segments, each with its own logical network address, that are connected with routers. The network segments are usually referred to as *subnetworks*. The routers know the address of each segment and how to transfer packets of information among the subnetworks. Internetworking is discussed in Chapter 7.

- **Campus network** A campus network extends to other buildings within a campus or industrial park. The various networks within each building are typically connected to a major cable run called the *backbone*. The organization usually owns the grounds on which the cable exists and is free to put in new cable as necessary without acquiring special permits. Campus networking and backbones are also covered in Chapter 7, "Expanding Networks and Building Internetworks."

- **Metropolitan area network (MAN)** A MAN is usually confined to a city and is subject to local regulations. It may be constructed with various public and private facilities, such as the public telephone system, local microwave systems, or in-ground optical cables. A local provider builds and maintains the network and makes it available to the public. You connect your networks into the MAN, pay a connection or transfer fee, and use it to transfer "packets" between networks at your other company sites in the metropolitan area. MANs are discussed in Chapter 8.

■ **Wide area network (WAN) and global network**   WANs and global networks span intercity, interstate, or international borders. WAN links are usually provided by public and/or private telecommunication providers that use microwave, optical cable, or satellite links, or a combination of these technologies. Currently, the usual method for connecting into a WAN is over standard telephone links, or telephone links that are "enhanced" and modified to provide fast *digital* service. WANs are also discussed in Chapter 8.

■ **Enterprise-wide network**   An enterprise-wide network is used to interconnect all the computer systems within an organization, regardless of geographic location, operating system, communication protocols, and hardware. As the Internet becomes more widespread, companies can use connections to a local Internet service provider (ISP) to achieve interconnectivity between remote offices. This is becoming very attractive to companies, as the costs associated with dedicated long line links are quite high. The network itself is viewed as a communication platform on which many different types of devices can be connected. Operating systems and applications help hide the differences between systems, so users can access any resource in a transparent manner.

Components of a Network

A computer network consists of both hardware and software. The hardware includes network interface cards and the cable that ties them together. The software includes the network operating system, communication protocols, drivers to support hardware components such as network interface cards, and network applications.

Network Operating System

As mentioned previously, the network operating system provides all the services that let users communicate over the network and share resources such as files and printers. In peer-to-peer networks like Windows 95 or Windows 98, the operating system running in the user's computer contains the network support. With dedicated server operating systems like NetWare, servers manage network traffic and file- or peripheral-sharing. Client software must be installed in the computers of users who need to access the server.

Server

Servers can provide the following services to users on a network. In Novell NetWare 5, these services are added in the form of modules to the network operating system running at the server and take advantage of all the features of the operating system, such as access control and communication.

- **File server**   This server provides file storage and retrieval services, including security features that control file access rights.

- **E-mail server or gateway**   An e-mail server or gateway provides local or enterprise-wide electronic mail services and translation between different mail systems.

- **Communication server**   This type of server provides connection services to the outside world or to remote users who need to connect into an organization's network. Banks of modems are usually attached to communication servers that people can dial out from or dial into.

- **Fax server**   This server provides fax services for the network. Fax modems are attached to the server. Incoming faxes are routed to appropriate users, and outgoing faxes are sent through the fax modems.

- **Gateway server**   This server provides connections to host systems such as IBM mainframes and DEC minicomputers.

- **Database server**   This type of server is a dedicated system that stores and processes large databases and provides users with access to the information in the database.

- **Backup and archive server**   This type of server performs data backups for other servers or user computers on the network.

- **Print server**   This type of server manages one or more printers, allowing any number of users to send print jobs at any time. A print queue system organizes print jobs in the order they were sent or by priority.

- **Directory services server**   This server provides information about users and resources on the network, similar to a White Pages or Yellow Pages directory. People can look up users or resources by keyword, location, availability, or other criteria.

- **Web server**   This server provides user access to Web pages created using the Hypertext Markup Language (HTML). It allows for the mixing of text, images, sound, and video into a nonsequential web of associations.

Note   *You'll find a discussion of selecting servers and server components in Chapter 13 .*

Client Systems

Client systems are user workstations that attach to the network via network interface cards. Software runs in the client system to handle network connection, login, server requests, and other network communication. The architecture of the client and server system is pictured in Figure 1-5. The client software directs server requests made by users or applications to an appropriate server on the network and receives responses from those servers.

Communication protocols provide the mechanism for transporting requests and responses over the network. The standard communication protocol in the NetWare 5 environment is the Transmission Control Protocol/Internet Protocol (TCP/IP) suite of protocols. It is designed for organizations that need to build wide area networks, support existing UNIX systems, and connect with the Internet. NetWare 5 also supports the earlier Internetwork Packet Exchange (IPX)/Sequenced Packet Exchange (SPX) protocols through the use of compatibility mode drivers. NetWare 3 and 4 systems rely on the Service Advertising Protocol (SAP) to locate network resources. SAPs have been replaced in NetWare 5 with a new Service Locating Protocol (SLP) to provide service discovery. Support for multiple protocols is now a requirement as organizations interconnect a variety of computer systems with networks. Using TCP/IP and SLP, Novell has made IP the default protocol and has provided a unique service referred to as *compatibility mode*. Using this mode the user can continue to use

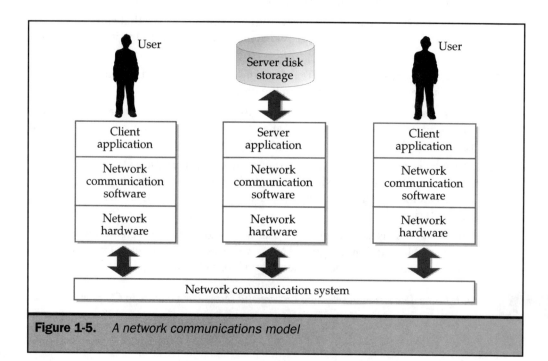

Figure 1-5.   *A network communications model*

IPX where it is needed and covert to IP at a later date. In the long run, the traditional IPX protocol will be replaced with the IP protocol. This will provide better network performance, especially over WAN links.

Network Interface Cards (NICs)

Network interface cards (NICs) are adapters installed in a computer that provide the physical connection to a network. Each NIC (pronounced *nick*) is designed for a specific type of network, such as Ethernet or Token Ring. A NIC has a connector for a specific type of cable such as coaxial cable, twisted-pair cable, or fiber cable. NICs for wireless LANs have an antenna for communication with a base station.

The physical connection and electrical specifications of a network interface card are based on the type of network it supports (Ethernet, Token Ring, etc.) and are defined by international standards. Multiple protocols can be supported concurrently as defined in the international standards. The electrical specifications define the methods for transmitting bit streams across the cable and the control signals that provide the timing of data transfers across the network. Standards also define the cable access method, which is a protocol that determines the order, priority, and amount of time that a computer can transmit on a shared cable.

Standards committees also define addresses for network interface cards so that no two cards share the same physical address. Every NIC manufacturer has a unique number onto which they attach an additional identification (i.e., serial number) for each card they manufacture.

Most network cards also come with a socket for a remote-boot PROM (programmable read-only memory) so that you can install the card in diskless workstations, which have no disk drives. This technology is used to reduce cost, eliminate an entry point for viruses, and improve security throughout the network. The PROM holds a program that directs the computer to get startup information from a network server, rather than a program stored on local disk.

You'll learn more about network cards in Chapter 6.

Cabling System

Choosing a type of cable for a network is a critical decision. Cable and cable equipment must meet current and future needs for data transmission, and physical layout (topology) and communication requirements. Recently, network cable standards have been enhanced to boost data transfer rates on relatively inexpensive copper twisted-pair cable. That makes the decision about which cable to use much easier because twisted-pair is less expensive than coaxial cable and has a higher data rate. Fiber-optic cable, which is a cable that interconnects many different networks within a building or campus area, is a good choice for backbones and environments where electromagnetic interference is a consideration.

To help managers make informed decisions and design workable cable systems, a new wiring standard has emerged from the EIA/TIA (Electronic Industries Association/Telecommunication Industries Association) called the EIA/TIA-568 Commercial Building Wiring Standard. This standard is a set of specifications for data communication wiring systems that the industry can follow. It is discussed further in Chapter 6.

Devices for Expanding the Network

Network cabling systems have distance limitations due to signal loss and other electrical characteristics. You can extend the distance of network segments by adding a repeater, which regenerates the electrical signal and doubles the allowable length of the cable, although it doesn't let you add to the network more computers than the defined number.

To increase the distance of a network and add more stations, you can add another network segment and link the stations with a *bridge*, or, if an existing network is bogged down because too many users are trying to access it, you can split it and then bridge the new segments together. This last technique lets you "filter" traffic between the two so that local traffic stays on the local segment.

Routers let you build internetworks, in which networks that use different topologies and protocols are interconnected. A router understands the network addresses created by network protocols such as IPX and IP. These addresses are *logical*, rather than hard-wired into any workstation. The advantage is that a workstation on one network (in a department or division of your company) can address a packet to a workstation on another network in your company (or even another company's network). IPX and IP handle all the functions of getting that packet from one network to the next. Some networks are very large, and a packet might need to cross many different networks before it reaches its destination. Routing protocols keep an "internal" map of the entire network so they can send the packet along the best path to its destination. Knowing the best route is especially important when networks are linked over expensive long-distance connections.

Hubs and *wiring centers* are used to build structured cabling systems. A hub is a concentrator that forms the center of a star-configured hierarchical wiring scheme. High-end hubs can support a variety of networks such as Ethernet, Token Ring, and optical networks. Workgroup hubs connect all the computers in a specific area or for a department and are linked to enterprise hubs that potentially interconnect an entire organization.

You'll find a discussion of bridges, routers, hubs, and other network expansion devices in Chapter 7.

Shared Resources, Peripherals, and Applications

Shared resources, peripherals, and applications are parts of servers, as discussed earlier. In a peer-to-peer environment, these components are spread around the network, but in dedicated server environments, they tend to be located in one place, although this is not a strict rule. Remember that peer-to-peer and dedicated server operating systems can coexist on the same network. Users might run Windows 98 at the desktop and share components on their systems with others. At the same time, network administrators may install application servers (database, communication, fax, etc.) at central locations and make resources available to authorized users.

Network Architecture

The architecture of a network is defined by its topology, the cable access method, and the communication protocols in use. Before any workstation can transmit on the cable, it must make sure that no other workstation is transmitting. Each type of network has defined cable access methods that prevent or reduce communication conflicts and that govern how information is communicated from one station to another.

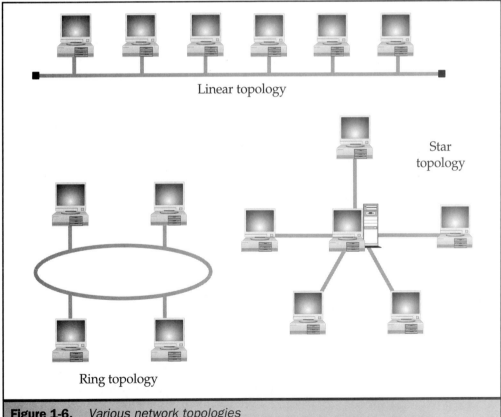

Figure 1-6.   *Various network topologies*

Topology

You can think of a network's topology as a map of its cable layout. Topology defines the basic configuration of how you connect workstations together and, in some cases, the signal path of a data transmission over the cable. Figure 1-6 illustrates the basic topologies. Each topology is discussed below, but keep in mind that modern networks are really hybrids, or combinations, of all three topologies, as discussed in a moment.

- **Linear topology**   A linear topology consists of a single cable that extends from one computer to the next in a daisy-chain fashion. The ends of the cable are terminated with a resistor. Ethernet coaxial networks use linear topologies. When a workstation transmits a signal, it is "broadcast" on the wire so that every other workstation can potentially receive it.

- **Star topology**   In a star topology, all wires branch from a single location, such as a file server or a central wiring hub. Star topologies require a cable to each workstation from a central hub, which requires more cable, but a break in a cable only affects transmission to the computer it is connected to.

- **Ring topology**   In a ring topology, the signal path on the network forms a loop, even though the physical cable layout looks more like a star topology. In Figure 1-6, note that computers branch from a central hub in a star-like configuration, but the hub itself contains an inner ring on which signals travel.

Modern networks are hybrids of the topologies just discussed. The EIA/TIA-568 Commercial Building Wiring Standard defines a hierarchical wiring scheme that can potentially interconnect every computer system in an organization.

Cable Access Method

Traditional local area networks are shared cable systems, meaning that computers are attached to the same cable, but only one computer can transmit at a time. Therefore, some method is needed to prevent simultaneous transmissions. *Cable access methods* define how a workstation gains access to the cable system. You will find a discussion of cable access methods in Chapter 6.

On a linear cable system like Ethernet, a workstation sends data by transmitting on the cable. Other computers on the network use a *carrier sensing* method to determine if a computer is already transmitting on the cable. If the cable is in use, a computer waits and tries to transmit later. If two computers do manage to broadcast at the same time, a *collision* occurs and both back off, wait for a random amount of time, and try again. If a lot of computers are attached to the network, the chance of collisions increases, which causes a degradation in the performance of the network. This type of cable system has an maximum throughput of 35 to 40 percent of the available bandwidth.

Token-passing methods are typically used on ring networks like IBM's Token Ring. In a token-passing system, a station only transmits when it has possession of a token. Think of a token as a temporary ticket or pass to use the network. When a station is ready to transmit, it must wait for an available token and then take possession of the token. This prevents two machines from using the cable simultaneously. Token-passing methods generally have a maximum throughput of 85 to 90 percent of the available bandwidth.

Communication Protocols

Communication protocols are the rules and procedures used on a network to communicate among nodes that have access to the cable system. Communication protocols can be compared to diplomatic protocols, in which diplomats at different ranks negotiate with peer diplomats at other embassies.

There are several "levels" of protocols. High-level protocols define how applications communicate, and low-level protocols define how signals are transmitted over a cable. In between the high- and low-level protocols are intermediate protocols that perform a number of other functions, such as establishing and maintaining communication sessions and monitoring transmissions for errors. Note that low-level protocols are specific to the type of network in use, such as Ethernet or Token Ring.

You can find a complete discussion of network protocols in Chapter 5 and in Chapter 9.

Essential Network Operating System Services

Early network operating systems provided simple file services and some security features. But user demands have increased, and modern network operating systems offer a wide range of services.

DIRECTORY SERVICES   Directory services are like Yellow Pages and White Pages directories that help people find other people or services on the network. They also provide important organization and management tools for network administrators and allow users to log on once to the network and gain access to any resources they have rights to without further logins. Refer to Part III of this book for more information on Novell Directory Services (NDS).

MESSAGING   Messaging is a communication service that can provide automatic data transfers across a network. Messaging in the NetWare environment supports popular mail client applications such as GroupWise and mail-enabled applications based on popular mail transport protocols.

MANAGEMENT AND ADMINISTRATION Centralized management is an essential feature of most networks. It allows administrators to monitor the network, maintain security, perform backup, and perform many other tasks much easier than if essential network components are in diverse locations.

SECURITY Security services are essential in a shared information environment. NetWare implements important security features such as RSA (Rivest, Shamir, Adleman) public key encryption, auditing capabilities, packet signatures, and government security certifications. NetWare provides security for the entire network.

FILE SERVICES A network operating system should support native file services for DOS, Microsoft Windows, Macintosh, UNIX, IBM OS/2, and OSI clients. Other important features are file compression to reduce file storage requirements, data migration to move unused data offline, system fault tolerance (SFT) to provide automatic backup, and a transaction tracking system (TTS) to provide data recovery in the event of a power outage. You'll learn more about NetWare 5 file services in Part V of this book.

PRINT SERVICES Print services are designed to allow many users to share printers on the network, no matter where those printers are located. Print services can handle multiple print jobs and provide ways to prioritize and manage those print jobs. Chapter 23 covers printing under NetWare 5.

BRIDGE, ROUTER, AND WIDE AREA NETWORKING SUPPORT As stated earlier, bridges and routers allow networks to interconnect with other networks. NetWare provides internal routing, which means that you can connect two networks simply by installing two network interface cards, one for each network in the server. Wide area networking requires appropriate communication protocols. NetWare 5 supports the TCP/IP and IPX/SPX communication protocols for connectivity. Part II covers these topics in detail.

The Complete Reference

NetWare 5

Chapter 2

Novell Networking Strategies

This chapter presents a brief outline of Novell's involvement in the network computing industry, and outlines some of Novell's strategies with its current product line and future product line. While this material is not essential for learning about NetWare, you might find it interesting if you are working in an environment that has existing NetWare products or plans to expand with future Novell products.

A Brief History of Novell and NetWare

Novell has been a major influence in the growth of the microcomputer industry. It developed Z-80–based microcomputers in the 1970s and created its first networking products in the early 1980s. Novell's main product during the emerging years of the personal computer was a file-sharing device based on the Motorola 68000 processor. In 1983, when IBM announced the IBM Personal Computer XT, which had a hard disk, Novell quickly responded with a product that converted the hard disk system into a file-sharing system. A star-configured cabling system, known as S-Net, was used to attach workstations.

A few years later, Novell introduced NetWare/86, which provided file server capabilities. The new server operating system not only let users share files, it provided access to those files through a security system and helped manage other features of the network. As NetWare grew in popularity, its designers improved its hardware independence. Novell stopped pushing its own LAN hardware and began providing support for products from many vendors. This was one of the most important strategies in the advancement of NetWare as an industry standard. In 1986, a new version of NetWare, called Advanced NetWare, provided even more support for LAN hardware by bridging different network types within the file server or an external workstation. For example, you could install both an Ethernet and Token Ring card in the server.

Advanced NetWare 286 was developed to take advantage of Intel 80286-based systems. It provided multitasking capabilities long before products like OS/2 and Microsoft Windows existed. In addition, it ran in the protected mode of the 80286, which allowed it to provide advanced features not available when running only under DOS, and it did not have the 640K memory constraints of DOS. Many users were getting better performance when accessing files on NetWare servers than when accessing files on their local hard drive! Up to four different types of network interface cards could be installed in an Advanced NetWare 286 server.

Eventually, Novell began splitting its product line. At the low end, it offered NetWare ELS (Entry Level System), which supported a small number of users. At the high end, it introduced NetWare SFT (System Fault Tolerance). NetWare SFT provided protection from disk failures by mirroring, or duplexing, the disk system. In this arrangement, two disks record the same information, and if one fails, the other can be put into use. Novell also began offering file storage support for Apple Macintosh computers on the NetWare server.

In 1989, Novell announced NetWare 386 3.0, an operating system that was completely rewritten to take advantage of features built into the Intel 80386 processor.

NetWare 386 is a full 32-bit operating system that was designed for large networks with massive data handling needs. It also provided enhanced security, performance, and flexibility. (Operating system changes were much easier.) In June of 1990, Novell shipped version 3.1 of the operating system, which provided enhanced performance, reliability, and system administration. In 1991, Novell announced NetWare 3.11, which supports DOS, Macintosh, Windows, OS/2, and UNIX file and print services. In 1994, Novell announced NetWare 4, which introduced Novell Directory Services (NDS). Instead of the traditional flat database bindery structure of the previous products, this new product relied on a X.500-based hierarchical tree structure.

In 1998, Novell introduced the NetWare 5 operating system. With this product, Novell completely rewrote the core operating system to use both the TCP/IP protocol and the traditional IPX protocol for all interprocess communications. Novell's premiere operating system accommodates both open standards and de facto industry standards while providing the "ten essential services":

- *Directory services,* so administrators can manage large internetworks and quickly locate users and resources; support for other operating systems such as Microsoft's NT products

- *Multiprotocol routing,* which supports internetworking with a variety of industry-standard communication protocols

- *DNS and DHCP,* support for traditional DNS and also the new Dynamic DNS (DDNS). A graphical-based DHCP management system for assigning Internet addresses based on container-level constraints

- *Network management,* using the new Zero Effort Networks (Z.E.N.works) management system so administrators can monitor, troubleshoot, and optimize servers, clients, and the entire network

- *Enhanced security,* using C2-based authentication services and Public Key Infrastructure Services (PKIS) to keep information safe and protected

- *File services,* to let users access and share files and resources on the network

- *Novell Distributed Print Services,* to let users access shared printers, which helps reduce equipment costs

- *Netscape FastTrack Server,* for creating, publishing, and serving Web documents

- *Oracle8 for NetWare,* to provide database capabilities to applications on the network

- *ConsoleOne,* a 100 percent Java-based server management application supporting local volume browsing and file copying

Novell's Computing Strategy

Novell is a major force in the network industry and it has implemented strategies to protect its future. These strategies are discussed here. Note that, in most cases, Novell's strategies parallel Microsoft's strategies, which are largely implemented in Windows 95 and 98 clients and Windows NT servers.

Surveys and estimates indicate that Novell NetWare is used at approximately 60 percent of existing network sites. The remaining 40 percent is divided among Microsoft Windows NT Server and other operating systems such as UNIX.

Novell is focusing on the *enterprise network,* which encompasses all the computing resources of an organization. The network itself can be thought of as a platform to which you attach any type of computer system. Computers can share information with other computers, even with computers that are running different operating systems, while maintaining the kind of performance, security, and reliability traditionally found in larger, centralized systems, at a much lower cost.

Enterprise networking is an evolutionary step beyond workgroup computing, which involved integrating desktop computers into networks. Enterprise networking is both local and wide area in scope. It integrates all the systems within an organization, whether they be mainframes, minicomputers, Windows based computers, Apple Macintoshes, UNIX workstations, or other systems. The goal is to provide network computing services to any user on the network. An interconnected network provides the communications platform, and Novell NetWare is the software that helps you bind it all together using components supplied with NetWare or available as optional products.

The driving force behind Novell's enterprise networking strategy is a plan to make NetWare as open as possible to integration with other systems and other vendors' products.

What Is Pervasive Computing?

In late 1994, Novell coined the term *pervasive computing*, which outlined plans for linking office-bound and mobile users to corporate information systems. It also included nonbusiness users, such as consumers who use home banking services, voice messaging, mobile paging, and home shopping. The primary strategy was to make information systems available to people no matter where they were. Networks were growing beyond the traditional configuration of a workstation connected to a server to include new devices such as cellular phones, notebook computers, and pagers. This strategy also included *collaborative computing*, in which groups of people at any location could work together on projects. Novell's *pervasive computing* strategy encompassed three primary areas:

- **Network services**   These are services that are distributed across multiple platforms and available to all users and/or applications. Services include Novell Directory Services (NDS), security, telephony, messaging, file, print, storage, backup, connectivity, and management.

- **Access**   Devices such as desktop computers, notebooks, personal digital assistants, telephones (wired and cellular), televisions, and pagers must have easy access to network resources. In addition, Novell is improving access to corporate data with products that give users access to legacy systems such as IBM mainframes.

- **Applications**   Network applications must implement built-in network features and provide users with access to network services so people can easily communicate and collaborate on projects.

In addition, programming tools with standard application program interfaces (APIs) had to be developed so that developers could create applications for network environments and management systems that would help administrators manage complex universal computing environments at a reasonable cost.

The corporation of today has become a "virtual corporation," with an increasing need to network and communicate in new ways. Several trends in the 1990s are influencing networking models:

- The ability to work where you want with seamless access to information and services.

- Applications that are designed to run on any hardware—the new "write once, run anywhere" strategy.

- Having instant connection to any network or information resource around the world.

- Services that adjust to the way you work when you're in your office or when you go on the road. Intelligent systems can detect when you've taken your portable computer on the road and adjust settings to match the peripherals or requirements at different locations.

- Public access services that help make up for network and communication deficiencies and provide expanded services for people. With the advent of the World Wide Web, even small companies or individuals have access to previously unavailable resources.

- Interactive services that provide new services and business opportunities.

- Document retrieval systems and information retrieval services that help people gain access to information in ways never before possible.

Novell sees the network as the point of convergence and primary link that will allow people to communicate in this new environment. The growing use of the Internet and online services is indicative of this. People use these services to communicate with one another with electronic mail and to acquire information. Novell believes that the network is the only logical way to connect and manage the countless computing devices, applications, and services that users need.

According to Novell, access devices and the computing environment have expanded in the following ways to meet the needs of user-centric environments:

- **Shared devices**   In the early days of networks, users primarily shared expensive printers and storage devices. Fax machines, scanners, backup systems, and video servers are now part of that environment.

- **Shared information**   Users now have a need to share many types of information, not just text. Multimedia operating systems like Windows 98 now let people easily work with and share sound and video in spreadsheet documents, memos, and electronic mail worldwide.

- **Corporate data processing**   There is an ever-increasing need to give users access to corporate data on legacy systems (minicomputers and mainframes) or data in different departments or organizations.

- **Interpersonal and commercial communication**   Interpersonal communication includes electronic mail, fax, telephony (integrated telephone and computer technology), and intersystem messaging. Electronic commerce includes company and individual requirements for billing, bank account access, security trading, and more.

- **Public networks**   Public networks, and most specifically the Internet, are filling the need for inexpensive access to information such as online magazines, documents, and news services. Research and intercompany communication are easier, faster, and less expensive.

Making It Happen

Novell's strategy is to position NetWare 5 as the core network operating system in this new universal network. NetWare 5 provides tight security and authentication features and includes Novell Directory Services (NDS) so users can easily locate resources and administrators can easily manage large global networks. Other advanced features include the following:

- Fault tolerance to provide data integrity is lifted to higher levels with inclusion of Vinca's Standby server software, which provides redundant server backup.

- Support for older IPX-based protocol systems is provided under a completely rewritten core operating system based on the TCP/IP protocol suite.

- Software distribution with NetWare Application Launcher (NAL) makes it easier to install and monitor applications over large networks from a central location.

- Document management, imaging, and multimedia support for new forms of information is provided by add-on products such as GroupWise.

- Remote access is easier with products like BorderManager, which provides basic "firewall" services and support for remote and mobile users.

Novell Directory Services (NDS) is the backbone service that lets organizations build large computing infrastructures. NDS can be compared to a Yellow Pages directory service that ties users, computers, groups, printers, modems, faxes, copiers, phones, pagers, files, documents, and applications into one common access and administrative framework. NDS is covered in more detail in Part III of this book.

The Complete Reference

NetWare 5

Chapter 3

NetWare 5
Feature Overview

NetWare 5 is a 32-bit network operating system that runs on Intel Pentium and above processors. It is a "brand-new animal" from Novell. NetWare 5 uses the basic logic and structure from the prior NetWare 4 product, but that is where all similarity stops. NetWare 5 offers an integrated set of tools and services that allow you to easily manage and control your entire heterogeneous networking environment. The basic operating system provides services to client workstations, and in this respect is a *client-server operating system*. The relationship between the server and workstations is illustrated in Figure 3-1. The client portion runs in a workstation and requests services from one or more servers. The server manages communications on the network by controlling access to network hardware and software. A *redirector* is installed as software at the client workstation, and it determines whether requests made by a user (or a running application) are for the local operating system or should be redirected to a server on the network. The network support software interfaces with the network hardware and communication system which, in turn, receives and sends messages across the network.

What Is NCP Anyway?

The core services provided by NetWare 5 use a communication mechanism referred to as the NetWare Core Protocol (NCP). The NCP defines connection control and service request/response encoding. It provides session and packet-level error checking in a very efficient manner. Each packet is comprised of a *sequence number, connection number, task number, function code,* and *service completion code*. The NCP packet structure is shown in Figure 3-2. The various components of each packet are defined as follows:

- **Sequence number**   Each NCP request packet on a given connection has a unique sequence number. When the server finishes processing a client request, a response packet is sent to the client with the same sequence number. This allows the client to verify that it has indeed received the expected response.

- **Connection number**   A unique connection number is assigned to each client when it establishes a connection with the server. These connection numbers allow the server to keep track of the clients for response and security purposes. Regardless of the number of applications running on the client, there is only one server connection.

- **Task number**   The server identifies each process running on the client by a unique task number. The server uses this task number to determine which files to close when the client closes an application. The server also uses this number to ensure record and file synchronization between multiple applications that may be competing for the same record or file.

- **Function code**   This code specifies the NCP function to be executed by the server. These functions are available to programmers through the use of application programming interfaces (APIs). This subject is beyond the scope of this book and is left to the realm of programmers.

■ **Service completion code**   This is a number returned by the file server as part
of the response header to a client requesting a service. Any nonzero completion
code indicates that an error occurred while processing the client request.

The NetWare 4 NCP was designed to use the IPX/SPX protocol for all
communication purposes. The NCP of NetWare 5 was rewritten and expanded to
support both the TCP/IP and IPX/SPX protocols. This allows the NetWare 5 NCP to
function in a pure TCP/IP environment without the associated overhead incurred in

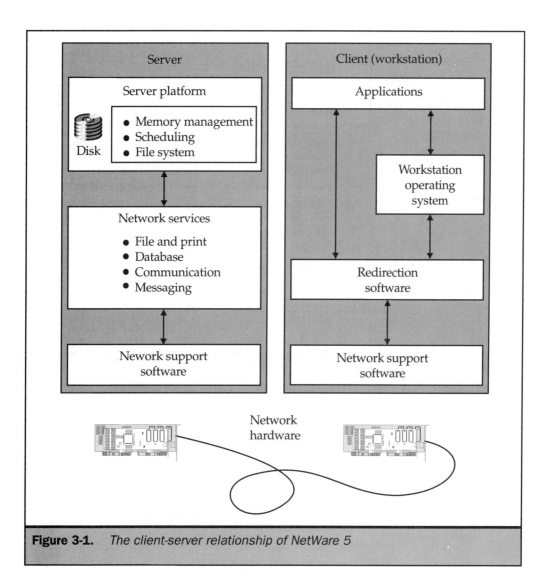

Figure 3-1. *The client-server relationship of NetWare 5*

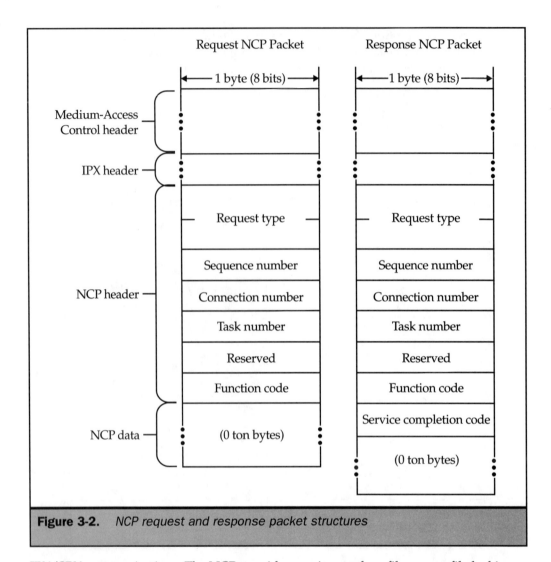

Figure 3-2. *NCP request and response packet structures*

IPX/SPX communications. The NCP provides services such as file access, file locking, resource tracking and allocation, event notification, and other services to devices that request them. A general overview of the basic core services available in a NetWare 5 environment is listed below.

■ **Login and authentication services** Users connect with NetWare 5 servers and log in by supplying their user name and password. This information is checked in the Novell Directory Services (NDS) database, and the user is authenticated and logged in.

- **Security**   The security system in NetWare 5 is robust. It prevents unauthorized access to sensitive and secure files and prevents users from accessing resources they are not authorized to use.

- **File services**   The NetWare file system is hierarchical and familiar to Windows and UNIX users. Users can be granted specific access to specific servers, directories, and files, and that access can be based on read-only rights, or rights that allow users to change content. Rights may also grant users the ability to manage the file system and other users' access to it.

- **Data protection**   NetWare 5 includes various features to help you protect data that might be lost through equipment failure. You can "mirror" the contents of one hard drive to another hard drive; or, with the Vinca Backup Server software, you can duplicate an entire server and its data contents to a duplicate backup server in real time.

- **Routing**   NetWare 5 includes built-in routing. A server can contain more than one network interface card (NIC), and NetWare will route information between users on those networks independent of the protocols in use on each segment.

- **Management**   NetWare servers include many utilities and applications for managing, monitoring, and optimizing performance.

- **Print services**   NetWare includes a full range of print services that let users share their printers with other users. Users can access and monitor printers from inside their applications.

- **Internet/intranet and mobile communications**   NetWare fully supports the World Wide Web, mobile users, and wide area networking.

NetWare 5 System Expandability

NetWare 5 is a sophisticated network operating system that combines high performance with a scalable and flexible architecture. NetWare 5 is an ideal platform for server applications because it is modular and expandable. You can install additional core services by loading Novell Loadable Modules (NLMs) or Java applications, as shown in Figure 3-3. NLMs are available from Novell and from third-party developers as off-the-shelf packages. Some are included as software support for add-on hardware peripherals. The following is a list of some of the services available in the form of NLMs:

- **Name space support** This support allows users of other operating systems to store files on NetWare servers as if the server were a local hard drive.

- **Internetworking** Novell's NetWare MultiProtocol Router (MPR) provides wide area connectivity. MPR runs as NLMs on a NetWare server and so takes advantage of the server as the router in an enterprise environment.

- **UNIX connectivity products** NetWare provides a platform for integrating UNIX servers and clients into the network environment. An optional product, NetWare Network File System (NFS) provides UNIX clients with access to NetWare services. The NFS Gateway gives NetWare users access to files stored on NFS servers in a UNIX environment.

- **Host connectivity** Novell provides a number of products that allow NetWare users to access data and applications on IBM and DEC host systems.

- **Groupware** Novell's GroupWise product is a family of collaborative applications that includes electronic mail, personal calendaring, group scheduling, task management, rules-based message management, Internet access, and workflow routing.

- **Java Novell Loadable Module (NLM)** Full Java support is provided by loading the java.nlm on the server. Java-based installation programs and Java applets can be run on the server console.

NetWare 5 features support for other operating systems. DOS, Windows 95/98, Windows NT, Macintosh, and UNIX workstations can access the services of any NetWare servers. The new NetWare management utilities are designed to run on Microsoft Windows 95/98 and NT workstations and servers.

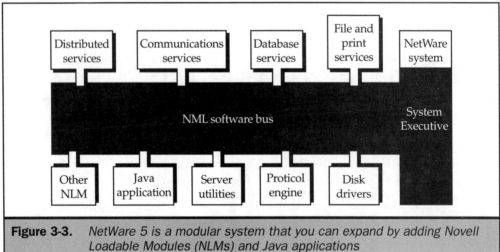

Figure 3-3.   *NetWare 5 is a modular system that you can expand by adding Novell Loadable Modules (NLMs) and Java applications*

NetWare 5's Core Services

Core services are those services that form the basis, or core, of an operating system. The NetWare 5 kernel provides many improvements, such as multiprocessor support, memory management, DHCP/DNS, security, and others as detailed here:

Multiprocessor Support

NetWare 5 provides integrated support for both single and multiprocessor server platforms with the new Multiprocessing Kernel (MPK). The MPK provides a clean execution environment for NLMs and Java applications. The MPK replaces the symmetrical multiprocessor (SMP) kernel that was used in NetWare 4 products. A new scheduling algorithm has been added that allows the administrator to scale applications using "fair-share" scheduling in both single and multi-processor environments.

Memory Protection

Memory protection provides each application running on the server with its own memory space. In this way, every loaded NLM or application is isolated from all other NLMs and applications. In this environment, if one or more modules fail, only the isolated address space associated with that module will be corrupted. The failed modules can be automatically reloaded and diagnostic core dumps can be created for the failed address space without bringing down the server. NLMs and applications that use the standard NetWare CLIB application programming interfaces (APIs) and do not modify the interrupts can be run with little or no loss of performance. The memory protection feature is a user-selectable option. If the option is not selected, all NLMs and applications will be run in kernel space without VM support, as in the existing NetWare 4 product.

Virtual Memory

Virtual memory (VM) allows applications running on the server to access more memory than physically exists on the server. The NetWare 5 VM swap file is much more dynamic than those incorporated into other VM operating systems. The NetWare 5 VM supports more than one swap file and each swap file can dynamically grow and shrink as needed. With VM, only the necessary and frequently accessed memory is kept in the system RAM. All other memory is swapped to the hard disk as needed. Most NLMs and other server-based applications use only a small percentage of the memory that they allocate upon startup. VM significantly decreases the physical memory requirements for a given NLM and frees the remaining memory for use by another application. VM is configured with a minimum and maximum size parameter and a location parameter specifying on which NetWare volume the swap file is to be located.

Scheduler

The scheduler provides the administrator with the ability to assign a weight to the importance of each application with respect to others operating on the server. This allows the various applications to be tuned for better responsiveness by allocating more or less processor time to the various tasks. NetWare 4 used a classic "round robin" scheme that scheduled processor threads in the order in which they entered the queue. The new scheduler provides for preemptive multitasking of application threads that are in an idle state. Once enabled by the administrator, all processor threads running in the selected NLM code address range can be preempted at 145 times per second. This allows scheduling to be defined on an application-by-application basis. Using various LOAD commands, an application can be defined as using the classic "round robin" scheduling algorithm or the new priority-based scheduling algorithm.

I2O Support

I2O is an industry standard that allows the server to offload the input/output functions from a host processor to a dedicated I/O processor. It provides greater server scalability by reducing the host processor utilization and hence supports more applications without degrading performance.

Compatibility Mode

The compatibility mode consists of three different technologies. Separate drivers are associated with the server and the workstation. The first technology is based on the rewriting of the NetWare Core Protocol (NCP) to support both the IP and IPX protocols. If an IPX-based application issues a request to the NCP, a response will be returned to the requesting application. This response will be via the IP protocol and not IPX if the client is TCP/IP-enabled. The second technology is the *Migration Gateway*. It has the ability to encapsulate IPX in an IP packet. Some older applications have their "dirty hooks" into the IPX stack and go around the normal Novell prescribed methods of communication. When this type of application is encountered, NetWare 5 will not compromise the IP-only environment, and instead captures the IPX traffic and encapsulates it in an IP packet. It is only needed when you want to link the two logical worlds of IPX and IP. The gateway provides emulation that prevents IPX protocol packets from populating the IP world. It replaces traditional SAP and RIP packets on behalf of IPX clients by using the information stored in the NDS database. The gateway uses the IPX and IP addresses as well as routing information contained in IPX packets to send the packet to the appropriate node. With this gateway, IPX-based applications on the local LAN can span the IP-based world of WANs without imposing any unwanted IPX traffic. The third technology is the *Bindery Gateway*. This allows for backward compatibility with the NetWare 3 bindery. With this gateway, dynamic objects are transformed into static ones and placed into NDS. In this way, applications that depend on the bindery can still find the object information they need to operate properly.

Novell Directory Services

Novell Directory Services (NDS) is an object-oriented distributed database that stretches across multiple servers. NDS represents users and resources such as file servers and printers as *objects* in the NDS tree. Each object in the database has various properties associated with it. This provides both users and network administrators with a single, integrated view of the entire network and all servers connected to it. Users log in once and gain access to the resources available on all servers (depending on their access rights). With NDS, network administrators assign access rights to the various objects and services on the network by changing a user's network-wide account permissions. In this way, NDS presents a hierarchical view of a network that can be organized by divisions, departments, locations, projects, or other operating units.

You'll learn more about NDS in Chapter 10. You'll also learn how to plan your NDS directory tree in Chapter 11, and how to implement security in Chapter 12.

Security

NetWare 5 provides three different mechanisms for network security:

- **Secure Authentication Services (SAS)** is the next generation in authentication services. It provides server-based user applications with controlled access to files and NDS objects based on the user's SAS authentication. SAS provides a framework for distinguishing between authentication mechanisms of various qualities as well as support for third-party authentication services. It is based on the current NetWare 4.11 C2-certified security system and is designed to provide support for new and evolving authentication mechanisms.

- **Public Key Infrastructure Services (PKIS)** is a set of services that enable the use of public key cryptography and digital certificates in a NetWare 5 system. These services allow an administrator to establish a certificate authority (CA) management domain within NDS. The CA is used to perform certificate and key management activities such as Secure Sockets Layer (SSL) security for Lightweight Directory Access Protocol (LDAP) servers.

- The **Audit** system provides the ability to monitor and record each user's access and track modification of network resources. The audit log files are represented and managed as NDS objects within the tree.

NetWare Time Synchronization Services

These services ensure that the internal clocks on all servers within the enterprise report time in a consistent and synchronized manner. Servers in an enterprise need to have their clocks synchronized because a number of programs, including NDS and other distributed databases, utilize timestamps. Unreliable timestamps will result in incorrect ordering, resulting in databases that have lost their integrity. NetWare 5 supports the new NTP protocol for time synchronization in a TCP/IP environment using the Internet.

DNS/DHCP Services

NetWare 5 provides the benefits of centralized management, replication, and fault tolerance to the industry standard DNS/DHCP utilities. The Dynamic Host Configuration Protocol (DHCP) provides unique IP addresses to clients and network devices upon request. It is fully integrated within the Novell Directory Services (NDS), allowing management of IP addresses throughout the enterprise. The Domain Name System (DNS) converts Internet domain names into numerical IP addresses. With the integration of DNS into NDS, each user can be automatically assigned an appropriate DNS server upon login. NetWare 5 also supports the new Dynamic DNS (DDNS). This allows DNS to discover and add new devices to the DNS tables without the administrator having to manually update HOST files.

Service Location Protocol (SLP)

This new protocol provides for automatic resource discovery and registration over TCP/IP connections. It replaces the older implementation of the Service Advertising Protocol (SAP) used in prior Novell products.

Lightweight Directory Access Protocol (LDAP)

Lightweight Directory Access Protocol (LDAP) is an industry-standard protocol that lets users easily access X.500-based directories such as NDS. It is becoming the de facto standard for accessing directory information over the Internet or intranets. LDAP services for NDS are fully compliant with the latest LDAP 3 standards.

Configuration Manager and Hot-Plug PCI

The configuration manager tracks all of the changes and modifications made to the hardware within the server. It includes Hot-Plug PCI , EISA, and PnP ISA hardware management. The configuration manager detects the hardware configuration of the server upon startup and compares it to the saved configuration information. If a change is detected, the operating system will automatically load the appropriate installation application (NLM or Java). When using the Hot-Plug PCI capability, the system will detect the removal of a PCI device and unload the associated drivers automatically. When a new PCI device is dynamically added to the operating server, the configuration manager will automatically load the appropriate installation application to deal with the configuration change.

NetWare 5 Utilities and Enhancements

NetWare 5 comes with a series of utilities and enhancements that are add-ons to the basic core services. Some of these are third-party products that have been adapted for use on a Novell platform. Others are utilities to help the network administrator perform day-to-day administrative tasks.

Novell Installation Service (NIS)

NIS provides a common utility to install all future Novell products with a consistent installation interface. It integrates GUI server technology to allow easy administration of the server and the network.

Novell Licensing Services (NLS)

NLS provides a consistent and efficient licensing service for all future NetWare products conforming to the new specifications.

NetWare 5 GUI Console

The server console is managed using a GUI interface similar to the X-Windows environment found on UNIX platforms. *ConsoleOne* provides administrators with flexible, role-based network management. It is Internet standards-based (Java, IP, LDAP, and SSL) and integrates Java applets and snap-ins into the server console. ConsoleOne supports features such as applet launching, local volume browsing and file copying, basic management and administration, graphical server monitoring, and other GUI-based management tools as well as server-based remote console functions.

NetWare Management Agents (NMA)

NetWare 5 includes a Simple Network Management Protocol (SNMP) agent that can supply SNMP-compliant management systems with information about resources on the network. You can use Novell's ManageWise or any other SNMP management system to access this information from SNMP agents and monitor the entire network.

Novell Storage Services (NSS)

Novell Storage Services (NSS) is a new file system designed to allow for the mounting of large server volumes in seconds. It is a 64-bit indexed storage system that redefines the current limitations in regard to file size and mount times. It allows for billions of volumes, and directories of up to 8 terabytes. It eliminates the restrictions on the number and size of files that can be stored in volumes and directories on the server. Currently, hard drives and CD-ROMs are supported. Future modules will be made available to support new storage type devices as they come on the market.

Novell Distributed Print Services (NDPS)

Novell Distributed Print Services (NDPS) provides a simplified, centralized administration for all printing resources throughout the network. NDPS supports automatic driver download for plug-and-print installation of new print devices. It provides for automatic printer discovery and configuration anywhere on the network. NDPS is configured and controlled through the use of the NetWare Administrator (NWADMIN32) program on a client machine. It provides support for bidirectional printer communications and is fully backward compatible with the legacy queue-based printing systems.

Storage Management Services (SMS)

Storage Management Services (SMS) is a new backup utility that is protocol independent. It supports multiple and repetitive scheduling and has support for new devices such as autoloaders. SMS is administered through a Windows-based GUI and takes full advantage of NDS by allowing central management of backup jobs across the network.

Oracle8 Database

NetWare 5 includes a five-user version of release 8.0.3 of Oracle's Relational Database Management System (ORDBMS). This version uses NDS to provide transparent authentication to any Oracle server on the network. Each database can be configured for single sign-on and privilege management through NDS. Oracle8 provides a variety of standard data access methods, which include ODBC Oracle Objects for OLE, JDBC, and native Oracle drivers.

Netscape FastTrack Server

NetWare 5 contains a fully integrated version of the Netscape FastTrack Server for creating, publishing, and serving Web documents. This product has been rewritten to make optimum use of the Novell operating system. It provides the highest security available for Web communications and offers LDAP support for centralized user and group management. These features provide a full-function Web server that is easily administered and controlled via NDS.

Zero Effort Networks (Z.E.N.works)

Zero Effort Networks (Z.E.N.works) is a collection of management utilities that assist you in managing workstations in an enterprise environment. Workstation objects and groups are defined as NDS objects and added to the NDS tree. With Z.E.N.works, administrators can leverage NDS by managing a few objects, rather than hundreds of workstations. When a user logs in, his or her workstation is configured according to an associated object. Remote observation and control of the workstation for troubleshooting can also be implemented. The administrator can manage desktop configurations, distribute applications, and remotely control user workstations.

JAVA Server Framework

The Java Server Framework allows developers to write programs that access the NCP application programming interfaces (APIs). These APIs provide the developer access to the directory, security, printing, and other network services. NetWare 5 supports applications that use the Common Object Request Broker Architecture (CORBA), ORB, VBScript, NetBasic, JavaBeans, JavaScript, and Perl 5.

The new enhanced kernel provides multiprocessor support, delivers high performance, adds new reliability features, and includes an improved debugger and compiler for developers.

WinSock 2 Support

WinSock 2 provides a common way for developers to access various protocol stacks. These stacks are used to provide communication services to an application program. By supporting this on the NetWare 5 platform, developers can access IPX/SPX, IPv4, and IPv6 transport protocols.

Basic Operation of the NetWare System

This section provides a general overview of how the basic kernel operates. It details some of the internal actions that are being performed using a file server with the traditional file system, not NSS. NSS is an advanced file system that cannot be used for the SYS volume and does not support the Transaction Tracking System (TTS). It is addressed in Chapter 20.

Dynamic Configuration

NetWare 5 dynamically configures itself to match current usage conditions on the network. The following features are dynamically configured:

- Memory usage
- Directory caching
- Number of volume directory entries
- Size of the open file table

- Turbo FAT indexing
- Active TTS (Transaction Tracking System) transactions

You can alter the limits and maximum values so that NetWare 5 is not constrained. You can also adjust how quickly the operating system configures itself, and you can set the maximum amount of resources that is used.

The File System

The basic file services in NetWare 5 provide many performance-enhancing features:

- **Elevator seeking**   This feature of the disk system prioritizes incoming read requests based on how they can best be accessed by the read head of the disk drive, given its current location. The operation of elevator seeking is analogous to that of a building elevator. A building elevator doesn't make random up and down trips among floors; it stops at floors on the way up or down to pick up passengers who need a ride. Elevator seeking minimizes disk head movement, thus improving access time and reducing hardware degradation.
- **File caching**   File caching minimizes the number of times the disk must be accessed. The files that are most often read are retained in the cache buffer, where they can be accessed if needed. This eliminates the need to go to disk for the information. Files in the cache are prioritized so that the least-used files are flushed from the cache to make room for new files.
- **Background writes**   Disk writes are handled separately from disk reads in NetWare. This separation allows the operating system to write data to disk during moments when disk requests from users have slowed. Background writes give users who need to read data from the drive the highest priority, which improves performance from their point of view.
- **Overlapped seeks**   This NetWare feature is available if two or more hard disks are present and each is connected to its own controller (disk channel). NetWare accesses all the controllers simultaneously. If two disks are attached to one controller, only one of those disks is accessible at a time.
- **Turbo FAT**   This feature is also known as the *index file allocation table*. The turbo FAT indexes the file allocation tables of files over 2MB so that the locations of their segments are immediately available to the operating system without the need to read the FAT.
- **File compression**   NetWare 5 can increase disk space up to 63 percent with its file compression feature. NetWare manages the compression in the background. Administrators and users can flag files to indicate that they should be compressed after use or that they should never be compressed.

■ **Block suballocation**   This feature maximizes disk space. If there are any partially used disk blocks (usually a block is 8K in size), NetWare divides them into 512-byte suballocation blocks for the storage of small files or fragments of files.

Files up to 4GB in size are allowed, and the basic file system supports more than two million directories and files per volume and 100,000 open files. Volumes can span multiple disk drives, and the size of the volumes can be increased dynamically by adding new drives.

NetWare's salvageable file system allows recovery of deleted files. You can set a minimum amount of time that a deleted file must be kept recoverable, and for security reasons you can mark files for immediate purging. You can also keep all deleted files until the volume runs out of disk space, after which the oldest deleted files are removed to free space for new files. Trustee rights to files are preserved after a file has been recovered, and rights can be set to control who can salvage files. Deleted files are preserved even if a directory is deleted.

Data Protection Features

The operating system provides several important features that ensure the survivability and quick recovery of data on the server:

■ **Read-after-write verification**   This feature reads every write to the disk at the time it is written to verify that it is correct. If an error occurs, the data is rewritten while it is still in the cache. An error can indicate a bad sector, which can be marked as unusable by the Hot Fix feature described shortly.

■ **Duplicate directories**   NetWare duplicates the root directory structure to provide a backup in case the main directory structure is corrupted.

■ **Duplicate FAT**   A duplicate of the file allocation table is maintained as a backup. If the original is lost, the disk remains accessible through the duplicate.

■ **Hot Fix**   This feature detects and corrects disk defects as the system runs. Data in defective sectors is moved elsewhere on the disk, and the sectors are marked as unusable.

■ **Transaction Tracking System (TTS)**   The Transaction Tracking System protects data files from incomplete writes. This can occur when a user is editing records in a database and the server goes down. When the server is restarted, it backs out the incomplete transactions so that the files remain the way they were before the transaction began. Transactions must be either wholly completed or wholly abandoned under this system.

- **UPS monitoring**   NetWare monitors the status of an uninterruptible power supply (UPS) to determine if the server is running on backup power. A NetWare-compatible UPS is capable of providing this signal to NetWare. If a power failure occurs, NetWare warns users (who must be out of the blackout area or on their own UPS), and then begins to save any open information (cache data) and safely shut down the system.

- **System Fault Tolerance (SFT)**   This feature allows you to provide redundancy for hardware in the system. You can install two disks and then *mirror* the contents of the main disk on the secondary disk, as shown on the left in Figure 3-4. Should the main disk fail, the secondary disk can be put into service. The disk controller can also be duplicated, or *duplexed*, to further protect from hardware failure, as shown in the middle of Figure 3-4.

Security Features in NetWare

The security features of NetWare are critical for large corporate-wide network environments. Security is provided at several levels:

- **Login/password security**   Users type the LOGIN command to gain access to the file system. They enter their user name and then a password. No access is allowed without the password. After they are logged in, users can access computers in an internetwork based on the access rights that have been assigned to them by the network administrator.

- **Account restrictions**   Under NetWare, each user has an account that is managed by the network administrator. Restrictions can be applied to accounts to control when users can log in, the workstations at which they can log in, and when their accounts expire. It's also possible to force users to change their passwords on a regular basis and to require a unique password that is not similar to one recently used.

- **Object and file security**   The network administrator grants users trustee rights to objects, directories, and files. These rights determine exactly how users can access resources on the network. Object rights determine whether a user can access physical devices like a server or printer. Directory and file rights determine how users can access file systems.

- **Internetwork security**   Novell Directory Services tracks all objects on an internetwork, including user objects and their access rights. Network administrators use NDS to create and manage user accounts, track network resources, and assign user access to network resources. Users log in once to gain access to all the network resources granted to them through the NDS system.

As mentioned earlier, Novell Directory Services allows users to log in once at any server on the network and have access to services over the entire network, based on

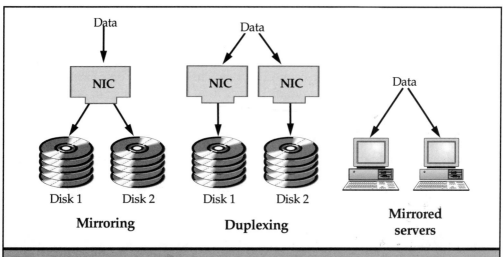

Figure 3-4. *System Fault Tolerance is provided by installing a second disk to mirror
the primary disk image*

their rights. An authentication feature verifies that users are authorized to use the
network. It works in conjunction with the Access Control List (ACL), which stores
information about how users can access an object on the network, such as volumes.

When a user logs into the network, the directory server requires that the user's
workstation authenticate that it knows the user's password. A special key encryption
technique is used to verify the user and to ensure that a user's password never passes
over the network wire. This ensures that the password is not captured and used for an
unauthorized login.

Users are not aware of authentication; it works in the background. Authentication
assigns a unique identification to each user for each login session. The identification,
not the user's password, is then used to validate requests for network services at any
location on the network.

Authentication guarantees that a user's password never goes beyond the login
process. It is immediately converted to a different code that identifies the user and the
station logged into during the user's current session. Authentication also guarantees
that messages are from the correct user at his or her workstation in the current session
and are not corrupted, counterfeited, or tampered with.

Auditing and Resource Accounting

In addition to authentication and access rights, NetWare implements auditing features
so that an independent person (an auditor) can monitor the activities on the network to
ensure that all persons, including system administrators, are performing their duties
and are not undermining security. The auditing features record selected network
events on any resources and present them to the auditor in a form that makes it easy to

determine if the network has security "holes" or has had a security breach. Note that the auditor can only access the network security reports and does not have management responsibilities that would compromise security.

Resource accounting features provide a way to charge users for their use of the network. You can base charges on connection time, the number of disk blocks read from or written to disk, the amount of disk space used, or the number of requests made by the workstation. Rates can vary based on the time of day and the day of the week.

NetWare 5 Command Changes from NetWare 4

Numerous changes and improvements have been made to the commands that can be entered at the server console. The following table highlights some of the command changes:

Legacy Command	NetWare 5 Command	Command Comments
INSTALL	NWCONFIG	NWCONFIG replaces INSTALL.
LOAD	LOAD	LOAD is now optional.
DOWN and RESTART SERVER	RESTART SERVER	RESTART SERVER combines the previous two-step process.
DOWN and EXIT	DOWN	DOWN replaces the previous two-step process.
[none]	RESET SERVER	RESET SERVER performs a warm reboot of the server.
SERVMAN	MONITOR	MONITOR provides the functions previously found in SERVMAN.
SET	SET	SET commands entered at the console are remembered after restarting the server.

Requirements for Running NetWare

The following list defines the hardware you need to install and run NetWare 5:

- A Pentium or higher system processor.
- A minimum of 64MB of memory is required. To run Java applets on the server, a minimum of 128MB of memory is required.

■ A hard drive with a minimum of 230MB of storage. You need 30MB for a DOS partition and 200MB for NetWare.

■ An ISO 9660-compliant CD-ROM reader (with drivers for DOS and Microsoft CD extensions). This is needed if you plan to install NetWare 5 from a CD-ROM.

■ One or more network interface cards (NICs). Although one network card in the server can support a large number of users, you'll get better performance if you install multiple network cards in a fast server and then split those users up over the cards. See Chapter 5 for a discussion of NICs. The cards you choose for servers should be of higher performance than the cards you choose for workstations.

■ Network cabling. The type of cabling depends on the type of network card used. Refer to Chapter 5 for more details.

■ To ensure job security, purchase an adequate power backup system and take measures to secure the hardware from theft, destruction, and other loss, as described in Chapter 11.

Additional information to help you evaluate and purchase equipment for your network is presented in Part III of this book.

The
Complete
Reference

Chapter 4

NetWare Enhancement Products

This chapter provides an overview of the various products available from Novell. The majority are add-ons loaded directly at the server as Novell Loadable Modules (NLMs). A brief description is provided for each product. You'll find a more complete description, including specifications, hardware and software requirements, and compatibility listings in the *NetWare Buyer's Guide*. Contact Novell at 1-800-NETWARE or at www.novell.com on the World Wide Web to order this guide.

Network Operating Systems

intraNetWare 4.11 is a powerful, flexible, and reliable server operating system. It provides a single point of network administration through the NetWare Administrator (NWADMIN32) utility. NWADMIN32 uses a point-and-click GUI for managing your network. It gives you access to Novell Directory Services (NDS), the hierarchical database that stores comprehensive information about network users and resources. Other features include flexible resource accounting and licensing management, easy installation and migration, multiprotocol routing, integrated TCP/IP protocol support, file and print services, and security.

NetWare for Small Business

NetWare for Small Business provides a solution for networks of 50 users or fewer. It offers simple installation, management, and provides Internet access capabilities. It comes complete with Novell GroupWise for E-mail, calendaring, scheduling, task management, and document management.

NetWare 3.2

NetWare 3.2 is an enhancement to the older NetWare 3.x server operating system. It includes all software updates since the release of NetWare 3.12, including Year 2000-compliance. NetWare 3.2 also includes a new GUI-based SYSCON program for network administration.

Personal NetWare

Personal NetWare is a peer-to-peer network operating system that supports up to 50 computers running Windows or DOS. Users can share hard disks, printers, CD-ROM drives, and other resources. It includes a scaled-down version of Novell Directory Services (NDS) referred to as Single-Network View. This database is a distributed, replicated database containing information about all objects on the network, such as users, groups, printers, volumes, and other network services.

NetWare for Macintosh

NetWare for Macintosh provides Macintosh users with full NetWare file and print services, Novell Directory Services (NDS), and AppleTalk routing. Macintosh users view files stored on the NetWare server in the familiar Macintosh form. Non-Macintosh users view Macintosh folders and files in the form native to the operating system they are using.

Advanced Network Services

Advanced network services are specialized products that are designed as enhancements to the NetWare operating system. These products range from data replication services to clustering technologies for server fault tolerance.

Novell Replication Services

Novell Replication Services (NRS) is server-based software that enables you to easily manage the distribution of shared information across multiple Novell servers. It enables you to copy volumes, directories, and files to geographically separate servers. NRS supports both one-way and two-way replication. It can automatically update the replicated files on each server it links when a change is made to the source file. The administrator-set access rights and security of the source files are also replicated to each server. NRS includes a snap-in to NetWare Administrator (NWADMIN32) for simple management of the replicated files. Updates can be scheduled to occur dynamically as a source file is changed or at selected times, such as after business hours.

SnapShotServer for NetWare/intraNetWare

SnapShotServer is a backup software product that allows you to backup open files and live databases to a secondary server. You can perform complete and entirely safe backups of the source server as often as every fifteen minutes. SnapShotServer provides system rollback capabilities for quick and easy data recovery. Backups can be stored on a secondary server or routed to a tape backup unit or other backup media for storage.

StandbyServer for NetWare/intraNetWare

StandbyServer is a software-only solution that creates a backup server from your primary server. This allows you to create a mirrored-server system that switches quickly to the StandbyServer in the event of primary server hardware or software failure. You can use any combination of Novell certified server hardware for the mirrored server pair. This eliminates the need to deploy identical server hardware. StandbyServer ensures that your mission-critical information is protected and always available to your users.

Orion Clustering Solutions

Orion Clustering Solutions is the code name for a series of products that will be released in three phases. Orion will provide unparalleled scalability for network growth and continuous access to network information and applications.

Internet Services

Novell has also created a suite of products designed to enable connection to the Internet reliably and securely. Within this suite are products that speed up your access to Web pages, provide e-mail capabilities, and allow you to publish documents on both your intranet and the Internet.

BorderManager

BorderManager is a unique combination of various open technologies and services. It is bundled as a stand-alone software solution for networks that connect to the Internet. It delivers a single point of security management, Internet and intranet access management at the user level, enhanced network performance, and reduced cost of operations. BorderManager is designed to meet the needs of "border services," as shown in Figure 4-1. BorderManager is comprised of the following technologies:

- **Firewall security architecture** defines a three-tiered model comprising packet filters, circuit-level proxies, and application-level proxies. Packet filters use routers to filter information coming to and from the corporate network. Circuit-level proxies provide a general virtual circuit relay between the Internet and intranet desktop applications. Application-level proxies intercept all traffic and apply content-based semantic access controls prior to relaying the data.

- **Proxy caching** brings Internet information closer to the user. It moves frequently accessed Internet information, such as Web pages, from the Internet to the BorderManager server.

- **IPX gateway services** allow IPX-based clients on the network to access IP services on the public side of the router. This is accomplished through a protocol conversion and address mapping within the gateway software. The client IP addresses can be nonregistered so long as they conform to the IP networking protocol. All access to the gateway can be controlled using NDS.

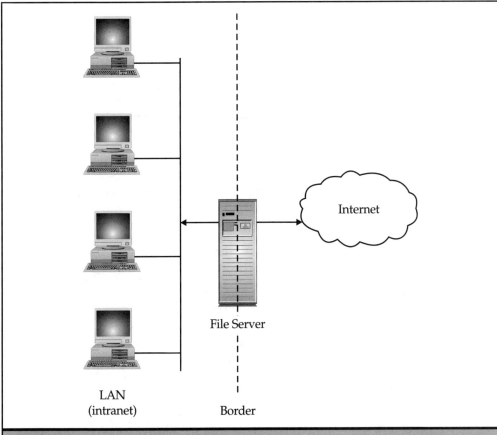

Figure 4-1.   *BorderManager provides a single point of connection between the
Internet and the corporate intranet*

- **Network address translator (NAT)** services convert the network client IP addresses to the IP address on the public side of the router. This service does not provide security controls via NDS.

- **Virtual private networks (VPNs)** allow users to establish secure, encrypted connections across low-cost Internet links without the need for custom software on the client. VPNs use the RC2 encryption algorithm for all communications.

- **Remote access** uses the Point-to-Point Tunneling Protocol (PPTP) for authenticating remote clients accessing a site from the Internet. This provides multiprotocol access using IP in either of two ways: Users can use PPTP-enabled clients to establish tunnels with intranet servers, or remote clients using Point-to-Point Protocol (PPP) can connect with standard dialers into an Internet service provider (ISP) that supports PPTP.

BorderManager FastCache

BorderManager FastCache is software that speeds up access to information stored on Internet or intranet servers. It is installed at the "border" and caches information that users request from various Web servers. It speeds up Web access by providing frequently accessed information from a local cache instead of retrieving information from a Web server. FastCache offers proxy caching, hierarchical caching, and Web server acceleration to all Web servers, regardless of manufacturer.

GroupWise WebAccess

This product has been incorporated into the GroupWise 5 product. See the section "GroupWise 5—E-mail, Calendaring, and Scheduling," later in this chapter.

GroupWise WebPublisher

This product has been incorporated into the GroupWise 5 product. See the section "GroupWise 5—E-mail, Calendaring, and Scheduling," later in this chapter.

Netscape Enterprise Server for NetWare

Netscape Enterprise Server is a high-performance Web and application server designed for enterprise performance and use. It provides advanced Web publishing capabilities through WebPublisher and offers full indexing and search functions. It supports rules that can be defined to notify users when a document is modified. Netscape Enterprise Server is tightly integrated into Novell Directory Services (NDS), allowing centralized management of one or more Web servers.

Netscape Messaging Server for NetWare

Netscape Messaging Server is designed for users who want to implement simple e-mail services. It supports basic e-mail services and therefore does not compete with Novell's GroupWise product family. It supports Post Office Protocol 3 (POP3) and Internet Message Access Protocol (IMAP). Netscape Messaging Server does not support messaging gateways, connectors, or translators. This makes it very easy and inexpensive to deploy and manage.

Netscape FastTrack Server for NetWare

Netscape FastTrack Server is designed for small- to medium-sized businesses that do not need the power of the Enterprise Server. It allows organizations to create, publish, and distribute Web documents quickly and efficiently over the Internet or intranet. It includes all of the same features as Enterprise Server except document revision control, automated link management, agent capabilities, full-text searching and indexing, SNMP agent, and cluster management.

LAN WorkPlace Pro for Windows 95 and NT

LAN WorkPlace Pro is an application suite that enables network users and remote users to transparently access a wide range of information and services. It includes the Netscape Navigator Web browser with integrated e-mail and news reader, TN5250, TN3270, and VT420 client terminal emulation, File Transfer Protocol (FTP) capabilities, file and print sharing between UNIX and PC systems, X-Server capabilities, and more.

LAN WorkPlace 5 for Windows and DOS

LAN WorkPlace 5 is a connectivity package that enables Windows and DOS users to support concurrent connections to NetWare, TCP/IP, and Internet resources. It gives you terminal emulation, drag-and-drop file transfer through File Transfer Protocol (FTP), and transparent UNIX NFS file sharing. It also includes an easy-to-use dialer for dialing in from remote locations over standard phone lines. The X-Server application allows you to run remote X-Windows applications from your desktop.

LAN WorkGroup 5 for Windows and DOS

LAN WorkGroup 5 is a server-based application that enables all network users to access TCP/IP resources. It provides for centralized administration of installation, workstation configuration, and maintenance. It includes the same applications that come with LAN WorkPlace 5 for Windows and DOS.

RADIUS Services for NDS

RADIUS Services for NDS is designed to manage the physical or hardware level of your network through modem banks, access routers, and access servers. Remote Authentication Dial-In User Service (RADIUS) is an emerging standard that has been adopted by Novell and many leading dial-in and router hardware vendors. Integrated with Novell Directory Services (NDS), it provides a centralized point of authentication as well as configuration information detailing the type of service to deliver (SLIP, PPP, Telnet, rlogin, etc.).

Business Internet Services

Business Internet Services (BIS) is a suite of technologies and services licensed to Internet service providers (ISPs). It is designed to add business-class services to their customers. It includes BorderManager, Novell Directory Services (NDS), GroupWise, ManageWise, and NetWare 5. ISPs can offer value-added services such as virtual private networks (VPNs), accelerated Web page access, managed network services, and other end-user services. In addition, they can offer gateways to messaging systems that enable their customers to exchange e-mail with any other e-mail service.

MultiProtocol Router (MPR)

Novell's MultiProtocol Router (MPR) provides routing of popular protocols on standard desktop computers. It runs as a Novell Loadable Module and is fully integrated with the NetWare environment. You can run MPR on stand-alone servers to get the best routing performance. MPR provides the following:

- On the protocol side, MPR will route IPX, TCP/IP, AppleTalk, and SNA protocols. It also provides source-route bridging for NetBIOS and LLC2 applications.

- On the communication side, MPR supports a wide range of LAN topologies and WAN connections, including dedicated leased lines, dial-on-demand voice-grade circuits, ATM, frame relay, X.25, ISDN, and SMDS. See Chapter 9 for a description of these technologies.

NetWare MultiProtocol Router is a family of products that includes the following components. Each component is purchased separately, based on an organization's requirements:

- *NetWare Enterprise Router* is the "enterprise" component that provides 16 WAN ports.

- *NetWare BranchLink Router* is the "branch office" component that provides two WAN ports.

- The *WAN Extensions* add-on package provides connection services to ATM, frame relay, and X.25 networks.

- The *SNA Extensions* add-on package enhances IBM SNA communications through Data Link Switching (DLSw) and Link/SNA.

MPR integrates well with other Novell communication products and allows you to build connections to branch offices in geographically separate locations.

| Note | *MPR is discussed in more detail in Chapter 9.* |

NetWare for SAA—Host Connectivity Products

NetWare for SAA gives NetWare workstations access to IBM mainframe and AS/400 host systems, as shown in Figure 4-2. The security, name services, and administration of NetWare are retained. Access to AS/400 applications is transparent to all NetWare workstations.

NetWare for SAA is an NLM you install in the NetWare file server to provide gateway services to network users. It eliminates the need for a separate gateway to the

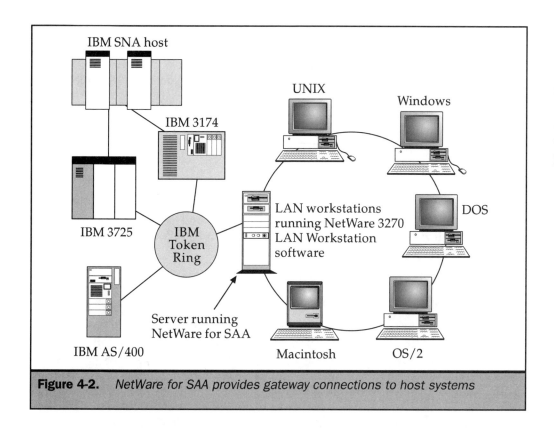

Figure 4-2. *NetWare for SAA provides gateway connections to host systems*

IBM systems. Alternatively, the product can run in a dedicated communications server when the NetWare Runtime application is used. NetWare Runtime is bundled with NetWare for SAA.

intraNetWare HostPrint

intraNetWare HostPrint is an NLM that runs on a NetWare for SAA server. It lets users send host print jobs to networked printers through server-based, IBM 3278 LU1 and LU3 printer emulation sessions. The software routes host print jobs directly from the host to NetWare print queues, which reduces network traffic. NetWare HostPrint 400 is a similar product designed for the IBM AS/400 environment.

intraNetWare HostPublisher

intraNetWare HostPublisher is an NLM that runs on a NetWare for SAA server. It lets users expand the use of their mainframe data by translating it into Web-accessible documents.

intraNetWare NFS Services—UNIX Connectivity

intraNetWare NFS Services is a complete suite of IP-based network services that enable transparent, bidirectional file and print sharing between NetWare and UNIX platforms. It provides a File Transfer Protocol (FTP) server and a gateway that allows FTP clients to transfer files from IBM hosts. It enables companies with mixed intraNetWare and UNIX networks to get the most from their network computing investment. It is included free of charge in the intraNetWare 4.11 product.

intraNetWare Print Services

intraNetWare Print Services is software that enables users on UNIX and intraNetWare networks to share printers while using their native commands and interfaces. It provides centralized administration of both the UNIX and NetWare user accounts. It is included free of charge in the intraNetWare 4.11 product.

NDS for NT

NDS for NT is software that enables administration of mixed Windows NT and NetWare networks. It integrates the Windows NT system and user information into the NDS database. Windows NT domains are treated as containers in NDS. Objects in a domain can be treated the same as any other object in NDS. Objects assume the hierarchical relationships within the NDS tree. This eliminates the need to administer and maintain complicated Windows NT trust relationships. It allows you to use either Novell's NetWare Administrator (NWADMIN32) or the familiar Windows NT tools to manage the domain.

GroupWise 5—E-mail, Calendaring, and Scheduling

GroupWise 5 is a fully integrated messaging system that offers a wide range of powerful communication and collaboration capabilities. It supports task and document management capabilities, native Internet addressing, calendar options, e-mail, group scheduling, automatic workflow, rules-based message management, electronic discussions, and vCard. It provides a Universal Mailbox as a single point of access for the user. GroupWise 5 supports LDAP, IMAP4, and POP3. It includes a Java and HTML 3.2-enabled version of GroupWise WebAccess that provides Web browser access to your Universal Mailbox. It also includes GroupWise WebPublisher, a document management tool that enables users to publish documents contained in the document store to Internet and intranet users. The GroupWise 5 Administrator is integrated into the NetWare Administrator (NWADMIN32) product as a snap-in utility. It also provides a snap-in utility for ManageWise that enables you to monitor GroupWise 5 agents, servers, and gateways that support SNMP.

GroupWise WorkFlow Professional

GroupWise WorkFlow Professional is workflow automation software that gives you tools for designing and managing project workflows. It provides graphical symbols that represent actions and participants in a workflow. You use these symbols to design a workflow that is added to the GroupWise 5 system as an automated series of instructions. These can incorporate tasks such as modifying, reviewing, and approving. GroupWise WorkFlow Professional comes as a stand-alone product or bundled with GroupWise 5.

GroupWise Gateways

GroupWise 5 has the ability to interconnect with existing e-mail systems through the use of various gateways. The available gateways are as follows:

- **GroupWise Async Gateway** provides connection to remote users and systems using modems connected to the standard telephone system. Available platforms are Novell NLM and OS/2.

- **GroupWise API Gateway** provides a series of application programming interfaces (APIs) for developing custom applications on a GroupWise 5 system. Available platforms are Novell NLM, OS/2, and DOS.

- **GroupWise Gateway for cc:Mail** provides interconnectivity between a GroupWise 5 system and a cc:Mail system. The available platform is OS/2.

- **GroupWise Fax/Print Gateway** has been replaced by the Cheyenne Software FAXserve Gateway product. It provides integration of FAX send and receive capabilities through the e-mail client interface. The available platform is Novell NLM.

- **GroupWise Internet Agent (GWIA)** provides access to the Internet using SMTP, POP3, and LDAP services. Available platforms are Novell NLM and Windows NT.

- **GroupWise Gateway of Microsoft Exchange 5** provides interconnectivity between a GroupWise 5 system and Microsoft's Exchange 5 e-mail system. The available platform is Windows NT.

- **GroupWise Gateway for NGMHS** provides interconnectivity between GroupWise 5 and the older Novell MHS e-mail system. Available platforms are Novell NLM, OS/2, and DOS.

- **GroupWise Gateway for Lotus Notes** provides interconnectivity between GroupWise 5 and Lotus Notes. The available platform is OS/2.

- **GroupWise Gateway for Microsoft Mail** provides interconnectivity between GroupWise 5 and the older e-mail system from Microsoft. The available platform is OS/2.

- **GroupWise Gateway for Office Vision/VM** provides interconnectivity between GroupWise 5 and IBM's Office Vision mainframe-based e-mail system. Available platforms are Novell NLM and OS/2.

- **GroupWise Pager Gateway** interconnects a paging service with the e-mail system. Users can be paged automatically upon receipt of an e-mail message. Available platforms are Novell NLM and OS/2.

- **GroupWise Phone Access Gateway** integrates a PBX phone system into the e-mail system. Users can send and receive voice-mail messages and access e-mail via a speech synthesis system. The available platform is Windows NT.

- **GroupWise SMTP/MIME Gateway** was replaced with the newer GWIA gateway detailed above.

- **GroupWise WebAccess Server** provides interconnectivity between a GroupWise 5 system and clients accessing the system via a Web browser on the Internet. Available platforms are Novell NLM, OS/2, UNIX, and Windows NT.

GroupWise SDK

The GroupWise 5 Software Developer's Kit (SDK) enables a programmer to develop third-party applications that integrate tightly with GroupWise 5. It includes sample source code and applications as well as the server-based API Gateway. With the Administration API, a programmer can create applications that add functionality to the GroupWise Administrator snap-in utility. It supports many industry-standard APIs and extensions, including HTTP, ODMA, DDE, and OCX/Active X controls.

InForms Designer/Filler

InForms is a two-part development tool that enables you to automate information gathering and sharing within your company. You create electronic forms and forms-based applications to integrate database information, workflow, e-mail, electronic signatures, and document management systems. You use InForms Filler at the client side to fill-in, route, receive, and sign the forms and applications generated by InForms Designer. InForms supports most common desktop and SQL databases. It enables you to create a database in any of the supported desktop databases, even if you do not have copies of those databases on your network.

ManageWise—Network Management

ManageWise is an integrated set of management services that works with Novell Directory Services (NDS), allowing you to monitor and control your network environment. It allows you manage Novell servers, print queues, Simple Network Management Protocol (SMNP) devices, and Windows NT servers. You can analyze network traffic, remotely control and manage networks and workstations, administer network applications, distribute software automatically, and prevent virus infection of workstations and servers. ManageWise automatically maps all network devices and provides a detailed inventory of each workstation and server on the network. ManageWise supports multiple operating systems and a variety of networking protocols such as TCP/IP, IPX/SPX, AppleTalk, DHCP, BOOTP, and FDDI. The product is sold and packaged like intraNetWare and runs as an NLM on the server.

ManageWise Agent for Windows NT Server

ManageWise Agent for Windows NT Server is software that allows you to manage a Windows NT environment from the ManageWise interface. It provides full configuration and remote management of Windows NT servers.

Zero Effort Networks (Z.E.N.works)

Zero Effort Networks (Z.E.N.works) is server-based workstation management software that lets you manage your network applications and workstations. It incorporates the Novell Application Launcher, Novell Workstation Manager, and a remote-control help request and troubleshooting solution. Z.E.N.works allows you to centrally create and manage Windows 95/98 policies and user profiles. Windows-based applications can be centrally distributed, managed, and updated across your network. Printing services can also be managed for each workstation. Printer drivers can be loaded automatically at the user's workstation with an option to automatically update them as new ones become available. Z.E.N.works also allows you to create hardware inventories for all of your Windows NT and Windows 95/98 workstations and store them in the Novell Directory Services (NDS) tree.

Novell Support

Novell offers several different options for help in troubleshooting your problems.

Electronic Support

The Novell Support Connection Web site is at http://support.novell.com. This site gives customers and partners immediate access to technical support information. It includes a site map with links to each product's support home page. It also contains profiles of locally certified Novell partners.

Novell Support CD

The Novell Support CD contains the same technical information as found on the Web site. It is updated monthly and is accessible from Windows, Mac OS, or DOS. It contains hyperlinks and has full text searching capabilities that simplify your search for information.

The Complete Reference

NetWare 5

Part II

Understanding Network Technology

The Complete Reference

NetWare 5

Chapter 5

Network Communication and Protocols

Computer networks are data communication systems that transmit data across copper wires, fiber-optic cable, and/or radio waves. To use these media and to successfully communicate with other devices, networks must follow established rules, or *protocols*. Protocols cover everything from the packaging of information into transmittable data packets to the timing of electrical signals on copper cable to the description of cable and connectors.

Communication Basics

There are two ways to move information from one place to another: parallel communication and serial communication. *Parallel communication* techniques use multiple lines between two points, like a multilane freeway. A parallel channel might consist of 8, 16, 32, or even 64 side-by-side lines for transmitting data. The transmissions on every line must be kept synchronized, so parallel connections are limited in distance and are used primarily for connecting peripherals such as printers and SCSI devices.

Serial communication transmits data as a stream of "bits" over a single line. A package of data is transmitted by a sender to a receiver. These bits travel across physical media as a series of electrical signals. Serial bit-stream communication is the primary method for transmitting information between systems in a network environment and in telecommunication. Figure 5-1 illustrates the usual physical topologies in this environment.

■ A point-to-point connection is a direct connection between two devices. In wide area networking environments, a point-to-point link is between two computers at different sites over telephone lines or other communication links.

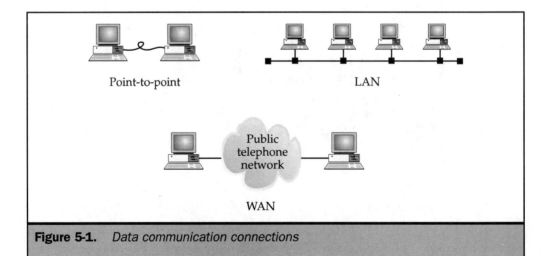

Figure 5-1.   *Data communication connections*

■ A LAN (local area network) is a shared data-communication facility. A number of computers can attach to the network, but only one can transmit at a time, in most cases.

■ A WAN (wide area network) provides connections between multiple sites and involves the telephone network or other communication providers.

Note   *Both LANs and WANs support point-to-point connections by establishing "virtual" links between two systems on a shared network.*

There are two primary methods for transmitting data over communication lines. In *asynchronous* communications, each character is coded as a string of bits and separated by a "start-of-character" bit and one or more "stop" bits. It does not have data clocking associated with the transmitted bit-stream and therefore incurs a lot of overhead. In contrast, *synchronous* communication relies on a data clocking mechanism to separate groups of bits. Synchronous communication is more efficient than asynchronous communication because you can transmit more data in the same amount of time. With synchronous transmissions there are no "start" and "stop" bits. It is the method used by the networks discussed in this book.

Transmitted data is subject to corruption caused by attenuation, outside interference, and other problems associated with transmission facilities. Error detection techniques are used to detect communication problems. In the past, extensive error checking was necessary over telephone links because they were generally unreliable. The underlying communication system performed this error checking. Today's reliable transmission facilities largely eliminate the need to perform extensive error checking. It is now common for the receiving station to handle most of the error checking. If received data packets are corrupted or any are missing, a retransmission is requested. This helps reduce overhead and increases transmission speeds.

A communication system has a certain *bandwidth*, which is a measure of data throughput, usually in bits per second (bps). Analog telephone circuits transmit in the thousands of bits per second (Kbits/sec) range, while LANs transmit in the millions of bits per second (Mbits/sec) range. New fiber-optic systems in the public telephone networks transmit in the billions of bits per second (Gbits/sec) range. Data transmission over *analog* voice telephone systems using modems is limited to 64 Kbits/sec. *Digital* lines are available that transmit at much higher rates (in the Mbits/sec or higher range).

In the network environment, a workstation sends data to a destination (receiver) in the form of packets. A *packet* (or *datagram*) is a package of data with header information that contains the source and destination address, error correction information, sequence numbers, and the data for the transmission. Each packet is limited in size, so a single transmission might include one packet or thousands of packets. The sequence number helps the receiving station put the packets back in order if they arrive out of order. Putting lengthy data transmissions into many small packets has the following advantages:

- A glitch in the communication link may only affect a few packets, not the entire transmission. These "corrupted" packets are easily retransmitted.

- Internetworks are constructed of many connected segments that may form a mesh of connection paths to a destination. Packets are independent data-carrying entities that easily traverse these paths. You don't need to set up a specific "circuit" between source and destination, although that can be done to improve performance.

- On shared networks, it is not feasible to allow one station to send one long transmission that could congest the network. Small packets allow many stations to transmit simultaneously by interleaving their packets on the network.

Local Area Networks (LANs)

The local area network (LAN) is the primary method of transmitting data among desktop computers at the department level in most organizations today. A cable system or wireless medium is deployed in a building, and computers are attached to it. A wide area network (WAN) typically involves a public switched telephone network (PSTN) or possibly a private communication facility that is built by the organization or leased from another organization.

LANs are shared communication systems that typically use twisted-pair cables, although wireless radio LANs are available. Because these networks are constructed with copper cable that has transmission distance limitations, they are called local area networks. In a typical twisted-pair cable system, computers are connected to a central box called a *concentrator*, or *hub*, as shown in Figure 5-2. Hubs are usually located in departments or workgroups, and you can interconnect hubs to provide intercompany communication, referred to as an intranet.

You might need the following devices if you experience distance restrictions, a limitation on the number of workstations, or a limitation on transmission speeds on your network:

- A *repeater* extends the distance of a cable segment by amplifying the input signal and retransmitting the signal.

- A *bridge* interconnects two LAN segments of the same network type so you can expand the network and add more stations. Unlike the repeater, bridges allow you to filter traffic between the bridged segments in order to keep traffic that belongs to one segment from crossing the bridge to the other segment.

- A *router* provides a way to interconnect many different types of networks (Ethernet, Token Ring, etc.). Routers understand higher-level network addressing, so you can build an internetwork-wide addressing scheme that is independent of the types of networks that are connected.

- A *switch* is a device used to segment a network into many smaller networks. It is basically a multiport device in which each port is a private network segment. The

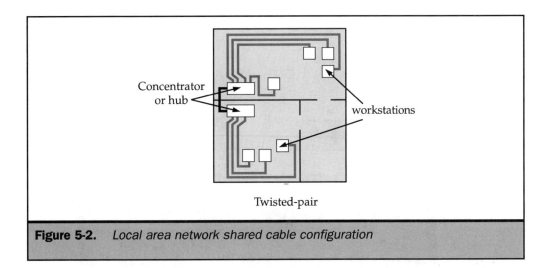

Concentrator
or hub

workstations

Twisted-pair

Figure 5-2. *Local area network shared cable configuration*

primary advantage of switching is that it eliminates the contention, collisions, and delays that are inherent with shared media networks. A switched network is shown in Figure 5-3.

Networks are shared media systems that provide connections for potentially hundreds of users. Because the media are shared, a mechanism is needed to ensure that only one workstation transmits data on the media at a time. These mechanisms are called *access methods*, and there are several, depending on the type of network:

- **Carrier sense multiple access**   Stations listen to see if the cable is in use and transmit only if it is available.

- **Token passing**   Stations take possession of a logical "token" and transmit only while they have possession of the token.

- **Demand priority**   A central hub determines which station can access the cable; it can grant some stations priority over others, depending on the time-sensitivity of the data to transmit.

- **Slotted bus**   A continuous stream of data slots (picture a train of boxcars) is available in which any station can place data for transmission to another station.

These methods for transmitting information on a network are discussed in Chapter 6.

Wide Area Networks (WANs)

When you want computers at different sites to communicate, you usually get involved with communication service providers like the telephone company or other companies

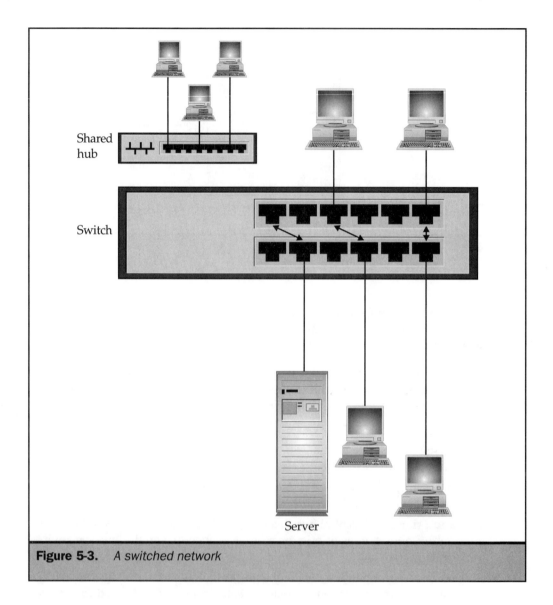

Figure 5-3. *A switched network*

that will lease you long-distance communication services. However, some large companies have created their own global networks by launching communication satellites or using other methods. Also, if the environment is a campus or industrial park setting, many organizations install their own high-speed "backbone" communication system among buildings.

Methods for communicating over the wide area are summarized below. Note that a *dedicated line* is a permanent connection leased on a monthly basis, while a *switched line* only accrues charges when used. *Any-to-any* connections provide links from one site to many different sites. Each of these types of connections is covered in more detail in Chapter 8.

■ A switched point-to-point connection is a link over the regular voice telephone network from your location to any other dial-up location.

■ A voice-grade dedicated point-to-point connection is a permanent link between two sites, but its analog nature limits transmission speeds.

■ A switched point-to-point digital line is a preconfigured dial-up link that you only pay for when you use it. Its digital nature provides high transmission speeds.

■ A dedicated point-to-point digital line is a line that you lease and pay for whether you use it or not. Its dedicated nature ensures that the line is immediately available for your use.

■ Any-to-any digital lines over circuit-switched networks let you create a temporary high-speed digital circuit between two sites of your choice.

■ Any-to-any digital lines over packet-switched networks let you connect into a public communication network and send packets to any destination.

Other methods for connecting systems over wide geographic areas include microwave and satellite systems. Microwave systems consist of transmitters on top of earth-based towers that transmit signals from one tower to the next. They usually are limited to "line-of-sight" due to the high frequencies used in transmission. Satellite systems transmit signals over large global areas.

Protocols in the NetWare Environment

The protocols supported in the NetWare environment are pictured in Figure 5-4. While this diagram may at first appear intimidating, it is relatively simple. At the bottom are the different types of physical networks (called *data-link* interfaces), such as Ethernet, Token Ring, and FDDI (Fiber Distributed Data Interface). Other media types are supported here as well, but they are not listed. Above this are transport protocols that package data for transmission and maintain connections between devices (including internetworks) such as IPX, TCP/IP, and AppleTalk. At the top are protocols that provide users with control over file systems and network commands. These three groups are summarized as follows:

■ **Application and service protocols**   These are the high-level protocols that define how applications use the underlying communication systems to interact with applications on other systems.

Understanding Network Technology

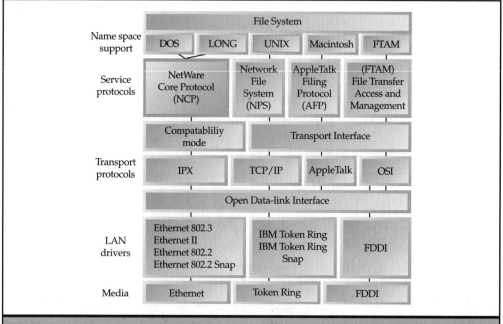

Figure 5-4.   *Protocol support in the NetWare 5 environment. Notice where the compatibility mode drivers and their interfaces are located*

- **Transport and network protocols**   These protocols define data packaging and addressing methods and help establish communication sessions so network nodes can exchange information.

- **Data-link protocols**   These are the protocols that control the flow of data on the physical network and define actual physical components such as connectors and cable and the electrical transmission of data bits between systems.

Communication protocols are generally described in the context of a layered environment. As you can see in Figure 5-5, there are lower layers and upper layers, and each layer must communicate its intentions to the layers just above or below it in order to communicate over the network. The International Organization for Standardization (ISO) has defined a standard model for describing communication protocols, as discussed next.

Open Systems Interconnection (OSI) Model

The OSI model defines a layered communication architecture as defined by the International Organization for Standardization (ISO). The OSI model (and any defined communication protocol, for that matter) was designed to help vendors create products

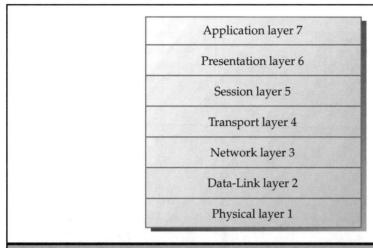

Figure 5-5.   *The Open Systems Interconnection (OSI) model as defined by the*
International Organization for Standardization (ISO)

that work with other vendors' products. This model is used to describe communication techniques and is pictured in Figure 5-5.

Figure 5-6 compares the OSI protocol stack to NetWare protocols and other protocols you are likely to encounter when connecting NetWare with other clients and servers.

Note   *Protocols are usually loaded into a computer as software drivers.*

Each layer of the protocol stack defines a specific set of functions. An application at the uppermost layer interacts with the layer below when it needs to send information to another system on the network. Each area between these layers is referred to as a *boundary layer*. The request is packaged in one layer and passed down to the next layer for outgoing transmissions, as shown in Figure 5-7. If a computer is receiving information, it is passed up through its protocol stack. This layered approach is defined further under "How Layered Architecture Works" later in this chapter.

The following sections describe each layer of the OSI protocol model so you can compare how the NetWare IPX/SPX, TCP/IP, AppleTalk, and Microsoft protocols fit into this scheme.

Application Layer

Applications access the underlying network services using defined procedures in this layer. It includes a range of applications that handle file transfers, terminal sessions, and message exchange (for example, electronic mail). OSI Application layer protocols are listed here:

■ The NetWare Core Protocol (NCP), which provides NetWare file, print, and other operating system services to clients

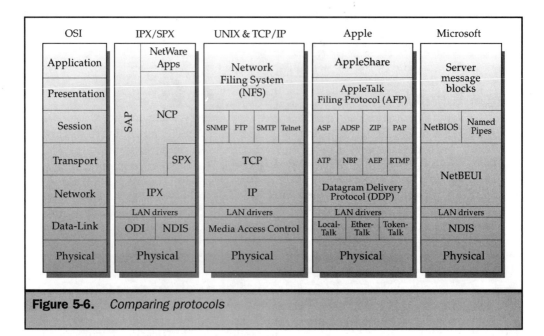

Figure 5-6. *Comparing protocols*

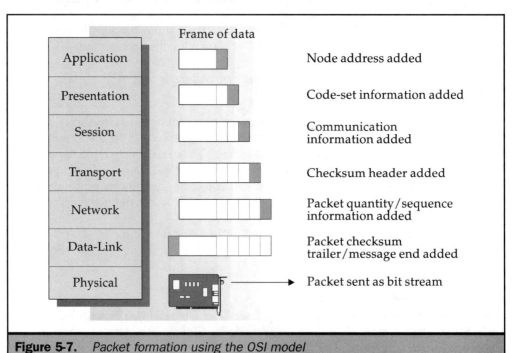

Figure 5-7. *Packet formation using the OSI model*

- NetWare applications and Novell Loadable Modules (NLMs)
- Directory services, such as Novell Directory Services (NDS)
- Message and electronic mail handling systems

Presentation Layer

Protocols at the Presentation layer are part of the operating system and applications that users run in a workstation. Information is formatted for display or printing in this layer. Codes within the data, such as tabs or special graphics sequences, are interpreted. Data encryption and the translation of other character sets are also handled in this layer.

Session Layer

The Session layer coordinates the exchange of information between systems by using conversational techniques, or dialog. Dialogs are not always required, but some applications may require a way of knowing where to restart the transmission of data if a connection is temporarily lost, or they may require a periodic dialogue to indicate the end of one data set and the start of a new one.

Transport Layer

The Transport layer provides a high level of control for moving information between systems, including sophisticated error handling, prioritization, and security features. The Transport layer provides quality service and accurate delivery by maintaining a "virtual connection" between two systems. That means it controls the sequence of packets, regulates traffic flow, recognizes duplicate packets, and looks for missing packets. For example, if a packet is missing, the transport layer protocol at the receiving system communicates with the transport layer protocol at the sending system and requests a retransmission. The SPX and TCP protocols provide connection-oriented transport layer services.

Network Layer

The Network layer defines protocols for transmitting packets over router-connected internetworks. It is concerned with data transmission and switching procedures, and it hides such procedures from upper layers. The Network layer can provide a "global" addressing scheme in which each node has a network address that is independent of the physical node address. This lets any node on the network send packets to any other node, regardless of the underlying physical topology. Routers and switches on the network are responsible for forwarding network-addressed packets to the proper node.

Data-Link Layer

The Data-Link layer defines the rules for sending and receiving information across the physical connection between two systems. This layer encodes and frames data for transmission, in addition to providing error detection and control. Because the Data-Link layer can provide error control, higher layers may not need to handle such services.

However, when reliable media are used, you can gain a performance advantage by not handling error control in this layer. This layer knows about physical network addresses for specific network segments. Bridges operate at this level and are thus only capable of forwarding packets between nodes on the same physical network.

Physical Layer

The Physical layer defines the physical characteristics of the interface, such as mechanical components and connectors, electrical aspects such as voltage levels representing binary values, and functional aspects such as setting up, maintaining, and taking down the physical link. Well-known Physical layer interfaces for data communication include EIA RS-232 and RS-449, the successor to RS-232. Well-known local area network (LAN) systems are Ethernet, Token Ring, and Fiber Distributed Data Interface (FDDI).

How Layered Architecture Works

Layering is a design approach that specifies different functions and services at levels in a "protocol stack." Developers use communication protocols to design products that interoperate with compliant products developed by other vendors. For example, if you want to create a network interface card that can connect to a network on which other vendors' cards are present, you would conform to the protocols defined for that network.

Each layer in the protocol stack communicates with the layers just above and below it. Note the following:

- Each layer has a set of services.
- Services are defined by standard protocols.
- Lower layers provide services to upper layers.

When systems communicate, peer protocols at each level in the protocol stack of each system coordinate the communication process. For example, the Transport layer in one system coordinates its activities with the Transport layer in the other system.

As an analogy, imagine the creation of a formal agreement between two embassies. At the top, formal negotiations take place between ambassadors, but in the background, diplomats and officers work on documents, define procedures, and perform other activities. Diplomats have rank, and each rank performs some service for higher-ranking diplomats. The ambassador at the highest level passes orders down to a lower-level diplomat and uses services provided by that diplomat. At the same time, the diplomat below the ambassador in rank is coordinating his or her activities with a diplomat of equal rank at the other embassy. Each diplomat follows established diplomatic procedures defined at each level of operation. For example, a diplomatic officer at a particular level may provide language translation services or technical documentation. This officer communicates with a peer at the other embassy regarding translation and documentation procedures.

In the diplomatic world, a diplomat at one embassy simply picks up the phone and calls a peer at another embassy. In the world of network communication, peer messages must be put in packets and passed down to lower levels where they are sent across the physical network to the other computer (see Figure 5-8).

Entities are analogous to diplomatic officers and reside in each protocol layer. When an entity needs to communicate a message to an entity in another computer, it formats the message information as *protocol control information* (*PCI*) and places it in a *protocol data unit* (*PDU*). Each layer then adds its PDU to a *packet* of information that is sent to the next lower layer.

Eventually, the packet reaches the lowest physical protocol layer, where it is *framed* into a stream of data bits and sent across the physical connection (Ethernet, Token Ring, etc.). When the packet arrives at its destination, it moves up through the protocol stack, and information for each entity is stripped off the packet and passed to entities in appropriate layers.

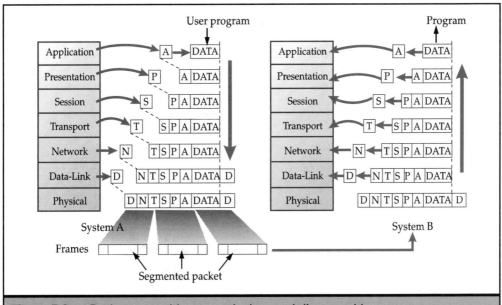

Figure 5-8.   *Packet assembly, transmission, and disassembly*

Some of the information added at each level is listed here:

Protocol Layer	Type of Information
Application	Destination node address information
Presentation	Code-set information added
Session	Communication session information added
Transport	Checksum header added
Network	Packet quantity/sequence information added
Data-Link	Packet checksum trailer/message end added
Physical	Convert to bit stream and transmit

Figure 5-9 illustrates *service access points (SAPs)*, the connection points that entities in adjacent layers use to communicate messages; they are like addresses, and any protocol layer may have several simultaneous SAPs active at one time.

We can describe this process by using the analogy of a communication procedure at the embassy (although, with all the paperwork involved, you might think it is wasteful). Assume an ambassador wants to send a message to an ambassador at another embassy. He or she creates the message and passes it to an assistant, who is a diplomat at the next rank down. This diplomat places the message in an envelope and writes instructions on the envelope addressed to his or her peer at the other embassy. This package then goes down to the next-ranking diplomat, who puts it in another envelope and writes

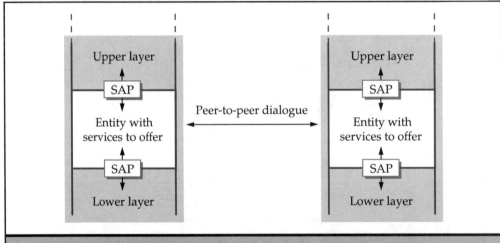

Figure 5-9. *Interlayer communication in a protocol stack*

instructions on this envelope for peers at the other embassy. This process continues down the ranks until it reaches the "physical" level, where the package is delivered by a courier to the other embassy. At the other embassy, each diplomat reads the message addressed to him or her and passes the inner envelope up to the next-ranking officer.

More About Packets and Frames

A *packet* is a package of data that is exchanged between devices over a data communication link. The data in the packet might be

- Messages and commands, such as a request for service
- Control codes for managing the session, such as codes that indicate communication errors and the need for retransmission
- Data, such as the contents of a file

One of the main reasons for packetizing and framing information is that any errors on the communication link only affect a small, discrete part of the transmission, which is easily retransmitted. In addition, you can interleave packets from several sources and simultaneously share a link between end points using a process called *multiplexing*. This is shown in Figure 5-10. Note that stations A, B, and C are transmitting over the same cable, but packets are intermeshed and sent one after the other. At the other end, which might be a router, the packets are separated out of the transmission and sent to an appropriate destination, which might be along another network path.

The terms *packet* and *frame* are often used interchangeably, but a *frame* is really a block of bit-stream data on a physical transmission medium. It might hold all or parts of a packet. The Data-Link layer communicates directly with the physical network

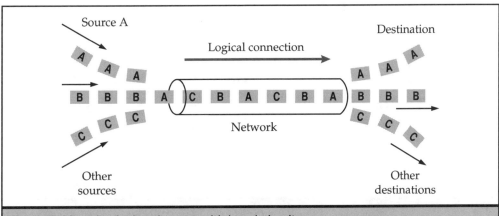

Figure 5-10.   *Logical paths on multiplexed circuits*

where the packets are broken up into frames for transmission over a network link, as shown in Figure 5-11. On a local area network, the type of network (Ethernet, Token Ring, etc.) defines the frame size and how much data you can put in each frame. For example, Ethernet defines frames that can hold up to 1,514 bytes of packet data. With some networks, the frame size is variable, but new high-speed networks define small fixed-size "cells" that are much easier to handle at switching points on the network. Note the following:

- The Data-Link layer is subdivided into the Logical Link Control (LLC) and Medium Access Control (MAC) layers.

- The lower MAC layer is where each type of network (Ethernet, Token Ring, etc.) resides. The LLC serves as a "switching" layer to direct packets to a specific network interface card if more than one exists in a computer.

Large interconnected networks may have many different paths (networks) that a packet can follow to get to its destination, as shown in Figure 5-12. These networks are interconnected with routers. As packets traverse the networks, routers use addressing information in the packets to direct them to their destination or to keep them off of networks where they don't belong, as follows:

- **Packet forwarding**   A process performed by a network node when it forwards packets to the next appropriate node or router in a network.

- **Packet filtering**   A way of sorting and selecting packets so that only packets of a specific type or with a specific address are transmitted.

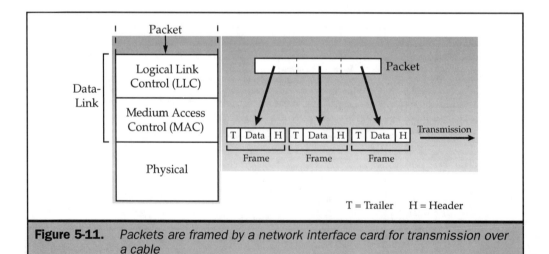

Figure 5-11.   *Packets are framed by a network interface card for transmission over a cable*

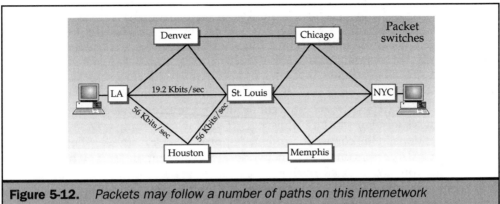

Figure 5-12.   *Packets may follow a number of paths on this internetwork*

Routers can determine in advance the best path that a packet should take to its destination and adjust the path if it becomes congested. Routers use algorithms to determine efficient paths in conjunction with other routers on the network. Administrators can also manually configure routers, based on the cost or speed of routes.

Connection-Oriented and Connectionless Protocols

Communication protocols are either *connection-oriented* or *connectionless*, depending on whether a program needs to contact and maintain a dialogue (connection-oriented) with the recipient, or simply send a message without any prior contact (connectionless) and expect the recipient to get everything in order.

■ In the connection-oriented method, two end stations set up a communication "session" with each other so they can "reliably" transmit data.

■ In the connectionless method, the sender just starts sending packets to a destination without any prior contact. No special session link is set up in advance that might allow for more reliable communication. The receiver must determine whether packets are corrupted as they arrive or if they are missing, and request a retransmission.

Assume you want to send a letter to a friend in another town. The letters are analogous to the packets of data sent across a computer network. You call your friend and tell him or her that you are sending a letter. Your friend waits for the letter and calls you if it doesn't arrive. This is a connection-oriented approach. The connectionless approach is more like sending a letter to someone you don't know and who doesn't know you are even sending a letter. If the letter doesn't arrive, you might not hear back from the person unless he or she really needs the information in the letter and calls you to request another mailing.

Connectionless methods are often called *datagram delivery services*. Each data packet is an independent entity that travels on its own over the network usually as a broadcast type message. There is no initial negotiation between the sender and receiver. The sender simply starts sending datagrams. There is also no acknowledgment that the destination received a packet. The destination must determine if a packet is missing (based on information in other packets) and request a retransmission.

When it comes to performance, the connectionless strategy usually wins if the transmission is short. For short transmissions, it's not worth setting up a session in advance as is done in the connection-oriented approach, so transmission begins immediately. Also, errors on modern networks are infrequent (unless you have a problem that you haven't fixed), so it's possible to do without some of the reliability features of the connection-oriented approach. For long transmissions, the connection-oriented approach is often better. This is mainly because a "virtual circuit" or path is set up through the network between the stations. This reduces the amount of header information required for each packet to direct it to its destination, and allows more data per packet.

 The programs you use determine which type of protocol is used. You don't normally make this decision.

In the NetWare 4 environment, the native SPX protocol provided connection-oriented services, and IPX provided connectionless services. In the NetWare 5 environment using the Transmission Control Protocol/Internet Protocol (TCP/IP) suite, TCP provides connection-oriented services, while User Datagram Protocol (UDP) provides connectionless transport services.

 NetWare IPX networks by default require that workstations acknowledge the receipt of a packet to the sender of that packet. This is not connection-oriented, but it is not fully connectionless either.

Novell NetWare 5 includes a remote monitoring program called RCONSOLE, which allows administrators to operate the NetWare server console from their own desktop computers. The connection between the server and the workstation usually lasts for minutes or hours or even days and produces a relatively steady stream of data as console screens are updated. This is an example of the need for a connection-oriented link and, in fact, the RCONSOLE program uses either the SPX or TCP protocol to maintain communication.

Virtual Circuits

Virtual circuits are connection-oriented communication links that are typically implemented in high-speed packet-switching technologies, as discussed in Chapter 8. They mimic a physical circuit such as the connection you get when you call another person on the telephone. However, the circuits are *logical* in nature. The focus is to keep two end stations in contact, even though the underlying physical communication path over which packets travel may change.

 This term logical *is used often when discussing network technology. Networks are often viewed as "clouds" with many interconnected pathways between systems. When a packet travels from sender to receiver through this network, its path is called a logical connection.*

Virtual circuits exist on large packet-switched networks that have been built by the telephone companies or other carriers. A company contracts to use this network to provide any-to-any connections among its distant offices. A virtual circuit is a path through this network that can provide the benefits of a permanent connection but that is much more cost-effective than a dedicated link.

Another advantage of virtual circuits is that the path through the mesh network is predefined, so most addressing information can be removed to make more room for data and improve transmission speeds.

You contract with a service provider and define the end points of a virtual circuit in advance. You then pay for what you use. A *permanent virtual circuit (PVC)* forms a permanent and guaranteed logical link through the network.

Protocols Supported by NetWare 5

Now we take a closer look at the protocols used in the network environment. First we look at the higher-level application protocols that form the core of NetWare 5, and then we look at the communication protocols. The native NetWare 5 communication protocol is now TCP/IP, but it is common to use the IPX/SPX protocol as well. Both protocols can be used simultaneously through the use of the Migration Gateway. NetWare 5 also supports the AppleTalk protocol, which lets Apple Macintosh users connect with a NetWare 5 server and use it for file storage.

NetWare Core Protocol (NCP)

The NetWare Core Protocol (NCP) is a set of service protocols that a file server's operating system follows to accept and respond to service requests from clients and other servers. Several services are provided by NCP:

- File access (opening and closing files; reading and writing data to and from files)
- File locking
- Security
- Tracking of resource allocation

- Event notification
- Novell Directory Services and synchronization with other servers
- Connection and communication
- Print services management
- Network management

Network "requester" software running at a client workstation redirects commands for network services to an appropriate server. For example, a user can request a file from a local drive or from a network server. The requester software directs local commands to the local operating system and commands for network services to an appropriate server on the network. However, to the user, the network drive appears as a local drive.

Network administrators or technicians can track what users are doing on the network by analyzing NCP with a protocol analyzer. You might do this to troubleshoot the network and monitor excess traffic loads from some workstations. Each NCP packet contains a code that identifies the type of service requested or being serviced. These codes are easily identified by most protocol analyzers, and you can use filters to see a particular type of service or traffic from one workstation. Following are brief descriptions of some of the calls:

- Login and logout requests
- Directory handling requests (such as create, list, rename, delete, and others)
- File handling requests (such as open, close, create, erase, and others)
- Server requests (clear connections, down the file server, get disk information, get file server information, send messages, and others)
- Messaging services (send or receive messages)
- Printer services
- File locking and unlocking services

This list only describes the general category of service requests and responses. There are hundreds of calls, each with a specific purpose and code. For example, the request "Create Directory" has a specific request type number (2222), a function code (22), and a subfunction code (10). These codes appear in packet listings during protocol analysis. For the purposes of this discussion, these codes are not important. However, they do point out how workstations communicate with servers and how you can track the activities with a protocol analyzer.

For example, you might want to track a user's activities because you suspect the user might be engaging in unauthorized activities, or you might want to track the activities of a user for auditing purposes. Using ManageWise, you can filter out the packets produced for a single user's workstation and produce a log of every service requested by the user. Alternatively, a network device might be flooding the network with excess packets and you need to determine which device it is.

By following the stream of NCP requests and responses between a server and its client, you can watch users log in and log out, start applications, access files on the server, communicate with other users, and perform a number of other activities. However, for the most part, you track packet flow to isolate problems or bottlenecks in communication.

NetWare Open Data-link Interface

NetWare provides simultaneous support for multiple protocols in clients and servers through its Open Data-link Interface (ODI) standard, as shown in Figure 5-13. This interface provides a way to support multiple transport protocols on a single network card, or to support one or more transport protocols over multiple network cards. The LSL (Link Support Layer) serves as a switching layer. It diverts any upper-layer transport protocol packet to any lower network, or vice versa.

ODI provides the following benefits:

- A single network card interfaces with different protocol stacks.

- A logical network board is created that processes packets from different systems. Those packets can be sent on the same network cabling system attached to a single network card.

- The workstation can use a different protocol stack without being rebooted.

- ODI allows NetWare servers and workstations to communicate with a variety of other systems, including mainframes that use different protocol stacks.

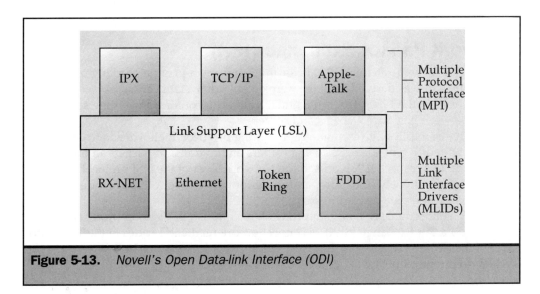

Figure 5-13. *Novell's Open Data-link Interface (ODI)*

■ ODI standardizes the development of network interface card drivers; vendors no longer need to worry about writing their drivers to fit a specific protocol stack. Instead, drivers are written to attach to the Link Support Layer (LSL).

You can see the component layers of ODI in Figure 5-13. At the bottom are the interfaces for different types of network interface cards. At the top are the protocols that interface with the NetWare operating system. In between is the Link Support Layer, which directs traffic between the components.

Multiple Link Interface (MLI)

The Multiple Link Interface (MLI) layer is an interface where device drivers for the network interface card are attached. The device drivers are written by vendors of network interface cards to match the Novell specification of the Link Support Layer. Drivers are referred to as Multiple Link Interface Drivers (MLIDs).

Link Support Layer (LSL)

The LSL provides a link for drivers at the bottom and protocols at the top. It acts as a switching board, directing network traffic from MLIDs to the proper protocol, and vice versa. When a packet arrives at a network interface card, it is processed by the card's MLID and passed to the LSL. The LSL determines which protocol stack the packet should go to and hands it to the protocol. The packet passes up through the protocol stack in the normal way, where it is handled by higher-level protocols.

Multiple Protocol Interface (MPI)

The Multiple Protocol Interface (MPI) provides an interface for the connection of protocol stacks, such as IPX, TCP/IP, and AppleTalk. Other protocol stacks such as OSI and SNA are also available.

Internetwork Packet Exchange (IPX)

Internetwork Packet Exchange (IPX) is the built-in peer-to-peer networking protocol for NetWare 4. It was derived from the Xerox Network System (XNS) protocol, which was developed in the 1970s. IPX is the underlying protocol for transmitting service requests between NetWare 4 clients and servers.

As its name implies, IPX is an internetworking protocol. It allows you to connect networks with different addresses using routers and to transmit packets among those networks. In this respect, IPX works in the Network layer of the OSI protocol model to create and maintain network addresses throughout the network that are independent of the physical and data-link addresses.

IPX is a connectionless datagram protocol. In contrast, IPX's sister protocol, Sequenced Packet Exchange (SPX), is connection-oriented and resides in the Transport layer of the OSI protocol model. It sets up communication sessions between two systems to monitor the flow of data.

Installing IPX

IPX/SPX is installed as an optional protocol when you install a NetWare 5 server. At workstations, the protocol is installed automatically. You install workstation support by installing the Client 32 software for either DOS or Windows. Current versions of the software include the Novell Open Data-link Interface (ODI), which provides a way to load multiple protocol stacks such as TCP/IP and IPX/SPX side by side.

The Client 32 software is basically a redirection utility that looks at commands issued by the user and either sends them to the local operating system or sends them out over the network to a NetWare server as appropriate. If requests are destined for the network, the requester software packages the requests in a TCP/IP packet and hands it to the network interface card, which sends the packet as a bit stream. Actually, packets can have several different destinations:

- A server on the same LAN segment
- A workstation on the same LAN segment
- A workstation or server on another LAN segment

The header information in the packet contains a network address, and when the packet is sent over an internetwork, routers see this information and forward the packet to an appropriate network segment.

NetWare 5 supports a wide variety of data links and the transmission of TCP/IP and IPX/SPX over them. Supported links include Ethernet, Token Ring, Fiber Distributed Data Interface (FDDI), and others.

In the NetWare environment, the following protocols rely on TCP for network services:

NetWare Core Protocol (NCP)

NCP is the principal protocol for transmitting information between a NetWare 5 server and its clients. NCP handles logon requests and many other types of requests to the file system and the printing system. TCP is the underlying protocol that carries these transmissions.

Transmission Control Protocol/Internet Protocol (TCP/IP)

Transmission Control Protocol/Internet Protocol (*TCP/IP*) is the traditional transport protocol suite for the Internet and UNIX systems. It has strong wide area networking capability, and its development is open and supported by the U.S. government. Due to this, it is now fully supported as a transport protocol in almost every network environment. With TCP/IP support everywhere, interoperability among different systems has also increased.

The development goals for the TCP/IP protocol suite were to allow communication among a variety of independent, multivendor systems. In 1983, TCP/IP protocols became the official transport mechanism for the Department of Defense Internet, which evolved into a system of interconnected networks spanning the globe.

Understanding Network
Technology

TCP/IP continues to evolve. One of the most important aspects of TCP/IP's development was the program of testing and certification carried out by the government to ensure that developers met published TCP/IP standards, which are published and available to the public free of licensing arrangements. This ensured that developers didn't alter the standard to fit their own needs, possibly causing confusion in the rest of the TCP/IP community. Today, the use of TCP/IP protocols virtually assures internetworking and interoperability among systems.

 TCP and UDP are sister protocols. TCP is a higher-level connection-oriented protocol and UDP is a lower-level connectionless protocol.

Transmission Control Protocol (TCP)

The Transmision Control Protocol (TCP) protocol sets up a two-way (duplex) connection between two systems using the *sockets interface*. A socket is one end of a communication that specifies the address of the computer and a "port" within that computer that a running application is using to communicate. You might think of this arrangement as you would a telephone within a building—the building has an address, and the telephone number is like a port within that building that connects you with a specific person. Likewise, a socket is a connection to an application or process running within a computer.

TCP communication sessions are connection-oriented and have the following features:

■ Flow control provides a way for two systems to actively cooperate in the transmission of packets to prevent overflows and lost packets.

■ Acknowledgment of packet receipt lets the sender know the recipient has received packets.

■ End-to-end sequencing ensures that packets arrive in order so the destination doesn't need to put them in order if they arrive out of sequence.

■ A checksumming feature is used to ensure the integrity of packets.

■ Retransmission of corrupt or lost packets can be handled in a timely and efficient manner.

User Datagram Protocol (UDP)

A TCP connection-oriented session requires a setup phase, a take-down phase, and a lot of monitoring and possibly more excess traffic from overhead than is necessary for some data transmissions. During the development of TCP, Denny Cohen at USC recommended splitting the TCP protocol to accommodate "timeliness rather than accuracy." He argued that all the flow control and error-checking features just described, as well as the overhead of setting up a connection-oriented session, were not always necessary. What was needed was a way to quickly get data to another system, and then let that system handle all the error checking and sequencing on its own. Thus, the User Datagram Protocol (UDP) was born. UDP was also created to provide a way for applications to access the connectionless features of IP.

Note   *Both TCP and UDP use IP.*

UDP is a connectionless communication protocol that by itself provides a datagram service. Datagrams, as mentioned earlier, are self-contained packets of information that are forwarded by routers based on their address and the routing table information contained in the routers. Datagrams can be addressed to single nodes or multiple nodes. There is no flow control, acknowledgment of receipt, error checking, or sequencing. Datagrams may traverse different paths to the destination and thus arrive out of sequence. The receiving station is responsible for resequencing and determining if packets are lost. UDP handles congestion by simply discarding packets. Resequencing and error handling are taken care of by upper-layer protocols, not by UDP. Thus, UDP is fast, efficient, and well-suited to modern networks and telecommunication systems that already provide relatively reliable service.

IP works on a number of local and wide area networks. When IP runs in the LAN environment on an Ethernet network, for example, the data field in the Ethernet frame holds the IP packet, and a specific field in the frame indicates that IP information is enclosed. IP uses an addressing scheme that works independently of the network addressing scheme. For example, every Ethernet adapter has a factory-assigned hardware address referred to as the Medium Access Control (MAC) address. IP does not use this address and instead uses an assigned address for each node, as described next.

IP Addressing and Naming

Every node on a TCP/IP network using IPv4 requires a 4-byte (32-bit) numeric address that identifies both a network and a local host or node on the network. This address is written as four numbers separated by dots; for example, 192.100.10.5. In most cases, the network administrator sets up these addresses when installing new workstations; however, software is available that lets workstations query a server for a dynamically assigned address using Dynamic Host Configuration Protocol (DHCP).

The assignment of addresses can be arbitrary within a company or organization, but if the company plans to connect with the Internet in the near future, it is wise to obtain registered addresses from the Internet Network Information Center (InterNIC) in Chantilly, Virginia, at (800) 365-3642. With the growth of the Internet, it is recommended that all organizations obtain registered addresses to avoid address conflicts in the future.

A service called the Domain Name System (DNS) is used to map IP addresses to easily remembered names. These are the Internet names you encounter when sending electronic mail or contacting Internet hosts. For example, the author's numeric address might be represented as:

    bpayne@kramerkent.com

where *bpayne* is the network name or handle, *kramerkent* is the host system, and *com* is a three-character domain identifier.

Application Protocols

The following applications have been built on top of the TCP/IP protocol suite, and you are likely to encounter them when working at TCP/IP installations, including the Internet:

- **Network File System (NFS)** A filing system for UNIX hosts that is shareable and distributed; originally developed by Sun Microsystems
- **Simple Network Management Protocol (SNMP)** A network management protocol that collects information about the network and reports it to administrators
- **File Transfer Protocol (FTP)** A protocol that enables file transfers between workstations and a UNIX host or Novell NetWare NFS
- **Simple Mail Transfer Protocol (SMTP)** A protocol that enables electronic messaging
- **Telnet** DEC VT100 and VT330 terminal emulation
- **Netscape and Microsoft Internet Explorer** Popular "browsers" that let you navigate on the World Wide Web

Chapter 6

Local Area Networks and Cabling

91

A network is a modular and adaptable communication system that can be customized to meet many different site requirements. Its modularity makes it easy to add new components or move existing ones, and its adaptability makes changes and upgrades easy. This chapter discusses the technology of local area networks (LANs), which are networks you install within offices, buildings, and in campus areas.

Primarily, we cover Ethernet, Token Ring, and wireless technologies. These topologies are considered LANs because they have signal and cabling limitations that restrict them to local areas. However, you can interconnect these topologies to build larger networks by using bridges, routers, and wide area networking techniques as discussed in the next few chapters.

 Each network type such as Ethernet and Token Ring uses a specific topology and method for accessing the network. Some people refer to "the Ethernet topology," while others refer to "the Ethernet media access method," or just "Ethernet networks."

LANs Are Data-Link Devices

As discussed in Chapter 5, the OSI (Open Systems Interconnection) model is a communication protocol standard that helps developers create interoperable networking systems. The OSI model defines a layered architecture for differentiating each of the communication processes required to transmit data between networked systems and applications. The bottom layer of this stack defines the actual physical components, such as connectors and cable and the electrical signals for transmitting data bits. Above this layer is the Data-Link layer, which defines how data is packaged for transport over the physical network. This chapter describes components of the Physical and Data-Link layers, such as network interface cards (NICs) and cable that you use to create local area networks. Similar Data-Link and Network layer components for creating internetworks and wide area networks are discussed in Chapters 7 and 8.

Because the Data-Link layer sits just above the Physical layer, it defines protocols for directly interacting with the physical components of the network. It controls the flow of information across the link, and it adds its own error checking to the packets it sends out across the links.

The Institute of Electrical and Electronics Engineers (IEEE) has defined two important sublayers in the Data-Link layer, as pictured in Figure 6-1:

- **Medium Access Control (MAC) sublayer**   This layer is where each of the different networking topologies such as Ethernet and Token Ring are defined. All of the specifications for how a network interface card (NIC) accesses the cable are handled here.

- **Logical Link Control (LLC) sublayer**   In some cases, a computer or server will have more than one NIC and these NICs might be for different network

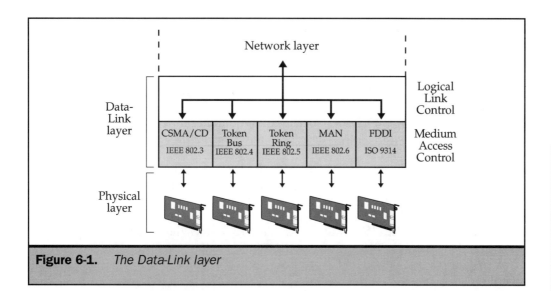

Figure 6-1. *The Data-Link layer*

topologies. For example, a server might have two Ethernet cards and one Token Ring card installed. When a packet is sent and travels down the protocol stack, it hits the LLC sublayer and is diverted to the correct network interface card.

Two interesting protocol standards that operate in the Data-Link layer are Novell's Open Data-link Interface and Microsoft's Network Driver Interface Standard:

- **Open Data-link Interface (ODI)**   This Novell standard provides a way to run two or more communication protocols in one computer on one network adapter or multiple network adapters. For example, it's possible to transfer both TCP/IP and IPX protocols over a single network card.

- **Network Driver Interface Standard (NDIS)**   This Microsoft standard provides the same multiple protocol support as the Novell ODI standard. The two standards essentially compete in the LAN world.

Types of Local Area Networks

The IEEE 802 committee, or Project 802, defines local area network (LAN) standards. Most of the standards were established by the committees in the 1980s when personal computer networking was just beginning to emerge.

Note   *Not all the standards are listed here, only the most popular for local area networking.*

802.1 INTERNETWORK DEFINITION   This standard defines the relationship between the IEEE 802 standards and the ISO Open Systems Interconnection (OSI) reference model. For example, this committee defines a 48-bit LAN station address for all the 802 standards so every adapter can have a unique address. That means you can install any NIC in your network without a hardware address conflict.

802.2 LOGICAL LINK CONTROL   This standard defines the IEEE Logical Link Control (LLC) protocol, previously described and pictured previously in Figure 6-1.

802.3 CSMA/CD NETWORKS   The IEEE 802.3 standard (ISO 8802-3) defines the carrier sense multiple access/collision detection (CSMA/CD) cable access method used in Ethernet.

802.5 TOKEN RING NETWORKS   This standard defines the access protocols, cabling, and interface for Token Ring LANs. IBM made the standard popular. It uses a token-passing access method and is physically wired in a star topology but forms a logical ring.

802.6 METROPOLITAN AREA NETWORKS (MANs)   This standard defines a high-speed protocol in which attached stations share a dual fiber-optic bus using an access method called Distributed Queue Dual Bus (DQDB). The dual bus provides fault tolerance to keep connections alive if the bus is broken. The MAN standard is designed to provide data, voice, and video services in a metropolitan area of approximately 50 kilometers at data rates of 1.5 (T1), 45 (T3), and 155 (OC3) Mbits/sec.

802.9 INTEGRATED DATA AND VOICE NETWORKS   The IEEE 802.9 working group defines the integration of voice, data, and video traffic to 802 LANs and Integrated Services Digital Networks (ISDNs). Nodes defined in the specification include telephones, computers, and video coders/decoders (codecs). The specification has been called Integrated Voice and Data, or IVD.

802.11 WIRELESS NETWORKING   This committee defines standards for wireless networks, such as spread-spectrum radio, narrowband radio, infrared, and transmission over power lines. The committee is also working on the standardization of wireless interfaces for network computing, in which users connect into computer systems using pen-based computers, personal digital assistants (PDAs), and other portable devices.

802.12 DEMAND PRIORITY (100VG-ANYLAN)   This committee defines the 100 Mbit/sec Ethernet standard with demand priority access method proposed by Hewlett-Packard and other vendors. The specified cable is four-wire copper twisted-pair, and the demand priority access method uses a central hub to control access to the cable. Priorities are available to support real-time delivery of multimedia information.

Network Interface Methods and Topologies

A network consists of workstations with network interface cards that are connected to cable or are part of a wireless networking scheme. The following sections describe the various topologies, access methods, and cabling techniques for the most popular networks, namely Ethernet and Token Ring.

Topology

The physical layout of the network is its topology, and this topology is defined by network standards. There are bus, star, star/ring, and star/bus topologies, as pictured in Figure 6-2. While these topologies are normally associated with local area networks, campus, metropolitan, and wide area networks may take on some of the same characteristics.

■ **Bus**   A single trunk cable connects each workstation in a daisy-chain topology. Signals are broadcast to all stations, but packets are received only by the station to which they are addressed. IEEE 802.3 Ethernet is the primary bus standard.

■ **Star**   Workstations attach to hubs, and signals are broadcast to all stations or specific stations from the hub.

■ **Star-configured ring (star/ring)**   A ring network in which signals are passed from one station to another in a circle. The physical topology is a star in which workstations branch from concentrators or hubs. IEEE 802.5 Token Ring is the primary star/ring topology.

■ **Star-configured bus (star/bus)**   A network that has groups of star-configured workstations connected with long linear bus trunks.

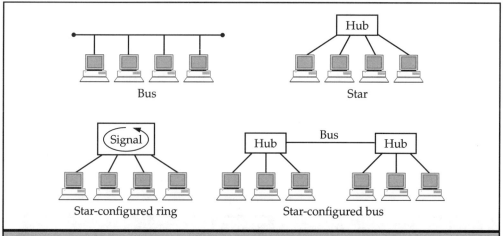

Figure 6-2.   *Local Area Network (LAN) topologies*

If all your workstations are in a row—such as in a classroom or down a hallway in an office building—then a bus topology using coaxial cable (Ethernet) is easy to install and manage. However, breaks in the cable can cripple the whole network. Ethernet 10Base-T is a star/bus topology that uses inexpensive twisted-pair cable to connect workstations to a central hub. A break in a cable only affects the workstation attached to the cable segment. On an Ethernet bus network and an Ethernet star/bus network, workstations signals are broadcast to all workstations in the same segment. Table 6-1 lists the various forms of network topologies and the maximum length of segments in each.

An internetwork consists of department or workstation LANs interconnected with translation bridges or routers. A backbone cable is often used in the local environment, such as a building, but public services like the phone company can provide metropolitan and wide area links. The three main topologies are pictured in Figure 6-3 and are discussed here:

- **Backbone network**   A backbone network is typically found in office or campus environments, in which department networks or networks in buildings are interconnected over the backbone cables. Bridges or routers manage traffic flow between attached network segments and the backbone.

- **Mesh network**   A mesh network contains multiple redundant pathways through interconnected networks. If one path fails or is congested, a packet

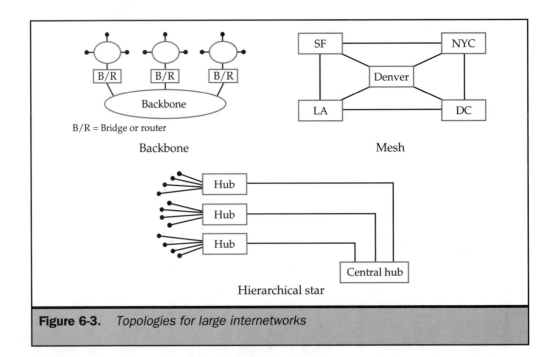

Figure 6-3.   *Topologies for large internetworks*

Network Topology	Maximum Segment Length
Thin Ethernet (bus)	185 meters (607 feet)
Twisted-pair Ethernet (star/bus)	100 meters (330 feet)
Twisted-pair Token Ring (star/ring)	100 meters (330 feet) from hub

Table 6-1. *Cable Segment Lengths for Various Topologies*

can use a different path to its destination. Routers are used to interconnect the separate networks.

- **Hierarchical star**   This is the new topological paradigm for structured wiring systems in buildings and campus environments. Departmental star-configured hubs are wired to a central hub that handles internetwork traffic.

Access Methods

One of the most important characteristics of LANs is that they are *shared networks* on which many workstations are attached but only one workstation can transmit at a time. The cable access method defines the protocol that a workstation must follow in order to transmit on a shared cable. The primary access methods are *carrier sense* and *token passing*, which basically define Ethernet and Token Ring networking, respectively. These methods and a new demand priority access method are described here:

- **Carrier sense multiple access/collision detection (CSMA/CD)**   In this scheme, nodes attached to the network listen for a carrier tone on the cable and send information when other devices are not transmitting. Multiple access means that many devices share the same cable. If two or more devices sense that the network is idle, they may attempt to access it simultaneously (contention), causing collisions. Each station must then back off and wait a certain amount of time before attempting to retransmit. The more nodes on the network, the greater the contention, but you can split networks into segments to reduce contention.

- **Token passing**   A token is a special packet on Token Ring, Token Bus, and Fiber Distributed Data Interface (FDDI) networks that controls access to the network. A node that takes control of the token packet holds the right to communicate on the network. Unlike contention-based networks (such as Ethernet), workstations do not attempt to simultaneously access the network. Only the station that obtains an available token transmits.

■ **Demand priority access method**   This is a relatively new access method for 100 Mbit/sec Ethernet. It turns over network access management to a central hub, rather than relying on individual workstations to determine when they should access the cable. Workstations request permission to transmit data based on priority, and the hub transmits the highest-priority data first. Demand priority access was proposed by Hewlett-Packard and AT&T for use in the Ethernet 100VG-AnyLAN (IEEE 802) networking scheme.

Carrier sense methods tend to be faster than token-passing methods, but collisions can bog down the network during heavy traffic loads. Token Ring does not suffer from cable contention problems. However, Token Ring is generally more expensive to implement.

Workstation and Network Addresses

Every node on a network has an assigned *workstation address*, which other nodes use when communicating with it. For Ethernet and Token Ring network adapters, unique addresses are assigned at the factory. For example, the address of an Ethernet and Token Ring network adapter consists of a six-byte address, half of which is a special number identifying the board's manufacturer. The last half of the address is a unique number for the board assigned at the factory. This strategy virtually guarantees that no two Ethernet or Token Ring cards from any vendor will ever have the same address.

A LAN is generally defined as a network cable segment with a specific network address that all nodes attached to the network share. If you need to extend the network or add more stations, you can use a repeater or a bridge. When two networks are bridged, they still share the same network address. The bridge provides some unique features that let you expand a network while controlling the amount of traffic on network segments.

If you want to join two networks that have different network addresses, you need a *router*. This is where the routing functions of TCP/IP and IPX/SPX come into play. They provide an addressing scheme that is above the hardware addressing scheme of Ethernet, Token Ring, or other Data-Link layer components. This addressing scheme helps workstations on one network identify a workstation it wants to communicate with on another network. With TCP/IP and IPX/SPX, you can create an addressing scheme that encompasses an entire internetwork of separately addressed subnetworks. Routers know where workstations are located based on their internetwork address, not their Data-Link address.

When you install a NetWare server, you load a driver for the network interface cards in it. You then "bind" a network protocol such as TCP/IP or IPX/SPX to the interface card and provide the network address. You can create a new address, or you can specify the address of an existing network to which the server is attached.

Network Interface Cards (NICs)

You purchase network interface cards (NICs, pronounced *nicks*) to fit the networking topology and cable type you have selected for your network. For example, if you are configuring an Ethernet 10Base-T twisted-pair network (described later), you need a 10Base-T–compatible card with appropriate telephone-style cable jacks and a hub device to interconnect all the workstations. This section covers some of the features you want to look for when purchasing network interface cards.

You evaluate network interface cards based on whether you plan to put them in a server or a workstation:

- **NICs for servers**   These cards must have the best features and provide the best performance, because servers handle traffic for hundreds or thousands of users. These NICs must be able to push packets through their channels at much faster rates than the NICs you install in client workstations. Spend more money on server NICs.

- **NICs for workstations (clients)**   You don't need the fastest and most expensive NICs in the client workstation unless the activities at the workstation require high performance.

This discussion focuses on performance-boosting features for server NICs, but you might want to also consider such features for client workstations that produce higher-than-normal traffic.

Differences in hardware design among interface cards on a network can slow performance. For example, a network card with a PCI interface can transmit faster than a 16-bit card. If the PCI card transmits to a workstation with an 8-bit card, the 8-bit card can get overrun with data. This can tie up the network transmission longer than normal. To alleviate this problem, vendors place memory buffers on interface cards to hold incoming data. The sender can then complete its data transmissions and free up the network much faster.

Performance bottlenecks are also introduced when moving packets in and out of a server or client workstation. The following techniques are usually implemented, some of which are more efficient than others. The price of a NIC depends on its packet-processing capability.

Types of NICs

There are four basic technologies associated with NIC cards. Each technology has pros and cons associated with it. The primary differences are the manner in which the NIC card communicates with the system processor and memory.

SHARED MEMORY   With the shared memory technique, NICs have their own memory that the system processor can access directly, or a block of memory is set aside in the server. If the memory is on the NIC, the CPU thinks the memory is part of its own system memory and accesses it accordingly. This can lead to problems if you are not careful to ensure that the memory area allocated to the NIC is not used by another card or process (a driver or application, for example). These cards are appropriate for clients but not for servers.

> **Note**
>
> *When you set up a shared memory card, you set switches on the card or set its startup commands to specify the memory area the card will use. The adapter's manual refers to these as base memory addresses. The shared memory starts at the base memory address and extends the length of the shared memory, which may be 8K, 16K, or 32K. You need to ensure that no other card or processor uses this memory. If so, you must change the base memory address of the NIC or the adapter that it conflicts with.*

DIRECT MEMORY ACCESS (DMA)   Some NICs implement a direct memory access (DMA) controller to take control of the bus and transfer data from the NIC's buffer directly into a designated memory area on the workstation or server. Some cards have built-in DMA controllers, and some rely on the workstation's DMA controller. These cards have been found to be slow and are not recommended for servers.

BUS MASTERING   With the bus mastering technique, a network adapter can transfer information directly to system memory without interrupting the system processor. Cards that use this method provide a form of enhanced DMA by assuming control of the system bus. Bus mastering is possible only on PCI, MCA, and EISA computers. Bus mastering techniques can increase performance by 20 to 70 percent for both workstations and servers.

INTELLIGENT BUS MASTERING   NICs that perform bus mastering with their own on-board processors are called *intelligent* NICs. They are primarily designed for server use. The on-board processor relieves the server's CPU of handling the I/O tasks of moving network data in and out of the server. The server CPU can then focus on processing NetWare Core Protocol (NCP) requests and running other processes. NIC cards designed to the new I20 specifications are based on this technology.

Remote-Boot PROMs

PROM stands for programmable read-only memory. Most network cards come with a socket for a remote-boot PROM. You use remote-boot PROMs on diskless workstations that can't boot on their own but instead boot from the network server. A diskless workstation is less expensive than a system with floppy disk and hard disk drives. It is also more secure, because users can't download valuable data to floppy disk or upload viruses and other unauthorized software. Be sure to order the boot PROM for your network cards because it is usually supplied separately.

Cabling

Managers who need to cable networks face critical decisions. Cable and cabling equipment must meet current and future requirements for data transmission, electrical characteristics, and topology. Fortunately, manufacturers have boosted data transfer rates on relatively inexpensive copper twisted-pair wire to where it should meet future demands for high bandwidth to the desktop. In fact, in the future, you will be able to boost throughput on copper cable even beyond the existing 100 Mbit/sec Ethernet technologies by upgrading NICs. Fiber-optic cable can provide high throughput, but it is more expensive than copper cable and harder to install. There are three cases where you might consider fiber-optic cable over data-grade twisted-pair copper cable:

- When linking networks over extremely long distances
- For security reasons (fiber cable does not emit an external signal)
- For extremely high-speed links between interconnected servers, superservers, supercomputers, and mainframes, or as a link to peripherals like disk arrays. Special interface cards are required, such as Fibre Channel link cards.

To help managers make informed decisions and design workable cable systems, a new wiring standard has emerged from the Electronic Industries Association/ Telecommunication Industries Association (EIA/TIA), called the EIA/TIA-568 Commercial Building Wiring Standard. This standard is discussed later in this chapter under "Types of Twisted-Pair Cable" and "Structured Wiring Topology."

There are two types of media for data transmission:

- *Guided media* include metal wire (copper, aluminum, and so on) and fiber-optic cable. Cable is normally installed within buildings or underground conduits. Metal wires include twisted-pair wire and coaxial cable, with copper being the preferred core transmission material for networks. Fiber-optic cable is available with either single or multiple strands of plastic or glass fiber.
- *Unguided media* refer to techniques for transmitting signals through air and space, such as infrared and microwave technologies.

Copper cable is a relatively inexpensive, well-understood technology that is easy to install. It is the cable of choice for the majority of network installations. However, copper cable suffers from various electrical characteristics that impose transmission limitations. For example, it is resistant to the flow of electrons, which limits its distance. It also radiates energy in the form of signals that can be monitored, and is susceptible to external radiation that can distort transmissions. However, new standards support Ethernet transmission at speeds of up to 100 Mbits/sec. In fact, AT&T is working on technology that will boost twisted-pair transmission rates above 500 Mbits/sec.

In contrast, fiber cable transmits light signals (photons) through a core of pure silicon dioxide that is so clear, a three-mile thick window of it would not distort the view. Photonic transmissions produce no emissions outside the cable and are not affected by external radiation. Fiber cable is preferred where security or distance is an issue.

One other overall characteristic of cable has to do with where it gets installed. In order to comply with the National Electrical Code (NEC), all cable installed in the plenum space, which is the airspace between the ceiling and the next floor or roof, must be installed in metal conduit or must meet local fire codes. If the cable should burn, it must not produce noxious or hazardous gases that are pumped to other parts of a structure through the plenum. Consequently, there are normal cable types that are insulated with polyvinyl chloride (PVC) materials, and plenum-rated cables that are insulated with fluoropolymers such as DuPont's Teflon.

The remainder of this discussion concentrates on copper cable and its use in hierarchical wiring structures that employ hubs, switches, and other equipment for emerging networking topologies.

Copper Cable Characteristics

Binary data is transmitted over copper cable by applying a voltage at one end and receiving it at the other. Typically, a voltage of +V volts represents a digital 1, and a voltage of –V volts represents a digital 0. The following cable characteristics directly relate to the type of cable specified in a network topology standard and the reasons for various distance limitations.

BALANCED AND UNBALANCED CIRCUITS   Metal cables that conduct electrical signals are either balanced or unbalanced. Twisted-pair cable is *balanced*: it consists of two wires that are individually surrounded by an insulator. Each wire in the pair has an equal current, but in opposite directions. A single twisted pair forms a circuit. The twisting helps reduce electrical noise as well as external interference, which tends to be canceled by the opposing currents of the wire pair. Coaxial cable is an *unbalanced* medium in which current flows through the signal conductor and returns on the ground. In coaxial cable, mesh shielding that surrounds the conductor serves as the ground and shield.

ELECTRICAL PARAMETERS   Copper cable is subject to the following parameters that are related to the materials used to create the cable and the construction design. These parameters are attenuation, capacitance, delay distortion, and noise. The longer a cable, the more likely you will find signal distortion caused by these parameters. In addition, increasing the frequency of the signal to boost data transfer rates will require a reduction in cable lengths to avoid signal distortion.

- ■ **Attenuation**   Signal transmissions over long distances are subject to attenuation, which is a loss of signal strength or amplitude. Attenuation can cause transmission errors, which in turn reduce performance due to retransmission attempts.

- ■ **Capacitance**   This parameter can distort the signal on a cable. The capacitance is controlled by the dielectric material separating the conductors, and varies as the inverse square of the distance between the conductors. For example, if the distance between conductors is reduced from 0.10 inches to 0.05, the capacitance will increase by four times. Capacitance is a measure of the energy (electric charge) stored by the cable, including the insulator. All cable has known capacitance values that are measured in pico Farads (pF).

- **Impedance and delay distortion**   A signal made up of various frequencies is prone to delay distortion caused by impedance, which is resistance that changes at different frequencies. Decreasing the cable length and/or lowering the transmission frequency can solve the problem.

- **Background noise**   Transmission lines will have some amount of background noise that is generated by the transmitter, adjacent lines, or external sources such as fluorescent lights, motors, microwave ovens, and office equipment such as computers, phones, and copiers. This noise combines with the transmitted signal. The resulting distortion may be minor, but attenuation can cause the amplitude level of the digital signal to decrease to the level of the background noise. Reducing cable length solves the problem.

STRAIGHT CABLE   Straight copper cable consists of copper wires surrounded by an insulator. It is used to connect various peripheral devices over short distances and at low bit rates. Serial cables used to connect modems or serial printers use this type of wire. This wire suffers from cross talk (signals emanating from nearby wires) over long distances. It is not suitable for networks.

TWISTED-PAIR CABLE   Twisted-pair cable consists of copper core wires surrounded by an insulator, as shown in Figure 6-4. Two wires are twisted together to form a pair, and the pair forms a circuit that can transmit data. A cable is a bundle of one or more twisted pairs surrounded by an insulator. Unshielded twisted pair (UTP) is common
in the telephone network. Shielded twisted pair (STP) provides protection against external cross talk. The twisting prevents interference problems. High data rates (100 Mbits/sec) are possible if *data grade* cable (Category 5) is installed. The twists must be maintained all the way to the connection points. The same twisted-pair cable is now commonly used in Ethernet, Token Ring, and other network topologies, making your decisions about cable much easier.

 Twisted-pair cable is discussed further under "Types of Twisted-Pair Cable" later in this chapter.

COAXIAL CABLE   Coaxial cable consists of a solid copper core surrounded by an insulator, a combination shield and ground wire, and an outer protective jacket, as pictured in Figure 6-5. In the past, coaxial cable had higher bit rates (10 Mbits/sec) than twisted-pair cable, but newer transmission techniques for twisted-pair cable equal or surpass coaxial cable rates. However, coaxial cables can connect devices over longer

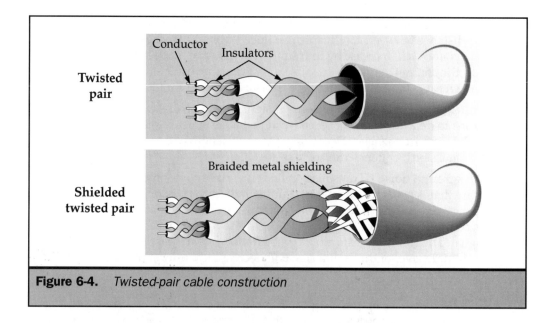

Figure 6-4. *Twisted-pair cable construction*

distances than twisted-pair cable. While coaxial cable is the traditional medium for Ethernet networks, twisted-pair and fiber-optic cable are common today. New structured wiring system standards call for data-grade twisted-pair cable wire that transmits at 100 Mbits/sec, ten times the speed of coaxial cable. This makes coaxial cable an all but dead cabling scheme for large office and internetwork environments.

Types of Twisted-Pair Cable

As mentioned earlier, twisted-pair cable is available as unshielded twisted pair (UTP) or shielded twisted pair (STP). UTP is the most commonly used twisted-pair cable.

The EIA/TIA has defined the EIA/TIA 568 specification to standardize the installation of premises wiring. It applies to all UTP wiring schemes that work with Ethernet 10Base-T, Token Ring, Private Branch Exchange (PBX), Integrated Services Digital Network (ISDN), and Twisted Pair-Physical Media Dependent (TP-PMD) networks. EIA/TIA-568 has benefits for customers because it standardizes network cabling and installation. The standard defines the following cable categories:

- **Category 1** Traditional unshielded twisted-pair telephone cable that is suited for voice but not data. Most telephone cable installed before 1983 is Category 1 cable.

- **Category 2** Unshielded twisted-pair cable certified for data transmissions up to 4 Mbits/sec. Similar to IBM Cabling System Type 3. This cable has four twisted pairs and costs less than 10 cents per foot. Plenum cable costs about 30 to 40 cents per foot.

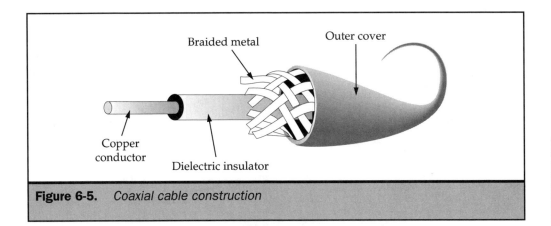

Figure 6-5.   *Coaxial cable construction*

- ■ **Category 3**   Supports 10 Mbits/sec transmission rates and is required for Token Ring (4 Mbit/sec) and 10 Mbit/sec Ethernet 10Base-T. The cable has four pairs and three twists per foot. Costs are around 7 cents per foot. Plenum cable costs about 50 cents per foot.

- ■ **Category 4**   Certified for 16 Mbit/sec transmission rates and is the lowest grade acceptable for 16 Mbit/sec Token Ring. The cable has four pairs and costs around 11 cents per foot. Plenum cable costs about 60 cents per foot.

- ■ **Category 5**   Defines 100-ohm, four-wire twisted-pair copper cable that can transmit data at 100 Mbits/sec to support technologies such as Ethernet and Asynchronous Transfer Mode (ATM), if installed according to specifications. The cable is low capacitance and exhibits low cross talk. It costs about 16 cents per foot. Plenum cable costs about 60 cents per foot.

The high transmission rates of Category 5 and other standards in the works that deliver hundreds of megabits per second are attributable to tighter twisting of copper pairs, better materials, improved hardware designs, and new access methods. All cables, patch panels, and terminations must conform to the specifications to eliminate cross talk between wire pairs.

Cabling Components

The components of a structured cabling system are illustrated in Figure 6-6. It consists of computers connected over horizontal cabling to a modular jack panel. Cables on the front of the panel then connect to network devices such as hubs and routers. The cabling components are discussed next.

Note   *Hubs and routers are discussed in Chapter 7.*

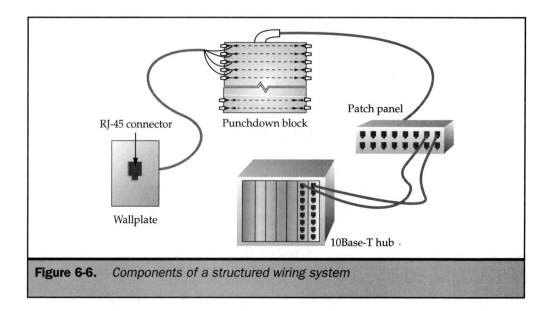

Figure 6-6. *Components of a structured wiring system*

Typical wall jacks and cable connectors for a Category 5 cable system are pictured in Figure 6-7. The right side of the picture illustrates the pin/wiring schemes for the two types of eight-pin jacks. The wallplate is a Siemens design that is oriented to keep debris out of the jack opening when a cable is not connected. It has both telephone and data connectors.

The EIA/TIA-568 standard calls for four twisted pairs in each cable in order to accommodate the diverse needs of current and future network and telecommunication applications. There are two pin configurations for the cable connectors, as shown in Figure 6-7. T568A should be used unless the T568B configuration is required to accommodate existing equipment.

Horizontal wiring extends from workstations to wallplates, and then to wiring closets and equipment rooms. A typical modular jack panel may contain 48 termination points for workstations. Wire pairs are connected to the back of the panel, while the front of the panel provides modular connector ports. Patch cables connect these ports with ports on network hub devices. Changes such as moving a workstation to a different workgroup on the local area network (LAN) are made by simply moving the patch cable.

Structured Wiring Topology

Structured wiring or cabling is a preplanned cabling system that is designed to implement future services and growth, thus making it easy to accommodate future moves and reconfiguration. The EIA/TIA-568 Commercial Building Wiring Standard provides a uniform wiring system and supports multivendor environments and products, as follows:

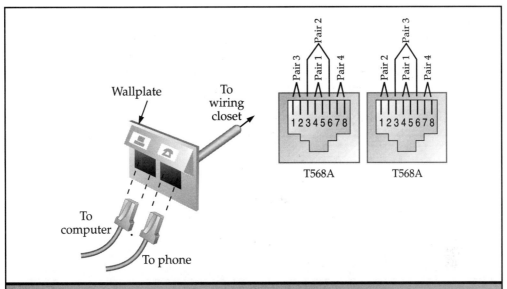

Figure 6-7. *Cabling system wallplate and pin configuration*

- A generic telecommunication wiring system for commercial buildings
- Defined media, topology, termination and connection points, and administration
- Support for multiproduct, multivendor environments
- Direction for future design of telecommunication products for commercial enterprises
- The ability to plan and install the telecommunication wiring for a commercial building without any prior knowledge of the products that will use the wiring

The EIA/TIA-568 specification calls for a hierarchical physical star topology, as pictured in Figure 6-8. Cables are pulled in a star topology from the telecommunication closet to the outlet on the wall where computer devices connect into the network. The telecommunication closets (TCs) on each floor are joined in the equipment room (ER), and each floor is interconnected at the main cross-connect (MC) facility. The maximum distance of the site is 3,000 meters (9,840 feet), covering one million square meters (about ten million square feet) of office space, and up to 50,000 individual users.

The entire system can be mapped as pictured in Figure 6-9.

Note   *Structured wiring systems depend on hubs and intelligent wiring systems, as discussed in Chapter 7.*

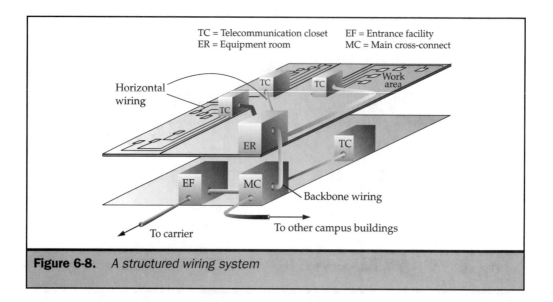

Figure 6-8. *A structured wiring system*

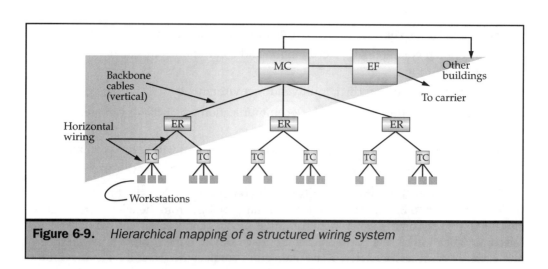

Figure 6-9. *Hierarchical mapping of a structured wiring system*

Ethernet

The Ethernet networking system was originally created by Xerox, but it was jointly developed as a standard in 1980 by Digital Equipment Corporation, Intel, and Xerox. The Institute of Electrical and Electronics Engineers (IEEE) 802.3 standard defines a similar, but slightly different, network that uses an alternate frame format. (The frame is the structure and the encoding of a transmitted bit stream across a link.) Because the IEEE 802.3 standard has been adopted by the International Organization for Standardization, it is discussed here.

Ethernet has 10 or 100 Mbit/sec throughput and uses a carrier sense access method in which workstations share a network cable but only one workstation can use the cable at a time. The CSMA/CD (carrier sense multiple access/collision detection) access method is used to arbitrate access to the cable.

There are several adaptations of the IEEE 802.3 standard, as listed below, that differ in speed, cable type, and transmission distance. Note that the first number in the name refers to the speed in Mbits/sec, and the last number refers to the cable length in meters per segment (multiplied by 100). *Base* stands for baseband and *Broad* stands for broadband.

- **10Base-5** Coaxial cable with maximum segment lengths of 500 meters; uses baseband transmission methods.

- **10Base-2** Coaxial cable (RG-58 A/U) with maximum segment lengths of 185 meters; uses baseband transmission methods.

- **10Base-T** Twisted-pair cable with maximum segment lengths of 100 meters.

- **1Base-5** Twisted-pair cable with maximum segment lengths of 500 meters and transmission speeds of up to 1 Mbit/sec.

- **10Broad-36** Coaxial cable (RG-59 A/U CATV type) with maximum segment lengths of 3,600 meters; uses broadband transmission methods.

- **10Base-F** Supports fiber-optic cable backbones of up to 4 kilometers with transmission at 10 Mbits/sec. The EIA/TIA has approved this cable for cross-connects between campus buildings in its Commercial Building Wiring Standard.

- **100Base-T (Fast Ethernet)** A new Ethernet standard that supports 100 Mbit/sec throughput and uses the existing CSMA/CD access method over hierarchical twisted-pair wiring configurations.

Understanding Network Technology

■ **100VG-AnyLAN**   A new Ethernet standard that supports 100 Mbit/sec throughput and uses a new demand priority access method over hierarchical twisted-pair wiring configurations.

The topology of 802.3 Ethernet networks, with the exception of those that implement the new 100VG-AnyLAN standard, is a linear bus with a CSMA/CD access method.

The twisted-pair version of Ethernet (10Base-T) is the most popular method for connecting Ethernet. It is configured as a star topology in which the cable to each station branches from a central wiring hub, as shown earlier in Figure 6-6.

Ethernet 10Base-T

A basic 10Base-T network consists of workstations attached to a central hub. Hubs can be attached to other hubs in a hierarchical formation, as pictured in Figure 6-10. The 10Base-T specifications are listed here. Note that some of these specifications are flexible, depending on the vendor.

Note   *Hubs can be as simple as repeaters, which extend transmission distances, or as complex as enterprise wiring and switching systems. See Chapter 7 for this discussion.*

■ Use Category 3, 4, or 5 unshielded twisted-pair cable.

■ Use RJ-45 jacks at the ends of cables. Pins 1 and 2 are "transmit" and pins 3 and 6 are "receive." Each pair is crossed over so that the transmitter at one end connects to a receiver at the other end.

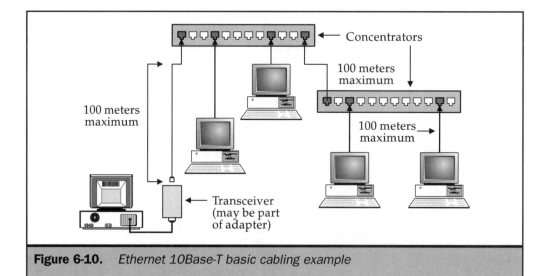

Figure 6-10.   *Ethernet 10Base-T basic cabling example*

- A transceiver and a 15-pin transceiver cable may be attached to each workstation. Most cards today have built-in transceivers.
- The distance from a transceiver to a hub cannot exceed 100 meters (328 feet).
- A hub typically connects 12 workstations.
- Up to 12 hubs can be attached to a central hub to expand the number of network stations.
- Hubs can be attached to coaxial or fiber-optic backbones to become part of larger Ethernet networks.
- Up to 1,024 stations are possible on a network without using bridges.

Ethernet Frame Formats

An Ethernet frame represents the structure of a data packet sent over an Ethernet network. It describes the position of headers, data bits, and the payload in the packet. Understanding frame types is important if you want to connect a protocol analyzer to a network and monitor the network's traffic. There are four frame types in Ethernet:

- **Ethernet_II**   The original Ethernet frame type. It assigns a unique packet header that is used on AppleTalk Phase I networks, networks connected to DEC systems, or to computers using the TCP/IP protocol.
- **Ethernet_802.3**   The frame type commonly used in older Novell NetWare networks.
- **Ethernet_802.2**   The frame type used in Novell NetWare 3.12 and 4.*x* networks by default.
- **Ethernet_SNAP**   The frame type used on AppleTalk Phase II networks.

NetWare 5 supports all of these frame types, but the default Ethernet frame type is 802.2. The Open Data-link Interface technology in NetWare allows stations with different Ethernet frame types to coexist on the same Ethernet cabling system. A workstation with one network board can communicate with other devices using different types of Ethernet frames.

Segmentation

Segmentation is the process of splitting an Ethernet segment into two or more segments, thus reducing the number of workstations attached to each segment and improving performance. Basically, a single segment is split and a bridge (or router) is used to join the segments. The bridge or router then manages and filters traffic between the network to keep local traffic local.

Segmentation becomes an important concern as new users join the network, especially those who require high bandwidth. Video and computer-aided design (CAD) applications require the most bandwidth. In addition, live video is time-sensitive and must be prioritized, which reduces performance for others. Users of video should share their own network segment.

NetWare has built-in routing capabilities, so you could subdivide a network by simply installing two network interface cards and placing some of the users on one network and some on the other network. Figure 6-11 shows a server with two installed network interface cards running star and bus topology Ethernets.

Filtering is an important part of the segmentation scheme. Once you've divided a network to reduce traffic and improve performance, you filter packets to reduce traffic on networks where those packets don't belong. One drawback to the bridging/routing approach of interconnecting networks is that bridges and routers introduce some delay in transferring packets between networks. Switching hubs can alleviate some of this delay problem.

Ethernet Switching Hubs

Switching hubs expand on the segmentation concept by providing *microsegmentation* in a box. Switching hubs implement matrix switches, as shown in Figure 6-12. Workstations are attached to ports on the switching hub and the hub is able to set up a dedicated connection between any two ports on an as-needed basis. Because only one workstation attempts to transmit on the connection, there is no contention for the line and transmission can reach the full 10 or 100 Mbit/sec bandwidth of Ethernet.

Many switching hubs also have high-speed dedicated connections for servers, such as a Fiber Distributed Data Interface (FDDI) 100 Mbit/sec interface. This is because standard Ethernet's 10 Mbit/sec throughput is usually inadequate for a server that must handle traffic from many nodes. It would not help to upgrade to a faster server if the network card is not able to process the throughput from the workstation. Consider the

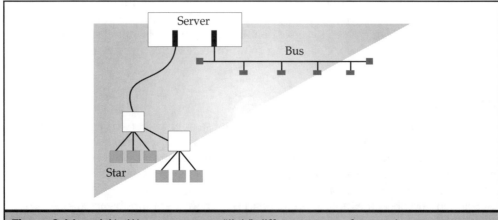

Figure 6-11.   *A NetWare server can "link" different types of network segments*

numbers. FDDI can provide 100 Mbits/sec. The switching hub in Figure 6-12 provides ten ports at 10 or 100 Mbit/sec each, so the 100 Mbit/sec bandwidth of the FDDI port can adequately handle ten workstations that are simultaneously transmitting.

Ethernet at 100 Mbits/sec

With the increasing use of multimedia, high-definition video, and real-time video—and electronic mail that incorporates these formats—there is an increasing need for higher bandwidth to the desktop. There are two new Ethernet standards that run at 100 Mbits/sec: 100VG-AnyLAN Ethernet and 100Base-T (also called Fast Ethernet).

Between the two, 100Base-T has become the more accepted standard because it uses existing cabling. However, many organizations have chosen to implement switching hubs instead of upgrading to 100 Mbit/sec Ethernet. In a switched environment, each client can potentially run at the full 10 Mbit/sec bandwidth on existing cable with little in the way of hardware upgrades.

Ethernet 100VG-AnyLAN (Voice Grade)

The 100VG-AnyLAN proposal is based on technology originally developed by AT&T and Hewlett-Packard. It is under the direction of the IEEE 802.12 committee. The standard uses four-wire twisted-pair cable and a new cable access method that replaces

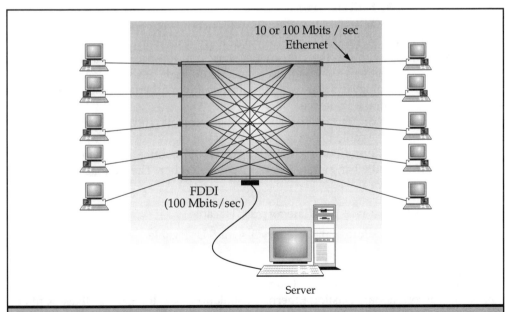

Figure 6-12.   *Switching hubs can provide direct port-to-port connection between systems*

the carrier sense multiple access/collision detection (CSMA/CD) access method used in existing Ethernet networks.

100VG-AnyLAN uses four pairs of Category 3 voice-grade cabling per station, but it can take advantage of the higher-grade Category 5 cable if it is installed. If so, cable distances are boosted from 100 meters to 150 meters.

The access method of the original Ethernet is changed, but the frame stays the same. The new access method is called *demand priority*. With the retained frame format, bridging can occur between existing Ethernet standards and the 100VG-AnyLAN standard. According to Hewlett-Packard, the Ethernet frame format, not CSMA/CD, is the component that defines interoperability and compatibility between different Ethernet standards.

In the demand priority scheme, the hub arbitrates when and how workstations get access to the network. A priority system can guarantee that time-sensitive applications such as real-time video get the access time they need to the network. The efficiency is improved with the hub approach because contention is basically eliminated. The hub determines which station gets access.

Because 100VG-AnyLAN is similar to 10Base-T in topology, adapters and other components share many of the same features. A computer with either 10Base-T or 100VG-AnyLAN can plug into the 100VG-AnyLAN hub and operate at the speed they are designed for. The star topology and structured cabling system approach are retained, as is the frame format of existing Ethernet. In addition, 10Base-T connector types are used.

100Base-T (Fast Ethernet)

Fast Ethernet was originally developed by Grand Junction Networks, 3Com, SynOptics, Intel, and other vendors. It modifies the existing Ethernet standard to support transfer rates of 100 Mbits/sec but uses the same carrier sense multiple access/collision detection (CSMA/CD) access method. However, users need to upgrade NICs, bridges, routers, and switches. The topology is a star configuration similar to Ethernet 10Base-T, with all wires leading to a central hub device.

100Base-T is based on the fact that CSMA/CD is scalable. 100Base-X scales up the speed by shortening the cable distance. The network is easily extended by building a hierarchical cable configuration that interconnects outlying hubs. This type of wiring fits into new structured wiring strategies as discussed earlier. The standard supports the following cable types:

- 100Base-TX uses two-pair Category 5 UTP cable

- 100Base-T4 uses four-pair Category 3, 4, or 5 UTP cable

- 100Base-FX uses fiber-optic cable

The primary concern of 100Base-T developers was to preserve the CSMA/CD standard to accommodate existing Ethernet installations. By doing so, 100Base-X fits into the IEEE Media Access Control (MAC) sublayer, which can bridge different IEEE network standards such as Token Ring, Fiber Distributed Data Interface (FDDI), and other Ethernet standards. A bridged network of 10 Mbits/sec Ethernet and 100Base-X would simply need to perform speed matching when exchanging packets.

Token Ring Network

Token Ring is the Institute of Electrical and Electronics Engineers (IEEE) 802.5 standard for a token-passing ring network that can be configured in a star topology. IBM made the standard possible by marketing the first 4 Mbit/sec Token Ring network in the mid-1980s. While the network physically appears as a star configuration, internally, signals travel around the network from one station to the next. Therefore, cabling configurations and the addition or removal of equipment must ensure that the logical ring is maintained.

Workstations connect to central hubs called *multistation access units (MAUs)*. Multiple hubs are connected together to create large multistation networks. The hub itself contains a "collapsed ring," as shown in Figure 6-13. If a workstation fails, the MAU immediately bypasses the station to maintain the ring topology of the network. Note that unconnected stations are bypassed.

MAUs are connected together to extend the ring by attaching connectors to special ring-in and ring-out receptacles on each MAU. Because the cable contains multiple wire pairs, a cut in the cable causes the ring to revert back on itself, as shown in Figure 6-14. Signals simply reroute in the opposite direction, creating a loop-back cable configuration. Repeaters are also available to extend the distance of a Token Ring network.

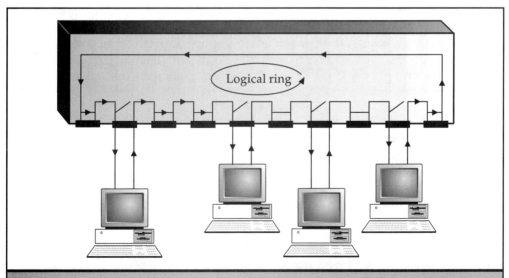

Figure 6-13.   *The multistation access unit (MAU) is a collapsed ring*

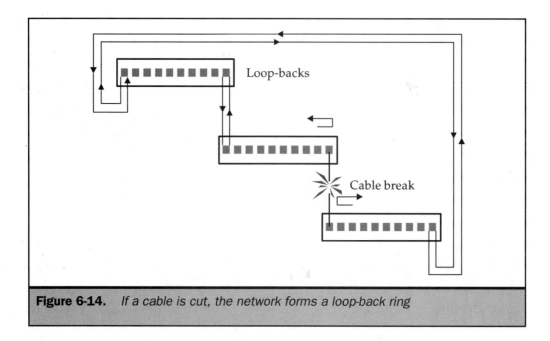

Loop-backs

Cable break

Figure 6-14.   *If a cable is cut, the network forms a loop-back ring*

Figure 6-15 shows how a Token Ring network might be configured in a large office or multistory building. The main ring connects all the MAUs in a circular formation.

In Token Ring networks, a station takes possession of a token and changes one bit, converting the token to a start-of-frame sequence. A field in the token allows workstations to indicate the type of priority required for the transmission. The priority setting is basically a request to other stations for future use of the token. The other stations compare the workstation's request for priority with their own priority levels. If the workstation's priority is higher than theirs, they grant the workstation access to the token for an extended period. Other workstations can override the priorities, if necessary.

Workstations attached to the ring transfer packets to their downstream neighbors. Thus, each workstation acts a repeater. When a new station is attached to the network, it goes through an initialization sequence to become part of the ring. This sequence checks for duplicate addresses and informs downstream neighbors of its existence.

The role of an active monitor is assigned to one of the workstations on the network, usually the first workstation recognized when the LAN comes up. The active monitor watches over the network and looks for problems, such as errors in the delivery of frames or the need to bypass a workstation at a MAU because it has failed. It sends out a special token every seven seconds that informs each node of its upstream neighbor. If the active monitor should fail, other workstations are available to take its place and basically bid for the job by transmitting "free tokens." The active monitor makes sure the network runs efficiently and without errors.

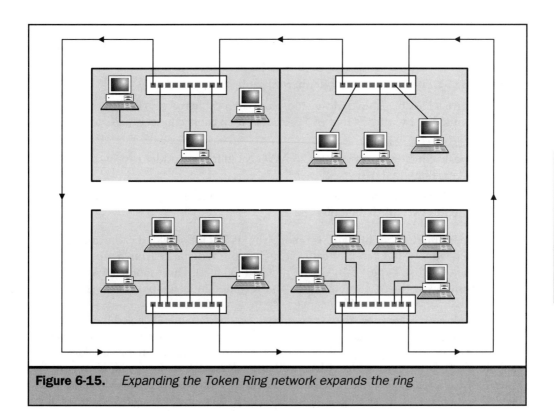

Figure 6-15.   *Expanding the Token Ring network expands the ring*

IBM Token Ring cards are available in a 4 Mbit/sec version and a 16 Mbit/sec version; however, if a network has both, it slows down to the 4 Mbit/sec rating. The faster version has an increased frame length that requires fewer transmissions for the same amount of data. Token Ring networks that follow the IEEE 802.5 standard and use connection methods that expand on the IBM design are available from many vendors. Unshielded twisted-pair cable and MAUs with 16 ports are common. In addition, two- and four-port hubs are available from some vendors. These hubs branch from an eight-port MAU and provide for the connection of two or more workstations in a cluster. Non-IBM vendors also make sophisticated MAU devices that contain additional ports, fault-detection features, and management features. Token Ring connections are also available on minicomputer and mainframe systems.

IBM Token Ring specifications allow for a variety of cable types:

- **Type 1**   A shielded cable containing two twisted-pair 22 AWG wires.

- **Type 2**   A voice/data shielded cable containing two twisted-pair 22 AWG wires for data with four twisted pairs of 26 AWG wires added outside the shield for voice.

- **Type 3**   Contains four solid, unshielded twisted-pair 22 or 24 AWG cables. A media filter is required for use with Token Ring networks. Do not confuse this with the EIA/TIA Category 3 cable. They are not the same.

- **Type 5**   Fiber-optic (100/140 micron) cable (two strands).

- **Type 6**   Flexible, shielded twisted-pair patch cables of 26 AWG wire. Distance is limited to two-thirds that of Type 1. A patch cable connects a PC to another device or a wall plug.

- **Type 8**   Shielded twisted-pair 26 AWG cable for use under carpets. Distance limits are half that of Type 1.

- **Type 9**   Shielded twisted-pair 26 AWG plenum firesafe cable. Distance is limited to two-thirds that of Type 1.

The maximum number of stations on one ring is 260 for shielded cable and 72 for unshielded telephone twisted-pair cable. The maximum distance from a workstation to a MAU when you use Type 1 cable is 101 meters (330 feet). This assumes that the cable is one continuous segment. If cable segments are joined by using patch cables, the maximum workstation-to-MAU distance is 45 meters (150 feet).

If multiple MAUs are used, they should be stacked together and cabled locally. Calculating the maximum distance of a Token Ring network can be complicated because of its ring nature. The total length of the LAN may vary as each station logs in. For example, if a station connected to a MAU with an 8-foot patch cable logs in, 16 feet are added to the total ring distance. This is because the signal travels from the MAU out to the workstation, and then back again to the MAU and on to the next workstation.

Wireless LAN Communication

Wireless communication falls into two categories: wireless local area network (LAN) communication, as covered here, and wireless mobile computing, which is not covered here. The primary difference between the two is found in the transmission facilities. Wireless LAN communication uses transmitters and receivers that are located within a company's premises and owned by that company. Wireless mobile computing involves telephone carriers or other public services to transmit and receive signals using packet-radio, cellular networks, and satellite stations for users who are "out of the office" and "on the road."

A wireless LAN transceiver (transmitter/receiver) is typically located in a fixed position within an office. Users with portable computers are allowed some mobility, typically within the immediate area of the transceiver. Wireless LANs can eliminate the need to run cable, especially if the LAN site is a temporary installation or serves a workgroup that might disband in the near future. With a wireless LAN, you save the wire and installation costs and, in some cases, avoid the need to get special permits to wire a building as is required in some areas.

A typical wireless LAN configuration consists of a transceiver unit connected to servers and other equipment using standard Ethernet cable. The transceiver broadcasts and receives signals from workstations around it, as shown in Figure 6-16. There are three primary techniques for wireless data transmission:

■ **Infrared light** This method offers a wide bandwidth that transmits signals at extremely high rates. Infrared light transmissions operate by line of sight, so the source and receiver must be aimed at or focused on each other, similar to a television remote control. Obstructions in the office environment must be considered, but mirrors can be used to bend infrared light if necessary. Because infrared light transmissions are susceptible to strong light from windows or other sources, systems that produce stronger beams might be necessary. Note that infrared light is not regulated by the government and there are no restrictions on transmission rates. Typical transmission speeds range up to 10 Mbits/sec. With the use of newer laser diode systems, speeds can go up into the hundreds of Mbits/sec.

■ **Narrowband (or single-frequency) radio** This technique is similar to a broadcast from a radio station. You tune in to a "tight" frequency band on both the transmitter and receiver. The signal can penetrate walls and is spread over a wide area, so focusing is not required. However, narrowband radio transmissions have problems with radio reflections (ghosting) and are regulated by the FCC. They must be precisely tuned to prevent interference from other frequencies. Motorola uses the narrowband radio transmission technique in its Altair series. The company received licenses for frequencies in the 19GHz range, which it allocates to customers based on geographic region. Motorola handles

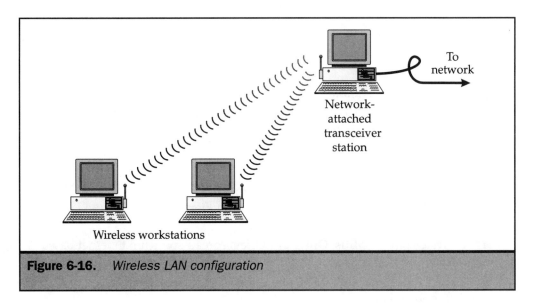

Figure 6-16. *Wireless LAN configuration*

all the FCC licensing for its products. Transmission speeds are in the 4,800 Kbit/sec range.

■ **Spread-spectrum radio**   This technique broadcasts signals over a wide range of frequencies, avoiding problems inherent in narrowband communication. A code is used to spread the signal, and the receiving station uses the same code to retrieve it. Coding allows the spread-spectrum signal to operate in a wide range of frequencies, even if other spread-spectrum signals are in the same range. Spread-spectrum radio does not interfere with conventional radio because its energy levels are too weak. Transmission speeds are in the 250 Kbit/sec range.

Another wireless LAN option is microwave, which is available in small, short-distance systems that can interconnect buildings in a campus environment or in a metropolitan area.

Black Box sells a wireless LAN bridge for connecting Ethernet networks up to three miles apart, eliminating the need for wide area connections such as T1 lines or fiber-optic cable. Transmission rates are in the 2 Mbit/sec range. It is an IEEE 802.1D-compliant Medium Access Control–layer bridge that provides protocol transparency. Spread-spectrum radio technology is implemented to provide secure data transmission, even in inclement weather.

The Black Box bridge connects to any Ethernet 10Base-2 (Thinnet) or 10Base-T network and automatically learns all the addresses on the LAN. Three antennas are available. A short-range antenna and a long-range antenna provide transmission distances of one half mile and three miles, respectively, in a point-to-point configuration. An omnidirectional antenna provides multipoint configurations with transmission distances of one half mile. Contact Black Box in Pittsburgh, Pennsylvania, at 412-746-5500.

If you're interested in wireless LANs, contact Motorola (800-233-0877) about its narrowband products; contact NCR (800-237-2870) about its spread-spectrum products; or contact Laser Communications (800-527-3740) about its infrared products. Other vendors are listed here:

■ **Altair (Arlington Heights, Illinois), a division of Motorola**   Provides Ethernet networks that use the narrowband 18GHz frequencies

■ **InfraLAN Technology (Cambridge, Massachusetts)**   Provides infrared 4 Mbit/sec and 16 Mbit/sec Token Ring networks with ranges of 24 meters (80 feet)

■ **NCR (Dayton, Ohio)**   Provides WaveLAN spread-spectrum-type systems

■ **Proxim, Inc. (Mountain View, California)**   Offers spread-spectrum LAN products

■ **Telesystems (Don Mills, Ontario)**   Offers spread-spectrum Ethernet-based networks

■ **Windata (Northborough, Massachusetts)**   Offers spread-spectrum Ethernet-based networks

NetWare
5

Chapter 7

Expanding Networks and Building Internetworks

A local area network, as discussed in Chapter 6, is a single network segment with its own network address that has certain "limitations." For example, a 10Base-T Ethernet segment is limited to 100 meters. Most organizations exceed these limits in just one department. To extend the distance and capacity of a network, you need bridges, routers, and switching devices to expand the network and build internetworks. This chapter describes these traditional internetworking devices and describes new devices you can use to build "enterprise" networks that span your entire organization.

Note   *The segments of LANs in an internetwork environment are called subnetworks throughout this chapter.*

An important point to keep in mind throughout this chapter is that routing can take place in NetWare servers. You don't need to buy separate devices in many cases. However, it is not recommended that you use busy file servers or application servers in a heavy routing environment, as this can reduce performance.

Why Use Bridges, Routers, and Switches?

Repeaters, bridges, routers, switches and, to some extent, hubs, are the devices you use to expand your network or to build internetworks, but what are these devices and when do you use them?

If you just want to increase the size and distance limitations of your existing network, buy a repeater and attach another segment of cable to it. A repeater boosts network signals so you can run a longer cable segment. Repeaters do not change any packet information or provide any type of filtering.

When your network becomes overloaded with traffic and performance starts to drop, you can do one or both of the following:

- Divide a network and link it together with bridges and routers
- Use a faster topology (i.e., 100 Mbits/sec)

Splitting a LAN reduces the number of workstations on each segment and improves traffic flow. But it may also reduce communication between users, which is both good and bad. Recall that all the workstations on a single network segment with the same network address can "hear" all the broadcasts that take place on that network. When you split a network, you can filter or block transmissions from propagating over the entire network. This will boost performance on the subnetworks, but you will also need the following devices to join the subnetworks:

- **Bridges**   Use a bridge to split an existing network into two network segments. The segments still have the same network address, but the bridge can filter traffic to reduce the load on both sides of the network.

- **Routers** Use a router to create an internetwork that consists of subnetworks, each with its own address. In a routed internetwork environment, traffic stays on local subnetworks, but if a node needs to communicate with a node on another subnetwork, it can get the address of that node from a router and begin transmitting. The routers handle all the internetwork traffic.

Note *You need routers to create an internetwork out of existing networks that already have their own separate network addresses.*

The second method of getting more performance out of a network is to upgrade your network topology and cabling system to handle higher bandwidth with networking technologies such as 100 Mbit/sec 100Base-T or FDDI. However, some organizations balk at this approach. Instead, they are keeping their existing Ethernet cabling and network interface cards and upgrading hubs to new switching technologies that reduce contention and boost throughput. Switching technology involves microsegmenting a network into segments with fewer and fewer nodes by attaching segments to ports on a switch.

It is often called *private networking*, because a port can support as few as one user who gets the full bandwidth of the network. Switching devices are like "bridges in a box." Bridges are discussed next.

Bridges and Bridging Techniques

A bridge is an internetworking device that provides a communication pathway between two or more network segments. Figure 7-1 illustrates how you can split a network with a bridge. Notice that both segments still retain the existing network address.

Bridges provide the following benefits and functions:

- You can expand the distance or number of nodes for the entire network.

- You can split a busy network into two segments, thus reducing the amount of traffic on each and improving performance.

- Bridges are protocol-independent, meaning that you can run multiple network protocols (TCP/IP, IPX, AppleTalk) on your bridged network (but the bridges don't recognize the protocols).

By default, bridges broadcast over the entire network. This is good if you need to expand a network over long distances (longer than is possible with a repeater). However, to fully realize the benefits of a bridge, you can apply packet filtering techniques that keep local network traffic within the segment where it belongs, rather than propagating out over the entire network.

As you expand a network by adding more bridged segments, you open up the possibility that loops or inefficient paths will appear in the network. Congestion may occur when too many workstations need to broadcast. That actually increases

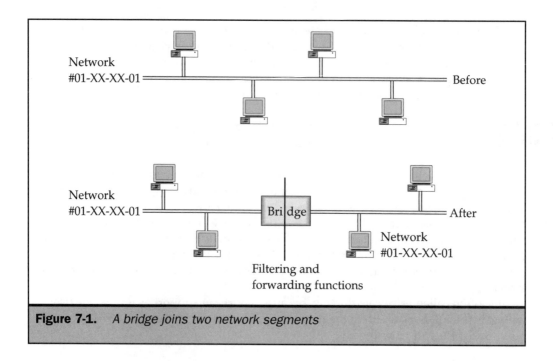

Figure 7-1.   *A bridge joins two network segments*

congestion further, because workstations start broadcasting more packets on the network in an attempt to recover from communication timeouts caused by congestion.

Bridge Functionality

There are generally two types of bridges: local and remote. A local bridge connects segments within the same building or area, as shown on the bottom in Figure 7-2. Remote bridges have ports for analog or digital telecommunication links to connect networks at other locations, as shown on the top in Figure 7-2. WAN connection types may be dial-up lines, dial-on-demand lines, dedicated voice lines, or high-speed digital lines. In any case, filtering is required to optimize the WAN link because it doesn't make sense to send packets addressed for local workstations across the WAN link to distant network segments.

A *translation bridge* can join two similar or dissimilar LAN segments. Basically, packets get repackaged and sent over another type of network segment. Any device that conforms to the medium access control (MAC) specifications of the IEEE 802 standard can be bridged with other IEEE MAC devices if you have a translation bridge. Ethernet, Token Ring, and Fiber Distributed Data Interface (FDDI) are examples of networks that conform to IEEE 802 standards for MAC-level bridging.

Functions provided by bridges include the following:

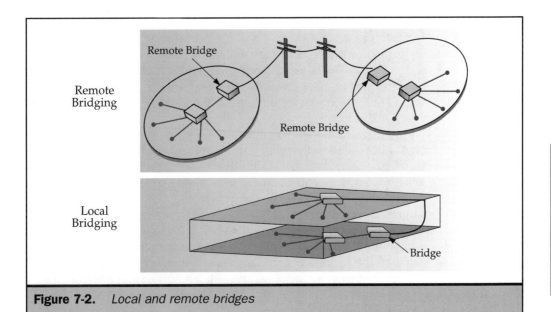

Figure 7-2. *Local and remote bridges*

- **Frame forwarding** When a packet arrives at a bridge, the bridge reads the destination address in the packet and determines whether it should forward the packet across the bridge. This processing might slow down network performance; however, most bridges today are well up to the task of bridging networks.

- **Loop resolution** Large-bridged LANs may have loops that could cause a packet to travel continuously. Some bridges will detect such looping packets and intercept them.

- **Learning techniques** Bridges build address tables that describe routes through the network. Tables are built by either examining packet flow or obtaining information from "explorer packets" that have learned about the network topology during their travels. The first method is called *transparent bridging*, and the second is called *source routing*. These learning techniques are discussed next.

Early bridges required that network managers hand-enter the address tables. This was a tedious task, and the tables had to be periodically updated if a workstation or user moved to another location. Today's advanced bridges can learn the address of other stations on the network using techniques discussed next. Note that transparent bridges are often called *learning bridges*, and they use the *spanning tree algorithm*, which is an IEEE 802.1 standard. Transparent bridging is found in the Ethernet environment, while source routing is found in the Token Ring environment.

Transparent Bridging

Transparent bridges automatically set about learning the topology of the network environment as soon as they are installed and powered up. As packets arrive on bridge ports, the address and the port number are added to a bridging table, as pictured in Figure 7-3. The bridging table is constantly updated as the bridge gathers new information about network devices.

Arriving packets are forwarded based on table information. A discovery process is initiated if an address is not found in the table. A frame is sent to all LAN segments except the one from which the frame originated. When the destination responds with a network address, the bridge makes a new entry in its bridging table. Given time, a bridge will learn the address of every node on the network.

The number of interconnected network segments is an issue in the learning process. If a bridge only connects two network segments, it is relatively easy to build a table that defines which stations are on one side and which are on the other. However, the bridge must first learn the address of each connected network by forwarding packets from one side of the bridge to the other and listening for a response from the destination.

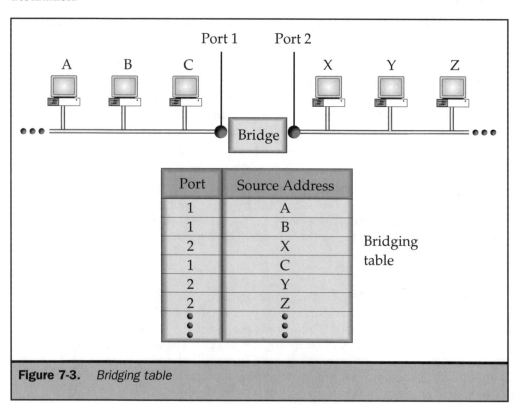

Figure 7-3.   *Bridging table*

How do you interconnect multiple LAN segments? The network at the top in Figure 7-4 must transmit packets from the left segment through the middle segment in order to reach the segment on the right. While this increases traffic on the middle segment, the configuration only requires two bridges. An alternate method is to bridge each LAN segment to a backbone network such as an FDDI ring, as shown at the bottom in Figure 7-4.

Creating redundant paths in a bridged network can provide fault tolerance, as shown in Figure 7-5. If the link between LAN A and LAN B goes down, an alternate link is still available indirectly through LAN C. The *spanning tree algorithm (STA)* provides a way to create multiple paths while preventing loops. However, STA does this by blocking one path until it is needed. This blocked path should be a switched analog or digital line that is put into service only when needed. An alternative strategy called *load sharing* solves this problem somewhat.

On large interconnected networks, multiple bridge paths are possible that can form a closed loop and cause packets to circle endlessly, reducing performance or crippling the network. In the worst case, *broadcast storms* occur when new packets are endlessly generated to correct the problem. Techniques for filtering traffic and monitoring long-lived packets help reduce the problem.

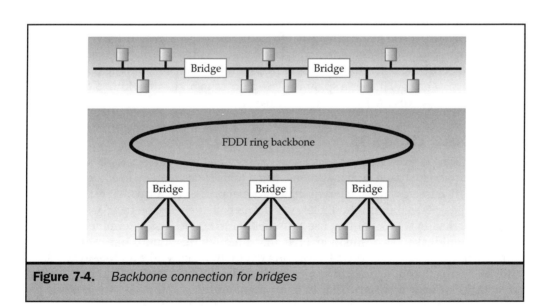

Figure 7-4. *Backbone connection for bridges*

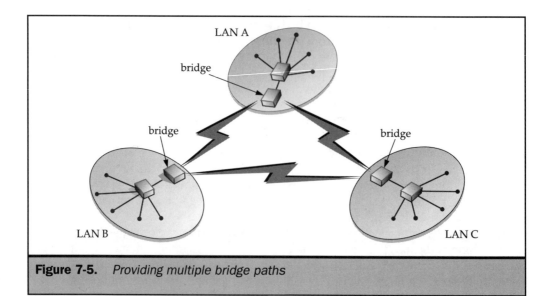

Figure 7-5.   *Providing multiple bridge paths*

Load-Sharing Bridges

A fault-tolerant, bridged network has redundant connections, some of which might only be used in the event that another connection fails. When bridges use leased lines to span wide areas, it is not economically feasible in the minds of most network managers to block the line and only use it for fault tolerance. Some bridge manufacturers provide load-sharing bridges that are capable of using the backup link to share the network load without causing loops. The load-sharing bridge is the most efficient form of bridge. It uses a spanning tree algorithm and a dual link to transfer packets. This improves internetwork performance.

Source Route Bridging

IBM Token Ring networks use a special *source routing* method that tells the bridge not only where packets should go but also how to get to their destination. In source routing, the packets themselves hold the forwarding information. Path information is placed directly in packets so they can find their way through the network on their own.

Bridges that do source routing use a discovery method to first determine the route a packet should take to a destination. Note that although this sounds like routing, the source routing bridge is simply a forwarding device that knows the addresses of other bridges. Best-path routing information is contained within the packet. This has advantages for wide area networks. In transparent bridging, it is necessary to block some links to prevent loops. In source routing, loops are avoided, so it is much easier and safer to create parallel redundant paths over wide area links to remote locations.

More About Routers

Routers are essential devices for creating internetworks in an environment that already has existing networks. An internetwork may consist of many different network types and many different communication links. Routers provide a way to rise above the hardware-specific network addresses and create an addressing scheme that encompasses an entire network. Because this addressing is independent of the type of network in use, a node on one network can obtain the network address of a node on another network (from its local router) and address packets to it.

In the NetWare environment, TCP/IP and IPX provide this type of independent addressing, but you need routers in order to transfer packets between networks with different addresses and topologies.

Routers are protocol-dependent packet switches. They read the information that is defined in the Network layer, as defined by the Open Systems Interconnection (OSI) protocol model. This information contains the source and destination network addresses. Data-Link layer information only contains specific hardware addresses on a single network.

Routers also provide valuable filtering and traffic control functions, which are critical on the type of mesh networks that are usually built with routers. When more than one pathway exists between two end points on the network, as shown in Figure 7-6, routers can direct packets along the most efficient or economical path.

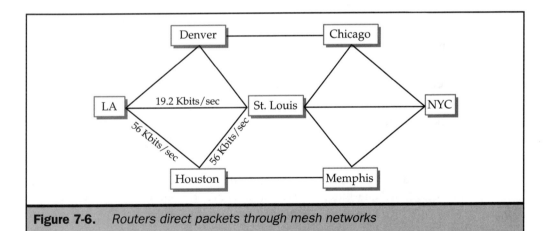

Figure 7-6. *Routers direct packets through mesh networks*

How Routers Work

Routers maintain tables of adjacent routers on the network. The following example will help explain the routing process. Assume that a workstation (we'll call it Node 1) wants to send a packet to a workstation (we'll call it Node 2) on a distant network. All the networks are connected via routers to the same backbone, as pictured here:

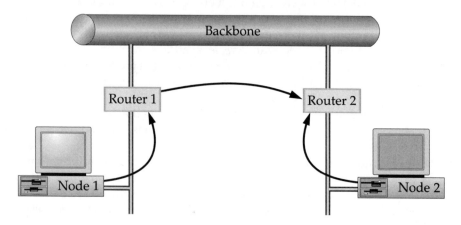

We only need to send a packet from Node 1 to its router (Router 1), which in turn sends the packet over the backbone to the destination network's router (Router 2), which finally forwards the packet to Node 2. The following steps explain how the packet is addressed as it moves through the network.

 Recall that a data-link address is a hardware-level address specific to a local network, while a network address is the media-independent address created by TCP/IP or IPX that identifies nodes throughout the network.

1. Node 1 broadcasts a SAP (Service Advertising Protocol) request so it can determine the network address of Node 2.

2. Router 1 knows this address and sends Node 1 a packet that contains its own data-link address and the network address of Node 2.

3. Node 1 builds a packet that has Router 1's data-link address and Node 2's network address.

4. Router 1 receives this packet because it is attached to the same network as Node 1 and because its data-link address is in the packet. It then rebuilds the packet by inserting the data-link address of Router 2 in the packet.

5. When Router 2 receives the packet over the backbone, it recognizes Node 2 as a workstation attached to its network and inserts Node 2's data-link address in the packet.

6. Node 2 receives the packet based on the address in the data-link header of the packet, not the network address, which is no longer used on the local network.

In the NetWare environment, you can set up a server as a router by simply installing two or more network interface cards. However, if there is a lot of internetwork traffic, it is best to avoid routing in busy file or application servers. You can set up a Novell NetWare MultiProtocol Router in a separate server to route internetwork traffic over TCP/IP, IPX, and AppleTalk networks. Multiprotocol routing is discussed further in Chapter 9.

Note	*Some protocols such as NetBIOS can't be routed. However, unroutable protocols can be carried across internetworks by encapsulating them in a routable protocol such as TCP/IP.*

Router Packet Processing

Routers handle packets that are addressed to them. When a router receives a packet, it begins a procedure that opens the packet and determines where the packet should be sent. Here are the packet procedures a router follows:

1. The packet is error-checked using the checksum value in the packet.
2. The information added by the Physical and Data-Link layer protocols of the sending device is stripped off.
3. The information added by the Network layer protocol at the source computer or router is evaluated.

The Network layer protocol information contains the destination address for the packet. The router may do one of several things:

- The packet might be addressed to the router itself, so the router receives the packet.
- If a packet is for a destination on the same network, the router simply forwards it.
- If the filtering list is available, the router checks a packet's address against the list and discards the packet if necessary. This keeps packets within or out of a network for security reasons.
- The packet is forwarded to the appropriate router, which may do any one of the above.

In some cases, if a router doesn't know a path or can't find the destination address of a packet in its routing table, it discards the packet and may return an error message to the source. Some packets (such as TCP/IP) contain information about the number of hops they have made on the network. If a packet exceeds a certain hop count, it is discarded by the router on the assumption that the packet is in a loop.

Understanding Network Technology

Choosing the Best Path

An internetwork is usually built with fault tolerance in mind. Several paths are created among routers to provide a backup path in case a link fails. Routers can send data over the best of these paths, depending on which is the least costly to use, the fastest, the most direct, or the one specified by an administrator.

Routing protocols (see the following section) can determine the best path through a network. A best path might also be a path that goes around congested LAN segments. You can also prioritize traffic. For example, high-priority packets can be sent over a 56 Kbit/sec digital communication link, and low-priority packets can be sent over a 19.2 Kbit/sec telecommunication link.

A private network built with leased or dial-up lines and routers is shown in Figure 7-6. If Los Angeles wants to send a message to St. Louis, the router can use the 19.2 Kbit/sec direct-connect line or the 56 Kbit/sec lines that connect through Houston to St. Louis. In another situation, if New York City wants to send a message to Los Angeles, that message may go through Chicago and Denver, or through St. Louis. Note that the New York City to Los Angeles connection makes two hops (passing through a router) if it goes through St. Louis, and three hops if it goes through Chicago and Denver. The router might base these decisions on the amount of congestion at Chicago or Atlanta or on the "hop/tick count," which is a value based on the number of routers between points and the amount of time in 1/18-second intervals it takes to get between them.

Routing Protocols

Routing protocols provide routers with the information they need to get packets to their destination over an internetwork. Routers share information about the network topology with one another in order to build routing tables that contain "best route" information.

A router device might have two or more ports on which it can send packets, so it needs to know which port is most appropriate for forwarding a packet. Early routers used static routing techniques in which a network administrator programmed the routing table. A better method, called *dynamic routing*, relies on the router to collect information about the network and build routing tables on its own.

Dynamic routers exchange routing tables with one another, and each router merges the routing information it receives to create new routing tables. Information obtained from other routers provides information about the number of hops or costs associated with pathways to destination networks. Over time, the routing tables in each routing device should contain roughly the same routing information. There are basically two types of routing protocols: distance-vector and link-state, as discussed in the next sections.

Distance-Vector Routing Protocols

Distance-vector routing protocols route packets based on decisions about the number of hops or the cost to the destination. This information is provided by neighboring routers. The technique generally follows the Bellman-Ford algorithm.

A router with a number of ports such as that pictured in Figure 7-7 has a cost assigned to each of its ports. These costs are assigned by the network administrator as a value that represents how much it actually costs to use a line, or as a way to indicate a preference for one line over another. In addition, neighboring routers inform routers of their costs to get a packet to the destination. The router adds these port costs to the cost of neighboring routers, as described here:

Port 1 cost 10 + neighbor cost 17 = 27

Port 2 cost 20 + neighbor cost 5 = 25

Port 3 cost 30 + neighbor cost 7 = 37

In this case, the router would send the packet through Port 2 because it represents the least cost to the destination. The neighboring router attached to Port 2 will then calculate additional pathways through other routers if necessary. If a particular port or path gets congested, the administrator can just raise its cost to lower traffic.

Information about routes, such as the address of the next hop, is stored in tables; and routers exchange tables with other routers approximately every 30 seconds. Initially, each network knows about the routers it is directly connected to. When a router gets a table, it compares entries in the table with those in its own table. From this

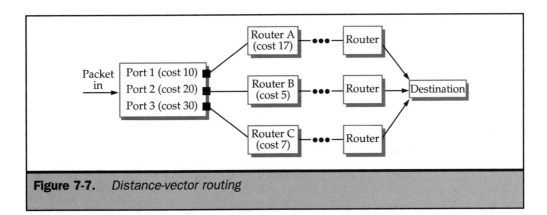

Figure 7-7.   *Distance-vector routing*

Understanding Network Technology

information, it updates its table with new routes or deleted routes. Information in this table includes the following:

- Network number
- Port number
- Cost metric
- Address of next hop

The *cost metric* is the value that allows the router to determine which route to use when forwarding packets to the next router in the network. Common distance-vector routing protocols are the following:

- *Routing Information Protocol* (*RIP*) is a distance-vector routing protocol that was first implemented in the Xerox Network System (XNS) and subsequently implemented in Novell NetWare. A different version of RIP is used in the TCP/IP environment, but newer routing protocols are now predominant.
- *Interior Gateway Routing Protocol* (*IGRP*) is a distance-vector routing protocol developed by Cisco Systems.
- *Routing Table Maintenance Protocol* (*RTMP*) is an Apple protocol that finds the best path between AppleTalk zones. Broadcasts occur every ten seconds.

Distance-vector routing is not suitable for large networks that have hundreds of routers or networks that are constantly updated. On large networks, the table update process can take so long that tables in distant routers may fall out of synchronization. Link-state routing protocols are preferable in these situations, as discussed next.

Link-State Routing Protocols

Link-state routing requires more processing power than distance-vector routing, but it provides more control over the routing process and responds faster to changes. Routes can be based on the avoidance of congested areas, the speed of a line, the cost of using a line, or various priorities. The Dijkstra algorithm is used to calculate routes, based on the following:

- Number of routers the packet must go through to get to its destination, or hops
- The transmission rate. Some routes use slow asynchronous connections, while others are high-speed digital connections.
- Delays caused by traffic congestion. If a workstation is transmitting a large file, a router might send packets along a different route to avoid congestion.
- Cost of the route, which is a metric defined by an administrator, usually based on the transmission medium. The cheapest route might not be the fastest but is preferable for some types of traffic.

The most common link-state routing protocol is the Open Shortest Path First (OSPF), which is used to route IP traffic on the Internet and TCP/IP networks. Novell's NetWare Link State Protocol (NLSP) for IPX/SPX traffic is based on OSPF. OSPF routing table updates only take place when necessary, rather than at regular intervals, and only the information that has changed is exchanged, thus reducing the amount of traffic required to keep routers up-to-date.

Autonomous Environments

Internet routing (TCP/IP) uses the concept of an autonomous system or administrative domain, which can simply be referred to as a domain. A *domain* is a collection of hosts and routers that use the same routing protocol and are administered by a single authority, as pictured in Figure 7-8. In other words, a domain might be an internetwork administered by a university or other organization. For example, the Internet is a set of linked autonomous systems consisting of educational institutions, government organizations, and companies.

Each of these organizations has its own interior networks connected to other Internet networks through *external gateways*. The Internet has interior gateway

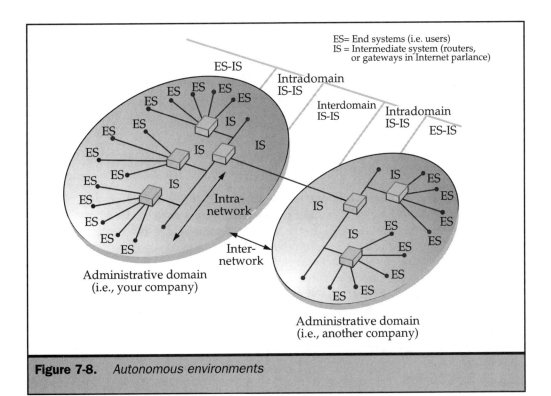

Figure 7-8. *Autonomous environments*

Understanding Network Technology

protocols and exterior gateway protocols. Any routing between domains is called *interdomain routing*.

The reason for these different protocols and the division of domains is because, on large networks, it is not practical for all routers to keep track of every system on the network. There are millions of addresses on the Internet! Routing information is organized in this hierarchical form so each routing device only needs to keep enough information to guide packets to the next most important router. You may want to follow similar designs when creating your own internal network.

Backbone Networks

A backbone is a network that connects two or more local area network (LAN) segments or subnetworks, usually over a long distance or between floors of a building. You connect a network to the backbone with a bridge or router, but routers are more appropriate if the network is large and you need to connect many different types of network topologies. Bridging to a backbone assumes that all the attached networks share the same address unless a translation bridge is used (but then you may as well use routers).

Backbones are usually implemented with a fast network topology so they can handle internetwork traffic from many sources. Fast Ethernet, Fiber Distributed Data Interface (FDDI), and Asynchronous Transfer Mode (ATM) switches are typically used as backbones.

- The backbone cable can extend throughout the premises, or you can create a "collapsed backbone" in a hub at a central location.

- Backbones handle internetwork traffic, while local traffic is handled within the subnetworks.

- You can attach a special server, backup devices, or other resources directly to the backbone so that all users can more easily access them.

A NetWare server-based backbone is illustrated in Figure 7-9. Each server contains two network adapters. One of the adapters connects the server to the backbone, and the other connects the local network to the server. The server acts as a router, forwarding traffic over the backbone to other networks.

Figure 7-10 illustrates how a backbone interconnects the LAN segments on each floor of an office building. The backbone cable extends through a conduit between the floors.

Figure 7-11 illustrates a centralized network design that can provide better management of network resources. Departmental servers are moved to a central management area and connected to a fast network topology such as FDDI. Department

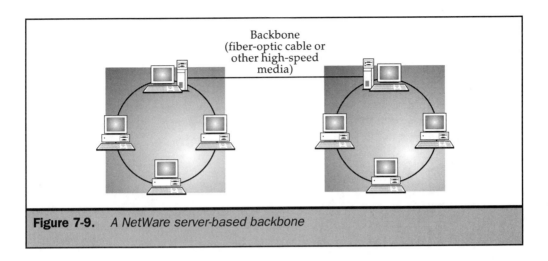

Figure 7-9.   *A NetWare server-based backbone*

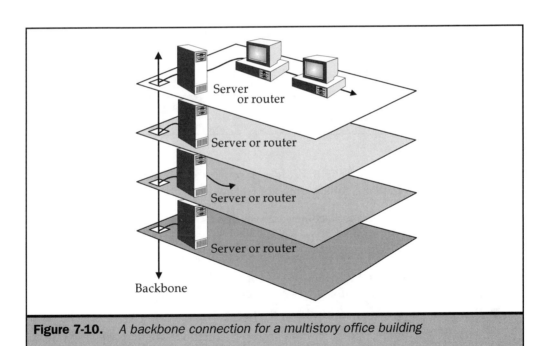

Figure 7-10.   *A backbone connection for a multistory office building*

Understanding Network
Technology

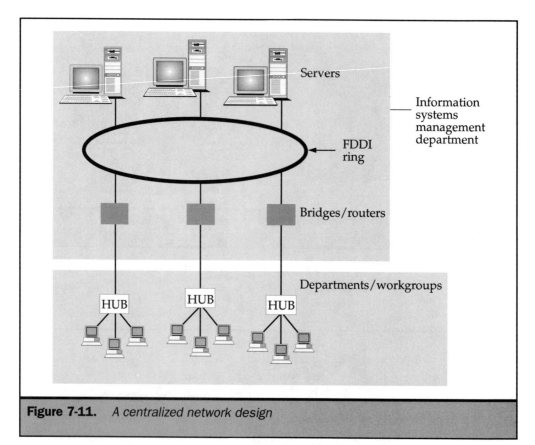

Figure 7-11. *A centralized network design*

LANs are linked to the backbone with bridges or routers. Centralized networks are easier to monitor and manage, for a number of reasons:

- Hardware repairs and replacements are easier, as all the parts and personnel are at the same location.
- Security is enhanced because the server area can be locked and fireproofed.
- Servers are not locked into individual departments where maintenance personnel may have trouble accessing them during off-hours.
- Performance can be optimized over the backbone.
- Backups, archiving, and other data protection methods are performed in one area by trained personnel.

- All hardware can take advantage of power and grounding enhancements.

- Connections to metropolitan area networks (MANs) and wide area networks (WANs) are simplified.

A *collapsed backbone* is a backbone that is reduced to fit within a single box. Instead of deploying the backbone cable between floors, you install a hub device at a central location, and then run cables from hubs located on each floor or in departments to the central hub. This may appear to require more cabling, but there is a great amount of fault tolerance in this scheme. Hubs are discussed in the next section.

While collapsed backbones and structured wiring systems provide in-house solutions, public carriers can help you create "backbones" over wide areas. Services like Switched-56, Frame Relay, Switched Multimegabit Data Service (SMDS), and Asynchronous Transfer Mode (ATM) are high-speed services that provide bandwidth-on-demand and pay-for-use features. Chapter 8 discusses these options.

Hubs

Simple hubs are concentrator devices to which you attach a number of workstations and servers. Ethernet 10Base-T uses hubs as signal repeaters between attached workstations and also lets you create a star topology. Token Ring multistation access units (MAUs) are hubs that include an internal ring for transmitting signals to any attached device. But hubs have grown from simple devices that you use to connect a group of workstations in a department to complex devices that include high-speed buses for transmitting data among a variety of networks connected into the hub. Hubs form the backbone of structured wiring systems, as shown in Figure 7-12. The logical configuration of the hubs is pictured on the left, and the physical layout is pictured on the right.

Hubs help companies manage the growth of their networks. They typically form the backbones of structured wiring systems to make it easy to plan for future growth. A typical "enterprise" hub will accommodate many different networking options, including Ethernet, Token Ring, FDDI, and wide area network (WAN) connections such as Frame Relay, SMDS, ATM, and others. You can centrally manage hub-based networks and build fault-tolerant cabling schemes.

Hub Evolution

The original Ethernet local area networks (LANs) were created by snaking cable through buildings and connecting each workstation in a daisy-chain fashion. When all of the stations were connected, you terminated each end of the cable and booted the network. Simple things could keep the entire network from working on the first try, like loose connectors, interference from outside sources, ground loops, and bent or crushed cables. Locating these problems was difficult. Hub-based topologies were designed to help solve these problems.

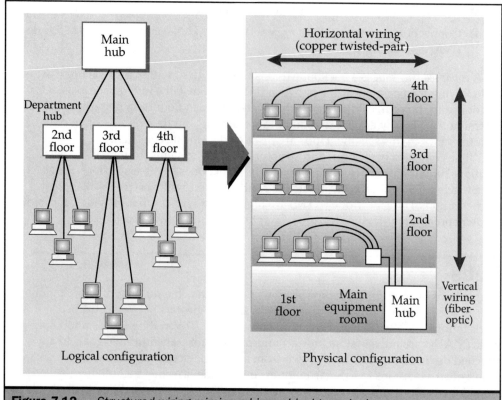

Figure 7-12.   *Structured wiring mimics a hierarchical tree design*

Hubs have evolved through several generations since the first simple repeating hubs. They are now the major components in structured wiring systems that support many local and wide area network topologies. A hub can serve as the wiring center for an entire floor, a building, a campus-wide area, or even a global network.

Hubs became popular in the LAN environment with the growth of star-configured 10Base-T. Large networks consist of many of these hubs, linked together to form departmental networks and internetworks.

The next logical step was to build a big box with expansion slots so you could just add multiport modules as you needed them. This single-box, "multislot" hub design centralizes power supplies and components and reduces their cost. The Cabletron MMAC hub pictured in Figure 7-13 accommodates up to eight different modules and up to 183 parts. It has a protocol-independent *backplane* that supports Ethernet, Token Ring, FDDI, SNA, and future ATM topologies.

Figure 7-13.   *Cabeltron's MMAC multiport hub*

Second-generation "smart hubs" include management features, fault-detection systems, and modules for bridging and routing. They also include features for collecting statistics about the modules in the hubs and each of the individual ports. You can manage the hubs from a remote console using SNMP management protocols. Still another feature is the ability to create logical LAN segments within a single hub. This feature allows managers, sitting at a remote management console, to divide a LAN into smaller segments for organizational and performance reasons.

Third-generation hubs are enterprise hubs, designed to support all the cabling and internetworking needs of an organization. They have intelligent features, high-speed backplanes, and are highly modular, supporting a number of plug-in modules, including wide area connections and advanced management.

The devices have extremely high-speed bus designs to handle all the traffic of the enterprise and advanced management features for monitoring and reporting on the condition of the entire network. Reliability is also an important feature—there are many redundant features to protect against the failure of components such as the power supply, bus, and wide area links. Many emerging hubs use Asynchronous

Transfer Mode (ATM) cell-switching backplanes that operate in the gigabit-per-second range. Additional features include the following:

■ Segmented backplanes to support multiple Ethernet, Token Ring, and FDDI LANs

■ High-speed internetwork bridging and routing

■ Switching capabilities for microsegmenting the network (see "Switching Hubs," later in this chapter).

■ Dedicated circuits between end-to-end nodes to support high-volume or time-sensitive traffic

■ Distributed management features built into each module to improve performance under heavy load conditions

Categorizing Hubs

You could categorize hubs into three main groups, defined by how they are used in a structured wiring system. The three categories are the workgroup hub, the intermediate hub, and the enterprise hub, as pictured in Figure 7-14.

■ **Workgroup hubs**   A workgroup hub connects a group of machines within its general vicinity. For example, it might connect eight computers in the art department. There may be several different workgroups on the same floor.

■ **Intermediate hubs**   An intermediate hub is typically found in the wiring closet located on each floor. Workgroup hubs are cabled to it, and it in turn is connected to the enterprise hub. Traffic among the local workgroup hubs may be handled by the intermediate hub, or the enterprise hub might handle all traffic for the internetwork, depending on your requirements or the design of the hubs.

■ **Enterprise hubs**   The enterprise hub is the central connection point for all the end systems connected to workgroup hubs. Enterprise hubs either form the backbone themselves or provide connections to a backbone. They may provide bridging, routing, and wide area connection services. Advanced management modules can be located in the enterprise hub.

You can start building a network with the workgroup hubs, and then add intermediate hubs and enterprise hubs later as required. Enterprise hubs must be designed to handle the mission-critical requirements of entire organizations and should be compatible with emerging technologies such as Asynchronous Transfer Mode (ATM).

Management Features

Management features are important in hubs. Most high-end hubs have their own microprocessor that can run programs to track data packets and errors and store this

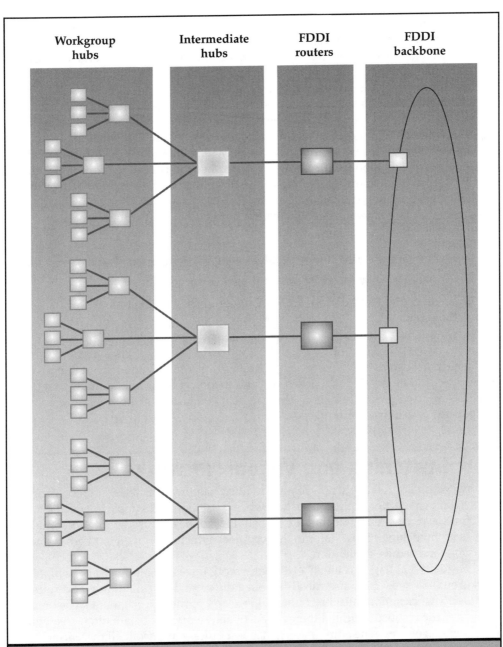

Figure 7-14.   *Types of hubs in a hierarchical wiring scheme*

information in a management information base (MIB). A management program running at a network administrator's workstation occasionally collects the information from the MIB and formats it for presentation to the administrator. The information is useful for tracking trends, troubleshooting problems, pinpointing congestion problems, and avoiding potential future problems. Alarms can alert administrators when various thresholds are met that might pose problems. For example, alerts can warn the administrator when network traffic exceeds a given level, so he or she can take corrective actions such as segmenting the LAN or moving a high-volume user to a dedicated segment.

Most vendors support the Simple Network Management Protocol (SNMP). SNMP runs on the Transmission Control Protocol/Internet Protocol (TCP/IP) protocol and uses TCP/IP as a transport for getting information from the workstation MIB to the management computer. If thresholds are met, SNMP uses TCP/IP to send warning messages (alarms) to the management computer. Following are other important features of SNMP:

- It automatically disconnects problem nodes that are disrupting the network.

- It provides a way to isolate ports for testing purposes.

- It will connect and disconnect workstations based on the time or day of the week.

- It supports off-site management of network components at remote locations.

Management software also provides a way to gather information about the network over a specific time period for analysis, or you can look at historical information for comparisons to current information. This can help you justify the need for new components or expansion modules.

Port Switching and Virtual Networks

Port switching is a relatively new feature in hubs that provides a way to reconfigure workstation connections quickly, such as when a user switches departments. Port switching is a management technique that should not be confused with switching hubs (see "Switching Hubs," later in this chapter), which allow you to microsegment a network and reduce contention.

Consider what happens when a company reorganizes, or the company is highly workgroup-oriented. Each user needs to join a different department or workgroup, and each user's workstation must be connected into an appropriate segment so he or she can access the resources located there. In particular, workgroups are often created for short periods of time. The administrator needs a quick way to join all these users, regardless of their physical location, into a segment so they can easily share common LAN traffic. When the workgroup breaks up, the workstations can be reconfigured into other segments.

In first-generation hubs, workstations were connected to a hub module and every port on that module was part of the same segment. In other words, modules were hard-wired to repeat signals only among the attached ports or to ports on other modules that were part of the same network. To move a user to a new LAN segment, you had to physically move the cable from one repeater module to another. Also, if a repeater module had ten ports, but a department or workgroup only had five workstations, five of the ports would go unused while another module might not have enough ports.

The latest hub designs use plug-in modules in which each port connects to a high-speed multisegment backplane, as shown in Figure 7-15. Each port basically has its own connection to the backplane, rather than to a hard-wired segment in the module itself. Managers configure segments at a management workstation by making a port a part of a *logical* segment. In Figure 7-15, note that LAN segment 1 consists of one or more ports on each of the plug-in modules. The shared backplane makes it possible to create segments that span multiport modules.

Hub devices that provide virtual LAN capabilities have high-speed backplanes. Encapsulation or translation is used to transfer medium access control (MAC) information across the backplane of the switch between virtual LANs. There is no standard for this process, and vendors typically use proprietary methods.

Why simulate LAN segments with virtual LANs? Virtual LANs promote workgroups and can keep traffic for a workgroup within that workgroup's logical boundaries. Virtual LANs also promote security and reduce congestion on the internetwork. But to achieve these objectives, you need to control traffic between the virtual LANs with routing techniques. There are several methods for doing this. In the backbone approach, routers are placed at the backbone and all network traffic goes to

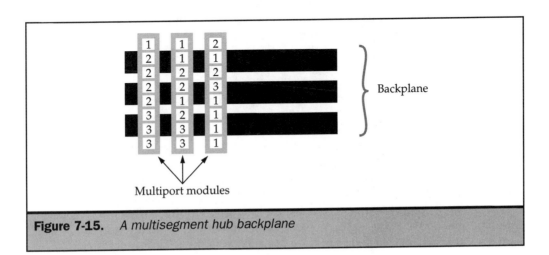

Figure 7-15. *A multisegment hub backplane*

the backbone, even if the destination is very close to the source. Routing is handled centrally. Bay Networks uses this design.

In another approach (Fusion, by Cisco Systems; High Performance Scaleable Networking, by 3Com), switches near workstations make some routing decisions, but they don't get involved in traditional router tasks like calculating routing tables. A route server builds all the routing tables and sends them to switches. However, the switches must understand the tables created by the route server, so this may require that all equipment be purchased from a single vendor or be compatible with that vendor's products. There is currently a lot of discussion going on about the advantages of creating virtual LANs and the best way to implement the technology. Virtual LANs are often difficult and time-consuming to set up, but provide management benefits later. Be sure to familiarize yourself with the current trends in this technology before committing to it.

Switching Hubs

A switching hub is a relatively new concept that takes advantage of star-wired topologies and hub designs to reduce contention on Ethernet network segments. Switching has also been developed in the Token Ring environment. Switching involves *microsegmenting* LANs so that there are as few as two workstations on a LAN segment, and thus no contention. The original switching hubs were designed for workgroups, but newer switching devices are modular units that fit into hubs.

Let's look at switching further. Assume you have a network with 200 nodes that is bogged down by excess traffic—you can split the network into two segments and bridge them. This reduces traffic and contention on each segment. If traffic is still a problem, you can split the LAN into four segments or six segments, and so on. A switching hub performs exactly this type of segmentation. It has a number of ports, each of which is a network segment designed for the connection of workgroup hubs or even a single workstation. Traffic is handled by an internal high-speed multiplexed bus. Switching is handled at the Medium Access Control (MAC) sublayer, which means that switches are basically multiport bridges.

The important point is that fewer workstations on each segment generate less traffic and less contention. Assume that one workstation is attached to one port and it needs to communicate with a workstation on another port. The switching device bridges the two ports, essentially creating a "private" network with no contention. It gets the full bandwidth of Ethernet for transmitting. High-speed switching hubs are also available that implement Asynchronous Transfer Mode (ATM), as discussed in the next section.

A switch handles the traffic between one port and another over a high-speed data bus, and the bus can handle simultaneous port-to-port data transfers. If a switch has 20 ports, it can handle ten simultaneous port-to-port (computer-to-computer) connections. A switch with 20 ports has an effective bandwidth of 100 Mbit/sec (ten port-to-port connections at 10 Mbits/sec each). Switches build a table of the MAC address of the workstation attached to each port.

Switched Ethernet is an easy upgrade for existing 10Base-T installations. You don't need to replace existing NICs in workstations or change the existing twisted-pair cable. All you have to do is upgrade the hubs to provide switching. Also, you can start by attaching 8-, 10-, or 12-port hubs to ports on the switch. This helps reduce contention by reducing the number of workstations on a segment.

Asynchronous Transfer Mode (ATM)

Hub design is moving toward the switching concept. Major hub vendors such as SynOptics, Cabletron, and Ungermann-Bass have announced products that let users implement switching of Ethernet, Token Ring, and FDDI frames. The trend is to also provide multiprotocol support, bridging, routing, wide area networking, management functions, and protocol analysis all in one box.

The bandwidth generated by all the components plugged into the hub will require the fast switching technology provided by *Asynchronous Transfer Mode* (*ATM*), which theoretically can deliver gigabit-per-second switching speeds. An ATM switch can potentially create a dedicated circuit between any two devices on a network. This is possible because ATM uses multiplexing techniques to move packets (called *cells* in ATM lingo) around the network.

ATM is not just designed for in-house networks. The major carriers have already incorporated ATM switching into their long-distance networks. That will make it easy for companies to interconnect their ATM-based divisions and branch office.

What Is ATM?

ATM is a data transmission technology that has the potential to revolutionize the way computer networks are built. Viable for both local and wide area networks, this technology provides high-speed data transmission rates and supports many types of traffic including voice, data, facsimile, real-time video, CD-quality audio, and imaging. The carriers such as AT&T and US Sprint are already deploying ATM over a wide area and offering multimegabit data transmission services to customers. ATM products include

- ATM routers and ATM switches that connect to carrier ATM services for building enterprise-wide global networks
- ATM devices for building internal private backbone networks that interconnect all the local area networks (LANs) within organizations
- ATM adapters and workgroup switches for bringing ATM connections to desktop computers

ATM takes advantage of the high data throughput rates possible on fiber-optic cables, although ATM networks to the desktop run much slower to take advantage of existing copper cable connections. The carriers are implementing ATM at transmission speeds from 155 Mbits/sec to 622 Mbits/sec.

ATM has the potential to become the standard data transmission method, replacing most of today's voice and communication methods. It is interesting to note that during early standardization, many assumed ATM would not be widely implemented until the next century. However, the need for high-bandwidth services in the carrier networks and in LAN environments has driven vendors to produce products well ahead of schedule.

ATM Technical Aspects

ATM is a broadband *cell relay* technology for transmitting voice, video, and data over LANs or WANs. Data is placed in cells, which are fixed-size frames that carry segmented packet data. The cells are small and easy to transmit through network switches. It is best to picture this with an analogy.

Think of an ATM switch as if it were a busy traffic intersection, and ATM cells as if they were cars passing through the intersection. All those cars are the same size, say Porsche 911s, so traffic flows like clockwork. Now picture a non-ATM network that places data in variable-length frames, not fixed-sized cells. That is like letting a semitrailer pass through our busy downtown intersection. Other traffic must wait for the truck to get through before proceeding. Variable-length packets can monopolize a switch for a relatively long period of time, and because the frame size is variable, traffic flow is unpredictable. This causes problems when you need to guarantee data throughput, such as when you want to transmit *live* video. ATM solves these problems by not allowing variable-length frames, only fixed-sized cells of 53 bytes each.

Conventional LANs like Ethernet, Fiber Distributed Data Interface (FDDI), and Token Ring use shared media in which only one node can transmit at any one time. ATM, on the other hand, provides any-to-any connections, and nodes can transmit simultaneously. Information from many nodes is multiplexed as a stream of cells, as shown in Figure 7-16. In this system, the ATM switch may be owned by a public service provider or be part of an organization's internal network.

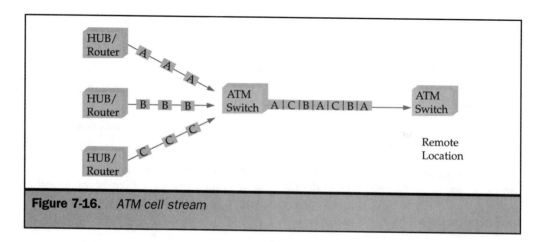

Figure 7-16.   *ATM cell stream*

ATM has been deployed in some of the carrier networks and is used to provide a high-speed backplane in some hubs. It will eventually be cost-effective for in-house networks. Meanwhile, Fast Ethernet technologies and switching hubs may be preferable and more cost-effective. ATM will deliver traffic from all popular LAN networks such as Ethernet and Token Ring by using "LAN emulation" techniques that are being standardized. LAN emulation simply provides a migration path for companies that want to invest in ATM technology now without scrapping their existing equipment.

Organizations considering a migration to ATM should follow a step-by-step approach to deploy a hierarchical distributed wiring structure. In a multistory office building, you would start by installing a main ATM switch as a backbone that links the connections from each floor. These connections might be existing Ethernet or FDDI backbones. In the next phase, you install ATM switches on each floor to connect the high-performance servers installed there. In the last phase, when ATM is relatively inexpensive, you connect end-user systems directly to the ATM switches.

Firewalls

Firewalls are designed to protect your internetwork from external access. They provide a barrier set up in bridges, routers, or gateways that filter packets based on the type of packet (TCP/IP, IPX, and so on) or destination address. Firewalls control traffic between the internetwork and the environment beyond it by controlling which packets pass through them. Most firewalls also implement some form of auditing. The best reason for implementing firewalls today is interconnection with the Internet. Without a firewall, you are opening your company network to millions of users throughout the world. Novell's BorderManager product provides security between your internal network and the Internet in the following four ways:

- Access to Internet services from the internal network (intranet)

- Access to internal networks (intranets) from remote locations

- IP/IP Gateway and IPX/IP Gateway, which can hide private networks and provide controlled access via NDS

- Links to geographically dispersed sites through the use of virtual private networks (VPNs) via the Internet

Chapter 8

Wide Area
Networking and
Telecommunications

This chapter covers methods for building wide area network links. All of the services discussed here are feasible with NetWare 5 using either the IPX or the pure TCP/IP services. The older IPX-only environment from NetWare 4 used the Service Advertising Protocol (SAP) and Routing Information Protocol (RIP). These can produce excessive traffic on WAN links. However, SAPs can be filtered and RIP can be replaced with Novell's NetWare Link Service Protocol (NLSP) routing protocol. In the TCP/IP environment, NetWare 5 uses the standard Open Shortest Path First (OSPF) routing protocol. These techniques are covered in Chapter 9, but keep them in mind as you read through this chapter.

WAN Communication Methods

A WAN is a communication system that interconnects geographically remote networks using services provided by public carriers or, in some cases, installed by the organization itself. A range of connection methods is available for building wide area networks. The services described here are offered by local exchange carriers, interexchange carriers, and value added carriers (VACs):

- **Dial-up telephone connections**   These are temporary connections over analog telephone lines between a user and a network or between two networks. Modems are required at both ends. You pay for services only when connected.

- **Dedicated analog circuits**   These circuits are similar to dial-up lines, except that they are always connected (do not require dialing and setup) and the carrier may provide a better grade of service (such as error-free lines). You pay a monthly rate based on distance.

- **Dedicated digital circuits**   Digital lines that are always connected, such as T1, T3, or Fractional T1. The lines are set up between two fixed points and you pay a monthly rate based on distance.

- **Switched digital circuits**   Digital lines that can be *switched* to create point-to-point links between a number of prearranged sites. Charges are typically on a per-use basis, but there are initial setup fees.

- **Packet-switching networks**   Packet-switching networks (also called public data networks) forward packets through a mesh of connections to their destination. Multiple virtual connections between multiple sites can exist simultaneously. Charges are based on packets sent and the maintenance of virtual circuits.

The carrier network that can provide analog and digital circuits is pictured in Figure 8-1. A local access and transport area (LATA) is a geographic area usually associated with a telephone area code. A local exchange carrier (LEC), which is one of the regional Bell operating companies (RBOCs), operates within LATA areas. Other non-Bell carriers may also operate within a LATA. A LEC is required to provide a

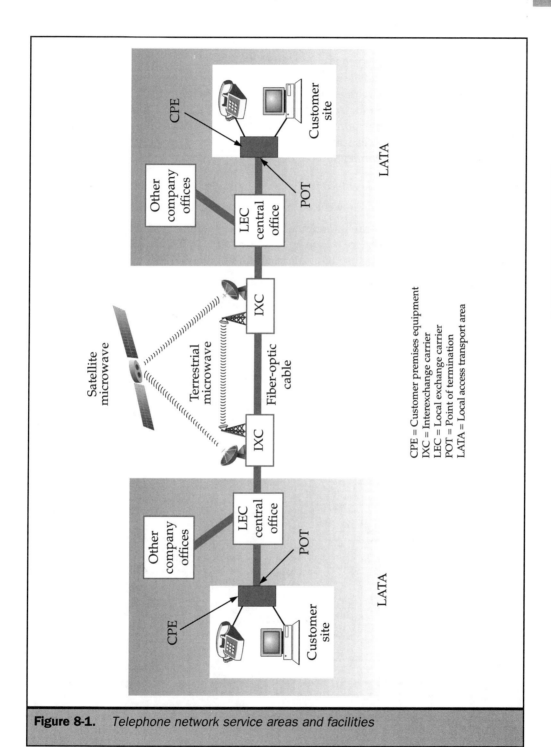

Figure 8-1. *Telephone network service areas and facilities*

point-of-presence (POP) facility for long-distance interexchange carriers (IXCs) such as AT&T, MCI, and US Sprint so customers can choose the IXC of their choice. Some long-distance carriers provide bypass facilities so customers can connect directly into their long-distance services, rather than going through the LEC.

The physical equipment for various point-to-point WAN connections is pictured in Figure 8-2. A bridge or router funnels WAN traffic from the local network over the wide area connection. Devices such as modems or a channel service unit/data service unit (CSU/DSU) provide connections to the lines or public data networks.

- In (A), modems connect two LANs over analog telephone lines.

- In (B), a CSU/DSU connects two remote lines over a digital line.

- In (C), multiple sites are interconnected over separate digital lines such as dataphone digital service (DDS) or T-carrier services (T1). A voice/data *multiplexor* can also be used to transmit both voice and data over the digital lines.

- In (D), a single connection into a Frame Relay network provides connections to multiple remote sites using the carrier's switching facilities and Frame Relay packet services.

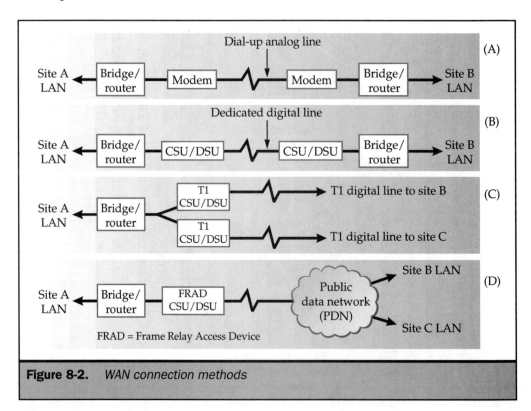

Figure 8-2.   *WAN connection methods*

It is usually not recommended that you use bridges to interconnect networks over WAN links unless one end of the connection is a small network with only a few users. Recall that bridges link networks that have the same address. Bridging is not practical if both networks are large, and is not possible if they contain many subnetworks with different network addresses.

Study the connection equipment pictured in Figure 8-2 and notice the link between the bridge/router and the carrier connection devices (modem, CSU/DSU, FRAD). In the case of modems, this link is made with a standard RS-232 cable connection between the bridge/router and modem. In the case of the digital connections (B, C, and D), the bridge/router requires a synchronous adapter that is linked to the CSU/DSU with a V.35 or RS-422 cable.

Point-to-Point Protocol

Any discussion of internetworking and wide area networks is incomplete without some mention of the point-to-point protocol (PPP). PPP is a relatively new protocol that defines a way to encapsulate and send high-level data protocols like IP and IPX across point-to-point links. Basically, PPP has its own packets and puts IP, IPX, or other packets inside of those packets for transmission across the link.

PPP is growing in importance for wide area links because it provides a *nonproprietary* way to connect multivendor routers over WAN links. In the past, router vendors used their own proprietary encapsulation and linking protocols, which in most cases required that you use devices from the same vendor on both sides of the link. Individual Internet users also use PPP to create direct links from desktop computers or LANs into the Internet.

PPP is based on an earlier protocol called SLIP (Serial Line Internet Protocol). PPP encapsulates other protocols such as TCP/IP, IPX, AppleTalk, and bridging for transport over a WAN link. SLIP, on the other hand, was limited to TCP/IP only.

 The PPP protocols are transparent across carrier networks. No processing is done to the data during transmission. Because of this, compression is easily implemented.

Point-to-Point Tunneling Protocol

Point-to-Point Tunneling Protocol (PPTP) is one of several new services that provide for virtual dial-up services. Using PPTP, a remote user can connect with the corporate LAN from a location that would normally require a long-distance telephone call. Instead, the remote user connects with a local ISP. The user then establishes a virtual connection across the Internet to the corporate network. Authentication and encryption can be added to the dial-up session to provide a private and secure connection. PPTP turns the Internet into a virtual private network (VPN), removing the costs associated with expensive leased lines and long-distance calling (see Figure 8-3).

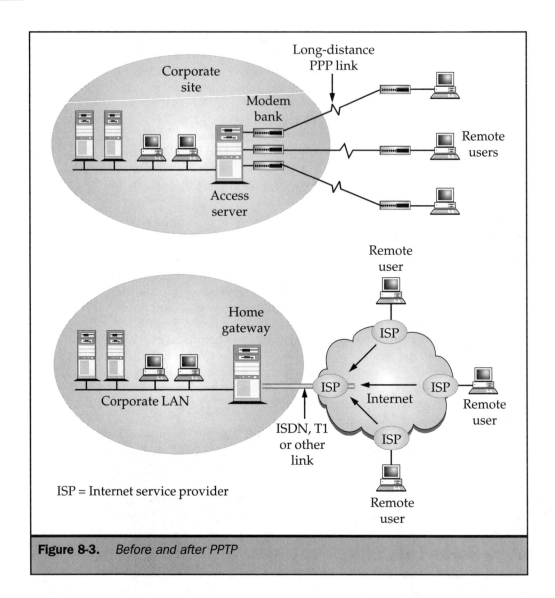

Figure 8-3. *Before and after PPTP*

In high-traffic environments, a point-to-point connection is usually made with dedicated digital T1 (1.544 Mbits/sec) or T3 lines (the equivalent of 28 T1 lines). Low volume point-to-point connections can be made over dial-up or dedicated voice phone lines.

Private or Public?

Organizations can build *private networks* or use *public networks*. A company that sets up a private network leases dedicated lines from a carrier to interconnect its network sites, and then buys and maintains its own connection equipment (customer premises equipment, or CPE). The dedicated lines are point-to-point links that provide guaranteed availability and throughput. They are not shared with other service provider customers, so the company gets the full bandwidth of the line at all times. Private networks let you maintain security and control over WAN traffic. A private network that connects four separate sites might look like Figure 8-4.

Private networks are usually built with DDS (56 Kbits/sec), T1 (1.544 Mbits/sec), or T3 (45 Mbits/sec) digital links (see "Dedicated Digital Services" later in this chapter for a description of these links). A switched (nondedicated) service called Switched-56 is

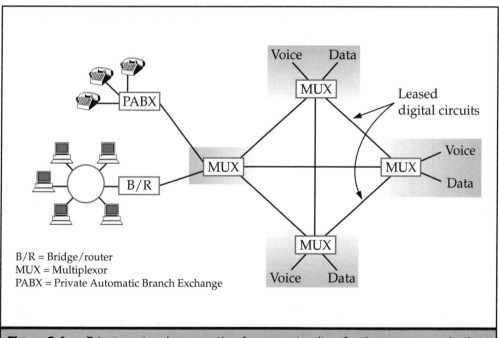

Figure 8-4.   *Private network connecting four remote sites for the same organization*

often used to create backup links in case a primary link fails. Here are some considerations:

- The cost of leased lines increases with distance, so they may not be feasible over long distances.

- Four or more hours of WAN traffic per day between two sites may justify a dedicated leased line, but distance costs may affect this calculation.

- Leased digital lines are feasible when interconnecting a few sites that have high traffic, but packet-switched networks are better if there are many sites and transmissions are sporadic.

- Voice calls and data transmissions can be multiplexed into T1 digital lines, so organizations can often justify such lines if a lot of voice and data traffic exists between sites.

A public data network (PDN) is a packet-switched network that provides services to many customers simultaneously. Packets are routed through the network by the carrier's equipment. Public networks are best for linking many remote sites and when you can't justify the cost of dedicated leased lines between sites. Also, public packet-switched networks are best if the distance between customer sites is far enough that distance costs make leased lines prohibitive.

Evaluating Volume

Managers must evaluate the volume of network traffic and its destination to determine the type of service to use. Table 8-1 lists the transmission requirements for various types of activities. If traffic is light, dial-up services are sufficient. If traffic is continuous between two points, dedicated lines are necessary. New "fast packet" switching services such as Frame Relay (data only) and Asynchronous Transfer Mode (ATM) may reduce your need for dedicated lines while filling volume requirements.

Application	Rate
Personal communications	300 to 9,600 bits/sec or higher
E-mail transmissions	2,400 to 9,600 bits/sec or higher
Remote control programs	9,600 bits/sec to 56 Kbits/sec
Database text query	Up to 1 Mbit/sec

Table 8-1.   *Common Data Transfer Rates*

Application	Rate
Digital audio	1 to 2 Mbits/sec
Access images	1 to 8 Mbits/sec
Compressed video	2 to 10 Mbits/sec
Medical transmissions	Up to 50 Mbits/sec
Document imaging	10 to 100 Mbits/sec
Scientific imaging	Up to 1 Gbit/sec
Full-motion video (uncompressed)	1 to 2 Gbits/sec

Table 8-1. *Common Data Transfer Rates* (continued)

Deciding which method to use, either dedicated, circuit-switching, or packet-switching, is based on the amount of delay that can be tolerated between the sender and the receiver. In a message-oriented system that delivers e-mail and data files, delays of seconds, minutes, or even hours are acceptable, and low-speed packet-switching systems provide the most economical service. For real-time applications such as online transaction processing and other interactive requirements, dedicated lines are best.

Bandwidth-on-Demand

Bandwidth-on-demand is a carrier service feature that accommodates bursts in data traffic and the need for additional bandwidth. Most network traffic does not flow in steady predictable streams, and therefore it is often difficult for managers to determine the type of wide area network connections they need. In this situation, an expensive dedicated line might not make sense. Bandwidth-on-demand provides a way to increase the bandwidth as traffic peaks. Because the lines are switched, customers only pay for services used.

Providers and Pricing

After you've decided on the type of service you need, you can begin contacting local and long-distance service providers. The local providers basically get you the link to the long-distance providers over the *local loop*, so your cost will encompass the equipment and services discussed next.

Understanding Network Technology

The estimates in the list below are extremely rough and should only be used for general comparisons between services. Your cost will vary with distance, type of service, and setup requirements (i.e., virtual circuit setup). Also, AT&T is the only provider that is required by the FCC to publish its rates, so you'll probably need to put your requirements out to bid before you can get an accurate cost for these services. The providers you contact will need the locations (area codes) of the sites you want to connect.

- **Premise equipment**   Routers in the thousands of dollars; DSU/CSUs in the hundreds of dollars; multiplexors (if used): $2,000 to $5,000.

- **Local loop charges**   In the $1,000 range per month for dedicated digital services. Note that you'll need a switched or dedicated digital line in the local loop to connect to a packet-switched network such as Frame Relay.

- **Local loop installation charges**   In the $500 to $1,000 range.

- **Interexchange carrier charges**   T1 digital point-to-point lines will cost approximately $3 per mile plus a base charge of $2,000. Lower speed digital will cost less than $1.00 per mile. Monthly pricing for packet-switched network services like Frame Relay is in the $400 to $500 range for a 64 Kbits/sec link into the network and in the $3,000 to $5,000 range for 1 Mbit/sec link rates into the network.

Dial-Up Analog Services

Dial-up lines use modems that can provide transmission rates as high as 56 Kbits/sec over switched lines (using new V.90 and X2 modem standards). Because the lines are switched, charges are incurred only during connection time.

Dial-up services are ideal for occasional links. These services can provide links for transferring electronic mail between company sites or enabling home or mobile users the ability to dial into the company database. In the case of a remote-control connection, a user dials into the company network and takes control of a computer attached to the LAN. The LAN-attached computer performs the processing but sends screen output to the remote user and accepts keyboard input from the remote user. This technique minimizes the amount of traffic transferred through the remote link.

Circuit-Switching Services

Basically, a circuit-switched service has the features of a normal voice telephone call that lets you create a circuit between any two sites. A dedicated channel set up between two points provides a specific amount of bandwidth for the duration of the call. Users pay for only the time they are connected, and their contract with the provider allows them to call many different sites.

- Circuit-switching services provide a fixed path between two points that is set up prior to information exchange.
- Circuit-switching services provide dedicated circuits with a known and guaranteed bandwidth.
- There is some delay required when setting up the circuit.
- The bandwidth may be fixed but may support bandwidth-on-demand to accommodate bursts in traffic.
- Downed lines can halt all transmission or require user intervention to route around the problem, although providers can guarantee reliable connections.

Circuit-switched lines are often used as backup lines for higher-speed dedicated lines. If a leased dedicated line fails, one or more circuit-switched lines are connected to handle traffic between sites until the dedicated lines are reconnected. If a dedicated line becomes saturated with traffic, circuit-switched lines are connected to handle excess traffic loads. This strategy provides an economical way for network managers to link sites without the need to acquire an excessive amount of dedicated service.

A circuit-switched service provides a temporary dedicated path through a carrier's switching systems. Customers can contract for various types of services, depending on their anticipated bandwidth needs.

Switched-56 Services

A common switched service is Switched-56, which operates at 56 Kbits/sec and requires a special Switched-56 channel service unit/data service unit (CSU/DSU) at each site. Switched-56 services were originally intended to provide an alternate backup route for higher-speed leased lines such as T1. If a leased line failed, a Switched-56 line would quickly establish an alternate connection. Switched-56 can still be used in this way, but it is also used to handle peaks in traffic, fax transmissions, backup sessions, bulk e-mail transfers, and LAN-to-LAN connections. Rates are calculated by the minute in most cases.

For higher data rates, carriers such as AT&T offer services such as Switched 384K and Switched T1. Customers are required to install Integrated Services Digital Network (ISDN) services, as discussed in the next section.

Integrated Services Digital Network (ISDN)

ISDN is a service that provides all-digital services on the *local loop*. The local loop is the so-called "last mile" in the telecommunication network that has not been fully converted to high-speed optical cable. It is the copper wire that runs between homes or businesses and the local exchange carrier's switching office. This loop is still largely copper twisted-pair wire supporting analog transmissions.

ISDN is offered in selected areas, and it is used in the same way as dial-up services. While it provides high-speed digital circuit-switched services between a customer and the telephone company, it also provides a range of integrated voice and data services on which many other offerings are built. For example, AT&T offers two services, Switched 384K and Switched T1, that require users to set up an ISDN interface between their site and the telephone company. In addition, Frame Relay is an outgrowth of ISDN.

Basic ISDN, which is called the Basic Rate Interface (BRI), has three channels: two provide 64 Kbits/sec, and a third provides 16 Kbits/sec signaling. The ISDN Primary Rate Interface provides extended services for those who need it. It consists of 23 voice or data channels at 64 Kbits/sec each, and one signaling channel at 64 Kbits/sec. In either interface, the signaling channel provides the important function of setting up calls. This provides microsecond call setup speeds and out-of-band signaling, which keeps the data channels free for data-only transmissions.

Emerging Circuit-Switching Services

Some emerging standards will boost data rates and lower prices on the local loop. *High-bit-rate Digital Subscriber Line* (HDSL) permits transmission over the existing copper-based lines between 784 Kbits/sec to T1 rates of 1.544 Mbits/sec. A related product, *Asymmetrical Digital Subscriber Line (ADSL)* works over twisted pairs, offering a 1.544 Mbit/sec circuit in one direction and a lower-speed (typically 16 Kbit/sec) data channel in the other direction. ADSL is designed for interactive video to the home using existing copper telephone lines. HDSL can offer the same services and provide a full-duplex line. A third encoding scheme, *Very-High-bit-rate Digital Subscriber Line (VHDSL)*, has been proposed that will provide 3 Mbit/sec to 6 Mbit/sec service over two twisted pairs. HDSL is being deployed, and ADSL is in the trial stages.

Dedicated Digital Services

Digital circuits provide data transmission speeds of up to 45 Mbits/sec. Currently, digital lines are made available at customer sites by "conditioning" normal lines with special equipment to handle higher data rates. The lines are leased from the telephone company and installed between two points (point-to-point) to provide dedicated, full-time service. You need bridges or routers to connect local area networks (LANs) to digital lines. T1 lines can carry both voice and data, so they are often used to provide voice telephone connections between an organization's remote sites. Voice and data *multiplexors (MUXs)* are required if you plan to mix both voice and data channels, as shown in Figure 8-5. Linking PABXs and setting up such services as teleconferencing on high-speed digital lines can help justify their costs, especially since teleconferencing can save travel costs.

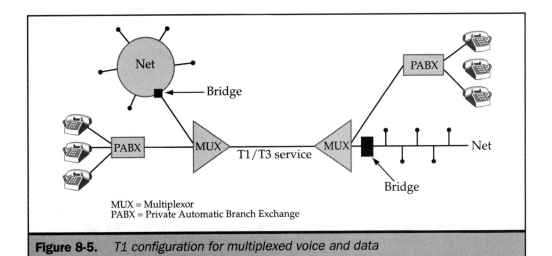

Figure 8-5.   *T1 configuration for multiplexed voice and data*

The standard digital line service is the *T1 channel*, which provides transmission rates of 1.544 Mbits/sec. The lines are *fractional*, meaning that they can be divided into channels for voice or data. T1 can be divided into 24 channels of 64 Kbit/sec bandwidth each, for example. Alternatively, a T3 line can provide the equivalent of 28 T1 lines for users who need a lot of bandwidth.

AT&T offers a number of digital services under its ACCUNET label. ACCUNET T1.5 provides a dedicated point-to-point digital T1 channel, while ACCUNET T45 service provides dedicated 44.736 Mbit/sec (T3) digital rates. T45 is equivalent to 28 NET also provides protection from line failures by immediately switching to another circuit, and it can provide temporary bandwidth for high-volume data transfers (bursts), which are common in LAN environments.

Not all leased lines are dedicated. An organization may temporarily lease a high-speed line for occasional use, such as end-of-month file transfers or weekly videoconferences. Such services are usually reserved in advance with the carriers. However, the switched digital services discussed next have reduced the need for these types of lines.

As mentioned, dedicated digital lines are often used to carry voice, video, and data. A digitized voice conversation requires 64 Kbit/sec bandwidth, so many T1 customers use digitizing and multiplexing techniques to merge both voice and data onto the same digital lines. In this way, a customer can lease a full T1 line and use some of the channels for voice calls between company sites. The remaining bandwidth is used for data. A multiplexor is required to merge the signals from voice, video, and data sources for transfer as a single stream of data over the T1 line. A demultiplexor at the other end then separates each individual channel.

Packet-Switching Services

A packet-switching network provides a mesh of connections through which data packets travel to reach their destination. Figure 8-6 compares a private network to a public packet-switched network. The packet-switched network is often viewed as a "cloud" because it contains any-to-any connections. Data from the source system is separated and placed into packets of a predefined size and delivered through the cloud to the destination. Public packet-switching services are X.25 and Frame Relay.

Organizations can use these services to create virtual data networks over wide areas that connect every site in the organization at a much lower cost than dedicated

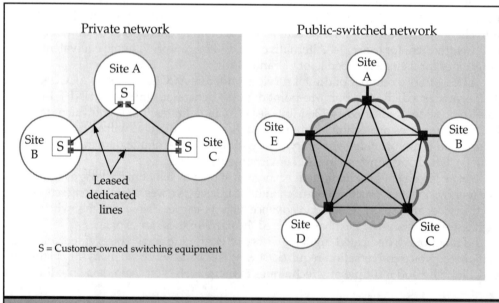

Figure 8-6. *Comparing private and public WAN services*

leased lines, assuming the strategy fits the bandwidth requirements. Packet-switched services provide bandwidth-on-demand and pay-for-use rates. Note the following:

■ Packets of information are routed through a mesh network based on destination address information in the packet header.

■ Packets travel through shared ports, where slight delays may occur, especially if packets are variable in length. Note that delays may be unacceptable for some data transmissions.

■ Logical, connection-oriented virtual circuits can be defined in advance.

■ Variable bandwidth capabilities support bursts in traffic.

■ The source can transmit at any time. It is not necessary to set up a session in advance.

■ The network automatically routes around downed lines or nodes. In the public networks, there are many "alternate" routes that can handle traffic from failed paths.

Because of the many possible connections and pathways, a packet-switched network is often said to provide any-to-any connections as opposed to point-to-point circuit-switched networks.

The traditional packet-switching service was X.25, but Frame Relay is growing in use as a way to build fast network connections over public-switching facilities. It is a "fast packet" service, as described next.

Fast Packet Services

The "fast" in fast packet technologies comes from the fact that error checking, packet sequencing, and acknowledgment are not handled by the network but by the end stations. This allows quick relaying of information. If the network loses a packet or drops a packet due to corruption, congestion, or link errors, it is the job of the receiving station to detect the missing packet and request a retransmission. Eliminating this error checking from the network improves performance. Because most modern telecommunication facilities are built on highly reliable media such as fiber-optic cable, they are inherently reliable and do not require extensive error checking. The error checking in X.25 was implemented to accommodate unreliable telephone lines, which were prevalent when the standard was implemented. Such lines are still prevalent in some countries, and X.25 is the only reliable service you can get.

More About Virtual Circuits

Because packet-switched networks transmit packets through a mesh of network connections, you establish logical or *virtual* circuits to create point-to-point links through the network. A virtual circuit is a connection-oriented link between sites that has some interesting characteristics. A path is defined through the network to improve performance. With a predefined path, some header information can be removed from packets, which leaves more room for data. Figure 8-7 illustrates virtual circuits between LAN users and remote sites.

There are *permanent* and *switched* virtual circuits:

- A *permanent virtual circuit (PVC)* is created when you order a switching service like Frame Relay from a provider. The provider programs the end points of your network connections into their switches. Currently, Frame Relay only supports PVC.

- A *switched virtual circuit (SVC)* is a service that lets you make connections to many different sites in a packet-switched network. So far, SVCs are available in X.25 networks but are still emerging in Frame Relay networks.

SVCs and PVCs are typically discussed in terms of the public data network, although organizations with in-house switching networks built around technology

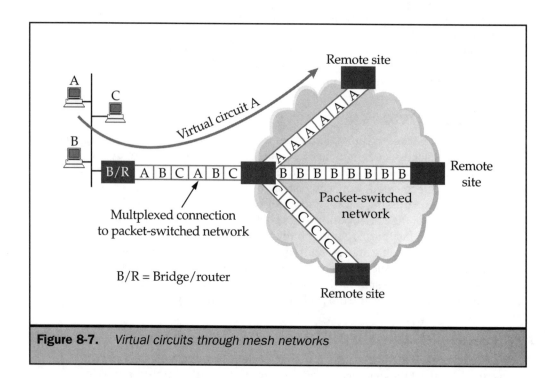

Figure 8-7.   *Virtual circuits through mesh networks*

such as ATM can define PVCs in advance to reduce network overhead. In terms of carrier services, customers are typically charged an initial setup cost for a PVC, and then charged on a monthly basis or on a per-packet basis.

PVCs are the traditional connection method in the Frame Relay environment, although SVC support was added to the specification in late 1993. PVCs have specific service characteristics. You define PVCs and the service characteristics listed here when setting up the service with a provider:

- *Committed burst size (CBS)* is the maximum amount of data (in bits) that the network provider agrees to transfer under normal network conditions during a time interval.

- *Committed information rate (CIR)* is the rate at which the network provider agrees to transfer CBS data during normal network conditions on a PVC.

- *Excess burst size (EBS)* is the maximum allowed amount of uncommitted data (in bits) in excess of CBS that the network will attempt to deliver during a time interval. EBS data is treated as discard-eligible by the network during congestion periods.

- *Frame size* is the size of the frame in which customer data is transferred through the packet-switched network.

X.25 Packet Switching

X.25 is a protocol that defines connections to a packet-switched public data network (PSPDN). Physical network connections and data-link connections are defined in the protocol. X.25 networks operate at speeds of up to 64 Kbits/sec. They perform extensive error checking at every node to ensure data delivery over unreliable telephone lines. However, as stated earlier, this extensive error checking is no longer as necessary on today's reliable networks. Faster services like Frame Relay obtain their performance improvement by reducing the error-checking overhead.

X.25 is a standard, well-tested, and often-revised protocol that has been a workhorse packet-switching service since 1976. It is suitable for light loads and was commonly used to provide remote terminal connections to mainframe systems. X.25 packet-switched networks are not suitable for most LAN-to-LAN traffic because they are slow and require a large portion of the bandwidth to handle error checking.

Frame Relay Services

Frame Relay provides services similar to X.25 but is faster and more efficient. As discussed earlier, Frame Relay is a "fast packet" technology that gains its performance by reducing error checking. Frame Relay is an excellent choice for organizations that need any-to-any connections on an as-needed basis. A customer connection into a public Frame Relay network takes the form of a switched or dedicated leased line.

Customer traffic is forwarded through this line to the Frame Relay provider and switched across the network.

Frame Relay is an innovation that emerged from the ISDN specification. It is a circuit-oriented service, although it is often discussed as a fast packet service. Frame Relay networks typically deliver 1.544 Mbits/sec of data throughput, although higher rates are being implemented. Figure 8-8 illustrates a typical Frame Relay network.

The overhead in X.25 is extensive compared to Frame Relay. For example, in X.25, every node along a packet's path must completely receive a packet and perform an error check on the packet before sending it on. Frame Relay nodes simply look at the packet header destination information and immediately forward the packet, in some cases even before it is completely received. Frame Relay does not require the state tables used in X.25 at each intermediate node to deal with management, flow control, and error checking. End nodes must detect missing frames and request a retransmission.

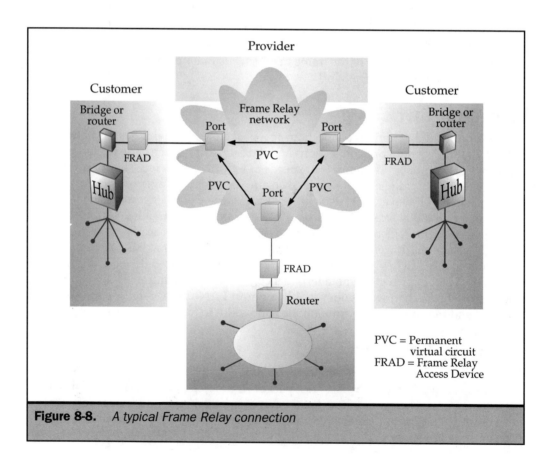

Figure 8-8.   *A typical Frame Relay connection*

Switched Multimegabit Data Service (SMDS)

Switched Multimegabit Data Service (SMDS) is a local exchange carrier (LEC) service that provides a way to extend local area networks in a metropolitan area. SMDS was developed by Bellcore. It uses the same fixed-sized cell relay technology as does Asynchronous Transfer Mode (ATM), and carriers are offering SMDS as a service that uses the cell relay technology.

As a switching technology, SMDS has advantages over building private networks with dedicated digital lines such as T1. Customers set up one line (of appropriate bandwidth) at each network site into the LEC's SMDS network. The network then provides any-to-any connections between the sites.

The switching technology of SMDS can provide customers with connection options that accommodate changing business needs. The cost of the service is typically based on a flat monthly fee, but it is ideal for customers who need to switch connections among many sites. Because the local exchange carriers are the primary providers of SMDS, there is usually no competition for the service in some areas. However, customers should weigh the use of SMDS against other switching services such as Frame Relay.

SMDS is one of the "fast packet" technologies that leaves error checking and flow control procedures up to the end nodes. If a packet is missing, the receiving node requests a retransmission. The network itself is not burdened with this type of error checking. While this places more work on end systems, again, that work is usually minimal because modern lines are relatively error-free.

Figure 8-9 shows the basic configuration of a customer connection to the telephone company's SMDS network.

SMDS is compatible with the IEEE 802.6 metropolitan area network (MAN) standard, as well as Broadband ISDN (B-ISDN). SMDS does provide management and billing services not specified in the MAN standard, however. The SMDS network is a dual bus design that forms an unclosed ring. Physically, it takes on the form of a star-configured network like Token Ring, in which all cables are connected at a central location. If the bus is spliced, the formerly unclosed portion is automatically joined to maintain the ring. The bus is filled with time slots into which any connected device or site can place data for transport. Think of boxcars attached to a train into which data is placed for transport to other locations. This technique provides a true multi-access bus technology, because all nodes can access the bus when they want until the network is saturated.

Some industry analysts feel that SMDS will fail to become popular due to Frame Relay and ATM technology. Carriers have been slow to adopt SMDS, and it is not available in every metropolitan area. Currently, equipment for Frame Relay connections is approximately one-sixth the cost of comparable SMDS equipment.

Understanding Network Technology

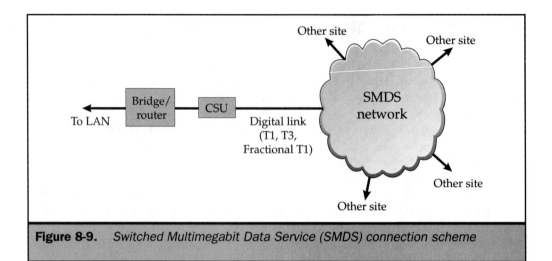

Figure 8-9.   *Switched Multimegabit Data Service (SMDS) connection scheme*

Gaining Access to Switched Services

The problem with any switched service is gaining access to the carrier facility that provides the service. The any-to-any connections from local LAN users to remote LAN users are not provided at the customer site for public networks but in the carrier's switching equipment. Customers must lease dedicated lines such as T1 or T3 with enough capacity to carry multiplexed local data traffic to the carrier's switching facility or use switched lines such as Switched-56 or the ISDN interfaces to reach the facility.

At first, leasing a dedicated line to reach the carrier facility may appear to defeat the purpose of using switched facilities, but keep in mind that the distance to the carrier's network is usually relatively short. The switched facilities then provide any-to-any connections over long distances at rates that are far less expensive than building private networks with dedicated lines over long distances.

The problem and expense of current WAN services is the requirement that customers route traffic through local exchange carrier (LEC) facilities in their area, where it is picked up by the long-distance carriers at the point-of-presence (POP) facility. As mentioned earlier, MCI and other long-distance carriers plan to alleviate this situation by building bypass facilities in major metropolitan areas.

Other Trends

It's worthwhile to look at some of the technologies and services that will support future global data, voice, and video networks. The amount of data traffic on networks will increase as the power and speed of computing systems improve. As demand grows, the data network will become as prevalent and transparent as the voice network. Synchronous Optical Network (SONET) is a transport network that enables this. It defines a multiplexing standard for fiber-optic cable transmission with data rates that range from 51 Mbits/sec to 2,488 Mbits/sec. Even higher rates are envisioned on existing optical cable by using different color bands to simultaneously transmit signals.

Asynchronous Transfer Mode (ATM) carries data on SONET networks. It multiplexes cells (fixed-sized packets) of data from many sources on the physical network (SONET). ATM provides virtual communication paths through the SONET network. A connection-oriented virtual circuit between two points can reach speeds from 45 Mbits/sec to 622 Mbits/sec, although 45 Mbits/sec is the current carrier limit. ATM switching is useful at the LAN level in wiring hubs. It is also useful as a switching technology for international and global telecommunication networks.

Above ATM is Broadband Integrated Services Digital Network (B-ISDN). ATM is the engine for B-ISDN. B-ISDN is a successor to ISDN, which defined how to provide circuit-switching communication to homes and offices in increments of 64 Kbits/sec. B-ISDN uses ATM technology and the SONET physical network to deliver data transfer speeds from 155 Mbits/sec to 622 Mbits/sec along with a variety of customer services.

The
Complete
Reference

NetWare
5

Chapter 9

Internetworking NetWare Networks

173

LANs have made it easy to share resources and information within departments or single-site companies, but as your company grows and builds branch or division offices, you need to internetwork in the local area and over wide areas. At the same time, with the proliferation of TCP/IP, internetworking has become easier, not more complex. New routing protocols, hardware devices, and support in the network operating system for large internetworks has also made internetworking much easier. Carrier services now offer a range of communication options that can provide full-time or part-time internetworking, so choosing a WAN service is simplified and you are more likely to find one that fits your budget.

This chapter looks at internetworking from the protocol perspective. When it comes to building internetworks, especially over WANs, some protocols such as TCP/IP are better than others. Novell's older IPX is not necessarily one of those protocols. However, Novell has enhanced IPX for organizations that need better WAN performance from it and are not ready to switch to TCP/IP. NetWare Link Services Protocol (NLSP) is one of those enhancements.

This chapter discusses Novell's older IPX, its inefficiencies, and ways that you can improve its performance. It discusses NLSP and techniques for building wide area networks, which may involve making the switch to TCP/IP. Novell has made this easier than ever with new built-in support for TCP/IP and with new add-on packages that help you implement and manage TCP/IP internetworks.

Goal of Building Internetworks

There are many reasons for building internetworks. The most obvious is that you need to interconnect the branch and division offices of your company. Other reasons include the following:

- To provide electronic mail services for the entire organization and include links to external mail services such as those provided on the Internet

- To provide an easy way to distribute information to people without resorting to printing and mailing the information

- To provide in-house bulletin board services so users can exchange information and create workgroup chat sessions

- To use electronic data interchange (EDI), in which you connect with customers and/or vendors to perform ordering, billing, and other business procedures online

- To manage all branches of the network from a central site

An internetwork can link all of an organization's offices and users to provide access to network services while physically locating those services anywhere they are best managed.

NetWare 5 Built-in Networking

A NetWare 5 server can connect with a variety of network topologies (e.g., Ethernet, Token Ring, and LocalTalk) and provide routing among popular network transport protocols (e.g., IPX, IP, and AppleTalk). By installing more than one network interface card in a NetWare server, as pictured in Figure 9-1, you automatically build an internetwork that potentially allows all the nodes on those networks to communicate with one another.

Not all computers attached to those networks will use the same transport protocols. Some of the computers on the Ethernet network might use NetWare's older IPX protocol, while others might use TCP/IP. Macintosh computers on the LocalTalk network use AppleTalk protocols. However, because the NetWare server supports multiple protocols, any client can access the server (assuming the server is running its protocols). In addition, NetWare servers act as routers and so participate in forwarding packets to an appropriate address on the internetwork.

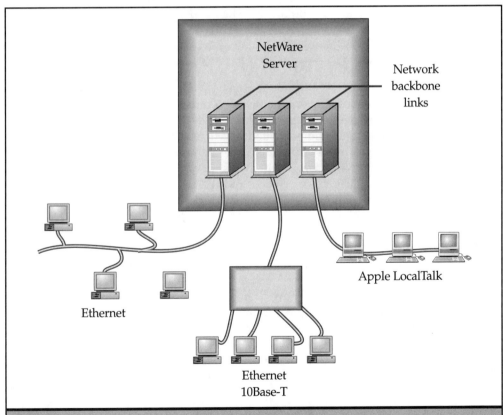

Figure 9-1. *NetWare servers have built-in internetworking features*

That means you can build a network with different data-link topologies such as Ethernet and Token Ring and attach computers using different protocol stacks, such as Apple Macintoshes running AppleTalk, DOS PCs running IPX, and UNIX systems running TCP/IP.

A busy NetWare file server or application server that also performs extensive routing functions may suffer a loss of performance. You may need to move the routing functions onto special routing servers such as the one that runs Novell's NetWare MultiProtocol Router (MPR). You install MPR on a separate NetWare server and let it handle all the routing functions, including routing packets over WAN links to branch offices.

When you install a NetWare 5 server, you select whether you want to run the TCP/IP protocol, the IPX protocol, or both. The appropriate protocol stacks will be assigned to your network interface cards. However, routing functions are not enabled for TCP/IP and IPX by default. You use a utility called INETCFG on NetWare servers to configure routing features and functions directly from the server's console. To monitor your networks and protocols, you use the MONITOR utility. It displays statistics and other information about the attached LANs and protocols in use.

NetWare Core Protocol (NCP) and WANs

The NetWare Core Protocol (NCP) provides the basic file, print, and other network services to NetWare clients. When a client needs services from a NetWare server, it sets up a connection-oriented session with the server, and NCP is used to manage the session. Because NCP is connection-oriented, server and client follow a request/reply procedure that basically consists of packets "ping-ponging" over the network between the systems. NetWare 5's NCPs were written to support both the IP and IPX protocols. They provide pure IP as the default protocol and IPX for backward compatibility.

All the requests and all the replies can generate a lot of network traffic, which can cause problems on a WAN. If a request or reply packet gets delayed on the WAN link, a timeout occurs, which may generate additional traffic if a correction is attempted. Novell has built "packet burst" technology into NetWare to take care of this problem to some extent. The Packet Burst protocol in NetWare allows you to transfer large files without all the acknowledgments from the receiver. Basically, there is an initial request to transfer a file, followed by an acknowledgment, which is then followed by a burst of data as the file is transferred. A single acknowledgment at the end of the transfer completes the transmission.

Note *Another way to avoid excessive NCP request/reply traffic is to avoid executing programs over a WAN link. If possible, execute all programs from a local hard drive.*

Building Internetworks with IPX/SPX

Routing takes place at the Network layer in the OSI protocol model. Novell's IPX network protocols operate at this layer. RIP (Routing Information Protocol) is commonly used to build information about the network, and SAP (Service Advertising Protocol) is used by servers to advertise the services they offer or by nodes to query for services. During installation of NetWare, you can "bind" the IPX protocol to one or more of the network interface cards in the server.

RIP is a distance-vector routing protocol that collects information about routes on the network and builds tables so routers can determine where to send packets. Versions of RIP are used in IP and AppleTalk networks.

RIP is also used in the TCP/IP environment, but the Open Shortest Path First (OSPF) routing protocol usually takes its place.

SAP is a legacy protocol that has been used in almost all versions of NetWare. NetWare servers send out SAP packets, which provide information about the type of services they offer. This information goes out as a database that other servers and nodes read. In NetWare 5, the use of SAP has been replaced with a system that dynamically adds the services into Novell Directory Services (NDS) as objects. Workstations locate services on the network by consulting NDS. Even so, SAP is still used on older IPX networks, including NetWare 4.*x* networks. Workstations using the older client software use it to initially find the closest NDS server and many older network devices require it.

The Problems with IPX

The problems with IPX are RIP and SAP, and these problems have become well-known as companies have tried to expand their networks. IPX with RIP and SAP were adequate when LANs were small and located within single departments or buildings, but RIP and SAP have some inefficiencies that can reduce performance, as discussed in the following sections.

RIP HAS INSUFFICIENT INFORMATION   Recall that the primary task of a routing protocol is to gather information about the routes on a network and build lookup tables for transmitting packets across an internetwork. These tables require periodic updating as the network changes.

A RIP process in a NetWare router gets summary information about routes on the internetwork from adjacent routers. It then builds a new routing table based on any new information it receives. The summary information indicates the next hop for the router (a hop is a jump to the next router). This "next hop-only" information limits the router's ability to make intelligent decisions about how to send a packet along the "best" route to its destination. The NLSP protocol, discussed later, solves this problem by maintaining a more complete map of the internetwork.

RIP PRODUCES TOO MUCH OVERHEAD RIP ties up the internetwork by transmitting a lot of unnecessary information. Each router periodically transmits packets that contain its entire routing table. These broadcasts occur on a periodic basis, even if the tables haven't changed. Routers running NLSP, on the other hand, transmit routing information only when things change on the internetwork, and then transmit only the information that has changed.

SAP ADDS TO THE OVERHEAD Older NetWare servers, 3.*x* and 4.*x*, use the Service Advertising Protocol (SAP). With SAP, a service will broadcast a copy of its service database to the entire network on a periodic basis so other servers and clients can know what the server has to offer. This is really an inefficient use of network bandwidth and can completely saturate a low-speed WAN link. There are ways to filter SAP traffic over WANs, and in NetWare 5, Novell Directory Services (NDS) removes the need for SAP because workstations can simply look up services in the NDS directory.

IPX HAS SCALABILITY PROBLEMS Packets on IPX internetworks cannot go through more than 15 hops when traveling from source to destination. If a packet crosses more than 15 routers, it is discarded. This is only a problem if your network consists of routers connected to routers connected to more routers. To avoid this problem, design or rebuild your networks around a backbone, and then connect each router directly to the backbone. Backbones are discussed in Chapter 7. On a backbone that supports directly attached networks, a node on one network is only two hops away from a node on another network. In addition, it's easier to filter network traffic and SAPs on specific networks.

Advantages of IPX

Even though RIP and SAP pose a few problems, there are still advantages to building IPX networks. IPX provides end-to-end data transport services that are easy to install and manage. You don't need to configure workstation addresses or configure routing information. IPX is also well-supported and is already installed in many existing LANs. Switching to another protocol like TCP/IP may not be cost-effective. Indeed, Novell has resolved most of the problems with RIP and SAP by creating NetWare Link Service Protocol (NLSP), discussed next.

NetWare Link Services Protocol (NLSP)

NetWare Link Services Protocol (NLSP) is a routing protocol that was developed by Novell for IPX internetworks. It is derived from IS-IS (Intermediate System to Intermediate System), the link state routing protocol developed by the International Organization for Standardization. Routers running NLSP exchange information about network links, the cost of paths, IPX network numbers, and media types. They use this information to build routing tables.

One of the most important features of NLSP is that it knows more about the entire internetwork, not just neighboring routers. This allows the router to make intelligent decisions about how to route a packet. A map of the network is constructed from information the router obtains from other routers. It then builds a table that is much more extensive than RIP tables, although this does take some time. In reality, the overhead of this process is actually quite small compared to the performance gains of NLSP. NLSP also provides other performance benefits:

- NLSP only transmits routing information when something has changed on the network, and it uses a multicasting method for transmitting the information. With multicasting, only specified routers bother to read the information. Other nodes do not waste their processing time accepting packets they don't need.

- NLSP provides a more efficient service advertising method than SAP. It sends out information about services that have changed on a server only when those changes take place.

- NLSP compresses the IPX header to reduce the size of the data packets. Compression helps to conserve bandwidth when IPX packets travel over low-speed WAN links.

- NLSP can forward packets through up to 127 hops and so is more scalable. It also uses hierarchical addressing of nodes, so you can deploy networks containing thousands of LANs and servers.

All of these enhancements add up to faster data transmissions over network links when compared to IPX with RIP and SAP. Figure 9-2 illustrates how IPX with NLSP can deliver more data over a line than IPX with RIP and SAP.

Some additional features of NLSP include the following:

- The optional ability to do *load splitting,* which is a way to split traffic across two or more equal-cost paths between two network routers. This feature lets you create fault-tolerant redundant links between sites and use all of those links for data transfer.

- You can manually assign the cost of a link. This provides a way to control which links are used. You could reduce traffic on an overloaded link by giving it a higher cost than a duplicate link you have to the same location.

- NLSP can automatically switch to alternate links if an existing link fails. It checks for failures on a periodic basis. After switching links, the NLSP routing tables are updated in each router so that packets are sent across the new paths if necessary.

This last point provides some insight into how you should build your internetwork. If you have three network sites, for example, you would create a ring as shown in Figure 9-3. In this configuration, a link exists between each site. If one of the links fails, network traffic can be diverted around the other links. For example, if the link between Site A and Site B fails, traffic from Site A to Site B can be routed through Site C.

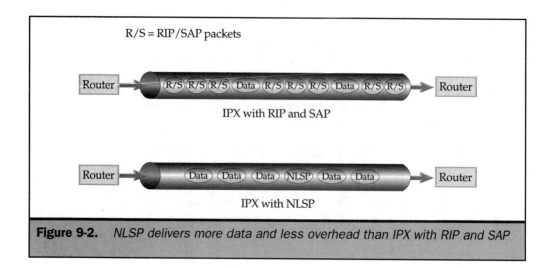

Figure 9-2. *NLSP delivers more data and less overhead than IPX with RIP and SAP*

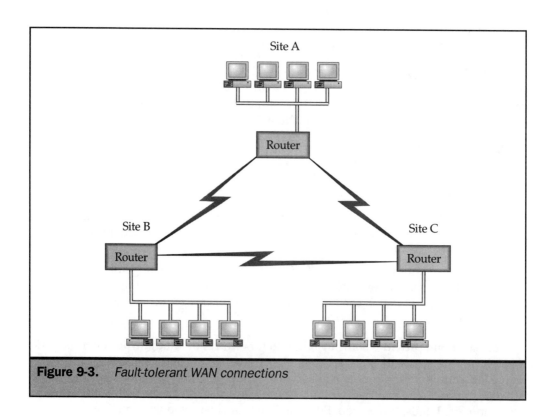

Figure 9-3. *Fault-tolerant WAN connections*

In another situation, assume that the link between Site B and Site C is a slow communication link that should only be used for backup in case one of the other two links fails. The other two links are high-speed connections, and you want all traffic to go through them. Even traffic between Site C and Site B goes through Site A. To prevent traffic from flowing through the Site B to Site C connection, you can manually assign it a high link cost. If one of the high-speed links fails, traffic is diverted through the backup link and all sites remain connected.

NLSP will eventually replace RIP and SAP; however, both are still included in NetWare for compatibility with Novell and third-party network devices that have not been upgraded to support NLSP and for communication between routers and workstations. Planners, managers, and technicians should note the following:

- NLSP works on Ethernet, Token Ring, and point-to-point links—basically all media supported by NetWare.

- Prior to NLSP, RIP and SAP filtering was used to restrict access to parts of the network and to keep RIP and SAP traffic from propagating throughout the network. Filtering is not required with NLSP except for security reasons. Novell is providing NLSP packet filtering that is based on source and destination addresses.

- NLSP- and RIP-based routers can coexist on the same internetwork. This helps you migrate from RIP to NLSP.

- NLSP can automatically detect non-NLSP routers and servers and generate the periodic RIP and SAP broadcasts they expect.

- You can manage NLSP from a management console that supports the Simple Network Management Protocol (SNMP). Novell's ManageWise is such a program.

NLSP is designed with smooth migration in mind. You can upgrade routers and servers one system at a time without disrupting the network. Segments converted to NLSP will realize immediate benefits over local and WAN connections. There are no modifications required at client workstations.

How to Design an NLSP Network

An efficient NLSP routing network requires a topology that may be different than your current IPX RIP/SAP internetwork. Novell recommends creating a mesh network topology for wide area connections. NLSP makes such a configuration practical and efficient. The advantages of a mesh WAN are pictured in Figure 9-4. Note that the configuration on the left is basically a WAN backbone network. If the link between any site and the main office fails, that site is cut off from the rest of the network. The configuration on the right provides fault tolerance in that each site has at least three links to the rest of the network.

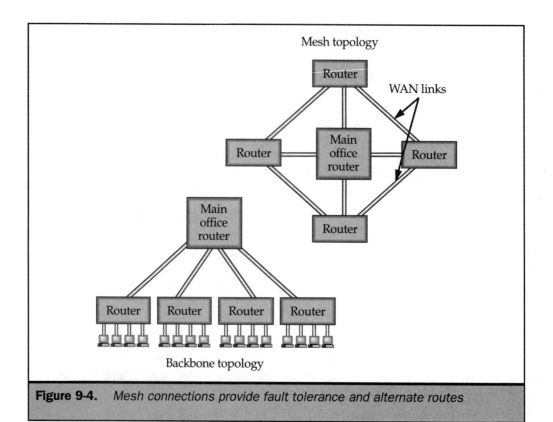

Figure 9-4.   *Mesh connections provide fault tolerance and alternate routes*

Note   *The reason that mesh topologies are not recommended for IPX RIP/SAP networks is that RIP and SAP packets can overwhelm the network.*

Novell has defined an NLSP routing hierarchy that looks similar to Figure 9-5. The hierarchy consists of local area networks within specific *areas* such as a floor or an office building, which are in turn connected together into a domain. Domains are then interconnected. If domains span large geographic areas, you can set up fault-tolerant WAN links, as pictured in Figure 9-5. The levels of routers are as follows:

- **Level 1 Routers**   These are the routers that LAN segments connect to. They are grouped within a specific area.

- **Level 2 Routers**   These are the routers that tie together the Level 1 routers to form routing domains.

- **Level 3 Routers**   These are the routers that tie together domains.

There are several advantages to this hierarchy. Level 1 routers only store link-state information (routing tables) for their own area. If the router needs to send traffic out of its area, it simply contacts the nearest Level 2 router. This reduces the amount of

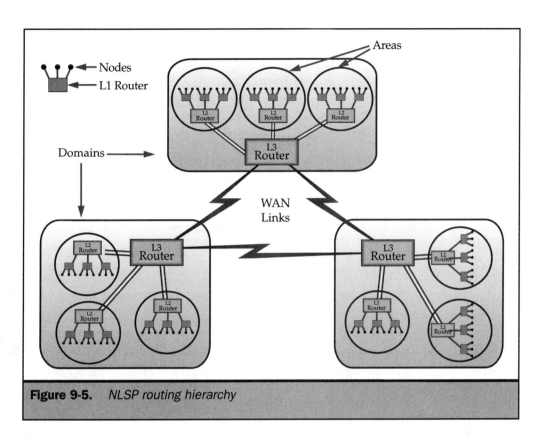

Figure 9-5. *NLSP routing hierarchy*

information that Level 1 routers must process and store. Level 2 routers need to advertise only the addresses for the areas they cover, not the entire link-state database. Likewise, Level 3 routers need to advertise only information about the domains they cover, greatly reducing the amount of information that can go over a WAN link. Note the following:

- Domains may be departments, divisions, or separate companies in the organization.
- Level 2 and Level 3 routing were not available at the time of this writing but are planned.

The hierarchical topology requires some foresight when it comes to assigning individual IPX network numbers to network segments and to the internal networks of routers and servers. You may need to plan your network addresses to accommodate splitting the network into separate areas in the future, a topic that is beyond the scope of this book. For further information, refer to "Migrating an IPX Network to NLSP" in Novell's NetWare 4.1 documentation. You can also contact Novell Network Registry at 408-321-1506 or send Internet e-mail to registry@novell.

Building Internetworks with TCP/IP

With all that was said about IPX and its NLSP enhancements in the previous section, you might not want to consider using TCP/IP on your network. However, current trends demand it. NetWare 5 is designed to use the TCP/IP protocols, so you can configure the server as an IP router and allow TCP/IP users to access the network and servers using their native protocol.

NetWare 5 provides a complete TCP/IP wide area network solution for large companies. It includes both server and client software (DOS and Windows clients), along with a number of features and utilities for managing the network. You can use NetWare 5 to integrate TCP/IP protocols into your current network or completely switch from the native IPX protocol to TCP/IP.

First note that TCP/IP provides the following transport functions that you will find in IPX:

- Transports data between end systems
- Provides routing functions between the subnetworks of a network

In addition, TCP/IP has the following advantages over IPX:

- TCP/IP is widely implemented.
- It is designed for internetworking and has become the protocol of choice for many organizations and systems that you may want to connect with.
- TCP/IP is now included with many desktop operating systems.

This last point makes the transition to TCP/IP much easier and virtually guarantees that TCP/IP will become the dominant protocol. In the past, you had to buy the TCP/IP software for every node, an expense that could be as high as $300. However, desktop operating systems like Windows 95/98 and Windows NT now include TCP/IP. Novell's optional LAN WorkPlace products, discussed in Chapter 4, provide workstation TCP/IP support.

There are some disadvantages to moving to TCP/IP, however. You must set up special IP addressing for every node, including the IP address, subnet mask, default router, and domain name server address. That means you have to plan ahead and designate administrators around your network who can configure the addresses in workstations, unless you implement various techniques to provide automatic configuration (say, for mobile users). Also, if you plan to connect with the Internet, you'll need a registered address.

 To obtain unique Internet addressing information, contact the Internet Network Information Center (InterNIC) in Chantilly, Virginia, at 800-365-3642.

Planning a TCP/IP Internetwork

The Internet is the prime example of a TCP/IP internetwork. It is a global network of interconnected companies and organizations. Local networks are connected to regional networks, which are in turn connected to backbone networks that take advantage of high-speed regional, national, and global connections. In this way, the Internet forms a hierarchical structure. You can connect your network into the Internet and use its communication facilities for exchanging e-mail among the users in your own organization and others and for other commercial activities. However, if you want private dedicated lines between your branch offices, you'll need to build your own TCP/IP network. A TCP/IP internetwork consists of *hosts*, *networks*, and *routers*:

- **Hosts**   A host is any computer that is attached to the TCP/IP network and that runs the TCP/IP protocols. The advantage of TCP/IP is that you can build internetworks with a diversity of computer systems that use different operating systems.
- **Networks**   A network is a collection of hosts that are interconnected with a physical and data-link media, such as Ethernet and Token Ring, or a WAN media.
- **Routers**   Routers are the devices that interconnect different networks and that transport packets from a host on one network to a host on another network.

Note   *A host is often called an* end system, *although a NetWare server that is set up as a router is both an end system that can send or receive IP packets and a router that can forward IP packets.*

The technologies for building the physical TCP/IP network are discussed in Chapters 6, 7, and 8. Any network that you build to run NetWare's native IPX protocol will also support the TCP/IP protocols. In doing so, you must develop a network addressing and naming scheme. It is important to define this scheme early because in many organizations, TCP/IP networks have simply evolved on their own. As TCP/IP is included in peer-to-peer desktop operating systems like Windows NT and Windows 95/98, it is possible to lose control of a company-wide network addressing scheme.

TCP/IP Addressing and Host Identification

There are three ways to identify a host computer system in a TCP/IP environment: by the host name, by the physical address, and by the Internet address of a node on a subnetwork.

Host Name

A host name is a name that makes it easy for people to identify a computer on a particular TCP/IP network. It is much less cryptic than the Internet address. In its simplest form, a host name can be a basic eight-character name, but you only use this form if the internetwork is small and it is easy to identify any computer with such a simple name.

On large internetworks, you create a hierarchical naming system that identifies different domains within the network. For example, Figure 9-6 illustrates the addressing scheme for CambrianCorp. It has subdomains for the sales, administration, and marketing departments. Hosts within each domain are then assigned host names. The host name is appended to the domain name and separated by periods, so that a computer (or user) in the sales department has a name like the following:

tsheldon.sales.cambriancorp

This is called the fully qualified domain name (FQDN). Every name within a domain must be unique. The hierarchical structure of the naming scheme allows a lot of flexibility in naming computers on your internetwork. If users need to refer to another host in their same domain, they can use the simple name or the fully qualified name.

Physical Address

The physical address is used by the data-link protocols to move packets from one computer to another on the same network. The physical address is the hardwired address that is assigned to a network interface card at the factory. The IEEE has devised a numbering scheme that network adapter vendors comply with in order to assure that no two network interface cards ever have the same unique physical address. However, with some cards, you can manually configure the address, so you need to make sure you don't create overlaps.

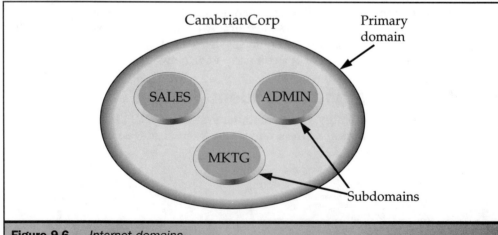

Figure 9-6. *Internet domains*

When one host wants to send a packet to another host, it creates an IP datagram that contains the IP address of the destination host. However, this address must be linked to a physical address. The Address Resolution Protocol (ARP) performs this task.

Recall from Chapter 7 that the physical address is used only when a packet is transferred within the confines of a single network. When a packet needs to traverse the internetwork, the physical address get "tucked" away in the packet and the network addressing scheme comes into play. The packet is directed from router to router based on the address of the network it is trying to find, not the physical address of the node. When the packet finally reaches the correct network, the physical address is pulled out of the packet and used on that network to send the packet to its destination.

Internet Address

An Internet address is a numeric address that uniquely identifies a host system within an IP network. The address, using IPv4, is a 32-bit (4-byte) binary number containing a network identifier and a host identifier. The *network identifier* indicates the network, and the *host identifier* indicates a specific computer on that network. An Internet address uses the dotted-decimal notation format similar to the following, in which a period separates each byte (often called an *octet*) of the 32-bit address:

192.100.10.5

 You can refer to a host system by its Internet address or by its domain name. The Domain Name Service (DNS) is the important Application layer service that performs the translation of a network address to a unique host name.

If you plan to connect with the Internet, then you first need to know about the *class* of a network address. There are basically A, B, and C networks, and each class allows a limited number of network addresses and a limited number of host addresses within each network. For example, Class A networks define 126 networks and an unlimited amount of hosts, while Class C networks define an almost unlimited amount of networks but only 255 hosts per network. When you install TCP/IP services, you'll also need to specify a *subnet mask*, which identifies the host identifier portion of the address based on the class of network. The addressing schemes and subnet masks are outlined as follows:

- **Class A**   The first byte is a number from 1 to 127. The last three bytes identify hosts on the network. Subnet mask: 255.0.0.0

- **Class B**   The first byte is a number from 128 to 191. The second byte is part of the network address and is assigned by the InterNIC. The third and fourth bytes uniquely identify hosts on the network. Subnet mask: 255.255.0.0

- **Class C**   The first byte is a number from 192 to 254. The second and third bytes are part of the network address and are assigned by the InterNIC. The fourth byte uniquely identifies up to 255 hosts on the network. Subnet mask: 255.255.255.0

InterNIC is allocating these addresses, and currently, only class C network addresses are available. All of the hosts on your network must use the same IP network address to contact the Internet. So assume InterNIC assigns you a class C network address of 192.01.01 (excuses to whomever owns this number). Your entire internetwork must use host addresses that look like the following in order to access the Internet, where *xxx* is a specific host address:

192.01.01.*xxx*

This poses a problem if your network consists of subnetworks that are linked by routers. Each of those subnetworks must have a unique network address, but the InterNIC demands that your entire organization only have one network address to connect with the Internet. What do you do? To get around this problem, you need to use *subnet masks*, which divide the network into *logical* subnetworks.

The subnet mask basically reserves the portion of the IP address that identifies the host. So if the subnet mask is 255.255.0.0 (a Class B address), the last two bytes are not masked and are used to identify a specific host. The number 255 converts to binary 11111111, so this subnet mask really looks like this:

11111111.11111111.00000000.00000000

Basically, when a binary 1 is present in the subnet mask, the identical digit in the IP address is reserved for the network address. When a 0 is present, the identical digit in the IP address is reserved as a host address. For your own internal network, you can change the subnet mask to allocate some portion of the host address identifier to a subnetwork. For example, assume you have a Class B network address using the subnet mask listed above. The two bytes (16 bits) on the right are all 0s and thus reserved for host addressing.

That's 16 bits, which means you can define over 65,000 hosts on this network! Because that number is probably excessive for your network, you can use a subnet mask to reserve some of those bits for subnetwork addressing. Assume you want to mask 6 bits for the network address. You go to your handy binary-to-decimal calculator and type in the number 11111100, and then convert it to decimal. The result is 252, so you create a new subnet mask that looks like this:

255.255.252.0

In binary, it looks like this:

11111111.11111111.11111100.00000000

Now you have 6 bits you can use to identify subnetwork addresses, which converts to potentially 62 different subnetworks. So now your internal IP addressing scheme can identify the following subnetworks, where *xxx* are hosts on those networks:

192.01.1.*xxx* to 192.01.62.*xxx*

Internet Routing

An Internet address uniquely identifies the point on the physical network where a host is attached. With this in mind, consider that a host can have two or more Internet addresses if it has two or more network interface cards installed that are running the TCP/IP protocol. A NetWare server that performs routing between TCP/IP networks will have multiple IP addresses, one for each of the network interface cards that it uses for IP routing.

Note *NetWare 5 includes the RIP and Open Shortest Path First (OSPF) routing protocols. OSPF is a link-state routing protocol similar to Novell's NLSP routing protocol used on IPX networks.*

Note that only the network identifier portion of the Internet address is used when routing packets between systems. The router only needs to know the destination network where a packet must be sent. Once the packet reaches that network, ARP is used to determine which host on the network should receive the packet. An ARP request is broadcast on the network, and the host with the target address responds with its hardware address.

The routing architecture of the Internet is a hierarchy of systems that consists of subnetworks with attached hosts. These subnetworks are attached to routers that connect them to other subnetworks within an autonomous system. An *autonomous system* (also called an *interior system* or *domain*) is a collection of subnetworks and routers that generally use the same routing protocols and are under the same administrative control. Autonomous systems are pictured in Figure 9-7.

Interior gateway protocols such as Routing Information Protocol (RIP) and Open Shortest Path First (OSPF) are used to exchange routing information within a domain. At the edges of domains are *border routers* that connect one domain to another. These routers use *exterior routing protocols* to exchange routing information. The Exterior Gateway Protocol (EGP) provides a way for two neighboring routers located at the edges of their respective domains to exchange messages and information.

INTERIOR GATEWAY PROTOCOLS   Interior gateway protocols are the protocols used within a domain for the exchange of routing information. Both routers and hosts use ARP to announce themselves. A router broadcasts packets that contain an IP address. The computer or device attached to a network with the address then returns its LAN address. The information is then placed in routing tables for future use. A similar protocol, called Reverse ARP (RARP), performs the opposite task; it obtains the IP address from a known network address. Both RIP and OSPF are used to exchange information about the state of the network between routers.

EXTERIOR GATEWAY PROTOCOLS (EGPS)   Exterior gateway protocols (EGPs) provide a way for two neighboring routers located at the edges of their respective domains to exchange messages and information. Each EGP exchanges routing information with interior gateways within the same domain using an interior gateway

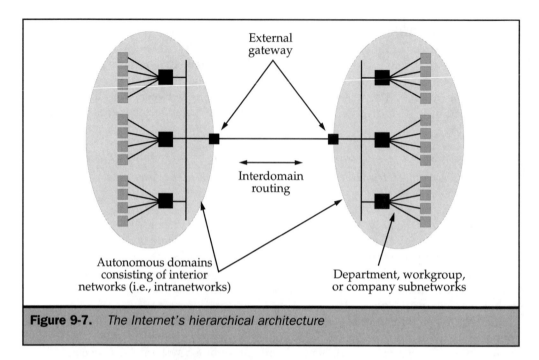

Figure 9-7.   *The Internet's hierarchical architecture*

protocol so that it knows the addresses of end systems (hosts) within the local domain. EGPs connect with EGPs in other domains and exchange routing information about the end systems in the respective domains. With this information, gateways know the best way to send information to other systems outside the domain.

INTERDOMAIN POLICY ROUTING PROTOCOLS   Several new interdomain routing protocols have been proposed for use on the Internet. As the Internet grows in size, existing exterior protocols don't provide adequate scaling capabilities. The new protocols that implement policy-based routing are more scalable (a requirement for the Internet) than EGP. Policy-based routing gives administrators more control over the network, allowing prioritization of traffic and the implementation of security features and service charges.

- *Border Gateway Protocol* (*BGP*) is an interim solution that provides some limited policy features but has limited scalability.

- *Interdomain Routing Protocol* (*IDRP*) is a distance-vector, policy-based routing protocol similar to the Internet Border Gateway Protocol (*BGP*). IDRP is an OSI-based protocol.

- *Interdomain Policy Routing* (*IDPR*) is a link-state routing protocol that implements source routing and policy-based routing between domains. In source routing, the packets themselves hold path information. Initially, paths must be discovered, but subsequent packets simply place the path in their headers.

About NetWare's Built-in TCP/IP

NetWare 5 includes a TCP/IP protocol stack that lets you set up the server to communicate with other servers or workstations using the TCP/IP protocols or to set the server up as an IP router. The following configuration options are set with the INETCFG utility that you run at the NetWare console:

- You must enable IP Packet Forwarding if you want to use the server as an IP router; otherwise, it is simply a TCP/IP end node.

- You must choose the type of routing protocol you want to use, either RIP or Open Shortest Path First (OSPF). OSPF is a link-state routing protocol that has many of the feature advantages of Novell's NLSP.

- You can set static routes in the router, which are useful for reducing routing traffic. Static routes also provide security, are useful for accessing isolated networks, and can serve as backup routers for LANs.

- You can set filtering options to control access to any services on the network or to control bandwidth consumed by routing traffic.

- You can configure router discovery to allow end nodes to find an IP router on their network. If your computer is operating as a router, it can advertise itself periodically as a router; if your computer is operating as an end node, it can send queries to locate a router.

- You can enable ARP or Proxy ARP. ARP is a LAN protocol that maps Internet addresses to physical addresses. IP routers and end nodes use ARP to determine a destination node's physical address. An IP router using Proxy ARP replies to ARP requests it receives through an interface on behalf of an end node on a network attached to another interface.

- You can enable the router to forward *directed broadcasts,* which are broadcasts intended only for a specific group of nodes, rather than all nodes on the network.

- You can configure the router or end node as a BootP forwarder, which enables end nodes to get an IP address at startup time. As a BootP forwarder, the router or end node accepts and forwards BootP requests to a BootP server, which assigns the IP address.

- You can configure multiple logical interfaces on a single board, which enables you to bind more than one IP network to a LAN board to operate as separate logical interfaces.

NetWare Compatibility Mode

NetWare 5's Compatibility Mode provides a link between the older IPX/SPX-based networks and newer TCP/IP-based networks. It is designed to provide a smooth

Understanding Network Technology

transition from IPX to IP. With Compatibility Mode, customers can run applications that have IPX dependencies in an IP-only environment. The rewriting of the NCP allows the use of pure IP without the older encapsulation methods used for transporting IPX in an IP network. The new NCP is shown in Figure 9-8. It has been modified to use both the TCP and UDP transports. This removes all IPX dependencies in NetWare 5. The Compatibility Mode consists of new drivers, a Migration Gateway, and a Bindery Gateway.

Compatibility Mode Drivers

The Compatibility Mode drivers consist of a server compatibility mode driver and a workstation Compatibility Mode driver. The server-side Compatibility Mode driver ensures that all routes and services from the IPX side of the network are communicated to and accessible from the IP side of the network and vice versa. The workstation compatibility mode drivers provide a means to encapsulate IPX in an IP packet. This is used for older applications that have been written using nonstandard interfaces to the IPX stack. NetWare 5 will encapsulate this traffic so as not to compromise the IP environment.

Migration Gateway

The Migration Gateway provides two types of translation services. The first service is a translation between the IPX and IP protocols. It provides a means to link the two logical worlds of IPX and IP. The second service is a translation between the older Service Advertising Protocol (SAP) and the new Service Location Protocol (SLP). It

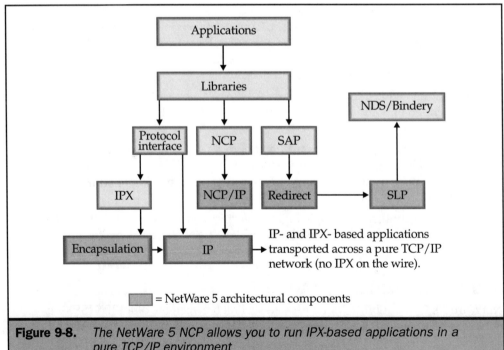

Figure 9-8.   *The NetWare 5 NCP allows you to run IPX-based applications in a pure TCP/IP environment*

replaces SAP and RIP packets on behalf of IPX clients. This prevents the chatty IPX protocol families from populating the IP world. The Migration Gateway has all of the functionality of an IPX router. It can route packets between an IPX segment and an IP segment.

Bindery Gateway

The Bindery Gateway provides backward compatibility with the NetWare 3 bindery. With this gateway, dynamic network objects are transformed into static network objects. These static objects are placed into the NDS tree. Legacy applications that depend on the bindery can find the information they need to operate properly via NDS. This minimizes the traffic on the network while still providing on-demand IPX functionality.

Service Location Protocol (SLP)

The Service Location Protocol (SLP) replaces the older SAP protocol that was used in previous versions of NetWare. It is based on the IETF Service Location Protocol, RFC 2165. It provides a naming and discovery service in a TCP/IP environment. SLP maintains a registry of all network services and registers a particular service's availability only once when that service becomes available on the network. It allows you to query the network and obtain a list of available services. This eliminates the traffic overhead that was characteristic of SAP in large network environments.

IPv4 and IPv6

The Internet Protocol is currently IP version 4, or IPv4. It is the underlying protocol for routing packets on the Internet and other TCP/IP-based networks. It is comprised of four octets separated by periods, *xxx.xxx.xxx.xxx*. IPv4 is limited to a 32-bit address space for both host and network. This worked fine until the recent explosion of more and more hosts connecting to the Internet. A solution was developed with the creation of Classless Interdomain Routing (CIDR), which allocated class C addresses as variable-sized blocks of addresses. CIDR was only a stopgap until a new protocol could be devised.

The IETF began working on a new IP protocol in 1990. The new protocol is called IPv6. It supports all the other Internet protocols but is not backwardly compatible with IPv4. Ipv6 is defined in RFC 1993 and RFC 1887, which are available at the IETF Web site (www.ietf.org). The most important feature of IPv6 is the longer address space. It is 16 bytes long, compared to the 4 bytes for IPv4. This 128-bit addressing scheme will provide enough IP addresses for every person and conceivable device on the planet. The full implementation of IPv6 may take up to ten years before it is in common use.

IPSec and Secure Sockets Layer (SSL) Security

IP Security (IPSec) is developing protocols for creating virtual private networks (VPNs) through the Internet. The IPSec protocol provides cryptographic security services supporting a combination of authentication, integrity, access control, and confidentiality. These services are located at the Network layer of the OSI protocol model. IPSec is based on the Internet Security Association and Key Management

Protocol (ISAKMP). This defines procedures and packet formats to establish, negotiate, modify, and delete security associations. A security association is a relationship between two or more entities that describes how they will utilize security services to communicate securely. ISAKMP cleanly separates the details of security association management and key management from the details of key exchange.

Secure Sockets Layer (SSL) is a Web protocol that sets up a secure session between a Web client and server. SSL encrypts all data being passed between the client and server at the IP socket level. It was originally developed by Netscape and then submitted to the IETF for standardization. With SSL, browsers and servers authenticate one another and then encrypt all data transmitted during a session. SSL consists of the SSL Handshake Protocol (SSLHP), which provides authentication services and negotiates an encryption method. SSL also consists of the SSL Record Protocol (SSLRP), which performs the job of packaging data so it can be encrypted. SSLHP operates in the Application layer of the OSI model. SSLRP operates in the Presentation layer of the OSI model.

IETF's Network Time Protocol

Network Time Protocol (NTP) is an Internet protocol that devices can use to obtain the most accurate time possible. The time sources are synchronized via radio or atomic clocks at various locations on the Internet. This protocol can synchronize the time of a workstation or server to another server or reference time source. The time provided by NTP servers is typically accurate within milliseconds.

NetWare MultiProtocol Router

When you need to build internetworks across wide area links, you can turn to Novell's NetWare MultiProtocol Router (MPR) and its family of products. MPR is a software-based router that can provide LAN-to-LAN, client-to-server, and client-to-host communication. As pictured in Figure 9-9, MPR runs on standard computers, routes IPX, TCP/IP, AppleTalk, and SNA protocols, and supports a wide range of LAN topologies and WAN connections, including dedicated leased lines, dial-on-demand voice-grade circuits, Frame Relay, X.25, ISDN, and SMDS. The NetWare MultiProtocol Router includes the following add-on components:

Add-On Component	Description
NetWare Enterprise Router	Provides 16 WAN ports
NetWare BranchLink Router	Provides 2 WAN ports
WAN Extensions	Provide connection services to Frame Relay and X.25 networks
SNA Extensions	Enhance IBM SNA communications through Data Link Switching and Link/SNA

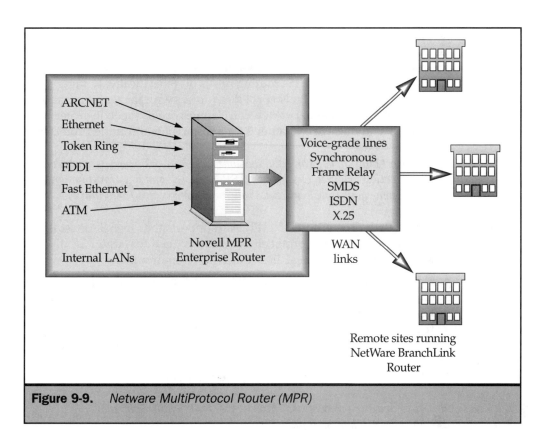

Figure 9-9.   *Netware MultiProtocol Router (MPR)*

The following are some of the important features of MPR:

- **Open Data-Link Interface (ODI)**   MPR runs on top of the NetWare 3, NetWare 4, or NetWare 5 operating system and takes advantage of the ODI interface. You can install many different network adapters such as Ethernet and Token Ring along with communication adapters that support Frame Relay, X.25, ISDN, SMDS, dedicated leased lines, and asynchronous lines.

- **Dial-on-demand routing**   An important feature is dial-on-demand routing, which is a way to provide temporary, nonpermanent links between network sites. This option saves leased line charges when branch sites do not need continuous connections. MPR will automatically make a temporary connection whenever it detects traffic that requires forwarding to another site. You can use this option over voice-grade and switched 56 Kbit/sec digital lines.

- **PPP support**   MPR also supports communication over dedicated leased lines using the industry-standard point-to-point protocol (PPP). Dedicated leased lines supported by MPR include voice-grade lines and digital circuits such as T1. You can use non-MPR routers on the other side of an MPR connection, such as those manufactured by Cisco, Bay Networks, and 3Com. Any PPP-compliant router will do.

■ **NetWare Link Services Protocol (NLSP) support**   MPR uses Novell's NetWare Link Services Protocol (NLSP) for IPX routing. NLSP is a link-state routing protocol that eliminates the excess traffic across wide area networks that was prevalent in previous IPX routing protocols (specifically, Routing Information Protocol, or RIP). It also provides routers with timely information about the current state of the network when changes occur due to its faster "convergence" techniques. See Chapter 7 for a discussion of routing protocols.

Note   *With NLSP support built in, you can build the same mesh network topology as previously discussed in the section "How to Design an NLSP Network" and illustrated in Figure 9-5. MPR can become your level 2 or level 3 routing system in this configuration.*

■ **Open Shortest Path First (OSPF)**   MPR also supports the Open Shortest Path First (OSPF) link-state routing protocol that was designed for large TCP/IP internetworks. OSPF is replacing RIP in the TCP/IP environment.

■ **Compression and filtering to optimize WAN performance**   MPR performs data compression and packet filtering to help reduce line charges on dedicated leased lines. Data compression can reach a four-to-one data ratio and works with all the supported protocols. Packet filtering helps to reduce unnecessary traffic over WAN links by filtering traffic per port, per packet, per protocol, per address, or globally (box level). For example, you can remove packets that are used to advertise the services provided by NetWare servers.

Note   *Use of the NLSP routing protocol also reduces excess traffic caused by the broadcast-intensive RIP and SAP protocols.*

■ **Management features**   Administrators can use built-in tools to manage and configure MPR from a central site. It is not necessary to maintain a manager at the MPR site or send an administrator to that site to perform configurations or updates. MPR uses SNMP-based consoles such as Novell's ManageWise. You can monitor alerts, alarms, and SNMP traps from the central management station.

The Complete Reference

NetWare 5

Part III

NetWare Planning and Installation

The Complete Reference

NetWare 5

Chapter 10

Introduction to Novell Directory Services

N ovell Directory Services (NDS) is an implementation of distributed directory services as defined by the International Organization for Standards (ISO) X.500 specification. The service keeps track of all network users, servers, and resources for small local networks or large global networks. This information is kept in a global database (called the *Directory Information Base,* or *DIB*), which network administrators and users access when they need to manage or use services on the network.

What Is NDS?

One way to think of NDS is as a giant telephone book for your network, and indeed you can store information such as telephone numbers, addresses, department locations, and other identifying information for every user on your network. Then any user or network manager can find a user by searching for the name or identifying information, such as ZIP code, department name, or job function. Take a look at Figure 10-1. It

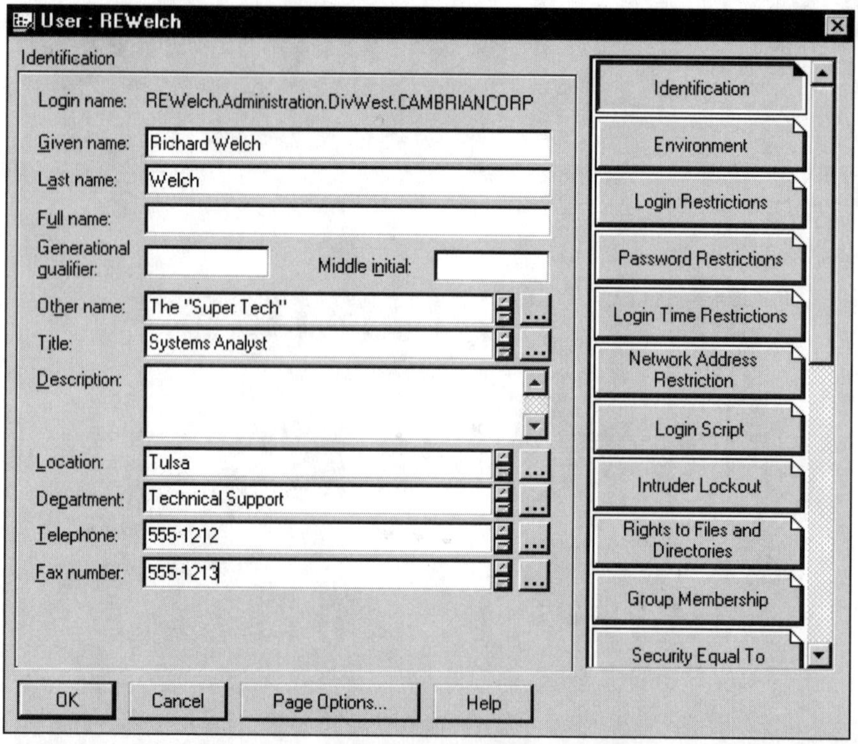

Figure 10-1. *Information about a user in the NDS database*

shows a picture of how NDS user information is presented in the Windows-based management tool called NetWare Administrator.

The information is a record in the NDS database and has fields such as Login Name, Title, and Telephone number. In NDS, the record is more properly called an *object,* and the fields are called *properties.* Note the buttons on the right side of the window. You click these buttons to view other "pages" of information about users, such as the type of restrictions they have to the network or their mailbox information.

Note *Typically, users can view but not change most of the properties of their own User object and other objects.*

NDS treats all network users and resources as objects and organizes them into a hierarchical directory tree. There are three types of objects:

- The *[Root]* object, which is the base of the directory tree and which usually has the same name as your organization
- *Container* objects, which hold other objects
- *Leaf* objects, which represent users and resources (devices) on the network and are contained in container objects

An NDS directory tree is often designed around the topology of the physical network, as shown in Figure 10-2. Note that the tree has container objects representing the company name (CambrianCorp), its regional divisions (Eastern and Western), and its regional offices. Under each regional office are leaf objects that represent users and physical network entities such as servers and printers.

Figure 10-3 illustrates how this directory tree appears when you use the NetWare Administrator utility. The tree can be expanded and collapsed so managers can view different parts of the network and work with objects in that area. In this example, the Administration container is expanded to show the users and network resources located in that department.

Users, devices, and other resources on the network are all represented by objects, although it's important to understand that an NDS object simply holds information about a real physical object in the same way that your driver's license holds information about you.

- The [Root] object is automatically created when you first install NetWare 5. You can name the root object anything you want.
- Container objects are *branches* in the directory that hold other container objects or leaf objects. You can grant your division, department, or workgroup managers control of the network at these branches (we will refer to these managers as subadministrators).
- The directory tree grows upside down, starting at the root, which is at the top.

NetWare Planning
and Installation

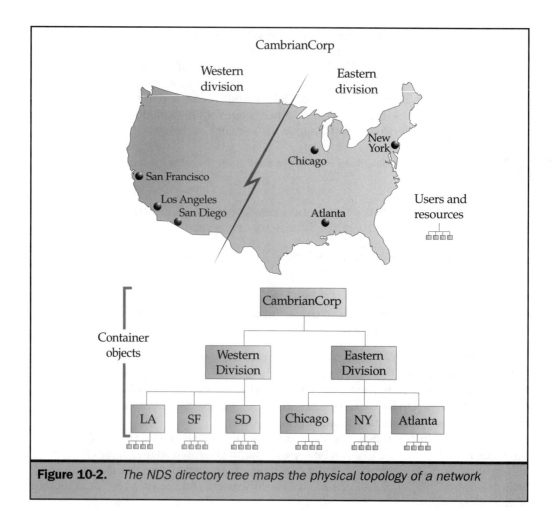

Figure 10-2. *The NDS directory tree maps the physical topology of a network*

■ A user called ADMIN with Supervisor (full) rights to the entire tree and server
  file systems is created during the installation process in the organization
  container, which falls directly under the root.

The structure of the directory tree is entirely based on an organization's structure
and/or location. You can create a directory tree that resembles the physical location of
users and resources in an organization, or you can organize it to reflect the management
structure. As stated earlier, the directory tree in Figure 10-2 is organized around the
geographic location of the network sites. Another method is to organize a tree based on
departments of the company, as shown in Figure 10-4. This model makes it easy for
department managers to manage their specific branch of the directory tree.

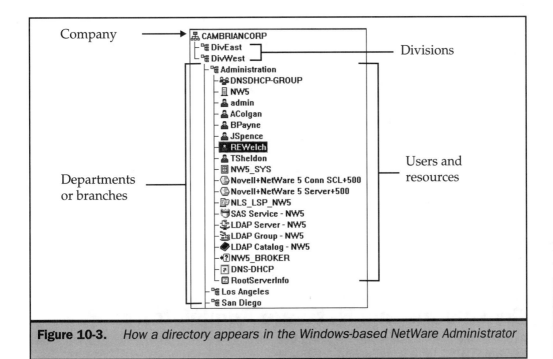

Figure 10-3. *How a directory appears in the Windows-based NetWare Administrator*

You should consider a number of things when designing a directory tree, and these are discussed in Chapter 12. One of the most important is protecting the NDS database from failure. It contains all the information that users need to log in, so it is important to replicate (copy) it to other servers so users can log in should the main database server go down. Using techniques called *partitioning* and *replication* (discussed later

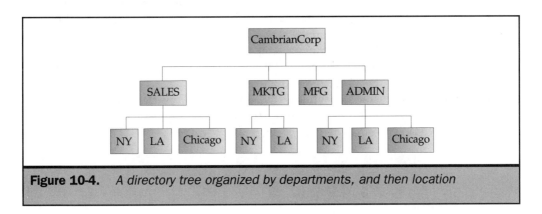

Figure 10-4. *A directory tree organized by departments, and then location*

under "NDS Partition Management"), you can split the database and copy parts of it to other locations so the database is more easily accessible to users at that location and protected from failure as well.

Another consideration when designing a directory tree is the administration of network access rights. Look at the Eastern Division in Figure 10-2. If a network administrator grants the NY container access rights to a file system directory on a server in another branch of the tree, then users in that container automatically obtain the same rights. This is because objects in a container automatically get the same rights to the container they belong to. Rights "flow down" through the container structure, so if you instead grant the rights to the Eastern Division container, those rights flow down to its subcontainers (Chicago, NY, and Atlanta). Now all the users in all of these containers can access the directory on the server. Good planning will make it much easier to manage the directory tree later.

Note *When you explicitly grant a user the right to access another object, the user becomes a trustee of that object.*

ConsoleOne and NetWare Administrator

ConsoleOne is a Java-based application that runs on any computer with a Java Virtual Machine (JVM). It is a GUI server console that allows you to perform basic NDS management tasks. Future versions of ConsoleOne will provide the same level of functionality as the NetWare Administrator utility. The ConsoleOne utility window is shown in Figure 10-5. ConsoleOne can be started either by entering C1START.NCF at the server console or by launching it from a workstation. It allows you to browse objects and manage objects from the server console. The left window frame allows you to navigate by expanding and collapsing objects. The right window frame displays the contents of the objects being browsed. Most server management tasks are located under the My Server object. When expanded, it shows volumes, configuration files, and tools. A Java-based GUI text editor and remote server access are contained in the tools object. ConsoleOne allows you to create Organization (O), Organizational Unit (OU), Group, and User objects within an NDS tree.

NetWare Administrator (NWADMIN32) is a Windows-based application used to manage Novell Directory Services as well as parts of the filing system. NetWare Administrator replaces many of the utilities and commands in previous versions of NetWare. It is easier to use and provides more functionality. Figure 10-6 shows a NetWare Administrator window.

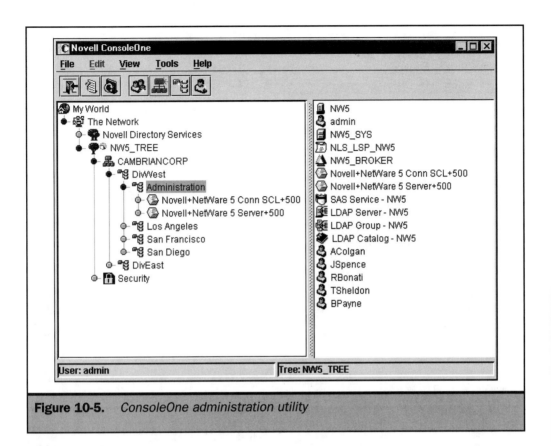

Figure 10-5.   *ConsoleOne administration utility*

NetWare Planning
and Installation

> **Note**   *A text-based version of NetWare Administrator called NETADMIN is also supplied with NetWare 5 to use at non-Windows workstations.*

Note that the NetWare Administrator window in Figure 10-6 has two open windows that present different views of the same directory tree. On the right is the top level of the tree showing the major Eastern and Western divisions. You can double-click on any container object to expand its list of containers or leaf objects. Note that DivWest is already expanded in this example to show its subcontainers, while DivEast is collapsed. The left window shows a view of the Administration department in the DivWest branch of the tree. Using multiple windows in NetWare Administrator makes it easier to access the objects in the tree you want to manage.

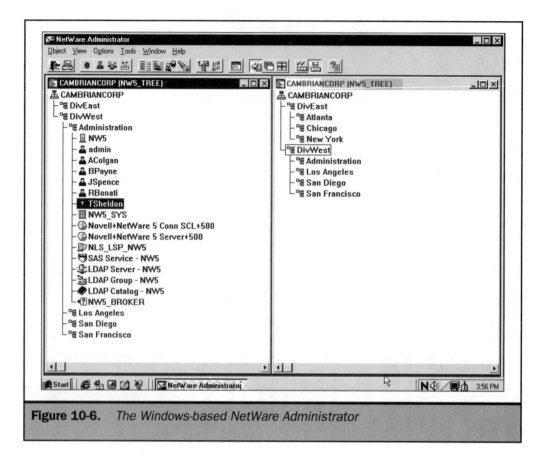

Figure 10-6.   *The Windows-based NetWare Administrator*

Once you've opened a container and expanded its objects, you can manage any object by double-clicking it. This displays a window of the object's properties, similar to the window you see in Figure 10-1.

A search feature lets you quickly locate similar objects. For example, you can list all users who live within a certain ZIP code area or who have a specific job description. Here's a list of things administrators can do with NetWare Administrator:

- Create additional objects, such as User and Printer objects
- Change the login restrictions of users
- Change users' access to resources
- Change users' access to directories and files
- Change the trustees of objects
- Grant other users Supervisor or subadministrator rights to objects on the network

- Specify groups of users and create login profiles for those users
- Create and edit system-wide and individual user login scripts
- Arrange and organize the structure of the Novell Directory Services tree and its partitions

Understanding the Directory Tree

The [Root] object is at the top of the tree (see Figure 10-7), and it holds the name of the tree. (It is named [Root] by default, but you can rename it during installation.) You'll rarely need to make reference to it after creating it during the installation process. Containers form the branches of the tree and are used to form divisions, departments, and workgroups within an organization.

There are four container objects, which are discussed later in the chapter:

- **Country** This is an optional object that you can use to split the tree into different countries if you have a multinational network.
- **Locality** You can use this object to designate regions of a network.
- **Organization** Use this object to define different companies within an organization or different divisions within a company. At least one Organization object is required in every tree.
- **Organizational Unit** Think of an Organizational Unit object as a subdivision or branch of the directory tree. You use it to organize leaf objects. Organizational Units typically define business Units, departments, or workgroups.

NetWare Planning and Installation

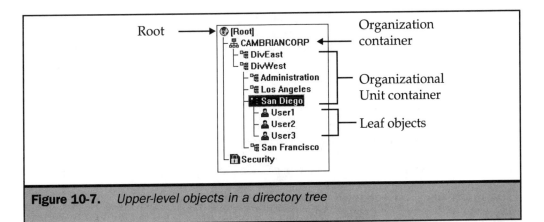

Figure 10-7. *Upper-level objects in a directory tree*

When you're planning your directory tree, you'll design the top layer of container objects first, based on geographic locations or the divisions and departments of your organization.

The Object-Naming Format

Every object has a specific context within the directory tree that forms a path from the object itself to the root of the tree. The context is the location of the object within the tree. This path to the root is called the *distinguished name,* and it specifies exactly where an object is in the directory structure, similar to a house address that specifies a street, city, state, and country. The path contains the name of the object itself and the names of the containers that hold it, each separated by periods. It is similar to the path name a file has in a hierarchical filing system, in which the true name of the file includes the drive where it is located, the directories where it is stored, and the name of the file itself.

The default name sequence is

Common Name.Organizational Unit.Organization.Country

Note	*The root of the directory tree is implied and you don't need to include it when naming objects.*

Here you can see that the name is constructed from left to right (the opposite of directory and file names in the filing system), starting with the leaf object name or common name. *Common name* (CN=) is the name of a leaf object, such as a user or server. If the tree contains multiple levels of organizational units, the name sequence could look something like this:

Common Name.Organizational Unit.Organizational Unit.Organization.Country

You might need to add the following name type abbreviations to help the operating system determine exactly what type of object a partial name represents. You'll also see these abbreviations used in print and in programs when referring to specific objects in the tree.

C = Country name
O = Organization name
OU = Organizational Unit name
CN = Common name (leaf object name)

For example, the complete name for the user AColgan in Figure 10-6 is as follows:

CN=AColgan.OU=Administration.OU=DivWest.O=CambrianCorp

Note	*Names are not case-sensitive, but the case is preserved. The system will determine what it is no matter what case you use.*

Because the object type identifiers are used in the name, this is called a *typeful* name. A *typeless* name, which eliminates the abbreviations, is shown here:

AColgan.Administration.DivWest.CambrianCorp

Your *context* is your current location in the directory tree. So if you are in the Administration container pictured in Figure 10-7, your current context is Administration.DivWest.CambrianCorp. From this context, you can refer to other objects in the same context by just their common name. For example, AColgan is in the same context and can be referred to as simply *AColgan*.

You specify a *relative distinguished name* to refer to an object in another part of the tree from your current location in the tree. In other words, your current context probably already makes up part of the path to the object. This is analogous to giving someone an address. If the address is in your same town, you just give the street address. If the address is out of town, you give the street address and city.

Note *The remainder of this discussion is important when you are typing names at the DOS prompt or in some program or utility to switch contexts or refer to another object. In most cases, you'll select objects by browsing a graphical tree, which makes things much easier.*

In NDS, if you're referring to an object that exists in a completely different path of the tree branching from the root, you'll need to specify the full root path of the object by placing a period before the name. Referring again to Figure 10-7, assume you want to refer to a user named JThomas in the DivEast container from your current context in the Administration container. You type **.JThomas.DivEast.CambrianCorp**.

Trailing periods move the context up the tree one level. If your current context is in the Administration container, a printer called LJ-PRN one level up in DivWest has this context (note the placement of the period):

LJ-PRN.

Navigating the Directory Tree

When you move from one container to another, you change context. If you are working with the Windows-based graphical administration utilities, you move from one context to another by using point-and-click techniques. If you work at the command level, you use the CX (Change Context) command and type out the path to the container you want to move to. Some examples of using the CX command are provided here.

You must be in your "home context" before you can log into the network. It is possible to browse the NDS tree with the CX command before actually logging in so you can move to your correct context. An alternative is to include the following statement in the NET.CFG file at a user's workstation, where the context name is the distinguished name of the user's container:

NAME CONTEXT = *"context name"*.

NetWare Planning
and Installation

There are a number of ways you can use the CX command to move around in the directory tree. The techniques will remind you of using the UNIX or DOS CD (Change Directory) command to move among directories in a file system. Referring again to Figure 10-7, assume your current context is the CambrianCorp container. You can switch to the DivWest container by typing

```
CX DivWest
```

The new container object name is added to the current context path and is displayed as follows:

```
DivWest.CambrianCorp
```

You can move back up the directory tree by using period qualifiers. For example, to move from the DivWest.CambrianCorp container back to the CambrianCorp container, you simply type

```
CX .
```

To move up multiple levels, just type a period for each level you want to move up. For example, type **CX ..** to move up two levels.

The CX command tries to add the context you specify to the current context, which can cause some confusion. Assume that your current context is the DivWest container, as pictured in Figure 10-7. You type **CX CambrianCorp** in an attempt to switch back to the CambrianCorp container. This produces the following:

```
CX CambrianCorp + DivWest.CambrianCorp =
CambrianCorp.DivWest.CambrianCorp
```

Because no such context exists, the operating system returns an error. There are three ways to get around this problem. First, you can add the /R option to the command so that the context you specify is treated as if it branches from the root.

```
CX CambrianCorp /R
```

Second, you can use a name type to indicate that CambrianCorp is the Organization object, as follows:

```
CX O=CambrianCorp
```

Third, you can precede the context with a period to indicate that the context name is relative to the root, as follows:

```
CX .CambrianCorp
```

A period can be used at the trailing end of a qualifier to control how the name context you type will be added to the current context. For each period added to the trailing end, an object name is removed. If two periods are added, then two object names are removed. If more periods are used than there are partial names, an error occurs.

For example, assume your current context is DivWest.CambrianCorp. You can switch to DivEast by typing

```
CX DivEast.
```

The period at the end removes DivWest from the previous context, adds the context you specify to CambrianCorp, and switches you to the DivEast.CambrianCorp container.

To avoid confusion with the NDS directory tree and context naming, it is best to minimize the use of multiple container levels in your NDS tree structure. It's also a good idea to create simple names and avoid the use of spaces or underline characters in container names. This reduces the amount of typing required to switch contexts.

Controlling Access Rights

Administrators assign *rights* to objects in the directory tree so that specific users can manage those objects. Administrators also assign directory and file rights in much the same way. When a user has rights to an object, directory, or file, he or she is a *trustee* of that object, directory, or file. Rights are covered in more detail in Chapter 12, but you should become somewhat familiar with how rights are administered in order to start planning your own NDS tree.

Note   *NDS rights give users the ability to work with objects in the directory, usually in a management role. File and directory rights are granted to regular (nonmanagement) users who just need to access information on servers. However, the two systems use similar techniques for granting these rights, so they are covered together.*

One way to assign rights is to individually grant a user explicit rights to an object or a directory in the file system. That means you make the user a direct trustee of the object (as opposed to user "inherited" rights discussed in the next paragraph). Granting each user explicit rights can get tedious if you have a lot of users. One solution is to make a user a member of a group and grant rights to the group, which simplifies the task of rights administration.

Another method is to take advantage of the *inherited rights* feature of the directory tree and the file system. Here's how it works. Referring to Figure 10-8, if you grant the Eastern Division manager rights to the DivEast container, those right also apply in the Sales and Mktg containers and all the objects in those containers, because rights "flow down" the directory tree. However, you can block rights at any container or for any object if necessary by using an *Inherited Rights Filter (IRF)*. This gives you complete control over what parts of the tree your managers control.

Some rights control access to objects and some rights control access to the file system:

- Administrators grant object rights to supervisors who need to manage all or part of the NDS directory tree.

- File system rights are granted to normal users who need to access directories and files on servers.

The most encompassing right is the *Supervisor right*, which gives a user complete control over an object in the directory tree or directories and files in the file system. For example, in Figure 10-6, you could grant the user JSpence Supervisor rights to the DivWest container. This would give JSpence the ability to manage all aspects of that branch of the tree. This is an important consideration if you plan to distribute control of your network to division or department managers.

Other, less-powerful object rights give users limited abilities to manage objects in the directory tree. For example, an assistant manager with the Create, Rename, and Delete rights to a container can add or remove user accounts.

Property rights give users the ability to view or change the properties of an object. Recall that properties are fields of information about an object, such as name, address, phone number, and administrative information. For example, you could grant a person

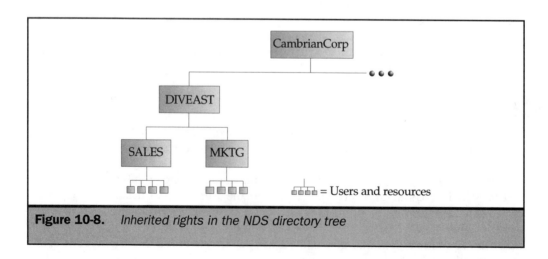

Figure 10-8. *Inherited rights in the NDS directory tree*

in the personnel department the ability to update addresses and phone numbers in user account objects but not to change any other fields.

More About Objects

Objects in Novell Directory Services help you track users and resources (like servers and printers) on your network and manage user accounts and how users access the network. In addition, you can use NDS to document the network. Objects that represent network resources like servers and printers can hold vital information about the objects, such as purchase dates, serial numbers, location, service requirements, and other information you might require. You can search for, sort, and list objects based on some of this information.

As pictured in Figure 10-7, an object can be a container object that holds other objects, or it can be a leaf object that is contained within a container object. A leaf object cannot contain objects of its own, and it is therefore sometimes referred to as a *terminal object*. Leaf objects represent physical entities such as users, printers, and servers. The only place where this rule is violated is with the GroupWise products. In GroupWise, a Post Office is a leaf object. Yet, it contains a Post Office Agent (POA), which is a leaf object to the Post Office object.

All NDS trees have a root that names the actual directory tree, and this root is usually given the name of the company. Because the root is the top of the tree, any rights assigned to it flow down through the entire tree. An object called Admin, which is created during the installation of the first NetWare server, has Supervisor rights to the entire tree. The person who installs the server is the initial Admin user and specifies the Admin login password. Admin is located in the container you create for your NetWare 5 server.

The objects available to you in NDS are shown in Figure 10-9. This list of objects will be extended in later chapters.

Basic Container Objects

You use container objects to organize the directory tree and hold other objects, including containers. The four basic types of container objects are as follows.

- **Country (C) container**   The Country container is the container that specifies which country a branch of the directory tree is located in. This object is optional and should only be used if you have a multinational organization. If you plan to connect your network into the information superhighway, you might also need to use this object. The name of the Country object must be two characters long, such as US for the United States.

- **Locality (L) container**   The Locality container object is optional. It can reside in other container objects, and you use it when you need to specify a location (such as a city or county for a government tree) for part of your network.

NetWare Planning and Installation

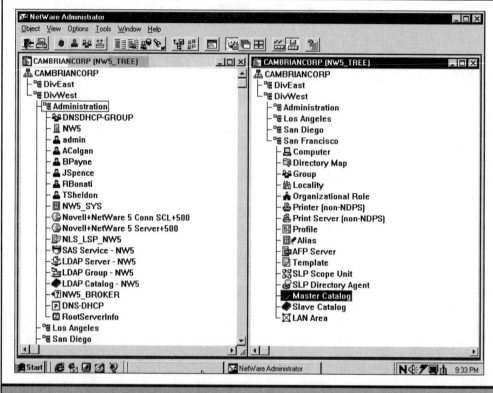

Figure 10-9. *The available NDS objects and their associated descriptive names*

■ **Organization (O) container** There is usually one Organization container, and it is given the name of your company. However, organizations with multiple business or operating units may want to create an Organization container for each. If the Country container is not used, the Organization container is the start of the directory tree.

Note

When you install a NetWare 5 server, you must specify an Organization container. If all servers belong to the same Organization container, you specify the organization's name when installing the first server and then use the same name when installing subsequent servers. To create different Organization containers, you specify a new name when installing the first server in that division or create the container later.

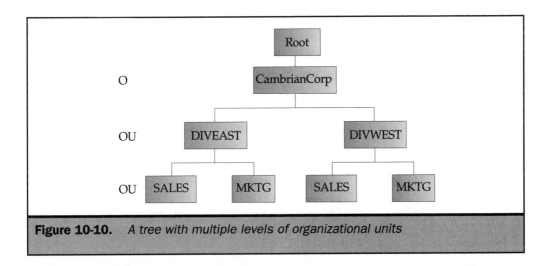

Figure 10-10.   *A tree with multiple levels of organizational units*

■ **Organizational Unit (OU) container**   Organizational Unit containers are typically used to organize units within an organization, such as departments or divisions. Organizational Units (OUs) are contained within Organization (O) containers. You use Organizational Unit containers to arrange the tree in a geographic or division/department organization. In Figure 10-10, a tree is organized first according to geographic location and then departments. Thus, there are two levels to the tree under the Organization container. To avoid confusion, it is not recommended that you create more than five levels in your directory tree—objects would be hard to find and reference.

Basic Leaf Objects

Once you've created the container structure for an organization, you can add leaf objects to containers that represent users and resources. The basic leaf objects are also shown in Figure 10-9. The names of each object are listed beside each object. The following list describes each object:

■ **Alias**   An Alias object points to an object elsewhere in the directory tree. You create an alias for an object in one branch of the directory tree that you often need to refer to in another branch of the directory tree. The Alias object is discussed further in the next section.

■ **AFP Server**   An AFP Server object is an Apple file server running the AppleTalk Filing Protocol.

- **Computer**   A Computer object holds information about a workstation on the network, such as its serial number, node address, users, and location or department.

- **Directory Map**   A Directory Map object specifies the locations of applications and simplifies the mapping of directories for a large number of users. Directory maps are used in login scripts to map directories for users. If the location of an application changes, you change the directory map, rather than change each user's login script.

- **External entity**   This is a reference to an object outside of the NDS directory tree. External entities are usually associated with users on other systems, such as Windows NT and GroupWise, who do not have an NDS account.

- **Group**   The Group object is used to group users into mail groups, project groups, management groups, or any other group of users. Groups simplify management because it's easier to work with a group of users than it is to work with an individual user in the group. When users are moved from one group to another, rights and privileges assigned to the new group will be applied to the user.

- **NetWare Server**   The NetWare Server object represents a NetWare server on the network.

- **Organizational Role**   The Organizational Role object is similar to the Group object in that you can make any user a member of it. The object is assigned rights and access to the system that define a role on the network, such as a department manager or a clerk that updates user account information. Then you can make users temporary members of the role when you want them to manage the position. You might create a role for temporary employees or a person who stands in for other managers.

- **Printer (non-NDPS)**   A Printer object represents a printer that is attached to a print server or workstation and is shared on the network.

- **Print Queue (non-NDPS)**   A Print Queue object represents a queue, which holds print jobs that are directed to one or more printers. Users send print jobs to queues.

- **Print Server (non-NDPS)**   A Print Server object represents a network print server. It can be part of the NetWare server or a stand-alone print server.

- **Profile**   A Profile is a special login script shared by more than one user. The profile script is executed after the script of the user's container but before the user's login script. Profile scripts make it easy to set up a network environment for a group of users who don't belong to the same containers (departments).

- **User**   A User object is an account that holds information about a user on the network.

■ **Volume**   A Volume object represents a physical volume on the hard drive of a file server. It also holds statistics about the volume. The name you assign to a Volume object does not need to be the same as the hard drive volume name.

New NDS Objects in NetWare 5

NetWare 5 is designed to operate in a pure TCP/IP environment. The emphasis of the product is to allow interoperability with the Internet. Services such as LDAP, DNS, DHCP, and others are designed for seamless integration with the Internet. Zero Effort Networks (Z.E.N.works) has been designed to provide network administrators with the ability to manage and control user workstations from a central location. Novell Distributed Print Services (NDPS) has been designed to provide a simple printing environment for the network user. Licensing Services has been designed to facilitate application metering and consistency of product licensing throughout a product mix. Each of these services has added new objects in NDS, which are available to the administrator. The following list describes these new objects:

■ **NSS Storage Group**   A Novell Storage Services (NSS) Storage Group object represents all the logical storage space residing on one or more storage devices. A storage group is organized by providers and consumers.

■ **DNSDHCP Group**   A DNSDHCP Group object contains servers that you designate as DNS and DHCP servers. They are automatically made members of this Group object.

■ **DNS-DHCP Locator**   The DNS-DHCP Locator object contains global defaults, DHCP options, and lists of all DHCP and DNS servers, subnets, and zones in the NDS tree.

■ **RootServerInfo**   The RootServerInfo object allows you to resolve domain names belonging to domains that you do not maintain in your NDS tree. It points to root server objects on the Internet.

■ **DHCP Server**   The DHCP Server object represents a DHCP server. It contains a listing of subnet ranges that the DHCP server is servicing. It also contains all server-specific configuration and policy information. It will have a line through it until it is actually running.

■ **Subnet**   The Subnet object is a container object holding IP address configuration information that can be assigned to nodes residing on the IP network segment.

■ **Subnet Address Range**   The Subnet Address Range object identifies a range of IP addresses available for dynamic address assignment. It can also be configured to exclude a range of addresses from the assignment range.

NetWare Planning
and Installation

- **IP Address** The IP Address object represents a single IP address. This object can only be created in Subnet object containers.

- **Subnet Pool** A Subnet Pool object allows you to assign multiple Subnet objects to service DHCP requests for a network segment that has more than one IP subnet address configured on it.

- **DNS Name Server** The DNS Name Server object is the DNS server that will respond to queries about the DNS zone. This object will have a line through it until it is running.

- **DNS Zone** A DNS Zone object contains all the data for a single DNS zone. It can represent three different kinds of zones: a standard DNS zone, an IN-ADDR.ARPA zone, or a IP6.INT zone. All DNS Zone objects must be configured as either a primary or secondary zone. It includes Resource Record Set objects and Resource Record objects.

- **Resource Record Set** A Resource Record Set object contains Resource Records. It is automatically created when the Resource Record object is created.

- **Resource Record** A Resource Record object contains the type and data of a single Resource Record. The most commonly used Resource Records are A, CNAME. MX, NS, and PTR.

- **NDPS Manager** The NDPS Manager object is a logical entity used to create and manage Printer Agents. A single NDPS Manager can control an unlimited number of Printer Agents.

- **Printer Agent** The Printer Agent object combines the functions previously performed by a printer, print queue, and print server into one intelligent entry.

- **NDPS Printer** A NDPS Printer object is a controlled access printer. The access permissions are defined in the object properties of the NDPS Printer.

- **Container Package** A Container Package object contains a single policy that allows you to configure a search for policies in effect in the container.

- **Windows 3.1 User Package** The policies in the Windows 3.1 User Package provide user-specific controls for the user.

- **Windows 95 User Package** The policies in the Windows 95 User Package provide user-specific controls for the user.

- **Windows NT User Package** The policies in the NT User Package provide user-specific controls for the user.

- **Windows 3.1 Workstation Package** The policies in the Windows 3.1 Workstation Package provide workstation-specific controls.

- **Windows 95 Workstation Package** The policies in the Windows 95 Workstation Package provide workstation-specific controls.

- **Windows NT Workstation Package**   The policies in the NT Workstation Package provide workstation-specific controls.

- **Workstation**   The Workstation object contains a workstation's address and various other parameters associated with a specific workstation.

- **Application**   The Application object is an application program that can be delivered to a workstation using the Novell Application Launcher (NAL).

- **License Certificate**   License Certificate objects are added to the Licensed Product container when an NLS-aware application is installed.

- **Licensed Product**   A Licensed Product container is created when you install a license certificate or create a metering certificate using Novell Licensing Services (NLS).

- **LDAP Group**   An LDAP Group object is required to use the LDAP services provided with NetWare 5.

More About Alias Objects

An Alias object provides a link so that users can easily access objects outside of their own organizational units. For example, in Figure 10-6, users in the San Francisco office often need to access files on the NW5_SYS volume in the Los Angeles office. By creating an alias in the San Francisco container (called LA_server in this case), users in San Francisco can more easily access the volume.

Administrators can use aliases to pool objects that are scattered throughout an organization. Printers, modems, and fax machines at various locations can be grouped on the network so they are easier to select, without regard for their locations. Users can choose an object that is not in use, one that provides the best service, or one that is close to their physical location.

> **Tip**   *Aliasing helps network administrators manage the network by organizing remote physical resources into logical groups.*

Properties of Objects

Every object has a set of properties (fields of information). The most obvious property is an object's name. You specify some or all of the properties of an object when you create it, and you can change them at any time by using ConsoleOne or the NetWare Administrator utility. You've already seen a typical property window in Figure 10-1. Figure 10-11 shows the properties of a volume in the file system. These are fields that

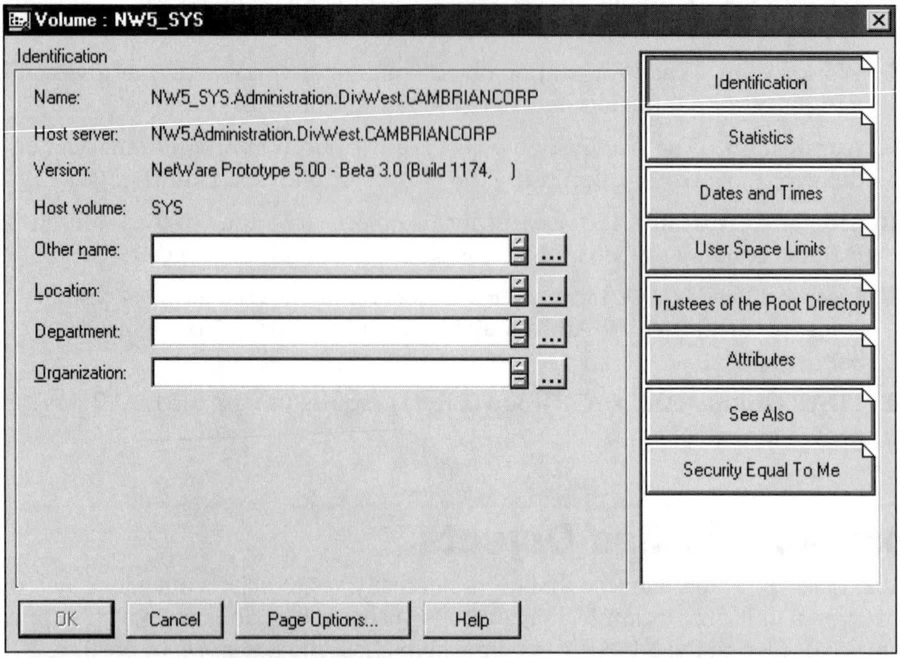

Figure 10-11. *The properties of a Volume object*

administrators can change. Normal users can view the information but cannot change it unless granted rights to do so.

You click the buttons on the right to view different fields. For the Volume object in Figure 11-11, you can view statistics about the drive, space limitations for users, and trustees. Any value can be changed with the proper rights. You can set up some users with full Supervisor rights to change any and all fields, or you can set up subadministrators who can change only some of the fields.

User objects are probably the most common objects you'll work with. Here's a list of properties for User objects:

- The user's name, address, phone number, and fax number
- Account information, such as the balance amount
- Login restrictions, such as the allowed time, the allowed workstations, and password requirements
- The default server of the user
- The groups the user belongs to

- The user's print job configuration and printer controls
- The Profile object used by the user
- The user's identification number

In contrast, here are properties for a physical object such as a server:

- The organizational unit name assigned to the server
- A description of the server, which is used for reference only
- The location of the server, which is used for reference only
- The network address of the server
- The trustees of the server, which is basically a list of users who can change the properties of the Server object
- A list of server operators
- Status information about the server's operation

You can search for specific values in the property fields of objects. For example, you could search for users based on the groups they belong to or telephone numbers. You can also search for resources such as printers based on their location. If you're going to a meeting in a different building and you need to get a print job done while you're on the way, you could search for a printer in that building to print the job and have it waiting when you get there (assuming you have rights to use the printer).

You must have rights to use an object like a printer. The network administrator can make any user a trustee of an object and set which of the object's properties that trustee can view and change. As mentioned earlier, department managers are usually granted rights to create and manage objects.

NDS Partition Management

Information about NetWare 5 users, devices, and other network resources is stored in the NDS database. When users log into the network, the database is checked to authenticate them and give them access to the resources they have been granted rights to use. Should the server or disk holding the NDS database fail, no users can log in. Therefore, it is essential that the database be stored on different servers to provide *fault tolerance*.

The NDS database is distributed, meaning that it can be partitioned and replicated (copied) to a number of servers. As pictured in Figure 10-12, partitions are *subtrees* of the entire NDS tree and are created at a specific container in the tree. The container where the partition is made is called the *root of the subtree*. However, the first partition of any tree includes the root object of the tree itself and is called *the root partition*. The root partition usually only contains the Organization object.

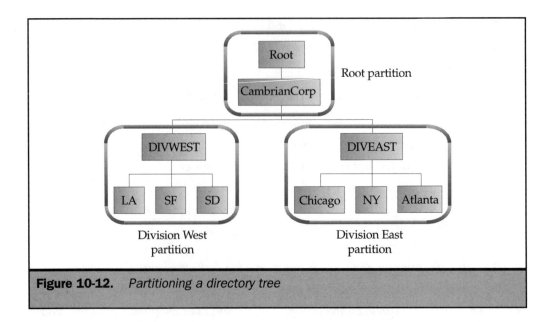

Figure 10-12. *Partitioning a directory tree*

Note *Directory replication only protects the NDS database. It does not provide replication for the file system.*

The partitions pictured in Figure 10-12 would normally be replicated to every other partition to provide fault tolerance and to provide partition information to users in other partitions who might need it. You should create three replicas of every partition; therefore, for example, you might replicate the DivEast partition to a server in its own partition as well as to servers in the DivWest and Root partitions.

One reason for partitioning and replicating the database is to put information about parts of the directory close to users who need it. This is most important when the network spans large geographic areas and is connected with wide area network (WAN) links that might restrict network traffic. It also ensures that users have NDS information locally if a link fails. Note the following:

■ If a network is within the same location (a building or campus area) and is relatively small (less than ten servers), you don't need to partition the database. Just replicate the entire database to at least two other servers.

■ If the network is large and spread over large geographic areas, partition the database and replicate it to servers throughout the network that need the information.

Even though a partitioned database is stored in different locations, it is still viewed as a single directory structure. If changes are made in one partition, the master database is eventually updated. This updating is called *synchronizing* the database. Synchronization can occur as required. For example, the Eastern division might not need immediate notification that a new user account has been added to the Western division. This update can be made later to reduce traffic on internetwork links. On the other hand, it's probably best to synchronize immediately unless this creates an excessive load on the WAN link between the divisions.

Replicating Partitions

Once you've partitioned a directory tree, you can replicate individual partitions to other NetWare 5 servers. The primary reasons for replicating partitions are to provide fault tolerance in the event of a disk failure and to reduce network traffic by locating part of the database close to users who need it. There are four types of database replicas:

- **Master read/write replica**   The master replica of a partition allows all partition operations, including create, merge, move, create a replica, delete a replica, and repair. There can only be one master replica for a partition.

- **Read/write replica**   There can be any number of read/write replicas of a partition stored on NetWare 5 servers. Writes can be made to the replica as long as a master replica exists on a NetWare 5 server somewhere else.

- **Read-only replica**   This is a replica containing partition information that can only be read. Read-only replicas are typically copied to remote sites to provide users at that site with NDS information they normally require. Read-only replicas cannot be used to authenticate a user. They are only useful for tree walking and viewing objects.

- **Subordinate reference replica**   Subordinate reference replicas cannot be modified and are automatically created by NDS for linking partitions of the tree. In some cases, you need to be concerned about how many there are and if they are affecting WAN traffic, as discussed in Chapter 11.

Transitive Synchronization

It is inevitable that a distributed NDS database will go out of synchronization. Partition replicas at various locations will not always have the same information. However, the contents of the replicas converge over time as changes to replicas are copied to other replicas. The NDS database is referred to as "loosely consistent." Some changes are sent immediately, while other less important changes are sent later.

This synchronization process involves contacting and updating all the locations where replicas requiring updates exist. During the synchronization process, only the properties that have changed are updated, not the entire object. In addition, changes made on a replica can be synchronized to other replicas via intermediaries. This eliminates the problem of NDS servers being unable to connect with one another.

Time Synchronization

NetWare 5 uses time servers to ensure that NDS partitions are properly synchronized. Time-of-day stamps establish an order of events and ensure that updates to partitions by administrators are handled correctly and in order. Time synchronization is important because computer clocks can deviate enough to cause different times on servers in the NDS system.

Because the NDS database is distributed, it is possible for changes to be made to the same object at different locations. When those changes are merged, a "collision" occurs, and the operating system must determine the correct sequence of events for the change. Because every change in the directory is time-stamped, it is possible to determine the correct order of events, but only if all the servers are time-synchronized.

NetWare 5 implements four types of time servers, as described below. During the installation of the server, you specify the type of time server. By default, the first server to be installed into a tree is a single reference. It never adjusts its clock. There can be one and only one single reference server in a tree. All subsequent servers installed in the same tree become Secondary. They adjust their time to the single reference server time.

Reference and primary servers are used to provide time provider groups (TPGs), and must be manually configured. There must be one and only one reference server in the group and there must be at least two primaries, a maximum of seven primaries per group. Both reference and primaries vote on the time, with the reference having a weight of 16 and each primary a weight of 2. Primaries adjust their time 50 percent (which provides stability); otherwise, they could be constantly hunting.

There can be multiple time provider groups within a tree. These groups are useful in trees covering large geographical areas such as Europe and the U.S. You can have a TPG in each continent and connect the Reference servers to the same external clock. Then only two servers exchange time synchronization information across the long distance. Time in each continent is then dispersed locally from its TPG.

- **Single reference time servers** Single reference time servers are typically implemented in geographically small networks and provide the only source of time on the network. They provide time to *secondary servers* and to their own client workstations. Secondary servers must maintain a link to the time server and provide time to their own clients.

- **Secondary time servers** Secondary time servers obtain their time from single reference time servers, primary time servers, or reference time servers. They then provide the time to their locally attached clients. All servers on the network that are not set up as single reference, primary, or reference time servers should be set up as secondary time servers.

■ **Primary time servers**   Primary time servers are typically implemented on large internetworks. A primary time server is set up in each geographically distinct area, and each primary time server communicates with all other primary time servers (or a reference time server) to synchronize the time. For example, a company might set up a primary time server at both its New York and Los Angeles offices. These servers then communicate over the link to ensure that the time on the network is synchronized. In the event of a time discrepancy, primary time servers "vote" to determine what the common network time should be (unless a reference time server with an accurate external time source is connected to the network). Once the new time is determined, the primary time servers automatically adjust their internal clocks appropriately. Installing primary time servers in different locations provides fault tolerance. If a primary server fails, secondary time servers and clients at that location can get their time from a primary time server at another location.

■ **Reference time servers**   Reference time servers provide a single source from which all other time servers and clients can get the time. Reference time servers get their time from an extremely accurate source, such as an *external* radio atomic clock or the Internet. Reference time servers only adjust their clocks based on the external time source, never on a "voted" time determined by other time servers. Primary time servers get their time from reference time servers. If multiple reference time servers are installed (to provide fault tolerance), they must all get their time from the same external source.

Chapter 18 provides more information on partition and time services management.

NDS Enhancements in NetWare 5

The enhancements in NetWare 5 focus on providing protocol independence among the IPX and IP worlds. This allows developers to utilize NDS for name resolution instead of using older technologies such as SAP and SLP.

Lightweight Directory Access Protocol (LDAP)

LDAP is a de facto standard for accessing directory information over the Internet. It is a protocol that lets users easily access X.500-based directories such as NDS. NetWare 5 LDAP Services are fully compliant with the latest standards (LDAP 3).

Directory Services (DS) Diagnostics

New functionality has been added to the DSDIAG Novell Loadable Module (NLM). It can report on status attributes on background processes, compare replica rings, allow tuned name reporting, and produce comparison reports between schemas.

WAN Traffic Manager

The WAN Traffic Manager is a general-purpose WAN traffic policy interpreter for use by NDS. It gives network administrators the ability to determine how often NDS should send changes over the WAN links. It allows the network administrator to select both the time for NDS synchronization to occur and which WAN links to use, if multiples exist.

WAN Policy Manager

The WAN Policy Manager is a GUI utility that provides the network administrator with control of the creation, deletion, and editing of WAN Traffic Manager policies. Policies are stored as text in NDS as attributes of server and LAN Area objects.

Catalog Services

Catalog Services provides the network administrator with the capability to create and access catalog databases. A catalog database is a flat file database that contains snapshot information from NDS. It provides for fast querying of a defined set of data from an entire NDS tree or a portion of the tree.

Catalog Services Manager

The Catalog Services Manager is a GUI utility that allows the network administrator to specify the search scope, match criteria, and extraction criteria for creating a catalog database. It allows the administrator to either schedule or run the Dredger operation manually to create and refresh the catalog. It includes a basic catalog browser that allows the administrator to perform queries against an existing catalog.

DSbacker

DSbacker was created in response to requests over the years for a method of archiving the NDS data and schema into a file that can be backed up by any backup application.

Organizing Your NDS Directory

You establish the initial organization of the NDS directory during NetWare installation. You specify the root name of the NDS tree, an optional Country container, and one or more Organization containers.

You can create Organizational Unit objects for additional departments after installing NetWare by using ConsoleOne or NetWare Administrator. However, if other departments have their own servers, you can create Organizational Unit objects for those departments when installing the servers. You would specify the same organization and then specify a different department name in the Organizational Unit field of the install screen.

You'll learn more about planning and organizing your directory tree and the network environment in Chapter 11. Then, in Chapter 12, you'll learn more about NetWare's security features and how users and managers fit into the security system.

NetWare Planning
and Installation

The
Complete
Reference

NetWare
5

Chapter 11

Novell Directory
Services Planning

ovell Directory Services (NDS) provides a way for network administrators to manage networks from central sites or to distribute management to the divisions or departments of the network. It can help reduce the cost of management, especially if the network spans large geographic areas. A single network supervisor can manage the entire network, or the management responsibility can be distributed to local administrators.

The NDS database is a critical component of a NetWare 5 installation because it authenticates users who are logging in and accessing network resources. This makes the partitioning and replication features of NDS a critical part of any NDS planning. This chapter looks at design considerations for NDS trees and helps you build a directory tree that fits your organization.

> **Note** *Be sure to familiarize yourself with Object, Directory, and File rights before finalizing a tree design. Refer to Chapter 12 for details.*

Assessing the Network

The first step in designing an NDS tree is to determine the goals of the company and to gather information essential to the design. Issues such as understanding the company's priorities, network performance, fault tolerance requirements, and network accessibility are just a few of the areas that need to be reviewed. The network assessment can be broken into the following three stages:

1. **Analysis and specification** In this stage, the overall scope of the NDS tree design is determined. The underlying business needs of the company must be recognized and stated. The high-level goals, constraints, and resource requirements must also be detailed. General information about the project must be gathered through interviews, surveys, and so on.

2. **Design** After the initial analysis has been performed, the next step is to design the NDS tree. The design phase should include the development of various generic solutions, the evaluation of these alternatives, and the design of a specific solution. NDS partitioning, replication, and time synchronization must be defined at this stage.

3. **Implementation** After a specific solution has been chosen, you can begin implementation. At this stage, you define specific milestones, develop and test a working solution, obtain customer acceptance, document the system, and train users.

The Implementation Team

The project team selected for the design and implementation of a NetWare 5 network is crucial. Each company or organization is unique. In a similar manner, each project team is also unique. The team members should include the following members:

- **IS Manager**   The IS Manager manages the project and helps move the team through each phase of the project. This person is the liaison between the design team and upper management.

- **NDS Expert**   The NDS Expert is a person who has experience working with NDS and NetWare 5. This person is most likely to be the team leader in the design process.

- **Server Specialist**   The Server Specialist is a person who works daily with the administrative tasks associated with a NetWare network. This is the person responsible for implementing upgrades to existing servers and implementing the rollout to other departments.

- **Workstation Specialist**   The Workstation Specialist is the person who works daily with the network users and their associated workstations. This is the person who is responsible for the login scripts on the file servers and who performs upgrades to network client software.

- **Application Specialist**   The Application Specialist is the person responsible for the applications running on the network and the workstations. This person tests the compatibility of applications and ensures the stability of those applications.

- **Printing Specialist**   The Printing Specialist is the person involved in providing access to the network printers, determining printer locations, and upgrading the printer drivers when needed.

- **Connectivity Specialist**   The Connectivity Specialist is the person who works daily with the internetwork backbone, telecommunications, WAN, and router placement. A key responsibility is to identify bandwidth issues for both LANs and WANs.

Design Considerations

Directory trees can model the organizational chart of a company, its geographic location, or its functional structure (workgroups and available services). Another option is to design the network to accommodate bindery services, which group users in the same containers as the bindery services they are most likely to use. Some of the most important considerations in designing any directory tree are discussed next.

Naming Standards

This section covers the rules for naming NDS objects and provides a few suggestions for developing a naming standard that you can use throughout your organization. NDS object names must follow two rules:

- They must be unique within the container.
- They must not exceed 64 characters in length.

You can use any special characters. You can use uppercase and lowercase for object names, but the case is not recognized. Thus NetWareServer and NETWARESERVER are considered the same name. Spaces and underscores are considered the same character. Thus NetWare_Server and NetWare Server are considered the same name. Try to avoid using spaces, because you must put quote marks around them when using command-line utilities.

Keep names as short as possible to make it easy for users to remember and type the names. While being short, they should also retain some meaning. Therefore, it is recommended that you develop naming standards that all users in the organization can refer to. Naming standards are important for two reasons:

- If you rely on division or department managers to manage parts of the network, naming standards help ensure that objects are assigned names that identify the object and provide other useful information, such as its location or purpose.
- Users must be able to search for and identify objects using standard names.

The directory database is searchable, so administrators and users can locate users and resources on the network. For example, assume a smart network administrator has implemented a naming strategy that uses PRN as the designator for printers and COL as a color designation. Color printers following this standard have names such as PRN-COL-ADMIN or PRN-COL-DESIGN. To list all the color printers in your area, simply search for PRN-COL*. The asterisk is a wildcard character to indicate a replacement of any trailing characters.

Upper-Layer Tree Design Stipulations

When designing a directory tree, it is best to plan the upper levels of the tree first. Start by creating the country name (if needed), and then the organization container (or containers) you'll need to name your organization or its divisions. Next, you can design organizational unit containers based on the physical network requirements or management requirements, or with a consideration for WAN links.

You create the root and first branches of the directory tree when you install the first NetWare 5 server. During the installation process, you're asked for the root name of the tree, the Organization object, and the Organizational Unit object where you want to place the server. As you install additional servers, you can add them to the context you've already created or you can create another container object. You can manipulate the directory tree at any time by running the Windows-based NetWare Administrator or the ConsoleOne utility from the server or a workstation. You also use these utilities to create directory tree partitions and manage replication.

You can use a number of other utilities to manage the directory tree. For example, you can merge two or more trees into a single tree with the DSMERGE utility.

> **Tip** *DSMERGE may be helpful when initially creating your directory tree. You can have department managers create their own trees on their own servers, and then you can merge all the trees into a single tree with DSMERGE. The utility is discussed in Chapter 18.*

The upper levels of the directory tree reflect the geographic or functional layout of the network. You start by defining the country name (if used) and the organization container. Then you create organizational unit containers for the geographic locations, divisions, or departments of the company.

Use the country and organization containers to create directory trees for organizations that span large geographic areas and international borders. Remember that every NDS tree requires at least one Organization container. If you have a single-site network, you typically create one Organization container with your company name, and then use Organizational Unit containers to create the divisions, departments, buildings, or workgroups of your organization.

Use the country name to fully comply with the X.500 naming standard and to exchange information with other X.500 services or on the Internet. Using a country name adds some complexity to naming and referring to objects in the directory tree, but the benefits of accessing other name spaces (if required) outweigh this complexity.

> **Note** *Multinational organizations can use the country name to build a tree based on every country in which the organization has an office.*

The organization name falls under the country name in the directory tree. If an organization consists of multiple companies or divisions, create an Organization container for each company or division. If a country code is not used, the Organization containers form the base of the directory tree.

> **Note** *Novell recommends that organization names be registered with the Internet and that ANSI-standard names be used to enable X.500 multiple tree and multiple name space operations.*

NetWare Planning and Installation

All users should be familiar with the Organization container to which they belong and Organization containers of other divisions in case they need to access objects there. Be sure to keep the names simple but descriptive.

The locality container is useful in NDS environments that have many city locations, such as state or local governments.

Lower-Layer Tree Design Stipulations

Once you have developed the country name and Organization container levels, you can begin creating Organizational Unit containers that reflect the geographic or functional divisions of the organization. Here are some guidelines for developing a tree that makes it easy for users to access objects:

- Think about the best way to define a path to a user on the network. This path should be easy for network users to comprehend and should minimize the use of too many Organizational Unit containers.

- Determine the workflow of the organization or its departments. It might be more beneficial to organize users into containers based on what they do, rather than on the departments to which they belong. However, keep in mind that you can add users to groups if you need to grant them access to common network resources.

- Be sure to place users and the resources they use in proximity in the tree. This eases administration and may reduce replication traffic on multisite networks.

- If users need to access resources outside of their immediate network segments, use aliases to make those resources more accessible and easy to find.

- Don't create a lot of excess containers in an attempt to subcategorize your network. You might just create confusion for users.

- Remember that rights flow down through the NDS directory tree. If you grant a right in a container, all the containers and objects under it will gain the right unless you block it. Use this technique to your advantage to help reduce the amount of time you or your administrative staff spend administering the network.

- Determine the placement of servers and other network resources in the NDS hierarchy. You can organize resources in one location to make administration easier, or you can keep resources at division or department levels to reduce network traffic. As a self-check, verify that the user can perform 90 percent or more of their work using resources in their home container.

- Use aliases when a resource is needed that resides in another container.

- Use Directory Map objects to provide access to needed portions of the file system. Make it appear to users that they can do everything in their container.

Partitioning and Replication

You partition and replicate the NDS database to provide fault tolerance and to provide NDS information close to users who need it. The NDS database is used to authenticate users onto the network. If the database becomes corrupted, it may not be possible for anyone to log in. Therefore, replicas of the database must be placed at local and/or remote sites to protect against failure. If a server holding the database fails, users can log in by being authenticated at a replication site.

Users should be able to access the database on a local server, rather than on a server at a remote site connected with a WAN link. Therefore, another reason for partitioning and replicating the NDS database is to bring NDS information closer to the users who need it. For example, if users in New York access resources at the Chicago network site, the Chicago partition of the NDS database should be replicated to the New York site.

However, partitioning and replicating the database over many sites can become a complex operation. If users at every site access resources at every other site, you'll need a replica of every partition at every site. As changes are made to the database, these replicas must be updated and synchronized throughout the network. You'll need to closely examine how database updates will be handled on the network and how they will affect network traffic. Excess network traffic on expensive WAN links may reduce performance for users, and you might need to install higher-throughput lines or develop hierarchical network topologies that tend to regionalize updates and synchronization.

When designing your directory tree, you need to keep partitioning and replication in mind. Some general points to consider are discussed here, but remember that every directory tree design is a balance between providing information to users and minimizing NDS's effect on network traffic. While some points may appear to be contradictory, you need to consider the impact of each for your own situation.

- Replicate the root partition and other partitions to at least three servers to provide fault tolerance and ensure that users can log in to the network should a server fail. Note that NetWare will attempt to create these replicas on its own.

- While more than three replicas may improve fault tolerance, the more replicas you have, the more network traffic increases to keep the replicas synchronized.

- If the network is a multisite regional network, replicate the root partition to each regional site. Try not to span physical locations with a partition.

- Use a pyramid design when partitioning the directory tree. Keep the root partition and other high-level partitions small. Then create regional or departmental partitions that tend to group resources and users in the same area.

- Replicate regional partitions to the major site or to other regional sites, but monitor for excess network traffic during synchronization of the database.

- Keep in mind that servers holding replicas must communicate with one another. Every server with a replica communicates with every other server with a replica. If the servers are connected via WAN links, this may cause excess traffic.

- If a server is down or a link is down among the synchronizing servers, synchronization cannot take place. As you add more servers and WAN links, the inability of the database to synchronize due to server or link failure increases.

- If mobile users access the network from different sites on a regular basis, it is useful to have replicas of the partitions they use at each regional site they visit.

- Centralize partition management, but distribute NDS directory tree object and file system management. If partition management is not centralized, simultaneous changes may affect the database.

Base your decisions on how often changes are made to the database and thus how often the database must be updated and synchronized. If there is high bandwidth between the regional sites of a large multisite network, it may be beneficial to create a directory tree based on the geographic location of each division of the company and then partition the database at each division. You can place replicas of each partition at servers in other divisions and at a main site.

Planning Time Synchronization

Time synchronization provides a service that maintains consistent timestamps for events across an enterprise environment. Time synchronization provides time information for the file system, messaging services, applications, and NDS. With time synchronization, NetWare servers in different time zones remain in sync with one another.

When you plan time synchronization you need to determine the time source, the time server type, and the time server communication method. NetWare 5 provides the capabilities of the prior NetWare 4.*x* product and includes the ability to synchronize time through the use of Internet time standards via the World Wide Web. This is covered in detail in Chapter 18.

Topology

Network environments generally fall into two categories: *single-site* or *multisite*. A single-site environment may encompass a single building or a group of buildings in the same geographic area. Single-site networks typically implement direct high-speed connections among network segments or rely on local service providers for these services.

A multisite network consists of individual network segments located in different geographic areas. A multisite network with regional and branch offices is pictured in Figure 11-1. Note that high-speed WAN connections are only between regional offices, not branch sites. The branch sites communicate with the regional sites over less expensive links with lower throughput.

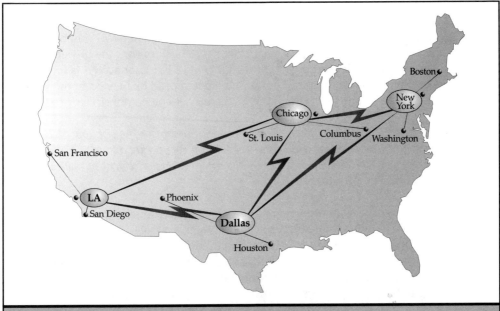

Figure 11-1. *A multisite network with regional and branch offices*

You need to consider the cost and throughput of the communication links that interconnect the network and how much NDS partition information is transferred across those links. Tree designs for multisite networks can reflect the geographic or functional (department/workgroup) organization of a company. Design considerations for these models are discussed in the upcoming section, "Examples of Tree Models."

Users intuitively understand an NDS tree design that reflects some aspect of an organization's geographic locations because the directory tree reflects the region or city where they work and where other people or resources are located. A functional design that reflects the departments, workgroups, services, or administration of the organization and network can also be easy to comprehend; and it supports a centralized or departmentally managed tree structure. However, a functional design is usually only appropriate for single-site networks.

A tree organized around departments may be difficult to use and expand if the organization grows to a multisite topology. The tree will most likely need to be reorganized, with containers for each geographic site and subcontainers for each department located at those sites.

Management Considerations

Networks can be centrally managed, or the management of the network can be distributed to departments or network sites, whichever best follows the physical design of the network and logical design of the NDS tree. The user accounts for any network managers other than the central manager should be located in the Organizational Unit container for which the managers will be responsible.

Note *In a decentralized approach, you can relinquish the Supervisor right of upper-level managers so that department managers have full control over their branch of the tree without any control from upper managers. This may be a requirement in some cases, such as in government networks.*

Other management considerations are login scripts and rights management. When users log in to the network, three different types of login scripts to execute commands and map the environment are potentially available: container, profile, and user. The container login script is unique because it executes for every user that belongs to a container. You might want to consider planning part of your directory structure to take advantage of this feature. These are discussed in detail later in the chapter.

You can grant rights by exception, which means that users then automatically obtain the rights of the container they belong to and any rights that are inherited from upper containers. You should organize the directory tree to take advantage of these features.

Design your tree with the future in mind. Remember that designing and building a tree will involve a lot of review and redesign, so don't hold tightly to your initial plans.

Examples of Tree Models

The following examples illustrate the upper container levels of the directory tree for CambrianCorp, the fictitious company used throughout this book. The network is discussed in a number of configurations, starting as a local-site network and then as a network that spans large geographic areas. Only container objects are discussed here because they reflect the layout of the tree and how it relates to the actual environment or physical topology of the network. Leaf objects, such as user accounts, servers, and printers, are not illustrated.

Keep in mind that one of the defining factors in designing any NDS tree structure is the cost and efficiency of WAN links and the amount of NDS information you need to transfer over those links. Two of the primary defining factors for the tree designs discussed here are the partitioning and replication of the directory tree.

Note *This section does not advocate one design over another. The benefits and disadvantages of each are discussed so you can find a design that fits your needs.*

Single-Site Network

Figure 11-2 illustrates CambrianCorp as a single-site network. Note that such a network may span a campus area, a city, or even a geographic region. But its main characteristic is that all the servers are connected by relatively fast and efficient connections so that internetwork throughput and cost are not major considerations in the partitioning and replication of the NDS database.

The design of the tree is based on the departments of the organization. The tree level directly under the Organization object (CambrianCorp) reflects the departments, rather than a geographic layout. Because the tree is organized by departments, you can make department managers responsible for managing their part of the tree. However, a tree organized in this way is difficult to scale if the company grows to include multiple geographic sites.

Because the tree is organized by department, most users can access the resources they use most often within their portion of the tree. This reduces the need to search other parts of the tree and reduces traffic outside their branch of the tree. If users do need to search for users (to address e-mail) or resources outside their department, locating the objects is intuitive because the tree is organized by department.

Users who need to access resources outside of their department will need to have rights granted to them for those resources, or an alias can be created to make the objects easier to access. However, this makes managing the tree difficult, especially if department managers need to manipulate objects for use by other departments.

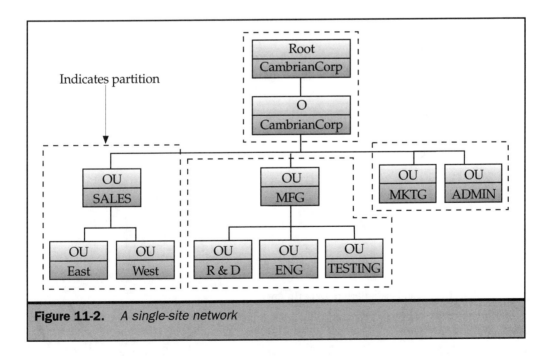

Figure 11-2. *A single-site network*

NetWare Planning
and Installation

Note *It may not be necessary to partition a single-site NDS tree if the network is small. Instead, simply replicate the entire tree to three servers in the same general area to achieve fault tolerance. This greatly simplifies your work and you might want to try it until your network demands multisite replicas.*

Multisite, Geographically Designed Tree

Refer to Figure 11-1 for a picture of a multisite network with regional offices in New York, Chicago, Dallas, and Los Angeles. Each regional site is interconnected with high-speed WAN communication links (such as T1 lines). Branch sites in each region are connected to the regional offices with lower-speed communication links. Figure 11-3 illustrates the directory tree for this environment.

Partitioning and replication of the database is a major consideration for this layout. Containers for branch offices are located under the containers for each regional site, and a replica of each regional partition is placed at these branch sites for fault tolerance and to provide local access to the database. A replica of each regional partition is also placed at every other region for protection and local access. Mobile users also benefit from having a replica of each regional database at every region. The root partition can be placed in every region.

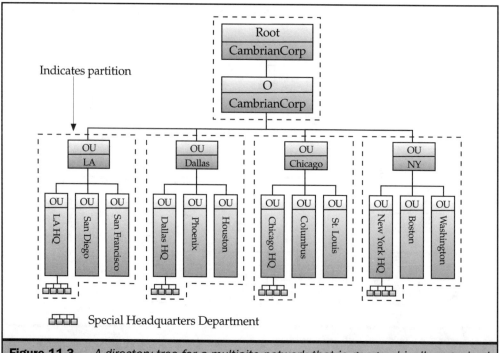

Figure 11-3. *A directory tree for a multisite network that is geographically organized*

This model keeps replication traffic minimized over just a few WAN links. The branch offices are contained within the regional partition, and that information is copied with the regional replica to other regional sites. However, if the database grows or changes often, WAN traffic may become excessive. Also, if a region contains many branch offices, there may be excessive traffic on the links between branches and the regional office site. One other thing to consider is that this plan may have too many replicas, which might create a synchronization problem across the network if a server or communication link fails.

Note that with this plan, users can quickly find other users or resources, because searching based on geographic location is intuitive. It's also easy to share resources in the same regions. In addition, each regional site and its branches can be managed by an administrator at that site. However, departments of the company are divided among regions, so department management becomes more complex. The tree design discussed next looks at this problem.

Multisite, Function-Based Network

The function-based network pictured in Figure 11-4 is designed around the departments (or workgroups) of an organization. This tree is useful because it supports both central management and department-level management techniques. However, as you'll see,

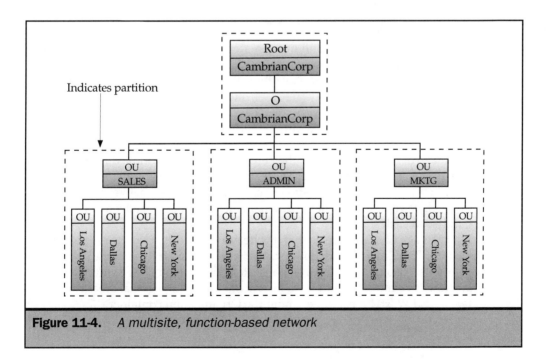

Figure 11-4. *A multisite, function-based network*

this tree design is not recommended for multisite networks with inefficient WAN links. We mention it here to help you understand the limitations of this model in that situation.

Note that because the tree follows the functional organization of the company, users can quickly locate other users and resources anywhere on the network. For example, if you want to send e-mail to someone in the New York sales office, you first go to the Sales container and then to the New York office. In addition, security and rights administration are simplified. While administrators can take advantage of inheritance and the flow of rights down the tree, resource sharing outside a department is difficult, especially if the resource is a server on which file and directory rights must be administered.

The disadvantage of this tree structure is in the way partitioning and replication are handled. Note that partitions contain information from each network site. It is necessary to replicate this information to almost every other site whenever the database is updated, which results in excessive WAN traffic. In this case, the WAN traffic would generate some hefty bills because the sites are in distant cities. This tree design is only manageable if only a few sites are involved. It is closer to the implementation you would configure for a single-site network. It requires partition replicas at almost every site, which makes it prone to synchronization problems if any of the communication links are down.

Multisite, Star-Configured Network

Organizations with a central office and many regional, branch, or satellite offices may want to design a tree similar to the one in Figure 11-5. In this example, management is centralized at the New York site, and all other sites physically connect to it over communication links. In the directory tree, each site is placed directly under the Organization container (CambrianCorp) to form a flat database structure. Replicas of each site are then placed at the central office and duplicated at each site as well for fault tolerance.

The advantage of this design is that the network is easily partitioned into small units that represent each satellite office. These partitions are then replicated to the central office. In this way, synchronization of each site is handled between it and the central office, which reduces complexity. Management can be centralized at the main office or handled at each site.

The disadvantage of this model is that it is heavily dependent on the central site for synchronization. There must be adequate servers and administrative staff to handle the central operations. Also, this model does not scale well if the number of satellite offices grows. An alternative model would be to insert containers for regional areas called East, Midwest, and West, for example, under the Organization container.

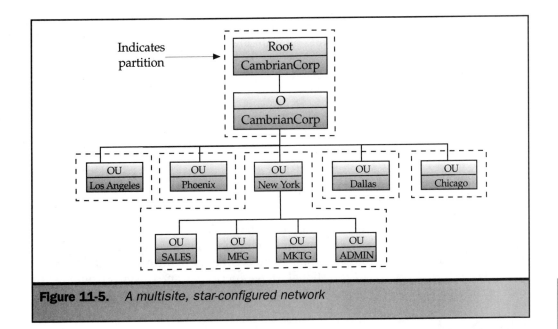

Figure 11-5.   *A multisite, star-configured network*

Planning Leaf Objects

After container objects are in place, you can begin planning the leaf objects for network users and resources. These objects are created in containers using the ConsoleOne or Windows NetWare Administrator utilities. You'll learn more about creating and assigning values to objects in Chapter 16. However, you should be familiar with a few objects when planning your directory tree.

Alias Objects

An Alias object represents another object in the directory tree and is essentially a shortcut to the object. Usually, an alias points to an object that you need to use outside of your current context. Alias objects are created by network administrators to make access to objects easier for both managers and users. For example, assume users in the Chicago office need to access a server in the New York office on a regular basis. A network administrator can create an alias in the Chicago office that points to the server in the New York office. Then users can see and access the server as if it were located in their own office.

Any network resource can be aliased. In addition, you can alias an Organizational Unit object in order to make all the resources contained in the object available to other users. For example, assume that the New York office has a group of servers in an organizational unit called Servers and you want to give users in the Chicago office access to the servers. You can simply alias Servers to the Chicago office, as pictured in Figure 11-6, to give those users access to the servers. Note that aliases inherit all the rights assigned to the servers in the Servers container.

Organizational Role Objects

For management purposes, you can create an Organizational Role object that has specific rights to various parts of the network. You can then assign users to the Organizational Role object. In this way, any users assigned to the organizational role have the same rights to the network as the organizational role and can manage those parts of the network.

An important characteristic of the organizational role is that you can easily add or remove users. If you need to make someone a temporary manager of a department or branch of the directory tree, simply assign them occupancy to the organizational role.

You can create as many organizational roles as necessary and assign any number of users as occupants to them.

Profile Objects

The Profile object contains a special login script that executes for anyone who has been assigned the Profile object. Profile object scripts can contain special login commands, drive mappings, or environmental settings, just like any other login script.

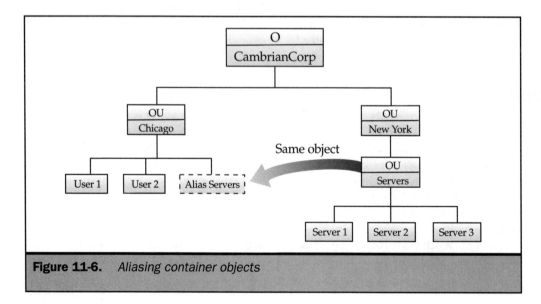

Figure 11-6. *Aliasing container objects*

Recall that there are three types of login scripts (which are covered in more detail in Chapter 24):

- *Container login scripts* execute when users belonging to the same container log in.
- *Profile login scripts* execute for any users that belong to the profile.
- *User login scripts* are specific to each user and execute when a user logs in.

The login scripts execute in the order shown when a user logs in. All are optional, but as a manager, you'll quickly learn that it's easier to create container and profile login scripts for groups of users than it is to create personal login scripts for each network user. In fact, user login scripts can be created and edited by the user, so you might want to avoid administering them altogether. Instead, you create container and profile login scripts to specify login parameters for users within specific containers or users who are assigned to a profile.

Group Object

Group objects are useful to consider when designing a directory tree, and they provide another unique way to manage a network. Group objects are similar in function to container objects like the Organizational Unit objects. Users that belong to a container obtain the same rights as the container through security equivalency. Likewise, members of a group obtain whatever rights the Group object has. However, you can be more selective in assigning users to groups because it is not dependent on the organization of a tree. For example, users who are scattered throughout a network's directory tree can be members of a group, such as department managers.

As mentioned previously, login scripts can execute commands based on the groups a user belongs to. The IF MEMBER OF GROUP statement can be used to evaluate whether a user is a member of a group, and if so, execute various login, environment, or mapping commands. For example, if a user is a member of a group called Managers, he or she can be assigned access to a special security server.

NetWare Planning
and Installation

The Complete Reference

NetWare 5

Chapter 12

NetWare 5 Hierarchy and Security

The NetWare 5 environment consists of a hierarchy of users who have access rights to objects in the NDS directory tree as well as directories and files in the file system. This chapter helps you understand the hierarchy of supervisors and users in NetWare 5 and how security is implemented.

Access rights determine what users can do on the network. Access rights are granted by network administrators. There are rights for managing objects in the directory tree and there are rights that grant users access to the file system. A right called the *Supervisor right* gives the user to whom it is granted "full" access to an object in the directory tree or a directory or file in the file system.

When a user is granted rights to an object, a directory, or a file, he or she becomes a *trustee* of that object, directory, or file. Rights differ from user to user, so while one user might only have the ability to open a file, another user might be able to change it or delete it. While administrators can grant rights to users on an individual basis, this can be tedious. An alternative method is to add a user to a group such as Managers or Clerks and then grant the rights to the group. Another method is to grant rights to the container the users are in. All rights applied at the container level flow down into the objects below.

The way that rights are administered for the directory tree and for the file system is similar; however, they are very different systems. This chapter helps you see the similarities and differences in those systems.

Administrative and User Hierarchy

A NetWare 5 network consists of a hierarchy of network administrators, subadministrators, operators, and users, as pictured in Figure 12-1. When you install the first NetWare 5 server, the ADMIN administrative user account is created with unrestricted access rights to the entire NDS directory tree and every server. You log in as ADMIN to set up a directory tree and to install the first servers for the network.

Note
The Supervisor object right is a specific right that you can grant to users to give them full control over a branch of the NDS directory tree. This is the only right that flows down into the file system of the server. The ADMIN account has the Supervisor right to the base of the tree and so has full control over the entire tree.

To help manage the network, you can create *subadministrators* who have full or partial rights to manage various parts of the directory tree and the file system. These managers are usually responsible for creating and maintaining user accounts and controlling access rights for their branch of the tree.

Under subadministrators in the hierarchy of users are *operators* or *managers*. We use the term *operators* loosely (it is not an official NetWare object or term) to refer to any user who has some rights to manage a device such as a printer or server. An operator might manage a print queue and be the person to notify if the printer runs out of paper. An operator might not be responsible for creating user accounts, but he or she might be responsible for updating information in user accounts.

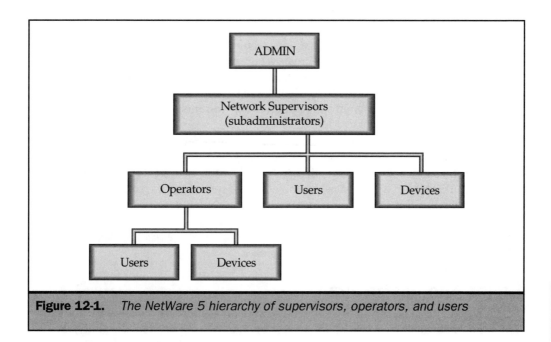

Figure 12-1.   *The NetWare 5 hierarchy of supervisors, operators, and users*

The ADMIN User

The ADMIN user account is created during the first NetWare 5 installation in the Organization object at the base of a directory tree. It has the Supervisor right to the [Root] of the tree and thus has rights to the entire tree. Keep the following in mind about ADMIN:

- The person who installs the first NetWare server in a directory tree specifies the ADMIN password and logs in as ADMIN.

- Because the ADMIN account has so much power, the person who is ADMIN should also have a normal user account to use when accessing the network for nonadministrative tasks. This can prevent accidents.

- Do not give out or lose the password to the ADMIN account. Doing so compromises the security of the entire network.

- The ADMIN account is critical for the maintenance of the entire network and cannot be deleted unless you create a backup administrator with the same rights.

Caution   *If you create a backup administrator and delete ADMIN, do not delete the user account of the backup administrator! You would lose supervisor access to the network. As a precaution against this, create an Organizational Role object, assign the Supervisor object right to [Root], and add administrators as occupants with their respective passwords. Use this to do the day-to-day administration. Leave the ADMIN account as a "back door."*

The system administrator's password is the master key to the system. It should be written down and placed in a locked safe or given to a trusted person of authority for safekeeping. Another suggestion is to create a backup ADMIN account with a two- or three-word password and then give a portion of the password to two or three people in the company. This "fail-safe" approach ensures that others can gain administrative access to the server should something happen to the administrator. To gain access, they must do so together.

Because the ADMIN account is created during the installation of the first NetWare 5 server, it receives the Supervisor object right to that Server object in the NDS directory tree and all other servers that are installed. In turn, ADMIN also gets the Supervisor right to the [Root] directory of all volumes attached to those servers and so can control all Directory and File rights for the entire network.

If ADMIN (or an equivalent account) is deleted, you need to either reinstall the tree or contact Novell Technical Support for assistance.

Container Administrators

Large internetworks require skilled users who can manage parts of the network at remote locations or manage the server equipment within their own departments. Initially, the ADMIN user can create *subadministrators* for various parts of the NDS tree by granting them the Supervisor right (or a lesser set of rights) to those parts of the tree as pictured in Figure 12-2. Users who are granted rights to a container in the NDS directory tree have the same rights for all subcontainers in that branch of the tree. Thus, the regional manager of the Los Angeles container has control over the Sales and Mktg containers. However, some or all of those rights can be blocked at lower levels if necessary.

The tasks of a network supervisor are listed here, but keep in mind that not all supervisors have the same tasks. Just as an organization has a management structure, the network may have different levels of management with supervisors, assistant supervisors, and operators.

- Set up servers and install the NetWare operating system in specific branches of the NDS directory tree.
- Administer specific branches of the NDS directory and create additional supervisors to manage subbranches of the tree.
- Create, manage, and delete User and resource objects.
- Create file system directory structures on the servers and Volume objects.
- Install applications and grant users the right to use those applications.
- Assign passwords to users or require them to periodically change their passwords.
- Monitor the performance and integrity of the network.

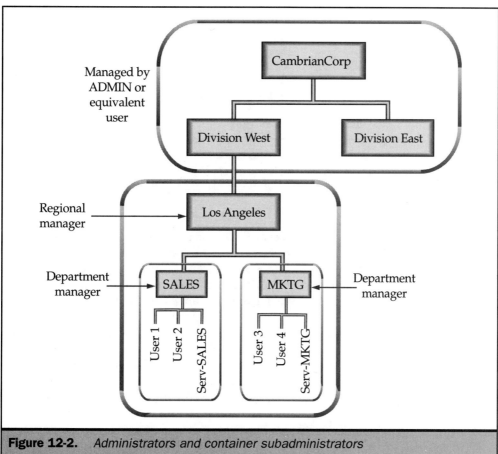

Figure 12-2. *Administrators and container subadministrators*

- Recommend new equipment or manage the expansion of the network when it becomes overloaded.

- Ensure that data is properly protected with backup procedures and System Fault Tolerance (SFT) features, as well as by physically securing servers.

ADMIN (or an equivalent user) initially creates the Organizational Unit objects for each division or department of the company, and then creates user accounts within those container objects for managers and gives them Supervisor rights (or some subset of rights) to specific container objects in the tree.

For example, assume you're the ADMIN user for our fictitious CambrianCorp company and you've just installed the network pictured in Figure 12-3. It consists of

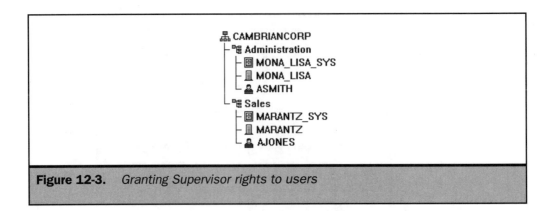

Figure 12-3. *Granting Supervisor rights to users*

an Administration container with a server called Mona_Lisa and a Sales container with a server called Marantz. To create supervisors for the Administration and Sales departments, you log in from a workstation and start NetWare Administrator. Then you create the User object ASmith in the Administration container and the User object AJones in the Sales container, as shown. Next, you grant each of these new users the Supervisor right (or a lesser set of rights) for their respective containers.

Now suppose that ASmith, with Supervisor rights to the Administration container, creates a new branching container called Personnel and creates a user in that container named TMalone, as shown in Figure 12-4. ASmith can grant TMalone the Supervisor right to the Personnel container so that TMalone can manage that branch of the tree and create new containers or users as required in that branch.

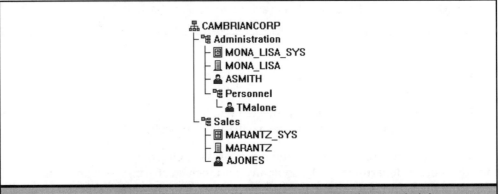

Figure 12-4. *Container administrator ASmith creates an assistant administrator named TMalone*

Keep in mind that TMalone's Supervisor right in the example encompasses only the Personnel container and not any upper-level containers.

Operators

An operator is a user who has responsibility for a system resource such as a printer or a server. You grant the user limited rights to the resource object so that he or she can change the object's property fields if necessary. For example, a print queue operator can be granted the rights to control who has access to a particular queue and thus access to send print jobs to a printer.

Operators can relieve network administrators of mundane tasks or of the need to drive to remote locations. Operators are typically on the list of users to notify or contact when there is a problem with a device. For example, if a user needs a special form in a printer, he or she can look up the operator's name in the object and call the operator. If a printer runs out of paper, the operator is notified automatically through the messaging system.

You might also want to create operators who manage user accounts, but limit their duties to working with user accounts in a single container and to changing only specific properties like addresses, telephone numbers, and e-mail addresses. A personnel clerk is a good candidate.

Users

Everybody who logs into the network is a user and is represented by a User account object in the NDS directory tree. A User object holds information about the user, such as name, location, phone number, personal login scripts, as well as management information such as login restrictions and account balances. The name of a user account can be up to 47 characters long, but a naming format that combines a user's first initial and last name (TSheldon, for example) is recommended.

Access to the network is based on the *trustee rights* that users have to specific objects and file system directories or files. These rights might come from a direct trustee assignment, from the user's membership in a group, or the container that the user account belongs to. There are other indirect ways of obtaining rights, as discussed later in this chapter under "NDS Rights Inheritance."

NetWare 5 has a special entity called [Public] that is not an object but a unique trustee. It is located at the root of the directory, and every user receives the same rights as [Public]. By default, [Public] has the Browse right, which is the right to scan through the directory tree and view objects. Even if you attach to the network but don't log in, you get [Public]'s rights.

Although you can assign additional rights to [Public], keep in mind that all users will get those rights. It is better to assign additional rights to individual containers (branches of the tree). Note also that some administrators may prefer to remove even the Browse right from [Public] to tighten network security.

The ADMIN user or a network supervisor creates new user accounts in specific containers of the directory tree. New accounts automatically obtain various rights on the system as follows:

- New accounts automatically obtain the rights associated with [Public].

- New accounts are security-equivalent to the container they belong to. *Security-equivalent* means that they get the same rights granted to the container.

- If a server is installed in a container, the container is granted the rights to list and open files in the SYS:PUBLIC directory of the server. In turn, any users added to that container get the same rights to the server.

- Users can change their own personal login scripts.

In addition, supervisors can create a home directory for new users where they can store personal programs and files. Users are typically granted full access rights to their own home directory so that they can create subdirectories and store files, but the amount of disk space they use can be restricted. Novell recommends setting aside a separate volume for home directories on large networks. A home directory usually has the same name as its user and branches from a root-level directory called USERS or HOME.

Here are some of the property rights and user restrictions that supervisors can apply to user accounts. User restrictions are discussed further in the next section.

- Login restrictions
- Password restrictions
- Login time restrictions
- Login scripts
- Security equivalence
- Rights to the file system
- Group memberships

Changing properties for individual users can be tedious. To ease this task, you can create multiple user *templates* in the container where you plan to create user accounts, and then define common properties for each template. Then when you create a new user account, you specify that you want to use the properties of that specific template.

User Restrictions

Supervisors can place a number of restrictions on a user's account. Restrictions are assigned in the ConsoleOne or NetWare Administrator utility by modifying individual user accounts or by creating templates as just described. You'll see how to apply these restrictions to user accounts in Chapter 17.

ACCOUNT BALANCE RESTRICTIONS   You can restrict a user's access to the system and its resources by specifying a credit limit. A credit limit is a balance in an account that depletes as time and resources are used. Once depleted, the user can't log into the system until given more credit.

EXPIRATION RESTRICTIONS   You can set an expiration date and time for a user account. The account is closed at the time specified. You might use this restriction for temporary employees.

PASSWORD RESTRICTIONS   The administrator or a supervisor can specify the length and uniqueness of login passwords. You can force users to change their passwords at regular intervals and to use passwords that they haven't used recently.

DISK SPACE RESTRICTIONS   Disk space restrictions prevent users from using too much of the server's disk space by loading unnecessary programs or files.

CONNECTION RESTRICTIONS   Connection restrictions can limit the number of stations a user can log into simultaneously.

TIME RESTRICTIONS   Time restrictions specify the hours, in half-hour blocks, that users can log into the system.

STATION RESTRICTIONS   Station restrictions prevent a user from logging in at any station other than the specified workstation. This prevents users from logging in at unsupervised workstations where their activities cannot be monitored.

Groups

Groups are collections of User objects. You create groups to simplify the task of managing large numbers of User objects. Rather than assigning directory and file access rights to individual users, one at a time, you include those users in a group and then assign the rights to the group. It is best to create groups for users, projects, and management purposes early on and then simply add users to the groups as necessary. Group members can be anywhere in the NDS tree. Here are two examples:

- Create a group that consists of managers at different network sites and then grant the group rights to a server that contains management information.
- Create a word processing group and then grant the group rights to run a word processing program and store files in its data directories.

Groups provide a convenient way to change or remove the rights of a large number of users. You can delete an entire group or remove individual users from the group. Once removed, the users no longer have the rights of the group.

NetWare Planning and Installation

Access Rights and Security

Let's take a closer look at rights. You've seen that network users need access rights to use resources on the network and to work with files in the file system. Rights determine exactly how a user can access another object and how a user can access directories and files in the file system.

Access rights and security are vital in a network operating system. When security is managed correctly, you can prevent unauthorized people from stealing or corrupting data and ensure that private files are secure. Login restrictions are the first line of defense against unauthorized users, but once a user is logged in, object and file system rights ensure that users don't go snooping around the network in places where they don't belong.

Logging In

Users must log in and be authenticated with Novell Directory Services (NDS). Access depends on login restrictions and a few other important features. When users log in, their password is encrypted before being sent across the wire to prevent hackers (who might capture it using various monitoring tools) from deciphering it. NetWare uses the RSA public key encryption technology, which provides encryption and authentication features.

Network administrators can force users to periodically change their password and use passwords with a minimum length of eight characters. Users can also be prevented from logging in at workstations other than the one to which they are assigned or from logging in outside of designated times.

Home Context

A user must be found in his or her "home context" before he or she can log into the network. This is the container where the user's account is located. Catalog Services provides a means of "contextless" login that allows the user to log in without specifying his or her context. It is possible to browse the NDS tree with the CX command before actually logging in so that users can switch to their correct context. However, a better solution is to define the user's context in the properties page of the NetWare Client.

Connection Types

There are three types of connections that users can have to NetWare 5. These connection types are a concern if you have a limited number of licenses available (additional licenses are available from Novell).

- **Connected (but not logged in)**   A user is still attached to a server but is not currently logged in. This is a typical situation if a user temporarily logs in, leaves the computer on, and goes out to lunch. No licenses are in use in this situation.

- **Authenticated**   The user has logged in and been verified by NDS but is not accessing resources such as servers or printers. The user may be browsing the NDS tree. A license is not used.

- **Licensed**   In this case, a user is logged in, has mapped a drive to a server and/or captured a network printer, and is using a NetWare license.

Managing NDS Security

NDS security is managed through the use of object and property rights. All objects within the NDS tree have one or more associated property pages. Through these pages, the administrator can control access to the file system and other NDS objects. This provides the ability to establish and maintain security across all users and the enterprise networking environment.

Object/Property Access Rights

The Object Rights and Property Rights fields are where you specify what rights each trustee will have. Remember, we're working with NDS objects here, not directories and files, so you don't see anything related to the file system (although assigning the Supervisor right would give Supervisor rights to any volumes in the Administration container). Let's study the object and property rights.

Object Rights

You grant object rights to users who will manage objects in the directory tree. The object rights are listed here:

- **Supervisor**   Users with this right have all the other object rights listed below and all property rights listed in the next section.

- **Browse**   This right allows users to see the object in the directory tree. By default, all users have this right because they are security-equivalent to the Public entity.

- **Create**   Users with this right (containers only) can create new objects in the container.

- **Delete**   This right allows users to delete objects in the tree.

- **Rename**   This right allows users to rename an object.

Note   *Remember, you only assign these rights to users who will manage some or all of the directory tree. Regular users don't need these rights. In fact, most regular users only need the default Browse right (which they get through the [Public] entity), rights to volumes in the file system, and rights to use printers.*

NetWare Planning and Installation

There are basically two ways to assign these object rights to trustees. First, you can grant the Supervisor right and give the new trustee full control over the object. Second, you can grant only Browse, Create, Delete, and Rename rights if the new trustee should have only limited management rights.

Property Rights

Recall that every object has a set of properties, and you can grant users (usually managers) the ability to change all or some of the properties for objects in the directory tree. For example, user accounts have name, address, phone number, and e-mail properties, and you might grant clerks in the personnel department the ability to change these fields. Other properties are more critical to the security of the network, and only higher-level managers should have rights to change them. Some of these properties are account restrictions, login restrictions, and security equivalence. Here is a description of property rights:

- **Supervisor**   This property right grants a user all the rights listed below. It does not grant object rights, although the Supervisor object right does grant the supervisor all property rights.

- **Compare**   This right returns true or false, depending on a comparison of two values. This right is implicit in the Read right.

- **Read**   This right lets users see the value of a property.

- **Write**   This right lets users change property values. This is the most important right to assign to managers unless you want to give them full Supervisor rights.

- **Add or Delete Self**   This right lets users add or remove themselves from a property and is implied if the user has the Write right. This right is used only when the user can add himself or herself to the value, such as a membership in a group or address list.

Here is a simple analogy to the differences between object and property rights. Wrapped birthday presents are objects. We can do things to the presents without knowing what is inside. We can add more presents to the stack, throw some away, or give some to someone else. These options are controlled by the object rights. Property rights let you open the presents and look inside. You can see the contents, change them, or do whatever the property rights will permit.

Assigning Object Trustee and NDS Rights

You're probably wondering just how you go about granting access rights to objects in the NDS directory tree and to directories and files in the file system. The Windows-based NetWare Administrator is the best tool to use for managing NDS (and to some extent, the file system), so we use it here to demonstrate how you create and manage trustees.

Remember, a trustee is a person with rights to another object. All objects in the NDS directory tree have an Access Control List (ACL), which contains the following entries:

- The object rights for each trustee of the object
- The property rights for each trustee of the object

Because each object has its own ACL that must be updated with trustee information, you normally go to the object to add a trustee or change trustee rights, as opposed to going to a trustee (or proposed trustee).

Note   *The file system uses the Directory Entry Table (DET) to store similar information about the trustees of directories and files.*

The directory tree for CambrianCorp showing the Administration container and the user AColgan as a member of that container is pictured in Figure 12-5.

NetWare Planning and Installation

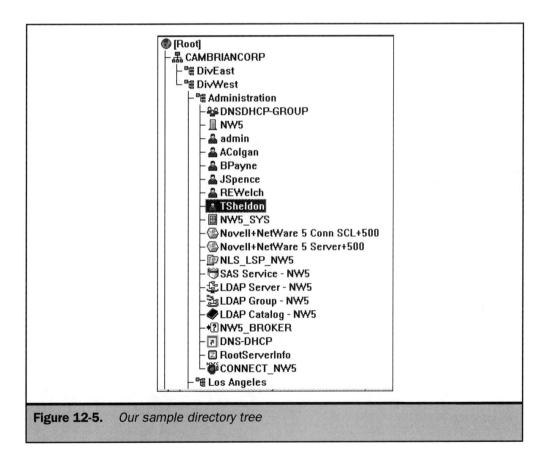

Figure 12-5.   *Our sample directory tree*

By default, AColgan has all the rights that the container has because she is a member of that container. This is due to a form of security equivalence. However, assume we want to make AColgan a manager of the Administration container with trustee rights to manage it. There are two ways to do this in NetWare Administrator:

- Right-click the Administration container and choose Trustees of this Object from the context menu that appears; then click the Add Trustee button in the Trustees Of dialog box.
- Click and drag the AColgan object over the Administration object.

Either way, the dialog box shown in Figure 12-6 appears. Take a close look at this dialog box—you'll work in this box most of the time when managing user access rights. At the top, in the Trustees field, is each user or object with explicit rights to the object (Administration, in this case). An *explicit* trustee right refers to someone who has been directly granted rights to an object, not someone who is a trustee through inheritance. If you want to view users who are trustees through inheritance, you click the Effective Rights button.

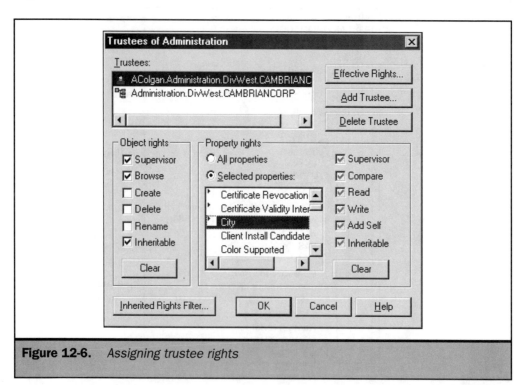

Figure 12-6. *Assigning trustee rights*

You can grant rights to properties either all at the same time or to each property individually. This sounds confusing at first, but just take a look at the Property Rights field in Figure 12-6. Under it are two buttons marked All Properties and Selected Properties.

- When you select the All Properties button, you can click one or more of the property rights in order to assign those rights to all the properties of the object.

- When you select Selected Properties, you can scan through the list, click a specific property, and then choose one or more property rights.

The normal procedure is to first assign global rights by clicking All Properties, and then click Selected Properties and assign (or revoke) any special property rights assignments.

Use caution when assigning the Write right to the property called Object Trustee (ACL). Assigning the Write right allows the person to change his or her own access to the object from what a higher-level manager had granted. See "Assigning Rights for Specific Users," later in this chapter, for special circumstances regarding this right.

Managing File System Rights

The rights for directories and files are listed in Table 12-1. You can assign these rights from the ConsoleOne or the Windows-based NetWare Administrator (NWADMIN32), or with other DOS commands as discussed in Chapter 19.

While the NDS directory and the file system are completely different, they share similar rights management techniques. There are two points of overlap between NDS and the file system:

- Any user who has the Supervisor right for a container has full Supervisor rights to the file system on the servers in that container. This includes ADMIN by default.

- All users have Read and File Scan rights to the SYS:PUBLIC directory on any servers.

Assigning file system rights with the NetWare Administrator is easy. You can assign rights to individual users, to groups, to containers that hold users, to directory maps, and to Organizational Role objects. Users then obtain these rights by being a member of the group or container, through inheritance of rights, or by being security-equivalent to an

Rights	For Directories	For Files
Supervisor	Grants all rights to the directory, subdirectories, and their files. Overrides any Inherited Rights Filter restrictions in subdirectories or files. Trustees with this right can grant others any rights in this directory or subdirectories, or files. The Supervisor right can only be revoked from the directory in which it was originally assigned because filters below that point are ignored.	Grants all rights to the file. The trustee can grant any right to another user and modify all rights in the file's Inherited Rights Filter. The Supervisor right cannot be blocked by an Inherited Rights Filter.
Read	Grants the right to open, read, and execute programs in the directory, unless other rights are set at the file level.	Grants the right to open and read the file.
Write	Grants the right to open and modify files in the directory, unless other rights are given at the file level.	Grants the right to open and write to the file.
Create	Grants the right to create files and subdirectories in the directory. If the Create right is the only right granted at the directory level and no other rights are granted below it, this right creates a DROP BOX directory, which allows users to open and write to a new file in the directory, but after the file is closed, users can't see or read from it. A user can copy files into the directory and retain ownership, but all trustee assignments are revoked.	Grants the right to salvage the file after it has been deleted.

Table 12-1. *Directory and File Rights*

Rights	For Directories	For Files
Erase	Grants the right to erase (delete) the directory and everything in it, including subdirectories and their files, unless other rights are assigned below it.	Grants the right to erase (delete) the file.
Modify	Grants the right to rename or change the attributes of the directory and all subdirectories and files below it. It does not give the right to see or modify any directory or file.	Grants the right to rename the file or change its attributes, but not to see or modify the file's contents.
File Scan	Grants the right to see files in the directory, unless other rights are in effect below the directory level.	Grants the right to see the file when viewing the directory, including the directory structure back to the root of the volume.
Access Control	Grants the right to change the trustee assignments and Inherited Rights Filter of the directory and any files or subdirectories below it. With this right, users can grant all rights, except the Supervisor right, to other users, including rights that they themselves have not been granted.	Grants the right to change the file's trustee assignments and Inherited Rights Filter. With the right, users can grant all rights, except the Supervisor right, to other users, including rights that they themselves have not been granted.

Table 12-1.   *Directory and File Rights* (continued)

object. To assign file system rights, you first double-click a Volume object in the directory tree. This displays its file structure, as shown in Figure 12-7.

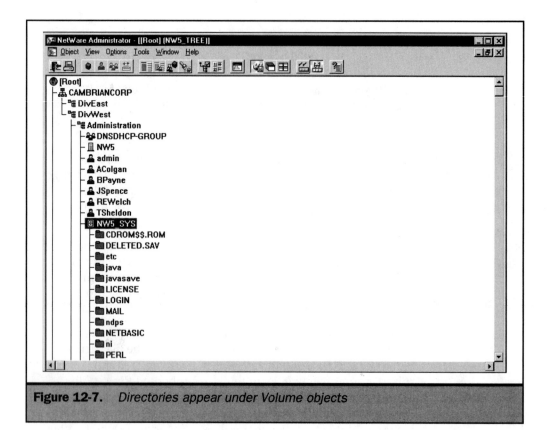

Figure 12-7.   *Directories appear under Volume objects*

Changing NDS Default Rights

If you right-click a directory (such as Public), you can choose Details from a context menu to display the Details dialog box for the directory. Next, you click the Trustees of this Directory button to display the dialog box shown in Figure 12-8. This is where you add new trustees (by clicking the Add Trustee button) or change the rights of existing trustees listed in the Trustees field. To change a trustee's rights, you select a trustee in the Trustees field, and then click Rights in the Access Rights field. The procedure for setting rights to files is similar.

 You can set directory and file attributes by clicking the Attributes button, as seen in Figure 12-8. This is covered in Chapter 19.

Special Considerations

Note the following with regard to trustee rights:

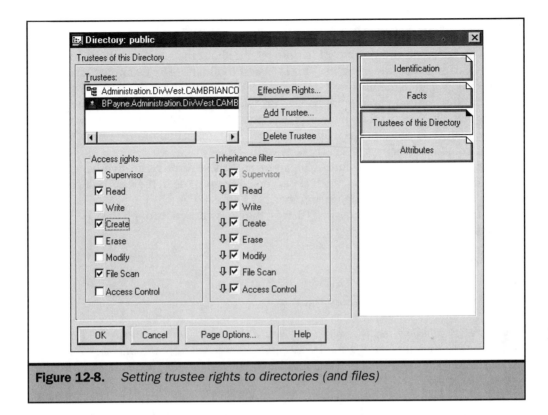

Figure 12-8. *Setting trustee rights to directories (and files)*

- Trustees of a file server's volumes, directories, and files can open, change, create, rename, and delete files, depending on the rights they have been granted.

- If a user is granted the Supervisor right to a container object in the directory tree, he or she has Supervisor rights to all objects and containers under that container unless those rights are blocked at another level.

- If a user is granted Supervisor rights to a container that holds Server objects, he or she has Supervisor rights to all the volumes on all the servers in the container.

- The [Public] entity has the Browse object right to the root of the NDS directory tree. All users obtain this right, giving them the ability to see objects in the directory tree.

- When installing a new NetWare 5 server, you must designate a container for the Server object and its Volume objects. This container is automatically assigned Read and File Scan rights to the SYS:PUBLIC directory on the server. If the container contains user accounts, those users get the same rights, due to security equivalence.

NDS Rights Inheritance

Perhaps the most important concept to understand about the NetWare object and file security system is the flow of rights. This is easiest to illustrate by example. Assume you make AColgan (a member of the Administration container in Figure 12-5) a trustee of the DivWest container and grant her the Browse, Create, Delete, and Rename object rights so she can create and manage user accounts. These rights flow down the tree to the Administration container as well as the other containers that branch from DivWest so that AColgan can manage users there as well.

Of course, you might not want AColgan to have these same rights to other objects in the Administration container, such as servers. As you'll see in the next section, you can block these rights by setting up an Inherited Rights Filter (IRF).

The following rights are inherited (that is, they flow down through the directory tree):

- Object rights
- File system rights
- The All Properties category right

Note   *Individual properties, as assigned by Selected Properties, are not inherited. A change made to a single property for a trustee only applies to the current container and is not passed down to the child container. See "Assigning Rights for Specific Users," later in this chapter.*

Inheritance works in the file system as well. If a user has Read, Write, and Create rights to a directory, that user has those same rights in its subdirectories, unless the rights are specifically changed. The rights flow down the directory structure.

You can use this feature when designing your tree. For example, assume you have servers or other devices that you want users in multiple containers to have access to. One way to grant this access is to place the device at the top level of a branch of the tree. Now any rights you assign to that container to the object flow down to the lower containers and the objects in them.

Blocking Inherited Rights

The Inherited Rights Filter (IRF) controls which rights users can inherit from parent container objects in the directory tree or parent directories in the file system. You can use the IRF to remove some or all of the rights a user inherits from the parent object or directory. The IRF applies to all users who access an object or directory with rights they have obtained from a parent object (or directory in the file system). Note the following:

- Every object or directory can have its own IRF.
- Objects in containers obtain rights from the container due to security equivalence. You cannot block these rights with an IRF.

- An IRF has no effect on the rights of a user who is granted explicit rights to an object (made a trustee of that object).

- In the file system, the Supervisor directory right is inherited in all subdirectories and by all files and cannot be blocked by an IRF.

- In the NDS directory tree, an IRF can block Supervisor object rights from above. This provides a way to give subadministrators complete control over their branch of the tree.

Determining an Object's Effective Rights

A combination of rights form what are called the user's *effective rights*. Effective rights are largely dependent on a number of default rights that NetWare automatically creates for users and containers. The actual rights that a user has to a directory or object depend on the following:

- Direct trustee rights to objects, files, or directories

- Security equivalence to another user or object

- Rights that are inherited from upper-level containers

- Rights obtained from group membership through direct trustee assignment or through inheritance

- The status of the target object's Inherited Rights Filter, which blocks some or all rights that might be inherited from a parent container or directory

Note *The rights that users obtain through group membership might not immediately be obvious.*

Another way to understand trustee rights is by remembering the following two points:

- If you are directly granted rights to any object, those are your rights and they can't be changed by an Inherited Rights Filter. Note that you might also have direct rights due to security equivalence or membership in a group.

- If you don't have direct rights to an object, all your rights to it come from inheriting rights from higher container objects (or the Public entity), and these rights are subject to being blocked by an Inherited Rights Filter.

Examining Default Rights

When you install a NetWare 5 server, some rights are automatically granted to supervisors and users. Understanding these default rights helps you determine the rights that users have to objects.

NetWare Planning
and Installation

Keep in mind that rights granted to objects at the root or in higher-level containers flow down the directory tree.

A special entity called [Public] has the explicit Browse trustee right in the [Root] of the directory tree. All users are security-equivalent to [Public] and so have Browse rights for the entire tree, even before logging in. The Browse right can be revoked for [Public] if you don't want unlogged users browsing your network. If you revoke the right, grant the highest-level organization container the Browse right so that users can browse the network *after* logging in.

 To change [Public]'s Browse right in NetWare Administrator, right-click the [Root] object and choose Trustees of this Object from the context menu that appears. Click [Public] and revoke the right.

Here are the other default object and file system rights:

- The ADMIN user has the Supervisor right to the [Root] object and thus has full supervisory control of the entire tree and file system through inheritance.
- Users get the Read right to all of their User object properties.
- Users get Read and Write rights to the Login Script and Print Job Configuration properties so they can change these fields in their user accounts.
- The ADMIN user has Supervisor rights to all server file systems due to inheritance via the Server object. This is the only NDS right that translates over to the file system.
- Containers that hold servers get the Read and File Scan rights to the server's SYS:PUBLIC directory. All user accounts in the container get these rights through security equivalence.

The [Root] object property right allow users or entities to view or change the properties of other objects. Here are the default property rights:

- The [Public] entity also gets the Read rights to all servers' Network Address properties.
- The [Root] gets Read property rights to the Network Address and Group Membership properties for user accounts.
- The [Root] receives Read property rights to the Host Server and Host Volume properties.
- The [Root] gets the Read property right to the Default Server user property.

Using Security Equal To

Security equivalence, or Security Equal To, is a property that gives the object (usually a user but sometimes a container) the same rights as the object that it has been made equal to. Security equivalence simplifies management. Making a user security-equivalent to another is considered a temporary convenience. You'll want to remove the equivalence as soon as possible. Note the following:

- When a user is made a member of a group, the group's name is added to the Security Equal To property of the user's account.

- The rights obtained through security equivalence are lost if the source object holding the original rights is deleted.

- All objects within a container are security-equivalent to the container. Any rights you grant to a container become the rights of any User object within the container.

It is not recommended that you use security equivalence as a regular means of assigning rights to a user account. If the source account is deleted, all the dependent accounts will lose the equivalent rights. However, it is a good idea to take advantage of *container* security equivalence. All the user accounts within a container obtain its rights, so you might want to plan your directory and security hierarchy around this feature by granting server, printer, and other rights directly to a container. Another method for assigning rights is to assign them to groups.

Security Equivalence is a button in the Details dialog box for User objects. A trustee of a User object can add other User objects to its security equivalence list. To do so, this trustee must have the Write property right to the Security Equivalence property of the object.

Note   *Do not grant users the right to change their own security equivalence properties as listed in their Trustees Of dialog box (see Figure 12-6). They could add an object that has the Supervisor right and thus gain access to areas of the network they are not authorized to access.*

Suggested Administrative Roles and Rights Assignments

This section defines how to create specific users and assign rights for the directory tree and file system. Several examples are presented. You'll get a chance to create these users or objects in Chapter 17.

Creating Network Supervisors

First, consider the many ways that a user can obtain rights to an object, as illustrated in Figure 12-9. Assume that AColgan needs to manage the Laser_PRN object in the Administration container. The following methods are available for granting those rights.

■ **Method #1**   A supervisor can explicitly grant AColgan a trustee assignment to the Laser_PRN object.

■ **Method #2**   Make the Administration container a trustee of Laser_PRN. Because AColgan is security-equivalent to the Administration container, she gets access to the printer as well. So do all the other users in the Administration container, which may or may not be what you want.

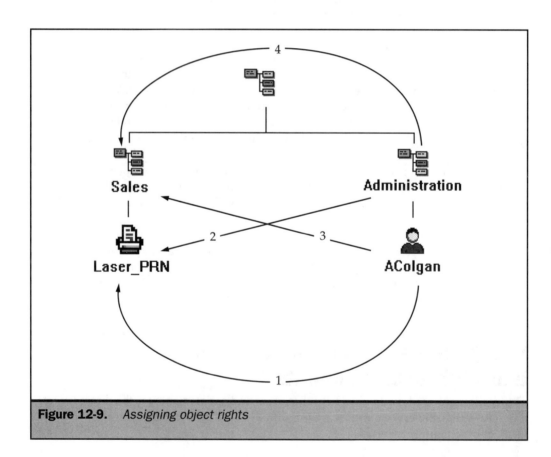

Figure 12-9.   *Assigning object rights*

- **Method #3**   Make AColgan a trustee of the Sales container. Through inheritance, she gets access to the printer. However, an Inherited Rights Filter at the printer can block those rights.

- **Method #4**   Make the Administration container a trustee of the Sales container. AColgan is security-equivalent to Administration and so becomes a trustee of Sales and obtains rights to the printer through inheritance. However, an Inherited Rights Filter at the printer can block those rights.

AColgan can also gain rights to the printer by being made security-equivalent to a user or group with rights to the printer.

Using the Organizational Role

The Organizational Role (OR) object defines a position or role within an organization that you need to assign to more than one person or to different people at different times. You create the OR and assign object, property, and file system rights to it as appropriate. You then add occupants to the OR object.

Users assigned to an organizational role receive all the rights of that role until they are removed from it or until the organizational role is deleted. The most common method for using Organizational Role objects is to create an OR under a container and assign rights to it for that container or specific objects in the container. Then you add users in the same container to the role. However, users from any location in the directory tree can be added to an OR and it can be assigned rights to any object in the directory tree.

The following example illustrates a typical management situation. Assume the directory structure pictured in Figure 12-10. Your goal is to let AColgan manage the users in Sales (but not the server), and to let RBonati manage the server in Sales.

The trick here is to give AColgan Supervisor rights to all the objects in the Sales container except for the server. Here's the procedure:

1. Create an Organizational Role and assign it Supervisor rights to the Sales container.

2. Make AColgan a member of the OR.

3. Add an Inherited Rights Filter to the server to block the Supervisor right of the OR.

4. Grant RBonati explicit trustee rights to manage the server or create another OR for this right and then make RBonati a member of the OR.

Figure 12-11 illustrates the control that each manager now has over the Sales department. Note the location of the IRF on Server, which blocks the Supervisor right from above.

NetWare Planning and Installation

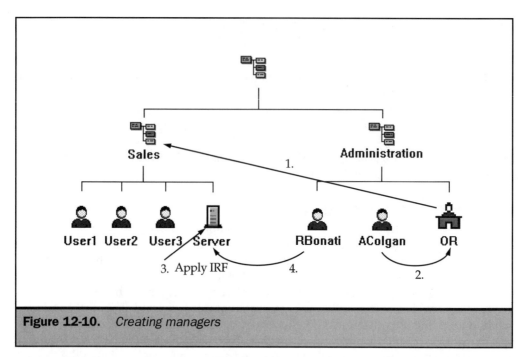

Figure 12-10. *Creating managers*

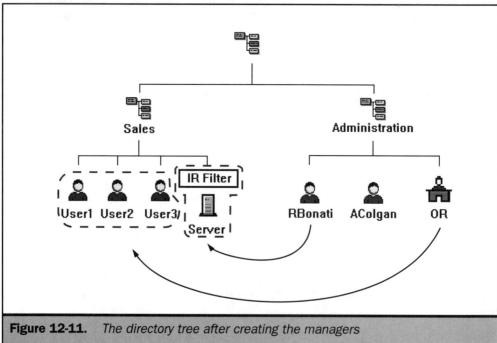

Figure 12-11. *The directory tree after creating the managers*

Guidelines for Implementing NDS Security

For most users, the default NDS rights provide adequate access to the necessary network resources. Users receive the Browse object right through the [Public] trustee, allowing them to see the objects in the NDS tree. User objects will require additional rights assignments to access network resources found in other containers. Only those users who need to manage NDS objects need additional rights. Most users do not need to create, delete, or modify objects and property values. If you do need to assign additional NDS rights to a user, refer to the following guidelines:

- Start with the default NDS assignments.
- Avoid assigning rights through the All Properties option.
- Use Selected Properties to assign property rights.
- Use caution when assigning the write property to the ACL of any object.
- Use caution when granting the Supervisor object right to a Server object.
- Granting the Supervisor object right implies granting the right to all properties.
- Use caution when filtering the Supervisor right with an Inherited Rights Filter (IRF).

Troubleshooting NDS Security

Most problems with NDS are rights-associated. The two most common involve finding users who have unauthorized access to objects and their properties and determining why users cannot access network resources. If a user has more access to a resource than they should have, you, as the administrator, must determine where the rights are coming from. To determine a user's effective rights use the NetWare Administrator (NWADMIN32) utility to complete the following steps:

1. Highlight the resource you want to check.
2. Right-click the object to bring up the Trustees of This Object menu.
3. Click the Effective Rights button.
4. Click the Browse button to the right of the Object Name field.
5. Click the User object in the Available Objects list.

You may also need to determine where the improper rights are coming from. To do this, check explicit rights assignments for the following:

- User object
- Groups the user is a member of
- Organizational Role the user is an occupant of

- Security equivalencies the user may have
- Containers the user is in up the tree to the [Root]
- Rights given to the [Public] trustee
- Rights given to the [Root] of the tree

Assigning Rights for Specific Users

You'll probably want to create a number of managers with very limited rights. For example, these managers might create and delete user accounts or only change specific properties in those accounts such as the e-mail address. The main point is that you don't want to let them change every property right for objects, just selected properties.

To create subadministrators with limited rights to containers and other objects, right-click the object and choose "Trustees of this Object" from the context menu to display the Trustees of Administration dialog box, as pictured in Figure 12-6. Next, you click the Selected Properties button, highlight a property you want to change, then choose appropriate rights, such as Read and Write. This gives the user the ability to change the fields for their own account or for other objects.

You should watch out for two things when creating these subadministrators:

- Don't assign the Supervisor object right. This would give the user full property rights for the object.
- Don't assign the Write right to the Object Trustee (ACL) property. This would allow the user to change his or her own rights to the object!

Remember, there is an inheritable right for both object and property rights in NetWare 5 and it is on by default. This is good if you want a subadministrator to have property rights in a container and in subcontainers. But it can pose a problem when you want to create a subadministrator with limited selected property rights in branches of the container. Because the rights are inherited by default, you'll need to go to each subcontainer and disable the inheritable right for both the object and property rights. This is both good and bad. It promotes a certain level of security, but makes it difficult to create subadministrators with selected rights.

Watch out for the following: Assume you grant a user the Write right to all property rights and then revoke the right for the Object Trustee (ACL) property, which prevents the user from changing his or her own rights. This works fine in the current container, but the selected property right change you made to Object Trustee (ACL) is not inherited, so the user has the right in lower containers through inheritance!

Centralized Versus Distributed Administration

NetWare 5 allows for both centralized and distributed administration. A tree can have one administrator for the entire tree, administrators for various branches of the tree, or a combination of administrators.

In centralized administration, one or more users have rights to the entire NDS tree. This is the NetWare 5 default. The Admin object has all rights to manage the directory tree through an explicit assignment of the Supervisor object right to the [Root] object. The ADMIN user inherits rights to the rest of the NDS tree unless an IRF is applied lower in the tree to block the rights. This type of administration is appropriate for organizations with small NDS trees or those that wish to retain a central administrator.

In distributed administration, specific users are given enough NDS rights to manage specific branches of the NDS tree. The user who is assigned the administrative tasks at the branch level (container) becomes the container administrator. This type of administration tends to allow administrators to respond more quickly, as control of the network does not reside with one person.

Creating Container Administrators

A container manager is a subadministrator who has Supervisor rights (or lesser rights) in a container. Through inheritance, these rights flow down to objects in the container and subcontainers. This section shows you how to create various levels of subadministrators. However, before proceeding, there are a few things you need to be aware of:

■ A user who is granted the Supervisor right to a container has full control over the container, including the ability to set up an Inherited Rights Filter and block any users with Supervisor rights in upper levels. This would effectively cut the ADMIN user off from the directory. This may or may not be beneficial, depending on your requirements.

■ If such a container supervisor did set up an IRF to block upper-level supervisors and that supervisor's account is deleted, no one will have supervisor access to that part of the tree. Use caution when deleting supervisor accounts.

■ NetWare protects you in some ways from removing the only user with Supervisor rights to a container. You cannot delete that trustee from the Trustees list or remove the Supervisor object right for that trustee. However, if the user's account is accidentally deleted, access to the container and its branch of the tree is lost.

■ Creating a user with limited rights who still has adequate control of a container can be a problem.

Keep a log of users who have Supervisor object rights in containers or at the root of the directory tree and make sure no one deletes these users so that you do not cut yourself off from any part of the directory tree.

Creating Group Assignments

Groups are useful for assigning rights or addressing users who are scattered about your directory tree. For example, members of your fantasy football league might be located in many different geographic locations. You can add them to a group and then address mail to the group.

You can create groups for people in your organization who work on special projects or who belong to special workgroups. These people are often scattered throughout the company but need similar access to the same files. First create the group; then make the group a trustee of a directory on your file system. Finally, add users to the group.

Creating File System Access

As mentioned, you can assign rights to users based on their membership in groups. Another method is to use the Directory Map object to give users access to applications or document directories as follows:

1. Create a directory map and assign it a path to a directory or file on a volume.
2. Assign users appropriate rights to the directory so they can access the files.
3. Refer to the directory map in user login scripts.

This method is really useful if all the users belong to the same container. Then you can add the directory map reference to the container login script so it executes for all the users in the container. Some other methods for assigning file system rights are listed here:

■ Add file system rights directly to the Directory Map object, and then make each user security-equivalent to it.

■ If the users are scattered about the tree but belong to the same workgroup or management group, create a profile login script and add the directory map reference to it.

■ A *user template* simplifies the creation of new User objects by allowing you to assign predefined property values and object/directory rights. You can create user templates in every container to which you plan to add User objects. Then, when you create a new User object, you can choose to give it the property values and rights of the user template, or you can specify those values and rights individually.

For a complete description of file system rights, refer to Part V.

The Complete Reference

NetWare 5

Chapter 13

Equipment Planning and Setup

This chapter will help you plan for, acquire, and obtain vital equipment that you need for your network. It will help you identify your network requirements and develop a plan for implementing the network, plan for growth, evaluate your hardware and equipment needs, understand server technology requirements for NetWare 5 networks, protect your equipment and data, and prepare the network site for NetWare 5 and the network's users.

The Planning Process

Planning is essential for any network. Although no network has a final plan that is set in concrete, preparing an initial plan is essential. Technology and user needs change constantly, so the plan is bound to change. You should develop your initial plan in the most professional and responsible way possible, regardless of the size of your network.

It's common to hire outside organizations to bring expertise to the planning stages. A systems analyst or consulting organization can work as an unbiased mediator with your users, managers, and system supervisors to determine hardware and software needs, budget requirements, policy implementation, and other concerns.

It's also common practice to interview the management staff and network users to identify problems and requirements. Many times, users will develop some sort of workaround to "make the system work anyway." Here are a few things to identify:

■ How well the current system is working

■ Whether the current system has sufficient storage capacity

■ A requirement for new applications or the need to support new types of clients, such as Windows 98 and Windows NT

■ New management requirements, such as a need to centralize equipment or have control over that equipment

■ New user requirements, such as those of mobile users or users at remote offices

■ New equipment requirements, such as for printers, backup devices, or file servers

■ Whether the network is providing adequate communication services (such as electronic mail and Internet capabilities) for users

Part of the planner's job is to develop technical specifications for the network that include server and other hardware requirements as well as software requirements. The plan must also include methods for implementation and a description of new procedures. If a major update or set of changes is being incorporated, make sure a pilot system or an adequate test phase is part of the plan. In addition, network supervisors and network users will need training.

You should work up your plan in stages and then present a report for each stage, so that management can decide whether to go ahead with the next phase of the project or rework it based on benefits and budgets. Be sure to document the project every step of the way so that management can track its progress.

Eventually, you can develop a request for proposal (RFP) to send to vendors, who can then provide pricing and configuration information. You should end up with a complete blueprint of the proposed network or upgrade that identifies each component and its cost, along with a time schedule for development. From this, you can evaluate the cost and the benefits with management for approval.

Once the project is approved, you can acquire equipment and services and begin the installation and testing phase of the project. During testing, you create logs to track equipment problems, technical difficulties, and potential future problems. Finally, you install applications and implement system security, bring the system online, and begin training users.

Identifying Network Requirements

To identify network requirements, familiarize yourself with the current system and its limitations. Here are some tips for assessing the current system, identifying problems, and developing solutions.

IDENTIFYING EXISTING EQUIPMENT   You should document any information known about the current systems, such as the types of computers, storage devices, backup systems, printers and plotters, and communication equipment, as well as computers and communication equipment at remote sites.

MAPPING THE POTENTIAL NETWORK ENVIRONMENT   Create a map of the complete network and include the locations of the computers and peripheral devices you defined when you identified existing equipment. Locate existing wiring closets, cable runs, cable tracks, and wire outlets.

EVALUATING USAGE   Determine the number of users on the network and the server and disk requirements of those users. If a company has multiple departments, involve the department managers. Will each department have its own network segments? How much disk space will each department require on shared servers, or will each department have its own server? If each department has its own server, will the servers be managed by each department, or will all the department servers be managed at a central location by special network managers and technicians?

ESTABLISHING PROCEDURES   All businesses require procedures. Some are manual and some are automated. You must identify existing procedures and specify new procedures to implement for the network. Procedures have a cost and they require personnel to implement them, so they should be figured into any network plan. You should also identify the procedures that users must follow to access the network and use its resources.

NetWare Planning
and Installation

LOCATING INTERDEPENDENCIES Identify the interrelationship among users and departments in a company so that you can physically connect them over the LAN and give them access to information on other systems. For example, sales and accounts receivable are dependent on each other. Although this relationship is obvious, other relationships might not be. Query users and department managers to identify the type of information they need and its location.

DETERMINING COST RESPONSIBILITIES When departments or workgroups manage their own budgets, you need to determine how to allocate the cost of shared resources. The NetWare 5 accounting system provides tools for gathering information about resource usage. You can track how much time or how many resources users or departments access on a system, and charge the departments based on that usage. The difficult task is determining these charge values in the planning stages so that you can establish how much each department must allocate in its budget for the network system. Also note that these values may not be measured in dollars. They may be accounting or trade-out values only.

Evaluating Hardware and Performance Needs

Network performance is affected by the number of users on the system and the type of work they do. It helps to closely evaluate who will access the network. A typical server these days has 64MB to 512MB of memory and more than 3GB of disk storage. Prices have fallen so much that this type of system is typically found on desktops. It's not worth your time to evaluate whether you need 64MB or 128MB of memory, because the difference in cost is low. The same holds true for disk storage. The cost of an ultrafast 4GB disk drive recently fell under the $1,000 range. Only a few years ago, such drives were in the $3,000 to $4,000 range.

If your network has thousands of users who access the same data and you want to place the servers in the same physical location, consider using so-called "superserver" systems that implement multiple processors, massive and redundant storage devices, and high-speed data buses. These systems will adequately handle new network communication technologies such as Fast Ethernet or ATM and the high throughput they deliver.

Your goal in selecting any server is to reduce bottlenecks. A *bottleneck* is a location or condition in the network environment that reduces throughput and reduces the speed of data access for users. Throughput may be affected by inadequate network topology, server components such as disk drives, or the performance of individual workstations. Initially concentrate on finding bottlenecks at servers, because their performance affects users on the network.

If the cabling system, network interface cards, or server are inadequate, performance drops when many users simultaneously access the network. On the other hand, a drop in performance can occur when only one user accesses the network if that user overloads a server with intensive computing tasks or uses up the cable bandwidth by transferring large data files. Here are some methods for improving network performance:

- Allocate applications to specific servers. If an application performs intensive computing tasks that tie up its processor for periods of time, put that application on a server that is separate from the server that most users access on a regular basis.

- Put users who require high-performance servers or high-bandwidth network throughput on their own LAN segments and install special servers for their exclusive use.

- Keep Novell Directory Services (NDS) traffic to a minimum by configuring and using the management capabilities of the WAN Manager in NetWare 5. It is designed to optimize partition replication across the network and provide users with easy access to the resources they use.

- Use high-capacity, high-performance hard drives. That means you should consider only SCSI drives. In today's marketplace, there is no reason not to use them in your system, as they provide much better performance than even the new extended IDE (EIDE) adapters and drives.

- Install high-performance network interface cards in the servers. Install multiple cards and subdivide your network if necessary.

- Use new 100 Mbit/sec Ethernet technology, or consider high-speed FDDI or ATM technology between a server and a network switching device.

- Consider the types of applications versus the number of disk drives. In some cases a database application may tend to hog the disk. Everyone on that server will be affected with slow response times. A better choice may be to use two smaller drives, with the database application on one disk and everything else on the other disk. With this approach, you will have two sets of heads accessing the disks. This will tend to reduce "head thrashing."

The NetWare 5 operating system uses memory extensively to increase its operating speed. Memory is used for file cache buffers, communication buffers, directory caching, and various other tasks. With the virtual memory capability of NetWare 5, disk swapping between the disk and memory may become excessive. This swapping will reduce the performance of the server. For simplicity, Novell recommends starting with a minimum of 64MB of memory and expanding from there. If your network has a hundred users, you may need more than 64MB of RAM. Plan to add more in your budget.

It is almost impossible to evaluate network and server requirements until you actually have the system in place and users accessing it. Proper planning and evaluation of system requirements can help you locate potential bottlenecks in advance and reduce their impact. Some other considerations are described next.

NetWare Planning and Installation

DISK STORAGE   Hard disk capacity and performance have improved greatly over the last few years, while prices have steadily fallen. Make sure you read the drive specifications provided later in this chapter to get just the drive you need. Many older technology drives are on the market at discounted prices. These drives probably don't implement the latest technologies in disk drive design that optimize performance. Disk space is almost always underestimated. User disk requirements might skyrocket or an electronic mail system might overburden the drive with thousands of archived messages. Fortunately, NetWare 5 uses compression techniques that can reduce a text or graphics file's size by as much as 50 percent. NetWare 5 also supports data migration, which automatically moves unused files to a secondary storage device. Don't forget to figure in multiple disk requirements for mirroring disks.

BACKUP SYSTEMS   Backing up server data is essential. You can centralize server backup to ease the task and designate a manager to implement the same backup procedure for all the servers at a designated time, preferably during evening hours. However, if file servers are not centralized, it might be better to have subadministrators handle backup near the server's physical location to reduce network traffic. Special considerations must be given to backing up the Novell Directory Services (NDS) database. The backup application software must be NDS-aware and someone must be responsible for backing it up on a regular basis.

One backup method is to install a dedicated high-performance, high-capacity backup system that provides backup services for a multitude of servers. Alternatively, you could use tape backup systems, optical disk backup systems, or real-time systems such as NetWare StandbyServer (an optional product) or other systems that duplicate not only data but hardware as well. Keep in mind that backup software must be specifically designed to recognize the file system and NDS requirements of NetWare 5.

DISKLESS WORKSTATIONS   Diskless workstations are inexpensive computers without floppy disk drives or hard disk drives. They provide users with network access at a reasonable price and offer data security because users can't download data to floppy disks. They also provide virus protection to the network because they don't have the ability to read or execute a floppy-based program.

You might consider using diskless workstations if your data is sensitive and you hire temporary employees. Diskless workstations require a network interface card that has a slot for a *remote boot PROM*. The PROM allows the workstation to boot from a boot file located on the network server, which means that cards that use PROMs immediately connect with the network cable and server when you turn them on. Most interface cards have this option, but it's a good idea to make sure. Remote boot PROMs cost about $50 and are added to cards as an option.

CABLING   You need to fully understand the cable requirements of a network. Managers and installers should be familiar with the way the cable is assembled and connected to network components such as repeaters, hubs, bridges, and routers. Make a detailed map of the network topology, including the location of all accessories. Plan for growth and mark the location of future workstations and servers. Refer to outside cabling companies for estimates on your cabling cost and rely on them for your cable installation in most cases. They have the equipment and expertise to do the job right and guarantee it.

SYSTEM PROTECTION EQUIPMENT   You'll need system protection equipment, such as an uninterruptible power supply (UPS), surge suppressers, and line filters. A UPS protects the server from blackouts or other power problems. It also allows the server to shut itself down properly, saving cache buffers, closing open files, and completing transactions.

Server Requirements

The Intel microprocessor is the traditional Novell NetWare platform. This section outlines some of the considerations you need to make in choosing servers for your network. When the first edition of this book came out in 1993, a typical workgroup server based on the Intel 80486 microprocessor with a rating of 50 MIPS (million instructions per second) cost about $3,000. In mid-1998, you could buy a Gateway 300MHz Intel Pentium II processor system with a 6.4GB hard drive, a monitor, 64MB SDRAM performance-enhanced memory, and a 32x CD-ROM drive for $1,295. That's $705 cheaper and it runs at 300+ MIPS! This radical reduction in price and boost in performance makes any discussion of server selection almost moot, especially if you look at Table 13-1. There is not much reason to purchase anything less than the fastest Pentium III system unless you are looking for superservers or non-Intel platforms.

To support the new high-speed processors, the entire computer industry has made a sweeping change to the PCI (Peripheral Component Interconnect) data bus technology. PCI is a full 32-bit data bus that runs at 33MHz and can transfer data at speeds of up to 132 Mbits/sec. Compare that to the speeds of other bus architectures, as outlined in Table 13-2.

Note   *The dual-bus PCI design supports a separate bus for I/O from network interface cards and other devices. It also supports multiprocessing system design.*

PCI bus speeds are so far above ISA, EISA, and Microchannel speeds that they are not worth evaluating. In fact, PCI removes a major decision factor. Only a few years ago, you had to weigh your budget against the cost of systems based on the inexpensive ISA (Industry Standard Architecture) bus systems or more expensive systems that implemented faster EISA (Extended Industry Standard Architecture) or IBM's Microchannel bus design. Today, PCI bus systems provide excellent performance at comparable prices.

Processor	MIPS/SPECint95 Rating
IBM PC (1981)/Apple Macintosh (1984)	Less than 1 MIP
Intel 80286 (8 to 12MHz)	1.2 to 2.66 MIPS
Intel386 DX CPU (16 to 33MHz)	5 to 11.4 MIPS
Intel486 DX CPU (25 to 100MHz)	20 to 70.7 MIPS
Intel Pentium 100MHz	166.3 MIPS, 3.30 SPECint95
Intel Pentium II 333MHz	14.1 SPECint95
Sun UltraSPARC-IIi 360MHz	15.2 SPECint95
Intel Pentium II 450MHz	17.2 SPECint95
Motorola G4 (used in Apple Macintosh)	18 SPECint95
Sun US-3 (600 MHz)	35 SPECint95
Digital (Compaq) Alpha 21264	40+ SPECint95
Intel IA-64, code-named Merced (projected)	50+ SPECint95
Digital (Compaq) Alpha 21264 1 GHz (projected)	100 SPECint95

Table 13-1. *Processor Speeds*

Bus Type	Bus Size	Transfer Rate
ISA (Industry Standard Architecture)	16 bits	1.5 Mbits/sec
IBM Microchannel architecture	32 bits	20 Mbits/sec
EISA (Extended ISA)	32 bits	33 Mbits/sec
PCI	32 bits	132 Mbits/sec
Dual-bus PCI (for P6 systems)	32 bits	264 Mbits/sec

Table 13-2. *Bus Data Transfer Rates*

What's Left to Evaluate?

With a market full of inexpensive, high-performance systems, what do you need to evaluate when it comes to servers? Novell likes to point out that CPU performance isn't the only consideration. You must consider workloads in the computer that don't necessarily rely on the CPU. For example, bus mastering network interface cards can read and write directly to the server's disk system, bypassing the CPU. In many cases, disk activity is almost 90 percent of a server's total workload.

A typical *file server* will produce more activity on its I/O channels (network interface cards and disk adapters) than on the CPU. A file server "serves up" files for users, and there is not much processor activity involved in that. Most of the work is done by expansion cards that move data between devices and server memory. With this in mind, you can obtain dramatic performance improvements by increasing the memory cache and improving the disk channel or disk storage device. With the advent of the new I2O standard, the use of intelligent I/O cards has become a reality. These intelligent cards offload the I/O work from the main processor to another processor on the I/O card.

On the other hand, *client-server applications* that run on NetWare servers as Novell Loadable Modules (NLMs) use the CPU intensively. User requests come in over the I/O channel, and those requests initiate a process that "drives" the server's CPU for a period of time. A client-server database *engine* is a good example of a server application that requires a high-performance processor or a multiprocessing system.

Evaluate the system and components you need based on whether the server will produce more I/O activity or CPU activity. For servers that use the CPU intensively, upgrade to the fastest processor system that fits into your budget and consider using "bus mastering" network adapters that handle their own workload, rather than relying on the CPU. For servers that are I/O-intensive, upgrade to PCI bus systems, use SCSI disk adapters (rather than IDE or EIDE), and implement I/O cards based on the I2O specifications. Also increase the memory in the server and consider using RAID disk storage systems. Some of these topics are covered in the next few sections.

Throughput and Bottlenecks

Throughput and bottlenecks refer to server performance and the degradation of performance caused by inefficient peripherals, software, or other factors. Picture the server as a sort of Grand Central Station. Data moves in and out of the server on network interface cards, and that data moves to and from system memory. Data also moves between memory, disk adapters, and disk drives. Throughput measures the combined performance of all components involved with data transfer. Bottlenecks, as pictured in Figure 13-1, are locations or conditions in the network environment that throttle back the throughput. Performance problems can occur outside the server. A fast server won't help users if the network is overloaded with traffic. Weak links that can affect overall performance are described next.

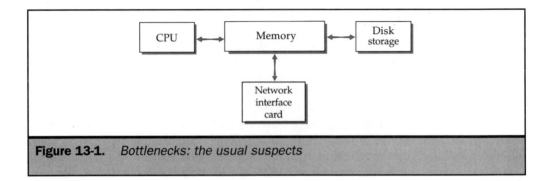

Figure 13-1. *Bottlenecks: the usual suspects*

SERVER As already mentioned, replace older technology servers with new systems that implement the Pentium II processors (or fast non-Intel processors) and the PCI bus.

 You need a special version of NetWare to run on a non-Intel processor.

BUS MASTERING USING I2O In a bus mastering scheme, the CPU is relieved of some processing tasks by shifting the execution of those tasks to a coprocessor on another board. A network interface card with an I2O design writes data directly to memory, which leaves the CPU free to handle operating system tasks.

CACHING Bottlenecks occur when data is not shuffled in and out of memory quickly enough. Caches can reduce bottlenecks caused by exchanges between the CPU and memory and between disk storage and memory.

DISK INPUT/OUTPUT One of the most important considerations when evaluating performance is the speed of disk input/output (I/O). You can reduce bottlenecks by upgrading disk adapters and drives.

NETWORK INTERFACE CARDS Use network interface cards with improved buffering techniques and bus mastering. For the server, use PCI-based 32-bit cards. For workstations, use the fastest cards you can afford.

WORKSTATIONS Workstations that demand too much server time or that produce too much network traffic produce bottlenecks for other users. One solution is to place these users on separate network segments or install special servers for their use.

NETWORK CABLING SYSTEM As more and more users access the network, performance drops. Consider upgrading your network topology to new (and now inexpensive) 100 Mbit/sec networks or switching technologies that reduce the number of users on a network segment.

Special Servers

Intel is prepackaging its Pentium II server processor with a motherboard design that includes up to a 450MHz version of the chip that is tightly coupled to 256K or 512K bytes of internal Level 2 cache. This will handle the majority of processing without involving the system bus. Low-end servers that implement this design can be purchases below $5,000. Vendors have also designed high-end multiprocessing systems that include two or more Intel Pentium II server processors.

An enhanced design includes a RISC i960 RP processor-based subsystem that handles I/O tasks using the I2O specifications. This frees up the main processor to handle application tasks while the i960 handles input and output functions. These systems provide benefits for high-throughput technologies and applications such as the following:

- RAID (redundant array of independent disks)
- 100 Mbit/sec Ethernet, FDDI, and ATM networks
- Multiprocessing systems in which the bus is capable of delivering anything the processors can handle, and vice versa.
- Server-based, mission-critical applications in client-server environments

Companies that are downsizing from mainframes and minicomputers will find such systems attractive. They provide high performance when many users need to access centralized applications and data. However, some organizations may benefit by building a server environment that consists of numerous low-cost servers. In this environment, applications and data are spread out among many servers, which reduces the number of users who access a server at any one time. For example, you might purchase servers specifically to store electronic mail, users' home directories, Web documents and applications, or word processing. Each workgroup might get its own server as well.

Many organizations are designing networks in which all data is stored at a central location but is also moved to servers at local sites where it is close to users who need it. This strategy may implement distributed databases that require partitioning and replication or that simply require frequent updates. This is easily achieved using Novell's Replication Services product.

Multiprocessing Systems

PC servers now commonly implement multiprocessing architectures, with two or more Intel Pentium II CPUs. There are two types of multiprocessing systems:

- **Symmetrical multiprocessing (SMP) systems**   In an SMP system, resources such as memory and disk I/O are shared by all the microprocessors in the system. The workload is distributed evenly to available microprocessors so that one isn't sitting idle while another is overworked with a specific task. The performance of

NetWare Planning
and Installation

symmetrical multiprocessing systems increases for all tasks as microprocessors are added. Because SMP systems share the same memory, their scalability is limited to the same system and they typically implement from four to eight processors.

■ **Asymmetrical multiprocessing (ASMP) systems**   In ASMP systems, tasks and system resources are managed by different microprocessors. For example, one microprocessor handles I/O, and another handles network operating system tasks. Asymmetrical multiprocessing systems do not balance workloads. A microprocessor handling one task can be overworked, at the same time that another microprocessor sits idle.

Of the two approaches, SMP has won out as an industry standard. Intel basically added its stamp of approval by implementing its Multiprocessing Specification (MPS) into the design of its chip sets. Both Novell and Microsoft support SMP in their network operating systems. NetWare 5 supports the newer ASMP specifications, which allow the administrator to assign the affinity of an application to a specific processor. In addition, NetWare 5 supports up to 32 processors. The upcoming Novell Distributed Parallel Processing (DPP) will provide *clustered* SMP systems, in which multiple servers can be connected and perform as a single logical server.

Superservers

Superservers provide speed, fault tolerance, scalability, and security for large networks. They are typically classified as systems that provide the following:

■ Multiple CPUs

■ A high-performance bus or multiple buses

■ One gigabyte of error-correcting memory or more

■ RAID disk arrays

■ Advanced system architectures that reduce system bottlenecks

■ Redundant features such as two power supplies

A superserver's multiple-processor architecture lets you add microprocessors within a single chassis, rather than buy additional servers. There are two situations in which you should consider a superserver system:

■ The server runs computing-intensive applications such as a client-server database that hundreds or thousands of users access.

■ There is a large traffic load on the network, and the current server is incapable of handling it.

The high-performance bus in a superserver can quickly move data among multiple network cards, disk controllers, and CPUs, as shown in Figure 13-2. Superservers typically use a proprietary high-speed bus or the PCI bus.

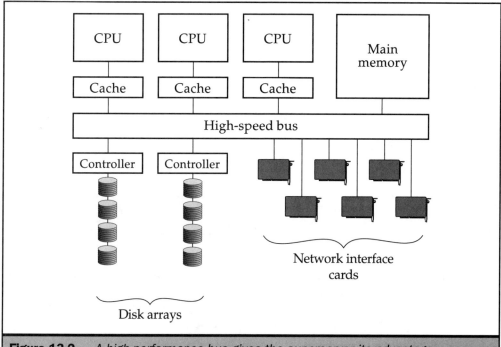

Figure 13-2. *A high-performance bus gives the superserver its advantage*

NetWare Planning and Installation

Server Disk Systems

You should carefully study disk system technology to get the best performance from your servers. Even if you decide to use the fastest SCSI disk system, you still need to evaluate the version of SCSI you are getting and the features of the drives such as spin rate and other factors that will affect performance. SCSI disks that spin at 7,200 rpm, as opposed to older drives that spin at 5,400, are now common. As prices fall, you should consider only 7,200-rpm drives for server use, which makes it much easier to compare and purchase drives.

The two primary types of disk interfaces for the server environment are IDE and SCSI, as described in the following sections. Also refer to Table 13-3 for performance features.

SCSI INTERFACE   The Small Computer System Interface (SCSI) is a system that consists of a host adapter and devices that you attach to the adapter, such as disk drives, CD-ROMs, optical disks, and tape drives. Primary SCSI features include the following:

- You can attach up to seven devices to a single adapter, which provides a shared data transfer bus between any attached device and system memory. Some of the newer adapters will support up to 16 devices.

Disk Interface	Maximum Throughput
IDE	4 Mbits/sec
Enhanced IDE (mode 3)	11 Mbits/sec
Enhanced IDE (mode 4)	16 Mbits/sec
SCSI-1	5 Mbits/sec
Fast SCSI-2 (16-bit)	10 to 40 Mbits/sec
SCSI-3 (Ultra SCSI)	40 to 100 Mbits/sec

Table 13-3. *Disk Interface Throughput*

- The SCSI host adapter provides bus services (a connection point) for intelligent devices. These devices have their own control circuitry, which allows the device to "disconnect" itself from the host adapter to perform some task, freeing the host adapter to communicate with other devices.
- SCSI devices are "intelligent," meaning that they can initiate commands on their own when necessary, rather than rely on CPU instructions.
- The bus can handle simultaneous reads and writes.
- Because the control circuitry is built into each SCSI device, configuration and compatibility issues are minimized. Theoretically, you can plug any SCSI device into any SCSI controller, but it's best to check compatibility and software drive requirements before doing so.

SCSI-2 is a refinement of the original SCSI interface and is backward compatible with SCSI-1. It specifies additional standards for implementing synchronous transmissions to boost the bus speed and wider data paths (16- and 32-bit) to improve data transfer rates.

- SCSI-1 is asynchronous, and handshaking takes place with every data transfer.
- Fast SCSI-2 is synchronous and removes some handshaking to boost data transfer rates.
- Wide SCSI-2 provides 16-bit and 32-bit data paths.

Table 13-4 outlines the different implementations of SCSI-2. The nomenclature can get confusing. Note that the synchronous 8-bit implementation is called Fast SCSI-2, while the 16-bit and 32-bit synchronous implementations are called Fast/Wide SCSI-2.

SCSI-2 Type	8-Bit	16-Bit (Wide)	32-Bit (Wide)
Asynchronous SCSI	5 Mbits/sec	10 Mbits/sec	20 Mbits/sec
Synchronous (Fast SCSI-2)	10 Mbits/sec	20 Mbits/sec	40 Mbits/sec

Table 13-4. *SCSI-2 Implementations*

Note *Wide SCSI-2 devices use 68-pin connectors.*

The SCSI-3 specification (also called Ultra SCSI) includes some improvements to the SCSI-2 standard and provides for the use of serial interface methods. There are basically three major SCSI-3 implementations:

- *Ultra SCSI* uses the parallel interface but provides some protocol extensions and improvements that offer some performance enhancements over traditional SCSI. It provides 40 Mbit/sec data transfer rates.

- *Fibre Channel Arbitrated Loop (FC-AL)* is a subset of the ANSI Fibre Channel standard and provides data transfer rates of up to 100 Mbits/sec. It also supports up to 126 disk drives on a single connection.

- *Serial Storage Architecture (SSA)* is an IBM serial interface technology that can provide SCSI-3 speeds of up to 80 Mbits/sec and is less expensive than FC-AL. IBM uses the interface for its highly acclaimed Ultrastar2 XP 8.7GB disk drives.

While the data transfer rates of SCSI-3 may seem excessive, they may be essential if you plan to implement multimedia and video on your network or if you plan to interconnect server, supercomputers, and high-performance peripherals. Also remember that the media is shared, so in the case of Fibre Channel, the connections are more like shared network topologies than simple peripheral connections.

IDE INTERFACE The Intelligent Drive Electronics (IDE) interface is a hybrid that combines features of the other interfaces and offers new features of its own. Like SCSI, IDE devices have their own control circuitry and attach to an IDE host adapter. The host adapter is inexpensive and is often built right onto the motherboard. Note the following:

- An IDE adapter supports only two devices, and disk capacity cannot exceed 528MB.

NetWare Planning and Installation

■ EIDE (Enhanced IDE), and its equivalent Fast ATA-2, are enhancements to the IDE interface. EIDE supports up to four disk devices (two each per dual channels), and those drives can be larger than 528MB in size.

The IDE and EIDE standards are primarily implemented on desktop systems to save costs. SCSI is recommended for server storage devices.

Disk Considerations

Besides the disk adapters, you must also consider the features of the disks you attach to them. Primary disk considerations include the following:

■ **Rotation speed** The speed at which the disk platters spin. Spin rates are typically 5,400 rpm and 7,200 rpm. As mentioned, accept only 7,200 rpm drives as prices continue to fall.

■ **Seek time** The amount of time it takes for the read/write head to move one-third of the way across the disk. Seek times for server drives should be in the 8-millisecond to 12-millisecond range.

■ **Data transfer rate** The amount of data transfer as divided by the access time. For comparison, a fast SCSI drive has a transfer rate of 5 Mbits/sec.

■ **Access time** The product of the rotation speed, seek time, and overhead of the drive system.

Note that actual data transfer rates are considerably less than the throughput ratings for disk adapters listed in Table 13-3. However, consider that adapters can cache incoming or outgoing data and can handle multiple drives.

Mirrored and Duplexed Drives

Disk mirroring and disk duplexing provide protection against disk failures. Mirroring continuously duplicates data on a primary drive to a secondary drive, as shown in Figure 13-3. If the primary drive fails, the secondary drive can be put into service until the primary drive is replaced. Disk duplexing implements a disk controller for each drive to protect against failure of a controller, as shown in Figure 13-4.

SCSI controllers provide attachments for up to seven drives. This means that you could add three primary drives and three mirroring drives to one controller. But this arrangement does not provide protection if the controller should fail, so it's recommended that you use two SCSI controllers: one to handle the primary drives and one to handle the mirroring drives. In Figure 13-5, Board 0 and Board 1 are identical duplexed disk

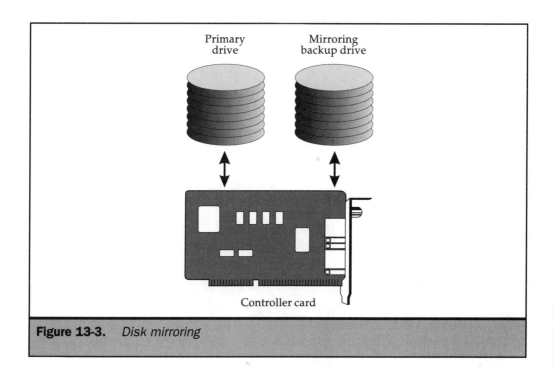

Figure 13-3.   *Disk mirroring*

controllers that support two drives each. The drives attached to each controller are
numbered Disk 0 and Disk 1.

    *Spanning a volume over several disks improves performance, but you must duplex
spanned volumes. If one drive in a spanned volume should fail, the entire volume
becomes inaccessible.*

Partitions on Duplexed Systems

You should be aware of the way partitions are established on a duplexed system.
Figure 13-6 shows a system that has two controllers and two drives attached to each
controller. The first controller and its two drives form the primary data storage area.
Note that a small DOS partition exists on the first drive. The second controller and its
drives form the duplexing system. Each drive has its own partition numbers. The DOS
partition is physical partition 0, and the remaining partitions are numbered from 1 to 5.
However, NetWare assigns logical partition numbers to mirrored drives, so partitions 1

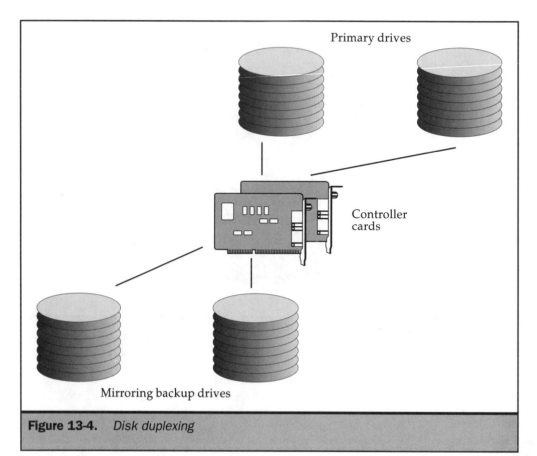

Figure 13-4. *Disk duplexing*

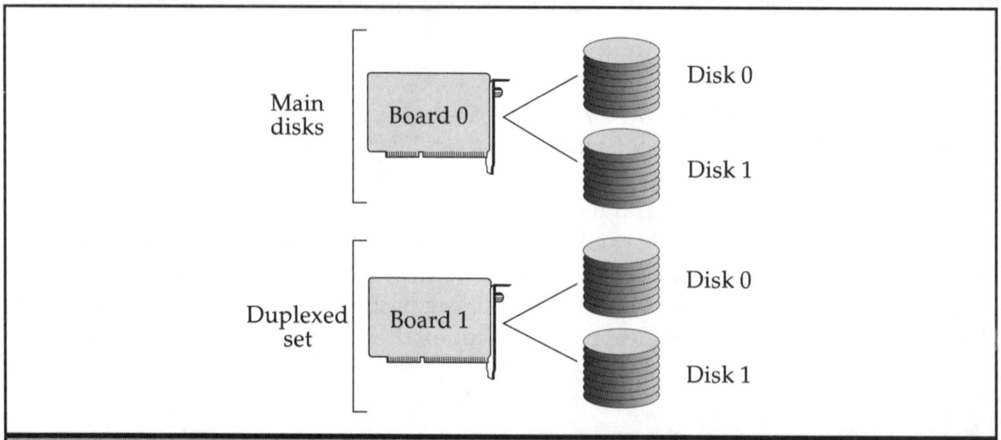

Figure 13-5. *Controller, adapter, and disk numbering schemes*

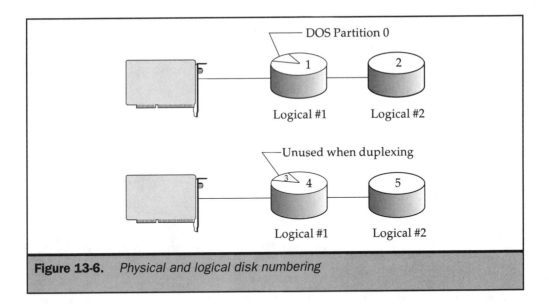

Figure 13-6.   *Physical and logical disk numbering*

and 4 are viewed as logical partition 1, and physical partitions 2 and 5 are viewed as logical partition 2.

These logical partition numbers are important when you are viewing information about mirrored disks. Logical mirrored partitions are listed in the NWCONFIG and MONITOR server utilities as follows:

Mirrored: Logical Partition #1
Mirrored: Logical Partition #2

However, the physical partitions that make up a mirrored set are listed as follows. Note the device number at the end of each line that identifies the driver, controller, and disk attached to the controller.

In Sync—NetWare partition 1 on Device #0 (20000000)
In Sync—NetWare partition 3 on Device #1 (20000100)

RAID (Redundant Array of Independent Disks)

A RAID (redundant array of independent disks) is a set of drives that appears as a single drive. Data is written evenly across the drives by using a technique called *striping*. Striping divides data over two or more drives, as shown by the crude example in Figure 13-7.

Data striping can occur at the bit level or on a sector level. A sector is a block of disk data. Striping improves throughput and provides a form of redundancy that protects

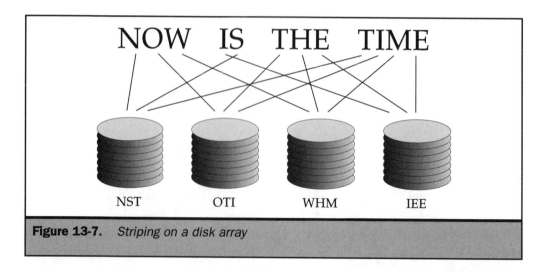

Figure 13-7.   *Striping on a disk array*

against the failure of one disk in the array by encoding the scattered data to a backup drive known as the *parity drive*.

RAID systems use SCSI adapters because of their performance. After issuing a read or write command to one drive, a SCSI controller can disconnect from it and turn its attention to another drive. The first drive then continues the operation on its own.

RAID provides redundancy (that is, mirroring and duplexing). The level of redundancy depends on the RAID level you chose, as described in a moment. In a normal mirroring configuration like that used by the standard NetWare mirroring method, one backup drive is matched to one primary drive. In RAID level 3, one parity drive provides mirroring for two or more primary drives. A coding scheme is used to write information to the parity drive that represents the data written to the other drives. If one drive should fail, the parity code and the data on the remaining drives are used to come up with the missing portion of the data.

Buying a single parity drive is much cheaper than buying a backup mirroring drive for each primary drive. However, a single parity drive provides adequate protection only if one drive fails at a time. If two or more primary drives fail, the parity code drive won't contain enough information to rebuild the data. RAID levels are available that provide disk mirroring as well as striping.

Many RAID systems allow hot replacement of disks, which means that disks can be replaced while the system is running. When a disk is replaced, the parity information is used to rebuild the data on the disk. Rebuilding occurs while the operating system continues handling other operations, so there is some loss of performance during the rebuilding operation.

There are several levels of RAID, as described next. When buying systems that use RAID, you need to check their levels against your system needs.

- **RAID level 0**   Data is striped over several drives, but there is no redundant drive. Level 0 provides RAID performance without data protection.

- **RAID level 1**   Data is striped to an array of drives, and each drive is mirrored to a backup drive. In a four-drive array, two are used as primary drives and two are used as mirroring drives. This level provides the performance benefits of striping and the highest level of protection by mirroring all primary drives.

- **RAID level 2**   This level is not normally implemented. It provides data striping at the bit level over all drives in the array. RAID level 3 is similar, but it is implemented more widely.

- **RAID level 3**   Data is striped at the bit or byte level (your choice) to all drives in the array except one, which becomes the parity drive. In a four-drive array, data is striped to three drives and parity information is written to the fourth. This level provides good read performance but relatively slow write performance, because the parity drive is written to with every write operation.

- **RAID level 4**   This level is similar to RAID level 3, except that data is striped in disk sector units rather than as bits or bytes. Read times are improved because each drive can retrieve an entire disk sector.

- **RAID level 5**   Data is written in disk sector units to all drives in the drive array. Error-correction codes are also written to all drives. This level provides quicker writes because the parity information is spread over all the drives, rather than being written to a single parity drive as is the case in RAID level 3. Disk reads are improved because each drive can retrieve an entire disk block.

Most RAID systems designed for server use on the market today use RAID level 5. You also need to weigh the price and performance of a RAID system against the standard disk mirroring and disk duplexing techniques that NetWare supports (or server duplexing provided by StandbyServer software). An additional consideration is that RAID systems are often proprietary, which ties you to the manufacturer for future support and service.

SCSI Controller Installation

The SCSI interface consists of a host bus adapter (HBA) to which you attach SCSI devices. Each device usually has an embedded controller mounted directly to it. However, some external subsystems have multiple devices attached to multiple controllers, which in turn attach to multiple host bus adapters. One HBA forms a channel, and NetWare can handle up to five host bus adapter channels. Up to four controllers can attach to each channel, and up to eight drives can attach to each controller, for a total of 32 drives. If you have large disk requirements, it's possible to run out of slots. If this is the case, consider a RAID system, which typically attaches to the server by using one controller.

Figure 13-8 illustrates the device numbering for embedded SCSI drives. Board 0 is the disk controller normally built-in to most off-the-shelf servers. Disks attached to this

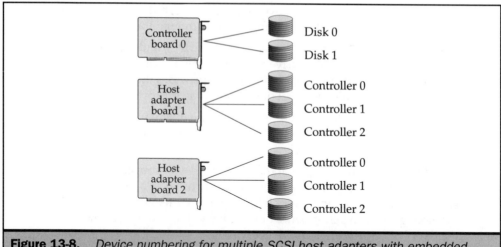

Figure 13-8. *Device numbering for multiple SCSI host adapters with embedded controller drives attached*

board are numbered 0 and 1. Host adapter boards 1 and 2 are add-in SCSI adapters. SCSI disks normally have built-in controllers, so the drives are numbered according to their controller number.

Figure 13-9 illustrates the device numbering for SCSI systems that use nonembedded controllers. In this case, each controller supports multiple drives, all of which are attached to a single host adapter.

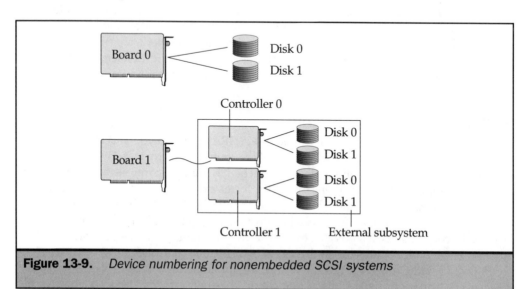

Figure 13-9. *Device numbering for nonembedded SCSI systems*

Protecting the Network and Its Data

The most important part of your network is the data in its storage devices. Everything else is replaceable at a cost. Most organizations accept the reality of backups. However, many are unprepared for the downtime that can occur if a critical system fails. Thousands or millions of dollars of revenue may be lost while network administrators bring the system back up. One solution is to completely duplicate the server in real time by using NetWare StandbyServer software. The following practices will help you guard against equipment and data loss.

PROTECTING AGAINST THEFT   You can use these methods to protect your server from theft:

- Bolt the server chassis to a table and lock the case to the chassis. This prevents removal of the hard drive, which could easily be carried out of the building.

- Lock the server in a protective case that contains an adequate cooling system to prevent the server from overheating.

- Lock the server and associated equipment in the wiring closet. Make sure the closet is adequately cooled.

- Create a data center that requires a keycard or fingerprint verification for access.

- Place the server in a central management facility that is staffed 24 hours a day.

- Ensure that your personnel are trustworthy, competent, and know the security procedures.

PROTECTING AGAINST FIRE AND NATURAL DISASTERS   Protecting valuable equipment and data against fire is a prime concern. Consider placing equipment in a vault or room that has internal or external fire protection. Many organizations already have filing cabinets in rooms with fire protection systems.

Protect equipment from natural disasters such as earthquakes and floods. You might need to reinforce or elevate the server area and develop plans so that users can access server data in case there is a disaster. For example, gas-powered generators can supply power to servers and workstations that must be accessed after a disaster that cuts off electricity.

CENTRALIZING MANAGEMENT   Move network resources such as servers, wiring centers, concentrators, routers, and even printers to central management areas.

PROTECTING AGAINST POWER LOSS AND POWER PROBLEMS   Don't consider the power supplied to servers and other equipment dependable. Refer to the "Power Problems and Solutions" section, later in this chapter, for more details.

USING FAULT TOLERANCE TECHNIQUES   Implement NetWare's disk mirroring and disk duplexing support or NetWare StandbyServer, which mirrors an entire server.

KEEPING ADEQUATE BACKUPS   Ensure that data is properly backed up. Implement a backup plan that rotates backup to off-site storage. Refer to Chapter 26 for additional information about backing up.

USING DISKLESS WORKSTATIONS   Use diskless workstations to prevent users from uploading or downloading data.

PROTECTING AGAINST VIRUSES   Computer viruses are everywhere and have the potential to infiltrate your network whenever a user logs in. This is especially true for users who work on a LAN remotely from their home systems or take laptop computers on the road. Bulletin boards, public domain utility disks, the Internet, and demonstration disks can carry viruses. It is essential that you have and use virus detection software. Viruses are sometimes even found in software that comes in shrink-wrapped packages. You should install all new software and updates on a test system and check for viruses before installing the software for use on the network server. You should also use appropriate file and directory rights to ensure that users can't alter executable files in program directories.

PROTECTING AGAINST INTRUDERS   Intruders can use various methods to gain access to a network. You can prevent intruders from accessing a local LAN by ensuring that your users log off. You can force users to log in at only specific stations and at only one station at a time. You can also add time restrictions to prevent access before or after normal working hours.

ADMINISTERING ACCESS RIGHTS   Directory and file access rights are one of the most important tools NetWare administrators and supervisors have to protect data against malicious or accidental loss or corruption by users. Users should never be given more rights than they need in program and data directories. Read and File Scan rights are usually adequate in program directories. Some applications create temporary files when invoked and erase them when finished. In this case, users will need Create and Erase rights, and possibly the Write right in addition to the Read and File Scan rights. One other precaution is to use the Execute Only attribute on the main application executable. This is a good hedge against viruses attaching to executable files.

Anything more opens program files to corruption and virus attack. Administering access to data directories is a little more complicated. Some users only need to look at files, such as databases; they only need Read rights in the directory or perhaps Read rights to only the database file within the directory. Users who need to update database files or other files need Read, Write, and File Scan rights. Use caution when granting other rights, such as Erase, Create, Modify, and in particular, Supervisor and Access Control rights.

TRAINING USERS   Train users to properly log in and log out of the network and to protect their passwords. If they need to leave their computers unattended, make sure they log out or know how to activate a password-protected screen saver that locks the computer (but maintains login) while they are gone. Screen savers also provide a way to run unattended tasks without possibility of disturbance. You can set options in user accounts that force users to change their passwords at a predetermined interval, prevent them from reusing recent passwords, or require passwords that haven't been used before.

TRACKING USERS   Keep track of users. Have department administrators inform you of users who have left the company or changed roles so that you can remove or alter their user accounts appropriately. Audit trails created by the NetWare auditing system can help you track users who disrupt the network either accidentally or on purpose.

Power Problems and Solutions

Electrical power is rarely supplied as a smooth wave of steady energy, as is evident when lights flicker or the TV goes haywire. Electrical connections are polluted with surges and spikes (collectively called *noise*). You can think of these surges and spikes as shotgun blasts of energy. The way electronic equipment handles this transient energy is unpredictable. There are four likely scenarios:

- **Data corruption**   Electrical disturbances can cause memory to change states or can disrupt the information in data packets traversing a wire. These glitches can alter a program in memory and cause it to fail. You might see general protection interrupt (GPI) errors and nonmaskable interrupt (NMI) errors. These errors, which are frequently mistaken for program bugs, are often caused by electrical noise.

- **Equipment failure**   If transient energy is high, it will cause permanent damage to equipment. Small microprocessor circuitry is especially susceptible to this energy. Surge suppressers should be used to protect equipment, but if the energy is high enough, the surge suppresser can burn out. As discussed later, however, some surge suppressers do not provide the right kind of protection against surges.

- **Slow death**   Equipment that is repeatedly subjected to low-energy surges will fail over time. The delicate circuits in a chip break down, and the equipment eventually fails for no apparent reason. Transients that cause this type of problem "sneak" through surge suppressers that are not designed to protect against them. After a period of abuse, the chips weaken and release the energy in unknown patterns throughout the chip, and the chip ultimately fails.

- **ESD**   Electrostatic discharge (ESD) is the silent killer for semiconductor devices. These discharges are the old familiar shocks you get when walking across some types of carpeting and touching another object. Repeated ESD hits will weaken semiconductor devices, cause excessive intermittent operation, and then finally destroy the devices. To control ESD, you can use wire in carpeted floors, install grounding wrist straps at workstations, or apply sprays that are designed to minimize the buildup of static electricity. The best deterrent to ESD is controlling the humidity where the computers are operated.

To clean up power problems, you need filtering and conditioning equipment. Improper grounding is another source of problems. In fact, surge suppressers are often the cause of grounding problems because it is in their design to route surges to ground. The surges then find their way back into the electrical system, where they can cause problems.

The electrical environment is noisy. Equipment such as air conditioners, elevators, refrigerators, and even laser printers cause transients when they are switched on and off. The electric company also causes transients when it switches grids to balance the system. In fact, any device that uses electricity in a nonlinear way can cause transients that affect other devices. Common electrical line problems include the following:

■ **Noise** Often referred to as surges, spikes, or transients. Noise problems, which are illustrated in Figure 13-10, cause slow or immediate damage to sensitive electronic equipment. Additional problems are caused by air conditioners, elevators, and other devices with electric motors. Most computer power supplies include built-in protection against low-level noise, but surge suppressers can protect against transients that are stronger than normal, such as those caused by lightning. In fact, cheap devices often block such surges by simply burning out and preventing any further flow of electricity.

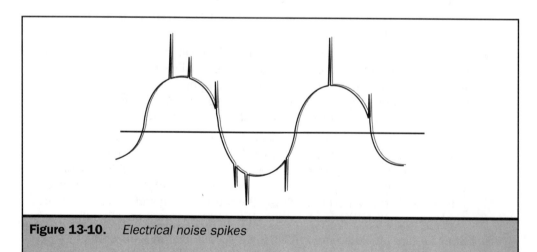

Figure 13-10. *Electrical noise spikes*

- **Sag**   When the power drops below the required level, a sag or dropout occurs, usually because the circuit is overloaded. A sag might continue for a period of time if the building is incorrectly wired or the utility company is having a problem. A long sag can cause damage to power supplies.

- **Swell**   A swell is the opposite of a sag and can also cause damage to power supplies.

- **Hum**   Hum is high-order harmonics caused by neutral-to-ground connection problems. Such problems indicate a defect in one of the electrical wires to ground. Hum can cause transmission errors in data communication lines. As errors occur, the communication software must check and resend incorrect packets, which causes a decrease in throughput.

Grounding Problems

In 1991, Novell Research published a report called "Power and Grounding for Distributed Computing," by David Fencl and Larry Fish of ONEAC Corporation. In this report, Fencl and Fish pointed out many problems and misconceptions about established power grounding methods.

Buildings contain a low-resistance ground connection to the earth to protect people from electric shock. A good ground basically drains electrical charges into the earth. If equipment is not properly grounded and a person touches the equipment, a charge will pass through the person to the earth. Fencl and Fish point out that current grounding practices are incompatible with the requirements of digital electronics. Connecting electronic equipment to earth grounds can subject the equipment to noise that seeks the shortest path to ground. In modern buildings, the shortest path to the ground is often through electronic equipment such as computers. Put simply, noise on the AC circuit can infiltrate sensitive electronics through the grounding circuit, not just through the hot lead.

Grounding problems are especially prevalent in a network environment, because the cabling system can provide a path for ground loops. Consider that devices on networks are usually connected to different sources of power, which are grounded. When these networks are interconnected, the cable bridges the two grounded systems together, which causes the potential for energy on the circuit to seek equilibrium by flowing from ground to ground. In doing so, it flows through the computer systems attached to the cable and causes noise problems. To solve ground-loop problems, according to Fencl and Fish, equipment on one power source must be isolated from equipment on other power sources.

On a large network, the creation of a single-point ground is usually impossible to achieve. Interconnected networks form links between close or distant points, any one of which can produce electrical problems due to poor wiring. These separate power sources might be in separate buildings or in a multistory office building that has separate power transformers on every floor or every other floor. Each transformer

NetWare Planning
and Installation

has its own electrical characteristics and should not be connected to equipment connected to other transformers.

Solutions

One solution to the problems of ground loops, line noise, and surges is to connect the entire network to one central power source and ground. However, this is usually impractical and defeats the purpose of a network, which is to spread computing resources to users at outlying locations. The only practical solution is to provide power conditioning and a proper ground point at the location of each network component.

Figure 13-11 illustrates the Fencl and Fish method for connecting network equipment within a single building or power source area. Note that a power conditioner and an uninterruptible power supply are used at the server. The power conditioner provides dedicated transformer isolation, a clean source of power, and a solid reference ground. Similar devices should be attached to workstations if your budget allows. Note that surge suppression equipment is placed at the feed to the electrical panel. If the surge suppressers are placed on the branch circuits, they will divert surges to ground and back into the circuits of other systems through the ground connection.

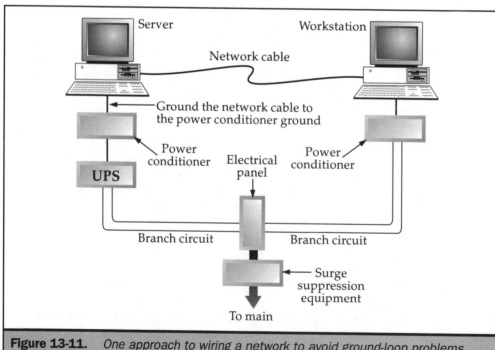

Figure 13-11.   *One approach to wiring a network to avoid ground-loop problems*

There are a few things to watch out for in this installation. You should not run electrical cables in parallel with power circuits or other sources of interference such as light fixtures and motors. If you do, electrical transients can enter the network through the cable systems. Some circuits improperly divert neutral to ground intentionally to solve noise problems.

They produce a repeating, low-frequency waveform on the network cable that can corrupt data. If you have this problem, have an electrical contractor check the line.

Caution *Ensure that a single LAN segment is connected to circuits that branch from a single power source and that no point in the segment shares a ground with other power sources. An electrical contractor can perform this service.*

Figure 13-12 illustrates the Fencl and Fish method for connecting an internetwork. Nonconductive fiber-optic cable is used to eliminate ground loops between the networks, which are on different power supplies. The primary reason for ensuring the separation of the power sources is that they will most likely have different ground potentials, which can cause problems in sensitive electrical equipment if they are linked together. In Figure 13-12,

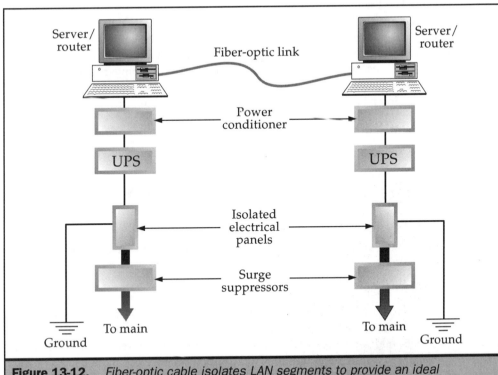

Figure 13-12.   *Fiber-optic cable isolates LAN segments to provide an ideal grounding solution*

each LAN segment is a self-contained environment in which you can more easily control grounding and noise problems. Note that internetwork devices are connected to power conditioning equipment. If fiber-optic interconnections are not possible, supplemental transient protection should be installed with the cable.

Uninterruptible Power Supplies

Your basic power and grounding system can be augmented by an uninterruptible power supply (UPS). A UPS provides electrical power to computers or other devices during a power outage. A UPS can be one of the following:

- A battery system
- A rotary UPS that uses the inertia of a large flywheel to carry the computer system through brief outages
- Internal combustion motors that run AC generators

UPS devices come in two forms: online and standby. A standby device kicks in only when the power goes down. It must therefore contain special circuitry that can switch to backup power in less than 5 milliseconds. An online device constantly provides the source of power to the computer. Because of this, it doesn't need to kick in. If the outside source of power dies, the batteries within the unit continue to supply the computer with power. Although online units are the best choice, they are more expensive than standby units. But because online units supply all the power to a computer, that power is always clean and smooth.

When purchasing a battery backup system, be aware of the following:

- The amount of time the UPS battery supplies power
- Whether the UPS provides a warning system to the server when the UPS is operating on standby power
- Whether the UPS includes power conditioning features that can clip incoming transient noise
- The life span of the battery and how it degrades over time
- Whether the device warns you when the batteries can no longer provide backup power
- Whether the batteries are replaceable

You also need to know the power requirements of the devices you'll hook to the UPS. For a server installation, this might include the CPU, the monitor, external routers, concentrator units, and wiring centers. You can find out the power requirements of these devices by looking at the backs of the equipment. Labels on the equipment list the power drawn by the unit in watts. Simply add the values of all the devices to come up with the requirements you'll need from the UPS.

Attaching a UPS to the File Server

A UPS attached to a file server requires an additional cable that alerts the file server when the UPS is running on standby power. The server will then proceed with shutdown procedures. One end of the monitor cable should have either a stereo phone plug (for plugging into the stand-alone UPS monitor board or the SS keycard in a non-PS/2 file server) or a 4-pin mouse plug (for plugging into the mouse port of an IBM PS/2 file server). The other end of the monitor cable should have the type of connector required by your particular UPS.

Some vendors have developed special power protection equipment. American Power Conversion's Smart-UPS series provides network managers with diagnostics information via a software control program called PowerChute. The software is installed on the server and communicates with the UPS over a cable. Managers can then track power quality, UPS operating temperature, line frequency, UPS output voltage, maximum and minimum line power, battery strength, line voltage, and UPS load. American Power Conversion can be reached in West Kingston, Rhode Island, at 401-789-5735.

Preparing the Site

Your first step when installing a network is to set up the environment. For this step, it's helpful to know where your servers will be located and who will supervise and maintain them. Typically, existing networks consist of LAN cable segments within departments. Under NetWare 5, these departmental LANs are brought under the global management of Novell Directory Services (NDS). However, those departmental LANs are still physically located in their respective departments, so you might want to retain the existing supervisors. The NDS system lets you grant Supervisor trustee rights for a departmental branch of the directory tree.

On large LANs or WANs, delegate the responsibilities of supervising users and maintaining equipment to other users, such as department managers. Define who will manage and monitor the following:

- Servers and workstations within a department
- Servers managed for departments by network specialists
- The cabling system
- Internetwork equipment, such as routers and switchboxes, and their associated cabling
- Wide area networking equipment, such as routers that handle connections to public and private data networks
- Remote services at outlying locations to which a support person might need to travel

After the network is installed and operating, hardware must be monitored for potential points of failure, overuse (such as a nearly full storage system), throughput, and general loss of performance.

Installing or upgrading a network can easily disrupt the normal activities of people at the sites. Make sure these people know who you and your staff are and what you are doing, especially if you need to crawl over and under desks to install cable or set up systems. It's best to develop a schedule of installation activities that you can present to department managers and employees. In addition, be sure to consider the department's needs. You won't win points if your installation takes place when employees need to meet sales quotas, get the payroll out, or do month-end posting.

You can approach the installation in several ways. One method is to set up and test equipment in your service department before installing it on-site. For example, many workstations in a network use the same components and setup parameters. You could connect one of these systems to a server in your service department to test the configuration and connection. This isolates any major problems up front, such as incorrect drivers or configuration file settings. It also helps isolate on-site cabling problems if you already know that workstation-to-network configuration parameters work.

If the installation must be completed as quickly as possible, you'll probably need to assemble teams who can install servers and workstations at different sites simultaneously. If you're not in a hurry, it's a good idea to work with the servers for a while before putting them into actual use. This gives you a chance to create user and resource objects, set up directory structures, install applications, and create the login environment for each user. This would also be a good time for you to test the backup system. Run an application program or two with some data copied from the production system. Back it up and restore it to an unused area of the disk. Then compare the original and the restored data. If the backup system is operating properly, both sets of data should match exactly. This gives you a chance to make sure everything works before you commit the company's data to the new server.

The upgrade of existing systems can pose logistical problems. You might find yourself working late at night or on weekends so that users can begin using the new system when they return to work. The upgrade of an existing server to NetWare 5 requires proper backup of its data, so you'll need to have your backup systems in place before beginning the upgrade. You should also be prepared to restore everything as it was just in case the upgrade doesn't go as planned. Consider upgrading a server on Friday night or Saturday so that you have plenty of time to get things in order or restore the old system before Monday.

The
Complete
Reference

Chapter 14

NetWare 5 Installation

309

This chapter prepares you for the installation of or upgrade to NetWare 5 and helps you gather the information you'll need during the installation process. The first two main sections describe what you'll need to know before running the installation program. The third section guides you through the actual installation.

The installation procedure for new servers is covered here. If you are upgrading an existing NetWare server or migrating from another operating system environment to NetWare 5, refer to Appendix A.

This chapter assumes that you have installed the server hardware and have the correct memory and disk configurations to begin the NetWare 5 installation, as discussed in Chapter 13.

As you read through this chapter, create log sheets that document the options you'll need to set and information you gather during the whole process, from planning to installation to postinstallation.

Installing NetWare 5 on New Servers

You can use two different methods to install NetWare 5 on a new server:

■ **Installing from a network drive**   This method requires that you connect to an existing server on a network on which the NetWare 5 files have been copied. This method is best if you are setting up a number of servers and do not have a CD-ROM drive installed in those servers, but it assumes you have a connection to the server with the installation files.

■ **Installing from a CD-ROM**   This method requires that you install a CD-ROM drive in the system that will be the server. This method is simple and intuitive and does not require that you make a client connection to an existing server.

You'll need an appropriate License diskette to successfully install NetWare 5, and you will be asked to insert this disk at a specific point in the installation procedure.

Preparing the Server

The first step to installing NetWare 5 is to install a CD-ROM (if you're using that installation method) and any other supporting hardware, then start the new computer. After you start the computer, you need to partition its drives, creating a small DOS partition to hold the NetWare 5 startup files for this server. You then install DOS and any drivers you need to support the CD-ROM, disk drives, or other hardware.

The DOS partition on the hard drive does not need to be large. It holds the NetWare 5 server startup file SERVER.EXE and associated files. Novell recommends at least 50MB for this partition, but you can create a large partition if you need it for additional drivers or software at the server. If you intend to capture core dumps on the local hard drive, you will need a DOS partition that is the size of your installed RAM memory plus the original 50MB.

Once you install the server and start it, the DOS partition is not used for normal use, although NetWare 5 startup files are stored on it. It can be accessed through the ConsoleOne utility on the server during normal operation.

After setting up the DOS partition, you start the normal NetWare 5 installation by running the INSTALL program on the NetWare 5 CD-ROM, or the server where the NetWare 5 files are installed. This startup procedure will be described step by step in the "Running the Installation" section later in this chapter. However, before running the installation, read through the following sections, which help you gather the information you'll need during the installation.

JAVA/GUI Versus Basic Text Install

The NetWare 5 installation program is comprised of two separate parts. The first part is a traditional DOS-based menu system that allows you to set up the basic parameters of the system. After this is completed, the JAVA-based GUI installation will start. This is where all similarities with previous versions of NetWare stop.

Gathering Information

During the installation process, you will be prompted for information regarding the hardware configuration of the server. You need to gather the following information and have it available.

Disk Drivers

During installation, you must specify the drivers that provide communication between your disk controller board and the NetWare server. NetWare 5 disk drivers are based on the NetWare Peripheral Architecture (NPA). The older disk drivers with the .DSK extensions are not supported.

NetWare Peripheral Architecture (NPA)

NPA is a disk driver architecture for SCSI and IDE disk controllers that all future releases of NetWare 5 will implement. It separates NetWare driver support into a Host Adapter Module (HAM) and a Custom Device Module (CDM). The HAM drives the host bus adapter, while the CDM drives the hardware devices attached to it. This design lets you easily connect a new device to the host bus adapter that is already installed in a server. For example, if you already have a host adapter installed and SCSI disk drives attached to it, you can easily attach and install other devices such as CD-ROMs or tape devices to the host adapter. Here is a list of HAMs you can load for specific devices:

- **IDEATA.HAM** Supports IDE host adapters for ISA and EISA computer architectures
- **SCSI154X.HAM** Supports Adaptec host adapters for ISA and EISA computer architectures
- **SCSIPS2.HAM** Supports IBM host adapters for Microchannel computers

Here's a list of CDMs for common devices:

- **IDEHD.CDM** Supports IDE hard disks
- **SCSIHD.CDM** Supports SCSI hard disks
- **SCSICD.CDM** Supports SCSI CD-ROMs
- **SCSIMO.CDM** Supports SCSI magneto-optical drives
- **SCSI2TP.CDM** Supports SCSI tape devices

Partitioning the Drive

During the installation, you are given the choice of manually creating partitions or having INSTALL automatically create them. Choose the automatic method if you want NetWare to create disk partitions. The automatic method creates a partition out of the remaining space on a disk. Choose the manual option in the following cases:

- If you want to configure your own partition settings
- If you need to install mirroring and/or duplexing options
- To change the size of the Hot Fix redirection area

Each partition is assigned a *Hot Fix redirection area* that is a fraction of a percent of the partition's space by default. The Hot Fix redirection area is part of NetWare's data protection strategy. By default, NetWare verifies all data it writes to disk to ensure that it matches the data in memory. If the verification fails, NetWare assumes the disk block is defective, stores the data in the redirection area, and marks the block as unusable.

 If you are using an older drive, you might want to increase the redirection area size, because the disk might be more susceptible to block failure than a newer drive and will need more space for redirection.

Disk Mirroring and Duplexing Options

Disk mirroring and duplexing provide redundancy in the disk storage system to protect against hardware failure. Mirrored drives are attached to the same controller, whereas duplexed drives are attached to separate controllers and provide a higher level of protection. If you installed a RAID system or if you're installing a second server using the Standby Server software, you won't need to set NetWare's mirroring or duplexing options.

You partition each disk separately, but a partition on one disk can be combined with a partition on another to form *volumes*. In each mirrored or duplexed set is a primary drive and a secondary drive. Typically, the partitions on the primary and secondary drives are the same size. NetWare makes adjustments to the partition sizes so that both partitions have the same disk space. For example, the primary disk usually includes a 30MB DOS partition. Assuming that the primary and secondary drives are the same model from the same vendor, 30MB of disk space on the secondary disk is not used because INSTALL adjusts its partition size to match that of the primary disk. Here are two duplexing options:

- **Two controllers with one drive each**   An example of this configuration is shown in Figure 14-1. If two controllers are installed with one drive attached to each, the first controller and its drive are the primary drive and appear as logical partition #1. This assumes that a DOS partition is logical partition #0 and that the disk contains no other partitions.

- **Two controllers with two drives each**   See Figure 14-2 for an example of this configuration. If two controllers are installed in the server and two drives are attached to each, the drives on the first controller are the primary drives and appear as logical partition #1 and logical partition #2, assuming a DOS partition is on logical partition #0. The drives on the secondary controller appear as

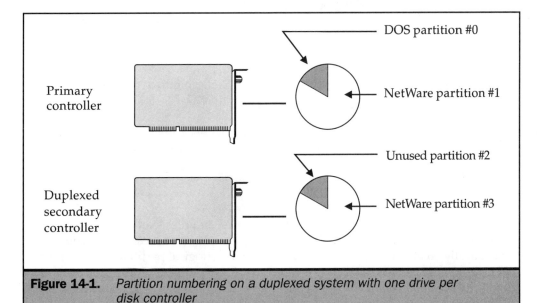

Figure 14-1.   *Partition numbering on a duplexed system with one drive per disk controller*

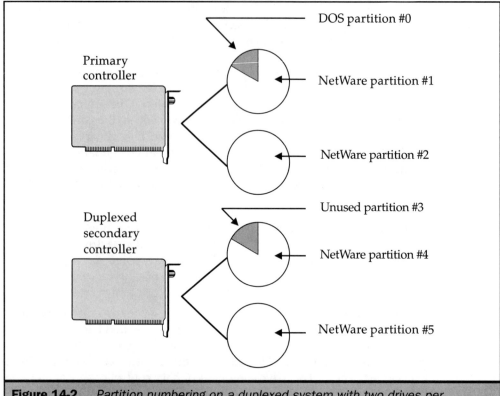

Figure 14-2.   *Partition numbering on a duplexed system with two drives per disk controller*

logical partition #4 and logical partition #5. You can mirror partition #4 to partition #1 and mirror partition #5 to partition #2.

 The load order of the disk drivers determines the logical partition numbering. If you want a particular drive to be logical partition #1, load its driver first during the installation process.

Volumes

Volumes are collections of directories, subdirectories, and files. NetWare allows more than one volume per server. The first volume on a server is called SYS and is automatically created in the free space of the first disk (logical partition #1, assuming that logical partition #0 is the DOS partition). The SYS volume is required on every server, and Novell recommends that you allocate 200MB or more of disk space for it.

INSTALL recommends using a disk's remaining free space for a single volume called VOL1, but you can subdivide it into two or more volumes. Additional volumes are assigned default names of VOL1, VOL2, and so on, but you can rename them anything you want. For example, you could name volumes DATA, USER, and MAIL.

SYS Volume

Novell recommends reserving SYS for the NetWare files and Novell Loadable Modules (NLMs) only. Do not store user data or applications on the SYS volume. This offers several advantages:

- Having these files in one volume makes them easy to back up.

- If the SYS volume is small, it takes less time to restore the drive (and the network attached to it) after a disk failure. You can quickly get the server back online and then begin the work of restoring the most important data.

- Security is improved. Except for the files in the PUBLIC directory, only supervisor-level users need object and directory/file access to the drive.

- If the SYS volume won't mount (possibly from virus corruption), even after trying to repair it by using utilities, you can re-create the SYS volume in the partition and reinstall NetWare without affecting data in other volumes.

Volumes can range in size from small to large. Multiple small volumes can fit on a single disk partition, as shown on the left of Figure 14-3. Large volumes can span several disk partitions, as shown on the right of Figure 14-3.

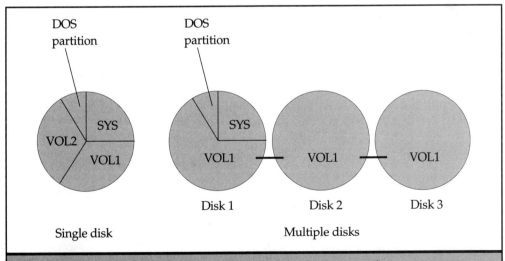

Figure 14-3.   *A single disk can contain multiple volumes, or volumes can span several disks*

Spanning volumes can provide improved disk performance. It is also the only way to increase the size of a volume if there is no free space on the disk. We recommend that not all of the free space on the disk be allocated to the NetWare partition at the time of installation. This way, you can add some of the free space to an existing volume as needed. You can never make a volume smaller than it is presently. That's called reinstallation!

To increase a volume, you add another drive and then create and attach the partition (or part of it) to the existing volume.

A spanned volume can provide faster file access, but you must mirror or duplex the volume to protect it from a disk failure. If a segment of the volume fails, the entire volume will not mount.

Volume Parameters

During the installation, you can specify the names of volumes and their parameters. The name you give volumes appears in the NDS tree under the container where the volume is located, along with an object for the server that the volume belongs to. Here are some of the parameters to have ready when you run INSTALL:

VOLUME NAME In the Volume Name field, you can specify a different name for the selected volume, unless it is the SYS volume. You might want to rename volumes according to the type of data stored on them or the name space they support. You'll need at least 200MB of disk space for the SYS volume, but you'll need more disk space if you plan to install additional services such as the NetWare 5 online documentation. You can find additional information about these services later in this chapter under "Step 23: Additional Products and Services."

VOLUME BLOCK SIZE For the sake of efficiency, a file is not stored in a block of disk space that exactly matches its size. Disk space is divided into blocks that are typically 32K to 64K in size, and files are stored in one or more of these blocks. If a file is smaller than the block size, part of that block is unused (unless you use block suballocation, as discussed shortly). Following are the block sizes available under NetWare. Note that the default block size depends on the volume size.

Volume Size	Block Size
0MB to 32MB	4K
32MB to 150MB	8K
150MB to 500MB	16K
500MB to 2,000MB	32K
2,000MB or more	64K

INSTALL sets a specific block size that depends on the size of the volume. Typically, you don't need to change the value. However, depending on the type of files you plan to store on the volume, you can increase or decrease the block size to improve performance. For example, assume you set aside one volume to store larger graphics files. It would make sense to set the block size on this volume to a large value that matches the size of a typical graphics file. Keep in mind, however, that large blocks require longer read and write times, which can affect performance. If a volume is used to store many small files, you might want to specify the smallest block size. Because the most efficient block size depends on the type of files stored on the volume, consider organizing volumes by file type.

FILE COMPRESSION   By default, the File Compression field is enabled. This means that files that have not been accessed for a certain period of time are automatically compressed. When a compressed file is accessed, it must first be decompressed, but the time to do so is usually negligible. In most cases, you should specify file compression, but check with vendors to ensure that compression is compatible with their applications. You might need to store some applications on volumes that don't compress files. In addition, you can flag a directory or file with a Don't Compress attribute. This will override the compression umbrella assigned to the volume and will apply to all subdirectories under the one to which the Don't Compress attribute was assigned.

BLOCK SUBALLOCATION   With the Block Suballocation field enabled, the volume can store files in smaller increments than the value set in the Volume Block Size field. Basically, any partially used disk block is suballocated into 512-byte blocks that can be used for other files. Block suballocation conserves disk space. For example, if the Block Suballocation field is turned off and the volume block size is 4K, a 6.5K file would require 8K of disk space. With Block Suballocation enabled, that file requires only 6.5K of disk space. Using both file compression and block suballocation maximizes the disk space on a volume.

DATA MIGRATION   NetWare's data migration feature lets you migrate seldom used files to an alternate medium such as an optical storage device to free up space on the server's disk storage system. Turn the Data Migration field on to enable the migration facility for the volume.

LAN Drivers

During the installation process, INSTALL displays a list of common network interface cards. You then pick an appropriate driver for the cards installed in your system from this list. If you don't see your card listed, you can load a driver from a floppy disk that you have obtained from the NIC's manufacturer. You must load a driver for each network card. You'll need to have interrupt (IRQ) and I/O addresses handy when installing the LAN drivers.

NetWare Planning
and Installation

You'll also be asked about the network protocols to use during the installation. IP is automatically bound to a network interface, but you can bind IPX as well.

NetWare automatically supports the following Ethernet frame types. These variations exist because of the different ways vendors have implemented the Ethernet standard.

- **Ethernet_802.2** The default standard for NetWare.

- **Ethernet_802.3** An alternate Ethernet standard (and former NetWare default standard). Do not use it on a network that uses protocols other than IPX.

- **Ethernet_II** Used to communicate with DEC minicomputers. Also used on TCP/IP or AppleTalk Phase I networks.

- **Ethernet_SNAP** The IEEE 802.2 frame standard with an extension added to the header to support AppleTalk Phase II.

While NetWare installs support for all these frame types, it binds only the frame types it finds on the network. If new frame types are added later, you will need to bind the frame type using the server management utility.

Specifying Novell Directory Services Information

During the installation, you must specify time zone and time server information for the server. You must also specify the root name of your Novell Directory Services (NDS) tree and the context for the server you are installing. The context is the organization container and organizational unit container where the server will reside.

> **Note**
>
> *If this is the first NetWare 5 server, the ADMIN user is created in the container where you place the first NetWare 5 server.*

When installing additional NetWare 5 servers, INSTALL looks at the network to locate the first server and then displays the directory tree you already created. It recommends the context of the first server for the new server you are installing, but you can choose (or create) a different context.

Naming the Novell Directory Services Tree Root

Most companies will have only one tree, and thus you will specify only one tree root name. However, some organizations might require two separate and distinct directory trees. For example, an organization with separate and distinct companies might be managed by one central authority.

Every directory tree has a root name. During installation of the first server, you are asked to name the root of the tree into which the server will be installed. This name can be simply ROOT or TREE_ROOT, or it could include your company name, such as

XYZ_CO. When installing additional NetWare 5 servers on the same network, the root you specified on the first server is suggested.

Other Information You'll Need

In addition to the preceding information, other information will be needed during the installation of the server.

Specifying the Time Zone

During the installation, you'll need to specify time zone information for the server. A screen appears on which you can select the time zone you are in. After selecting the time zone, a menu with the following options appears.

STANDARD TIME ZONE ABBREVIATION   This field contains the abbreviation for the time zone you selected. The commonly used time zone abbreviations for the United States are listed here, but you can enter your own abbreviation if you prefer:

Abbreviation	Time Zone
EST	Eastern Standard Time
CST	Central Standard Time
MST	Mountain Standard Time
PST	Pacific Standard Time

STANDARD TIME OFFSET FROM UTC   UTC stands for Universal Time Coordinate, which was formerly Greenwich Mean Time. The offset is the number of time zones you are away from UTC and whether you are ahead or behind it. These are the settings for the United States:

Abbreviation	Offset
EST	Offset of 5 and behind
CST	Offset of 6 and behind
MST	Offset of 7 and behind
PST	Offset of 8 and behind

DST TIME ZONE ABBREVIATION   If your time zone switches to daylight saving time and back to standard time during the year, the daylight saving time abbreviation for your time zone is in this field. If you don't specify an abbreviation, daylight saving time will be set by default to occur. You can enter your own abbreviation or a commonly used abbreviation.

DST OFFSET FROM STANDARD TIME   This field holds the difference between standard time and daylight saving time. It is usually one hour ahead.

- **DST Start**   The date daylight saving time starts.
- **DST End**   The date daylight saving time ends.

Specifying the Time Server Type

Novell Directory Services must ensure that servers on an internetwork are time-synchronized so that time stamps can accurately track the order of events. Time synchronization is important, because internal computer clocks can deviate from one another. It ensures that all systems know the correct time so that updates to the same data from various parts of the internetwork are handled correctly.

 For more details on time servers and time synchronization, refer to Chapter 18.

Recall that there are four time server types:

- **Single reference server**   The sole source of time on the network. Any time changes are set on this server, and then others synchronize with it. A single reference server should not be used if a primary time server is used. This time server type is usually for single-site networks or networks that are in the same geographic location.

- **Primary time server**   Synchronizes time with other primary time servers or a reference time server, and provides the correct time to secondary time servers. If there are multiple primary servers on a network, they "vote" on what the common network time should be.

- **Reference server**   A reference server gets its time from an external source (such as a radio clock or the World Wide Web) and is a contact to what the outside world says the time should be. A reference server does not use or change its internal time clock. A reference server helps primary time servers set a common time by using a "voting" procedure. Eventually all time servers are set to the time indicated by the reference server's outside time source.

- **Secondary server**   All other servers on the network can be secondary time servers. They merely get the time from single-reference, primary, or reference time servers and do not participate in the establishment of a common time over the network.

During installation, specify the type of time server based on whether the inter-network covers large geographic areas. Secondary servers should get their time from a local primary or reference server, rather than use a WAN link to access a distant time server. If this is the first server in a tree, it will default to a single reference server. If this server is installed into an existing tree, it will default to a secondary server. Primary and reference servers must be created manually. Also note that each reference server must have at least two, but not more than seven, primary servers.

Use multiple primary time servers on internetworks that span large geographic areas. This provides fault tolerance and redundant paths for secondary time servers: If one primary time server is offline, secondary servers can get the time from another primary time server. Place primary time servers in each geographically distant location so that other servers can access them without having to use expensive wide area links. Install one server as a reference time server and attach an external time source to this server. All other servers not participating in the establishment of a common time on the internetwork should be set up as secondary time servers.

Use single reference servers on small networks that are not connected by WAN links. If you set up a NetWare 5 server as a single reference time server, do not install a primary server or a reference server. If you do, you will get error messages every two minutes at the server consoles.

Defining the Network Administrator

When installing the first server, you can specify the name and password of the administrative user if you do not want to use the default name ADMIN. INSTALL recommends the name ADMIN. To change the name and password, simply type new values. You can change this name at any time in the future by using the ConsoleOne or NetWare Administrator utility.

Write down the context of the administrator (for example CN=ADMIN.O=CambrianCorp) for future reference. You'll need it to log in as the administrator and if you want to specify this user as the administrator for other servers.

IP Addressing Information

Because NetWare 5 operates in a "pure" TCP/IP environment, you need to have the IP address and IP submask ready during the installation. If you are not familiar with IP addressing, you will find some information in Chapter 5 and Chapter 9, but you can also call the Defense Data Network (DDN) Information Center in Chantilly, Virginia, at 800-365-3642. They administer IP addresses and will assign you an address configuration that can be used on the Internet.

Optional Files You Can Install

You can install optional files during the installation process to support other Novell applications and UNIX print services. Make sure you have enough disk space to handle the options. For example, the UNIX utilities require approximately 1MB of additional disk space.

NetWare Planning and Installation

Running the Installation

This section guides you through the installation by briefly describing each step. You should have gathered the information you need to perform each step as discussed in the previous sections. This discussion assumes you are installing NetWare 5 on a new server.

Step 1: Preparing the New Server

The first thing you must do is install all the components in the server, such as the disk controller, network interface card, CD-ROM drive, and others. You then boot the server with a DOS disk.

INSTALL needs to access the NetWare files from either a local CD-ROM or from a server at another location that holds the files. This last option requires that you are running as a client on the existing network. The first option requires that you start the server with DOS.

If you are installing from a local CD-ROM, you need to start the computer and create CONFIG.SYS and AUTOEXEC.BAT files that load the drivers and CD-ROM support files for the CD-ROM. This enables you to access the NetWare CD-ROM. Reboot the computer after creating the files. Refer to your CD-ROM drive manual for details.

Step 2: Creating a DOS Partition

Use the standard DOS FDISK and FORMAT utilities to create at least a 30MB DOS partition on the disk drive to hold the NetWare 5 server startup files.

Step 3: Running the INSTALL Program

Switch to the CD-ROM drive or network server that holds the NetWare installation files and type **INSTALL**. You're on your way. The CD-ROM loads up a run-time version of the server and begins the install process.

Step 4: Selecting the Install Language

The first menu to appear is the one that allows you to select the installation language to be used. The available choices are English, French, German, Spanish, Portuguese, or Italian. Highlight the selection and press ENTER.

Step 5: Accepting the License Agreement

The screen will fill with the Novell licensing agreement. You must agree to the terms of the agreement or the install will terminate. Press F10 to accept and continue.

Step 6: The NetWare Welcome Screen

Figure 14-4 displays the NetWare 5 welcome screen. Here you specify whether this is an upgrade or a new server installation. In addition, this is where you define the DOS

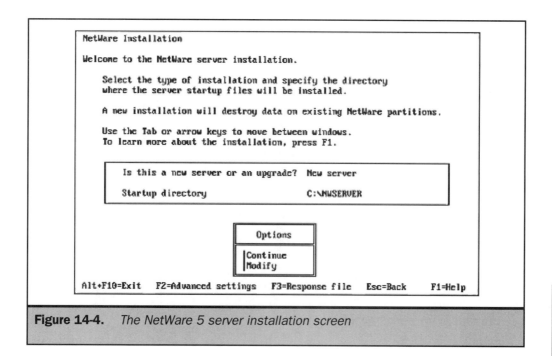

Figure 14-4. *The NetWare 5 server installation screen*

directory where the server startup files will be installed. Please take notice that a new installation of NetWare 5 will destroy all data on any existing NetWare partitions.

 The quality of Figures 14-4 through 14-39 is poor because there is no screen capturing utility available to create quality screen shots during NetWare installation.

Step 7: Regional Settings for the Server

The country, code page (unicode), and keyboard mapping are configured on the screen shown in Figure 14-5. To change a setting, highlight Modify and use the TAB key to select an entry to change. Press ENTER, and a list of available options appears in a pop-up window.

Step 8: Selecting the Mouse and Video

The default mouse type is a PS/2 mouse. To change the mouse type, select Modify and tab over to the Mouse Type field, as shown in Figure 14-6. Press ENTER and select the mouse interface from the pop-up menu list. The display defaults to a super VGA for supporting the GUI stage of the installation program. If desired, you can change this to a standard VGA.

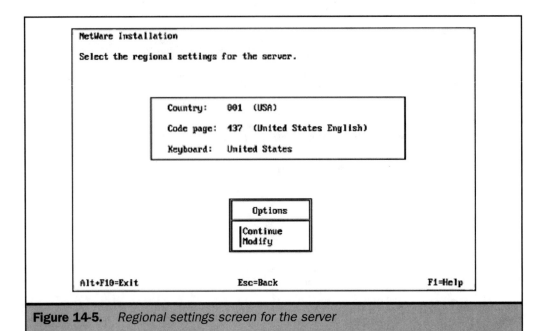

Figure 14-5.   *Regional settings screen for the server*

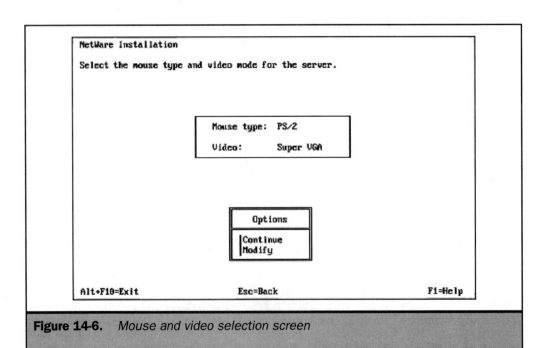

Figure 14-6.   *Mouse and video selection screen*

Step 9: Hardware Device Detection

The installation program automatically detects the various hardware parameters on the computer. If the computer supports multiple processors, you will be presented with a Platform Support Module selection. If the computer supports the new PCI-HotPlug technology for storage and network boards, the HotPlug Support Module field will have various selections available for you. If these fields are displayed as optional, then the installation program did not detect these capabilities in the hardware, as shown in Figure 14-7.

Step 10: Device Driver Detection

The installation program automatically detects and loads the appropriate drivers for the storage system and the network boards, as shown in Figure 14-8. The NetWare Loadable Modules selection is for the loading of NLMs that are required by the hardware for proper initialization.

Step 11: NetWare Partitions and Volumes

Any existing NetWare partitions on the server will be detected at this stage and displayed, as shown in Figure 14-9. If you want to preserve the existing data on the partition, exit the installation and select the upgrade procedure. If you continue, all existing NetWare partitions and volumes will be destroyed.

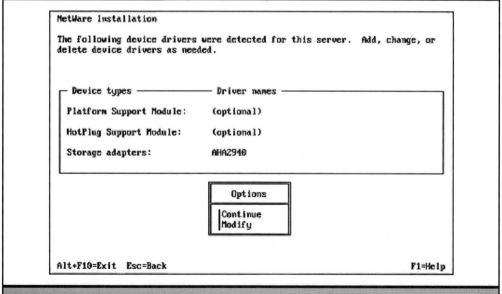

Figure 14-7.   *This screen displays what the installation program found during the hardware detection phase*

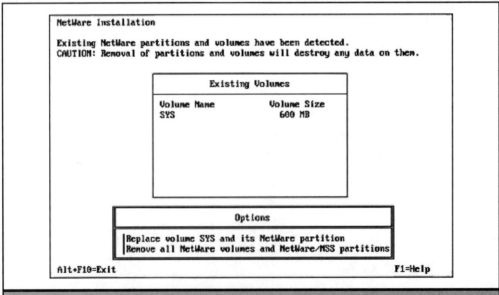

NetWare Installation

The following device drivers were detected for this server. Add, change, or delete device drivers as needed.

┌─ Device types ──────────── Driver names ──────────────┐
│   │
│ Storage devices: SCSIHD   │
│   │
│ Network boards: 3C90X   │
│   │
│ NetWare Loadable Modules: (optional)   │
│   │
└──┘

            ┌──────────────────┐
            │   Options   │
            ├──────────────────┤
            │ Continue   │
            │ Modify   │
            └──────────────────┘

Alt+F10=Exit   Esc=Back   F1=Help

Figure 14-8. *This screen displays the drivers that the installation has selected for the hardware in the computer*

NetWare Installation

Existing NetWare partitions and volumes have been detected.
CAUTION: Removal of partitions and volumes will destroy any data on them.

        ┌──┐
        │   Existing Volumes   │
        ├──┤
        │ Volume Name   Volume Size   │
        │ SYS   600 MB   │
        │   │
        │   │
        │   │
        │   │
        └──┘

      ┌──┐
      │   Options   │
      ├──┤
      │ Replace volume SYS and its NetWare partition   │
      │ Remove all NetWare volumes and NetWare/NSS partitions │
      └──┘

Alt+F10=Exit   F1=Help

Figure 14-9. *The installation program will detect if any existing NetWare partitions exist on the computer*

Step 12: Creating a NetWare Partition and SYS Volume

The installation program will default to using the entire NetWare partition for the SYS volume. If you want multiple volumes, or room for NSS volumes, select Modify, and change the size of the SYS partition, as shown in Figure 14-10. The following list gives approximate disk space requirements for the various install options:

Installation Option	Disk Space Required
NetWare 5 Operating System	250MB
NetWare 5 OS with defaults	350MB
NetWare 5 OS with all (no docs)	450MB
NetWare 5 OS with all (all docs)	600MB

Step 13: Volume Information Screen

The SYS volume parameters are shown in Figure 14-11. If you want to change things such as the volume block size or the suballocation settings, this is where you do it.

This completes the DOS menu phase of the installation process. The rest of the installation is performed through the JAVA-based GUI installation program.

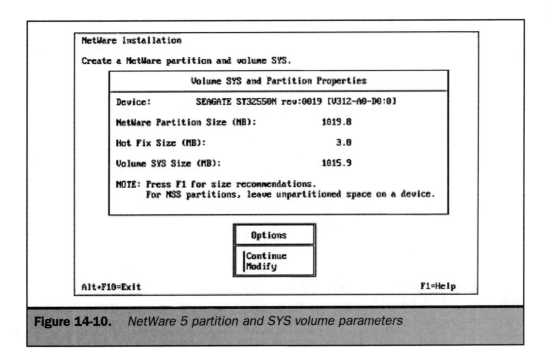

Figure 14-10.   *NetWare 5 partition and SYS volume parameters*

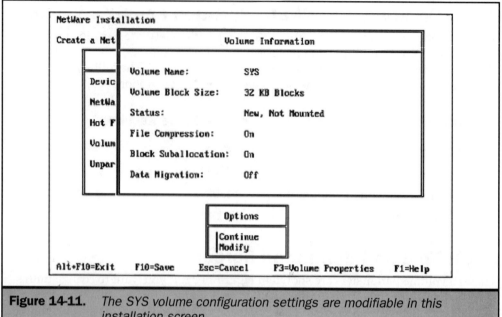

NetWare Installation

Create a Net

                         Volume Information

Devic   Volume Name: SYS

NetWa   Volume Block Size: 32 KB Blocks

Hot F   Status: New, Not Mounted

Volum   File Compression: On

Unpar   Block Suballocation: On

        Data Migration: Off

Options
Continue
Modify

Alt+F10=Exit   F10=Save   Esc=Cancel   F3=Volume Properties   F1=Help

Figure 14-11. *The SYS volume configuration settings are modifiable in this installation screen*

Step 14: Setting the Server Name

This screen displays a field in which you type the name of the new server. In Figure 14-12, you will also notice that you move to the next screen by using the mouse to click the Next button.

Step 15: Configuring the File System

Figure 14-13 displays the current configuration of the hard disks within the system. You can select an existing volume and change various parameters from the GUI interface. If you select the free space on the system, the screen shown in Figure 14-14 will pop up to allow you to name and configure the new volume.

Step 16: Volume Mounts

The screen shown in Figure 14-15 allows you to mount all the new volumes immediately or to have them mount when the server restarts.

Step 17: Network Protocols

This screen allows you to select which protocols will be bound to the network cards. Figure 14-16 shows only one NE2000 network card in the server. If others are detected, they will appear in this window also.

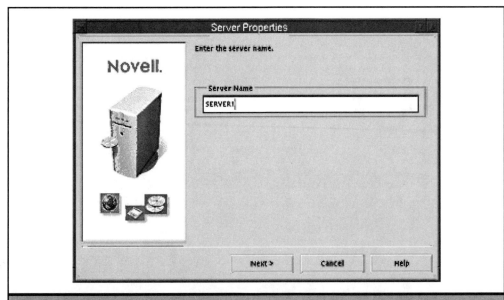

Figure 14-12.   *Enter the server name in the text field*

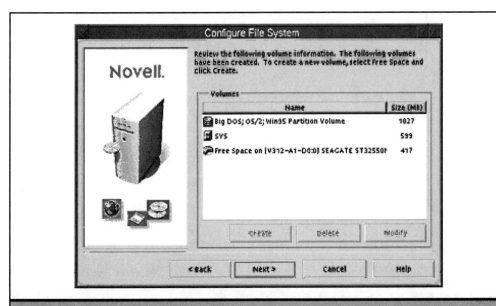

Figure 14-13.   *The currently configured volumes on the hard disks are displayed*

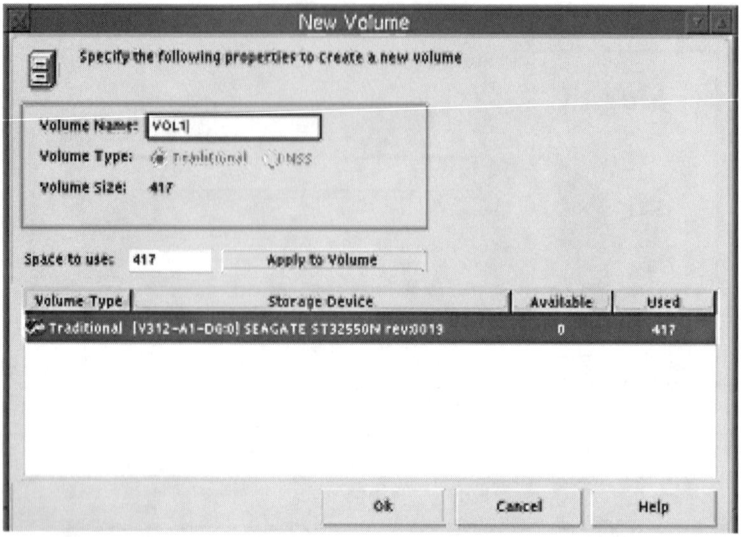

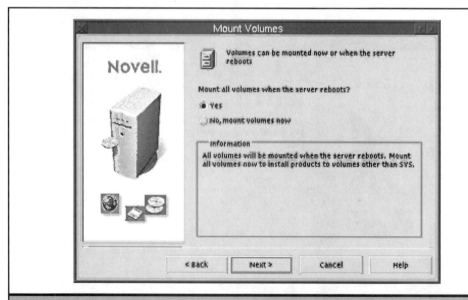

Figure 14-14. *If you decide to make a new volume from the existing free space, this screen will appear for you*

Figure 14-15. *The new volumes can be mounted at this stage of the installation or delayed until the server is restarted*

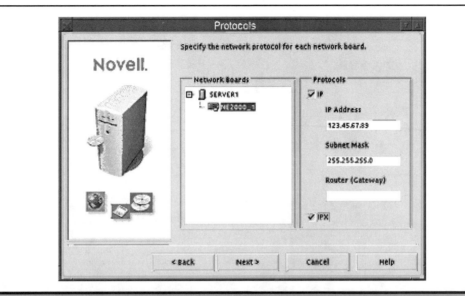

Figure 14-16.   *The Protocols selection screen allows you to select either the IP protocol, the IPX protocol, or both. See the text for specifics as to their operation*

If you select only the IP check box, you are operating in a "pure" TCP/IP environment. This provides passive support for IPX traffic using the Compatibility Mode drivers. With this mode, IPX packets destined for another LAN across the TCP/IP connection will be encapsulated into IP packets. IPX SAPs will be replaced with a lookup feature in the new NCP using NDS lookups. If you want to disallow the Compatibility Mode drivers, remove the LOAD SCMD line from the AUTOEXEC.NCF file.

If you select both the IP and IPX check boxes, the server will handle all TCP/IP traffic using the IP protocol. The server will also broadcast and respond to all IPX requests using the IPX protocol.

Whenever the IP check box is selected, you will be prompted for an IP address, a subnet mask, and a router (gateway) address. The gateway address will be the IP address of your gateway to an Internet connection or router on your WAN.

Step 18: Time Zone Selection

The time zone for the server is defined in the screen shown in Figure 14-17. It is very important for NDS to know which time zone it is in for synchronization purposes. The Daylight Saving Time check box is available for those areas and countries that use it.

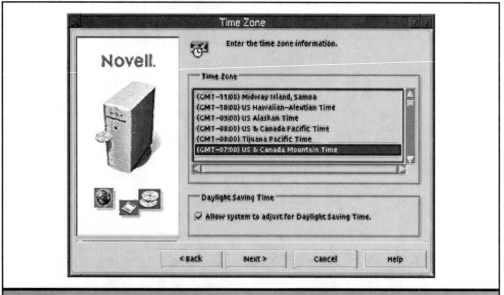

Figure 14-17.   *The Time Zone selection screen displays different time zones from across the globe*

Step 19: NDS Installation

The new server can be installed into an existing NDS tree or a new tree can be defined. The default is into an existing tree. You can change this by selecting the second radio button to create a new NDS tree, as shown in Figure 14-18. Remember that if you install the server into a new tree, the resources on the server will not be available to users on other trees unless they log in to your new tree.

Step 20: NDS Configuration and Admin Installation

Figure 14-19 shows the screen in which you define the name of the new NDS tree. You also define where to place the Server object into the tree structure. Any containers you define here will be created for you. You also define the name of the administrator for the server. The default name is ADMIN. We do not recommend that you change the name, but you can if you desire. A new feature of NetWare 5 allows you to define the context in which to place the Admininistrator object. In prior versions of NetWare, it defaulted to the context of the first organization container.

Step 21: NDS Summary

After the server has installed NDS, a summary screen like the one in Figure 14-20 is displayed. This screen shows the NDS tree name, the server context, and the

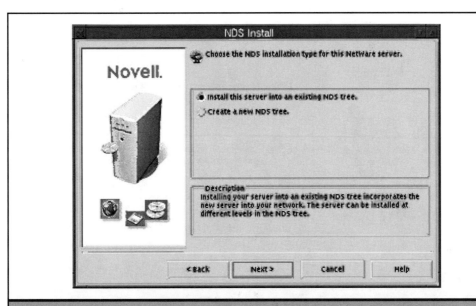

Figure 14-18. *The NDS Install screen allows you to select installation into an existing tree or the creation of a new tree*

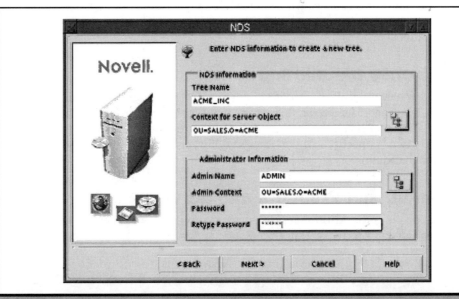

Figure 14-19. *This figure shows the NDS tree naming and context selection screen. The Administrator object is also defined on this screen*

NetWare Planning and Installation

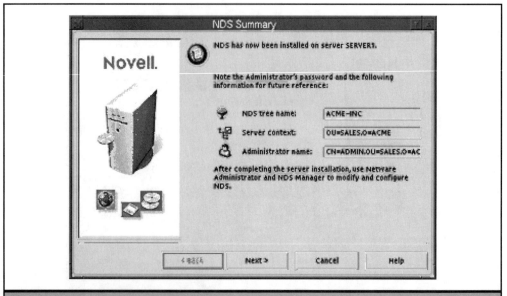

Figure 14-20. *The NDS Summary screen displays the configuration options for the newly installed NDS*

administrator name and context. After the installation is completed, you can use the NetWare Administrator (NWADMIN32) utility or the NDS Manager to change the configuration.

Step 22: License Installation

The NetWare 5 server requires a license to operate properly in a network environment. You can put the license disk in the floppy drive or browse the network for it, as shown in Figure 14-21. If you check the Install Without Licenses check box, the server will allow for only two connections. If you are installing this server with a run-time version only, this will be adequate.

Step 23: Additional Products and Services

Figure 14-22 displays the additional products and services that can be installed on the server. The following products and services are available:

- **LDAP Services** This service provides client access to information stored in the NDS database through the Lightweight Directory Access Protocol (LDAP).

- **NDS Catalog Services** This service stores information about the various objects in NDS in the catalog database. It allows for contextless logins and

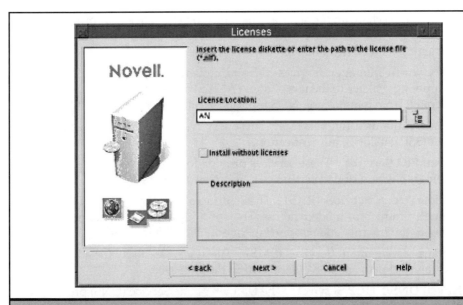

Figure 14-21. The Licenses screen prompts you for the license disk or the network location of the license files

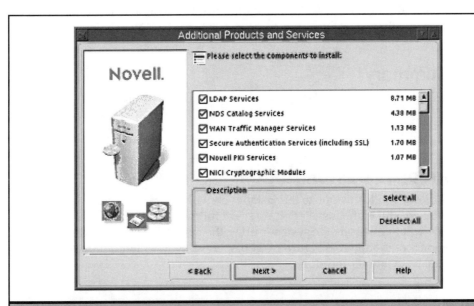

Figure 14-22. This screen displays the additional products and services that can be installed on the server

provides a mechanism for older applications to extract object information from the database. This eliminates the traditional SAP broadcasts that caused traffic problems in IPX environments.

- **WAN Traffic Manager Services** The administrator can control WAN traffic by applying policies to the use of the WAN links. This includes the traffic generated from maintaining NDS replicas on other servers in the WAN.

- **Secure Authentication Services** These services include the Secure Sockets Layer (SSL version 3) authentication.

- **Novell PKI Services** These services provide for the use of public key cryptography and digital certificate generation and management.

- **Remote Access Services (RAS)** These services are based on the NetWare Connect product for modem access. They provide a means for connecting the server to the Internet and supporting dial-up client connections.

- **Storage Management Services (SMS)** These services allow the administrator to create and manage SMS objects within the NDS tree.

- **Novell DNS/DHCP Services** The Domain Name Service (DNS) provides a means to resolve host names to IP addresses. The Dynamic Host Configuration Protocol (DHCP) provides the ability to dynamically assign IP addresses to clients as they access the network.

- **Novell Documentation CD-ROM** The NetWare 5 documentation can be stored on the server. This allows the administrator to assign access to various documents through permission assignments to various NDS objects.

Step 24: Summary

The screen shown in Figure 14-23 displays a summary of the products and services selected for the example installation. The next series of screens are generated by selecting the Customize button.

Step 25: Product Customization

NetWare 5 allows you to customize the installation with a variety of screens. Keep in mind that you are still in the installation program for the operating system. These screens allow you to fine-tune the system during the installation. The Product Customization screen shown in Figure 14-24 displays the overall options selected thus far in the installation procedure.

NetWare Operating System Properties

The Operating System Properties screen is displayed by clicking the NetWare Operating system icon in the Product Customization window, as shown in Figure 14-24. This brings

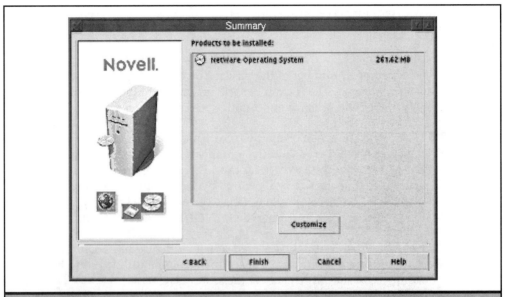

Figure 14-23.   *The Summary screen for the selected products and services to be installed on the server*

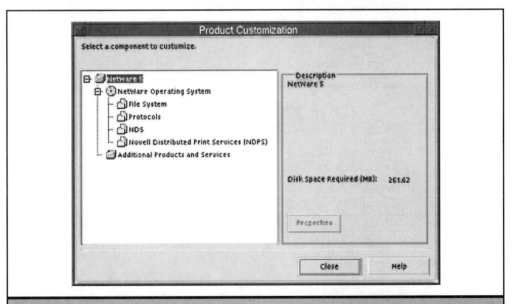

Figure 14-24.   *The Product Customization screen displays the overall system configuration and allows you to modify each aspect of the operating system*

up a window with tabs for Server Properties, Language, ConsoleOne, License, and Components. Each of these screens is detailed as follows:

SERVER PROPERTIES TAB   The Server Properties screen shown in Figure 14-25 shows the internal server ID number of the server. You can change this number and reassign a new one if desired. The ID number will be written to the AUTOEXEC.NCF file. The new ID number will not take effect until you restart the server.

LANGUAGE TAB   The Language properties screen shown in Figure 14-26 displays the selected languages for the server and the administration utility. The server language is the language that the server console and error messages will use. The Admin language is the language that will be used by the administration programs to create and manage NDS objects. The language selected for the server can be determined at the server console by typing the **LANGUAGE /?** command.

CONSOLEONE TAB   The ConsoleOne screen shown in Figure 14-27 controls the startup options for the ConsoleOne server-based management utility. If the check box is checked, the utility will start up whenever the server is restarted.

LICENSE TAB   The License screen shown in Figure 14-28 displays the serial number or numbers of the installed NetWare 5 licenses on the server. It also displays the

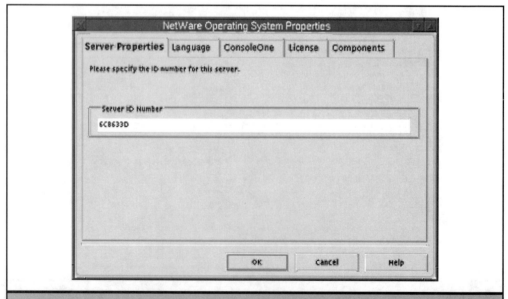

Figure 14-25.   *The Server Properties screen displays the server ID number*

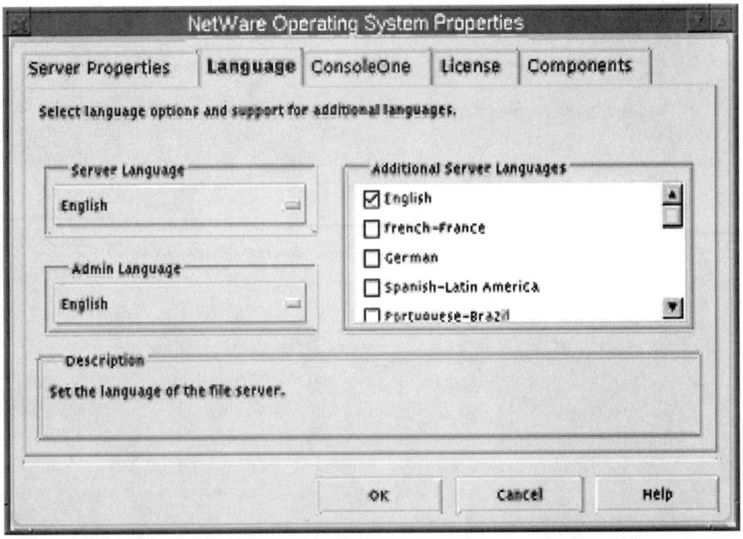

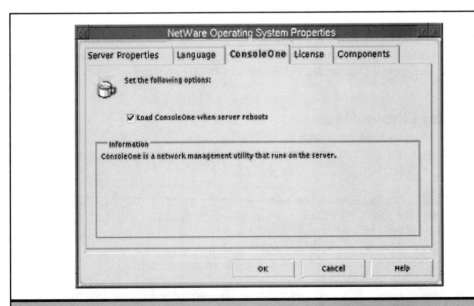

Figure 14-26.   *The Language tab displays the selected languages for the server and the administration utilities*

Figure 14-27.   *This setting controls the startup operation of the ConsoleOne management utility*

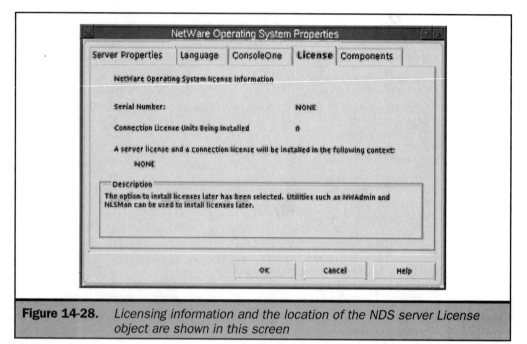

Figure 14-28. Licensing information and the location of the NDS server License object are shown in this screen

number of connections allowed and the NDS context in which the server License object will be placed.

COMPONENTS TAB The Components screen shown in Figure 14-29 displays the currently selected components to install. If you uncheck any of the selections, it will not be installed. The Novell Distributed Print Services (NDPS) check box is not shown in the figure.

File System Properties

The file system properties are configured by highlighting the File System icon shown in Figure 14-24. Once selected, click the Properties button to review the configuration settings and to make changes.

FILE SYSTEM The File System screen shown in Figure 14-30 displays the current configuration of the hard disks in the system. The DOS partition and the SYS volume cannot be deleted from this screen. All available free space on the disk or disks is displayed. You can create, modify, and delete both partitions and volumes from this screen. In addition, you can mount the volumes from this screen.

NEW VOLUME If you decide to create a new volume from the available free space on the hard drive, the screen shown in Figure 14-31 will be displayed. You fill in the name for the volume and the size in megabytes. You also have the ability to select

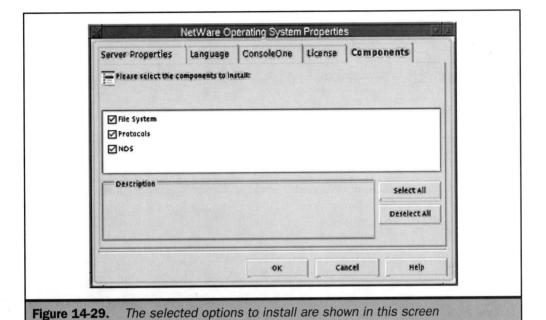

Figure 14-29.   *The selected options to install are shown in this screen*

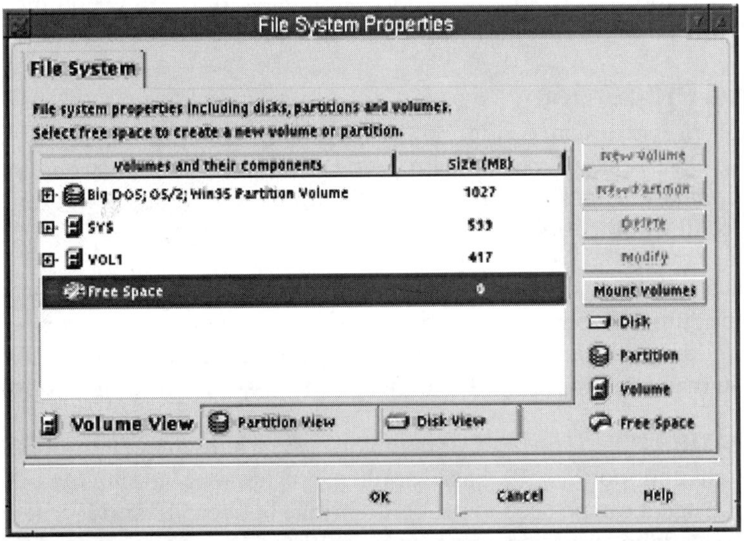

Figure 14-30.   *The partitions and volumes on the hard disks are shown. This is the volume view for the drives. You can also select to view the information using the partition view or the disk view*

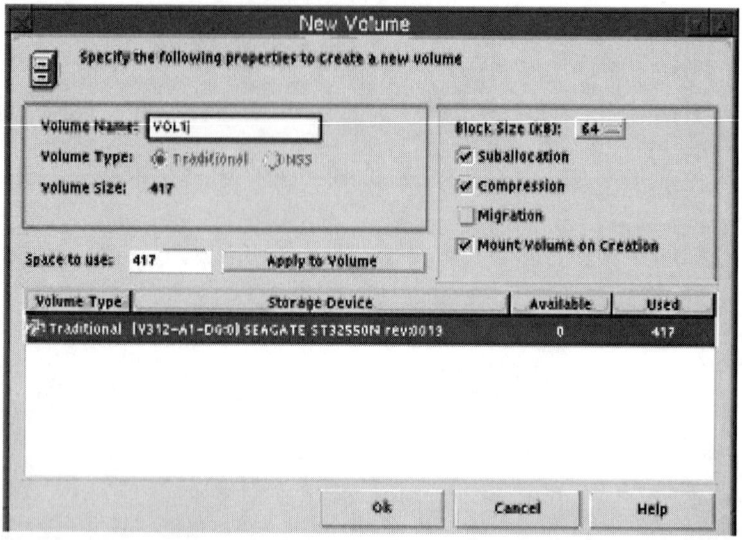

Figure 14-31. *The new volume name, size, and various other parameters can be configured from this screen*

suballocation, compression, and migration parameters for the new volume. In addition, you can choose to have the volume mount upon creation.

Protocols Properties

The protocols properties are configured by highlighting the Protocols icon shown in Figure 14-24. Once selected, click the Properties button to review the configuration settings and make changes. There are three separate tabs relating to configuration of the protocols: IPX Compatibility, Domain Name Service, and SNMP.

PROTOCOLS When the screen shown in Figure 14-32 pops up, select each network board to configure the operating parameters. If IP has been selected, you will need to enter the IP address, the subnet mask, and the gateway for the server. If IPX has been selected, you may need to change the network addresses for the various protocols.

IPX COMPATIBILITY The IPX Compatibility screen shown in Figure 14-33 provides you with passive support for IPX-based applications without binding the IPX protocol. The migration agent can be used to provide a bridge between IP and IPX network segments. To load the migration agent, both the IP and IPX protocols need to be selected.

DOMAIN NAME SERVICE The Domain Name Service (DNS) screen is used to configure the server for DNS. Figure 14-34 shows the domain name and the name

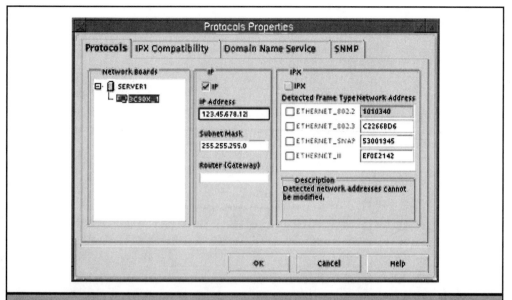

Figure 14-32.   *The various protocols configured for each network adapter on the server are displayed*

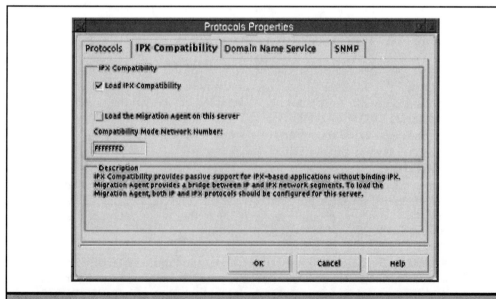

Figure 14-33.   *The IPX compatibility mode allows older IPX-based systems to communicate via IP between network segments*

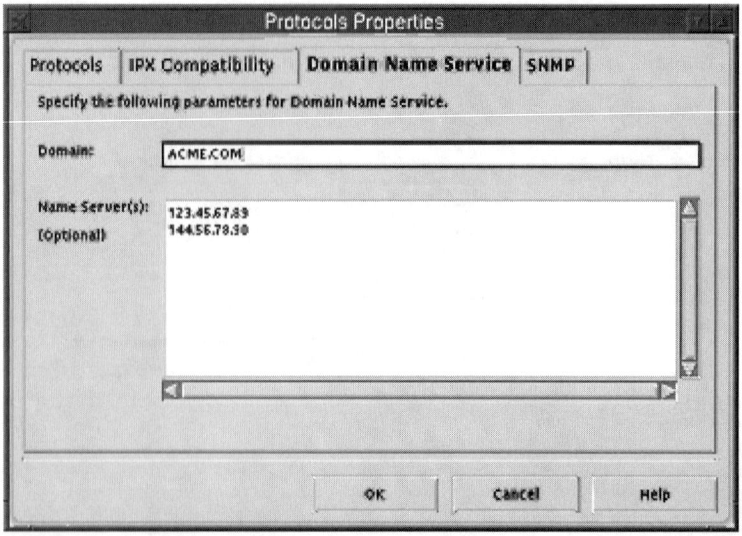

Figure 14-34. *The domain name and associated name servers are displayed in this screen*

servers used to resolve host names to IP addresses. If you did not select DNS services in the prior configuration screens, you will have to return to the Summary screen shown in Figure 14-23 and install DNS/DHCP services.

SNMP The Simple Network Management Protocol (SMNP) screen is used to record and communicate information about devices on the network. You can set and monitor threshold levels and specific events for SNMP-enabled devices. In the screen shown in Figure 14-35, you can configure the devices to receive this information when an SNMP event occurs. Both IPX and IP device addresses can be configured.

NDS Properties

The NDS properties are configured by highlighting the NDS icon shown in Figure 14-24. Once selected, click the Properties button to review the configuration settings and to make changes. There are three separate tabs relating to the configuration of the NDS: NDS Summary, Time Zone, and Time Synchronization.

NDS SUMMARY The NDS Summary screen shown in Figure 14-36 provides status information as to the state of the NDS installation, the NDS tree name, the server context, and the name and context of the Administrator object. Use the NetWare Administrator (NWADMIN32) or NDS Manager utility to modify and configure NDS after completing the server install.

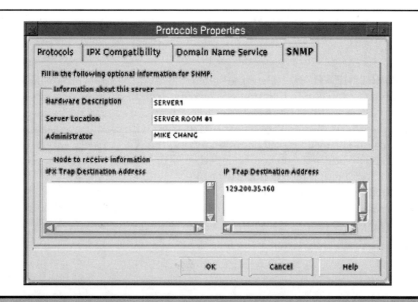

Figure 14-35. *The SNMP screen is used to define the devices to receive Simple Network Management Protocol (SNMP) information when an event occurs on the network*

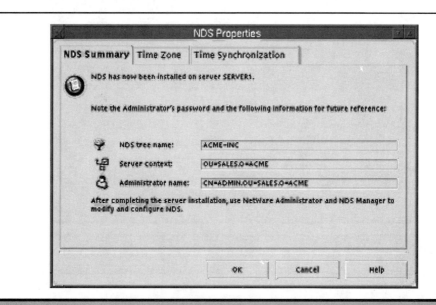

Figure 14-36. *The NDS Summary screen displays the status and contexts for the Server and Administrator objects within the NDS tree*

NetWare Planning
and Installation

TIME ZONE   Figure 14-37 displays the time zone information that was entered earlier in the installation program. All of the configuration options can be modified on this screen.

TIME SYNCHRONIZATION   The time synchronization settings are displayed in Figure 14-38. You can change the time server type from this screen, if necessary.

After the customizations have been completed, you are returned to the Summary screen shown in Figure 14-23. When you are satisfied with all of your settings, click the Finish button. The system will begin analyzing the NDS objects, upgrading the volumes into NDS, adding security if needed, and preparing for the system file copy. When this is completed, the screen in Figure 14-39 will be displayed.

Congratulations! You have completed the NetWare 5 installation. If you are not sure whether an option was set correctly, don't worry. You can go back into INSTALL at any point to correct individual settings.

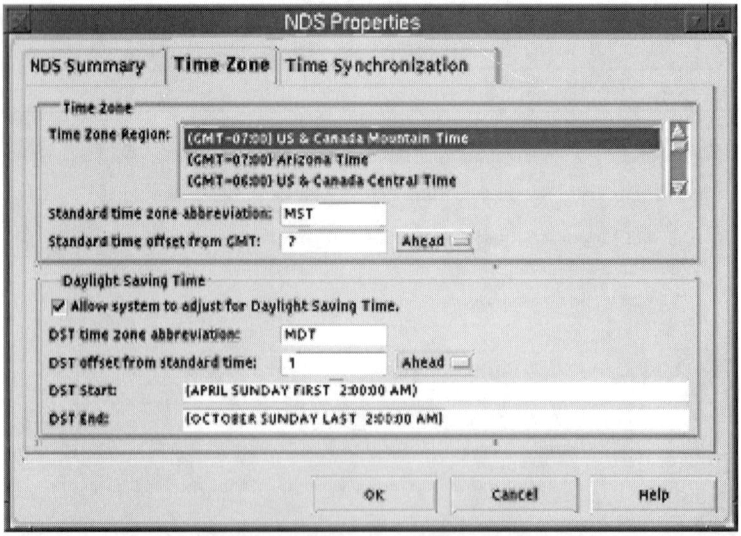

Figure 14-37.   Server time zone settings and daylight saving times are configurable from this screen

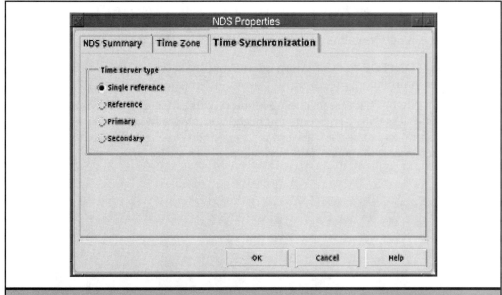

Figure 14-38.   *Time server type settings are configurable from this screen*

Figure 14-39.   *This screen is displayed after you successfully complete the installation*

NetWare Planning
and Installation

At this point, you need to verify the current installation. Press ENTER to restart the server. You see the server console screen, which displays the name of your server as a prompt. You can perform a number of actions at the console, including the following:

- Type **MONITOR** to view information about the server, such as disk and LAN driver information, processor utilization, and memory utilization.

- On the MONITOR screen, choose Memory Utilization. If the Percent Free field indicates less than 20 percent, you need to add more memory. On a new server this is unlikely to be the case, but it's a good idea to check this field periodically as users access the server and loadable modules are installed.

The
Complete
Reference

NetWare
5

Chapter 15

Post-Installation
Procedures

This chapter covers mandatory and optional tasks you perform after installing the NetWare 5 operating system on the server. It is divided into two main sections:

■ **Post-Installation Tasks at the Console** This section covers things you do at the NetWare 5 server's console, such as loading additional NLMs, installing uninterruptible power supplies, configuring name spaces, setting password security at the console, and shutting the server down (if necessary). You don't need to be at a logged-in workstation to perform these tasks, although that is also possible, as discussed in the second main section of this chapter.

■ **NetWare 5 Server Console Commands and Utilities** This section covers the console commands and utilities you can run either at the server itself or from the remote administrator workstation you set up in the prior section.

Post-Installation Tasks at the Console

The following information describes essential tasks you need to perform at the physical server site, especially if you plan to manage it from another location. For example, you need to secure the console with a password to prevent unauthorized access and to set up the REMOTE.NLM, which lets you connect with the server from your administrator workstation.

Starting the Server

If you have downed the server, you need to know the command to restart the server. The command SERVER.EXE is located in the NWSERVER directory (or another directory if you renamed it) on the DOS partition of the server hard drive. To run the command, you need to switch to the directory. You can also include it in the AUTOEXEC.BAT file to start NetWare 5 when the server computer starts.

The NetWare startup information file called STARTUP.NCF is located in the same directory as SERVER.EXE. The commands in this file are automatically executed when you run SERVER.EXE. In most cases, the file contains commands to load disk drives so the disk containing the NetWare server software can be properly accessed.

The SERVER command has several startup parameters that you can use to test or troubleshoot the server:

■ **–S** Use this option, followed by a filename, when you want to load an alternate STARTUP.NCF file. Include a path if the file is in a directory other than the current boot directory. For example, to execute commands in a file called ALTSTART.NCF instead of STARTUP.NCF, you would type the following:

    SERVER –S ALTSTART.NCF

■ **–NA** Using this option prevents the commands in AUTOEXEC.NCF from executing. Use this option to prevent a driver you want to replace from loading.

- **–NS**   Using this option prevents the STARTUP.NCF and AUTOEXEC.NCF files from executing. As with the –NA option, use this option to change the way the server boots.
- **–NL**   Use this option to prevent the server splash logo from displaying while the server components are loading in the background.

About the Server Console

The server console displays the name of the server and a flashing cursor. As with the DOS prompt, you issue commands to the operating system from it. The console is very similar to a workstation connection. At a workstation, you can access programs that run on your workstation. At the NetWare console, you can issue NetWare console commands that set server parameters and options, run JAVA applets if the JAVA support modules are loaded, and load Novell Loadable Modules (NLMs).

Editing the Startup Files

This chapter discusses how to load various NLM modules or execute various commands directly at the NetWare console. However, you might want to put those commands directly in the STARTUP.NCF or AUTOEXEC.NCF files. You can edit these files by typing this:

```
[LOAD] EDIT AUTOEXEC.NCF
```

or this:

```
[LOAD] EDIT C:\NWSERVER\STARTUP.NCF
```

If you don't know the exact path to the file, you can press the INSERT key when prompted for a filename. This will allow you to search through the server for the specific file. The STARTUP.NCF file is usually in the NWSERVER directory on the DOS volume, so you need to enter its path. Add commands to the files mentioned in the following sections as appropriate.

   Most commands go in AUTOEXEC.NCF. If you need to execute a command immediately before or after loading disk drivers, put it in STARTUP.NCF.

Novell Loadable Modules

Novell Loadable Modules (NLMs) are programs that run on the NetWare server operating system. NLMs you run at the console might include management utilities, such as those discussed in the "NetWare 5 Server Console Commands and Utilities" section, later in this chapter, or server-based applications such as a database engine that users on the network access. You load NLMs by typing the name of the module. It is no longer necessary to type LOAD before the module name. Note the following:

- Press ALT-ESC to switch among loaded modules and the console command prompt.

- Press CTRL-ESC to display a list of all running modules on the server.

- You can keep loading additional NLMs until you run out of server resources and memory.

- You can quit many NLMs and remove them from memory by simply pressing the ESC key until you exit.

- Type **UNLOAD**, followed by the name of the NLM, to remove NLMs (unless the NLM has an onscreen exit option).

- You can place the command to automatically start NLMs in the STARTUP.NCF or AUTOEXEC.NCF file.

If you put NLMs in directories other than SYS:SYSTEM, you need to specify the path to the directory when typing the command. To avoid the need to type this search path every time you load the NLM, type the following command, replacing *servername:path* with the name of the server and the path to the NLMs:

SEARCH ADD *servername:path*

If the NLM uses a message file of a language other than English, set up the language before loading the NLM, using the LANGUAGE command, as shown here:

LANGUAGE *xx*

replacing *xx* with a language number that you can obtain by typing **LANGUAGE LIST** at the console. For example, the language number for Latin American Spanish is 14, so you would type **LANGUAGE 14** to load support for that language. You can also change the keyboard type used at the console from the U.S. English default. Type **LOAD KEYB** and then pick a different keyboard type from the list that appears.

To see the modules that have been loaded on the server, type **M**—the alias for the **MODULES** command—at the server prompt. Note the various colors of text displayed on the server screen when loading the server software. These colors each have a specific meaning:

- **BLUE**   These are NLMs loaded from a hard-coded internal list that is called when SERVER.EXE executes.

- **RED**   These are NLMs bound in SERVER.EXE but loaded from the startup partition at C:\NWSERVER.

- **PURPLE**   These are NLMs that are autoloaded by another NLM. Examples include LONG.NAM, CLIB, and STREAMS. They are purple during the initial load but may be displayed as red when listed using the M command.

- **WHITE**   These are NLMs loaded from the Novell Configuration file, from any .NCF files (e.g., AUTOEXEC.NCF or STARTUP.NCF), or from the server console prompt.

- **YELLOW**   These are informational messages that refer to symbol information about the module being loaded.

- **GREEN**   These are informational messages about the modules being loaded.

Installing Support for JAVA Applications on the Server

NetWare 5 supports the execution of applications written in Java on the server itself. It provides a graphical user interface (GUI) for applications that require user interaction through a mouse and a graphical display. The GUI support on NetWare 5 is provided by an implementation of X-Windows. With NetWare 5, you can dynamically load and unload the Java GUI support. GUI support on the server can be loaded in one of two ways. The first way is to type **STARTX.NCF** at the server console prompt. This will automatically load the JAVA.NLM and the mouse and video class drivers. The second way is by loading a Java class or applet that requires GUI support.

NetWare 5 supports applications written using the Java AWT or Java Foundation Class. In order to run these applications, the server must have a minimum of 128MB of memory. The mouse can be either a serial mouse or a PS/2 mouse that conforms to the Microsoft Mouse protocol. The video card must conform to the Video Emulation Standards Association (VESA) specification 1.2 or later. NetWare 5 will automatically detect your mouse and video during the installation of the server software. If you change them or need to redetect them, type **VESA_RSP** at the server console prompt.

Java applications exist as either Java classes or Java applets. A Java class is a compiled program that runs in a Java Virtual Machine (JVM). It is very similar to an NLM written in the C language. A Java applet is a compiled program designed to function within a Java-compatible browser. The JAVA.NLM is a port of the JavaSoft JVM interpreter for Java classes. Java class names are case-sensitive and require long name support. To load the JVM on the server, type this command at the console prompt:

```
[LOAD] JAVA
```

To run a Java class from the console prompt, type the following command:

[LOAD] JAVA [*–options*] *path_to_Java_class*

To view a list of the available run-time options when starting a Java class, type the following command at the server console:

```
[LOAD] JAVA -help
```

NetWare 5 can execute both Java classes and applets. Java applets are executed through an applet viewer on the server. The applet viewer will run any applet that has been defined as part of a Hypertext Markup Language (HTML) document. The applet runs as an application on the NetWare 5 server. To run a Java applet as an application on the server console, enter either of the following commands:

APPLET HTTP://*URL*

or

APPLET *path_to_local_filename_of_HTML_document*

The APPLET console command will only execute the commands contained within the <APPLET> </APPLET> tags within the HTML document. All other HTML code in the document will be ignored.

Installing Name Space Support

As mentioned in Chapter 13 and Chapter 14, you can store files created in non-DOS operating systems on the NetWare server in special *name space* areas. To support these files, you first need to load a name space support module at the server where the files will be stored, and then add the name space to a volume on that server using the ADD NAME SPACE command.

Each name space support you load increases the size of the directory tables on the specified volume. To load name space support, type one of the following commands, depending on the name space support you need. You should also put these commands in the STARTUP.NCF file to load the support the next time the server boots.

```
[LOAD] MAC.NAM
```

for Apple Macintosh support included with NetWare 5, and

```
[LOAD] NFS.NAM
```

for UNIX File System included with NetWare 5.

After loading the name space module, you need to add the name space to a volume. Do this with the ADD NAME SPACE command. You specify the name space to add and the name of the volume you want to add it to, using the following form:

ADD NAME SPACE *name* TO *volume*

Here, *name* is the name of the name space and *volume* is the name of the volume you want to add the name space to. For example, the following command adds Macintosh name space support to a volume called MACVOL:

```
ADD NAME SPACE MAC TO MACVOL
```

You don't need to include the ADD NAME SPACE command in the AUTOEXEC.NCF file. Once you execute it, it is permanent. You can list currently loaded name spaces by typing **ADD NAME SPACE** by itself. To see the name spaces attached to a specific volume, type the **VOLUMES** command at the console prompt.

 You may need more memory to support name space volumes.

Installing Uninterruptible Power Supply (UPS) Support

A UPS provides backup power to the server, usually long enough for users to log out of the system, for files to close properly, and for disk caches to write to disk. However, the server must "know" that the UPS is supplying it with backup power. Typically, a cable connection between the UPS and the server provides the signal the server needs to begin its shutdown procedure. UPS_AIO.NLM provides the software that allows the server to monitor the UPS's signals.

Most UPSs connect to the mouse ports on the server. Some models provide more elaborate features and their own server interface cards. If you are installing a UPS that comes with its own interface card, you will have to load the drivers that came with the UPS. Some UPSs come with their own NLMs. Copy the NLMs to the SYS:SYSTEM directory on the server; then follow the instructions in the UPS manual.

To install a UPS, execute the LOAD UPS_AIO command, as shown next, or put the command in the AUTOEXEC.NCF file. Note that the command should be typed as one continued line. The command is a long one that will automatically wrap at the server console prompt.

[LOAD] UPS_AIO DOWNTIME=*number* MSGDELAY=*number*
MSGINTERVAL=*number* DRIVERTYPE=*number*
BOARD=*number* PORT=*number* SIGNALHIGH

Here are the replacement values for the parameters in the LOAD UPS_AIO command:

- **DOWNTIME=*number***   Replace *number* with the amount of time to run on the battery before the system shuts down. If a low battery condition occurs before this time elapses, an immediate shutdown will occur. This value defaults to 300 seconds.

NetWare Planning
and Installation

- **MSGDELAY=*number*** Replace *number* with an elapsed time value before a broadcast message is sent to all users connected to the server. The default value is 5 seconds.

- **MSGINTERVAL=*number*** Replace *number* with the time interval to be used between broadcast messages to all connected users. The default value is 30 seconds.

- **DRIVERTYPE=*number*** Replace *number* with the AIO device driver type. The supported values are 1, 2, and 3. The default value is 1, which represents the AIOCOMX driver. Other drivers may be supported by other driver type values. See your UPS driver documentation.

- **BOARD=*number*** Replace *number* with the AIO board number. To determine the board number, read the driver information when the AIOCOMX driver is loaded. The default is 0.

- **PORT=*number*** Replace *number* with the port number. The supported values are determined by the driver manufacturer. To determine the port and board number, read the driver information that appears when the AIOCOMX driver is loaded.

- **SIGNALHIGH** This parameter is used to change to signaling state used by the UPS on the interface leads. Because most UPSs use low values, this value can be eliminated in the command. The default is the low signal value.

Installing a Remote Console Utility at the Server

NetWare 5 provides two remote console utilities that allow you to use a workstation as a server console. The first one is a DOS-based utility. The second one is a Java-based utility. Remote consoles allow authorized users to execute console commands from a location other than the server's console. Remote consoles simplify the management of servers that are scattered throughout an organization. To determine which utility best fits your needs, refer to Table 15-1.

DOS-Based Remote Console Utility

If you want to monitor and maintain a NetWare server from a remote workstation using the DOS-based utility, you'll need to install REMOTE.NLM.

By connecting a workstation to a server with a direct serial connection, you can maintain a workstation-type logon session with the server, even if the network fails.

There are two basic steps to installing the remote console software:

1. Install the REMOTE.NLM module and associated NLMs at each server you want to manage from an administrative workstation.

Function	DOS-Based	Java-Based
Use console commands	Yes	Yes
Scan directories and edit files	Yes	Yes
Transfer files to the server	Yes	No
Control the server using an IP connection	No	Yes
Control another server from the server console	No	Yes
Stop or start a server	Yes	Yes
Install or upgrade NetWare operating system	Yes	No

Table 15-1. *A comparison of DOS-based and Java-based remote console utilities*

2. At the administrative workstation, execute RCONSOLE.EXE, which is located in the SYS:SYSTEM directory of the server you are logged into.

Once the connection is made, you see a screen that looks just like the console at the server. In fact, the console screen at the server duplicates your workstation screen as you issue commands and display information. There are three possible remote console setups:

- **Network link** This setup runs the remote console from a workstation on the network, using the network communication protocol.
- **Modem link** This setup manages the console from a workstation linked by modems over a telephone line. This method has the advantage of letting you access the server even if the network cabling fails. It also gives you the freedom to travel.
- **Cable link** This setup lets you directly connect a workstation to the server using a null-modem cable so you can manage the server in case the normal administrative workstation attached to the network goes down.

You can place the commands that load remote console support in the server's AUTOEXEC.NCF file. You encode the required password and store it in this file so that the server will start and load remote support without asking for the password. When the password is encoded, you will get a keyword to use to access the console.

As previously mentioned, before you can move to your administrator workstation and use the remote console software, you must first load the support modules at the servers. The next two sections describe how to do this for network-attached workstations and for modem-attached workstations.

NETWORK-ATTACHED WORKSTATION SETUP   This section describes how to set up the remote console support at the server if you plan to use a network-attached workstation. Refer to the next section for modem-attached or directly attached workstations. Perform these steps at each server you want to manage remotely:

1. Type the following command to load the REMOTE module:

     [LOAD] *path*\REMOTE *password*

    where *path* is the drive or directory where REMOTE.NLM can be found if it is not in the SYS:SYSTEM directory, and *password* is the keyword that lets you access the console from a workstation. You will be asked for a password if you do not specify it in this command.

2. Now type the following command to load the RSPX remote SPX support module, replacing *path* with the drive or directory where RSPX.NLM can be found if it is not in the SYS:SYSTEM directory:

     path\RSPX

3. (Optional) NetWare 5 remote software implements packet signatures to prevent forgery of packets. It is not compatible with NetWare 3.11. If you run NetWare 3.11, set packet signatures OFF when you load RSPX. To set packet signatures OFF, type **RSPX SIGNATURES OFF**.

The remote console is now ready for you to run at a network-attached workstation.

REMOTE MODEM SETUP   This section describes how to set up remote console support in the server if you plan to manage the console from a modem-attached remote workstation. Note that you can also use this method if you want to use a workstation that is attached to the server via a null-modem cable.

1. Type the following command to load the REMOTE module:

     path\REMOTE *password*

    where *path* is the drive or directory where REMOTE.NLM can be found if it is not in the SYS:SYSTEM directory, and *password* is the keyword that lets you access the console from a workstation. You will be asked for a password if you do not specify it in this command.

2. Load the NetWare communications port interface, the communications board driver, and the asynchronous communications NLM by typing the following commands:

```
[LOAD] AIO
[LOAD] AIOCOMX
[LOAD] RS232
```

 AIOCOMX is a generic driver supplied by Novell, but you might need to obtain a specific communication driver from the vendor of your serial interface card and copy it into the SYS:SYSTEM directory of the server.

NetWare 5 provides the capability to interact directly with the communications port and the attached modem. With these commands, you can query the modem, issue commands, and perform functions as if connected to the modem with a terminal emulator program. The various commands are as follows:

- **RS232**   This command is used to view the current settings of the communications port.
- **MODEM** *modem_command*   This command is used to send commands directly to the attached modem.
- **MODEM** *@filename*   This command directs the server to read the file specified in *filename* for the specific modem commands.

CALLBACK SUPPORT   A callback feature ensures that the user calling in is at a site authorized to access the network. It checks the caller's ID against a list of phone numbers and then calls the user back at that site. Intruders calling from an unauthorized site will not be able to access the network. To use this feature, you need to create a callback file that contains a list of phone numbers authorized to call into the network. Use a text editor such as EDIT.NLM to create the file. Name it **CALLBACK.LST** and store it in the SYS:SYSTEM directory. Type an authorized phone number on each line of the file.

STARTING REMOTE CONSOLE FROM AUTOEXEC.NCF   You can place any of the commands listed in the previous sections in the AUTOEXEC.NCF file, but you must first encrypt the password for security reasons. The password is replaced by an encrypted keyword in the file. Follow the procedure listed next, which assumes you have already loaded REMOTE.NLM at the server.

1. Type the following command to encrypt the password:

```
REMOTE ENCRYPT
```

2. Type in the password you want to use to start the remote console session.

3. An encrypted keyword appears at the console. Write down this keyword.

NetWare Planning
and Installation

4. Edit the AUTOEXEC.NCF file by using EDIT.NLM. Add the following line to the file to load REMOTE.NLM, replacing *key* with the keyword you wrote down in step 3:

```
[LOAD] REMOTE —E key
```

Java-Based Remote Console Utility

The Java-based remote console has two connection requirements. You must have an IP connection to the network and be logged into a NetWare 5 server. The remote console utility is referred to as RConsoleJ. It consists of two primary components. A third component is necessary when managing an IPX server remotely. These components are as follows:

- RConsoleJ running on a client or server
- Agent software running on the target server
- Proxy software running on a proxy server if the target server uses the IPX protocol to communicate

Note *The proxy server must have both the IP and IPX protocols loaded.*

This section describes how to set up the remote console support at the server. Perform these steps at each server you want to manage remotely:

1. If the target server is using the IPX communications protocol, you must type the following command at the console prompt:

```
[LOAD] SPXS
```

2. At the server console prompt, type this command:

```
[LOAD] RCONAG6
```

You will be prompted to enter the password that will be used to establish a remote console session. This will be the password used by network administrators to access the target server.

3. You will be prompted to enter a TCP port number. This is the TCP port number on which RCONAG6 will listen for either RConsoleJ or a proxy server. The default port number is 2034. If the server communicates using only the IPX protocol, enter −1 to disable TCP listening. If the server is using a dynamically assigned port number, enter "0" to enable listening.

4. Enter the SPX port number on which RCONAG6 will listen for a proxy server. The default port number is 16800. If the server communicates using the IP protocol only, enter −1 to disable SPX listening. If the server is using a dynamically assigned port number, enter 0 to enable listening.

PREPARING A PROXY SERVER   If the target server communicates using the IPX protocol, a proxy server must be established, which will translate between the IP and IPX protocols. The steps necessary to establish a proxy server are as follows:

1. If the target server communicates using only the IPX protocol, type the following command at the server console prompt:

   `[LOAD] SPXS`

2. Type the following command to enable the proxy capabilities on the server:

   `[LOAD] RCONPRXY`

You will be prompted for a TCP port number on which RCONPRXY will listen for RConsoleJ. The default TCP port number is 2035. If the server is listening over a dynamically assigned port number, enter **0** to enable listening. RConsoleJ can communicate with a target server running the IPX protocol after the proxy server is running.

RUNNING RCONSOLEJ FROM A NOVELL CLIENT   There are two ways in which RConsoleJ can be run on a workstation. The first way is by starting the utility from within the NetWare Administrator utility (NWADMIN32). To do this from the main menu, select TOOLS | Pure IP Remote Console. The second way can be invoked on a Windows 95/98 or NT workstation. The following steps are required:

1. Ensure that you have a drive mapped to the root of the SYS volume on the NetWare 5 server.

2. In the Windows Start | Run dialog box, run RCONJ.EXE from the PUBLIC directory on the SYS volume.

3. Select a remote server from the list and enter the appropriate password.

4. If the target server is running only the IP protocol, enter either the DNS name or the IP address of the target server. If the target server is running only the IPX protocol, enter either the name or the IPX address of the target server, separated by a colon, as follows:

   IPX_Address:xxxxxxxxxxx

5. When prompted for the password, enter the password you entered when RCONAG6 was loaded.

6. If you entered a nondefault TCP port number or are using a proxy server, you must click the ADVANCED tab. Enter the TCP port number you used when you loaded RCONAG6 on the target server. Skip this step if you are using a proxy server.

7. Enter the SPX port number you used when you loaded RCONAG6 on the target server. If you are connecting to an IPX-only target server, check the Connect Through Proxy check box.

8. When prompted for the server address, enter the proxy server's DNS name or the proxy server's IP address. Remember, DNS names are case-sensitive.

9. Enter the proxy server's TCP port number in the Port Number field. Set the Agent Protocol to SPX if the target server communicates using the IPX protocol.

10. Click the connect box.

Graphical screens on the target server are not displayed on the remote console. If a graphical screen is displayed on the target server, the system console screen will be displayed on the remote console. If someone at the target server switches the screen to a graphical screen, the screen will not be reflected to the remote console.

RUNNING RCONSOLEJ ON A NETWARE 5 SERVER   RConsoleJ can be started in two different ways on a NetWare 5 server. The only requirement is that you have an IP connection to the network. To start RConsoleJ from the ConsoleOne utility, select MyServer | Tools | RConsoleJ. To start it from the console server prompt, follow these steps:

1. Type **RCONJ.NCF** at the server console.

2. Click on Remote Servers and select a server from the displayed list.

3. Enter the appropriate password that was entered when you started RCONAG6 on the target server. If the requested target server does not show up in the displayed list, you can enter the address manually.

4. Enter either the DNS name or the IP address of the target server if you are connecting to an IP-based server.

5. Enter the IPX address for a target server that is running only the IPX protocol and select the Connect Through Proxy option.

STARTING RCONSOLEJ FROM AUTOEXEC.NCF   You can place any of the commands listed in the previous sections in the AUTOEXEC.NCF file, but you must first encrypt the password for security reasons. The password is replaced by an encrypted keyword in the file. Use the following procedure:

1. Type the following command to encrypt the password:

```
[LOAD] RCONAG6 ENCRYPT
```

2. Type in the password you want to use to start the remote console session and enter the required port information.

3. An encrypted keyword appears at the console. Write down this keyword. The system will prompt you with a message asking if the LOAD CONAG6 command should be written to the SYS:\SYSTEM\LDRCONAG.NCF file. To include the command with the encrypted password, enter **YES**.

4. Edit the AUTOEXEC.NCF file by using EDIT.NLM. Add the following line to the file to load LDRCONAG:

```
LDRCONAG.NCF
```

Securing the Server

In most cases, you set up a server and then lock it in a secure room or closet and return to your office to manage it from your desktop administrative workstation. Before you leave the server, you must secure it as described here. Type the following command at the server console prompt to set some preliminary console security measures:

```
SECURE CONSOLE
```

This command does the following:

- It prevents someone from loading an NLM not located on the SYS:SYSTEM directory of the server. This prevents intruders from walking up to a server and loading an NLM from diskette or running an NLM if they are accessing the server from a remote console.

- It prevents intruders from accessing the operating system debugger, which they could use to look at data on the server.

- It prevents intruders from changing the date and time at the server, which they might want to do to bypass time restrictions for login or to affect the time recorded in server accounting logs. Only users with Console Operator rights can change the date and time.

 Note *Put the SECURE CONSOLE command in your AUTOEXEC.NCF file so it loads every time the server starts.*

To establish password-only access to the console and fully protect it from intruders, you can lock the server console and display a screen saver. The screen saver and the console locking features were formerly part of the MONITOR.NLM in earlier NetWare products. The new SCRSAVER utility protects the console by using the stronger security of NDS authentication. Type the following command to invoke the SCRSAVER utility:

SCRSAVER [*option*][*;option*][*;option*][…]

The available options for the SCRSAVER command are as follows:

- **(No parameters)**   Sets the configuration to the default values (AUTO CLEAR DELAY=60 seconds, ENABLE, ENABLE AUTO CLEAR, and ENABLE LOCK)
- **ACTIVATE**   Overrides the delay interval and activates the screen saver immediately
- **AUTO CLEAR DELAY**   Sets the number of seconds to wait before clearing the unlock dialog box
- **DELAY**   Sets the number of seconds to wait before activating the screen saver. The range is from 1 to 7,000 seconds (default is 600 seconds)
- **DISABLE**   Disables the screen saver and prevents it from activating
- **DISABLE AUTO CLEAR**   Disables the automatic clearing of the unlock dialog box
- **DISABLE LOCK**   Disables the console lock
- **ENABLE**   Enables the screen saver
- **ENABLE AUTO CLEAR**   Enables the automatic clearing of the unlock dialog box after the specified number of seconds of keyboard inactivity have elapsed
- **NO PASSWORD**   Unlocks the console without requiring a password
- **STATUS**   Displays the current status of the screen save feature and command options

Shutting Down the Server

If you need to shut down the server for maintenance or other reasons, read through this section. Shutting down a server is a simple one-step process. Never simply turn the server off without following this step. Type the following command:

```
DOWN
```

The DOWN command properly closes the filing systems and, most importantly, saves data in cache memory to disk. The directory and file allocation tables are also properly updated. Note that the file system of a server that has been shut down is no longer available for network use, but the file server is still available as a network node and can handle network traffic. Also, from the server console, you can issue console commands. The EXIT command is now integrated with the DOWN command. Therefore, it is no longer necessary to issue a separate EXIT command.

Using Remote Console

After you access the server console by using one of the remote console utilities, you can access the server console as if you were sitting at the console itself.

Remember that all activities performed at the remote console are mirrored on the screen of the file server. If you lock the file server's console, the remote console locks as well, so you'll need to physically lock the server's keyboard or secure the server system in a safe place to prevent users from accessing the console or viewing your activities.

RConsoleJ Keyboard Shortcuts

- **ALT-F1**   Access the drop-down list of target server console screens
- **ALT-F2**   Cycle forward through the target server screens
- **ALT-F3**   Cycle backward through the target server screens

Remote Console Keyboard Shortcuts

The following keys are available in the remote console session:

- **ALT-F1**   Access the Remote Console Available Options menu
- **ALT-F2**   Exit Remote Console
- **ALT-F3**   Cycle backward through the target server screens
- **ALT-F4**   Cycle forward through the target server screens
- **ALT-F5**   Show the current workstation address

You access the Remote Console Available Options menu, shown here, by pressing ALT-F1:

```
                  Available Options

Select A Screen To View
Directory Scan
Transfer Files To Server
Invoke Operating System Shell
End Remote Session With Server
Resume Remote Session With Server (ESC)
Workstation Address
Configure Keystroke Buffering
```

The options on this menu are described next.

SELECT A SCREEN TO VIEW   When you choose the Select A Screen To View option, a list of available screens appears. If you loaded MONITOR at the console,

MONITOR SCREEN and SYSTEM CONSOLE appear in the Available Screens menu. To enter console commands, select SYSTEM CONSOLE. The console colon (:) prompt appears so that you can execute any console command as you normally would at the file server. Of course, you wouldn't want to dismount volumes, down the server, or make other changes that would affect network operations unless they are vital and you have warned network users.

DIRECTORY SCAN Select the Directory Scan option to view directories and files on the file server. Type the drive letter and/or path of the directory you want to view. You can use wildcard characters to list specific files, the same way you would use them with the DOS DIR command. Press the PAGEUP and PAGEDOWN keys to scan long lists.

TRANSFER FILES TO SERVER Select the Transfer Files To Server option to transfer files from a workstation drive to any drive on the server. Two menus appear. The first asks for the source files, and the second asks for the destination directory on the server. As with the DOS COPY command, you can use wildcard characters to specify groups of files. Make sure your remote session is secure. Unauthorized users could transfer viruses or cause damage to the file system by using the file transfer feature.

INVOKE OPERATING SYSTEM SHELL Select the Invoke Operating System Shell option to temporarily return to the operating system prompt. You can then execute DOS commands on local drives or network drives. Because of the amount of conventional memory used by Remote Console and the secondary environment it invokes, you might not be able to run some utilities and programs.

END REMOTE SESSION WITH SERVER Select End Remote Session With Server to end a remote console session. You are returned to the Available Servers menu, where you can select another file server or press the ESC key to return to DOS.

RESUME REMOTE SESSION WITH SERVER The Resume Remote Session With Server option simply removes the Remote Console menu and returns you to the console prompt.

WORKSTATION ADDRESS Select the Workstation Address option to display the network address of your current workstation.

CONFIGURE KEYSTROKE BUFFERING This option lets you configure how keystrokes are sent to the server and is useful if more than one user is accessing the server with a remote console.

NetWare 5 Server Console Commands and Utilities

You can run the following commands if you are seated at the NetWare server console or if you are attached to it with a remote console link as discussed in the last section. All the commands described here provide useful information about the server, and some let you change its settings.

Viewing Server Information

Console commands that display useful information about a server are listed here in alphabetical order. Additional information on these commands is available in the NetWare 5 documentation.

ABORT REMIRROR   This command stops the remirroring process on a logical partition.

ADD NAME SPACE   This command allows the server to store non-DOS files on a NetWare volume.

ALERT   This command manages NetWare alerts. You can enable or disable the logging and display of specific events, limit the amount of information displayed, and control other aspects of alert messages.

ALIAS   This command allows you to use a user-defined keyword to represent another command string.

ATCON   This command monitors the activity of AppleTalk network segments.

ATMCON   This command allows you to verify the configuration of the AppleTalk router and the connectivity to the rest of the AppleTalk network.

BIND   This command links a communications protocol to a network board and its LAN driver.

CAPITRCE   This command debugs a problem with the PPP protocol over an ISDN connection.

CDROM   This command allows a CD-ROM to function as a Novell Storage Services (NSS) volume. This version replaces the version found in earlier NetWare releases. The previous version of CDROM is now named CDINST.

CHARSET   This command changes the code page currently in use by the NetWare 5 server.

CLEAR STATION   This command clears a client workstation connection to the server.

CLS   This command clears the console screen and moves the console prompt to the top of the screen.

CONFIG   This command displays useful information about the server, such as its name, protocol configuration, LAN configuration, and NDS information, as shown in Figure 15-1.

CONLOG   This command captures all console messages generated while CONLOG is loaded to a log file. This includes NDS messages, the console output of all commands executed, and messages that announce remote console connections and disconnections.

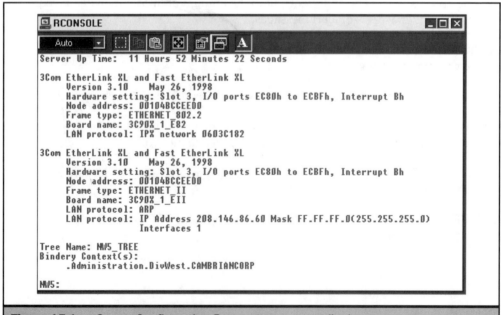

Figure 15-1.   *Server Configuration Parameters screen display*

CONSOLEONE   This command invokes the graphical Java application for centrally managing and administering all network resources.

CPUCHECK   This command displays per-processor information such as processor number, processor clock speed (MHz), processor ID, processor version, amount of L1 and L2 cache, and the current processor revision number.

DISABLE LOGIN   This command prevents users from logging into the server.

DISMOUNT   This command dismounts a mounted volume on the server.

DISPLAY ENVIRONMENT   This command displays the current search paths and current values of the settable server parameters, along with their default values and the range of valid values.

DISPLAY INTERRUPTS   This command displays the currently assigned hardware interrupts, interrupt handlers, and interrupt statistics.

DISPLAY MODIFIED ENVIRONMENT   This command displays all server parameter settings that have been modified from their default values.

DISPLAY NETWORKS   This command lists all networks and assigned network numbers that the server's internal router recognizes.

DISPLAY PROCESSORS   This command displays the status of all processors installed in the server.

DISPLAY SERVERS   This command displays a list of all IPX servers and services being advertised by Service Advertising Protocol (SAP) packets on the network.

DOWN   This command executes an orderly shutdown of the server. It now incorporates the EXIT command.

DSDIAG   This command documents the current NDS configuration, checks the health of the NDS tree, and diagnoses or pinpoint problems with NDS.

DSMAINT   This command saves NDS information, restores NDS information, or restores server information after a hardware failure.

DSMERGE   This command merges two separate NDS trees into one tree.

DSREPAIR   This command repairs and corrects problems in the NDS database such as record, schema, bindery object, and external reference problems.

NetWare Planning
and Installation

EDIT This command invokes a text editor that can create or modify a text file on either the DOS partition or a NetWare partition. The file size cannot exceed 8K.

ENABLE LOGIN This command re-enables the login function for the server.

ENABLE TTS This command starts the Transaction Tracking System (TTS) software on the server. Use this command only if TTS has been disabled.

FILTCFG This command sets up and configures filters for the IPX, TCP/IP, and AppleTalk protocols.

FRCON This command lets you view the Link/Frame Relay interface configuration and statistical information.

FRTRACE This command invokes the Frame Relay Trace utility.

HELP This command lets you view the syntax of a console command, including a brief description and an example.

INETCFG This command sets up and customizes the internetworking configuration for the IPX, IP, and AppleTalk protocols.

INITIALIZE SYSTEM This command enables the multiprotocol router configuration by executing all commands in the NETINFO.CFG file. Executing this command on a server that has already been initialized may produce errors.

IPCU This command moves or copies an existing NetWare volume to a Novell Storage Services (NSS) volume.

IPXCON This command invokes the IPX monitor. It is used to troubleshoot and monitor IPX routers and network segments, view the status of an IPX router or network segment, view all paths through which IPX packets can flow, and locate all active IPX routers on the network.

IPXPING This command allows you to check the IPX connectivity of workstations and servers on the network.

IPXS This command provides the IPX protocol to NLMs that require STREAMS-based IPX. If you don't specify a filename when loading the command, the parameters defined in the IPSPX.CFG are used.

JAVA This command loads the Java Virtual Machine (JVM) at the server and allows Java-based applications and applets, including multithreaded applications and applications that use a graphical interface, to run on the server.

JEDITOR This command invokes a graphical Java application for editing text files.

KEYB This command changes the console keyboard language on the server. To use this command, first unload KEYB and then reload it using the appropriate selection.

LANGUAGE This command sets the console language for subsequently loaded modules.

LIST DEVICES This command displays a list of storage devices on the server and registers new devices with the server's Media Manager database.

LIST STORAGE ADAPTERS This command displays a list of registered storage adapters and the devices they drive. The information is read from the Media Manager database.

LIST STORAGE DEVICE BINDINGS This command displays a list of all Custom Device Modules (CDMs) bound to a particular device.

LOAD This command is optional unless a .NCF file exists with the same name as the module being loaded. This command can load application modules in their own protected memory space if desired. It can also be used at a workstation running the Novell client to load client modules.

MAGAZINE This command responds to screen prompts that refer to media magazines.

MEDIA This command responds to screen prompts that refer to media magazines.

MEMORY This command displays the total amount of installed memory that the operating system can address. If you have loaded a memory manager, such as HIMEM.SYS, the operating system will not be able to access memory beyond 64MB.

MEMORY MAP This command displays the amount of memory allocated to DOS and to the server, in bytes.

MIRROR STATUS This command displays the status of all mirrored disk partitions and the percentage of mirrored data on each partition.

MODULES This command displays a list of all currently loaded modules on the server. Color coding, as defined at the beginning of this chapter, indicates the module's functional group. You can use an asterisk as a wildcard to display selected modules. For example, the command MODULES DS* will display all modules currently loaded whose first two characters are DS.

NetWare Planning and Installation

MONITOR This command invokes the MONITOR utility, which is described later in this chapter.

MOUNT This command is used to make a volume available to network users.

NAME This command displays the name of the server.

NCMCON This command invokes the Novell Configuration Manager Console (NCMCON) at the server to control and monitor PCI Hot Plug devices.

NCS DEBUG This command displays and saves a record of all NCS port activity in an ASCII file named NCSTRACE.LOG in the SYS:SYSTEM directory. The file size is limited to 800K.

NIASCFG This command enables you to configure the Novell Internet Access Server (NIAS) software. You can set up and customize your configurations for PPP, IPX, IP, AppleTalk, and the Source Route Bridge (SRB).

NPRINTER This command is used for supporting legacy, queue-based print services.

NSS This command is used to unload NSS, display NSS module or volume information, check NSS volume statistics, change NSS caching, and modify other NSS parameters.

NWCCON This command invokes a utility to configure remote access options.

NWCONFIG This command is used to modify the server's configuration, perform server maintenance operations, and install additional products. This is the new name for the NetWare 4.*x* install utility.

NWCRPAIR This command invokes a troubleshooting utility that recovers corrupted Btrieve files.

NWCSTAT This command displays the remote access status.

ORBCMD This command enables the Novell Object Request Broker (ORB) on the server. This is necessary to develop and distribute CORBA-compliant distributed object applications.

PING This command sends an ICMP echo request to an IP node on the network.

PPPCON This command displays the Point-to-Point Protocol (PPP) interface configuration and statistical information.

PPPRNCON   This command invokes the utility to configure Point-to-Point Protocol Remote Node Services (PPPRNS) options.

PPPTRACE   This command allows you to debug PPP data link problems. It fully decodes and displays PPP exchanges.

PROTECT   This command loads an NLM program into a protected address space.

PROTECTION   This command displays a list of protected address spaces and allows you to add or remove restart functionality from an existing address space.

PROTOCOL   This command displays the registered protocols on the server and allows you to register new protocols and frame types.

PSERVER   This command is used with legacy, queue-based print services.

QMAN NEW   This command creates the queues needed for the backup program.

RCONAG6   This command allows console access by using the RConsoleJ utility.

RCONPRXY   This command creates an RConsoleJ proxy server on a NetWare 5 server. It allows access to target servers using the IPX protocol.

RCONSOLEJ   This command allows a server to gain access to a local or remote target server's console through an IP connection.

REBUILD   This command recovers corrupted Novell Storage Services (NSS) volumes.

REGISTER MEMORY   This command configures the operating system to recognize installed memory above the amount of memory automatically registered. NetWare 5 can address up to 4GB of memory.

REINITIALIZE SYSTEM   This command enables configuration changes made since commands in the NETINFO.CFG file were executed.

REMIRROR PARTITION   This command starts the remirroring process of a logical partition.

REMOTE   This command allows remote access to the server from a workstation.

REMOVE NETWORK ADAPTER   This command unloads one LAN driver when the LAN driver has been loaded multiple times to support multiple boards.

REMOVE NETWORK INTERFACE   This command unloads one frame type when multiple frame types are loaded with one LAN driver.

REMOVE STORAGE ADAPTER   This command removes one instance of a storage driver.

RESET ENVIRONMENT   This command lists all server parameters with the option of resetting the current values to their defaults.

RESET NETWORK ADAPTER   This command resets a network adapter.

RESET NETWORK INTERFACE   This command restarts a logical board that has been shut down using the SHUTDOWN NETWORK INTERFACE command.

RESET ROUTER   This command resets the router table in a file server.

RESTART SERVER   This command brings down the server and then restarts it.

ROUTE   This command enables NetWare frame packets to pass through IBM-compatible source route bridges on a token ring cabling system.

RS232   This command sets up a communication port for remote management over a modem or a null-modem cable.

RSPX   This command loads the SPX driver for REMOTE and advertises the server to workstations.

SBON   This command invokes the backup software for the server. It can be used to back up the server or attached workstations.

SCAN ALL   This command scans all LUNs of all SCSI adapters in the server or all LUNs associated with a designated SCSI adapter.

SCAN FOR NEW DEVICES   This command forces a scan on LUN0 of all SCSI adapters and registers new devices with the Media Manager so that they are available to the operating system.

SCRSAVER   This command locks the server console.

SEARCH   This command tells the server where to look for NLM and NCF files. It is also used to add and delete search paths to the current search path.

SECURE CONSOLE   This command increases network security, as described in this chapter.

SET   This command allows you to view and configure various operating system parameters.

SHUTDOWN NETWORK INTERFACE   This command shuts down a logical board without removing its resources.

SPEED   This command displays a rating of the server's processor speed, along with some comparable values. A 50MHz 80486 processor will have a speed of 1370, a 100MHz Pentium processor will have a speed of 5490, and a 400MHz Pentium II processor will have a speed of 30070.

SPFCON   This command enables you to monitor Sequenced Packet Exchange (SPX) spoofing statistics.

SPXCONFG   This command configures certain SPX parameters.

SPXS   This command provides STREAMS-based SPX protocol services.

START PROCESSORS   This command starts one or more processors when the operating system is running on a multiprocessor computer.

STATICON   This command opens a connection to a remote IPX router and allows you to configure static routes and services at each end of the connection.

STOP PROCESSORS   This command stops one or more secondary processors in a multiprocessor computer.

SWAP   This command displays information about swap files and allows you to add or delete swap files, and to specify parameters of the swap files.

TCPCON   This command invokes a utility that allows you to monitor activity in the TCP/IP segments of your network.

TECHWALK   This command walks through the server configuration parameters and generates a report for the user.

TIME   This command displays the server's current date and time, daylight saving time status, and time synchronization information.

TIMESYNC   This command monitors the time on a server to ensure that the time reported by all servers across the network is consistent and synchronized.

TPING   This command sends an ICMP echo request packet to the IP target node. If it does not receive a reply from the target node, the request is resent a specific number of times. When the requester receives a reply, it stops sending requests and displays a message that the target node is reachable.

TRACK OFF   This command prevents the server console from displaying the RIP Tracking Screen.

TRACK ON   This command allows the server console to display the RIP Tracking Screen.

UNBIND   This command can be used to disable communications on a specific board or remove a communication protocol from the LAN driver of a network board.

UNICON   This command invokes the management utility for Print Services for UNIX and FTP services.

UNLOAD   This command is used to unload a previously loaded module.

UPS_AIO   This command enables an Uninterruptible Power Supply (UPS) to be connected to the server through a serial port.

VIEW   This command allows you to view a file from the server console.

VOLUME   This command displays a list of volumes mounted on the server.

VREPAIR   This command is used to correct volume problems and remove name space entries on Directory Entry Tables for non-NSS volumes.

X25CON   This command accesses the interface configuration and statistical information for all X.25 interfaces reported by the specified host.

X25DISP   This command provides a way to analyze the output of the X25TRACE utility.

XLOG   This command is used to help diagnose ISDN-related connection problems with Eicon Technology ISDN adapters.

Controlling Server Access

You can use the following commands to control access to the server:

```
DISABLE LOGIN
ENABLE LOGIN
CLEAR STATION
```

Use the CLEAR STATION command to remove a specific node connection to the network. Type **NLIST USER /A /B** at the workstation to determine the node's connection number, and then type **CLEAR STATION** *x*, where *x* is the node number.

Before you clear a station connection, down the server, or disable login, you might want to send messages to users with the following commands:

- **BROADCAST**   To send a message to all users, type this command followed by the message you want to send. For example,

  BROADCAST Please log out as soon as possible. We are downing ADMIN-SERVER in 30 minutes.

- **SEND**   Use this command in the same way you use BROADCAST.

 Users cannot block BROADCAST messages from appearing on their screen, but they can block SEND messages.

The NWCONFIG Utility

You can make changes to the NetWare operating system, even after NetWare has been installed. For example, you can modify the size of volumes or change their names. You can also expand a volume by adding a drive, and then run NWCONFIG to partition it and add it to an existing volume.

To take a look at NWCONFIG's maintenance features, type the following at the server console:

```
[LOAD] NWCONFIG
```

In a moment, the INSTALL configuration options menu appears, as shown here:

```
                        Configuration Options
    Driver Options          (load/unload disk and network drivers)
    Standard Disk Options    (configure NetWare partitions/volumes)
    NSS Disk Options         (configure NSS storage and volumes)
    License Options          (install or remove licenses)
    Copy Files Options       (install NetWare system files)
    Directory Options        (install NDS)
    NCF files Options        (create/edit server startup files)
    Multi CPU Options        (install/uninstall SMP)
    Product Options          (other optional installation items)
    Exit
```

The options on this menu are discussed next.

DRIVER OPTIONS   Select this option to load a new disk driver after installing a new disk controller, or to change the configuration of an already installed disk driver. You can also select this option to load a new LAN driver after installing a new LAN card, or to change the configuration of an already installed LAN driver.

STANDARD DISK OPTIONS   Select this option to do any of the following:

- Create a new partition on a disk you've just added to the system
- Change the partitioning of an existing disk
- Change the Hot Fix redirection area of an existing disk
- Delete a partition
- Mirror and unmirror partitions
- Test the surface of a disk

You can also use this option to change the volume configuration of existing partitions (doing so destroys data on those volumes), or to allocate the space on a new disk partition to existing or new volumes.

NSS DISK OPTIONS   Select this option to create, view, and rename storage groups and NSS volumes. The Storage option allows you to locate available free space on any disk drives in the network and place them into a pool for NSS to use.

LICENSE OPTIONS   Select this option to install additional licenses on the server so more users can access it.

COPY FILES OPTIONS   Use this option to install or reinstall the NetWare system files.

DIRECTORY OPTIONS   Use this option only when necessary to reinstall Novell Directory Services.

NCF FILES OPTIONS   Choose this option to manually create or edit the NetWare startup files AUTOEXEC.NCF and STARTUP.NCF.

MULTI CPU OPTIONS   Use this option to install a Platform Support Module (PSM) to enable multiprocessing support.

PRODUCT OPTIONS   Choose this option to install additional products on the server.

Monitor Utility

MONITOR.NLM is your window on the performance and reliability of the server. While some of the information MONITOR displays tends to be technical, it provides information that can help you locate the source of server, disk, and LAN problems.

The MONITOR screen is composed of two separate windows, as shown in Figure 15-2. One contains the server's General Information display and the other one contains the Available Options menu. General Information displays statistics about the server, including the following.

Note   *When viewing monitor statistics, you should look at a sustained level and not read the peak values. Try to form a mental chart of the information and think of the average value. In general it is best to form a baseline of the statistic before drawing any conclusions, as the variations can be extensive.*

■ **Processor Utilization**   This displays what percentage of the server's CPU is in use. This number changes as users log in or out and work with applications or files. This value should remain below 80 percent; otherwise, you may need to upgrade the processor or move some processes, applications, or heavy users to another server.

■ **Server Up Time**   The amount of time the server has been up is significant. NetWare adjusts its settings over time to match the load placed on it by workstations and internal processes. The longer the server is up, the more likely the settings will match those required for everyday use. If a server has been up only a few hours or days, operating information displayed is not likely to be representative of your system's normal requirements.

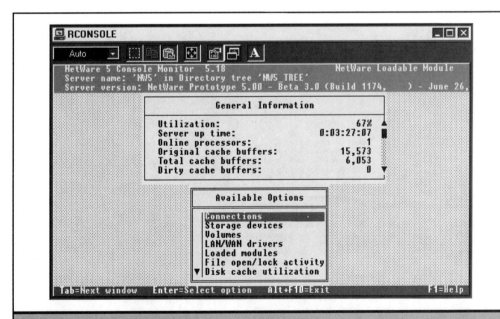

Figure 15-2.   *The MONITOR screen allows you see how well the operating system is functioning*

Checking Server Memory

All the memory in a NetWare server that is not used by NLMs and other processes is used to cache the disk storage system. A large cache improves performance, because information can be obtained from memory, rather than disk. As NLMs are loaded at the server, the amount of memory available for the cache is reduced. You can check whether a reduced cache is affecting performance by checking the cache hits value, as described here:

1. Use the TAB key to change the display, as shown in Figure 15-3.

2. Note the Long Term Cache Hits value.

A cache hit occurs when information is found in the cache and does not have to be read from disk. The cache hits value must be evaluated over time. A new server without any attached workstations will show a high percentage, but you should write this value in a log for future reference. As you add NLMs and users begin to access the server, continue to monitor the cache hit. It should remain at about 90 percent. If it drops below 90 percent, add more RAM to the server or add other servers to take up some of the load.

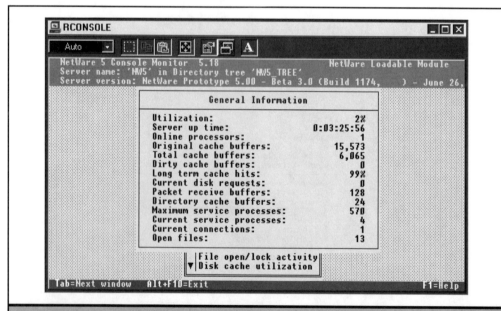

Figure 15-3. *MONITOR screen showing extended general information*

Checking Utilization

After you've loaded NLMs and set other features at the server, you should make sure the server can handle the new processing loads adequately. Start by loading MONITOR as described earlier. In the General Information display, note the Utilization percentage. If it is equal to or greater than 80 percent, one of the loaded modules or other processes may be monopolizing the system.

To investigate further, you can view the utilization of each process. Choose Kernel from the Available Options menu, and then select Applications to view a list of loaded processes and the percentage load that they put on the system. If you locate a module that seems to monopolize the system, you can unload it. However, if the module is necessary, you might need to move it or other modules to another server on the network, or upgrade the existing server with a more powerful processor.

If you choose the Server Parameters option in the Available Options menu, a menu appears from which you can choose other options for changing the parameters of the NetWare 5 operating system. These parameters, shown in Figure 15-4, are discussed in the following sections. You can open any menu option to view a list of possible settings. To get information about a setting, highlight it and press the F1 key. This displays a Help screen that includes a description and information about how you might set the option.

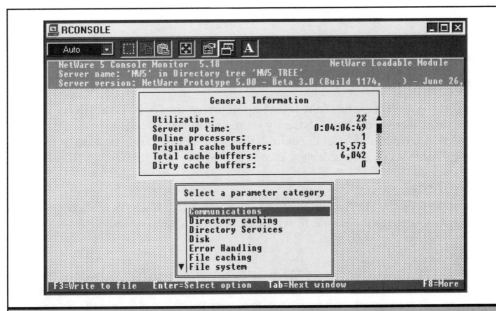

Figure 15-4.   *The Available Parameters selection window*

Communications

The Communications settings allow you to control the size and quantity of the communications buffers in order to improve server performance (by increasing the values), to correct problems, or to free memory for other uses.

Directory Caching

Directory caching ensures that files are easily located by keeping the directory tables in memory. Note that directory caching and file caching must be balanced. If you provide too many directory caches, memory is taken away from file caches, and vice versa. You can check memory and cache statistics with MONITOR and then make changes to the settings in the Directory Caching menu option.

Directory Services

Choose this menu option to set parameters for Novell Directory Services (NDS). In particular, you can set options for tracing NDS events.

Disk

The most important setting on the Disk menu is Enable Disk Read After Write Verify. When this setting is on (the default), data written to disk is checked to make sure it was written correctly. Turning this feature off exposes your data to possible corruption but also almost doubles disk write speed. You can safely set this feature off if your disk controller verifies on its own, as most SCSI drives do.

Error Handling

Choose this option to change settings for the error logs, such as overflow size.

File Caching

The file caching system is one of the most important features of NetWare. It ensures that files are available on a timely basis by keeping the most frequently used information in memory. Most of the default file cache settings are adequate, but you can change some settings by accessing these options.

File System

Use the options on the File System menu to set warnings for low volumes, to control what happens to purged files, and to set file compression parameters.

Locks

Applications may fail to run because they cannot open enough files or because there are not enough record locks. If this is the case, try doubling the four settings in the Locks menu. In some cases, you may need to reduce their values below the default settings. For example, a workstation may continuously request too many resources from the server.

Memory

Memory settings let you adjust the way memory is used in the server.

Miscellaneous

There are a number of miscellaneous settings, some of which enable the display of warning messages. Scan through the options under the menu, watching the Help menus as you go.

■ Set Display Disk Device Alerts on to display activity messages about disk drives, such as when they have been added, activated, deactivated, or shut down. Such messages can help you isolate disk problems.

■ Set Display Lost Interrupt Alerts on to display a message whenever a driver or board makes a request for service that is dropped. These alerts indicate problems with a driver or board.

■ Set Display Spurious Interrupt Alerts on to display alerts whenever one board creates an interrupt that is defined for another device. A board that creates these messages typically must be replaced.

NCP

Settings on this menu control the NetWare Core Protocol (NCP). An important option in this category is Set NCP Packet Signature Option. It sets the level at which a packet signature option protects against packet forgery. Refer to the NetWare 5 manuals for more details.

Time

The settings on the Time menu are for the time synchronization system, which ensures that all servers on a Novell Directory Services tree use the same time to record events. The file TIMESYNC.CFG holds commands that set the time system parameters when the server boots. Time commands do not belong in the AUTOEXEC.NCF file or in the STARTUP.NCF file.

Transaction Tracking

The Transaction Tracking System (TTS) protects database files that might otherwise be corrupted if a server crashes during an incomplete transaction. The incomplete transaction is completely backed out and must be reentered. When you reboot the server after a crash, the TTS will ask if you want to back out the transactions. You can set Auto TTS Backout Flag to on if you want the backouts to occur automatically when the server starts. Some supervisors prefer to monitor the backout process themselves, and leave the Auto TTS Backout Flag setting off. However, you can store the information in a log file called TTS$LOG.ERR (in the SYS:SYSTEM directory) by setting TTS Abort Dump Flag to on.

NetWare Planning
and Installation

Note *Check with database vendors to make sure their products support TTS.*

Tasks Ahead for Administrators and Supervisors

In the next few chapters, you'll learn more about NetWare security and object management. You'll also see how to create objects for users, groups, and supervisors. In addition, you'll learn how to change the properties of these User objects, such as how to change their login or workstation restrictions, and learn how to grant users, groups, or containers access rights to objects, directories, and files.

The Complete Reference

NetWare 5

Part IV

Managing Novell Directory Services

Chapter 16

Using NetWare Administrative Tools

NetWare 5 includes two primary utilities that you can use to work with and control access to resources. Specifically, these utilities are used to manage Novell Directory Services and the NetWare file system.

- **NetWare Administrator for Windows**   A Windows 95/98/NT utility that helps you manage the NDS tree and the objects in it. It displays the tree in graphical format and displays commands and options on pull-down menus.

- **ConsoleOne**   A graphical utility written in Java that runs on the NetWare 5 server. It allows you to manage the NDS tree and perform limited administrative functions from the server console. This is a proof-of-concept product that may run slowly on some server machines.

Be sure to differentiate between the NetWare Administrator, which is a Windows-based utility, and ConsoleOne, which runs on either the server console or a workstation. The first main section of this chapter covers NWADMIN32, and the second section covers ConsoleOne. You learn the basic interface and functions of the utilities in this chapter, and then learn about using them for specific management functions in the next two chapters.

NetWare Administrator (NWADMIN32)

This section assumes you are familiar with basic Windows techniques, although you will be guided through most of the steps. If you're not familiar with Windows, refer to the following Osborne/McGraw-Hill publication:

Windows 98 Made Easy, by Tom Sheldon and Dan Logan (ISBN 0-07-882407-9)

This book is written for beginning and intermediate Windows users. It discusses basic operating techniques and how to use the Windows accessories and utilities.

Creating Startup Icons

The NetWare Administrator is not installed by default. NetWare administrators and supervisors need to manually set up the Windows icon for this utility. You will learn how to do that next.

Setting Up Windows Utilities

This section explains how to create a startup icon for the NetWare Administrator and assumes you are the ADMIN user (or equivalent user) with rights to the SYS:PUBLIC directory on the NetWare 5 server.

The first step is to log into the network before you start Windows. The default login script maps the search drive letter Z to the SYS:PUBLIC directory on the NetWare server. The NetWare Administrator files are located in the WIN32 subdirectory. A search drive is like specifying a path in DOS. It means you can run programs in the directory if you are working from another directory. It also means you can type **Z:** and press ENTER to quickly switch to the SYS:PUBLIC directory on the server.

*The SYS:PUBLIC directory might be mapped to a letter other than Z. Type **MAP** at the DOS prompt to see the list of drive mappings or select Novell Map Network Drive from the pop-up menu.*

Once you're logged in and know the search drive mapping for the SYS:PUBLIC directory, you're ready to create the shortcut. In Windows, follow these steps:

1. Right-click in a blank area on the Windows background screen.

2. Choose New from the pop-up menu.

3. Choose Shortcut from the pop-up window.

4. Browse to the location of the NWADMIN32.EXE program in the SYS:PUBLIC\WIN32 directory and click Next.

5. Enter a name for the shortcut and click Finish. NWADMIN32 will be the default name.

6. Right-click the new icon and select Properties. The information should appear as shown in Figure 16-1.

The contents of the Command Line field and the Working Directory field might need to specify a different path on your computer, depending on how SYS:PUBLIC has been mapped. Notice also that UNC pathing is used.

Using NetWare Administrator

You use NetWare Administrator to manage objects, directories, and files. To start NetWare Administrator, double-click its shortcut icon. A window similar to that shown in Figure 16-2 appears. In this example, the directory tree starts at the root object. From it branches the CambrianCorp Organization container and from that branch the DivEast and DivWest Organizational Unit containers.

Container objects form the branches of the directory tree. They can hold other containers or leaf objects. Normally, when you start NetWare Administrator, leaf objects in the directory tree are *collapsed* under their respective container objects. You

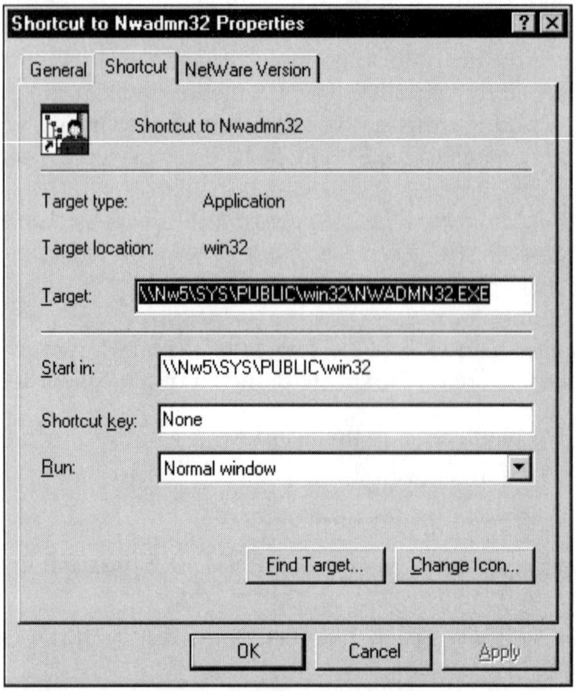

Figure 16-1.   *Checking the properties of the NWADMIN32 shortcut*

double-click a container to expand it and view the objects within it. In Figure 16-3, DivWest is expanded to show its branching container objects.

You can then double-click the Administration object to show the leaf objects within it, as shown in Figure 16-4. In this case, there are User, Server, and Printer objects, but no other branching container objects. Note also that the Admin object is in the container where you installed the server.

Now you're ready to work with objects within the container. By double-clicking a leaf object, you open its details dialog box, as shown in Figure 16-5. In this case, the dialog box for the user REWelch is displayed. This is where you control everything about the object, but the fields you see in the dialog box will be different depending on the type of object. In the case of a User object, you see fields related to the user's name, title, and location in the company. You also see buttons on the right that display fields

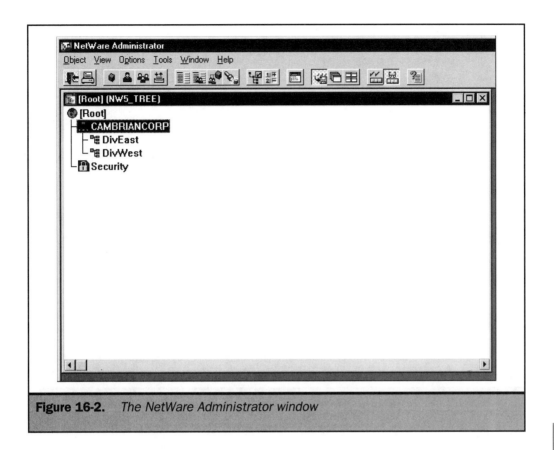

Figure 16-2. *The NetWare Administrator window*

for changing login restrictions, password restrictions, print job configurations, and login scripts. Network administrators are responsible for maintaining most of the information in the details dialog box, but users can change some of the information, such as user login scripts.

Note *You can't double-click to open the details dialog box for a container object. Double-clicking a container object either expands or collapses its contents. Instead, click the container with the right mouse button and then choose Details from the context menu that opens.*

Browser Windows

The "document" window (using Microsoft's lexicon) called [Root] that you see in Figures 16-2 through 16-4 is a browser window (Using Novell's lexicon). You can open multiple

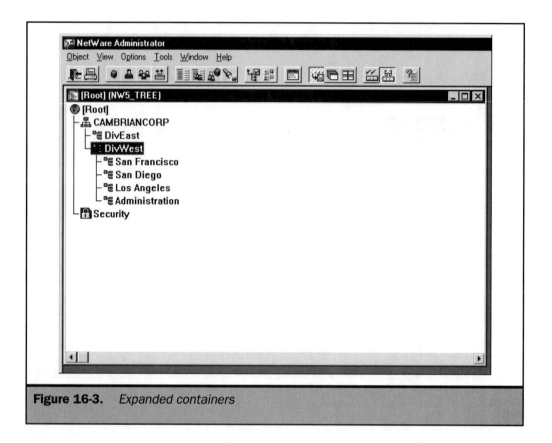

Figure 16-3. *Expanded containers*

browser windows at the same time to view different parts of the tree and compare or move objects from one place to another. You might do this if you are reorganizing users or the tree itself. Figure 16-6 shows multiple browser windows open at the same time.

To open additional windows, choose NDS Browser from the Tools menu. Once you've created a new browser window, you can do several things:

■ Change context and expand the contents of a container by double-clicking container objects.

■ Choose Set Context from the View menu to set the beginning context for a window. By setting a specific context in the tree, you can see containers or objects above it. This is just a convenience that keeps you from accidentally changing a particular view in a browser window.

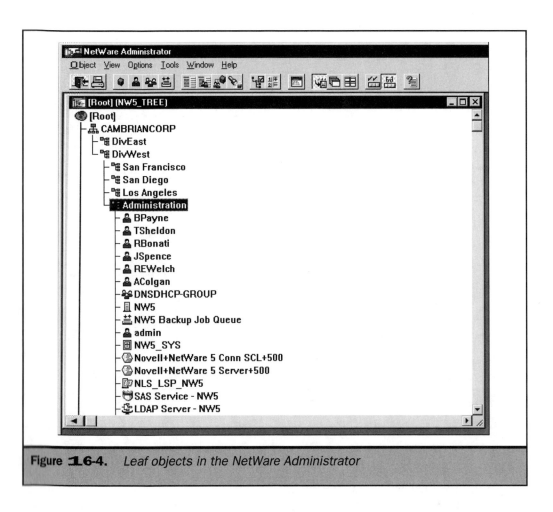

Figure 16-4. *Leaf objects in the NetWare Administrator*

■ Filter the contents of a window so you see only specific types of objects. For example, you could open two windows on the same context, and then display only user accounts in one window and only printers in the other window.

What Administrators Can Do in NetWare Administrator

As an administrator, your first duties will probably encompass the following tasks:

■ Create new branching containers for the departments and workgroups of your organization.

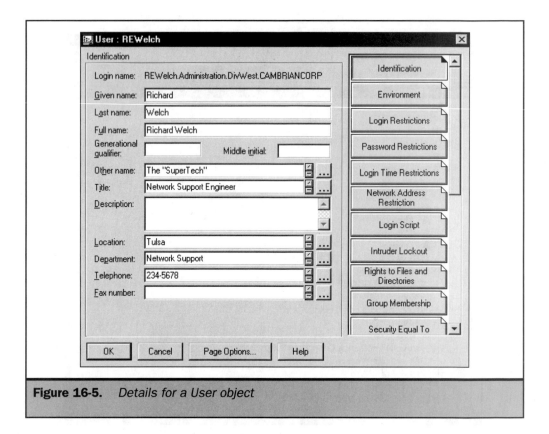

Figure 16-5.   *Details for a User object*

■ Create new user accounts, and make some of those users NDS managers so they can manage parts of the directory tree.

■ Create objects in the tree for network resources such as computers.

■ Organize and reorganize the directory tree.

■ Create partitions and manage replication.

Some objects such as Printer objects are automatically created by other utilities. For example, you run the NDPS utility as described in Chapter 23 to create Printer objects in the directory tree.

Chapter 10 contains a description of each object you can work with in the directory tree. Some objects are created for you during the NetWare 5 server installation, such as the root objects, the Organization objects, the Server object, the server Volume object(s), and the Admin objects.

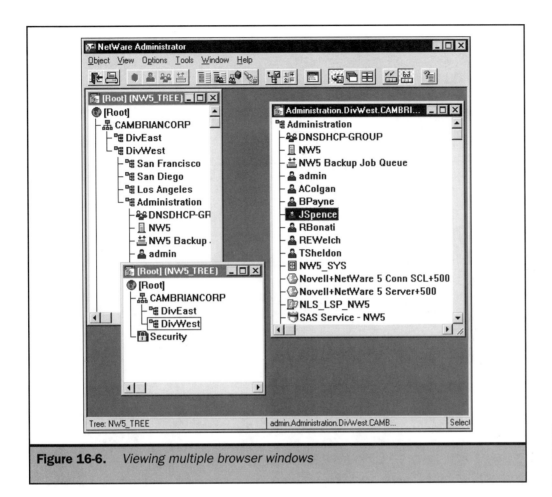

Figure 16-6. *Viewing multiple browser windows*

When you want to work with an object, you can do one of the following:

■ Right-click an object to display its context menu, as shown in Figure 16-7. From this menu, you can view or change details, rights, or trustees. See the next section, "Commands and Options," for more information.

■ Double-click the object to work with its details unless it is a container object, in which case you right-click and choose Details from its context menu.

■ Click an object and choose Options on NetWare Administrator's Object menu.

Administrators can also access the Pure IP Remote Console and manage server licenses from the NetWare Administrator by choosing appropriate commands on the

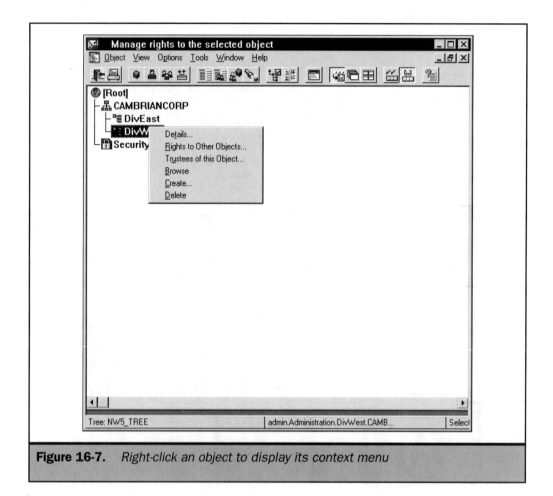

Figure 16-7.   *Right-click an object to display its context menu*

Tools menu. The next section briefly describes the commands on the NetWare
Administrator menus.

 *Regular users can also use the NetWare Administrator, but their default rights are very
limited. They can view properties of other objects and change their login scripts. That is
about it; however, you can give users additional rights, making them subadministrators
if necessary.*

Commands and Options

Most of the NetWare Administrator menu commands work on objects. Other
commands control the view you have of the directory tree and the way NetWare

Administrator operates. To work with an object, click it with the mouse. Note the following:

- When you right-click an object to see its context menu, some of the menu options are the same options you see on the Object menu.

- Some menu options are unavailable, depending on the object selected. For example, the Salvage option is available only when a Volume object is selected.

- To display a description of a menu option, open a menu and click the down arrow button until the option is highlighted, rather than click it with the mouse.

Object Menu

The Object menu contains commands for creating and modifying objects in the directory tree, as shown in Figure 16-8. You can also expand a Volume object and work with its directories and files by using some of the options on the Object menu.

- **Create**   Select this option to create a new object. This option is unavailable if a leaf object is selected. If selected, a list of objects appears from which you select the type of object you want to create.

- **Details**   Select this option to display details about a selected object, directory, or file. A details dialog box similar to that shown in Figure 16-5 appears. You can also simply double-click an object (except a container) to display its details dialog box.

- **Rights to Other Objects**   Select this option to see what rights a user has to other objects. Note that this option shows explicit trustee assignments, but you can click a button called Effective Rights to view rights on specific objects that are gained through inheritance or other means.

- **Trustees of this Object**   Select this option to see who has trustee rights to the currently selected object. Figure 16-9 shows trustees of a container object. By selecting a specific trustee in the Trustees field, you can view object and property rights in the lower fields. Note that this box only shows objects that have explicit trustee rights to the object. Click Effective Rights to view information about trustees that have rights through inheritance or other means.

- **Move**   Choose this option to move one or more objects. If you are working with a Volume object, you can move directories and files.

- **Copy**   Choose this option to copy an object from one location to another; or, if you are working with a Volume object, choose it to copy one or more directories or files to another location in the file system.

- **Rename**   Choose this option to rename a selected object, directory, or file.

- **Delete**   Choose this option to delete a selected object, directory, or file.

Managing Novell
Directory Services

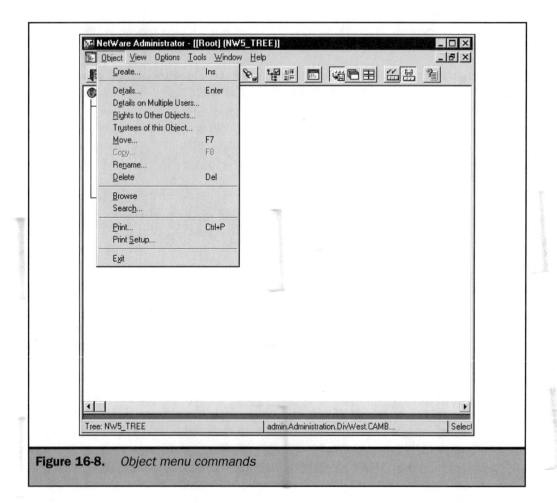

Figure 16-8. *Object menu commands*

- ■ **Browse** This option opens a new browser window.
- ■ **Search** This option helps you locate specific types of objects in the directory tree, starting at the currently selected container.
- ■ **Print** This option lets you print the tree structure currently displayed in the browser window. Print Setup is the standard Windows command for setting printing parameters.
- ■ **Print Setup** This option lets you select the output device.

View Menu

View options help you organize your view of the directory tree, and they become more important as the tree grows larger. The View menu options are shown in Figure 16-10.

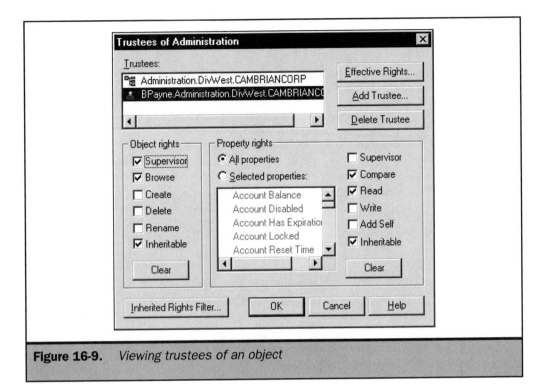

Figure 16-9. *Viewing trustees of an object*

- **Configure Toolbar and Status Bar**   This option allows you to customize the toolbars and status bars.

- **Set Context**   This option opens a dialog box that allows you to change which part of the directory tree you are viewing.

- **Sort and Include**   This option opens a dialog box that allows you to select exactly which object to show in a browser window, either by name or by object class. If you're working with a volume, you can limit by name the files and directories listed in the window. It also lets you select the order in which objects are listed in a browser window. You can choose to list servers first, and then volumes, users, and so on.

- **Expand**   This option opens the container object you have selected. This is the same as double-clicking a collapsed container.

- **Collapse**   This option closes the container you have selected. This is the same as double-clicking an expanded container.

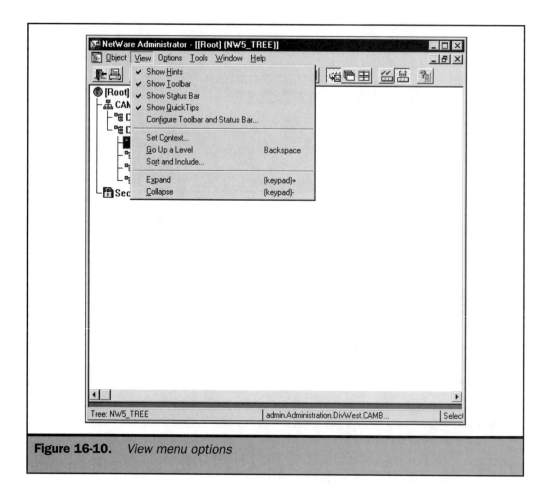

Figure 16-10.   *View menu options*

Options Menu

The options on the Options menu let you choose preferences for working in NetWare Administrator. A check mark appears in front of options that are selected. These options are shown in Figure 16-11.

- **Save Settings on Exit**   When this option is enabled, the current settings are saved for use in the next session, including sort preferences, browser filters, and the context of your active browser screens.

- **Confirm on Delete**   When this option is enabled, message boxes appear to confirm that you want to delete objects, files, or directories.

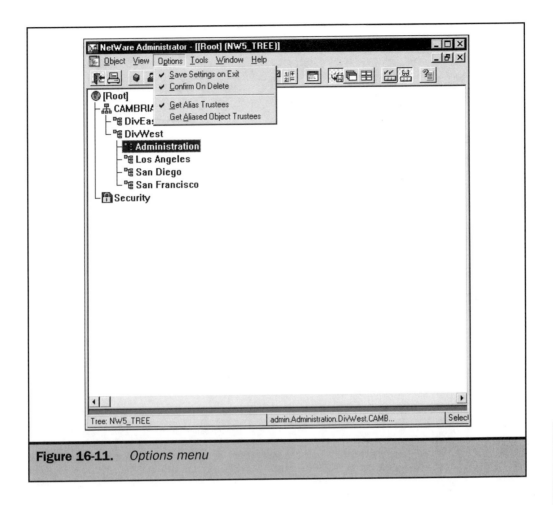

Figure 16-11.   *Options menu*

- ■ **Get Alias Trustees**   An alias points to another object. When this option is enabled, it allows administrators to manage the trustees of the actual Alias object, not the object the alias points to.

- ■ **Get Aliased Object Trustees**   When this option is enabled, you manage objects that the alias object points to, not the Alias object.

Tools Menu

The Tools menu has options for starting additional utilities or creating browser windows. This menu is shown in Figure 16-12.

- ■ **Internet Connections**   This option takes you to your favorite Internet sites via the World Wide Web.

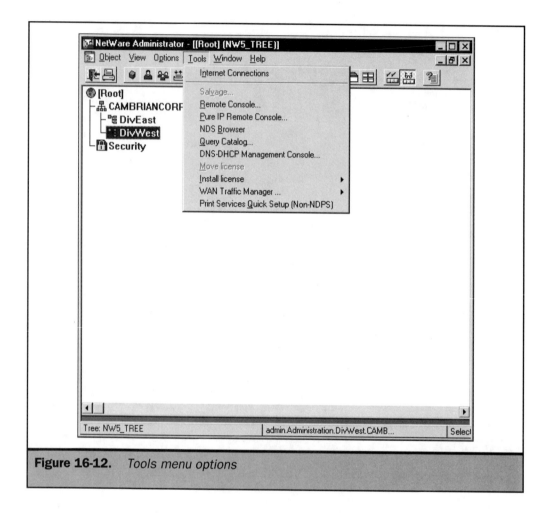

Figure 16-12. *Tools menu options*

- **Remote Console** This option starts the RCONSOLE.EXE program for remote access to a server console.

- **Pure IP Remote Console** This option starts the RConsoleJ program for remote access to a server console using IP communications.

- **NDS Browser** This option opens a new browser window.

- **Query Catalog** This option builds a query to extract data from a catalog.

- **DNS-DHCP Management Console** This option starts the DNS-DHCP Management Console utility.

- **Move License** This option allows you move a license certificate from one server pool to another server pool.

- **Install License**   This option allows you to install a license certificate.
- **WAN Traffic Manager**   This option allows you to add or remove the schema extensions to NDS for this utility.
- **Print Services Quick Setup (Non-NDPS)**   This option allows you to set up legacy queue-based printing on a NetWare 5 server.

Window Menu

Choose options from the Window menu to organize the windows that are open in NetWare Administrator. If you used the Browse command to open several windows, choose Cascade or Tile to arrange them, or choose Close All to close all the windows at once. If you can't see a window, choose its name from the list at the bottom of the menu.

Help Menu

Options on the Help menu provide useful information about the operation of NetWare Administrator, terminology, and error messages. Choose About NetWare Administrator to view its version number in case you need to call Novell Technical Support about a problem.

Creating and Working with Objects

This section walks you through the basic steps of creating a User object. Detailed steps that describe advanced features are covered in Chapter 17. The purpose of this discussion is to familiarize you with NetWare Administrator. You can delete the sample objects you create here when you're done with the chapter.

Creating an Object

This section assumes you have an existing directory tree with an organization and at least one Organizational Unit container branching from it. You'll create the sample User object in the Organizational Unit container. Your directory tree may look similar to the one in Figure 16-13 at this point if you just installed the first server. An Organizational Unit container called Administration branches from the DivWest Organizational Unit container. It holds the server and Volume objects (in this example NW5 and NW5_SYS respectively) where the initial copy of NetWare 5 is installed. DivWest branches from the CambrianCorp Organization container.

We'll start by creating a User object in the Administration container, but you can choose any container in your own directory tree.

1. With the right mouse button, click the container object where you want to create the new user. Choose Create from the context menu to display the dialog box shown in Figure 16-14.

2. Scroll down the list of objects, click the User object, and then click OK. The Create User dialog box appears, as shown in Figure 16-15.

Managing Novell
Directory Services

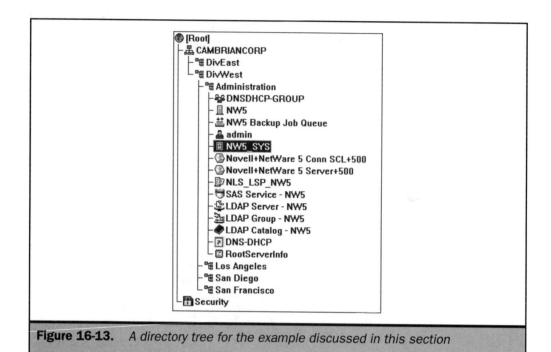

Figure 16-13. *A directory tree for the example discussed in this section*

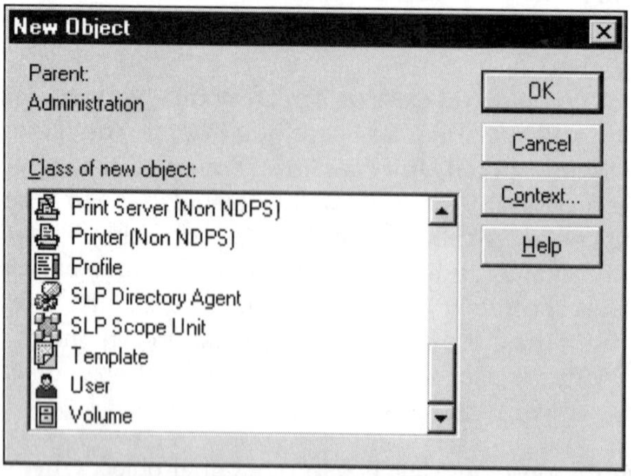

Figure 16-14. *The New Object dialog box*

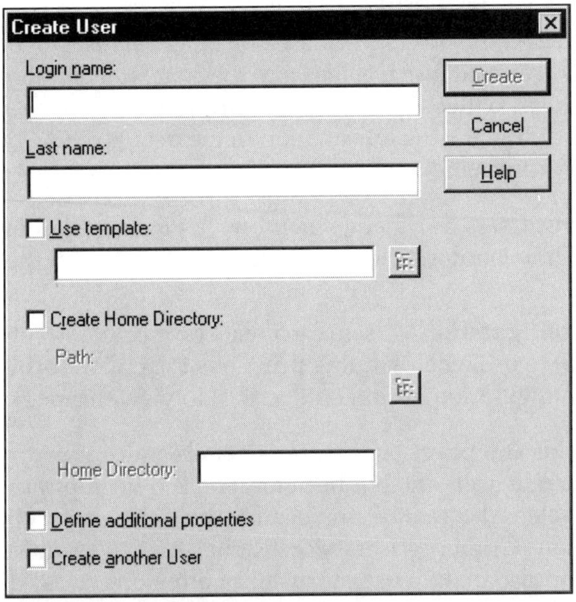

Figure 16-15.   *The Create User dialog box*

In the Login Name field, type a user name (TBones is the name in our example). This is the name the user must type to log in; first initial, last name format is usually appropriate. In the Last Name field, type the user's last name. You can search by this name later, so when you create User objects, don't enter any uncommon abbreviations or first name initials in this field; just enter the last name exactly as it's spelled.

Note   *The options in the Create User dialog box are covered in Chapter 17. In this chapter, we're just interested in creating a User object and experimenting with it for management training purposes.*

3. Click the Create button to create the User object.

Now look in the directory tree to find the new object and work with it, as discussed next.

Note   *Later you can delete this sample object if you no longer need it.*

Examining Object Details

Now that you've created the object, you can look at its details. Double-click the User object, or right-click it and choose Details from the context menu that appears. You'll see a dialog box similar to the one shown in Figure 16-5.

By default, users can view the information in the details dialog box for their own User object and they can change two fields:

- **Login Script**   Users can change their own login script if they have access to NetWare Administrator. Click the Login Script button on the right to view this page.

- **Print Job Configuration**   Users can create new print job configurations (Non-NDPS) to use when sending print jobs to network printers. Click the Print Job Configuration button on the right to view this page.

All the other fields and pages on the user's details dialog box can only be changed by the ADMIN user or a user who has been granted the appropriate rights to create User objects in the selected container and change the rights of the objects. This is covered in the section "Granting Users More Rights to Their Own User Object," later in this chapter. You can also make a user a trustee of other objects, as discussed under "Creating Trustees."

DIRECTORY AND FILE RIGHTS   You can view the rights a user has to directories and files in the file system and change those rights in the details dialog box. Click the Rights to Files and Directories button in the user's details dialog box to display the dialog box shown in Figure 16-16.

In this dialog box, you can view the user's current file system rights, make them a new trustee of directories and files, or remove them as a trustee of directories or files. The procedures for doing this are covered in Chapter 19.

Creating Trustees

Now let's make the user a trustee of another object. That means we'll grant the user specific rights to work with another object. In this example, we'll make our new user, TBones, a trustee of the Administration container, with some selected rights. You can do the same thing with the User object you created in previous steps. There are two ways to assign these rights:

- Right-click the target container and choose Trustees of this Object from the context menu.

- Click and drag the User object over the Administration container object and release the mouse button.

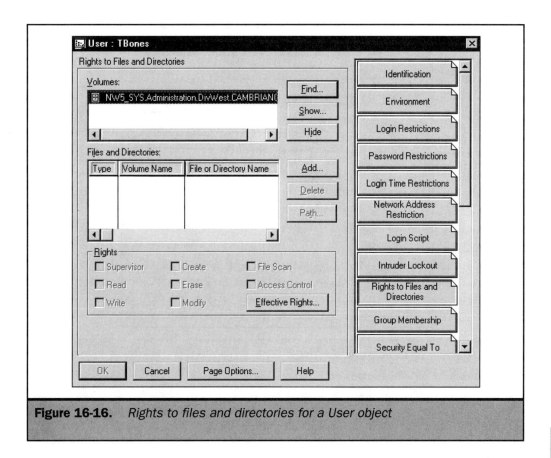

Figure 16-16.   *Rights to files and directories for a User object*

In either case, the same dialog box appears, similar to the one shown in Figure 16-17. We recommend that you become familiar with using the drag-and-drop method (the second method listed above).

Note *You can create additional trustees while the dialog box is open by clicking the Add Trustee button. You can also delete existing trustees by selecting the trustee and clicking the Delete Trustee button.*

The object you just added as a trustee appears in the Trustees field at the top of the dialog box. Click it to see the rights this trustee has to the container object. Object rights are listed on the left and property rights are listed on the right. Note that initially, new User objects will have the Browse and Inheritable rights. You need to assign additional rights using the techniques discussed in the next few sections. Keep in mind that if you

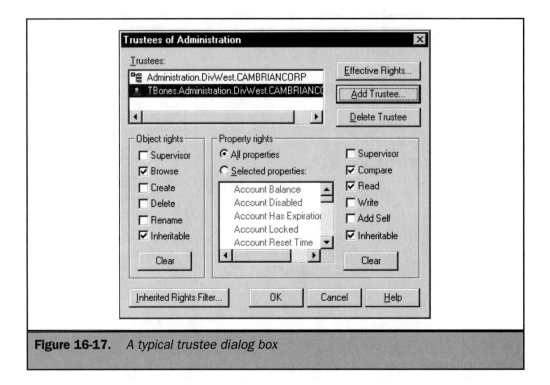

Figure 16-17.   *A typical trustee dialog box*

still have the Trustees of... dialog box open, you are working with a trustee list of a specific object, so you need to first select a trustee in the Trustees field.

CREATING A SUPERVISOR   To assign the Supervisor right to a trustee, first select the trustee in the Trustees field (see Figure 16-17). You can also click the Add Trustee button to add a new trustee. Now click Supervisor in the Object Rights field to grant this trustee full Supervisor rights for the container and all objects in it. The Supervisor rights also grant the trustee rights to branching subcontainers and the ability to block the Supervisor rights of higher-level users like ADMIN. Grant this right with caution.

CREATING AN ADMINISTRATOR WITH LIMITED RIGHTS   If you just want to grant the trustee partial subadministrator status to create new objects, delete objects, and rename objects, check Browse, Create, Delete, and Rename in the Object Rights field. Note that this is a less powerful version of the container supervisor discussed previously. If only these rights are assigned and not the Supervisor right, the trustee can't block the rights of higher-level administrators in the container.

CREATING A PROPERTIES ADMINISTRATOR   You can create a trustee that can manage property rights for the container and objects in it but cannot create, delete, or rename objects in the container. In the Object Rights field, check the Browse right and make sure the other rights are not marked. In the Property Rights field, check All Properties, and then click the Supervisor option. Alternately, you can mark Compare, Read, Write, and/or Add Self and unmark the Supervisor right to create a non-Supervisor trustee. Remember that the All Properties rights are inherited in subcontainers by default. The trustee will have these same rights in all sub-branches of the tree unless the rights are blocked with an Inheritance Rights Mask or the check mark is removed from the Inheritable check box.

CREATING A LIMITED PROPERTIES ADMINISTRATOR   If you check Selected Properties, you can choose a property and grant the user rights for that specific property. Note that these rights are not inherited, so they only apply to the container you are working with. For example, you could give this user the right to change city, department, description, and other nonsecurity-related information for the container. You check Selected Properties, scroll through the list until you find a property, check it, and then check one or more of the rights check boxes on the right. We recommend selecting Compare, Read, and Write in most cases.

As you can see, you can create many different types of trustees for objects in the directory tree. Have fun trying to make up names for each different type of administrator, based on the rights they have. However, keep in mind that the rights you set for Selected Properties are not inherited. They apply only to the specific object you are making the user a trustee of.

When you're done, click OK to save your changes. We'll look at those rights again later.

Granting Users More Rights to Their Own User Object

Now let's take a look at the object properties of specific User objects. One thing to note is that users are listed as trustees of their own account. You can see this by right-clicking any User object that currently exists in your directory tree and choosing Trustees of this Object. The Trustees of... dialog box appears for the User object you selected. The user's name appears in the Trustees field. Click the name to view the user's specific rights. Note the default rights for new user accounts:

- There are no object rights.
- The Read right is selected for All Properties.
- Check Selected Properties, and then scan the list to see the selected property rights. You'll see a check mark in front of properties that have specific rights. Click the property to see what those rights are.
- The Inheritable property right is selected by default. This allows the rights to flow down the NDS tree. The purpose of this property right is to provide compatibility with versions of NetWare prior to NetWare 5.

To grant a user additional rights for his or her own User object, check Selected Properties, and then scan through the list, highlight a property, and change the rights. For example, you might want to grant users the Write right for addresses, telephone numbers, and e-mail addresses.

Do not grant users the Write right to properties related to security features like Account Balance, Login Time Restrictions, and Security Equal To! This would allow users to dictate their own security rights. Likewise, don't grant users the Write right to All Properties.

Examining Rights That Objects Have to Other Objects

Now let's find out what objects our user TBones is a trustee of. Previously, we went to an object and looked at who was a trustee of that object. Here, we want to find out what objects a specific user has been granted trustee rights to.

Remember that a user (or another object) can be granted explicit trustee rights to an object. They then appear in the Trustees list when you view the trustees of an object, as shown in Figure 16-17. However, users might have rights to an object that they have inherited from higher-level containers.

Let's create a container called Test that branches from the container you are working in (the container where you previously created the new User object) so we can see how inherited rights work. Create a new container object as follows:

1. Right-click the container object that the new user belongs to (the Administration container, in our example).

2. Choose Create from the context menu.

3. Double-click the Organizational Unit object.

4. Type a name (**Test** is used in this example) and click the Create button.

The new container object now appears as a branching object of the container. Now let's look at the rights that the new user inherits for this new Test container.

1. Right-click the User object and click Rights to Other Objects on the context menu. The Search Context dialog box appears as shown here:

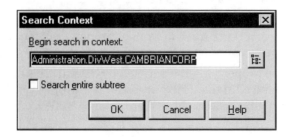

For this example, we're going to select the Test container directly, but in other cases, you can use this dialog box to search an entire directory tree for objects that the user might have rights to. You would click the Browse button to choose a starting location, and then mark the Search Entire Subtree option to search the containers in that branch of the tree.

2. To select the Test container, click OK to open the Rights to Other Objects dialog box, and then click the Effective Rights button to open the Effective Rights dialog box pictured in Figure 16-18.

3. From the Effective Rights dialog box, you click the Browse button to display the Select Object dialog box. Click the Test object in the Available Objects field, as pictured in Figure 16-19.

Note *Other actions that you can perform in this dialog box to move around in the directory tree are called out in Figure 16-19. Remember these for future use, or try experimenting now to see how browsing works.*

4. Click OK to display the Effective Rights dialog box, as pictured in Figure 16-20.

The Effective Rights dialog box now shows the Test container in the Object Name field and shows the effective rights that our new user has in this container. Remember that these rights are inherited from the parent container only if the Inheritable right has

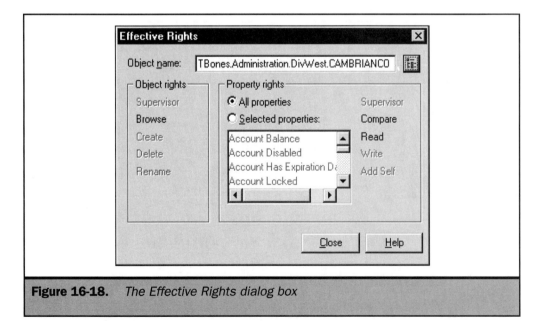

Figure 16-18. *The Effective Rights dialog box*

Managing Novell
Directory Services

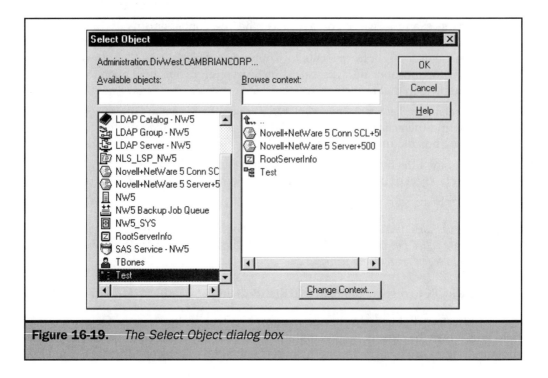

Figure 16-19.   *The Select Object dialog box*

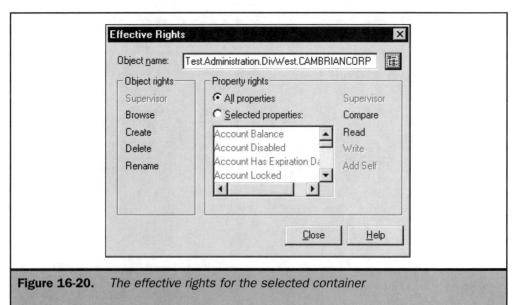

Figure 16-20.   *The effective rights for the selected container*

been granted. This user has the Browse, Create, Rename, and Delete object rights in a parent container, and thus has these effective rights in this container.

 Recall that effective rights are the rights that users inherit that are not blocked by an Inherited Rights Filter.

Looking at Trustee Rights

Remember that you can view trustee rights in a number of places:

- You can right-click an object and choose Trustees of this Object from the context menu to view the trustees of the object.

- You can right-click a specific object, and then choose Rights to Other Objects to see what objects it is trustee to.

- To view the trustees of a directory or file, open the Volume object where the directory or file exists, and then select it. Choose Details from the Object menu.

In the first case, only objects that have been granted explicit trustee rights are listed in the Trustees field. You need to click the Effective Rights button to view trustees that might have rights through inheritance. This opens the Effective Rights dialog box (as shown previously in Figure 16-20); you can click the Browse button to choose a specific object for which you want to see rights.

Note *The complete set of property rights a user has to an object is not immediately apparent when looking at a Trustees of... dialog box. Click Selected Properties, and then use the arrow keys to scan the list to see selected property settings.*

You should also keep the following in mind as you create new users and work with objects:

- Users with Supervisor rights to an object can control who can change and who can view the properties of the object. The user can also block the rights of higher-level supervisors. This may be useful in some management situations, but you can also lose control if you're not careful. A better method is to assign specific rights (Create, Rename, and Delete), rather than the Supervisor right.

- By default, all users have the Read property right to all properties in their own User object. This means that if a user has access to NetWare Administrator, they can open the details dialog box for their User object and look at the contents of fields.

- By default, all users have the Read and Write property rights to the Login Script and Print Job Configuration properties, which means they can change these properties.

■ Selected property rights are not inherited, so you'll need to assign them to each object individually. For example, granting AColgan the right to change the telephone numbers of a container object doesn't give her the right to change the telephone number for another object in the container.

Inherited Rights Filters

An Inherited Rights Filter (IRF) blocks the rights that users inherit from higher-level containers. For example, earlier we made new user TBones a trustee of the Administration container with Browse, Create, Rename, and Delete rights. We then created a subcontainer to Administration called Test. TBones gets these same rights in the Test container due to inheritance. Recall that rights flow down the tree unless blocked with an Inherited Rights Filter. Follow these steps to place an Inherited Rights Filter on the Test container:

1. Right-click the Test container, and then choose Trustees of this Object on the context menu.

2. Click the Inherited Rights Filter button to display the dialog box shown in Figure 16-21.

   The down-pointing arrows on the Inherited Rights Filter dialog box indicate that rights in parent containers are allowed to flow down into the current container. By default, all the rights are allowed. Use caution when blocking the Supervisor right, as this would block the ADMIN user from accessing the object and its subtree; however is useful in some cases.

3. To block rights, remove the check mark from the appropriate boxes.

After blocking rights, you can still make a user an explicit trustee of the container as discussed earlier. Right-click the object and choose Trustees of this Object. Then click the Add Trustees button and locate the user you want to make a trustee of the object. Grant the new trustee rights as appropriate. These trustee rights are not affected by the Inherited Rights Filter you applied to the object.

NetWare Administrator will not let you block the Supervisor right unless another user has been granted explicit Supervisor rights directly to the container.

Moving Objects

You can move any object in a container to a new container by holding down the CTRL key and dragging the object to the new container. If you can't see the destination container because there are too many objects in the window, try collapsing part of

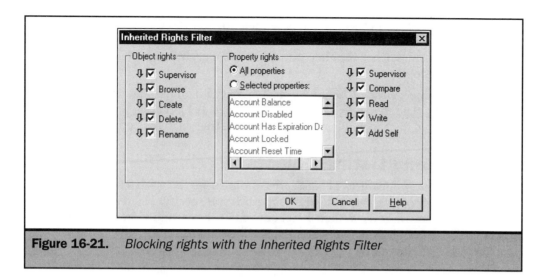

Figure 16-21.   *Blocking rights with the Inherited Rights Filter*

the directory tree, or choose Browse from the Tools menu to create another window. Place the two windows side by side, and then drag the icon from one to the other.

    To display a list that shows only containers into which you can then drag and drop objects, open a new window by choosing Browse from the Tools menu, and then choose Include from the View menu. Click the Exclude All button, and click OK.

If the mouse techniques seem like too much trouble, just choose Move from the Object dialog box, and fill out the fields as appropriate. Be sure to select the icon you want to move before choosing the Move option.

You cannot move a container object using the NWADMIN32 utility. You must use the NDS Manager utility to perform this operation. This utility is discussed in Chapter 18.

Changing the View

Once you've created a lot of objects, you probably want to change the view. Recall that you can click Browse on the Tools menu to create a new browser window. This lets you create multiple side-by-side views of the directory tree if you want to reorganize the tree. You can also do the following:

■ **Set Include options**   Choose Include from the View menu to display the Include dialog box, and then hold down the CTRL key and click the types of objects you want to view. You can also type wildcard characters in the

Directory Services Object Name Filter field to filter objects by name; or, if you are listing files, you can specify wildcards in the DOS File Name Filter field to filter filenames. Click the Help button for some useful examples of how to use this option.

■ **Sort by object class** Choose Sort by Object Class on the View menu to sort objects by class in the directory tree. You click an object class, and then move it up or down to change where it is listed in the tree relative to other objects.

Searching for and Listing Objects

One of the most useful features of NetWare Administrator is its search capability. You can search for objects that have the properties you specify. The results are listed in a separate window. You can then select one of the objects and view or change its properties. For example, you could search for all users who have a title of Printer operator or Server operator.

To start a search, choose Search from the Object menu. The dialog box shown in Figure 16-22 appears.

Note that your current context is listed in the top field. This is where the search starts. You can change the context by clicking the Browse button on the right. You can

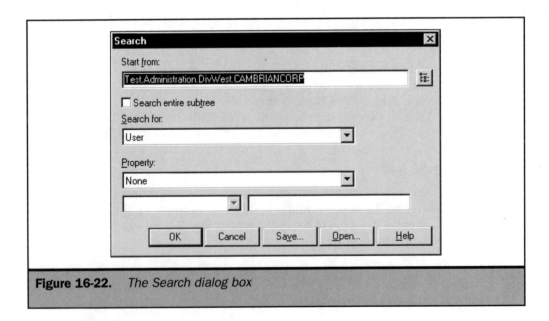

Figure 16-22. *The Search dialog box*

also click an appropriate container in the directory tree before starting a search. Here are the procedures for using the Search option:

1. To search all the containers that branch from this context, make sure the Search Entire Subtree check box is marked.

2. In the Search For field, click the down arrow button to select from a list of objects, such as User, Server, Printer, and Computer (the Top option lists all objects). Click Help to get a description of some nonstandard objects. Once you've selected an object, you can click OK to list all objects of that type, or you can further refine the search, as described in step 3.

3. Jump to the Property field by pressing TAB, and then press the UP ARROW and DOWN ARROW keys to view a list of properti es. Choose a property, and then define the two lower fields. For example, you could select Title in the Property field, select Equal To in the field below it, and type **Print Operator** in the lower-right field to display a list of users who have the Print Operator title.

4. Click OK to start the search. When complete, a list of found objects appears. You can double-click any listed object to view or change its properties.

ConsoleOne

ConsoleOne is a Java GUI application that runs on both the NetWare 5 server and a Windows workstation. It provides the ability to browse the NDS tree and create and modify User, Group, Organization, and Organizational Unit objects. You can also perform full rights management within the directory structure. ConsoleOne allows you to perform certain file system functions from the server console. This includes creating, deleting, renaming, moving, and copying files. You can also view the contents of DOS volumes. It is important to remember that the minimum requirements for running ConsoleOne on the server are 128MB of memory and at least a 200MHz Pentium processor. After 15 minutes, the program and the common GUI shell are written to virtual memory disk to conserve physical memory and other resources. When you change between screens on the server console, it may appear to hang while reloading the program and the GUI shell. The main screen is shown in Figure 16-23.

Creating an Object

This section assumes you have an existing directory tree with an organization and at least one Organizational Unit container branching from it. You'll create the sample User object in the Organizational Unit container. Your directory tree may look similar to Figure 16-23 at this point if you just installed the first server. An Organizational Unit container called

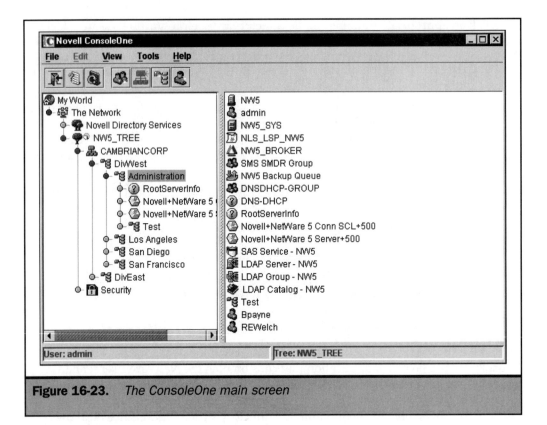

Figure 16-23.   *The ConsoleOne main screen*

Administration branches from the DivWest Organizational Unit container. It holds the
Server and Volume objects where the initial copy of NetWare 5 is installed. DivWest
branches from the CambrianCorp Organization container.

We'll start by creating a User object in the Administration container, but you can
choose any container in your own directory tree.

1. With the right mouse button, click the container object where you want to
   create the new user. Choose New | User from the context menu to display the
   dialog box shown next. Enter the login name and last name of the new user.

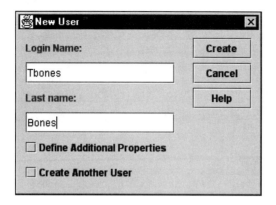

2. The Create Authentication Secrets dialog box is displayed, as shown next. Enter the tree name, context, and new password in this dialog box.

Managing Novell
Directory Services

The options in the Create User dialog box are covered in the next chapter. In this chapter, we're just interested in creating a User object and experimenting with it for management training purposes. Later you can delete this sample object if you no longer need it.

Examining Object Details

Now that you've created the object, you can look at its details. Right-click the User object and choose Properties from the context menu that appears. You'll see a dialog box similar shown in Figure 16-24.

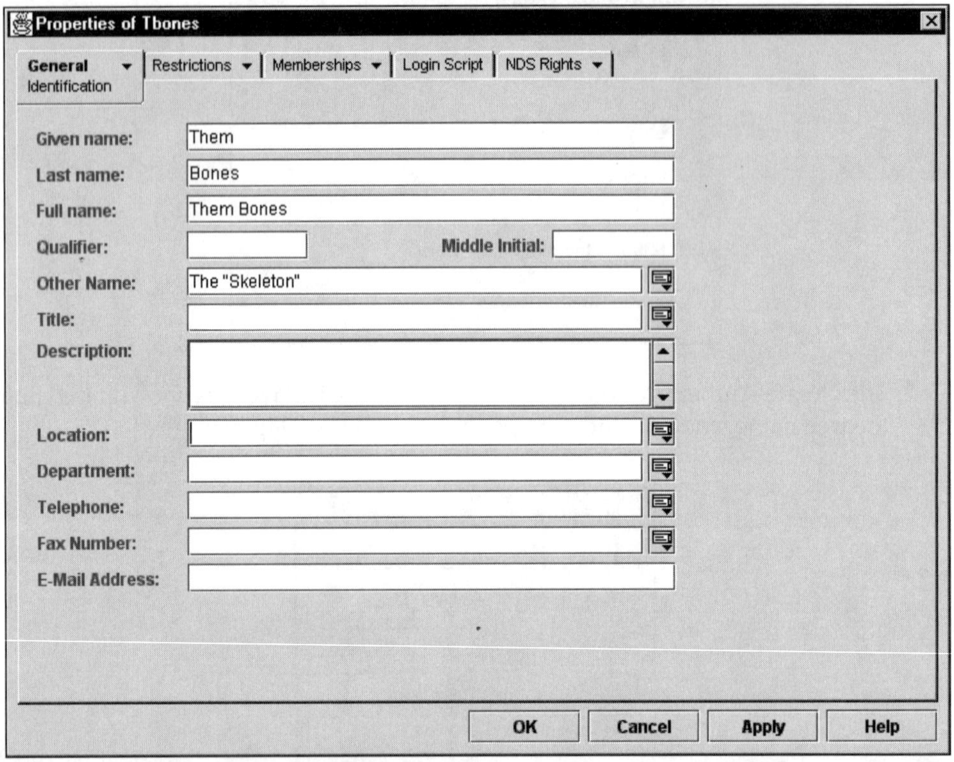

Figure 16-24. *The user properties screen*

By default, users can view the information in the details dialog box for their own User object and they can change one field:

- **Login Script** Users can change their own login script if they have access to the ConsoleOne utility. Click the Login Script tab to view this property page.

All the other fields and pages on the user's details dialog box can only be changed by the ADMIN user or a user who has been granted the appropriate rights to create User objects in the selected container and change the rights of the objects. This is covered in the section "Granting Users More Rights to Their Own User Object," earlier in this chapter. You can also make a user a trustee of other objects, as discussed previously under "Creating Trustees."

The Complete Reference

NetWare 5

Chapter 17

Managing Users and Objects

his chapter explores creating and modifying objects in the NDS directory tree. You learn procedures and important points for creating container, user, and other objects. You also learn about *templates*, which are special User objects you create in an individual container to hold default values to assign to User objects you create in that container.

All examples in this chapter use the Windows-based NetWare Administrator, but keep in mind that the procedures covered here translate over to the Java-based ConsoleOne utility if you find yourself working at the server. This chapter assumes you are logged in as the ADMIN user or equivalent user. This chapter also shows you how to create various types of managers and subadministrator accounts so other people can manage parts of the directory tree.

> **Note**
>
> *As you work with objects in this chapter, note the fields in the details dialog boxes that you might want to let other managers change. For example, you might create a user in the Personnel department who has rights to change e-mail, address, and telephone information for user accounts. You would make the user a trustee of the object and grant him or her selected property rights for those fields.*

You can arrange your view of objects before you begin working with NetWare Administrator and any time you need to work with a special set of objects. Here are some tips for arranging the directory tree:

- Choose Browse from the Tools menu to open additional browser windows, and then set the view for those windows as described next.

- To work with a specific branch and remove the clutter of other tree branches, choose Set Context from the View menu and then specify the container you want to work with.

- To view only certain types of objects, choose Sort and Include from the View menu and then choose the type of objects you want to see.

- Use the Search option on the Object menu to search for objects at any point in the directory tree and display them in a separate browser window. You can then work with any listed object without changing your context.

Working with the Details Dialog Boxes

When you open the details dialog box for any object, you see a specific page of information about that object. An example of the details dialog box for a container object is pictured in Figure 17-1. You click buttons on the right to view other pages of information.

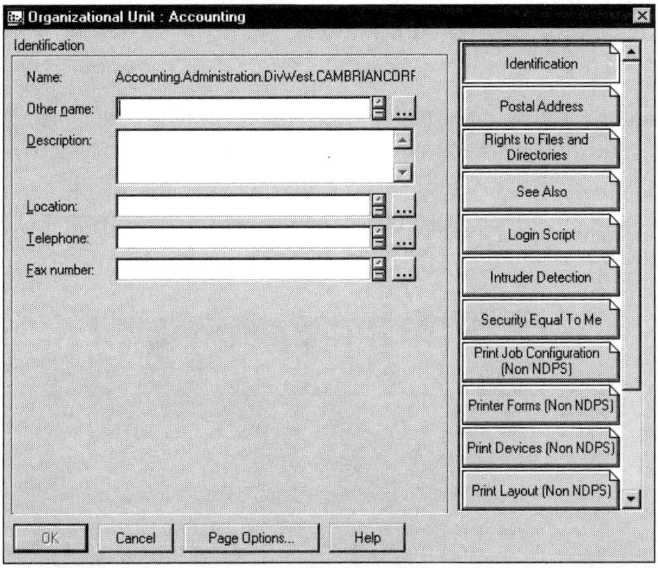

Figure 17-1. *The details dialog box for an Organizational Unit object*

The changes you make to any page in the dialog box are not saved until you click the OK button. If you make changes to a page and switch to another page, those changes are retained, but they are not permanently added to the object's properties until you click the OK button. If you decide you don't want to make any changes, click the Cancel button, but keep in mind that you will lose all of the changes on all of the pages.

You need to know about two buttons on the details dialog boxes:

- **Ellipsis**   Click the Ellipsis (...) button to select from a list of previously entered values. For example, the Location field holds previous locations you have entered, so you just choose from a list.

- **Browse**   Click the Browse button to browse for the complete name of an object in the directory tree.

Creating Container Objects

Containers are branches of the directory tree that hold other containers or leaf objects. With the organizational plan for your directory tree in hand, you can start creating the container objects that represent the divisions or departments of your company. Your directory tree will already have some containers, which were added when you installed NetWare 5 servers.

1. Right-click the container object where you want to create a new branching container and choose the Create option from the context menu.

2. When the New Object dialog box appears, select Organizational Unit in the list of objects and click the OK button. The Create Organizational Unit dialog box appears, as shown here:

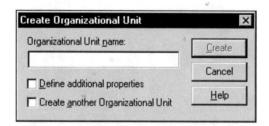

3. Type a name in the Organizational Unit Name field. Keep it short if users will need to type the context of this container often.

4. Click the Define Additional Properties check box.

Click the Create Another Organizational Unit check box only when you need to create a set of containers at the same time.

5. Click the Create button to create the container.

The details dialog box for the Organizational Unit (Figure 17-1) appears so that you can edit the properties of the object, as discussed next.

After you make changes to the details dialog box of any object, click OK to save the changes, or click Cancel if you decide not to make the changes.

Filling Out the Details Dialog Box

The following sections describe each of the *pages* in the details dialog box. You click a button on the right side of the dialog box to access different pages, and then set property values. Note that the buttons have a small foldover tab at the upper right. When you change any field in a page of properties, this tab turns black to remind you that you've made changes to that page.

Keep in mind that almost all of the fields in the details dialog box are optional and many are for documentation purposes only. On the other hand, you can enter values that you later use to search for objects when you're managing the tree.

Identification

The Identification page for containers is pictured in Figure 17-1. Enter field values that help you identify the object and search for it later. You can't change the Name field. In the Other Name field, either type another name to describe the container or enter the name of the person who manages it. In the Description field, you can briefly summarize what the container represents, who manages it, or its organizational purposes. In the Location field, you might enter the physical location this container object represents, if any. For example, in a campus environment, the location could be North Hall. In the remaining fields, supply the phone numbers and fax number of the person to contact for more information about the container.

 You can search by any field to display specific objects, so it is useful to create naming standards for the information you put in these fields.

Postal Address

Use this page to enter postal information for the object so you can send mailings to the person who manages the container or the department/location it represents. You can also search by the information you enter here. Fill out the fields at the top of the page, and then click the Copy to Label button to add the information to the Mailing Label Information field. Third-party programs can access the mailing label information to create mailing lists for the users and objects in your directory tree.

Rights to Files and Directories

Click this page's button if you want to assign the container object rights to the file system on a particular server. If you are just creating this container, you can only assign rights to volumes in other containers until you install servers in this container. See "Assigning File and Directory Rights to Objects," later in this chapter, for more information.

See Also

You use the See Also page to include the names of other objects in the directory tree that are related to this container. A supervisor or manager can use it to record information about this object. Click the Add button to select from a list of objects to add to the See Also field. The contents of this field are purely informational and have no effect on the object.

Login Script

The Login Script page for container objects is very important. The commands you place in a container's login script execute for all the users that you create in the container. Login scripts are covered in Chapter 24.

Intruder Detection

Intruder Detection provides a way to guard against unauthorized logins. An intruder might try several passwords to gain access. You can limit the number of incorrect attempts a user can make to gain access to the system. If a specified number of incorrect login attempts are detected, NetWare 5 assumes that an intruder is trying to log in and locks the account.

 The intruder detection limits you set in the container become the defaults for all user accounts you create in the container.

To set intruder limits, click the Detect Intruders box, which makes other options available. Now set the other fields as follows:

- **Incorrect Login Attempts**   Set this field to the number of incorrect login attempts you will allow. This value becomes the default for all user accounts in the container as well.

- **Intruder Attempt Reset Interval**   Set this field to the length of time you want to record incorrect login attempts before resetting the counter back to zero. You set the time in the Days, Hours, and Minutes fields located directly beneath this field.

- **Lock Account After Detection**   In this field, specify whether to lock a user's account when the specified number of incorrect login attempts occurs in the time designated in the Days, Hours, and Minutes fields.

- **Intruder Lockout Reset Interval**   In this field, set how long a user's account remains locked after an intruder is detected (the incorrect login attempts number is exceeded). You set the time in the Days, Hours, and Minutes fields located directly beneath this field.

Security Equal To Me

This is an NDS feature that allows a user to possess all the rights of another object. Only users can have security equivalence. A user is automatically granted security equivalence to the containers, groups, and organizational roles that the user belongs to. All users are automatically security-equivalent to the [Public] trustee. A user is explicitly security-equivalent to each object listed in the user's Security Equals property, as well as each object whose Security Equal To Me property lists the user.

Print Job Configuration (Non-NDPS)

The Print Job Configuration page lets you create customized print job configurations that users in the container can select when printing to Printer objects in the container. Print job configurations help users print specific types of jobs or automatically connect with a printer that will print a specific type of job, such as mailing labels or letters on company letterhead. Click the New button on the dialog box to see the options available for print job configurations. This option is discussed in more detail in Chapter 23.

Printer Forms (Non-NDPS)

The Printer Forms page lets you specify one or more printer forms. A printer form sets up a printer for a specific paper size. The forms are used when printing to a Printer object in the container. To add a printer form, click the Create button and then specify a name and number for the form, along with the length and width of the paper. This option is discussed in more detail in Chapter 23.

Print Devices (Non-NDPS)

The Print Devices page can contain a list of printing device definitions (called *printer definition files,* or *PDFs*). For example, the device driver HP3.PDF is required when printing to a Hewlett-Packard LaserJet III printer. To add this driver to the list and make it available to all User objects in the container, click the Import button. This option is discussed in more detail in Chapter 23.

Print Layout (Non-NDPS)

This page will show a map of the printing setup after you set up printers as discussed in Chapter 23. It lets you see the interrelationship of printers and objects and view the status of printers. Once printers are installed, they appear in a tree structure, and you can double-click a Printer object to expand or collapse the tree of objects below that object.

- A Trouble icon indicates printing problems. Expand the printer layout tree completely to see exactly which object is not functioning.

- A dashed line between objects means the connection is established only for the current print server session, rather than configured to connect every time the print server is loaded.

- Click the Update button to refresh the tree and show any changes.

- Click the Status button to see printer details, but keep in mind that you can see more details by finding the printer in the directory tree and opening its details dialog box.

- You can right-click an object to view its status.

Remote Access

This dialog box allows you to modify the remote access parameters for the container. You can specify the NDS Idle Timeout and both the IPX and IP communication parameters. These settings apply to the container and all objects within the container.

NDPS Printer Management

This dialog box allows you to install printers remotely on workstation clients. You can also remove printers or assign a default printer. This is covered further in Chapter 23.

Managing Novell
Directory Services

Creating and Changing User Objects

To create a User object, you first locate the container object in the directory tree where you want to add the object. But before creating any specific User object, it is a good idea to first create a *User object template* within the container. A template contains almost all the same fields as a User object, but the values that you enter into the fields of the template can apply to all User objects associated with that template. Templates save you time if you need to create a lot of users in a container who will have the same values. NetWare 5 supports multiple templates in each container. You can create templates based on departmental needs, user needs, or any other needs that a group of users has in common. When you create a new user, you can choose whether you want to use the values of the template or not. You can even use a template when creating a User object, and then change individual properties as necessary.

First we will discuss the procedure for creating a user template and explain the fields in the template. They are the same fields you see in a User object. Then we will discuss the technique for creating a User object, in which you use the template and make custom changes to properties as well.

The UIMPORT Utility

You can use the UIMPORT (User Import) utility to create a large number of users at the same time. You put information about users in an ASCII file, then run UIMPORT, which reads the information out of the file and creates user accounts from it. The information in the ASCII file can be exported from a database program that holds information about your users. It can include information such as the user's name, location, departments, group membership, and home directory path.

An additional "control" file must be created that contains the names of each field included in your ASCII file. UIMPORT uses the control file to separate each field and to know where the field information goes in the User object. For more information on running UIMPORT, refer to "Importing User Information into the Directory Services Database" in the NetWare 5 Documentation.

User Templates

As mentioned, user templates let you specify default rights that you can assign to any new User object you create. The details dialog box for user templates has almost all the same fields as the details dialog box for User objects. Following are some points to keep in mind.

Note *The following description of the pages on the user template details dialog box also applies to the User object details dialog box.*

- You can create multiple user templates in every container object.

- When creating a new User object, you can decide whether you want to use user template values or not.

- If you use the user template values, you can still individually change the default values in any user account.

- After you create the user template, it becomes an object itself.

- The Intruder Lockout page and Rights to Files and Directories page are not located on the user template. The intruder detection parameters can only be enabled at the container level. The Intruder Lockout page for the user shows the status for the specific user only. The rights to files and directories can be set for the container or individually for each user.

Container objects have the Intruder Detection page, which is slightly different than the Intruder Lockout page on User objects.

- When creating a user template, fill out fields with information that all users in the container have in common.

To create a user template within a container object, click the container and then choose Template from the Object menu. The Create Template dialog box for the template appears, as shown here:

Enter a name for the template and click the Create button. Notice that you can associate this template with an existing template or user, define additional properties, or create another template.

The details dialog box appears, as shown in Figure 17-2, after you click the Create button. A description for each page is provided in the following sections.

Identification

On the Identification page, you can optionally change all the fields except Name. The contents of the fields does not affect the access a user has to the network. However, it's highly recommended that you fill out this information, especially when creating the

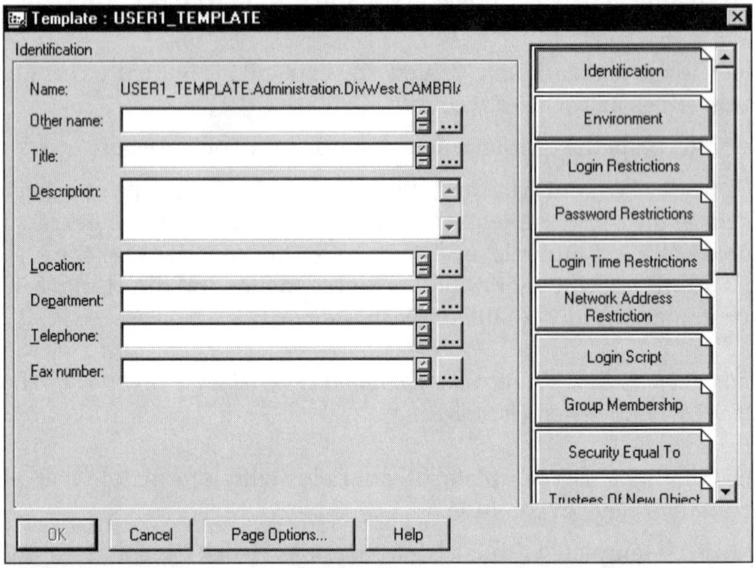

Figure 17-2. *The User template details dialog box for a container*

user template. You'll be able to search by it later. For a description of each field, click the Help button.

Note *Leave the word "template" in the Last Name field for the user template. That way, when creating User objects with a template, you'll be reminded that you are working with template values.*

Environment

The Environment page displays other properties of the User object:

- **Language** lists the languages, in order, in which the user prefers to work.
- **Default/Host Server** allows you to specify the NetWare server that the user will receive messages from when a message is sent using the SEND utility. Normally, you would set the default server to the server specified in the Preferred Server field of a user's client properties at the user's workstation. The Default/Host Server field is also the name of the server that the workstation authenticates to when the user logs in.
- **Home Directory** shows the Volume object and directory path of this user's home directory. The parent directory of the user's home directory must already exist, but the user's home directory itself will be created when the user is

created using the template. You can change the parent directory, but it must already exist. You can switch to Windows Explorer to create the directory, and then switch back and add it.

- **Run Setup Script** indicates whether the template's setup script will run as part of the user creation process.

- **Setup Script** specifies a setup script for the Template object. The setup script can perform user setup tasks that are not taken care of by the other properties of the template. As an example, you can copy files to the user's home directory when you create a new user. The setup script is processed on the workstation by the script processor immediately after each new User object is created.

Login Restrictions

The fields of the Login Restrictions page are shown here:

They determine when a user account expires and the number of simultaneous connections a user can have. It is best to specify login restrictions on the user template, rather than set them individually for each user. The Account Disabled check box is the one exception to this rule. There is little reason to check this on the user template unless you want user accounts to be disabled when they are first created. This might be useful if you are creating a new user workgroup and you don't want anybody to log in until preparations are complete. Locking an account is like shutting down an account without fully removing the account from the system. You might want to reactivate it later.

- If the User objects you create in the container should exist for only a certain period of time, check the Account Has Expiration Date box and then specify the range of time. Use this option when creating User objects for temporary employees or for an employee who is leaving the company.

- To prevent users from logging in at more than one workstation simultaneously, check the Limit Concurrent Connections box and then type in the number of concurrent connections that the user can have. Set this value to 1 for maximum security.

Password Restrictions

The fields of the Password Restrictions page are shown here:

```
☑ Allow user to change password
☐ Require a password
   Minimum password length:        [      ]
☐ Force periodic password changes
   Days between forced changes:     [      ]
   Date password expires:
   [  /   /    ] [▲▼]    [   :   :   ] [▲▼]

☐ Require unique passwords
☐ Limit grace logins
   Grace logins allowed:            [        ]


☐ Set password after create
```

To simplify your management task, it is best to fill out this page on the user template.
You can still make changes to individual accounts if necessary.

- **Allow User to Change Password**   Check this box if you want to let users
  change their own passwords.

- **Require a Password**   Check this box to require passwords for login. Doing
  so makes the remaining options available. Specify the minimum number of
  characters that passwords must contain in the field below the box. This
  heightens security by ensuring more diverse passwords.

- **Force Periodic Password Changes**   If users are creating their own passwords,
  you can force them to change their passwords after a specific period of time.
  Check the box, and then fill out the subfields either with the number of days
  between changes or with the date when the current password must be changed.

- **Require Unique Passwords**   When checked, NetWare remembers the eight
  previous passwords a user has created and does not let the user reuse one of
  these passwords.

- **Limit Grace Logins**   Check this box if you want users to be able to log in using
  expired passwords for a specific number of logins. You specify how many times
  users will see a message telling them to change their password before they can't
  log in using the old password anymore.

■ **Set Password After Create** When checked, you will be prompted to enter a password for each new user you create with this template.

Login Time Restrictions

The Login Time Restrictions page lets you specify the exact times that users can log into the system. You can set this for all users on the user template or set it for each user individually. The page includes the following box:

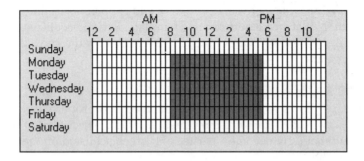

Click and drag a box around the block of time that you want to let users log in. In this example, users can log in Monday through Friday from 8:00 A.M. to 5:30 P.M.

Network Address Restrictions

The Network Address Restrictions page shows the network workstation addresses that a user can log in from. Do not specify this information on the user template. Set it on each user's individual account, as described in "Creating User Objects," later in this chapter.

Login Script

You can create a personal login script for users on the Login Script page. For the user template, create a login script that applies to every user. Remember that by default, users can change their personal login script. The Login Script page includes the Profile field. In this field, you can specify a profile object as a login script. See the section "Profile Objects," later in this chapter, for more information.

If you need to run "global" login commands for every user in a container, put them in the container login script. You can also create profile login scripts to assign to groups of people who don't belong to the same container.

Group Membership

On the Group Membership page, click the Add button and then choose a group that all the users you create by using the user template will belong to. If no groups have been created, there will be no groups to select.

Security Equal To

You use the Security Equal To page to specify other users that a user is equivalent to. You should not specify security equivalence on a user template, because security equivalence is usually only a temporary status for individual users who need to share rights. To grant multiple users trustee rights to objects, directories, and files, make them members of a group and then assign those rights to the group.

Trustees of New Object

This property page allows you to set up trustees and explicit object and property rights to User objects that will be created from this template. Each object listed on this page will automatically become a trustee of the new User object and receive the rights in the associated assignment.

New Object's DS Rights

This property page allows you to set up explicit object and property rights assignments for the User objects created from this template. Each User object created from this template will automatically become a trustee of each object listed on this page. They will receive the rights specified in the associated assignments.

New Object's FS Rights

This property page allows you to set up explicit file system rights for the User objects created from this template. Each new User object created from this template will automatically become a trustee of each file and directory listed on this page. They will receive the rights specified in the associated assignment.

Volume Space Restrictions

This property page allows you to limit the disk space each user can have on one or more volumes.

Postal Address

Click the Postal Address button to create address information for users. On the user template, you only need to fill this page out if there are fields that all users in the template have in common, such as the city and ZIP code. If mail will go to users at their department and they all share the same department, fill out the entire box. Remember that you can change these fields individually for any user. Once you fill out the upper address area, click the Copy to Label button. Third-party programs can access this information to create mailing labels.

Account Balance

The NetWare accounting system lets you specify credits for user accounts by setting the fields illustrated next.

```
Account balance:        [0]

☑ Allow unlimited credit

   Low balance limit:    [            ]
```

As users log in and log out of the system, they use up credits. Administrators use credits to help control user access in several ways. First, you can charge them for services rendered if they are students or nonemployees. You can also keep tabs on users who might be wasting the network's resources and time. You can give users a limited amount of credit and then review their operating procedures if they run out of credit too soon. Accounting and account balances are discussed in Chapter 21.

Members of Template

This property page displays a list of all User objects that have been created from this template. You can add and delete members from the list.

Security Equal To Me

This property page displays a list of users who will gain security equivalence to each new User object created from this template.

See Also

The See Also page contains an informational field that you can fill out on the user template if all User objects must have the same information. You could create a list of objects related to this object, or you could record information about the template.

Finishing Up

After you've modified all the necessary fields on the user template, click its OK button. The user template is added as an object to the container. If you ever need to change the template's properties, click the User Template object by using the right mouse button, and choose Details from its context menu.

Creating User Objects

Now that you've created the user template, you can begin creating User objects within the container. If you are the ADMIN user, you can start creating the subadministrators of your network to manage the divisions or departments in the organization. First, go through the following procedures to create a user in a container that the user will manage or that is most appropriate for the user. Then follow the steps in the section "Object Access Rights," later in this chapter, to assign subadministrator rights to users who will help you manage the network.

Follow these steps to create a User object:

1. Right-click the container object where you want to add a User object, and then choose Create from the context menu.

2. When the New Object dialog box appears, choose User in the list and click OK. The Create User dialog box appears, as shown here:

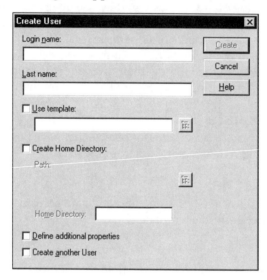

3. Fill the box out as follows:

   ■ Type a login name for the user in the Login Name field.

   ■ Type the user's last name, exactly as it's spelled, in the Last Name field. Don't use an abbreviation.

   ■ Check the Use Template box to assign template properties to the new User object. Then click the Browse button to scan for the template.

   ■ Check the Create Home Directory box if you want to specify a directory where the user can store personal files. Then click the Browse button to scan for the directory.

   ■ Check the Define Additional Properties box if you want to define the properties for the User object immediately. This disables the Create Another User field.

   ■ If you didn't check the Define Additional Properties box, you can check the Create Another User box to create another User object after creating this User object.

You can create a directory called Home or Users on a server, and then choose this directory by clicking the Browse button. A subdirectory is created for the user with the name entered in the Home Directory field. Users get all rights except supervisor to this directory.

4. Click Create to create this User object when the fields are set the way you want. NetWare Administrator creates a new User object in the container and creates a new directory at the location you specified in the Create Home Directory field. It then displays the details dialog box for the new User object (similar to the box shown Figure 17-1). If you selected the Use Template option, some of the fields will be filled out with values from the user template you created earlier.

To fill out the details dialog box, refer to the previous section, "User Templates." Most of the pages in the dialog box are discussed there; additional information is provided in this chapter. When you are done filling out the pages of the dialog box, click the OK button to save your changes.

Clicking the Cancel button will cancel all changes you've made on any page of the User details dialog box.

Network Address Restrictions

The Network Address Restrictions page shows the network workstation addresses that a user can log in from. Set this information on each user's individual account, not on the user template. If multiple protocols exist on the network, click the button of a protocol to see addresses for it. If no addresses are listed, there are no restrictions, and the user can log in from any workstation.

Security Equal To

You use the Security Equal To page to specify other users that a user is equivalent to. You should not specify security equivalence on a user template, because security equivalence is usually only a temporary status for individual users who need to share rights. To grant multiple users trustee rights to objects, directories, and files, make them members of a group and then assign those rights to the group.

If you make a user security-equivalent to another user and then delete or change that user, the security-equivalent user will be changed accordingly

Security Equal To Me

The Security Equal To Me property page displays a list of users who will gain security equivalence to this user. Be careful when assigning this property.

Postal Address

The Postal Address property page displays the address information for the user. Once you fill out the upper address area, click the Copy to Label button. Third-party programs can access this information to create mailing labels.

Rights to Files and Directories

This property page is discussed later in this chapter under the heading "Assigning File and Directory Rights to Objects."

Intruder Lockout

This property page is only a status page where you can view information about intruders, such as the number of times they incorrectly tried to log in or the network address of the computer on which they attempted to log in.

E-Mail Addresses

This property page contains a list of Internet e-mail addresses that are returned when an LDAP client requests a user's e-mail address. Figure 17-3 shows a user configured with an e-mail address of ttuser@netware5.com. See "Understanding Lightweight Directory Access Protocol (LDAP)" later in this chapter.

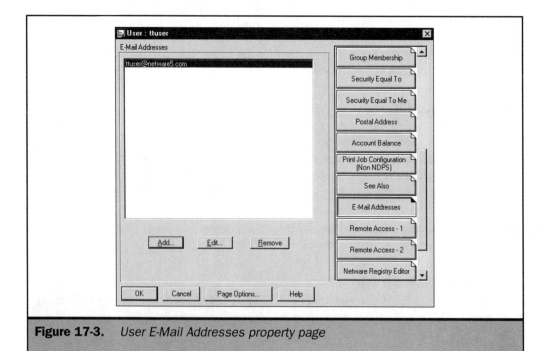

Figure 17-3.   *User E-Mail Addresses property page*

Remote Access - 1

The Remote Access - 1 property page, shown in Figure 17-4, enables you to configure remote access user parameters including the Remote Client password, connection time, idle timeout, and dialback. The various parameters on this page are detailed here:

- **Allow User To Change Remote Client Password**   Select this check box to permit users to change their own remote client passwords.

- **Disable Remote Client Password**   Select this check box to invalidate the remote client password after a specified number of days. Enter the number of days in the text box.

- **Use Default Maximum Connect Time**   Select this check box to select the default connect time of no limit. If you do not select this check box, enter the number of minutes between 1 and 100,000 in the Maximum Connect Time text box. A value of –1 indicates no limit.

- **Specify Idle Timeout**   Select this check box to specify an idle timeout period. The timeout can be between 1 and 100,000 minutes. A value of –1 indicates no limit.

- **Dialback**   The selected mode specifies the actions to take with remote connections from clients. Figure 17-5 shows the available modes.

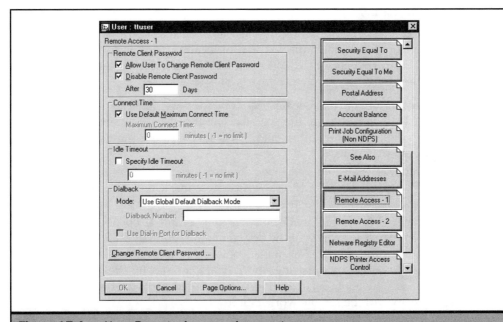

Figure 17-4.   *User Remote Access - 1 property page*

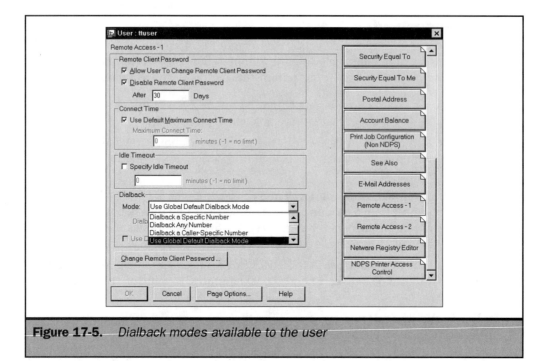

Figure 17-5. *Dialback modes available to the user*

Remote Access - 2

This property page allows you to configure the remote access service parameters for a user, organization, organizational unit, country, or locality. You can configure the AppleTalk Remote Access Service (ARAS) zone, IPX/IP parameters, and idle timeouts as shown in Figure 17-6. The parameters are as follows:

■ **User Restrict Zone** The User Restrict Zone for the AppleTalk Remote Access Service (ARAS) is entered in the text box. The ellipsis (…) can be clicked to bring up a dialog box for adding and deleting zones. This parameter is only applicable to User objects.

■ **IPX Parameters** Select this check box to create a virtual network containing remote IPX nodes. An IPX address, IPX address mask, and a home server to which remote nodes can attach is required.

■ **IP Parameters** Select this check box to enable remote IP clients access to the server. The network address of the domain name server and the domain name are required. If the Set Boot Parameters box is checked, enter the network address of the server that provides the Trivial File Transfer Protocol (TFTP) used to access the boot file. In addition, enter the name of the boot file that the clients use to start the remote workstations.

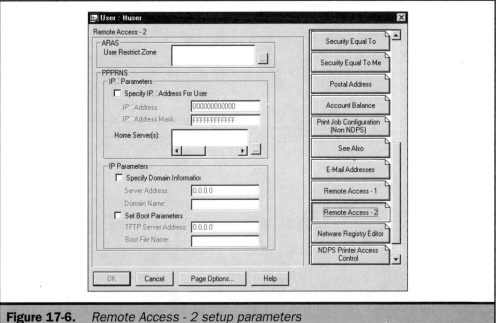

Figure 17-6.   *Remote Access - 2 setup parameters*

Remote Access - 3

Select this property page to configure remote access IP filtering parameters for a user, organization, organizational unit, locality, or country. You can set IP filtering by primary or secondary address pools so that the users can access only the Internet, only the Novell Internet Access Server (NIAS), or the Internet and limited locations on the NIAS server.

NetWare Registry Editor

This property page, shown in Figure 17- 7, allows you to edit the preferences that are stored for this user in the Windows registry. These properties are under the NRD Registry Index and the NRD Registry Data keys.

NDPS Printer Access Control

This property page allows you to configure Novell Distributed Print Services (NDPS) printers for the user to access. The access control level and the notification properties can be selected within this page as shown in Figure 17-8.

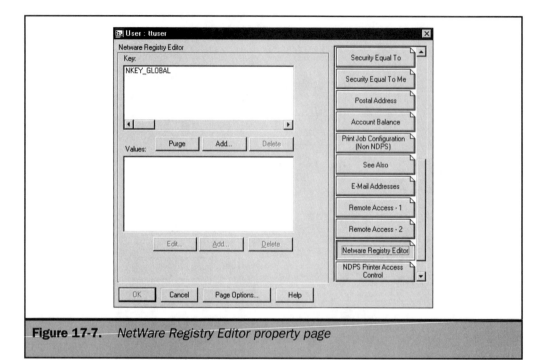

Figure 17-7. NetWare Registry Editor property page

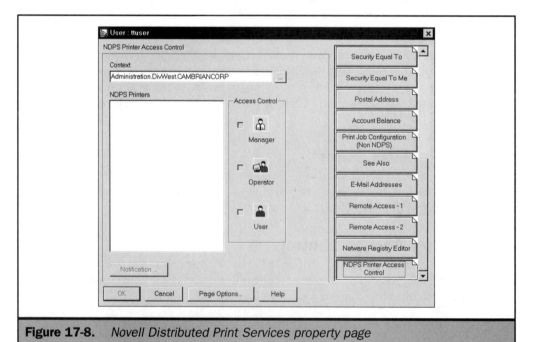

Figure 17-8. Novell Distributed Print Services property page

Creating Other Objects

The following sections describe how you create other objects in containers, but keep in mind that some of these objects are covered in more detail in other chapters, as follows:

- Directory Map objects are covered in Chapter 19.
- NetWare Server and Volume objects are created during installation, which is covered in Chapter 14. However, you should open the details dialog box for these objects and add information for documentation purposes.
- You create printer agents, gateways, brokers, and managers using Novell Distributed Printing Services (NDPS) as discussed in Chapter 23.

Group Objects

A group is a collection of User objects within a single container or from many different containers. You create a group so you can quickly assign rights to all the members of the group, send them e-mail, or perform other group tasks.

To create a group, locate the container object in the directory tree where you want to put the group, and then follow these steps:

1. Right-click the container where you want to put the group, and then choose Create from its context menu.

2. Choose the Group object on the New Object dialog box and click OK. The Create Group dialog box appears, as shown here:

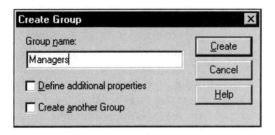

3. Fill out the dialog box as follows:
   - In the Group Name field, type the name for this group.
   - Check the Define Additional Properties box if you want to fill out the details dialog box for the new group immediately. Checking this box disables the Create Another Group box.

- If you didn't check the Define Additional Properties box, you can check the Create Another Group box to create another group as soon as you've created this one.

4. Click the Create button to create the new group. In a moment, the details dialog box appears. You fill out the fields on the Identification page in the same way you fill them out for container and User objects. Note the following:

   - Group objects have the Owner identification property, where you can specify the person who is responsible for the group.

   - Group objects have the Department identification property, where you can specify the department to which the group reports.

   - Group objects have the Organization identification property, where you can specify the organization to which the group belongs.

5. Click the Members button to add users to the group. A list of current members appears; you can click the Add button to add new members. Use the dialog box that appears to move up and down the directory tree to find the users you want to include in the group.

6. Click the Rights to Files and Directories button to assign file system rights, and then refer to the section "Assigning File and Directory Rights to Objects," later in this chapter, for more information.

7. Click the Security Equal To Me button to list users who are security-equivalent to this object.

8. When you are done specifying properties for the group, click the OK button.

Alias Objects

An Alias object is an object that refers to another object, such as a Volume or Server object somewhere else in the NDS directory tree. Users in one part of the tree who need to access a resource in another part of the tree on a regular basis need to have a local alias for that object to make it easier to refer to. Without an alias, they need to browse through the directory tree or type long context names every time they want to use the object.

For example, assume you have created a container called Info Systems that contains user accounts for all your NDS managers. However, the servers they manage on a regular basis are located in containers throughout the directory tree. To make their job easier, you can create an alias for every server scattered throughout the directory tree in the Info Systems container. Now they can refer to any server within their own container context. You could also establish similar arrangements for managers of communications equipment, printers, computers, groups, and other objects.

The steps for creating an Alias object are outlined here:

1. Locate the container where you want to place the Alias object. Right-click the container and choose Create from its context menu.

2. Choose Alias from the New Object dialog box and click OK. The Create Alias dialog box appears.

3. In the Alias Name field, type a name for this alias. Be descriptive with the alias name. You might want to include the name of a department or a code that identifies the location of the object the alias refers to. For example, names like "Alias of Engineering's Server" or "Alias of Marketing's Printer" are helpful.

4. Click the Browse button to the right of the Aliased Object field to locate the object this alias will refer to. The standard Select Object dialog box appears. Scan through the directory tree in the Directory Context field. When the object appears in the Objects field, click it, and then click OK.

5. When the Create Alias dialog box then reappears, you can choose to create additional aliases by clicking the Create Another Alias box.

6. Click the Create button to create the alias.

The alias in the container now represents an object in another container. You can now view and change details about the object represented by the alias by right-clicking the alias and choosing Details from its context menu. The properties on the details dialog box are exactly the same as if you had selected the actual object in its home container and viewed its properties.

Server, Volume, and Computer Objects

Server, volume, and computer objects represent physical devices on your network. All have interesting properties, which are described in the following sections.

Server Objects

A Server object is created when you install a NetWare 5 server. At that time, you specify which container will hold the Server object. The details dialog box, as shown in Figure 17- 9, displays useful information about the server, such as accounting information and network addresses, as described in the following list. You can fill out the other informational fields of Server objects at this time.

Note	*Many of the pages and fields in the Server object have no operational effect on the network or the server. They are for documentation only.*

- The **Identification** page lists the server's network address and version number.

- The **Error Log** page displays a list of errors that have occurred on this server. The file grows in size, so you might want to click the Clear Error Log button occasionally after viewing the log.

- The **Operator** page lets you record a list of operators who are in charge of this server.

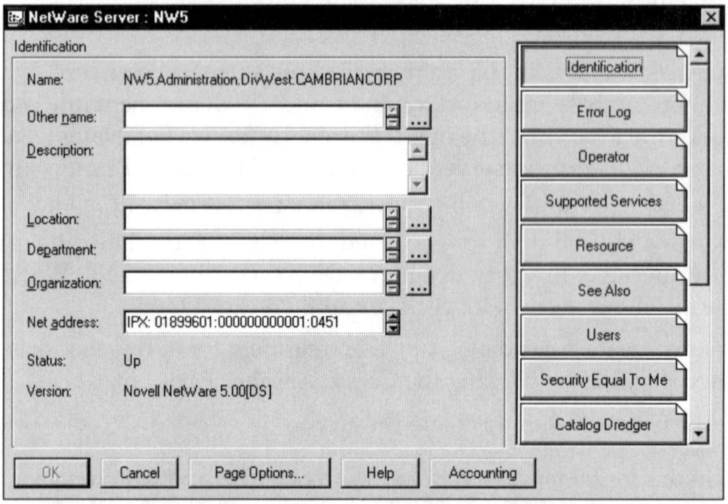

Figure 17-9. *The NetWare Server properties page*

- On the **Supported Services** page, you can create a list of services provided by this server.

- On the **Resource** page, you can create a list of resources available at this server, such as volumes and printers.

- The **See Also** page and **Users** page provide lists of other information and users who access this resource.

- The **Security Equal To Me** page displays a list of objects that are security-equivalent to this object.

- The **Catalog Dredger** page displays the catalogs on the server that are refreshed by the dredger service.

- The **SLP Directory Agent** page displays the Service Location Protocol (SLP) agent that will be used by the NCP server.

- The **LAN Area Membership** page allows you to add the server to a LAN Area object in the NDS tree. Once servers are added to a LAN Area object, you can apply WAN Traffic Policies to all of the included servers by defining and applying the policy to the object.

- The **WAN Policies** page is used to load predefined WAN Policies as described in Chapter 18.

- The **Cost** page allows you to display, add, or delete destination factors representing the relative expense of WAN traffic.

Note the Accounting button at the bottom. This is where you view and change charge rates for file services, such as disk block reads and writes, server connection time, and disk storage. If you click this button and the NetWare accounting features are not installed, you are asked if you want to install them. Refer to Chapter 21 for more information.

If you plan to install a new NetWare server in a new container object, use NetWare Administrator to create the container object before installing the server. This eliminates some problems that might occur otherwise.

Volume Objects

Volume objects provide vital information about the file systems in your servers. The Identification page displays the name of the volume and the server on which it is located. The Statistics page displays information about usage of the volume, as shown in Figure 17-10. On this page, you can view statistics about available disk space, deleted files, compressed files, and other information.

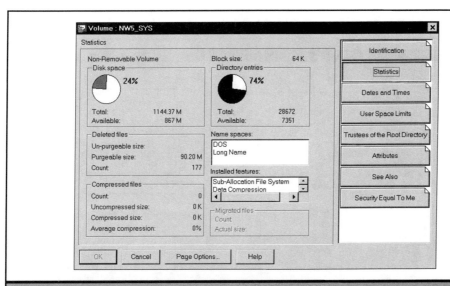

Figure 17-10.   *The Statistics page for a volume*

The Dates and Times page shows the date and time the volume was first created, the date the information was last updated, and archive information, such as the last time the volume was partially or completely backed up.

On the User Space Limits page, shown in Figure 17-11, you can specify how much disk space is available to individual users. For example, you can limit temporary employees to 20MB to store personal work files. You browse for a container in the tree, and a list of all users in that container appears with information about their current file usage.

Click a user and then click the Modify button to change his or her disk space usage limits. When the Volume Space Restriction dialog box appears, check the Limited Volume Space box and change the value in the field; then click OK.

The Trustees of the Root Directory page displays a standard Trustees dialog box where you can view, add, delete, or change the rights of trustees.

■ If a user has trustee rights to a higher object in the directory tree, such as the container holding the volume, that user will have those same rights for the volume, by inheritance. Users who have inherited rights are not listed in the Trustees field of the dialog box. To view the rights of a specific user in the volume, click the Effective Rights button and then browse for the User object of interest.

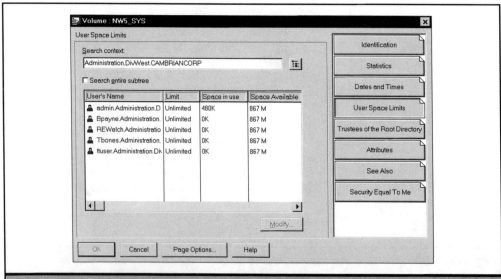

Figure 17-11.   *The User Space Limits page for a volume*

- Inherited rights that users have from higher-level containers can be blocked by clicking rights in the Inherited Rights Filter.

- Rights you grant to users in the root of a volume apply to all subdirectories of the volume unless blocked with an Inherited Rights Filter.

- The Supervisor right cannot be blocked by an Inherited Rights Filter in the file system.

To add new trustees to the root directory of the volume, click the Add Trustee button, and then browse for User objects in the directory tree. To delete a trustee of the root, highlight the user's name in the Trustees field and click the Delete Trustee button.

The Attributes page displays a list of directory attributes. Mark the box of any attribute you want to set for the directory. If you need an explanation of these attributes, click the Help button. Use the See Also page to add information about relationships that this object has with other objects. What you type on the page is for informational purposes only. Finally, the Security Equal To Me page is where you set other objects security equivalent to the Volume object.

Computer Objects

The Computer object is designed to help you manage the workstations on your network. The main purpose of the object is for documentation, because the properties are informational only and do not affect the network or the computer.

- On the **Identification** page, type useful information about the computer, such as its serial number, location, and other descriptions.

- On the **Operators** page, include a list of people who use this system.

- On the **Network Addresses** page, view and add network addresses for the workstation for each of the protocols listed, if they exist on the network. Click each protocol button to view its network addresses in the upper field.

- On the **See Also** page, include additional information about the computer or the resources attached to it, such as shared printers.

- On the **Security Equal To Me** page, include any objects for which you want security equal to the Computer object.

Legacy Print Server, Printer, and Print Queue Objects

You use the Print Server, Printer, and Print Queue objects to track shared legacy network printers. A print server is the core of the legacy printer management system. It keeps track of *shared* legacy printers on the network and manages the queues that network users submit print jobs to. Any number of print queues may exist for a single printer, or you can create one print queue that sends jobs to two or more printers. Use two or more printers for busy queues so that users can easily identify a single queue and not have to wait for their print jobs. The legacy printing environment has been replaced with Novell Distributed Print Services (NDPS). The printing system is described in Chapter 23.

Profile Objects

A Profile object contains a login script that executes for a set of users or groups who are not part of the same container object. The profile login script is optional and can be assigned to any user. You assign a profile login script to a user by specifying the name of the profile as part of the User object's property information. Specifically, you select the Login Script page of the User object's details dialog box and browse to locate a Profile object. This profile name is then entered in the Default Profile field.

Click the Login Script button to create the login script for the profile, and then refer to Chapter 24 for more information.

Organizational Role Objects

The Organizational Role object defines a position or role within your company. Use it as you would a Group object to define special access rights to the system for users who don't necessarily fit into any group context. For example, you could create an organizational role called Update Clerk and grant the Update Clerk object rights to program directories on a server. Then when a program needs updating, you make a user a temporary trustee of the Update Clerk object so that he or she can update programs in the directory.

The details dialog box of the Organizational Role object includes the Identification page, Postal Address page, Rights to Files and Directories page, See Also page, and the Security Equal To Me page, all of which have been discussed in this chapter.

Assigning File and Directory Rights to Objects

The following objects can be assigned rights to the file system by clicking the Rights to Files and Directories button on the object's details dialog box:

- Group object
- Organization object
- Organizational Unit object
- Organizational Role object
- Profile object
- User object

This section describes how to assign file system rights to an object. When you click the Rights to Files and Directories button, the dialog box shown in Figure 17-12 appears.

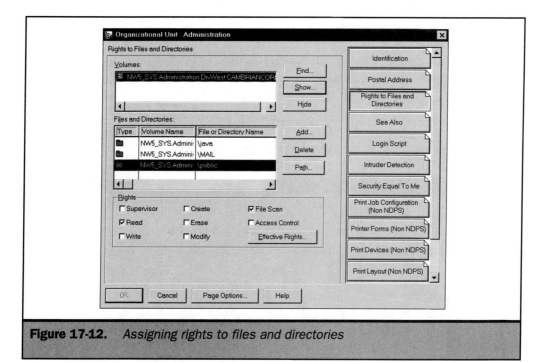

Figure 17-12. *Assigning rights to files and directories*

> **Note**   *If you assign directory and file rights in a container, all user accounts you create in the container obtain the same file system rights as the container. We recommend that you assign directory and file rights to the container first, and then to all groups, organizational roles, and finally the user. You can assign individual rights by working with a User object account.*

The dialog box is divided into two areas. At the top is a field where you select volumes to view. Initially, this field will be blank, but you can click the Find or Show button to add volumes to the list. Then when you click a volume, a list of files or folders and the assigned rights appear in the lower fields. Here's a description of buttons on the dialog box:

- **Find**   Click this button to search for a Volume object from a context you specify.
- **Show**   Click this button to add a Volume object to the Volumes list. Not all assigned volumes will appear in the list, so click this button to display specific volumes that you know have assignments.
- **Hide**   Click this button to remove a Volume object from the Volumes list.
- **Add**   Click this button to create a new trustee assignment for this object to a directory or file.

■ **Delete**   Click this button to delete this object's trustee assignment to the directory or file.

■ **Effective Rights**   Click this button to see this object's effective rights to a directory or file. Recall that effective rights are rights that the object obtains through inheritance from higher-level objects in the directory tree.

The steps for assigning rights to files and folders are as follows:

1. Click the Add button to display the Select Object dialog box:

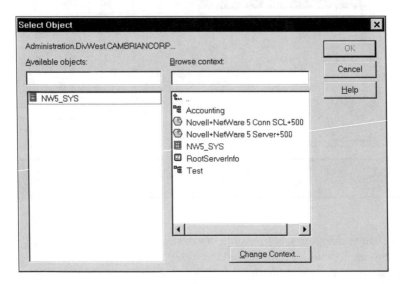

2. In the Select Object dialog box, scan through the directory tree in the Directory Context field until you locate the volume that contains the directories or files you want to make assignments to.

3. Once you find a volume, double-click it in the Browse Context field to display its folders (directories) and files. Select a folder in the Available Objects field and click the OK button.

You can select an entire volume and grant users rights to it, but that is usually not recommended, because users will then have rights to the root of the volume and all subdirectories of the root.

When you double-click a volume, a list of folders appears in both fields. You can then pick a folder in the Files and Directories field or, if you need to locate a subfolder or file within a folder, continue scanning in the Browse Context field until you locate the correct folder or file.

After selecting a file or folder and clicking OK, it appears in the Files and Directories field of the details dialog box (Figure 17-12). Now click it and select appropriate rights in the Rights field.

4. Click OK to complete the operation or click the Add button to continue adding more directories or files.

To view the effective rights the object has to the volume, folder, or file, click the Effective Rights button. Recall that effective rights are a combination of trustee rights, inherited rights, and security equivalence. From the Effective Rights dialog box, you can click the directory tree button to select other directories and view effective rights.

 You can rearrange the columns in the Files and Directories field to make information easier to see. Point to a column header, and then drag the header to the right or left over another header. The column assumes the new position. You can also change the width of the column by clicking the border between headers and dragging left or right.

An Alternate Method of Assigning File Rights

Another way to assign file system rights is to create a Directory Map object that has a path to a directory on a volume, and then assign file system rights directly to the Directory Map object. This is a good way to refer to directories whose location may change in the future. For example, if a server becomes overloaded and an application is moved to another server, all drive mappings associated with that application would have to change, and each user's login script drive mappings would have to be modified. If a Directory Map object is used in the drive mappings, then only the details as to where the application was moved would need to be changed for the Directory Map object. User login scripts would not have to change. Each user would have to be made security-equivalent to the Directory Map object.

Object Access Rights

In this section, you learn how to view and change access rights objects have to other objects. This section is really about creating subadministrators for your network, because it explains how to grant trustee rights to other objects. Object trustees may have the right to create or delete objects, or the right to change specific properties of objects. Recall that you can create trustees using two methods:

- Right-click the object that you want to make a user a trustee of, and then choose Trustees of This Object from the context menu.

- Click and drag the object you want to make a trustee over the object that you want to make the object a trustee of.

In either case, the same dialog box appears, and you can create new trustees by following the procedures discussed under "Creating Trustees" in Chapter 16. To create subadministrators for your directory tree, in most cases you drag a User object over a container to make that user a trustee of the container, its resources, and its subtree. However, some subadministrators manage resources such as servers or printers, so you may find yourself clicking and dragging a User object over a server or printer to create such trustees.

The NDS tree can grow quite large, so you may not have any choice but to create subadministrators to help you manage various parts of the tree. This may be imperative if the tree is structured geographically and containers represent parts of the organization that are far apart.

Autonomous Subtree Administrators

In some organizations such as state and local governments, it is often necessary to completely hand over control of a branch of your NDS directory tree. That means you give the director or manager Supervisor rights to the container where the subtree starts, and that person immediately applies either an Inherited Rights Filter or disallows inheritance to block higher-level supervisors (such as ADMIN) from the container. Thus, the subtree administrator takes complete control of the subtree.

To create this user, follow these steps:

1. Grant the subtree administrator Supervisor rights to his or her own User object. You right-click the object and choose Trustees of This Object, and then click the user's name in the dialog box and grant that user Supervisor rights.

2. Make the user a trustee of the container object he or she will manage.

3. In the Trustees of... dialog box, click the user in the Trustees field, then assign *all* rights, not just the Supervisor right.

4. To block the Admin rights in the container, revoke all inherited rights except the Browse object right and the Read property right. This allows ADMIN and other users to still view objects in the subtree.

5. Remove any existing explicit trustee rights to the container as appropriate.

The first step is important because it grants another user Supervisor rights to the branch of the tree. Without doing this, it would not be possible to create the IRF in step 4 and could cause a total loss of control in the subtree if the trustee's account were deleted. It is a good practice wherever possible to have a second account within the container that also has an explicit assignment of supervisor. Then if one account becomes corrupted, you can use the other.

Multiple Subtree Administrators

It may be necessary to create more than one administrator for a branch of the tree, especially if you plan to revoke the ADMIN user in the subtree. To create multiple subtree administrators, follow the preceding steps, but do the following as well:

■ Grant each subtree administrator the Supervisor right to his or her own account.

■ Make sure that a subtree administrator does not have explicit trustee rights for another subtree administrator.

■ Block any inherited rights that might give one subtree administrator control over another subtree administrator's object by using an Inherited Rights Filter.

Nonautonomous Subtree Administrators

In most cases, it is important to maintain the ADMIN user's (or equivalent) control over subtrees of the NDS directory tree. The preceding steps cut off ADMIN. Follow the steps in this section to create subtree administrators who can manage a branch of the tree but cannot cut off the ADMIN user. This is important in situations where a manager might leave the company under unfavorable conditions.

1. Make the manager an explicit trustee of a container and grant that person the following rights:

■ Object rights: Browse, Create, Delete, and Rename

■ Property rights: Compare, Read, Write, and Add Self

■ In the Selected Properties field, search for Object Trustee (ACL) and grant only the Create and Read rights.

Note *Step 1 prevents the manager from changing his or her own trustee assignments in the container!*

2. Make sure that the ADMIN user has all rights to the container, not just the Supervisor rights.

3. Assign the ADMIN user explicit trustee rights to the subtree administrator's object and grant all rights.

4. Revoke all inherited rights except browse to subtree administrators so they can't inherit rights to manage their own account.

5. Right-click the subtree administrator's object, and then click the subtree administrator's name in the Trustees field and assign the following rights. This prevents the subtree administrator from assigning more rights to himself or herself.

■ Object right: Browse

■ All properties: Read

■ In the Selected Properties field, locate Login Script and Print Job Configuration and assign Read and Write rights.

■ In the Selected Properties field, locate Object Trustee (ACL) and grant only the Create and Read rights.

All of this work prevents the subtree administrator from changing trustee assignments for a container that would allow the subtree administrator to gain more control over the container. Removing all but Create and Read rights to the Object Trustee (ACL) property achieves this.

Changing Default Rights

Recall that a special entity called [Public] has the explicit Browse trustee right in the root of the directory tree. All users are security-equivalent to [Public] and so have Browse rights for the entire tree even before logging in. The Browse right can be revoked for [Public] if you don't want unlogged users browsing your network. If you revoke the right, grant the highest-level organization container the Browse right so that users can browse the network *after* logging in.

To change [Public]'s Browse right in NetWare Administrator, right-click the [Root] object and choose Trustees of this Object. Click [Public] in the Trustees fields, and then revoke the Browse right in the Object Rights field.

Using Security Equal To

Security Equal To is an interesting property of User objects (it is a button on the details dialog box) that lets you quickly grant a user the same rights as another user. Also, when you add a user to a group or make a user a member of an organizational role, you are making that user security-equivalent to the object. The user is granted all rights that the other object has. Making users security-equivalent to other objects is usually only a temporary assignment.

To add an object to a user's Security Equal To list, a subadministrator must have at least the Write property right to the ACL (access control list) property of the object to be added to the list. It is not necessary to have rights to the Security Equal To property of the user, only the Browse object right.

Note *Objects within containers are security-equivalent to the container, but the containers do not appear on the Security Equal To list of a User object.*

Be careful when making an object security-equivalent to other objects. Don't give users the ability to add names to their own Security Equal To list. They might add the network supervisor to the list and gain supervisor status for the whole network! To avoid this problem, don't give users the Write or Supervisor right to the Security Equal To property in their User object. You can block the right in the Inherited Rights Filter of each User object.

Clerks

We use the label *clerks* to identify managers who have very limited rights to change object properties such as the address and phone number information in User objects. One way to do this is to create an organizational role in each container with the appropriate property rights, and then add a user in that container to the role. This makes sense if your tree follows the functional organization of the company, because a departmental secretary would be in the same container as the users he or she must manage.

Note that it is not difficult to create a manager with only selected property rights in NetWare 5. The inherited right has been added to the list of available rights. If it is checked for property rights, then the selected property rights will flow down the tree. It is no longer necessary to modify each user in a subcontainer.

> **Note** *Do not give the user the Write right to all properties. This would give the user the ability to change his or her own rights.*

Operators

An *operator* is a user who has control over a specific device on the network, such as a printer. You can grant a user this control by simply dragging his or her User object over the device, and then choosing the rights you want to assign to the user. In most cases, you should carefully evaluate the selected property rights.

Also note that you add some operators to lists within the object itself. For example, if you open the details dialog box of a Printer object, you see the Operators button. Click it to add names to the list. Printer operators manage the print server and the printers serviced by the Printer object. These duties include downing the print server, viewing its status, and controlling the printers serviced by the Printer object.

Understanding Lightweight Directory Access Protocol (LDAP)

LDAP is a comprehensive directory service and a standard method for accessing information located in the directory. It is a developing Internet communications protocol that allows client applications to access directory information. LDAP is based on the X.500 Directory Access Protocol (DAP). It is less complex than a traditional client and can be used with any directory service that follows the X.500 standard. The most popular use of LDAP is to allow clients to access directory services that store and publish telephone numbers and e-mail addresses. For more information on LDAP, refer to www.umich.edu/~drisvcs/ldap/ldap.html.

LDAP Services for NDS

LDAP Services for NDS is a server application (NLDAP.NLM) that allows LDAP clients to access information stored in the NDS database. Using NetWare Administrator, you can define the directory information you want to make accessible and grant the rights to the LDAP clients you want to have access to the directory. You can give different clients different levels of directory access, or you can access the directory over a secure connection. This allows you to make some types of directory information available to the public, other types available to your organization, and still other types available only to specific groups or individuals.

The directory features available to LDAP clients accessing information on a NetWare 5 server allow clients to read and write data in the NDS database. This is dependent upon the permissions granted to the individual clients.

LDAP clients can perform the following actions from the NDS database:

- Look up and retrieve information about a specific user, such as an e-mail address or phone number

- Look up and retrieve information for all users with a given last name, or a last name that begins with a certain letter

- Look up and retrieve information about any NDS object

LDAP Versus NDS Syntax

LDAP and NDS use different naming syntaxes. The important differences are the use of commas, typeful names, escape characters, and multiple naming attributes. Each of these is discussed in the following sections.

Commas

LDAP uses commas as delimiters. NDS uses periods. For example, a distinguished name in NDS is as follows:

CN=bpayne.OU=Administration.OU=DivWest.O=CAMBRIANCORP

The equivalent name using LDAP syntax is as follows:

CN=bpayne,OU=Administration,OU=DivWest,O=CAMBRIANCORP

Typeful Names

LDAP uses only typeful naming syntax with commas as delimiters. NDS uses both typeful and typeless naming syntax. For example, both of the following names are equivalent in NDS:

.bpayne.Administration.DivWest.CAMBRIANCORP
CN=bpayne.OU=Administration.OU=DivWest.O=CAMBRIANCORP

Using LDAP syntax, the name must be as follows:

CN=bpayne,OU=Administration,OU=DivWest,O=CAMBRIANCORP

Escape Character

The "\" character is used in LDAP as an escape character. It is used to allow other characters such as "+" or the "," to be used in an LDAP name. For example, a container with the name "Research + Development" would be represented as follows using LDAP syntax:

Research\+Development

Multiple Naming Attributes

Objects within NDS can be defined with multiple naming attributes in the schema. In both NDS and LDAP, the User object has two attributes: common name (CN) and organizational unit (OU). The plus character, "+", separates the naming attributes in the distinguished name. If the naming attributes are not explicitly labeled, the NDS schema determines which string goes with which attribute. For example, the first attribute would be the common name (CN) and the second attribute would be the organizational unit (OU). Using LDAP, you can reorder the attributes in a name if you manually label each attribute. For example, here the implied naming attribute is common name (CN):

bpayne

And here the implied naming attributes are the common name (CN), bpayne; and the organizational unit (OU), DivWest:

bpayne+DivWest

Both of the relative distinguished names can exist in the same context because they must be referenced by two completely different relative distinguished names.

LDAP Objects in NDS

When LDAP Services for NDS are installed on a NetWare 5 server, three objects are created in the NDS tree: the LDAP Server, the LDAP Group, and LDAP Catalog objects. Each of these objects is discussed next.

LDAP Server Object

The LDAP Server object stores the configuration data for the LDAP service that runs on the server, as shown in Figure 17-13. It contains the following server-specific properties:

- **Host Server**   This is the name of the server that is hosting the LDAP Services for NDS.

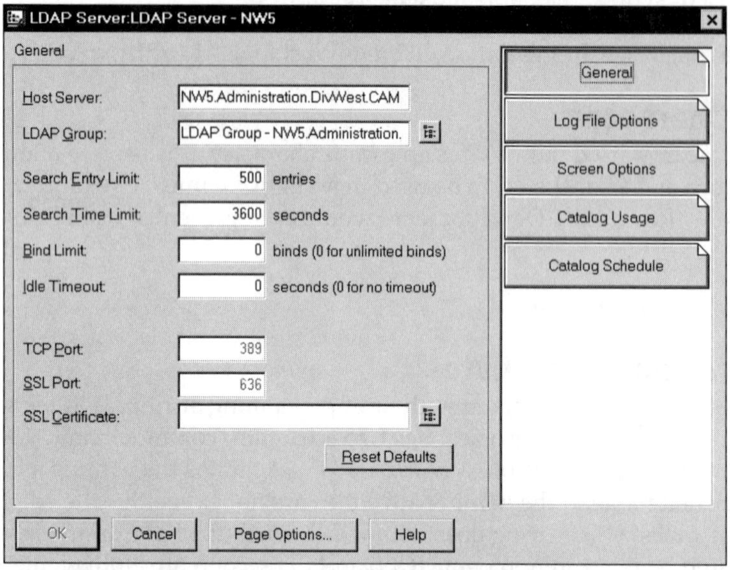

Figure 17-13.   The LDAP Server configuration dialog box

- **LDAP Group**   This is the object that contains the configuration settings used by this LDAP server. It is covered in detail later in this chapter.

- **Search Entry Limit**   This is the maximum number of objects for which the LDAP server will return data. The range is between 1 and 2,147,483,647. The default number of objects returned is 500.

- **Search Time Limit**   This is the maximum amount of time in seconds that the LDAP server will use to find objects. The range is between 1 and 2,147,483,647 seconds. The default is 3,600 seconds (one hour).

- **Bind Limit**   This is the maximum number of simultaneous client connections the LDAP server can support.

- **Idle Timeout**   This is the maximum number of seconds that an LDAP client connection can be inactive.

- **TCP Port**   This is the TCP port number for LDAP services on this server. The default value is 389 and should be changed with caution. The TCP port number should not be the same value as the SSL port number.

- **SSL Port**   This is the Secure Sockets Layer (SSL) port number for LDAP services on this server. The default value is 636 and should be changed with caution.

- **SSL Certificate**   This specifies the Key Material object for storing the Secure Sockets Layer (SSL) certificate for this LDAP server. The LDAP server will only use the certificate defined by this parameter for SSL connections, even if others exist.

The LDAP Server dialog box contains four other buttons in addition to the General button:

- **Log File Options** This page allows you to choose the types of events that are recorded in the log file, as shown in Figure 17-14. Logging is enabled when you enter a name or a value in the log filename text box.
- **Screen Options** This page allows you to choose the types of events that are displayed on the console of the LDAP server. To enable a log event, select the corresponding check box. The available events are the same as those shown in Figure 17-14.
- **Catalog Usage** This page, shown in Figure 17-15, defines how the LDAP clients will be able to search for information in the catalogs. You can limit the search to NDS only, the LDAP catalog only, or both.
- **Catalog Schedule** This page defines when you want to update or refresh the information in the Catalog object, as shown in Figure 17-16.

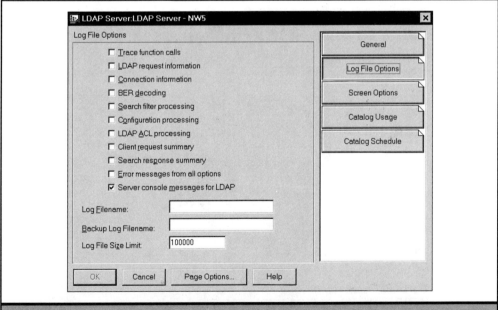

Figure 17-14. *LDAP Server Log File Options dialog box*

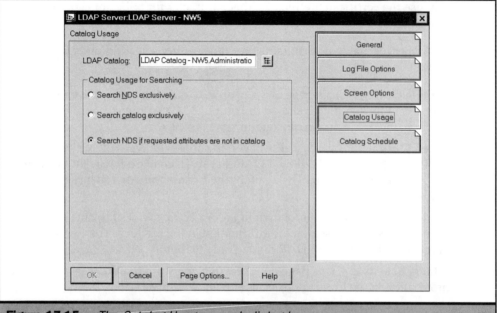

Figure 17-15.   The Catalog Usage search dialog box

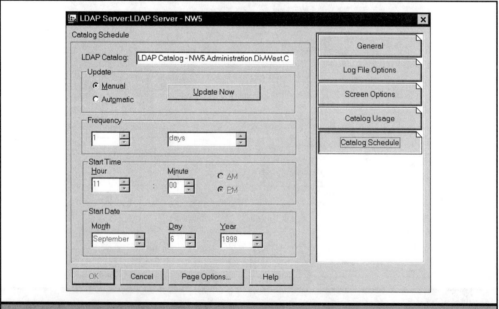

Figure 17-16.   Select how and when you want the information in the LDAP
Catalog refreshed

LDAP Group Object

The LDAP Group object stores the configuration data for the LDAP groups that will be accessing the server, as shown in Figure 17-17. It contains the following group-specific properties:

- **Suffix**   This defines the subtrees that NDS makes available to LDAP clients. If the LDAP client requests access to areas outside of the subtrees defined by the suffix, an error is returned to the requesting client.

- **Referral**   This text box specifies the URL of an alternate LDAP server that handles requests that are not valid within any of the subtrees defined in the suffix option.

- **Allow Clear Text Passwords**   This check box allows the transmission of bind requests that include passwords over non0encrypted connections. By default, only passwords exchanged over SSL connections are encrypted. If this option is not checked, the LDAP service will reject all binds that include passwords on non-SSL connections.

- **Proxy Username**   This option allows you to configure a separate identity for anonymous binds to the LDAP server. The name must be a valid NDS User object. It should not require a password and is assigned to all anonymous binds. If a proxy username is not defined, all anonymous LDAP clients are validated to NDS as the [Public] user. The typical NDS User object name is LDAP_PROXY.

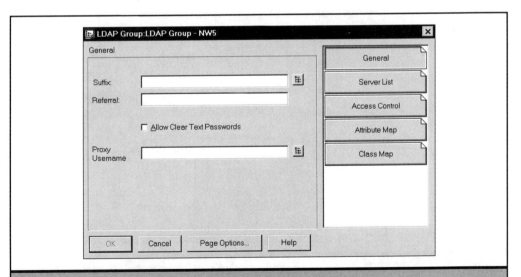

Figure 17-17. *The LDAP Group dialog box*

The LDAP Group dialog box contains four other buttons in addition to the
General button:

■ **Server List** This page, shown in Figure 17-18, allows you to view, add, and
   remove the servers that use the configuration data stored in this object. LDAP
   access to the servers in this list is logically equivalent to the same security
   restrictions and class and attribute mappings.

■ **Access Control** This page, shown in Figure 17-19, allows you to create Access
   Control Lists (ACLs) that create an additional layer of security between LDAP
   clients and NDS. You can implement LDAP client access restrictions for all
   LDAP servers in the Group object.

■ **Attribute Map** This page defines a relationship between the LDAP attributes
   and the NDS properties associated with each NDS object. When an LDAP
   client requests an LDAP attribute from the server, the server returns the
   corresponding NDS property. You can map multiple LDAP attributes to the
   same NDS property, as shown in Figure 17-20.

■ **Class Map** This page defines a relationship between an LDAP class and an
   NDS object class, as shown in Figure 17-21. When an LDAP client requests an
   LDAP class from the server, the server returns the corresponding NDS class. As
   a result of the differences between the LDAP and NDS schemas, many classes
   and attributes are not mapped in the default configuration. You should
   reconfigure them as needed.

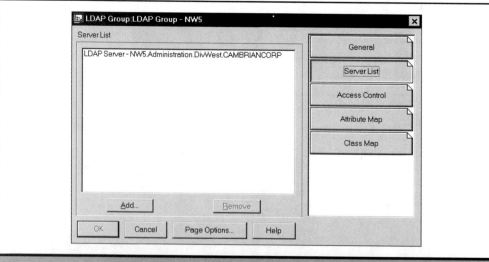

Figure 17-18.   *LDAP Server List displays servers that use the same configuration
data as this server*

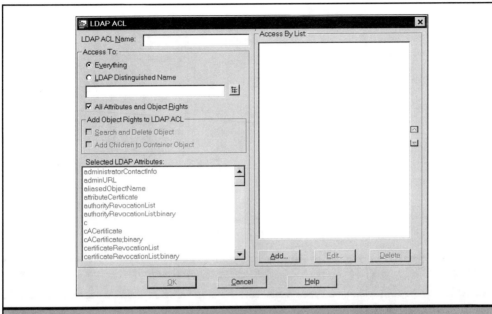

Figure 17-19.   *LDAP Access Control Lists (ACLs) allow you to create an additional layer of security between LDAP clients and NDS*

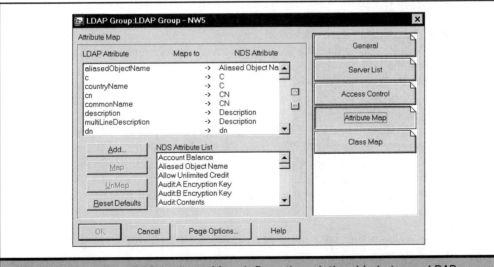

Figure 17-20.   *The LDAP Attribute Map defines the relationship between LDAP attributes and NDS properties*

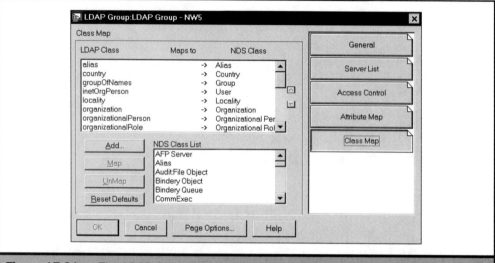

Figure 17-21. *The LDAP Class Map defines the relationship between LDAP classes and NDS classes*

LDAP Catalog Object

The LDAP Catalog is a flat database that contains a snapshot of information from the NDS database. A catalog can contain information from an entire NDS tree or a portion of the NDS tree. It only stores objects and properties that you specify. It lets you find information about various objects without a time-consuming search of the entire NDS database.

Catalogs are useful in networks in which some NDS objects are accessible only across a WAN link. A search of the local catalog negates having to search the NDS database across the link. Some applications create their own catalogs in NDS. For example, Novell's Contextless Login creates a catalog containing users' common names and their telephone numbers. The catalog is stored as an NDS object within the tree.

For each catalog you create, you create one Master Catalog. You can also create multiple slave catalogs if needed. The slave catalog is a copy of the Master Catalog. The Master Catalog receives its information from the dredger and then replicates this information to the slave catalogs. Querying and indexing a catalog allows you to retrieve information from it.

The Master Catalog dialog page is shown in Figure 17-22. It contains the following fields:

- **Name**   This is the object name of the catalog when it was created in the NDS database.

- **Host Server**   This is the NDS name of the server that is running the LDAP Services for NDS.

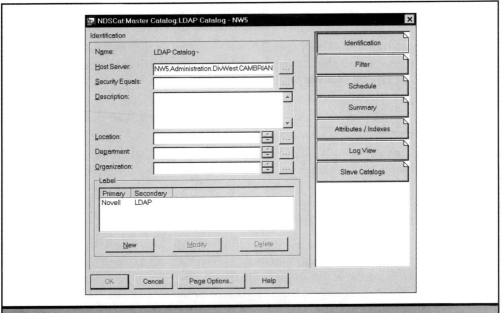

Figure 17-22.   *The Master Catalog dialog page*

- **Security Equals**   This field lets you specify the object that you want the Catalog object to be security-equivalent to. Browse and Read rights for the NDS tree are necessary for the catalog to become populated.

- **Description**   This is an optional field in which you can enter a description of the catalog.

- **Location**   This is an optional field in which you can enter the physical location of the catalog.

- **Organization**   This field allows you to associate the catalog with a specific organization.

- **Primary**   This field specifies the name of the catalog. This is an attribute of the Catalog object and can be used to specify the application with which the catalog is associated.

- **Secondary**   This field allows you to further specify the name of the catalog.

The Master Catalog also has six buttons for additional configuration options:

- **Filter**   This page allows you to specify the information that you want to retrieve from NDS and place into the catalog.

- **Schedule**   This page allows you to manually refresh the catalog or schedule automatic catalog refreshes.

■ **Summary**   This page displays information about the catalog such as date and time of the last update. It also is used to display the Query Catalog dialog box.

■ **Attributes/Indexes**   This page allows you to choose the object attributes that are to be included in the catalog. In addition, you define the attributes by which the catalog will be indexed.

■ **Log View**   This page displays the information returned to the console by the dredger. It includes the time of dredge (search), confirmation that the dredge was completed, and any error conditions reported.

■ **Slave Catalogs**   This page displays a list of catalogs that are slaves to the selected catalog, and allows you to add or delete catalogs from the slave list.

License Object

NetWare 5 includes a new license manager utility that allows you to manage Novell Licensing Services (NLS) on one or more servers. It can be started as a stand-alone utility or invoked from the NetWare Administrator. The NLS Manager is located in the \PUBLIC\WIN32 subdirectory on the SYS volume of the server. The NLS Manager screen is shown in Figure 17-23.

Installing a License Certificate

Novell Licensing Services (NLS) adds a License container object to the NDS tree and a License Certificate object when an NLS-aware application is installed. You select

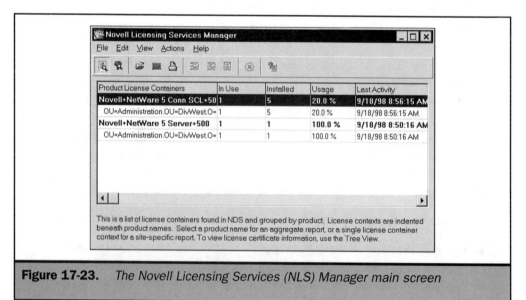

Figure 17-23.   *The Novell Licensing Services (NLS) Manager main screen*

the context in the NDS tree where you want these objects to be placed. Any additional licenses you purchase will be added to the NDS tree as objects in the License container object.

You can install a license certificate using either the NetWare Administrator utility or the NLS Manager. To install a license using the NetWare Administrator, select Tools | Install License | Install License Certificate. To install a license using the NLS Manager, perform the following steps:

1. Select View | Tree View from the main menu. A screen like the one shown in Figure 17-24 will be displayed.

2. Select Actions | Install License Certificate.

3. Enter the path and filename of the certificate or click the Folder icon to browse the directory structure. The .NLS file is linked to an activation password file (key) and automatically retrieves the password.

4. Select the NDS context where the Certificate object will be installed. If you are installing an additional certificate in an existing License container object, select the container's parent, not the License container object.

5. Click OK to install the license certificate.

6. Click OK to acknowledge the "need to update" message.

7. Click OK to acknowledge the successful installation.

8. If required, enter the key you received for this license in the Activation Key window.

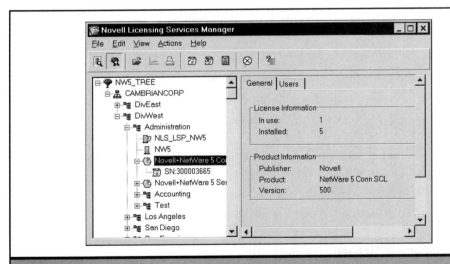

Figure 17-24.   *Novell Licensing Services Manager tree view screen*

A license certificate requires an activation key. If the file containing the activation key is in the same directory as the license file, it will be read automatically. If the activation key cannot be found, an Activation Key window will display, allowing you to enter a key. To browse for the file containing the activation key, click Import.

The activation key is like a password. It is a code that allows you to complete the installation of a license for a product you purchased. Activation keys allow you to install additional licenses for products you have already purchased via electronic purchases and distribution.

Creating a Metered Certificate

Metered certificates allow you to track the usage of applications even when they are not written to the Licensing Service Application Programming Interface (LSAPI) specifications. Through the use of metered certificates, you can allow users to continue to use non-NLS-aware applications while you track and manage the licenses for those applications. You can also configure Z.E.N.works to function as the NLS client for non-NLS-aware applications. Z.E.N.works will then request licenses on behalf of those applications.

To create metered certificates using the NetWare Administrator utility, select Tools | Install License | Create Metered Certificate. To create the metered certificates using NLS Manager, complete the following steps:

1. Select View | Tree View from the main menu.

2. Select Actions | Create Metered Certificate.

3. Enter the publisher's name of the software being metered.

4. Enter the version number of the software. If a period is part of the version number, the License container object will add a backslash to its NDS name.

5. Choose the NDS context for the certificate.

6. Enter or select the number of licenses for the certificate.

7. Enter or select the number of grace licenses you will allow.

8. Select an update interval. This determines how often an application is to check whether a license is still being used and to inform LSP of the status.

9. Select whether or not users use a single license when launching an application multiple times from the same workstation.

10. Click OK to acknowledge that Quick View must be updated.

11. Click OK to acknowledge that the certificate installed correctly.

Installing an Envelope

An envelope is a file that contains one or more license certificates. Envelopes allow you to install more than one license certificate at a time into a License container object. For example, you may have purchased a suite that contains four products. An envelope allows you to install license certificates for all four products at one time.

To create an envelope using the NetWare Administrator utility, select Tools | Install License | Install Envelope. To create an envelope using the NLS Manager, complete the following steps:

1. Select View | Tree View from the main menu.

2. Select Actions | Install Envelope.

3. Follow the onscreen prompts from the Envelope Installation Wizard.

Assigning Licenses to Users

Access to license certificates is determined by the location of the license certificate and whether any assignments have been made to the certificate. The owner of a license certificate is the NDS object that installed the certificate. As the owner, you can assign users, groups, organizations, organizational units, and servers access to the licenses.

If you assign access to a container object, all users in and below that container will have access to the licenses. Only those objects that have been assigned access to the licenses can use them. You can add and delete access assignments through the Assignments property page, as shown in Figure 17-25.

To assign access to license certificates using the NetWare Administrator utility, select a certificate in the Browse window and right-click the certificate. Select Details |

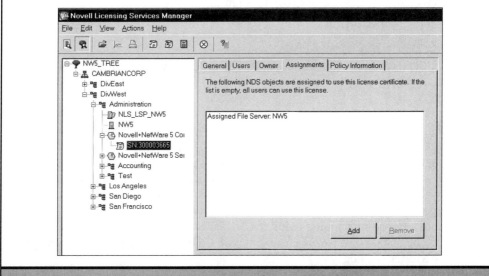

Figure 17-25.   *Assignments property page for a selected license*

Assignments | Add. Select an object and click OK. To assign access using the NLS Manager, perform the following steps:

1. Select View | Tree View from the main menu.

2. Select the license certificate you want users to access.

3. Select the Assignments property page (see Figure 17-25).

4. Click Add.

5. Locate and select the object that allows the users to access the licenses.

6. Click OK.

Assigning a New Owner to a License Certificate

The NDS object that installed a license certificate is the owner of the license certificate. Sometimes it may become necessary to reassign ownership of the license certificate.

Note *Only the certificate's owner can reassign ownership of the certificate.*

To assign ownership to another object using the NetWare Administrator utility, select a certificate in the Browse window and right-click the certificate. Select Details | Owner. Select an object and click OK. To assign ownership using the NLS Manager, perform the following steps:

1. Select View | Tree View in the main menu.

2. Select the license certificate.

3. Click the Owner property page.

4. Click the tree icon and select the NDS object you want to assign ownership to.

5. Click OK.

Creating a Licensing Catalog

A Licensing Catalog is an object in the NDS tree that "walks" the tree to discover License container objects within the tree. When you start the NLS Manager utility, you can direct it to get information from the Licensing Catalog object or to "walk" the tree. A Licensing Catalog object may be temporarily inaccurate because it will not contain recent changes in the NDS tree until it rewalks the tree.

You create a Licensing Catalog using the NetWare Administrator utility. Catalog Services must be installed in NDS before your can do this. Perform the following steps to create the Master Catalog:

1. No. BillSelect Object | Create | NDSCat:Master Catalog.

2. Name the new catalog Licensing Catalog.

3. Click Define Additional Properties | Create.

4. In the Host Server field, enter the name of the server where DSCAT.NLM will run.

5. In the Label field, set the Primary and Secondary parameters.

6. Select the Filter page.

7. In the Filter field, enter **"Object Class"="NLS:Product Container"**.

8. Select the Schedule page.

9. Select Automatic and set the frequency for updates.

10. Select the Attributes/Indexes page.

11. From the available attributes list, select the following: NLS:Product, NLS:Publisher, and NLS:Version.

12. Click OK.

13. Click OK again.

Add the new Licensing Catalog as a trustee of the [Root] object.

1. Select the [Root] object.

2. Right-click and select Trustees of This Object.

3. Click Add Trustee and browse to the new Master Catalog's context and select it.

4. Select Object Rights and select only the Browse right.

5. Select Property Rights and select only the Read right.

6. Click OK.

Making Server Assignments

A file server assignment allows you to designate which servers can grant requests for licenses. One server can carry the file server assignments for several license certificates. Each new license certificate is added to the previous license certificate for the total number of allowed connections.

To make server assignments using the NetWare Administrator utility, select the certificate you want to assign. Right-click the object and select Details | Assignments and browse to the file server you want. To make server assignments using NLS Manager, complete the following steps:

1. Select View | Tree View from the main menu.

2. Select the License Certificate object you want to assign to a server.

3. Click Assignments | Add.

4. Locate the Server object you want to assign as owner of this License Certificate object.

5. Click OK.

Creating and Using Reports

The NLS Manager utility tracks data about licensed and metered products. You can create reports that monitor usage and license compliance for these products. The reports provide data covering the past 15 months.

You can create aggregate reports or reports for license containers in a specific context. An aggregate report provides information about all license certificates being used for a given product. Create an aggregate report by completing the following steps:

1. Select View | Quick View.

2. Select a product license container.

3. Access the Usage Report Wizard by double-clicking the License container object.

4. Follow the onscreen prompts from the Usage Report Wizard.

Security Objects in NDS

NetWare 5 offers security services that include Public Key Infrastructure Services (PKIS), Novell International Cryptographic Infrastructure (NICI), and Secure Authentication Services (SAS). These security features are fully integrated with Novell Directory Services (NDS). Each of these security services is described in the following sections.

Public Key Infrastructure Services (PKIS)

Public Key Infrastructure Services (PKIS) enables public key cryptography and digital certificates in a NetWare environment. PKIS allows you to establish a Certificate Authority (CA) management domain within NDS and manage certificates and keys for Secure Sockets Layer (SSL) security for LDAP servers. PKIS within the NetWare 5 environment offers the following:

■ Integrity of certificate and private key storage using the inherent security in NDS

■ The ability to manage automated artificial certificate creation using the local CA

■ Single point of administration using the NetWare Administrator utility

■ Standards support for the generated certificates according to the X.509 v3 standard

■ Standards support for PKCS #10 certificate signing requests

■ The ability to securely manage the private keys for server applications

■ Worldwide exportable public key management capabilities

PKIS allows you to build a public key infrastructure on your network. You can create a CA local to your organization and use the services of external CAs. With PKIS you can generate unlimited key pairs and issue unlimited public key certificates through the local CA at no charge.

Novell stores all keys and certificates generated or obtained from external CAs in NDS. This security allows public keys to be openly published, while private keys are protected.

Novell International Cryptographic Infrastructure (NICI)

Novell International Cryptographic Infrastructure (NICI) is a technology that provides strong cryptography for worldwide use. It is designed to meet the needs of customers while complying with diverse national policies on the shipment and use of cryptography.

It delivers confidentiality, integrity, authentication, and nonrepudiation using a modular software design. New modules can be dynamically added as security requirements and standards change. All cryptographic services are available to the software engineer via the Novell Software Developer's Kit (SDK).

The key features that NICI provides to NetWare 5 are as follows:

- Software developers are free from having to integrate cryptographic code in their products.

- The dynamically bound cryptographic library delivers controlled cryptographic services to applications wherever they are used.

- It provides for international applications to receive expedited U.S. export approval.

- The integrity of key management is maintained through the integration with NDS.

- It provides a uniform set of cryptographic service APIs for software developers.

- It provides NetWare 5 with security services built on NICI.

NICI is the foundation for future network cryptographic services. It ensures that new software applications will be compliant with international cryptographic import and export laws. It has been the case in the past that software applications had to provide their own services if they wished to employ cryptography. This is now provided by the Novell SDK. Novell ensures compliance with international import and export laws, leaving developers free from these concerns.

Secure Authentication Services (SAS)

Secure Authentication Services (SAS) provides authentication services for existing applications and evolving authentication mechanisms in the future. It provides Secure

Sockets Layer (SSL) support for Novell's LDAP services. Server applications use the SAS API set to establish encrypted SSL connections between the client and the server. SAS is built entirely on NICI and therefore inherits the modularity of this technology.

PKIS provides the key management services for the SSL services. Any application written to the SAS interface inherits the ability to have PKIS manage its certificates. NDS is used to define the Access Control Lists (ACLs) that manage access to the private keys that enable SSL. SAS is a service, not an API library. Thus, applications do not have access to the protected authentication materials or the user's protected data. It also provides for worldwide exportable cryptographic services for authentication.

Requirements for PKIS

In order to use PKIS, your server and the workstation from which you administer the services must meet the following requirements:

- A NetWare 4.11 or NetWare 5 server with Novell's BorderManager product installed in the NDS tree
- Novell Secure Authentication Services (SAS) installed on the server that has the Certificate Authority (CA) defined in NDS
- Novell PKIS installed
- The NICI Cryptographic modules installed on the server
- NWADMIN32 installed on the workstation

SAS adds additional security functionality and creates the Security container within the NDS tree for PKIS to use. When you install SAS, the Secure Sockets Layer (SSL) protocol is also installed. It creates a SAS object in the NDS tree.

You can install SAS, PKIS, and the NICI Cryptographic Modules through the Product Options menu using the NWCONFIG utility at the server.

The server that owns a Key Material object must be able to communicate with at least one other server holding a writable copy of the Key Material object. You must ensure that both servers are running the same communications protocol. In addition, all of the components on the preceding list must be installed and running on the server.

The Complete Reference

NetWare 5

Chapter 18

NDS Tree and Partition Management

The NDS (Novell Directory Services) database contains all the information about your network, its servers, its users, and the security of the network. This database can be stored in a central location or distributed throughout your network to make it more accessible to users at those locations. Partitioning (dividing a tree into subtrees) and replication (copying subtree information) are the processes you use to distribute the NDS database.

This chapter describes how to partition the NDS database and how to set up replication. Chapter 11 provides information about planning your NDS tree with partitioning and replication in mind. Recall that if your network is large and located in many different geographic areas, you need to replicate the database so users at those locations can have more convenient access to it. However, replication can tie up network bandwidth and WAN links, so there is a trade-off in providing users with convenient local access that might reduce network performance. This performance trade-off can be minimized through the use of WAN policies established with the WAN Traffic Manager utility.

You create replicas of the NDS database to provide fault tolerance. A centralized strategy for a small network (10 servers, 1,000 users) is to replicate the entire database to at least two other servers in the local area. In a distributed approach, the entire database is still stored on at least two other servers, but parts of it are also replicated to users at other locations.

Note   *Keep in mind that a replicated partition is not a separate database. It is just an "image" of all or part of the master database.*

This chapter also describes the NDS Manager utility you can use to monitor and troubleshoot NDS, and it contains information about configuring and maintaining time servers in a time-synchronized environment.

Management Concepts for Partitioning and Replication

The partitioning utilities in NetWare 5 let you create partitions and decide where you want to store those partitions. All partitions are automatically linked by NDS so that data is shared among them.

The root partition is automatically created when you install the first NetWare 5 server [Root]. Consider the following illustration:

On the left, the root partition includes the [Root] of the directory tree, the Organization object specified during installation, and the container that holds the first NetWare 5 server. As your directory tree grows, as shown on the right, you can create new partitions. For example, you can create a partition at the Administration and Sales containers.

There can only be one [Root] partition. Each additional partition of the directory tree forms a distinct subtree that has its own *partition root object*. In the preceding illustration, the Administration and Sales containers form the partition root object of the partitions you create there. The partition root object is always the *topmost* container in a partition.

When the NDS database is partitioned and replicated, it must be synchronized on a regular basis to ensure that every replica of the database has the latest NDS information. Partition root objects are given the following attributes, which are used by NDS to synchronize the database:

- **Replica Pointer**   This attribute holds the location of all the copies of the partition in a list, which is usually called the *replica ring*. This list is referenced during a synchronization event.

- **Synchronized Up To**   This attribute holds a timestamp for each replica, which gives an indication of how up-to-date a replica is in relation to all other copies of the replica.

- **Inherited ACL (Access Control List)**   This attribute summarizes all the access rights from the root object down to the partition root object.

The replica pointers are also put to use when a user is browsing a replica of the NDS tree. When a user is browsing for an object that is not in a local replica, NDS uses the pointers to locate the information in replicas on other servers. Those servers might be linked with WAN connections, so searches might take a little longer than if a user were looking up information already in the local replica. If users look outside of their local replicas often, you may need to replicate other partitions of the directory tree to their local environment to reduce network traffic, especially if it is over a WAN link. However, creating more replicas also increases traffic when replicas are synchronized, so you need to find a balance between the two strategies.

The process of looking in other replicas for NDS information may occur during a user login. If a user is already attached to a NetWare 5 server and logs in, NDS first looks for the user's name in that server. If it is not found, NDS starts "walking the tree" to locate the user's account. Fortunately, this process is relatively easy for NDS, and it allows a user to log into the network from any server, not just the server that holds the replica for the User object.

Understanding the Replication Process

When changes occur to the NDS database, all the replicas affected by the change must be updated. This process is called *synchronization*. Only the changed information in the database is sent across the network to the replicas, which helps to reduce network traffic.

As soon as information in a master or read/write replica (described below) changes, the replica begins a process of propagating its new information to the other replicas. User information is typically updated in ten seconds, while less critical updates may take place in as long as five minutes. All the replicas of a partition on different servers form a *replica ring* (the pointers to these replicas are in the Replica Pointer attribute), and each server holding a replica is contacted one after the other until the replica ring is fully synchronized.

Note that there is a window of time in which a partition is not synchronized across the replicas, especially if the replicas are located across WAN links. Before you start any process that manipulates partitions, you should make sure that all replicas are communicating. In other words, you want to make sure that no server in the replica ring is down or can't communicate with the others. A way to check this using the DSTRACE command is covered later in this chapter under "NDS Utilities."

Recall from Chapter 10 that there are four types of replicas:

- **Master replica** Every partition has one master replica that is created when the partition is defined. This replica has read and write attributes and is the primary replica that NDS strives to keep as up-to-date as possible. All partition operations are performed on the master replica, so if you want to partition the directory tree, you must have access to the master replica, which locks other replicas during the operation.

- **Read/write replica** This replica is basically the same as the master replica, but you can't use it to partition the database or move partitions. This is a copy of a partition that can be changed (it has the read and write attributes), which is necessary for users to log in and be authenticated. You will most likely always create read/write replicas (as opposed to read-only replicas, discussed next).

- **Read-only replica**   Use this replica where users only need to retrieve information. It cannot be used for login and authenticated because a timestamp cannot be written. This replica might be useful in some locations to look up information about users and objects such as e-mail addresses and phone numbers.

- **Subordinate reference replica**   This replica is used internally by NDS to link child partitions (the subordinate) with parent partitions when the child partition is on another server. The subordinate reference replica does not contain the complete partition database, only information about the root object of the child partition, including the attributes discussed earlier (Replica Pointer, Synchronized Up To, Inherited ACL). This information contains a list of servers where replicas of the child partition are stored, as well as addresses and replica types.

> **Note**   *You cannot rebuild an NDS tree with subordinate reference replicas, because they do not hold a complete set of partition information—they hold only pointers to replicas.*

Any NetWare 5 server can "host" any number of partition replicas, but only one copy of each replica. This means that a NetWare 5 server at a branch office might have a partition replica from every division office. It also implies that you can replicate a partition to many different locations to provide fault tolerance and to provide the partition information to users at the locations.

Problems occur during synchronization if any server holding a replica is not available. NDS will continue to contact the downed server, flooding the network with update requests. The synchronization process cannot complete until the server is brought back online. As a general rule, never shut down servers that hold replicas unless you need to service the device. Remove the server from the replica ring and remove all partitions on the server. Make sure all NDS activities have completed before taking the server down.

Managing NDS Partitions and Replicas

Part of NDS management is handled automatically when you install the first NetWare 5 server. The root partition is created, and the container holding the first server is made part of the root partition. After installation, you can use the NDS Manager utility to manage the NDS partitions and perform other tasks as described below.

NDS Manager is designed to run on both Windows 95/98 and Windows NT workstations. It can be started either as a stand-alone executable or from the Tools menu in NetWare Administrator:

- To start the stand-alone executable, create a shortcut to the NDS Manager utility (NDSMGR32.EXE) found in the \SYS\PUBLIC\WIN32 subdirectory.

■ To start NDS Manager from the Tools menu in NetWare Administrator, copy the NMSNAP32.DLL file located in the \SYS\PUBLIC\WIN32 directory to the \SYS\PUBLIC\WIN32\SNAPINS directory. The next time you launch NetWare Administrator, you should see NDS Manager as an option under the Tools menu.

You can see the NDS Manager dialog box pictured in Figure 18-1. Note in this figure that a partition already exists at the DivWest container. The partition information is displayed in the right side of the dialog box when you select the partition.

Before you begin managing partitions, make sure all other servers that hold existing replicas are up and running.

Working with Partitions

The following sections describe working with the NDS Manager utility to place partition boundaries in your NDS tree and to view partition data. To work with replicas, refer to the section "Working with Replicas," later in this chapter. Before you start manipulating partitions, make sure that all the servers that hold replicas of partitions are running and communicating with other replica servers. You can do this with the DSTRACE command at each server, as discussed under "NDS Utilities," later in this chapter. You also should perform partition operations with the latest version of DS.NLM on each of the servers. Be aware that some partition operations may take considerable time to fully synchronize across the network.

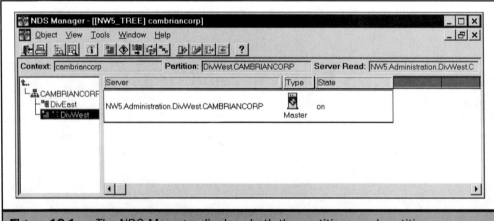

Figure 18-1. *The NDS Manager displays both the partitions and partition information for the selected partition*

Create as New Partition

A partition is a logical division of your NDS tree. Each of these divisions can be replicated and distributed among different servers in your network. When you create a new partition, you split the parent partition and end up with two partitions. The new partition becomes a child partition of the parent. To create a new partition, perform the following steps from within NDS Manager:

1. Click the Tree View icon.

2. Select from the browser the container you want to create as a partition.

3. Click the Create Partition icon.

4. Confirm your request.

NDS Manager will inform you that the Create Partition command has been issued to NDS. You will receive a message telling you that the partition is busy if you attempt another partition operation while the partition is being created.

Partitions cannot overlap. If you create a partition lower in the tree and then create another partition above it, the new partition does not include the lower partition.

Merge Partitions

Merging or joining partitions is a process of combining a child partition with its parent partition. This operation might take some time and affect network traffic, depending on the placement of partition replicas. If a server has a replica of the child partition but not the parent partition, then NDS must replicate the parent partition to that server to complete the operation. This occurs on every server that has either only a child or only a parent partition replica, so the more extreme this situation, the longer it will take to merge the partitions. Perform the following steps to merge a child partition with its parent:

1. Select the partition you want to merge with its parent partition.

2. Click the Merge Partition icon.

Check the partition synchronization of both partitions before merging the partitions. Fix all errors before proceeding.

View Partitions on a Server

To view a list of replicas stored on a particular server, browse through the directory tree in the NDS Manager dialog box until you find the desired Server object. Then, highlight the Server object by clicking it. The partitions as well as the partition's replica types stored on the server are displayed in the replica pane on the right side of the browser. To display information as to the status of the partition, as shown in Figure 18-2, right-click the replica displayed in the replica pane of the browser.

Abort Partition Operation

You can stop an operation such as creating, merging, or moving a partition, or when changing a replica type. This assumes that the operation takes some time and that you can abort an operation before the replicas of the partition are in their final state. You might need to do this when a partition operation won't synchronize because a replica is corrupted or because a server that holds a replica is not available. Use the following procedure to back out of a partition operation:

1. Select the partition where the operation has begun. If this is a merge operation, select the child partition that is merging with the parent.

2. Right-click the partition.

3. Select Abort Operation.

4. Confirm your request.

Delete Server

This operation will permanently remove a Server object from your network and remove its data and resources from the network. Select this option from the Object

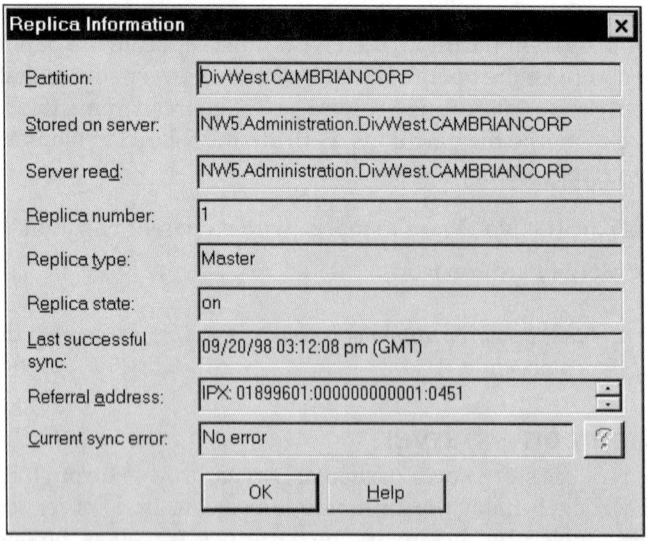

Figure 18-2.   *This displays the status information for the selected partition*

menu with caution. Deleting a server may corrupt your NDS database if the server holds a replica. Before you can delete a server, you must first move the replica from the server to another server, and then bring the server down.

Change the master replicas stored on the server to read/write replicas and then delete all replicas on the NetWare server you plan to delete. Once all the processes are complete, you can delete the NetWare Server object. Select the server in the browser window. Then, select Delete from the pull-down Object menu.

The preferred way to remove a server is by loading the Install utility at the server console and then selecting the Remove Directory Services option. This will prompt you to place master replicas on another server, clear replica rings, and so on.

Move Partition

You may occasionally need to move a partition from one context in the NDS directory tree to another context. You can move a container object only if it has no subordinate partitions. When you move a container object, Novell Directory Services (NDS) changes all references to the container. Although the object's common name remains unchanged, the context name of the container (and of all its subordinates) changes.

Note

Even if you just want to move a container and its subtree, you still need to make that container a partition before you move it.

Moving a partition can cause some confusion for users if they don't know it has been moved. To avoid problems, create an Alias object that points to the partition at its new location. Then users can log in as normal and locate objects that they accessed in the partition before it was moved. Some clients may also have the NAME CONTEXT parameter in their client setup parameters set to the original location of the partition in the directory tree. You can use the NCUPDATE (NetWare Client Update) utility to automatically update users' client configuration files with a new name context for the partition. To move a partition, follow these steps:

1. Open the NDS Manager dialog box and select the partition you want to move. Note the following:

   ■ If a partition has child partitions, you can merge them with the parent partition before moving the tree. Select a child partition in the browser window. Right-click it and select Merge Partitions.

   ■ If you want to move a container that is not already a partition, select the container and right-click to bring up the menu. Select Create New Partition.

   You might need to refresh the screen by collapsing and expanding the tree to see the new partition or use the Refresh command in the window drop-down menu.

2. To move the partition, click the Move Partition icon.

3. In the dialog box that appears, click the Browse icon to locate the container in the directory tree where you want to move the partition.

4. Click Create Alias for This Container Object to automatically create an alias where the container was located.

5. Click Yes.

6. Confirm your request.

The operation may take some time, and you won't be able to perform other operations until it completes.

Working with Replicas

Creating multiple partitions does not, by itself, increase fault tolerance or improve the performance of NDS. Strategically creating multiple replicas does, however. Note the following:

- You must have Supervisor rights in the container that is the partition root.

- Only one master replica can exist. All other replicas must be read/write or read-only.

- Only one replica of a partition is allowed per server.

- Most replicas should be read/write replicas, because they accept changes and send those changes to other replicas. Read-only replicas are not often used.

The following sections describe the actions that can be performed on partition replicas.

Adding Replicas

Perform the following steps to create a replica for a partition:

1. Select the partition that you want to replicate on a server.

2. Click the Add Replica icon.

3. Click the browse button to select the server to place the replica on.

4. Select the Server object from the browser and click OK.

5. Select either Read/Write or Read-Only.

6. Click OK.

7. Confirm your request.

Deleting Replicas

You may need to delete and recopy a replica that is corrupted. Before deleting a replica, make sure that copies of it are available on other servers. Also, keep the following in mind:

- You cannot delete a master replica. If the replica you want to delete is a master, go to a server with a replica of the master and make it the new master replica (see the "Changing Type" section, next, to do this). This automatically changes the old master replica to a read/write replica, which you can then delete.

- Deleting a replica deletes a copy of part of the NDS database. The database can still be accessed on other servers in the network, and the server that the replica was on still functions in Novell Directory Services.

Perform the following steps to remove a replica from a server:

1. Select the partition that has a replica you want to delete.
2. Select the replica you want to delete from the replica pane on the right side.
3. Right-click the replica and select Delete.
4. Confirm your request.

Changing Type

You might need to change the type of a replica; for example, from read/write to master. As mentioned above, you can delete a master replica only after making another replica the master replica. You cannot change the replica type of a subordinate reference. A subordinate reference is not a complete copy of a partition. It is created automatically by NDS when the server contains a replica of a partition but not of that partition's child. Perform the following steps to change the replica type:

1. Select the partition that has the replica you want to change.
2. Select the replica you want to change from the replica pane on the right side.
3. Right-click the replica and select Change Type.
4. Confirm your request.

Sending Updates

The Send Updates command is selected by right-clicking the desired partition, as shown in Figure 18-3. The command immediately sends update information in one replica to other replicas, even though Novell Directory Services will eventually do this automatically. Think of this operation as "manually" synchronizing the database. Note that this might create a lot of network traffic, so you might want to do the operation during off-hours. In addition, this will override any WAN policies that you have established to limit NDS bandwidth across a WAN link.

Receiving Updates

The Receive Updates command is used to manually update a selected replica with information from the master replica. This is also shown in Figure 18-3 and can cause the same problems as described in the preceding section for sending updates.

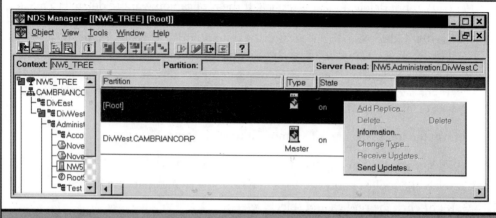

Figure 18-3. *The various commands associated with each replica are accessed by right-clicking the desired replica*

WAN Traffic Manager

The WAN Traffic Manager allows you to manage NDS synchronization traffic between servers. The servers can be on a LAN, a WAN, or both. It can restrict traffic based on cost of traffic, time of day, type of traffic, or any combination of these. It controls periodic events initiated by NDS such as replica synchronization, the Janitor process, and the Limber process. It does not control events initiated by you, users, or non-NDS server-to-server traffic such as time synchronization. The WAN Traffic Manager consists of three elements:

- **WTM.NLM** This is a Novell Loadable Module (NLM) that resides on each server in the NDS tree. It reads a WAN Traffic Policy to determine whether the traffic will be sent.
- **WAN Traffic Policies** These are rules that control the generation of NDS synchronization traffic. Each WAN Traffic Policy is stored as an NDS property value in the Server object, the LAN Area object, or both.
- **NetWare Administrator Snap-in** This snap-in allows you to create or modify policies, create LAN Area objects, and apply policies to LAN Areas or Servers. When the WAN Traffic Manager is installed, the NDS schema will be extended to include the LAN Area Membership, WAN Policies, and Cost property pages.

Creating a LAN Area Object

A LAN Area object allows you to manage WAN Traffic policies for a group of servers. Using the NetWare Administrator utility, you create the objects as you would any other NDS object. You can add or delete servers from the LAN Area object as needed. LAN Area objects are recommended if you have multiple servers in a LAN that are connected to other LANs via WAN links. To create a LAN Area object, perform the following steps:

1. Start the NetWare Administrator utility.

2. Select the container where you want to create the LAN Area object.

3. Right-click the container and select Create.

4. Select the LAN Area object and click OK. A screen like the one shown in Figure 18-4 will be displayed. If the LAN Area object is missing from the object list, the NDS schema has not been updated. Make sure you installed the WAN Traffic Manager snap-in and run Tools | Add WANman schema.

Adding Servers to a LAN Area Object

The LAN Area object allows you to manage WAN traffic for a group of servers, rather than individually. Each WAN policy you apply is automatically applied to all servers belonging to the object. A server can belong to only one LAN Area object. If the server you are adding belongs to another LAN Area object, it will be removed from that object

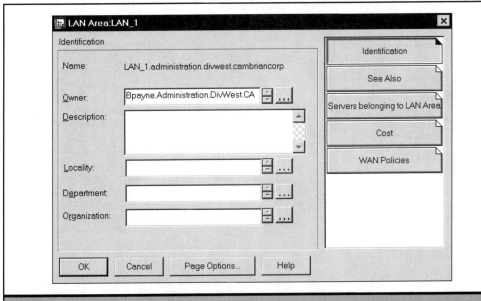

Figure 18-4.   *The LAN Area dialog box allows you to group servers into a common container*

and added to the new object. To add servers to a LAN Area object, perform the following steps:

1. Start the NetWare Administrator utility.

2. Select the server you want to add to the LAN Area object.

3. Right-click and choose Details. Then select the LAN Area Membership property page. The page shown in Figure 18-5 will be displayed.

4. Click the ellipsis (...) to find the LAN Area object you want to add the server to.

5. Click OK in the Select Object dialog box.

6. Click OK in the LAN Area Membership dialog box.

Assigning Cost Factors to LAN Objects

You can assign cost factors to network destination address ranges or default cost factors to servers or LAN Area objects. These cost factors allow the WAN Traffic Manager to compare the cost of network traffic with certain destinations and manage

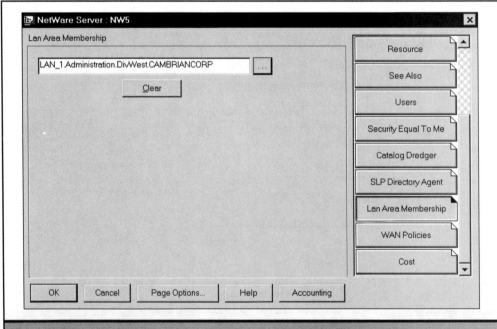

Figure 18-5.   *The LAN Area Membership property page allows you to add servers to the object group*

them using WAN policies. There are several predefined Policy Groups on the NetWare 5 server, including the following:

- 1-3AM.WGM
- 7AM-6PM.WGM
- COSTLT20.WGM
- IPX.WGM
- TCPIP.WGM
- SAMEAREA.WGM
- ONOSPOOF.WGM
- OPNSPOOF.WGM
- NDSTTYPS.WGM

Each one of these predefined polices can be modified. This is covered later in the chapter. To assign Cost Factors, perform the following steps:

1. Start the NetWare Administrator utility.
2. Select the server of the LAN Area object that will be the source of network traffic.
3. Right-click the object and select Details.
4. Click the Cost property page. Enter a value in the default cost field if you want to assign a default cost to the object.
5. Click the Add button if you want to add a cost to a destination address range.
6. Select either TCP/IP or IPX/SPX. Figure 18-6 shows the dialog box that will be displayed.
7. Specify the start and end addresses of the range.
8. Specify the cost as a non-negative integer.
9. Click OK.
10. Click OK again.

Note   *You must either enter **WANMAN REFRESH IMMEDIATE** at the server console or reload WTM.NLM before the new cost factors take effect.*

Writing New WAN Policies

The WAN Traffic Manager uses WAN policies to control network traffic between servers. It can use a predefined policy, a predefined policy that you have modified, or a new policy that you create yourself. Perform the following steps to create a new WAN policy.

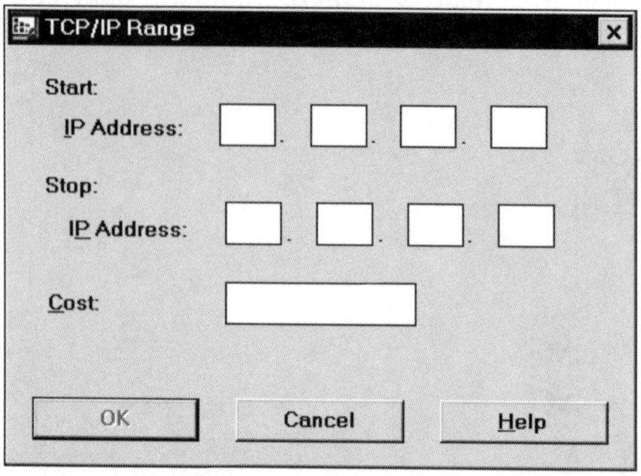

Figure 18-6. *The TCP/IP address range dialog box for the LAN Area object*

1. Start the NetWare Administrator utility.

2. Select the server or LAN Area object for which you want to write a WAN policy.

3. Right-click the object and select Details.

4. Select the WAN Policies property page.

5. In the Policies dialog page, enter the name of the policy and click the New button.

6. A simple text editor appears for you to write the new policy. Enter the text for the new policy as described in the Help manual. A sample policy is shown in Figure 18-7. This policy limits server NDS traffic to between 1:00 A.M. and 3:00 A.M.

7. Check the new policy for errors by selecting Check Policy from the Policy drop-down menu.

8. Save the new policy by selecting Save from the Policy drop-down menu.

9. Close the policy editor.

10. Click OK on the WAN Policies page.

Applying WAN Policies

WAN Policies can be applied to individual servers or a LAN Area object. Policies applied to an individual server manage the NDS traffic for that server only. Policies

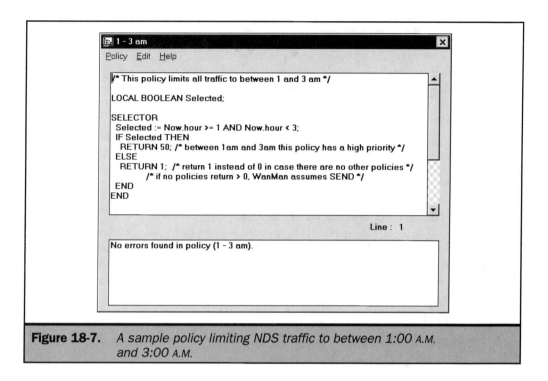

```
1 - 3 am                                                    ×

Policy   Edit   Help

/* This policy limits all traffic to between 1 and 3 am */

LOCAL BOOLEAN Selected;

SELECTOR
  Selected := Now.hour >= 1 AND Now.hour < 3;
  IF Selected THEN
    RETURN 50;  /* between 1am and 3am this policy has a high priority */
  ELSE
    RETURN 1;   /* return 1 instead of 0 in case there are no other policies */
              /* if no policies return > 0, WanMan assumes SEND */
  END
END

                                              Line :  1

No errors found in policy (1 - 3 am).

```

Figure 18-7.   *A sample policy limiting NDS traffic to between 1:00 A.M.*
                  and 3:00 A.M.

applied to a LAN Area object manage the NDS traffic for all servers that belong to the object. To apply WAN policies to an individual server or a LAN Area object, perform the following steps:

1. Start the NetWare Administrator utility.
2. Select the Server object or LAN Area object to which you want to apply the policy.
3. Right-click the object and select Details.
4. Select the WAN Policies property page.
5. Select the policies that you want applied to the object.
6. Click the Close button.
7. Click the OK button to confirm the policies you have applied.

Note   *The WAN Traffic Manager will look in the WANMAN.INI file for a WAN policy group section. This section will contain a* key=values *statement.* Key *is the policy name selected and* values *is the path to the text file contained the policy.*

Transitive Synchronization

Transitive synchronization reduces replica synchronization traffic on the network. With it, a server does not have to synchronize its replica with all the other servers in the replica list. Instead, the server checks a list on the target server to find when the other servers in the replica list synchronized with one another. If the target server has synchronized with the other servers more recently than the source server, it is not necessary for the source server to synchronize with the other servers in the list. This allows for larger replica lists and works well in mixed protocol environments. Transitive synchronization is automatically enabled on the NetWare 5 server when you set it up to run multiple protocols.

Viewing Transitive Synchronization

The Transitive Synchronization view displays the replica list of each server that holds a replica of the chosen partition. Each row represents the replica list of that server, as shown in Figure 18-8. This view uses the purge vector to evaluate whether synchronization has taken place within the NDS inactivity synchronization setting on each individual server. To display the Transitive Synchronization view, perform the following steps:

1. Start the NetWare Administrator utility.
2. Select NDS Manager from the Tools menu.
   (The snap-in was described earlier in this chapter.)
3. Select the partition you want synchronization on.
4. Select Partition Continuity from the Object menu.
5. Select Transitive Synchronization from the View menu.

NDS Utilities

The NDS utilities described in this section help you monitor and manage NDS. There is not enough space in the book to fully describe the utilities. You should refer to the NetWare 5 online documentation for full instructions. The following information will help you get started with the utilities.

DSREPAIR

DSREPAIR is an NLM that runs at the NetWare server; it provides you with status information about the NDS database and helps you repair problems. You can start the remote console as discussed in Chapter 15 and run DSREPAIR from your workstation.

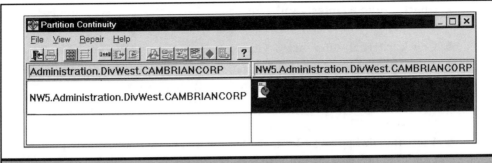

Figure 18-8.   *The Transitive Synchronization view provides you with synchronization status information on each partition on each server*

Once you're in the remote console, type **[LOAD] DSREPAIR** to start the utility. The main menu has the following options:

- **Unattended Full Repair**   Automatically performs all possible repair operations that do not require operator assistance and records all actions in the log file

- **Time Synchronization**   Collects time synchronization information and server status from all servers known to the local database

- **Report Synchronization Status**   Retrieves the synchronization status of all partitions from every server that contains a replica of the partition and displays any errors that occur

- **View Repair Log File**   Lets you view and edit the log file created during repair operations

- **Advanced Options Menu**   Displays a list of manual repair operations you can perform, as described in the following list:

    - **Log File and Login Configuration**   Configures options for the DSREPAIR log file and logs into the directory services tree, which is required by some operations

    - **Repair Local DS Database**   Repairs the Directory Services database files stored on a server

    - **Servers Known to This Database**   Lets you perform options to servers in the database, such as time synchronization, network address repair, and schema updates

    - **Replica and Partition Operations**   Provides functions to repair replicas, replica rings, and Server objects; also dynamically displays each server's last synchronization time

- **Check Volume Objects and Trustees**   Checks all mounted volumes for valid objects and valid trustees on the volumes
- **Check External References**   Checks for illegal external references
- **Security Equivalence Synchronization**   Allows user to synchronize security equivalence attributes throughout the global tree
- **Global Schema Operations**   Provides functions to update the schema in the tree
- **View Repair Log File**   Edits the log file that is optionally created when repair operations are performed
- **Create a Database Dump File**   Copies the Directory Services database files to disk in compressed format to be used for offline repairs and diagnostics; not to be used as a backup method

DSTRACE

DSTRACE allows you to view the current operations being performed by the operating system and allows you to diagnose errors. The complete list of available events to display is shown in Figure 18-9. For example, to verify that all partitions and replicas are fully synchronized, type the following at the NetWare 5 server console:

```
SET DSTRACE = SCREEN
SET DSTRACE = PART
SET DSTRACE = ON
```

This turns on the DSTRACE screen and lets you see current replica synchronization activity. Press ALT-ESC to toggle screens at the server console. Press ALT-F3 if you are using RCONSOLE. You can also type the following to save trace information to a file called SYS:SYSTEM\DSTRACE.DBG:

```
SET NDS TRACE TO FILE = ON
```

Before you start any process that manipulates partitions, you should make sure that all replicas are communicating and that no server in a replica ring is down or can't communicate with the others. Type the following commands at each replica server to check its status:

```
SET DSTRACE = ON + SCREEN + PART + *H
```

Now look for the statement All processed = YES. This indicates that the partition is healthy. If you see errors listed, you need to resolve them before continuing with any partition manipulation.

```
DSTRACE Configuration:

Trace mode is JOURNAL.  Trace Screen is OFF.  Trace File is OFF.
File Size: 0 (unlimited). File Name: DSTRACE.LOG.

*Key: [OFF]  [SCREEN]  [FILE]  [BOTH]

TAGS: Show Event Tags       TIME: Show Event Times    ABUF: Agent Buffers
ALOC: Memory Allocation     AREQ: Agent Requests      AUMN: Audit
AUNC: Audit NCPs            AUSK: Audit Skulk         AUTH: Authentication
BASE: Base Set              BEMU: Bindery Emulator    BLNK: Backlinker
CBUF: Client Buffers        CHNG: Change Cache        COLL: Collisions
DRLK: Dist Ref Links        FRAG: Packet Fragmenter   INIT: Initialization
INSP: Inspector             JNTR: Janitor             LMBR: Limber
LDAP: LDAP                  LOCK: Locking             LOST: Lost Entries
MISC: Miscellaneous         MOVE: Move                NCPE: NCP Engine
PART: Partition             PURG: Purger              RECM: Record Manager
RSLV: Resolve Name          SAPM: Srvc Advertising    SCMA: Schema
SPKT: Server Packets        SKLK: Skulker             STRM: Streams
SYNC: Inbound Sync          THRD: Threads             TVEC: Time Vector
VCLN: Virtual Client        WANM: WAN Traffic Mgr
NW5:
```

Figure 18-9.   *The list of available events to monitor with the DSTRACE server utility*

DSTRACE has many options. Type **SET** at the server console, and then choose option 13 to display Directory Services parameters. There you will see the status of DSTRACE and other options you can set. You can also look under the SET command in the utilities reference manual of the NetWare 5 online documentation.

Note   *DSTRACE was originally used by Novell as a development tool but is now available for advanced troubleshooting of Novell Directory Services.*

Setting Directory Service Parameters

You can set parameters for Novell Directory Services by loading the MONITOR utility at the server console or at a remote console. Setting up a remote console is discussed in Chapter 15. The procedure for setting parameters using MONITOR is discussed here.

1. At the NetWare server console or at a remote console, type **[LOAD] MONITOR** to display the menu shown in Figure 18-10.

2. Choose Server parameters from the Available Option menu and press ENTER to display the menu shown in Figure 18-11. Scan down the list and select the Directory Services option.

3. The menu shown in Figure 18-12 appears. Press the UP ARROW and DOWN ARROW keys to scan through the list.

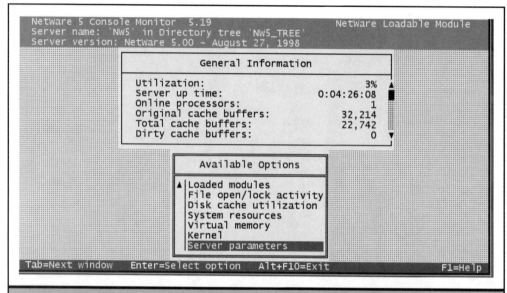

Figure 18-10. *The general MONITOR screen lists the available options*

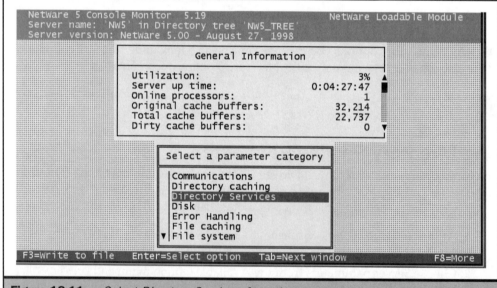

Figure 18-11. *Select Directory Services from the parameter category menu*

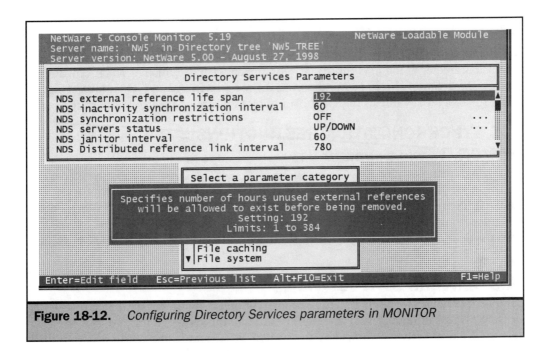

```
NetWare 5 Console Monitor  5.19                    NetWare Loadable Module
Server name: 'NW5' in Directory tree 'NW5_TREE'
Server version: NetWare 5.00 - August 27, 1998

                        Directory Services Parameters

   NDS external reference life span          192
   NDS inactivity synchronization interval   60
   NDS synchronization restrictions          OFF              . . .
   NDS servers status                        UP/DOWN          . . .
   NDS janitor interval                      60
   NDS Distributed reference link interval   780

                     Select a parameter category

      Specifies number of hours unused external references
          will be allowed to exist before being removed.
                         Setting: 192
                         Limits: 1 to 384

                     File caching
                     File system

Enter=Edit field    Esc=Previous list    Alt+F10=Exit              F1=Help
```

Figure 18-12. *Configuring Directory Services parameters in MONITOR*

As you highlight each line, a description for the option appears, along with default and suggested settings. The next section also provides a description of each SET parameter.

 Note *You rarely need to change the parameters discussed here unless you need to control NDS in special environments or you are having problems with it. Novell technical support may direct you to use one or more of these special parameters.*

You can also type the SET commands at the server console or insert them in the NetWare startup files. Descriptions of SET commands are provided next.

NDS EXTERNAL REFERENCE LIFE SPAN = *number in hours*

Set this parameter to specify the number of hours unused external references are allowed to exist before being removed. External references are local IDs assigned to users when they access other servers. When users no longer have access, the external references should be removed. The default is 192 hours and supported values are 1 to 384 hours.

NDS INACTIVITY SYNCHRONIZATION INTERVAL =
number in minutes

Set this parameter to the maximum elapsed time between exhaustive synchronization checks. The default value is 60 minutes and the range is from 2 to 1,440 minutes. For WAN links, set this value as high as 240 minutes (4 hours) to reduce WAN traffic.

NDS SYNCHRONIZATION RESTRICTIONS =
OFF/ON, *version number list*

Set this parameter to specify which versions of Novell Directory Services the server can synchronize with. To determine what version is currently loaded on a server, type **MODULES** at the server prompt and look under the heading "DS.NLM." When OFF (default setting), the server synchronizes with all versions available. When ON, the server synchronizes only with those versions specified as parameters to the ON value (for example, ON,420,421).

NDS SERVERS STATUS = *value*

Set this parameter to mark the status of all Server objects in the local namebase as UP or DOWN. This parameter can reset the status of all the servers if the status of one server isn't accurately recognized by the system. For example, if a server is up but the system recognizes it as down, set this parameter to mark all servers as up. The system would subsequently reassess the status of all servers and change the status to down for those servers that were truly down.

NDS JANITOR INTERVAL = *number in minutes*

Set this parameter to the interval in minutes at which the *janitor process* is executed. The janitor process cleans up unused records, reclaims disk space, and purges objects flagged for deletion. The process executes as soon as you change this value and then recurs at the specified interval. The default value is 60 and the range is from 1 to 10,080 minutes.

NDS DISTRIBUTED REFERENCE LINK INTERVAL =
number in minutes

Set this parameter to the interval in minutes at which distributed link consistency checking is performed. This process creates needed distributed reference links and deletes unnecessary ones. A distributed reference link indicates that an object in a partition has an ID in that partition where the actual object does not exist. The process executes as soon as you change this value and then recurs at the specified interval. The default value is 780 and the range is from 2 to 10,080 minutes.

NDS BACKLINK INTERVAL = *number in minutes*

Set this parameter to the interval in minutes at which backlink consistency checking is performed. A backlink indicates that an object in a replica has an ID on a server where the replica doesn't exist. This process creates needed backlinks and deletes unnecessary ones. Backlink consistency checking is executed as soon as you change this value and recurs at the specified interval. The default value is 780 and the range is from 2 to 10,080 minutes.

NDS TRACE FILE LENGTH TO ZERO = ON

Set this parameter to ON if you want to delete the contents of the trace file, but not the file itself. After the file is cleared, this parameter resets to OFF. To use this parameter, you must also set the NDS trace file parameter to ON, because the trace file must be open for the system to delete its contents.

NDS BOOTSTRAP ADDRESS = *address*

Set this parameter to allow NDS to operate properly in the absence of the Service Location Protocol (SLP). The local server uses this address to set the bootstrap address that the server uses to find its tree and authenticate to it.

BINDERY CONTEXT = *context; context*

Set this parameter to the containers to be used by Novell Directory Services when it provides bindery services. You can type multiple container names, separated by semicolons. To set multiple contexts, you must have a writeable replica of the container you specify in the context on the same partition. Be sure to specify the complete context of a container. Note that this parameter can be set in the STARTUP.NCF file.

NDS TRACE FILENAME = *path\name*

Set the parameters to specify the path and name of the NDS trace file. The default is SYSTEM\DSTRACE.DBG.

NDS TRACE TO FILE = ON/OFF

Set this parameter to ON to send messages about NDS events to the console screen and to the NDS trace file called SYSTEM\DSTRACE.DBG. If you want to change the name of the trace file, refer to the NDS Trace Filename option above. By default, the trace file has a maximum length of 500K; then it starts overwriting itself.

NDS TRACE TO SCREEN = ON/OFF

Set this parameter's value to ON to enable the NDS trace screen, which displays information about NDS events on the monitor.

Managing Novell
Directory Services

Time Synchronization

Time synchronization is essential in the Novell Directory Services environment when replicas of the database are copied to many different servers. Time synchronization ensures that all servers are time-synchronized, and it helps to establish the order of events when changes are made to the NDS database. Events are marked with timestamps to help resolve multiple changes to the same object in the NDS database. Time synchronization also helps to ensure that all files are marked with the correct time as well.

Time synchronization sets the clocks of servers to the Universal Time Coordinate (UTC), which was formerly Greenwich Mean Time (GMT). All servers are set to the time zone in which they are located relative to UTC, with an adjustment for daylight saving time if necessary. The most accurate way to ensure that all servers are synchronized with UTC is to attach an external time source service to the reference time server. This may be a radio clock or even an atomic clock, or a time source obtained from the Internet.

Even if you don't use an external time source, NDS will still synchronize the time on the network by using a "voting method" in which time servers "agree" on the most accurate time.

Caution *Time synchronization is handled by the TIMESYNC.NLM module. Do not unload this module.*

You can view time synchronization information by typing **TIME** at the NetWare 5 server. The information that is displayed tells you about the time zone of the server, the time synchronization status, and the current date and time.

Do not change the time in a NetWare 5 time-synchronized environment by using the TIME command. Instead, use the following command at a reference time server to adjust the clock forward or backward as appropriate.

```
SET TIMESYNC TIME ADJUSTMENT=[+/-]HH:MM:SS
```

For example, to adjust the clock one minute ahead, type this:

```
SET TIMESYNC TIME ADJUSTMENT=+00:01:00
```

The adjustments you make with this command do not take effect for one hour. During that time, you have the opportunity to cancel the time adjustment by retyping the command with a CANCEL parameter after the equal sign.

About Time Servers

Time synchronization in the NetWare 5 environment can be classified as follows:

■ A *single reference environment*, in which a stand-alone time server provides time to all other servers. This is the simplest setup, because the single reference time server is the only time server on the network, but it should only be used on small "local" networks.

■ A *voting environment*, in which primary time servers (and optionally, reference time servers) vote to determine the most accurate time.

> **Note** *There must be only one reference server and at least two primary servers, with no more than seven primary servers, in each time provider group. The reference has a vote of 16, and each primary a vote of 2.*

■ A *reference environment*, in which one or more reference time servers are connected to an external time source, such as an atomic clock or the Internet. Note that voting also takes place in this environment, but reference time servers have more weight in determining the time.

With these environments in mind, read over the descriptions of time servers provided in the "Time Synchronization" section of Chapter 10.

Setting Time Server Type

You control the settings of the time server by changing time values in the MONITOR utility or by specifying the following command in the STARTUP.NCF file:

SET Default Time Server Type = *type of time source*

Replace *type of time source* with reference, primary, secondary, or single reference. SET commands for time server environments are discussed later in the section, "Time Synchronization Console Commands."

Creating Time Server Environments

To set up time server environments, you may need to make some changes to the time server status of your servers. For example, the first NetWare 5 server in a new NDS directory tree is automatically set up as a single reference time server. Any additional servers added to the network are configured as secondary time servers. Thus, if you haven't done anything yet to change time services, you currently have a *single reference environment*.

> **Note** *The problem with a single reference environment is that the single reference time server is a point of failure that can lead to inaccurate times throughout the network.*

Time servers use one of two methods to find each other: Service Advertising Protocol (SAP) or Custom Configuration. SAP broadcasts about the services they offer every 60 seconds. It is the default method for broadcasting and is also the protocol time servers use to locate time providers. SAP can adversely affect network performance on large networks, because each time server broadcasts SAP packets at the intervals.

 The SAP method is easy to set up and is adequate for small networks (30 servers). Use the alternate configuration method, described next, for larger networks.

The alternative to using SAP is to run the MONITOR utility at the server to create a special TIMESYNC.CFG file containing a list of time servers that a time server should contact when it needs to check or update its time. Here's the procedure:

1. At the NetWare server console or at a remote console, type **[LOAD] MONITOR** to load the MONITOR utility.

2. Choose Server Parameters and press ENTER; then scan down the list and select the Time option.

3. The menu shown in the following illustration appears. You press ENTER in the top field to add the names of servers you want the current server to contact when it needs to update its time.

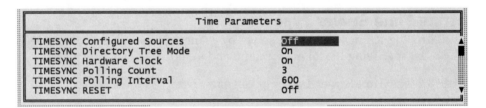

Move to the TIMESYNC Configured Sources field and press ENTER to set the field to ON. This ensures that the server does not listen to time sources that use SAP.

 When you exit MONITOR, you are asked if you want to save the updates to the TIMESYNC.CFG file. Press ENTER to select the option.

Recall that a "voting environment" consists of primary and reference time servers that vote to establish the most accurate time based on their own clock settings or the settings of an external reference. Reference time servers have more voting power than primary and secondary time servers, because they get their time from an accurate external source (and not their own internal clock).

To set up a time server environment, you start the MONITOR utility at each time server and change the time parameters. Follow the instructions at the beginning of this section to start MONITOR at the console. When the MONITOR main menu appears, choose Server Parameters and press ENTER, then choose Time from the list to display the Time Parameters menu shown in the previous illustration. In the Time Parameters menu, you can scan down the list to view each parameter. A description appears when you highlight a parameter. Change a parameter by pressing ENTER. If it is a toggle (Yes or No), the option toggles when you press ENTER. In particular, look for the TIMESYNC Type parameter to change the server to a single, reference, primary, or secondary time server. Note the following:

- On large networks (more than 30 servers), you should set up one primary time server in each location. Other servers in the location should be secondary time servers. An optional reference time server can be located anywhere, but all time servers must have a relatively fast link to it.

- The distance between time servers might affect synchronization due to network traffic. The minimum time difference between time servers to still be considered synchronized is 2,000 milliseconds (two seconds).

- Place primary time servers at main sites that are interconnected with relatively high-speed WAN links.

- If you have remote sites that are relatively small, place secondary time servers at those sites.

- On very large global networks, you might consider setting up two or more reference time servers at different global locations.

- Do not use the SAP communication method on large networks (more than 30 servers). Use the configuration method described in this section.

If you are having problems with time synchronization, type the **TIME** command at a server console. You may see a message that reads "Time is NOT synchronized to the network." This may indicate that a single reference time server was brought up after the secondary time servers, or the single reference time server is down.

In a voting environment, it is possible that one of the time servers is down or there is a communication problem. Type the following commands at the server to get a list of servers and networks that the current server can see:

```
DISPLAY NETWORKS
DISPLAY SERVERS
```

If you don't see one of the time servers or networks in the lists, you'll need to bring the server back online or correct the network problem.

Time Synchronization Console Commands

You run the following commands and set the following options at the NetWare server console to manage and control the time synchronization environment.

TIMESYNC

TIMESYNC.NLM loads automatically when the server boots in order to control time synchronization. It gets information from the TIMESYNC.CFG file located in the SYS:SYSTEM directory of the server. This file is optional, but you can add the following TIMESYNC parameters to it if necessary. You can use NetWare's EDIT (type **[LOAD] EDIT**) to edit the TYMESYNC.CFG file. Do not put time synchronization parameters in the STARTUP.NCF file.

*Normally, you will need to reboot the server to initialize the new time synchronization parameters you have placed in the TIMESYNC.CFG file. If you want the new settings to take effect immediately, type **SET TIMESYNC RESTART FLAG=ON** at the server console.*

Setting Time Synchronization Parameters

You can set parameters for Time Synchronization Services by loading the MONITOR utility at the server console or at a remote console. Setting up a remote console is discussed in Chapter 15. The procedure for setting parameters using the SET commands at the server console is discussed here. You can also insert them in the NetWare startup files. A description of the available SET commands follows.

TIMESYNC ADD TIME SOURCE = *server name*

Use this command to add a server to the list of servers that are contacted when a secondary server needs to update its time.

TIMESYNC CONFIGURATION FILE = *path*

This parameter specifies the path where the TIMESYNC.CFG configuration file is located. By default, it is located in the SYS:SYSTEM directory.

TIMESYNC CONFIGURED SOURCES = ON/OFF

Set this parameter to ON if you want the server to ignore SAP time sources and rely on time sources that are listed in the TIMESYNC.CFG file. Relying on specific time sources, rather than having the server listen to SAPs, can help reduce network traffic. By default, this option is OFF, which means the server listens to any advertising time source.

TIMESYNC DIRECTORY TREE MODE = ON/OFF

This parameter specifies how the server listens to SAP packets in the directory tree. When set ON (the default setting), time synchronization ignores SAP packets that don't originate from within the directory tree the server is on. When set OFF, the server can receive SAP packets from any time source on the network. Using OFF could corrupt the time synchronization for this server's directory tree.

TIMESYNC HARDWARE CLOCK = ON/OFF

This parameter controls hardware clock synchronization. When set ON (the default setting), the primary and secondary time servers set the hardware clock, and the single reference and reference servers set their time from the hardware clock at the beginning of each polling interval. Set this option OFF only if this server uses an external time source (such as a radio clock).

TIMESYNC POLLING COUNT = *number*

This parameter specifies how many time packets to exchange while polling. The default is 3 and the range is from 1 to 1,000. Note that increasing the number of packets adds unnecessary traffic to the network.

TIMESYNC POLLING INTERVAL = *number*

This parameter specifies the polling interval, which is the frequency in seconds at which time synchronization polling occurs. All time synchronization servers must be set to the same value. The default is 600 seconds (10 minutes) and the range is 10 seconds to 2,678,400 seconds (31 days).

TIMESYNC REMOVE TIME SOURCE = *server name*

This parameter deletes the server specified in the *server name* field as a time source. It is the opposite of the SET TIMESYNC ADD TIME SOURCE option.

TIMESYNC RESET = ON/OFF

This parameter resets time synchronization and clears the time source list when the ON value is used. Instead of using this command, you should edit the TIMESYNC.CFG file to edit or remove the time source list from the file.

TIMESYNC RESTART FLAG = ON/OFF

This parameter controls restarts of time synchronization. Type this parameter with the ON value only if you want to reload TIMESYNC (usually after changing values in the TIMESYNC.CFG file) without rebooting the server.

TIMESYNC SERVICE ADVERTISING = ON/OFF

This parameter controls time source advertising. When ON (the default setting), the single reference, reference, and primary time source advertise using SAP. Set this value to OFF only if you are using a custom-configured list of time sources.

TIMESYNC SYNCHRONIZATION RADIUS = *number*

This parameter controls the maximum time adjustment (in milliseconds) a server is allowed while still being considered synchronized. The default value is 2,000 and the range is 0 to 2,147,483,647 milliseconds. Increase this parameter to allow a wider margin of error for time synchronization between servers. If you lower this value, you may increase the chance of servers losing synchronization due to randomness between clocks. Set the synchronization radius for under two seconds only if you are using an application that uses synchronized timestamps that do not tolerate a two-second deviation between time sources.

TIMESYNC TIME ADJUSTMENT = [+ or −] *hour: minute:second* [at *month/ day/ year hour: minute:second* AM or PM]

This parameter specifies when a time adjustment will take place. You cannot use this parameter on a secondary time server. Set this parameter only to correct network-wide time errors. Default date and time is 6 polling intervals or 1 hour (whichever is longer) from the current time. Misuse of this parameter can corrupt time synchronization and the order of events on your network.

TIMESYNC TIME SOURCE = *server name*

This parameter specifies a server as time source. If no server name is entered, the parameter will display the list of configured servers. Set this parameter in the TIMESYNC.CFG file.

TIMESYNC TYPE = *type of time source*

This parameter specifies the default time source type. You should make this setting in the TIMESYNC.CFG file. The values are Reference, Primary, Secondary, and Single Reference.

TIMESYNC WRITE PARAMETERS = ON/OFF

This parameter specifies whether parameters specified by the TIMESYNC WRITE VALUE (see the following command) parameter are written to the configuration file. This option is OFF by default.

TIMESYNC WRITE VALUE = *number*

This parameter controls which parameters are written when the TIMESYNC Write Parameters (see previous command) option is set to ON. Supported values: 1 = Write internal parameters only; 2 = Write configured time sources only; and 3 = Write both parameters and configured time sources. This option is set to 3 by default.

TIME ZONE = *time zone string*

Use this option to specify the abbreviation for the server's time zone, the number of time zone offsets from the Universal Time Coordinate (UTC), and the abbreviated time zone name used when daylight saving time is in effect. This parameter causes UTC time to be recalculated from local time. You can set this parameter in the STARTUP.NCF file. Following is the syntax of the SET TIME ZONE command:

SET TIME ZONE zone +/– *hr:min:sec daylight*

where you see the current time zone settings if you don't type any parameters, or where you can replace the parameters with the following:

- Replace zone with a standard time zone abbreviation (EST, CST, MST, or PST, for example).

- Type a plus sign (+) or a minus sign (–) to specify the number of hours east or west of the Universal Time Coordinate (UTC) meridian (formerly Greenwich Mean Time, or GMT). If you don't enter this parameter, the default is +.

- Replace *hr:min:sec* with the time difference between UTC and the local time zone. You can just type the hours, or you can be more accurate and specify hours, minutes, and seconds.

- Replace *daylight* with the standard abbreviation for the time zone during daylight saving time (DST). For example: EDT (Eastern Daylight Time), CDT (Central Daylight Time), MDT (Mountain Daylight Time), PDT (Pacific Daylight Time).

DEFAULT TIME SERVER TYPE = *type of time source*

Set this option to specify the default time synchronization server type. This option can be overridden by other time synchronization settings. The support types are reference, primary, secondary, and single reference. The default is secondary. This option can be set in the STARTUP.NCF file.

START OF DAYLIGHT SAVING TIME = *date and time*

Set this option to specify the local date and time when the change to daylight saving time should occur. You must set both the start and end of daylight saving time before either date is actually scheduled.

END OF DAYLIGHT SAVING TIME = *date and time*

Set this parameter to specify the local date and time when the change from daylight saving time should occur. You must set both the start and the end of daylight saving time before either date is actually scheduled.

DAYLIGHT SAVING TIME OFFSET = [+ or –] *hour:minute:second*

Set this parameter to control the offset applied to time calculations when daylight saving time is in effect. This parameter causes UTC time to be recalculated from local time. You can place this SET command in the STARTUP.NCF file. The default setting is +1:00:00.

DAYLIGHT SAVING TIME STATUS = ON/OFF

Use this setting to configure whether daylight saving time is in effect. If set to ON, you should also set the Daylight Saving Time Offset parameter. Note that changing this option does not change the local time. You can place this command in the STARTUP.NCF file.

NEW TIME WITH DAYLIGHT SAVING TIME STATUS = ON/OFF

Use this parameter to control the adjustment of local time when daylight saving time is in effect. When set to ON, you can adjust the local time with the DAYLIGHT SAVING TIME OFFSET parameter.

SET TIME

SET TIME is a server console command that you can use to set the date and time at a NetWare server. You must use caution when setting time on time-synchronized servers because other servers may get their time from the server. The command has the following syntax:

   SET TIME *mo/day/yr hr:min:sec*

where *mo/day/yr* specify the date and *hr:min:sec* specify the time. You can type the date as 12/25/98, December 25, 1998, or 25 December 1998. You can enter the time in either standard or 24-hour clock format. Use the SET TIME reference or single reference time server because these time servers supply the time to other servers, but you can also set the time on primary time servers. Doing so causes all the time servers to converge to the new time.

Interoperability of NTP with TimeSync

NetWare 5 always uses TimeSync for time synchronization between servers, whether using IP, IPX, or both protocols. The TIMESYNC.NLM module is automatically installed during the installation of the operating system. The NTP.NLM module must be loaded manually when the network is using the IP protocol. TimeSync will operate as an NCP request responder only and NTP will manage and set the clock when the IP protocol stack is loaded. NTP becomes the main source of time for both the IP and IPX networks. The IPX TimeSync servers become secondary time sources and point to NTP through the Migration Agent for the primary source of time.

NTP is configured with the NTP.CFG configuration file located in the \SYS\ETC directory. A default NTP.CFG file is created during installation of the operating system. The default NTP.CFG file specifies the local clock (127.127.1.0) as the time source.

The following two commands specify the mode and time server host name to be used:

- **Peer address**   The PEER command specifies that the local server is to operate in symmetric active mode with the remote server. In this mode, the local server can be synchronized to the remote server and the remote server can be synchronized by the local server. This is useful in a network where either the local or a remote server is a better source of time. The time server address can be either a DNS name or an IP address.

- **Server address**   The SERVER command specifies that the local server will operate in client mode with the specified remote server. In this mode, the local server can be synchronized to the remote server, but the remote server can never be synchronized to the local server. On a local network without Internet access, the server can use its own clock as the reference clock using the local IP address (127.127.1.0). When there are no synchronization sources, the local reference clock can use the local hardware clock as a last resort. The time server address can be either a DNS name or an IP address.

The
Complete
Reference

Part V

The NetWare File System

The
Complete
Reference

Chapter 19

Administering the
Traditional File System

515

This chapter provides information about Novell's traditional file system. You learn about the structure of the file system and about using the NetWare Administrator and Windows Explorer utilities to manage the file system. You also learn useful techniques for manipulating files and managing the security of the file system.

Traditional NetWare Filing System Organization

The traditional NetWare filing system consists of servers that have one or more volumes. The first volume on each server is always called SYS. The default names for additional volumes are VOL1, VOL2, and so on, but you can give them custom names, such as MACVOL, USERS, or EMAIL, to describe what is stored on the volume and who might use it. Each volume has its own directory structure.

The name context that you use to refer to files is based on the Universal Naming Convention (UNC) standards. If you need to refer to a file on a server other than your default server, you type the full context of the filename using the UNC. A backward slash separates server, volume, directory, and subdirectory names.

For example, the following refers to a file called BUDGET.XLS in the BUDGDOCS directory on the APPS volume of the ACCTG server:

```
\\ACCTG\APPS\BUDGDOCS\BUDGET.XLS
```

NetWare Volumes

The *volume* is the highest level of storage in the NetWare filing system. It is a physical amount of hard disk storage space that is fixed in size, although you can expand a volume by adding more physical disk space. Volumes appear as objects in the NDS directory tree. Most volumes are created when you install the NetWare 5 operating system on a server. NetWare 5 servers support up to 64 volumes.

A volume is organized into a root directory and branching subdirectories. The first NetWare volume on a server must be named SYS. It contains the NetWare system and public files, unless they have been moved. Physically, volumes are divided into volume segments that can be stored on one or more hard disks. Logically, volumes are divided into directories containing files or subdirectories.

You can use both the NetWare Administrator and Windows Explorer utilities to view and work with volume information.

Creating a Volume

You use the NWCONFIG command at the server console to create a volume on any hard drive that has a NetWare partition. By default, the new volume will consume all of the free space in the NetWare partition unless you assign a new volume size. You can leave free space available for future volumes by specifying the volume size.

You must have free space available on the hard disk where you want to create the new volume. You must also have an existing SYS volume on the system. Supervisor rights are required to perform the creation operation, which includes the following steps:

1. Type **NWCONFIG** at the server console prompt.

2. From the Installation Options menu, choose Standard Disk Options and then NetWare Volume Options. The existing volumes will be listed as shown in Figure 19-1.

3. Press INSERT and the volume disk segment list appears, as shown here:

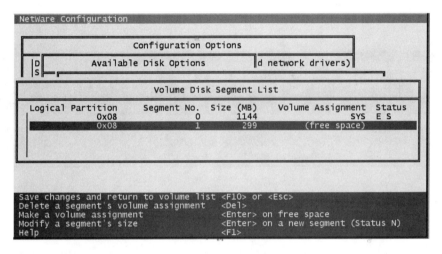

4. Select any existing free space on the list and press ENTER.

5. Select Make This Segment a New Volume from the dialog box, as shown here:

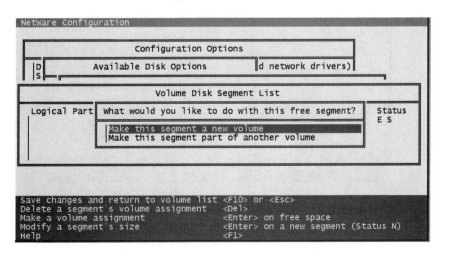

The NetWare File System

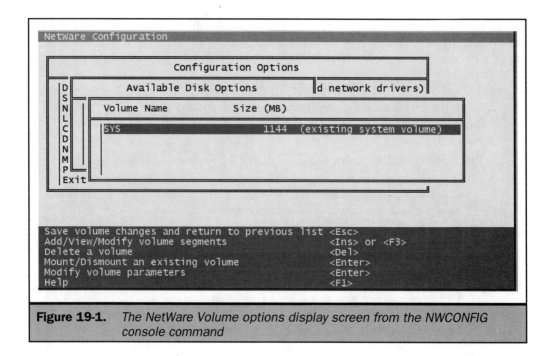

Figure 19-1. *The NetWare Volume options display screen from the NWCONFIG console command*

6. Enter a name for the new volume and specify the disk segment size in the dialog box, as shown here:

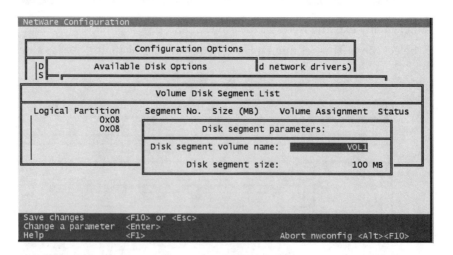

7. Press ESC or F10 to return to the volume segment list.

8. Press ESC or F10 to save the changes. The newly created volume will appear in the volume disk segment list, as shown here:

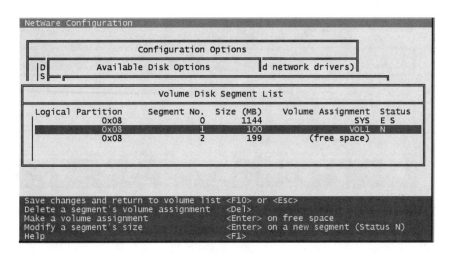

9. Save the volume changes by selecting Yes in the dialog box, as shown here:

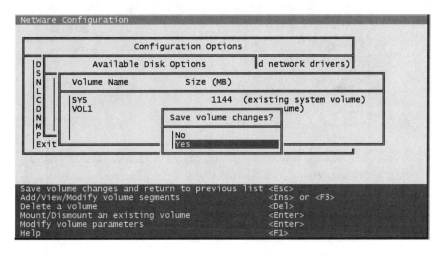

10. Authenticate to the network with Supervisor rights to add the new volume to the tree. Notice that you must use the full path name to the Supervisor object, as shown next.

```
NetWare Configuration

                     Configuration Options
    |D|              Available Disk Options        |d network drivers)|
    |S|_____|
    |_____|
                   Directory Services Login/Authentication
    Administrator Name: .cn=admin.ou=administration.ou=divwest.o=cambriancorp
    Password:                    ******

    |P|__|__|
    |Exit|__|__|

    Password Help

    Enter the password for the Administrator Name above.

    _____(To scroll, <F7>-up <F8>-down)_____
    Save field data  <Enter>                    Abort field entry   <Esc>
    Help             <F1>                        Abort nwconfig <Alt><F10>
```

The newly created Volume object will appear in the NetWare Administrator
browser window (see Figure 19-2) with the default object name of *file server
name*_VOL1.

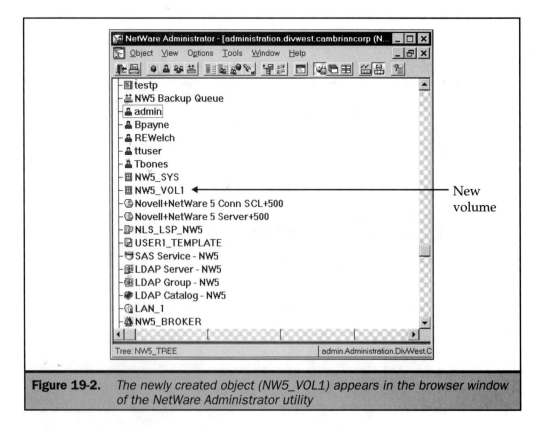

Figure 19-2. *The newly created object (NW5_VOL1) appears in the browser window of the NetWare Administrator utility*

Mounting and Dismounting a Volume

Volumes must be mounted before they can be accessed. The volume's File Allocation Table (FAT) is loaded into memory, and each file block of data takes up one entry in the FAT. Because of this, volumes with a smaller block size require more server memory to mount and manage. On the other hand, using large block sizes on a volume will waste disk space if you store a lot of small files.

There are two ways that you can mount and dismount volumes. This simplest way is to enter the MOUNT [volume name] and DISMOUNT [volume name] commands at the server console. The second way is a little more complex. To mount and dismount volumes using the NWCONFIG command, perform the following steps:

1. Type **NWCONFIG** at the server console prompt.

2. Select Standard Disk Options.

3. Select NetWare Volume Options.

4. Select the volume you want to mount or dismount and press ENTER. The Volume Information screen appears, as shown in Figure 19-3.

5. Use the arrow keys to highlight the status field and press ENTER.

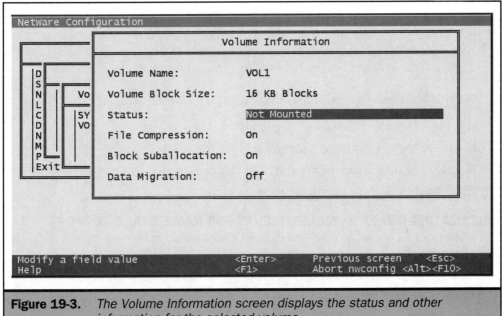

Figure 19-3.   *The Volume Information screen displays the status and other information for the selected volume*

6. Select the desired operation from the list, as shown here:

```
NetWare Configuration
┌──────────────────────────────────────────────────────────┐
│                        Volume Information                   │
│ ┌───┐                                                       │
│ │D  │           Volume Name:           VOL1                 │
│ │S  │                                                       │
│ │N  │  ┌──┐     Volume Block Size:      16 KB Blocks        │
│ │L  │  │Vo│                                                 │
│ │C  │  ├──┤     Status:                 ▓Not Mounted▓       │
│ │D  │  │SY│                                                 │
│ │N  │  │VO│     File Compress ┌─ Choose an action: ─┐       │
│ │M  │  └──┘                   │                     │       │
│ │P  │           Block Suballo │▓Mount▓              │       │
│ │Exit│          └─────────────│ Dismount            │       │
│ └───┘           Data Migratio └─────────────────────┘       │
│                                                             │
└──────────────────────────────────────────────────────────┘
Modify a field value              <Enter>    Previous screen    <Esc>
Help                              <F1>       Abort nwconfig <Alt><F10>
```

Storing Non-DOS Files on a Volume

By default, NetWare 5 volumes support both the DOS 8.3 and Long file naming conventions. To store files from systems such as Macintosh or UNIX, you must load the appropriate name space Novell Loadable Module (NLM) and add the name space support to that volume.

Each name space that you add to the traditional NetWare volume requires additional server memory. If insufficient memory is an issue, consider using Novell Storage Services (NSS) volumes. Each NSS volume uses only 1MB of memory to mount any size volume no matter how many name spaces the volume supports.

The following name space NLMs are included with NetWare 5:

- MAC.NAM (for Macintosh file storage)
- NFS.NAM (for UNIX NFS file storage
- LONG.NAM (automatically added to volumes created using NWCONFIG)
- FTAM.NAM (third-party name space module)

CALCULATING MEMORY REQUIREMENTS FOR NAME SPACE SUPPORT The following formula is used to calculate the additional server memory required for each added name space:

$0.032 \times volume\_size(MB) \div block\_size(MB)$

Round the result to the next highest megabyte. Remember, this is in addition to the memory required by the basic operating system.

ADDING A NAME SPACE TO A VOLUME   To add a name space to an existing NetWare volume, perform the following steps:

- Load the appropriate name space NLM by typing **[LOAD]** *name_space* at the server console prompt. For example, to load the Macintosh name space type **[LOAD] MAC.NAM**.

- Add name space support to the volume by typing the following:

  ADD NAME SPACE *name* to *volume_name*

  Replace *name* with the name space NLM and replace *volume_name* with the name of the volume to receive the added name space. Name space is added only once to a volume. It autoloads each time the server comes up after that.

- To view a list of the current volumes and name spaces on the server, type the following command at the server console prompt:

  VOLUME(s)

REMOVING A NAME SPACE FROM A VOLUME   The name space added to a volume can be removed either by deleting the volume and recreating it or by using the VREPAIR utility as described below. Be careful with this utility, as it works directly with the volume File Allocation Table (FAT) and the Directory Entry Table (DET). Perform the following steps to remove the added name space from a NetWare volume:

1. Type **[LOAD] VREPAIR** at the server console prompt. A screen like the one shown in Figure 19-4 will be displayed.

2. Select option 2, Set VRepair Options.

3. Select option 1, Remove Name Space Support from the Volume, as shown in Figure 19-5, and follow the onscreen prompts.

| Note |

The volume must be dismounted before any VREPAIR operations can be performed.

Mounting a CD as a NetWare Volume

You must load the CDROM.NLM to use a CD-ROM device on the server as a NetWare volume. The CD-ROM device will automatically be mounted when you load the CDROM.NLM module. This version of CDROM.NLM replaces the version used in the previous NetWare operating system releases. The old version of CDROM.NLM is now named CDINST.NLM and should only be used when installing the NetWare 5

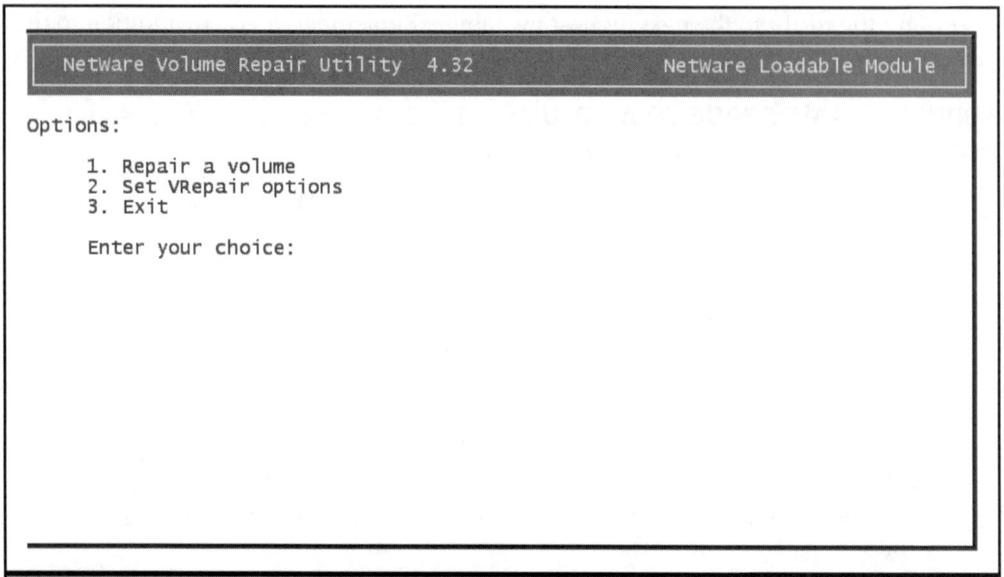

```
┌──────────────────────────────────────────────────────────────────────┐
│ ┌────────────────────────────────────────────────────────────────┐   │
│ │  NetWare Volume Repair Utility   4.32        NetWare Loadable Module │
│ └────────────────────────────────────────────────────────────────┘   │
│  Options:                                                              │
│                                                                        │
│        1. Repair a volume                                              │
│        2. Set VRepair options                                          │
│        3. Exit                                                         │
│                                                                        │
│        Enter your choice:                                              │
│                                                                        │
│                                                                        │
│                                                                        │
│                                                                        │
└──────────────────────────────────────────────────────────────────────┘
```

Figure 19-4.   *The main VREPAIR utility screen*

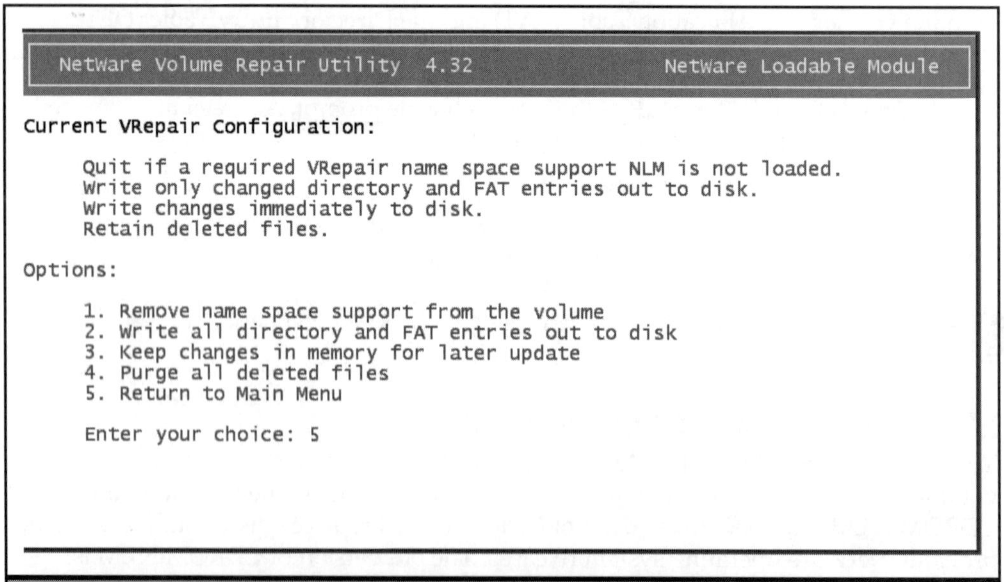

```
┌──────────────────────────────────────────────────────────────────────┐
│ ┌────────────────────────────────────────────────────────────────┐   │
│ │  NetWare Volume Repair Utility   4.32        NetWare Loadable Module │
│ └────────────────────────────────────────────────────────────────┘   │
│  Current VRepair Configuration:                                        │
│                                                                        │
│      Quit if a required VRepair name space support NLM is not loaded.  │
│      Write only changed directory and FAT entries out to disk.         │
│      Write changes immediately to disk.                                │
│      Retain deleted files.                                             │
│                                                                        │
│  Options:                                                              │
│                                                                        │
│        1. Remove name space support from the volume                    │
│        2. Write all directory and FAT entries out to disk              │
│        3. Keep changes in memory for later update                      │
│        4. Purge all deleted files                                      │
│        5. Return to Main Menu                                          │
│                                                                        │
│        Enter your choice: 5                                            │
│                                                                        │
└──────────────────────────────────────────────────────────────────────┘
```

Figure 19-5.   *Select option 1 to remove name space support from a dismounted volume*

operating system. The CD-ROM device will be loaded as a NSS volume. It will not be loaded unless you have loaded the NWPA.DSK NPA driver that interfaces with the Media Manager. Do not enable block suballocation or use file compression on the volume. The CDROM.NLM loads the following modules:

- **NSS**   This module loads the Novell Storage Services (NSS) modules.
- **CD9660.NSS**   This module loads support for High Sierra and ISO 9660 format CD-ROM devices.
- **CDHFS.NSS**   This module is loaded to support the Apple HFS file system for CD-ROMs.

Using Block Suballocation

Block suballocation enhances the use of space on the hard drive. It divides any partially used block into suballocation blocks of 512 bytes. These suballocation blocks can be used by files as needed. Block suballocation can only be enabled when creating a traditional NetWare volume. Figure 19-3 shows the dialog box where this option is configurable.

Using Spanning to Enhance Disk Response Time

You can improve the disk response time of heavily used volumes on the server by distributing volume segments across two or more hard drives. This technique takes advantage of the hard disk controller access times. Instead of having to wait for one disk access to complete, multiple accesses can be handled by the disk controller simultaneously.

The down side to this is that if one disk fails, the entire volume then becomes unavailable. You should mirror or duplex the disk drives containing the spanned volumes. The entire volume must be restored from a backup if a disk containing a spanned volume fails.

To effectively use this technique, you should distribute volume segments equally across all the disk drives. Do not simply fill up one disk and then start filling the next.

Changing Volume Size

The size of a volume can be easily expanded by adding any available free space to the volume. This can be from free space on the current hard drive or free space on a new hard drive. Reducing the size of a volume is another matter. You must delete the entire volume and then re-create the new smaller volume. Back up all data on the volume before deleting it. The following requirements must be kept in mind before expanding a NetWare volume:

- The maximum number of segments allowed per volume is 32.
- The maximum number of segments you can create on one hard disk is 8.
- The maximum number of volumes allowed is 64.

The NetWare File System

Follow the basic steps in creating a volume to extend a volume. Step 5 under "Creating a Volume," earlier in this chapter, shows the screen where you select "Make this segment part of another volume" to add free space to an existing volume.

Deleting a Volume

NetWare volumes can be easily deleted by using the NWCONFIG command at the server console. Be careful! Deleting one volume segment deletes all existing data on the volume. You cannot delete only part of a volume. Perform the following steps at the server console to delete a volume:

1. Type the NWCONFIG command at the server console prompt.
2. Select Standard Disk Options.
3. Select NetWare Volume Options.
4. When the screen depicted in Figure 19-1 appears, select the desired volume and press DELETE.
5. When the Delete Existing Volume prompt appears, select Yes and press ENTER.

Renaming a Volume

You can rename any volume on a NetWare server. But do not change the name of the SYS volume. It is mandatory for the operating system to have a SYS volume. Perform the following steps to change the name of a volume:

1. Dismount the volume you wish to rename.
2. Type the NWCONFIG command at the server console prompt.
3. Select Standard Disk Options.
4. Select NetWare Volume Options.
5. Select the volume whose name you wish to change from the screen shown in Figure 19-1 and press ENTER.
6. Use the arrow keys to highlight the Name field and press ENTER.
7. Backspace to erase the old name and enter the new name.
8. Press the ESC key twice and press F10 to save the new name.

Repairing a Volume

You can repair a damaged volume with the same utility you use to remove name spaces from a volume. A damaged volume will not mount even if it has minor damage. You use the VREPAIR utility to correct volume properties or to remove name space entries from the file allocation table (FAT) and directory entry tables

(DETs). VREPAIR can be run on a damaged volume without dismounting the other volumes on the server. Some of the typical instances in which running VREPAIR can help are as follows:

- A hardware failure either prevented a volume from mounting or caused a disk read error.
- A power failure or improper shutdown of the server corrupted a volume.
- The server console displays a mirroring error when the server boots. This mirroring refers to the two copies of FATs and DETs that the operating system keeps.

If a volume fails to mount when the server is coming up, VREPAIR will load automatically and attempt to repair the volume. When this occurs, VREPAIR will use the default options. If the default options are not acceptable, load VREPAIR manually to change the options before starting the utility.

If you do not want VREPAIR to automatically repair a volume that will not mount, use the SET parameter AUTOMATICALLY REPAIR BAD VOLUMES to change the default.

Viewing Volumes on the SERVER

You can view information on server volumes by using the NetWare Administrator or the Windows Explorer utilities. The information contained in the various screens is equivalent. The difference is only in the way that the information is presented to the user.

The NetWare Administrator volume information display is shown in Figure 19-6. Each of the property pages displays further information on the volume.

The Novell Client provides snap-ins to the Windows operating system. These snap-ins provide added functionality to the basic information displays in the Windows Explorer utility. Figures 19-7, 19-8, and 19-9 show the information that is available on a selected NetWare volume using Windows Explorer.

NetWare Directories

The NetWare directory system is similar to the DOS directory system. Each volume has one root directory. Directories can branch from the root, and subdirectories can branch from these directories. The NetWare installation program creates the directory structure of the SYS volume as shown in Figure 19-10. All of these directories are automatically created during installation of the operating system. Each directory pertaining to the file system is described in the following paragraphs.

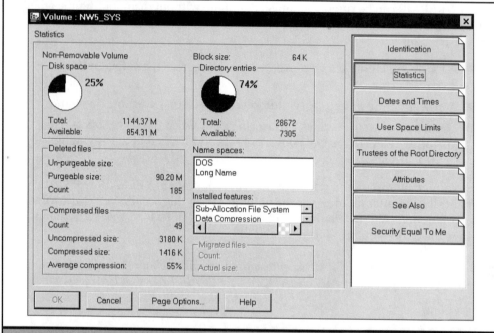

Figure 19-6. The NetWare Administrator utility displays information on the server volume using various property pages

SYS:DELETED.SAV   The DELETED.SAV directory contains files that have been deleted from deleted directories. Salvageable files are usually stored in the directory from which they were deleted. If a directory is deleted, the salvageable files from the deleted directory are moved to this directory. Deleted files can be salvaged if they have not been purged.

SYS:ETC   The ETC (pronounced *et-see*) directory contains configuration files for various Internet and communications programs. These are discussed in other chapters later in the book.

SYS:LOGIN   The LOGIN directory contains the programs necessary for users to log into the network. The NLS subdirectory contains subdirectories for login message files for each supported language. The LOGIN directory is mapped to the first network drive at workstations before logging in.

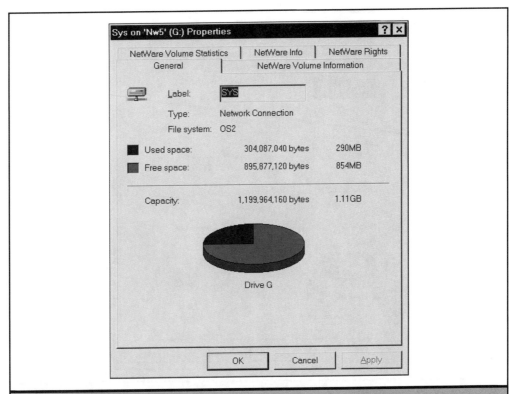

Figure 19-7.   *The Windows Explorer utility displays general information on the NetWare volume*

SYS:MAIL   The MAIL directory is a remnant of previous NetWare versions. NetWare used to create a subdirectory in MAIL for each user and store their login scripts in these subdirectories. Login scripts are now stored as part of each User object in the Novell Directory Services (NDS) tree. However, MAIL is retained for applications that require it.

SYS:PUBLIC   The PUBLIC directory holds NetWare utilities typically accessed by all users. Users are automatically granted Read and File Scan rights to the PUBLIC directory of a SYS volume that is at their context level. It contains subdirectories for Windows 95/98 utilities, Windows NT utilities, and an NLS subdirectory that contains the message files for the utilities. A default login script automatically maps a search path to this directory.

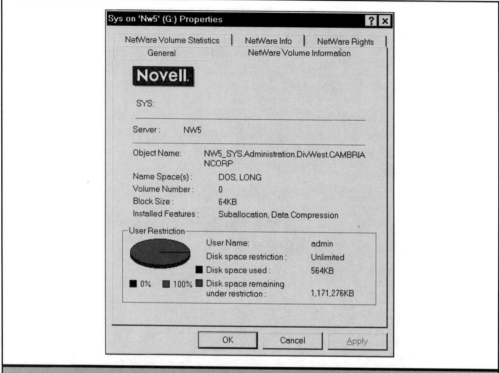

Figure 19-8. *The Windows Explorer utility displays the NetWare Volume Information, including the installed volume features*

SYS:SYSTEM The SYSTEM directory contains the NetWare operating system files as well as utilities and program files used for administering the network. It has an NLS subdirectory that contains subdirectories for each supported language for message files. It also contains hidden directories and files in the SYS volume where NDS information is stored on the server.

Planning the Directory Structure

The directory structure on your volumes should be optimized to improve performance and simplify administration. A number of tips are listed in this section to help you with organization. You should separate document files from program files to organize the directory structure in a way that makes backups easier. Program files don't need to be backed up every day because they typically do not change. Data files, however, usually require daily backup. Storing data files in the same directory as the programs used to create them would force you to back up all the files, which could take a considerably longer time and require more backup media.

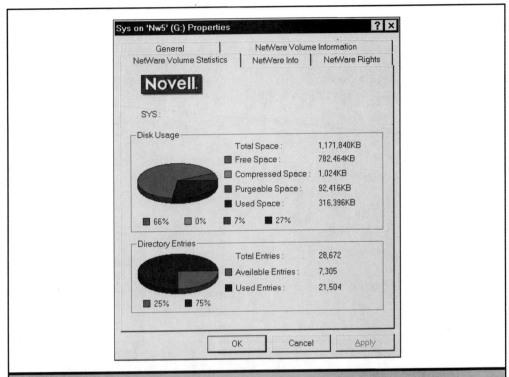

Figure 19-9. *The Windows Explorer utility displays the NetWare Volume Statistics for the selected volume*

Remember that rights flow down the directory structure, so you should organize directories to take advantage of this and make rights administration easier. Figure 19-11 illustrates a directory structure that makes backup and rights administration easy. The APPS directory has subdirectories in which applications are stored. You can back up this branch every week. The DOCS directory has subdirectories in which users can store shared document files (assuming they store personal files in their own home directory). You back up this branch every day.

To let users run programs in the LOTUS and WORD directories, grant them Read and File Scan rights in the APPS directory. Because rights flow down, they can run the programs in the subdirectories as well. To let a user run Lotus 1-2-3, but not Word, assign rights for that user only in the LOTUS directory. You would follow the same strategy to assign rights in the DOCS directory, except that users might have different rights to the document files. For example, users who can change files get Read and Write rights, while users who can only read files get the read-only right. Rights are discussed in more detail later.

The NetWare File System

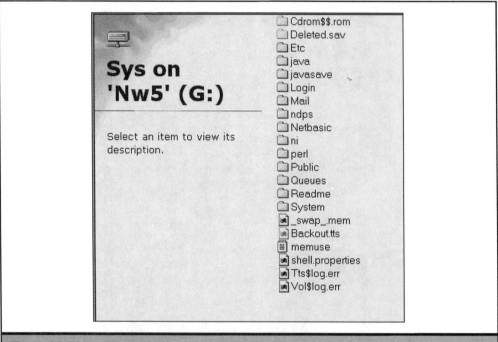

Figure 19-10.   *This is the directory structure created for the SYS volume when you install NetWare 5 on the server*

Note   *Trustee rights assignments granted to a user in a directory override any rights inherited from directories higher up in the directory structure.*

Figure 19-11 shows a rather simplified directory tree, but it illustrates the basic structure for program and data files. Large organizations will have entire servers

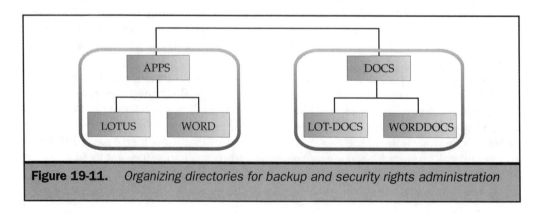

Figure 19-11.   *Organizing directories for backup and security rights administration*

dedicated to just one program and its data files, or entire servers for storing just shared data files. Here are a few points to keep in mind when organizing directory structures:

■ Place name space support for other file types, such as UNIX and Macintosh, on separate volumes.

■ If you have hundreds of users, install a separate server to hold users' home directories. This minimizes traffic on servers that must provide application support.

■ Some files require auditing, as discussed in Chapter 21. Group these files together if possible.

■ Files that need to be compressed should be organized into separate directories. Files targeted for migration should ideally have their own volume.

■ Applications use executable files that are prone to virus attack. Keep these files separate so that you can apply security features to them that prevent attacks. Never give casual users any rights in program directories except Read and File Scan.

User Home Directories

When you create a new User object, you can specify a directory that the user can use for personal files. These users get all file rights except the Supervisor right to this directory by default, so they can create subdirectories and even grant other users the right to access the directory.

You can limit each user's allowable disk space by opening the details page for a Volume object and clicking the User Space Limits button. Then select a user and set the disk space limits. The volume space limit applies to all storage used by that user in that volume.

You can set disk space limitations for all users in the user template of a container. These techniques are discussed in Chapter 17.

You can also limit the size of a directory using the Facts page for the directory. This can limit the size of the directory and its subdirectories regardless of who uses the directory.

The best way to organize user directories if you decide to use them is to create a directory called USERS or HOME, and then attach all user directories to it. If your network has a lot of users in different departments, create directories such as SALES/USERS and ACCTG/USERS to further separate and organize the directories. If hundreds of users are accessing files in their user directories, consider separating user directories from applications by placing user directories on a separate server so that user traffic doesn't decrease the performance of the application server.

Creating a Directory

You create new directories in NetWare Administrator or in your desktop application by first going to the volume and folder where you want to put the new directory. You must have the Create right for the directory to which the new directory will be added. If you choose to create a directory at a volume, it is created at the root level. Here are the techniques. In the NetWare Administrator utility, perform the following steps:

1. Select the Volume object where you want to create the new directory.

2. Right-click the volume and select Create. The dialog box shown here will be displayed:

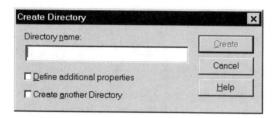

3. Enter the new directory name in the dialog box and click Create.

In Windows Explorer, perform the following steps:

1. Start the Windows Explorer utility.

2. Select the network drive that contains the volume where you want to create the new directory.

3. Select New Folder from the File menu.

4. Enter the name of the new folder (directory) at the blinking prompt, as shown in Figure 19-12.

Creating a Directory Map Object

A Directory Map object is used to represent a particular directory in the file system. It is a leaf object in the NDS tree that represents a path on a volume. It allows users to map a drive to a resource without knowing its physical location. If the path to the resource changes, only the directory map needs to be updated. The users' MAP commands remain the same.

To create a Directory Map object, perform the following steps in the NetWare Administrator utility:

1. Select the Organization or Organizational Unit object where you want to create the Directory Map object.

2. Select Create from the Object menu.

3. Select the Directory Map object from the New Object dialog box and click OK.

4. Enter the name for the Directory Map object in the dialog box, as shown in Figure 19-13.

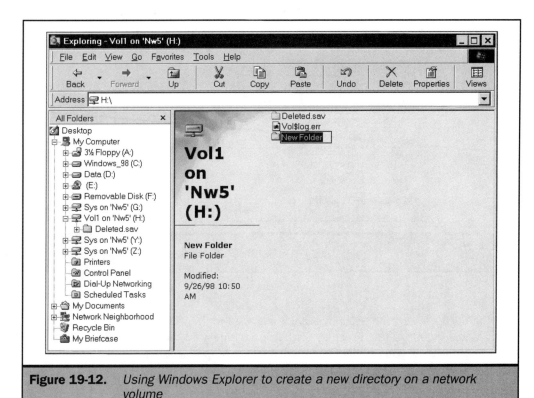

Figure 19-12.   *Using Windows Explorer to create a new directory on a network volume*

5. Enter the name of the volume this object will point to. You can use the Browse button to search through the NDS tree if desired.

6. Enter the path in the directory structure that this object will point to. Leave this field blank if the object points to the root of the specified volume.

7. Click the Create button to create the Directory Map object.

Using Directory Map Objects

Directory Map objects are designed to simplify your job administering the network. You create a Directory Map object to point to application programs or data that users can access simply by mapping a drive to the Directory Map in their login scripts. By using a Directory Map object, you avoid having to make changes to every user's login script when you relocate the directory to another location within the NDS tree.

For example, assume that you create a Directory Map object named JAVA_MAP, as shown in Figure 19-13. In your users' login scripts, you map a search drive to the Directory Map object, rather than to the specific directory as follows:

```
MAP INS S2:=.JAVA_MAP.Administration.DivWest.Cambriancorp
```

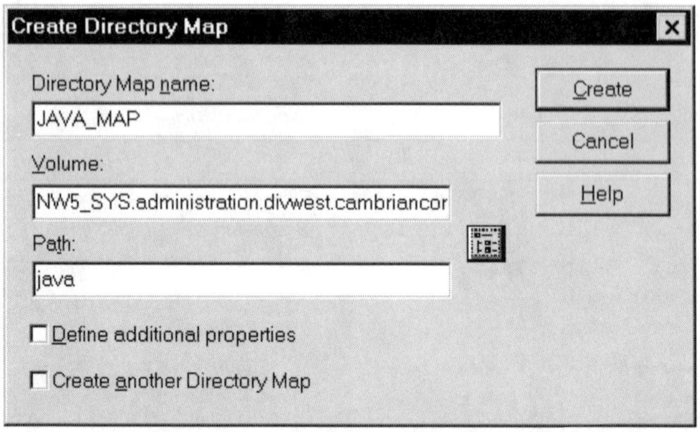

Create Directory Map   ✕

Directory Map name:

JAVA_MAP   Create

Volume: Cancel

NW5_SYS.administration.divwest.cambriancor   Help

Path:

java

☐ Define additional properties

☐ Create another Directory Map

Figure 19-13. *The Directory Map object dialog box*

When users log in, their search drive is mapped to the JAVA_MAP Directory Map object, which points to the directory containing the desired files. If you change the location of the files, you only change the Directory Map object to indicate the new path. The MAP command is covered in detail in Chapter 24.

Remember that the user (or group or container) must have the read path property right to the Directory Map object and rights in the file system where the Directory Map object is pointing.

Viewing Directory Information

You can view extended information about a directory by using either the NetWare Administrator or the Windows Explorer utilities. Both of these utilities present the same basic information but in different formats. To view the extended directory information using the NetWare Administrator utility, perform the following steps:

1. Start the NetWare Administrator utility.

2. Select the volume that the directory is located in.

3. Click the Volume object to display the directories associated with that volume.

4. Select the desired directory and right-click on it.

5. Select Details to view directory information, as show in Figure 19-14.

To view the extended directory information using the Windows Explorer utility, perform the following steps:

1. Start the Windows Explorer utility.

2. Select the network drive that the volume is mapped to.

3. Click on the volume to expand the view.

4. Select the desired directory and right-click to bring up the selection menu.

5. Select Properties to display the NetWare Info tab, as shown in Figure 19-15.

NetWare Files

Files are the basic building block of any directory structure. They can contain data such as spreadsheet values, word processing text, or any other type of information. They can also be application programs that allow the user to perform some useful function or to play a game.

Distributing Applications on the Network

The reason for a network is to allow multiple users easy access to shared information and applications. You install various types of applications, such as word processing,

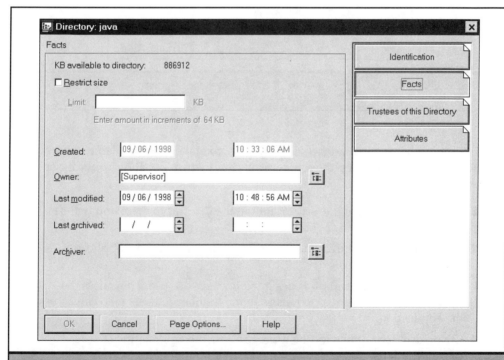

Figure 19-14.   *The Facts property page of the selected directory object*

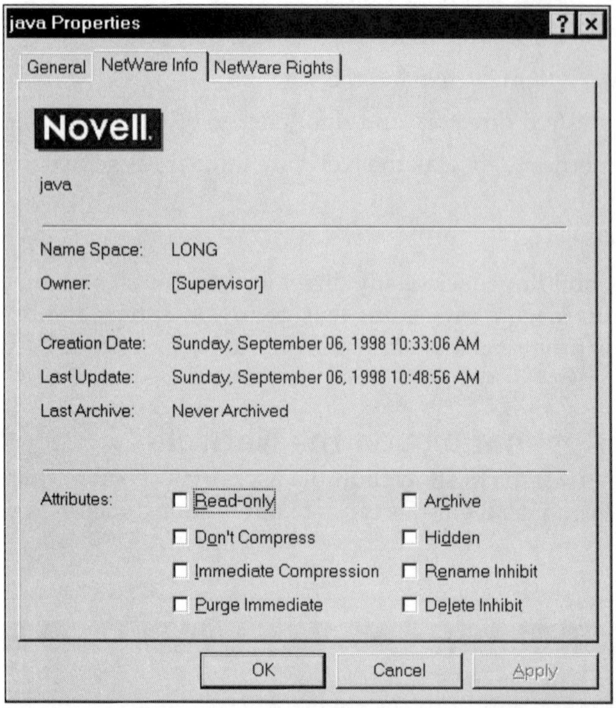

Figure 19-15. *The NetWare Info tab of the Windows Explorer utility*

graphics programs, and spreadsheet applications, to make them available to users attached to the network. Keep the following in mind when installing applications on the network server:

- Ensure that you have the Create right in the directory where you will be installing the application.

- Follow the manufacturer's documentation for installing the application on a network.

- Ensure that the application is designed for network use. This raises the issue of any licensing restrictions as to the number of users who can access the application.

- Create drive mappings for the users to allow the workstations to see the applications.

■ Consider creating a Directory Map object to simplify administration of the application.

■ Set up and manage network applications through NDS using the Application Launcher. This is a component of the Z.E.N.works product and is covered in Chapter 28.

■ Keep program files separate from data files to simplify application management, virus prevention, and backup.

Viewing File Information

You can view extended information about a file by using the NetWare Administrator or Windows Explorer utilities. Both of these utilities present the same basic information but in different formats. Perform the following steps to view extended file information using the NetWare Administrator utility:

1. Start the NetWare Administrator utility.

2. Select the volume that the directory is located in.

3. Click the Volume object to display the directories associated with that volume.

4. Select the desired directory.

5. Select the desired file and right-click on it.

6. Select Details to view directory information, as shown in Figure 19-16.

To view extended directory information using the Windows Explorer utility, perform the following steps:

1. Start the Windows Explorer utility.

2. Select the network drive that the volume is mapped to.

3. Click on the volume to expand the view.

4. Select the desired directory.

5. Select the desired file and right-click to bring up the selection menu.

6. Select Properties to display the NetWare Info tab, as shown in Figure 19-17.

File and Directory Compression

Compression is a means to getting more file and directory space from the physical size of the NetWare volume. You can set attributes on specific files and directories to compress the files when they are not needed. This allows you to store more files in the same physical space.

By default, file compression is enabled at the volume level when you create a new volume. If you disabled it when you created the volume, you can use the SET utility to

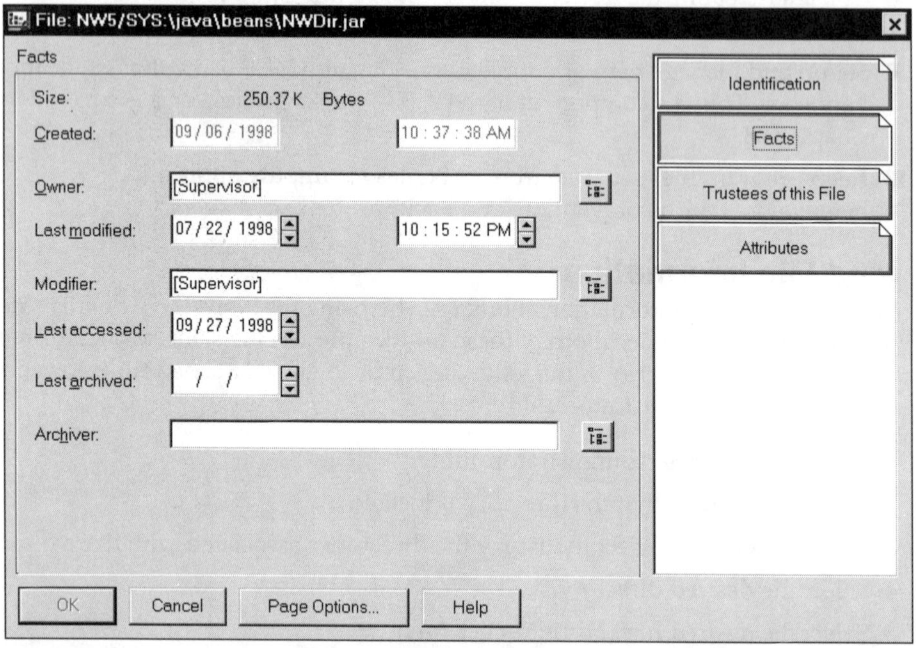

Figure 19-16.   *The Facts property page for the selected file*

enable it at a later time. File compression must be enabled for the volume before you can set individual file compression attributes.

To avoid the overhead of decompressing files that do not compress well, the operating system calculates the compressed size of a file before compressing it. The file will not be compressed if no disk space will be saved by the compression or if the file's compressed size is larger than the value specified in the SET parameter named MINIMUM PERCENTAGE COMPRESSION GAIN.

There must be enough free space on the volume to accommodate the decompressed file size before a file will be decompressed.

Setting Compression Attributes for a Volume

The SET utility is used to set the file compression attributes for an entire volume. The operating system will ignore individual file and directory compression settings if compression has not been enabled on the volume. The following ten SET parameters are used to manage file and directory compression on a NetWare volume.

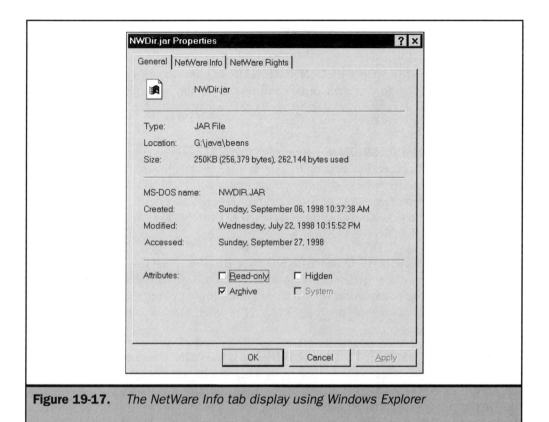

Figure 19-17. *The NetWare Info tab display using Windows Explorer*

We recommend that you use the Server Parameters option on the MONITOR screen to make these types of changes. It automatically creates the SET command in the appropriate NCF file.

COMPRESSION DAILY CHECK STOP HOUR = *number* Set this parameter to specify when you want the file compressor to stop scanning enabled volumes for files that need to be compressed. The default is hour 6 using a 24-hour time format. The supported values are between 0 (midnight) and 23. This parameter can be set in the STARTUP.NCF file.

COMPRESSION DAILY CHECK START HOUR = *number* Set this parameter to specify when you want the file compressor to start scanning enabled volumes for files that need to be compressed. The default is hour 0 (midnight) using a 24-hour format. The supported values are between 0 and 23. The file compressor will start and run as long as necessary if this parameter and the Compression Daily Check Stop Hour are set to the same value. This parameter can be set in the STARTUP.NCF file.

MINIMUM COMPRESSION PERCENTAGE GAIN = *number*   Set this parameter to the minimum percentage that a file must compress to remain in a compressed state. The supported values range from 0 to 50 percent. This parameter can be set in the STARTUP.NCF file.

ENABLE FILE COMPRESSION = *value*   Set this parameter to specify whether file compression is suspended. Setting this parameter to ON allows file compression on compression-enabled volumes. Setting this parameter to OFF suspends file compression on the volume. All compression requests will be queued until this parameter is reset to ON. This parameter defaults to the ON value and can be set in the STARTUP.NCF file.

MAXIMUM CONCURRENT COMPRESSIONS = *number*   Set this parameter to specify the maximum concurrent compressions on the server. Concurrent file and directory compressions can occur only if there are multiple volumes with compression enabled. The supported values are from 1 to 8. This parameter can be set in the STARTUP.NCF file.

CONVERT COMPRESSED TO UNCOMPRESSED OPTION = *value*   Set this parameter to specify what the operating system does with a decompressed version of a file after it has been decompressed. There are three supported values: 0 = always leave the file compressed; 1 (default) = leave the file compressed until the second access if it is read only once during the time specified by the DAYS UNTOUCHED BEFORE COMPRESSION parameter; and 2 = always leave the file decompressed. This parameter can be set in the STARTUP.NCF file.

DECOMPRESS PERCENT DISK SPACE FREE TO ALLOW COMMIT = *number*   Set this parameter to specify the percentage of free disk space required on a volume for decompression to permanently change compressed files to decompressed files. This parameter prevents newly decompressed files from filling up the volume. The supported values are from 0 to 75 percent. The default is 10 percent. This parameter can be set in the STARTUP.NCF file.

DECOMPRESS FREE SPACE WARNING INTERVAL = *number*   Set this parameter to specify the time between alerts when the file system is unable to decompress files due to a shortage of volume space. The supported values are from 0 to 2,562,603.8 seconds. The default is 1,878.5 seconds. This parameter can be set in the STARTUP.NCF file.

DELETED FILES COMPRESSION OPTION = *number* Set this parameter to specify whether and when deleted files are compressed. There are three supported values: 0 = do not compress deleted files; 1 (default) = compress deleted files the next day; and 2 = compress deleted files immediately. This parameter can be set in the STARTUP.NCF file.

DAYS UNTOUCHED BEFORE COMPRESSION = *number* Set this parameter to specify the number of days the operating system waits after a file was last accessed before compressing it. The supported values are from 0 to 100,000 days. The default is 14 days. This parameter can be set in the STARTUP.NCF file.

Viewing and Setting File and Directory Compression Attributes

You can view extended information about directory and file compression by using the NetWare Administrator or Windows Explorer utilities. Both of these utilities present the same basic information but in different formats. To view the extended directory compression information using the NetWare Administrator utility, perform the following steps:

1. Start the NetWare Administrator utility.
2. Select the volume that the directory is located in.
3. Click the Volume object to display the directories associated with that volume.
4. Select the desired directory.
5. Select Details to view directory information.
6. Select the Attributes property page, as shown in Figure 19-18.

To view the extended file compression information using the NetWare Administrator utility for a selected file, perform the following steps:

1. Start the NetWare Administrator utility.
2. Select the volume that the directory is located in.
3. Click the Volume object to display the directories associated with that volume.
4. Select the desired directory.
5. Select the desired file and right-click on it.
6. Select Details.
7. Select the Attributes property page to view directory information, as shown in Figure 19-19.

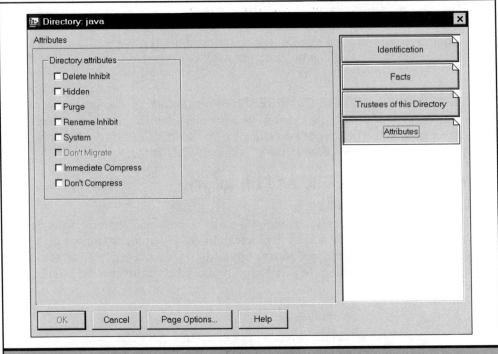

Figure 19-18. *The Attributes property page in NetWare Administrator shows the directory attributes for the selected directory*

To view the extended file compression information for the selected file using the Windows Explorer utility, perform the following steps:

1. Start the Windows Explorer utility.

2. Select the network drive that the volume is mapped to.

3. Click on the volume to expand the view.

4. Select the desired directory.

5. Select the desired file and right-click to bring up the selection menu.

6. Select Properties to display the NetWare Info tab (see Figure 19-20).

Saving Disk Space with Purging

NetWare automatically purges deleted files and directories beginning with the first ones deleted when the server runs out of disk space. You might decide you don't need

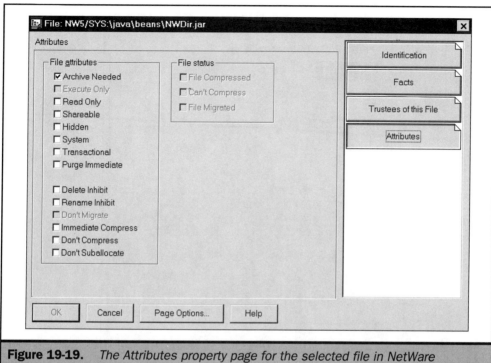

Figure 19-19. *The Attributes property page for the selected file in NetWare Administrator*

the capability to salvage deleted files. Perhaps the deleted files are taking up too much room on your volume and you have adequate backup of important files. Also, there is a slight increase in performance when the salvage feature is disabled. You can make NetWare immediately purge single files, groups of files, or all files in a directory by assigning the files or directory the Purge attribute. You can set the system to purge all deleted files immediately in three different ways:

- Use the SET Immediate Purge of Deleted Files = ON option at the server. This increases performance at the cost of losing the salvageable file feature.

- Set the Purge attribute for individual files and directories. A file is purged when it is deleted if it is flagged with the Purge attribute. All files in a directory are purged when it is deleted if it is flagged with the Purge attribute. These attributes can be set in the screens shown in Figures 19-15, 19-18, 19-19, and 19-20.

- Use the NetWare Administrator | Tools | Salvage screen to manually purge individual files and directories.

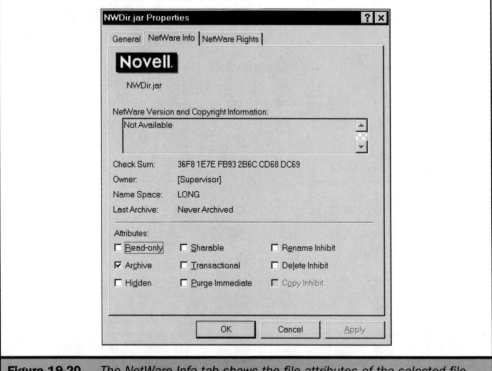

Figure 19-20.   The NetWare Info tab shows the file attributes of the selected file using Windows Explorer

   If you set the Immediate Purge of Deleted Files option to ON, all deleted files are immediately purged on the entire server and its volumes. You might wish to be more selective by marking volumes, directories, or individual files with the Purge attribute instead.

Salvaging Deleted Files and Directories

When a user deletes a file, NetWare keeps a copy of the file around for a while in case you need to recover it. The file does not appear in directory listings and is not available for use, but it is kept in a salvageable state until you restore or purge it. Deleted files are kept in the directory where they were deleted. If a directory is deleted, its files are saved in a file called DELETED.SAV, which is located in the root directory of the volume.

   NetWare Administrator lets you view a list of deleted files and recover files from that list. You can also permanently remove deleted files to save disk space by purging them from the volume. Keep in mind that when the volume becomes full, NetWare purges recoverable files from it on a first-deleted, first-purged basis. Also, if you assigned the Purge attribute to a file or directory, the file or the directory's files will be purged immediately when deleted, and these files are not recoverable by using NetWare Administrator.

To salvage deleted files by using NetWare Administrator, select the directory where the salvageable files are located and then choose Salvage from the Tools menu. The dialog box shown in Figure 19-21 appears. At the top, you can change the following options:

- **Include** Type a wildcard parameter in this field to specify the search pattern for the files you want to display.

- **Sort Options** Click the down arrow button and choose one of the sorting options on the drop-down list box.

- **Source** Click the down arrow button to get the files from the current directory or from a deleted directory.

After you set the options, click the List button. A list of salvageable files appears. Click the files you want to salvage, and click the Salvage button to recover the files. Note the following:

- You can select multiple files for salvaging.

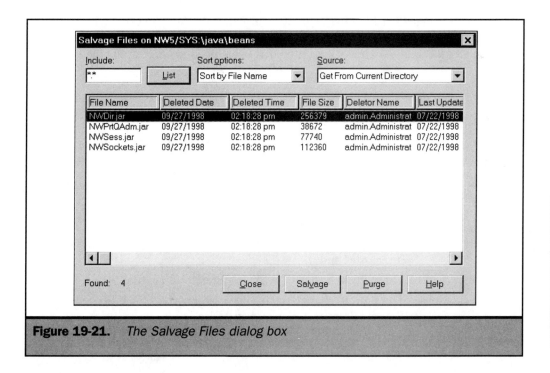

Figure 19-21.   *The Salvage Files dialog box*

- Click the Purge button to permanently remove files.
- You must have the Create right for a file to salvage it.

File and Directory Security

Assigning network users rights to the file system is one of the most important tasks of a network administrator. Recall from Chapter 17 that you can grant file system rights to the following objects:

- Group object
- Organization object
- Organizational Unit object
- Organizational Role object
- Profile object
- User object

In NetWare Administrator, you simply right-click the object, and then choose Details from the context menu and click the Rights to Files and Directories button. From there, you can make the object a trustee of a directory by scanning the file system and choosing volumes and folders. See "Assigning File and Directory Rights to Objects" in Chapter 17, for details about this operation.

This section describes how to assign directory and file rights to users while you're working with a folder or file. It also shows you how to set Inherited Rights Filters in the file system. Table 19-1 shows the rights that users need to work in the file system.

Right	Description
Supervisor	All rights to a directory, its files, and its subdirectories
Read	The right to open files
Create	The right to create new files and subdirectories in a directory
Write	The right to open and change files
Erase	The right to delete directories and files
Modify	The right to change the attributes (see Table19-2) or names of directories and files
File Scan	The right to browse the filing system and list files
Access Control	The right to change the trustee assignments and Inherited Rights Filters of directories and files

Table 19-1.   *Directory and File Rights*

Rights to Files and Directories

Rights that are granted in parent directories of the file system flow down the directory structure and are inherited by subdirectories and files within subdirectories. You use an Inherited Rights Filter (IRF) to block these rights if they are not appropriate in a directory or for a file.

Note, however, that any user or object can be granted explicit rights to a directory or file, which override any rights that might be inherited or that you try to block with an IRF. This is a useful feature because it means you can put up an IRF in a directory to block the rights that a large group of people might inherit to it, and then assign explicit rights to just the people you want to access the directory.

Basically, the Inherited Rights Filter cannot grant rights to anyone; it can only revoke rights from a user or group that has more rights to an object than you want it to have. Note the following:

- The Supervisor right cannot be blocked by the Inherited Rights Filter for directories and files in the file system if the Supervisor right is assigned at a higher level. Even a reassignment in a subdirectory or lower-level file will not revoke the Supervisor right in that branch of the directory structure. The only option is to revoke the Supervisor right at the higher level, and then reassign it at a lower level in a branch.

- For objects, the Supervisor object right can be blocked by the Inherited Rights Filter.

Managing File System Trustees

To assign a user or object trustee rights to a directory or file in the NetWare Administrator, first locate the directory or file, right-click it, and choose Details from its context menu. When the details dialog box appears, click the Trustees of this Directory button to display a dialog box similar to the one shown in Figure 19-22. You can do one of the following:

- Add a new trustee by clicking the Add Trustee button. A dialog box appears so you can scan through the directory tree and locate a user or object.

- In the Trustees field, click an existing trustee to view or change their rights in the lower Access Rights field.

- Click the Effective Rights button to view the rights that users or objects have through inheritance. These users may not appear in the Trustees field.

- Remove a trustee by clicking the trustee and clicking the Delete Trustee button.

- You can block the rights that are inherited by the directory or file by clicking the options in the Inheritance Filter field. Note that if a box is marked with a check, the right is inherited. Removing the check blocks the right.

The NetWare File System

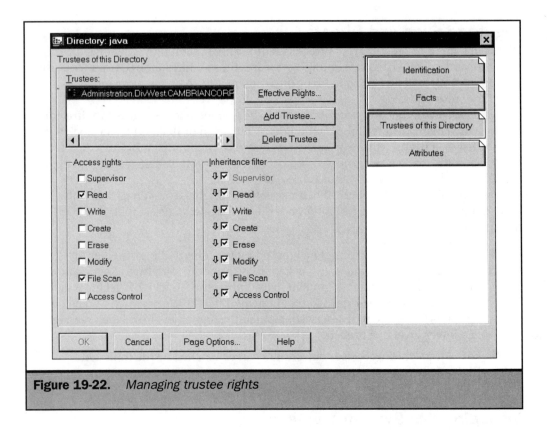

Figure 19-22. *Managing trustee rights*

After you make changes to the dialog box, click the OK button to save those changes.

Setting File and Directory Attributes

NetWare 5 uses various attributes to control access to the file system or to indicate the current status of files. Table 19-2 lists the attributes that can be applied to directories and files to control access or the status of a directory or file. Table 19-3 describes three status attributes for the compression and migration system that you may see when viewing file attributes.

You set the root directory attributes in the NetWare Administrator or Windows Explorer utility. To set attributes of the root directory for the volume using the NetWare Administrator utility, follow these steps:

1. Right-click the volume and choose Details.

2. Click the Attributes button on the Details page. A page similar to the one shown in Figure 19-23 will be displayed.

Attribute	Where Used	Description
A (Archive Needed)	Files	When set, this attribute indicates that a file has been modified and needs backing up. It has no effect on directories.
CI (Copy Inhibit)	Files	When set, it prevents Macintosh users from copying the file. Not used for directories.
DI (Delete Inhibit)	Directories/Files	When set, it prevents users from deleting a file or directory.
DC (Don't Compress)	Directories/Files	When applied to a file, it prevents the file from being compressed. When applied to a directory, it prevents files in the directory from being compressed.
DS (Don't Suballocate)	Files	This attribute prevents an individual file from being suballocated, even if suballocation is enabled for the system. Use this attribute for files that are enlarged or appended frequently, such as certain database files.
DM (Don't Migrate)	Directories/Files	When applied to a file, it prevents the file from being migrated to a secondary storage device such as an optical disk jukebox. When applied to a directory, it prevents files in the directory from being migrated.
X (Execute Only)	Files	This attribute prevents a file from being copied. Only the supervisor can set this file attribute; once set, it cannot be removed. It should be set only if you have a second copy of the file. Backup utilities don't back up a file marked Execute Only, and some program files that have this attribute set don't execute properly.

Table 19-2. *Directory and File Attributes*

The NetWare File System

Attribute	Where Used	Description
H (Hidden)	Directories/Files	It hides a file or directory in DIR listings and prevents the file or directory from being copied or deleted.
IM (Immediate Compress)	Directories/Files	When it is applied to a file, the file is compressed as soon as possible. When it is applied to a directory, the files in the directory are compressed as soon as possible.
P (Purge)	Directories	When it is applied to a file, the file is immediately purged from the system when deleted. When it is applied to a directory, the directory and any files it holds are purged when deleted. Purged files and directories cannot be recovered by using NetWare Administrator or FILER.
PI (Purge Immediate)	Files	A file with this attribute is purged immediately.
RO (Read Only)	Files	When set, this attribute prevents users from changing, deleting, or renaming a file. The DI and RI attributes are also assigned when RO is applied. It has no effect on directories.
RI (Rename Inhibit)	Directories/Files	When set, this attribute prevents users from renaming a file or directory.
S (Shareable)	Files	When set, it allows multiple users to access the file at one time. It is usually set on record-locking database files. It has no effect on directories.
SY (System)	Directories/Files	When set, it prevents users from seeing the file or directory in a DIR listing.
T (Transactional)	Files	When it is applied to a file, the transaction tracking system will protect the file. It has no effect on directories.

Table 19-2. *Directory and File Attributes* (continued)

Attribute	Description
Cc (Can't Compress)	This status attribute indicates that a file cannot be compressed due to lack of disk space. It is not used for directories, and you cannot assign this attribute.
C (Compressed)	This status attribute indicates that a file has been compressed. It is not used for directories, and you can't assign this attribute.
M (Migrated)	This status attribute indicates that a file has been migrated to a secondary storage device such as an optical disk jukebox.

Table 19-3. *Compression and Migration Status Attributes*

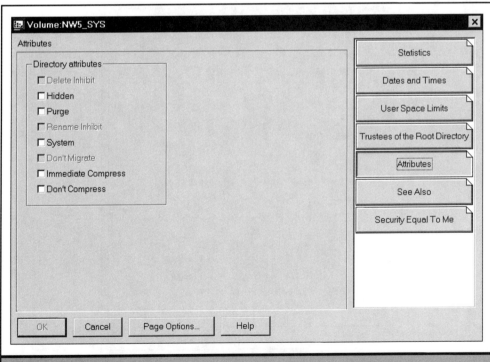

Figure 19-23. *The directory attributes for a root volume in the NetWare Administrator utility*

3. Set the attributes, which are listed here:

■ **Hidden** Hides the volume

■ **Purge** Purges files as soon as they are deleted

■ **System** Prevents users from seeing the files and directories with the DIR command

■ **Immediate Compress** Compresses files on the volume immediately

■ **Don't Compress** Prevents file compression on this volume

To set attributes of the root directory for the volume using the Windows Explorer utility, follow these steps:

1. Select the network drive for the desired volume.

2. Right-click and select the Properties option.

3. Select the NetWare Info tab. A screen similar to the one shown in Figure 19-24 will be displayed.

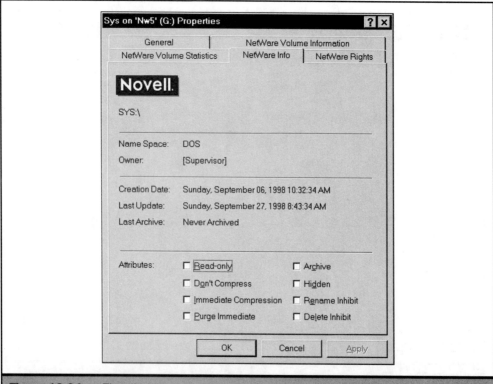

Figure 19-24.   *The directory attributes for a root volume in the Windows Explorer utility*

4. Set the attributes, which are listed here:

- **Read-only** This attribute prevents a file or directory from being deleted, renamed, or modified. When set, it automatically sets the Rename Inhibit and Delete Inhibit attributes.

- **Don't Compress**   This attribute prevents compression of files and directories. In the case of a directory, individual files marked with the Immediate Compress attribute are unaffected by this attribute.

- **Immediate Compression**   This attribute compresses files on the volume immediately.

- **Purge Immediate**   This attribute purges the files as soon as they are deleted.

- **Archive**   This attribute indicates that the file has changed since the last backup. This attribute cannot be set by the user.

- **Hidden**   This attribute hides the volume.

- **Rename Inhibit**   This attribute prevents the volume name from being changed.

- **Delete Inhibit**   This attribute prevents the volume from being deleted.

The Complete Reference

NetWare 5

Chapter 20

Novell Storage
Services (NSS)

Novell Storage Services (NSS) is an optional file system that can be installed on a NetWare 5 server. It is fully compatible with the traditional NetWare file system. NSS is a high-performance file storage and retrieval system that greatly expands the capabilities of NetWare 5. It was developed to meet the anticipated storage needs of users into the next decade.

File size limitations have been a problem to NetWare 4 users for quite some time. The traditional file system makes use of a 32-bit interface that limits file sizes to 2GB. A maximum of 16 million directory entries per volume and up to 64 volumes per server are available. The use of file allocation table (FAT) technology for file system organization required server memory roughly linear to the number and sizes of the files.

Advantages of NSS

NSS gives you the ability to store large objects and large numbers of objects without degrading your system performance. It gives you rapid access to data; volumes can be mounted and repaired in seconds, rather than hours; and it maintains full backward compatibility with the traditional file system.

The internal and external interfaces to NSS are all 64 bits wide. This allows huge numbers of entities, and entities are not constrained to size within the file system. NSS completely separates the amount of memory needed by a server from the amount of disk storage it maintains.

The key improvements provided by NSS include the following:

- The ability to store large files up to 8 terabytes each
- The ability to create, access, and store trillions of files in a single directory
- Rapid access to data regardless of file size
- Faster volume mounting and repair than in the traditional file system
- Low server memory requirements: mount on NSS volume of any size on a server with as little as 32MB of RAM
- Support for new types of storage devices as the technology evolves
- The ability to treat free space on multiple storage devices as a single volume
- Enhanced CD-ROM support by automatically mounting the device as a read-only volume
- Up to eight NetWare partitions per disk
- Unlimited volumes allowed per NetWare disk partition

NSS cannot fully replace the traditional NetWare file system. This is due to the following limitations of NSS:

- NSS cannot create its own SYS volume.
- NSS does not support the Transaction Tracking System (TTS).

- NSS does not support disk striping.
- NSS does not support disk mirroring.
- NSS does not support hierarchical storage management (HSM).
- NSS does not support real-time data migration (RTDM).
- NSS does not support the VREPAIR utility. Instead, it uses the new REBUILD utility.

NSS Storage Concepts

NSS is designed to make use of free space located anywhere on the network. It is comprised of three basic elements: the provider, the consumer, and the storage group. Figure 20-1 shows each of these entities, which are described in the following sections.

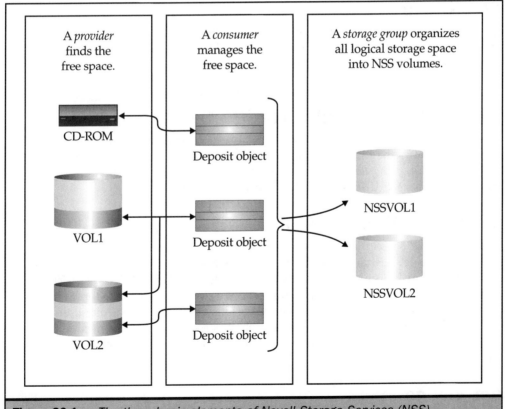

Figure 20-1. *The three basic elements of Novell Storage Services (NSS)*

Provider

The NSS provider scans a server's storage devices to identify and register usable free space. These devices can be hard disk drives, CD-ROM drives, and so on. Free space may be found in previously defined NetWare partitions or on other IBM-formatted, non-NetWare partitions. Two providers are included in NetWare 5. The NSS Media Manager (MMPRV) is designed for IBM-formatted partitions and file systems. The NSS File Provider (NWPRV) is designed for use with existing NetWare volumes.

Consumer

The consumer is an internal NSS component that manages the registered free space. It creates a Deposit object that represents a store of free space. It also builds logical internal file input and output paths to help NSS find stored data. In addition, it registers itself in the free space to prevent other consumers and the traditional file system from accessing the same space. Deposit objects can be formed into NSS storage groups.

Storage Group

An NSS storage group is a single object that represents all the logical storage space residing on one or more storage devices organized by providers and consumers. Each NSS storage group is organized into an NSS volume.

Structure of Novell Storage Services (NSS)

This section describes the internal NSS structure and explains how NSS works. Figure 20-2 shows the four basic sections of the NSS system: the Media Access Layer (MAL), the Object Engine, the Common Layer Interface, and the Semantic Agents. Each of these parts is discussed in the following sections.

Media Access Layer (MAL)

The Media Access Layer (MAL) provides connections to a wide range of storage devices. These devices can be hard drives, CD-ROMs, Digital Versatile Disk (DVD) media, virtual disks implemented as network clusters, and even RAM disks. The MAL lets you view the storage on your server as a simple quantity of storage blocks. It frees you from the details of enabling the various devices. The modular design of the MAL allows new storage devices and technologies to be added as needed. The MAL provides the interfaces used by the Object Engine to interact with the available storage devices.

Object Engine

The Object Engine is the NSS storage engine. It provides significantly higher levels of efficiency than the object engine used in the traditional file system. Through the use of

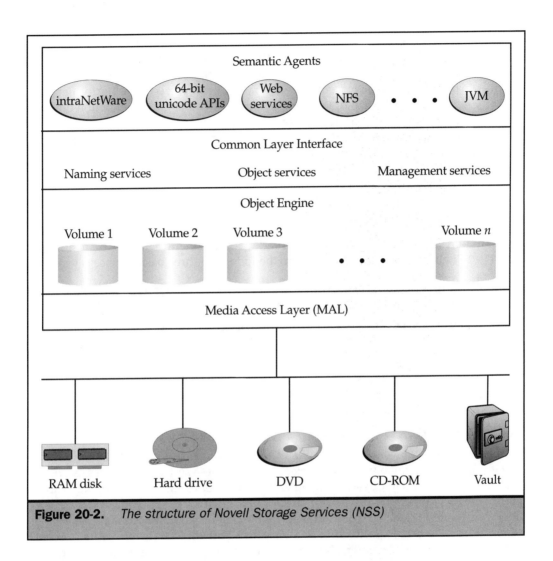

Figure 20-2.   *The structure of Novell Storage Services (NSS)*

sophisticated and highly efficient mechanisms to manage the stored objects, it achieves high levels of performance, scalability, robustness, and modularity. The Object Engine uses 64-bit interfaces to eliminate the NetWare 4.*x* file system limitations.

The Object Engine stores objects on the disk in balanced trees referred to as B-Trees. The B-Tree structures guarantee that the system can retrieve an object from the disk in no more than four I/O cycles. B-Trees improve memory management by allowing the system to locate an object anywhere in storage without loading the entire Directory Entry Table (DET) into memory.

The Object Engine improves disk space usage by sharing name spaces. The name spaces, such as NFS and DOS, no longer store a name for each name space in a single object. The name spaces now share a common name if no naming conflicts exist.

The Object Engine maintains a journal that records all transactions written to disk and all transactions waiting to be written. In the event of a system crash, the Object Engine can locate an error on a disk by referencing the transaction journal, noting the incomplete transaction, and correcting the error. This error correction is performed either by reprocessing the incomplete transaction or by backing the transaction out. Either of these processes is completed without searching the volume.

The Object Engine's modularity allows you to define new objects and plug them into the storage system as they become available. This modularity allows you to use hard links, symbolic links, and authorization systems not previously available through the traditional NetWare 4.x file system.

Common Layer Interface

The Common Layer Interface defines the interfaces the Semantic Agents use to access the Object Engine. These interfaces fall into the following three basic service categories:

- **Naming services**   These services include basic object naming and lookup operations as well as name space management services.
- **Object services**   These services provide direct bidirectional access to and from objects. They also provide for other operations on objects such as Create, Delete, and Truncate.
- **Management services**   These services cover a variety of tasks such as object locking, volume operations, and the addition and registration of new objects.

Semantic Agents

The Semantic Agent layer contains separate software modules that define the client-specific interfaces available to stored objects. Each of these software modules can be loaded or unloaded without affecting other modules. For example, the intraNetWare File System Semantic Agent is a client-specific interface to the legacy file system. It interprets requests received from IntranetWare 4.x clients and passes them to the Object Engine for execution. The HTTP Semantic Agent allows Web browsers to access data stored by the Object Engine. New Semantic Agents can be created and added to the system at any time. Semantic Agents for HTML, NFS, and Java Virtual Machine (JVM) will provide a single storage solution for all common object types. This will eliminate the need to develop new solutions as storage technology evolves. These new agents will not impact any Semantic Agents currently loaded.

Setting Up Novell Storage Services (NSS)

The majority of storage groups and volumes you create will use physical hard disk space. This space may already be allocated to existing DOS or NetWare partitions. You have the following three options if the hard disks on your server are already fully partitioned:

■ You can convert an existing NetWare partition to NSS using the NSS in-place upgrade utility. Remember, the SYS volume and any volume using the Transaction Tracking System cannot be upgraded.

■ You can repartition your server's hard disk drive to allow for free space. This free space can become part or all of an NSS storage group and NSS volume.

■ You can install a new hard disk on the server and dedicate the disk to NSS.

Creating NSS Components

Perform the following steps to create a NSS storage volume:

1. Type **[LOAD] NWCONFIG** at the server console prompt.

2. Select NSS Disk Options, as shown here:

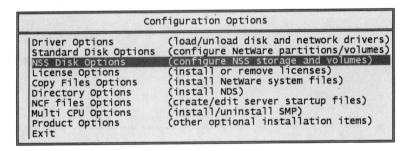

3. Select Storage from the available NSS options as shown here. This option allows you to locate any available free space and place it in a pool for NSS to use.

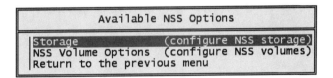

4. Select Update Provider Information from the menu options, as shown here:

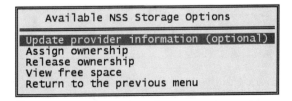

5. Select the NSS Media Manager Provider as shown in the following illustration. The storage provider determines which devices make up a Storage Deposit

object. These new Storage Deposit objects then become available to NSS for new volumes. The MMPRV provider is used with IBM-compatible disk partitions.

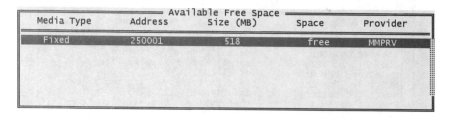

6. Press ENTER to continue. In this example, we added a new 520MB hard drive to the system. This new drive did not contain a NetWare partition. It had been formatted using the FORMAT utility in Windows 98. The 518MB of free space are displayed here, as well as the media type and the name of the provider:

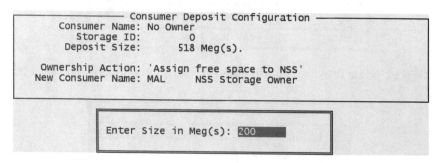

7. Select Assign Ownership from the menu options. A list similar to the one shown in the following illustration will appear, showing the free spaces registered with the provider. We have elected to use only 200MB of the available free space for the NSS volume. Notice the Ownership Action label. It states the action that will be taken with the selected free space.

```
========= Consumer Deposit Configuration ==========
    Consumer Name: No Owner
       Storage ID:          0
     Deposit Size:        518 Meg(s).

  Ownership Action: 'Assign free space to NSS'
  New Consumer Name: MAL      NSS Storage Owner


        Enter Size in Meg(s): 200
```

8. Select Yes from the Confirm Action dialog box, shown in the following illustration. The confirm message states that this action will modify the media

in your system. This is the only warning that you will receive before allocating the free space selected to a new storage group.

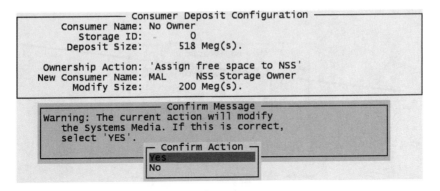

9. Log in to the NDS tree as the administrator, as shown in Figure 20-3. This is required to allow NSS to create the new Storage object in the NDS tree. The administrator's name must be entered with the complete NDS path, starting from the object location all the way back to the [Root].

```
NetWare Configuration

                    Configuration Options

 |Driver Options        (load/unload disk and network drivers)
 |                                        itions/volumes)|

                 Directory Services Login/Authentication

 Administrator Name:
 Password:

 |Product Options       (other optional installation items)   |
 |Exit                                                         |

 Administrator Help

  Enter the complete name of the user object that will manage this server and
  its associated objects.  This user name can correspond to any object that
  has supervisor rights on or above the context into which you want to
                        (To scroll, <F7>-up <F8>-down)

 Abort login        <Esc>
 Help               <F1>                    Abort nwconfig <Alt><F10>
```

Figure 20-3. *You must log into the NDS tree to create a new NDS Storage object*

The NetWare File System

10. Select Create from the menu, as shown in the following illustration. This menu allows you to manipulate the NDS Storage object within the tree. You can create, modify, delete, and view the Storage objects within the NDS tree using this menu.

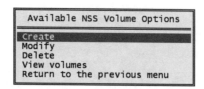

```
      Available NSS Volume Options
    Create
    Modify
    Delete
    View volumes
    Return to the previous menu
```

11. Select Storage Group from the menu shown here:

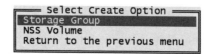

```
    ═══ Select Create Option ═══
    Storage Group
    NSS Volume
    Return to the previous menu
```

This is where you actually assign the selected free space to a Storage Group object in NDS. The managed objects available to NSS are displayed, as shown here:

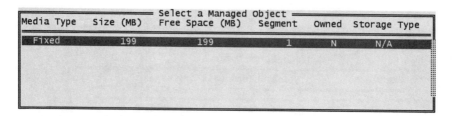

Media Type	Size (MB)	Free Space (MB)	Segment	Owned	Storage Type
Fixed	199	199	1	N	N/A

12. Confirm the action by selecting Yes in the dialog box shown next. Again, this action will modify the system media in the selected servers.

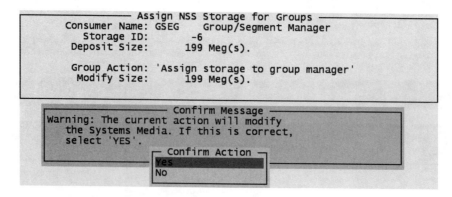

```
         ─── Assign NSS Storage for Groups ───
      Consumer Name: GSEG    Group/Segment Manager
        Storage ID:      -6
      Deposit Size:      199 Meg(s).

      Group Action:  'Assign storage to group manager'
        Modify Size:       199 Meg(s).

              ─── Confirm Message ───
    Warning: The current action will modify
       the Systems Media. If this is correct,
       select 'YES'.
                ─ Confirm Action ─
                Yes
                No
```

13. Enter a name for the new NSS volume, as shown next. The Volume Action shows that you are creating a new volume at this time.

```
─────────── NSS Volume Configuration ───────────
      Consumer Name: ZLSS    NetWare's Object Store
         Storage ID:  N/A
       Deposit Size:      199 Meg(s)

       Volume Action:  'Create a new volume'
         Modify Size:      199 Meg(s)



 Enter Name: NSSVOL
```

14. Press any key to continue after NSS has successfully created the new volume and added it to the NDS tree. This is shown in Figure 20-4, along with the new volume name and size. Figure 20-5 shows the new volume as it appears in the NetWare Administrator utility. The associated property pages for the volume are accessed by right-clicking the NW5_NSSVOL object, and are shown in Figure 20-6.

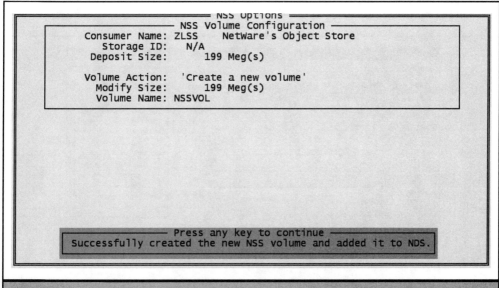

```
══════════════ NSS Options ══════════════
    ─────────── NSS Volume Configuration ───────────
        Consumer Name: ZLSS    NetWare's Object Store
           Storage ID:  N/A
         Deposit Size:      199 Meg(s)

         Volume Action:  'Create a new volume'
           Modify Size:      199 Meg(s)
           Volume Name: NSSVOL




          ──────────── Press any key to continue ────────────
          Successfully created the new NSS volume and added it to NDS.
```

Figure 20-4.   *This screen indicates that the system has successfully created a new NSS volume*

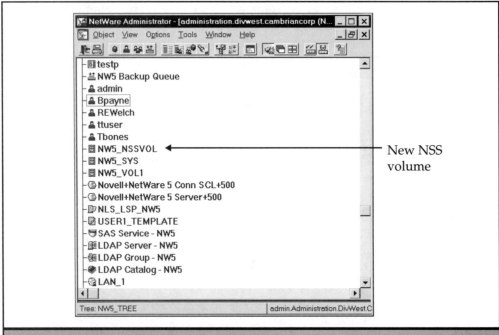

New NSS
volume

Figure 20-5.   *The new NSS volume as it appears in the NetWare Administrator utility browser screen*

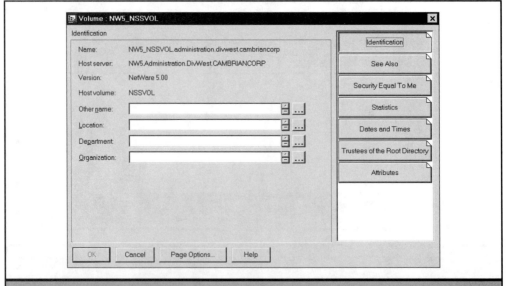

Figure 20-6.   *The new NSS volume, NW5_NSSVOL, has the same property pages as any other Volume object*

Chapter 21

Accounting and Auditing

Netware's accounting and auditing systems let you track the activities of users on specific servers so you can evaluate their use of resources and charge them if necessary. For example, departments might need to charge other departments for the use of resources, such as disk storage, for budgeting purposes. Or a department might need to track the distribution of payments on a contract. Educational institutions and time-sharing services often track the use of system resources and then charge users for the time.

Accounting System Overview

You install the accounting system separately at each server on the network. If you don't need accounting at a server, don't install it, because it takes up disk space and processing time.

Although accounting is typically associated with billing users for the time and resources they use on the system, NetWare's accounting system also provides useful information about user logins and logouts. Supervisors can monitor usage logs to determine exactly how resources are being used and by what users. This information is useful when you need to determine whether additional equipment and storage systems are necessary and when you need to justify their purchase.

The accounting system charges users for their time or the resources they use with a point system. Points can have monetary value, or they can be thought of as "tokens" or "credits" that users can spend. A supervisor may allocate a certain number of points to a temporary user. When the user depletes those points, he or she may ask for more, which alerts the supervisor to the usage patterns and resource needs of that user. Points can be limited or unlimited, depending on how the supervisor needs to manage the system.

At an educational site, students can be given a certain amount of resources and charged for the resources they use. A report, produced at regular intervals, can help you establish charge rates based on usage. Conversely, students may buy a block of time and space at the beginning of the school term. When the block runs out, they can buy more. Students who are aware of their limits will not waste system resources.

Determining exactly what to charge for account usage is the first step. The best strategy is to establish a test period by installing the accounting feature and then tracking system usage with users who have unlimited credit. At the end of the test period, you should have enough information to determine rates.

The ATOTAL utility is used to view accounting information. The utility compiles the accounting information and provides a list of connect times, service requests, block reads and writes, and disk storage requirements.

Types of Accounting

When you install the accounting feature at a server, user login and logout tracking is automatically done. Each user has an account of charges for the system resources he or she uses. Each file server designated as a chargeable system makes entries into user accounts.

Charges incurred by users fall into two main groups:

- Charges for the server's disk file space
- Charges for work performed by the server

If you charge for disk space, you'll need to come up with a rate and determine how often and at what times the file server should measure the disk space accessed by the user. The types of charges associated with a server are listed next. You can use one or all of these methods for charging:

- The amount of resources consumed not only from file servers but also gateways, print devices, and database servers
- The amount of time a user is logged on to the file server
- The amount of information read from the file server disk
- The amount of information written to the file server disk
- The number of requests made to the file server for services

Installing the Accounting System

The accounting feature must be installed before it can begin tracking logins and logouts and before you can use it to charge users for resources. Use the NetWare Adminis trator utility to install the system.

To install accounting on a server with NetWare Administrator, locate the server in the directory tree and click it with the right mouse button. Choose the Details option to display the details dialog box for the server, and then click the Accounting button. You are asked if you want to install accounting for this server, as shown in Figure 21-1. Click Yes to install accounting.

Once accounting is installed, the buttons shown next appear on the server's details dialog box. You click any of these buttons to set charge rates for the types of services listed on the buttons.

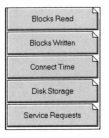

If you ever want to remove accounting from the server, click the Accounting button. You are asked if you want to remove accounting. All tracking services and file updates are suspended.

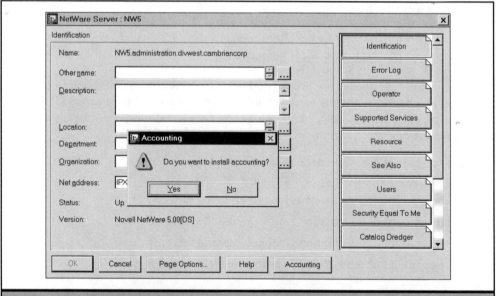

Figure 21-1. *Installing NetWare's accounting system in NetWare Administrator*

Types of Charge Rates

There are several categories of rates you can charge users for services provided by a network server. Each option is described in the following sections.

Blocks Read Charge Rates

The Blocks Read option sets the charge rates for the amount of information read from the server drive. This is not the same as the charge for storing blocks on the disk, which is covered later under "Disk Storage Charge Rates." Charges are specified in half-hour increments and are assigned per blocks read, with one block being equal to 4,096 bytes, or 4K.

> **Note** *The Blocks Read amounts can be misleading, because every time a database is opened and read, charges are compiled, even if no work is done.*

Each read from the drive is charged to the user's account. The Blocks Read option is important for servers that supply information to other users; for example, online services or database systems. Keep in mind that this option may inhibit users from using the system accurately or productively if they fear they may run out of credits.

Blocks Written Charge Rates

The Blocks Written option is similar to the Blocks Read option, except that users are charged for the amount of information written to the disk, rather than read from the disk. Charges for blocks written to disk are not the same as charges for blocks of disk storage (covered under "Disk Storage Charge Rates," below). Charges are specified in half-hour increments and are assigned per block written, with one block being equal to 4,096 bytes, or 4K.

Each write to the drive is charged to the user's account. Be careful when using this option because some programs write to the disk continuously, and you would be unfairly charging users of the program. For example, when Windows is installed on the file server, it writes temporary files to the server and updates those files regularly. In addition, users may be less productive if they know they are being charged every time they write to the disk.

Connect Time Charge Rates

The Connect Time option charges users for each half-hour of time they are logged into the server. It is important to consider the type of user and the resources available on the system before establishing this rate, however. If network usage is high, you may want to charge a higher rate to encourage users to perform their tasks on the system efficiently and not tie up the system for too long. This may not be appropriate for some systems, however, especially if the system is new and there are many first-time users.

Disk Storage Charge Rates

The Disk Storage option allows you to set up charge rates for each block of disk storage. A block is 4,096 bytes, or 4K. A charge rate is established for every half-hour increment of disk storage use and is assigned on a block-day basis, which measures the number of blocks stored in a day. If the network has limited disk storage, charges can be established to encourage users to be more efficient in the way they store files and to keep their storage area clear of unnecessary files.

Service Requests Charge Rates

The Service Requests option establishes charge rates for general use of the server. Every time a request is made to the server for any operation, the user is charged. Charge rates are specified in half-hour increments, and the user is charged per request received. Users are charged for services from the moment they log in to the moment they log out.

 This charge rate adds numerous entries to the accounting file, because any server activity makes service request calls. Watch the size of the accounting file when using this option.

Setting the Accounting Charge Rates

You must determine the types of charges and the rates you want to charge users for services provided by a network server. In addition, you must set up an initial account balance and view the existing accounting information, either to help establish the initial rates or to bill users for usage.

Charge rates are established by specifying a *multiplier* and a *divisor*. The multiplier is the rate you want to charge, usually in cents; and the divisor is the number of units you want to charge for, usually 1. In addition, there can be up to 20 charge rates. This way, you can charge different rates for different times of the day. For example, you might want to charge a higher rate for connect-time charges during the day than at night. Setting charge rates is a two-step process:

1. Create one or more charge rates.
2. Select a block of time, and then specify the charge rate that will be in effect during that time.

Setting Up Initial Account Balances

You set up the initial account balances for users by accessing their Account Balance dialog box. In NetWare Administrator, double-click a User object, and then click the Account Balance button on the dialog box. You can then do one of the following:

- Specify a limited balance amount in the Account Balance field.
- Select Allow Unlimited Credit.
- Disable Allow Unlimited Credit and specify a low balance after which the user is denied access to network resources.

To monitor the use of the system for each user, set unlimited account balances. Keep in mind that users will be logged out when they reach their account balance limits. This may cause a lot of extra work on your part if you need to assign new balances.

Specify account balances in units. You can assign a specified amount of credit by typing **No** in the Allow Unlimited Credit field and then entering a balance in the Low Balance Limit field. If you enter a negative number in the Low Balance Limit field, users will receive services until the charges have been used up. If you enter a positive number in the field, users must maintain some value in the field. Users can always go to the supervisor and request additional services.

Note *Account balances can also be assigned to the default user account in each container.*

Using NetWare Administrator's Charge Rate Dialog Boxes

The basic NetWare Administrator charge rate dialog box is pictured in Figure 21-2. This box is for Blocks Read charge rates, but it has the same features as the Blocks Written, Connect Time, Disk Storage, and Service Requests dialog boxes.

Setting Charge Rates

To set a new charge rate, click the Add Charge Rate button. The Add Charge Rate dialog box appears, as shown here:

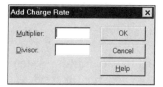

You type the multiplier and the divisor in the dialog box fields and press ENTER. Methods for determining these values are discussed later under "How to Calculate Charge Rates."

If you want to change a charge rate, you delete the rate and re-create it. This poses a little problem, as you cannot delete a rate if blocks of time are marked to use that rate. First undo any time blocks using that rate, and then highlight the rate and click the

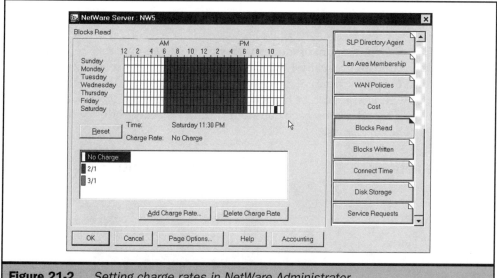

Figure 21-2.   *Setting charge rates in NetWare Administrator*

Delete Charge Rate button in the Charge Rate dialog box. Create the new rate following the procedure just given.

Specifying a Rate for a Block of Time

Click one of the charge rates you created. Then, in the upper part of the Charge Rate dialog box, click and drag through the time block you want to assign this charge rate to. A hollow box outlines the time blocks as you drag. When you let up on the mouse button, the block of time takes on the color assigned to the charge rate.

How to Calculate Charge Rates

Different charge rates can be established for each server on the network, although the network administrator should ensure that each system uses the same basic formula to establish rates. That ensures fairness when one department charges another for the use of its resources.

Initially, it's a good idea to set the accounting system on and track server usage. This will give you an idea of how to charge for services. After you have run the test for a week or two, use the server console-based ATOTAL utility to view the usage information and establish charge rates.

Accounting information is stored in the NET$ACCT.DAT file, which can get quite large. You should view a printout of its contents periodically or compile it with the appropriate accounting application (available from third-party developers), and then delete it from the system. A new file is then created by the accounting system as soon as a new user logs in.

Charge ratios are calculated with the following formula:

Charge rate multiplier ÷ Charge rate divisor

The multiplier is the amount of money you want to charge for a service, such as Blocks Read. The divisor is usually 1, which specifies one unit of that service. This ratio is assigned to specific times of the day, and up to 20 different ratios can be applied. In this way, charges can be higher during the day than in the evening, for example. Charges are shown for each half-hour during a weekly period and are applied in the following ways:

Charge Rate	Charged by (Unit)
Blocks Read	Block
Blocks Written	Block
Connect Time	Minute
Disk Storage	Block-day
Service Requests	Request received

Assume you want to charge two cents for every unit of services requested or used. The multiplier is then 2 and the divisor is 1, or 2 ÷ 1. For this charge rate, you type **2** in the Multiplier field and **1** in the Divisor field.

Charging fractional amounts requires a few more steps. Assume you want to charge $1.50 for one unit of service. You need to get rid of the decimal, so you multiply it by 100 to come up with 150. Likewise, you need to multiply the divisor by 100 to come up with 100. The charge rate is 150 ÷ 100, so type **150** in the Multiplier field and **100** in the Divisor field.

Another way to decide how to charge for services is by how much money you want to make on the service. For example, assume you have determined with AUDITCON that 500,000 blocks of space are normally in use, and you want to receive a $1,000 fee for that use. Also assume that each charge point is equal to one cent. The $1,000 weekly charge is converted to 100,000 and becomes the multiplier. The 500,000 blocks of disk space becomes the unit value, and thus the divisor, as follows:

100,000 ÷ 500,000 = 1 ÷ 5

If you just want to track usage, you must set up a rate for each category you want to view information on, even if it's just a 1 to 1 rate. Also, make sure there are no restrictions on the account balances.

Compiling Accounting Totals

You use the ATOTAL utility to compile the accounting information into a list you can display on the screen or send to a printer or file. Switch to the SYS:PUBLIC directory or map a search drive to it, and then use the ATOTAL command to run the utility.

To direct the listing to a file, type the following command, replacing *filename* with an appropriate filename:

ATOTAL > *filename*

The NetWare Auditing System

The NetWare auditing system provides a way for a specially designated network user known as the *auditor* to track events on the network. The events fall into two categories: volume tracking and container tracking. Each auditing group can have a distinct password, so that, for example, the auditor who tracks volume events cannot track container events. However, one auditor can track everything if you choose to set it up that way.

Volume Events Auditors Can Track

The auditor first selects a volume to track and then enables the tracking of events. Alternatively, the auditor can track the activities of individual users, files, or directories. The following events can be tracked for a selected volume:

- Creating and deleting directories
- Creating, opening, closing, deleting, renaming, writing, and salvaging files
- Modifying directory entries
- Queue activities
- Server events, such as changing the date and time, downing the server, and mounting or dismounting volumes
- User events, such as login, logout, connection termination, space restrictions, granting of trustee rights, and disabling of accounts

Directory Services Events Auditors Can Track

Directory Services events are tracked for individual containers. The auditor first selects a container and then enables the tracking of the following events in that container:

- Directory Services events; for example, when passwords change, when security changes, when restrictions change, and when entries are moved, removed, or renamed
- Activities of a specific user, such as the supervisor

Overview of the Auditing Procedure

The network administrator makes a user an auditor, gives the user a password, and then relinquishes control of audit tracking to the auditor, who immediately changes the password. From that point on, only the auditor can set up auditing features, view audit logs, and work in the designated audit directory. Auditing is set up at container levels and at volume levels. If container-level auditing is enabled, it only applies to the current container, not subordinate containers.

The auditing system keeps a record of each activity designated for tracking. Auditors can view these text files in AUDITCON and apply filters to produce reports that show specific activities. The following types of filters are available for producing reports of auditing events:

- Report within a specific date and time range
- Report only specified events
- Include or exclude specific file and/or directory events
- Include or exclude specific user events

Once a filter is created, the auditor can send the report to a specific file, open the file in a word processor, edit it if necessary, and print it. The auditor can also view the report directly onscreen while working in AUDITCON. The auditor also needs to manage the disposition of the auditing log files, which can grow quite large.

Installing the Auditing System

The procedures in this section are for the administrator who creates the auditing user. Once the auditor is created, the administrator starts AUDITCON, creates an initial password, and then gives the password to the new auditor. The new auditor then immediately changes the password to prevent the supervisor from accessing the auditing system.

The procedure for setting up an auditor is similar to setting up a user. You create a User object and make sure to specify a personal directory for that user to access. The directory is used to store the files the auditor creates. Be sure to map a search path to the SYS:PUBLIC directory as well, and grant the auditor rights to the directory if his or her User object was created in the directory tree above the Volume object.

To set up the initial auditor password, log in as administrator and start the AUDITCON utility by typing **AUDITCON** at a workstation. The AUDITCON menu appears as shown here:

```
┌─────────────────────────────────────┐
│ Available audit options              │
│ ┌─────────────────────────────────┐ │
│ │ Audit directory services        │ │
│ │ External Auditing               │ │
│ │ Change current server           │ │
│ │ Change current volume           │ │
│ │ Enable volume auditing          │ │
│ └─────────────────────────────────┘ │
└─────────────────────────────────────┘
```

You can change the current server or change the volume with the options on this menu. You can also enable external auditing which allows you to record workstation events. The top and bottom options are of interest here:

- **Audit Directory Services**   You can assign an auditing password for each container in the Directory Services tree. Choose Audit Directory Services from the AUDITCON menu; then choose Audit Directory Tree. You can then browse the directory tree for a container and press F10 to select it. Choose Enable Container Auditing on the menu that appears, and then specify a password. The menu now displays the Auditor Container Login option. The auditor would select this option to view and change the auditing features of the container.

- **Enable Volume Auditing**   Choose this option to enable auditing for the current volume. Look at the top of your screen for this information. You are asked to enter and reenter a password. The AUDITCON menu now appears as shown in Figure 21-3.

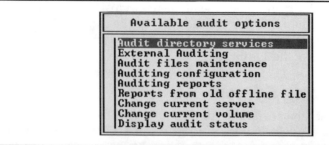

Figure 21-3.   *The available audit options are displayed and selected from this screen*

You should now provide the container or volume passwords to the designated auditors and refer them to the "Activities for Volume Auditors" section, next, or the "Activities for Container Auditors" section later in this chapter.

Activities for Volume Auditors

This section is for auditors assigned to track volumes. Type **AUDITCON** to start the auditing utility. Choose Audit Volume Login, and then type the password you were given by the supervisor. The menu shown in Figure 21-3 will appear.

Change the password you use to access the volume auditing options. To do this, choose Auditing Configuration, and then choose Change Audit Password.

Enabling Volume Auditing Events

To audit events on the volume, you must first specify which events you want to audit. Choose Auditing Configuration from the Available Audit Options menu to display the following menu:

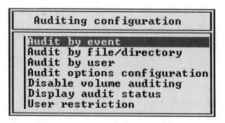

Some of the options on this menu are discussed below. Press F1 if you need help setting these options.

■ **Audit by Event**   Choose this option to select the events you want to track. Choose an option from the menu that appears to see a lists of events you can track. To enable an event, highlight it and press F10.

Event options are either Global, and, *or* or. *Global records all the designated events throughout the volume; and records events only for users being audited; and or records events for all users.*

- **Audit by File/Directory**   Choose this option to select a file or directory you want to track activities in. Browse the directory tree to highlight a directory or file, and then press F10 to enable tracking.
- **Audit by User**   Choose this option to track a user's activity. Highlight the user and press F10 to enable tracking.

The remaining options on the Auditing Configuration menu are used to change the configuration or status of auditing. Press F1 to view Help for the options on the menu.

The Audit Options Configuration option on the Auditing Configuration menu has important settings that determine what to do if the auditing file becomes full. The volume can be dismounted or audit tracking can stop, depending on your selection.

Activities for Container Auditors

This section is for auditors assigned to track volumes. Type **AUDITCON** to start the auditing utility. You see the menu pictured in Figure 21-3. Choose Audit Directory Services, and then choose Audit Directory Tree. Browse the directory tree to locate the container you want to audit and press F10; then choose Auditor Container Login. Type the password you were given by the supervisor. The menu shown here appears:

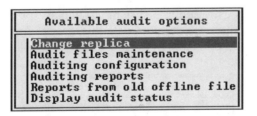

If you don't see the Auditor Container Login option, you need to choose Enable Container Auditing and follow the instructions under "Installing the Auditing System," earlier in this chapter.

The first option is used to select the replica with which to work. This would occur if the currently selected replica is not up-to-date. The second option is used to manage the auditing files once they become full or need to be removed. The third option is used to enable auditing events. The fourth option is used to view and report on the auditing events. The fifth option, Reports from Old Offline File, extracts reports from old files that have been copied offline. The last option displays the current status of auditing in this container.

To change your password, choose Auditing Configuration from the Available Audit Options menu, and then choose Change Audit Password.

Enabling Container Auditing Events

Choose Auditing Configuration from the Available Audit Options menu to enable auditing events. Choose one of the following options among those that are available:

- **Audit by DS events** Choose this option to select the Directory Services events possible in the container you want to track. Highlight an event and press F10 to enable it.

- **Audit by user** Choose this option to select a user from a list. The user's activities in the container are tracked. Auditors will probably want to track the supervisor's activities.

The remaining options on the menu are used to change the auditing configuration for the container and the password, or to view the current status. You can also disable auditing for the container.

  The Audit Options Configuration option on the Auditing Configuration menu has important settings that determine what to do if the auditing file becomes full. The volume can be dismounted or audit tracking can stop, depending on your selection.

Viewing and Reporting Auditing Information

You can create and view auditing information for volumes and containers and create reports for the events once the auditing system has had an appropriate amount of time to track the auditing events you selected. To do this, choose Auditing reports from the Available Audit Options menu (shown in Figure 21-3). The following menu appears:

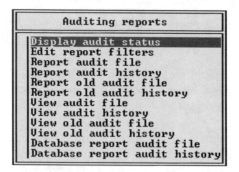

Choose the first option, Display Audit Status, to check the current status of the auditing files. You should do this periodically to ensure they don't overrun their specified sizes. You can send auditing information to a report file, and then start over with a new auditing file if necessary.

Other important options on the Auditing Reports menu include the following:

■ **Edit Report Filters** Choose this option to specify filters for the display and reporting of auditing information. Initially, you see "no filter." Press INSERT to create a new filter and display the following menu. Press F1 to get a description of the options on the menu. To add an option, press ENTER, and then choose an existing setting, or press INSERT to create a new setting.

```
            Edit report filter

     Report by date/time
     Report by event
     Report exclude paths/files
     Report exclude users
     Report include paths/files
     Report include users
```

■ **Report options** Choose one of the report options to send the current (or old) audit data file or the audit history file to a standard text file for editing and printing.

Note   *Audit File and Old Audit File contain auditing information. Audit History File contains information about the auditor's activities.*

■ **View options** Choose one of the View options to immediately view the information specified by the Report option filter.

Managing the Auditing Files

From the main AUDITCON menu, choose Audit Files Maintenance to close, copy, delete, or display information about the auditing files. If you are working in a container object, choose this option from the Available Audit Options menu for the container object.

The Complete Reference

NetWare 5

Chapter 22

Other Directory and File Commands

The commands described in this chapter are commands that you execute at the command prompt. They provide useful information for system administrators, supervisors, and network users. The commands include a number of options used to display network information, directory and file rights, and User objects. Whether or not users can use any command that changes settings depends on their access rights to objects, directories, and files.

Command-line utilities provide an excellent way to perform a file maintenance task in a hurry. You should browse through this chapter and mark or write down the commands and the command options you might need to use.

The FILER Utility

The FILER utility is a DOS-based utility for working with the NetWare file system. If you are at a non-Windows workstation, you might need to use it in place of the NetWare Administrator. Note that you can do almost everything in FILER that you can do in NetWare Administrator with regard to the file system.

To start FILER, type **FILER** at the command prompt. The Available Options menu (also called the main menu) appears, as shown in Figure 22-1. Your computer will show additional information at the top of the screen that indicates your current context in Novell Directory Services, the current volume, and the directory you are working on in that volume.

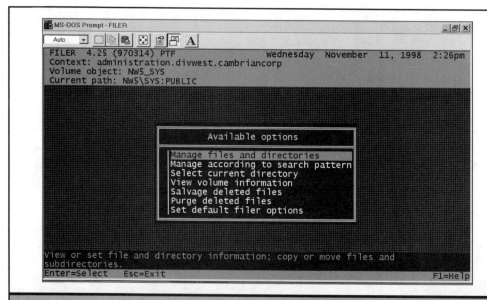

Figure 22-1. The FILER Available Options menu screen

The following sections describe how to use FILER and navigate the filing system using its menu options.

Setting FILER's Default Options

You can choose Set Default Filer Options on the FILER main menu to make changes to the way FILER works. The Filer Settings dialog box appears, as shown in Figure 22-2. Set options as follows:

- **Confirm Deletions**   If this option is set to Yes, you must confirm every file deletion, which can be time-consuming when deleting large groups of files or directories. You might want to set this option to No when you are sure you want to delete a group of files, and then set it back to Yes to protect against accidental deletions.

- **Confirm File Copies**   When set to Yes, you must confirm that you want to copy files.

- **Confirm File Overwrites**   Set this option to Yes to prevent files from being overwritten without a warning. Set this option to No only temporarily when you are sure you want to copy over files.

- **Preserve File Attributes**   Choose Yes to preserve extended attributes when copying files. These attributes are set to Normal when this option is set to No.

- **Notify If Name Space Information Is Lost**   When you copy files that have extended attributes (for example, copying OS/2 files), the extended file attributes and long name are lost. If you want to be notified each time a file's extended attributes and long name are lost, choose Yes. If you don't want to be notified, choose No.

- **Copy Files Sparse**   This determines whether extended file attributes are preserved when you copy files from an OS/2 system. If set to No, the file attribute is set to Normal.

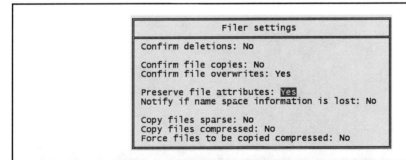

Figure 22-2.   *The Filer Settings dialog box*

- **Copy Files Compressed** If the medium receiving the file to be copied will support compressed files, you can choose whether to copy a compressed file in that format. Set to Yes if you want the compressed files to stay compressed when copied, or No if you want the compressed file to be decompressed at the destination.

- **Force Files to Be Copied Compressed** Set to Yes if you want compressed files to be copied compressed even if the medium they are being copied to doesn't support compression.

Changing Directories and Context

The current context, volume, and directory path are listed at the top of the screen above the FILER main menu. You can choose other directories, volumes, and servers to work on by choosing the Select Current Directory option from the main menu. A dialog box appears that displays your current directory path.

You can type a new directory in this box, or you can press the INS key to choose a new directory from a list, as shown in Figure 22-3. You can do one of the following:

- Select the double-dot entry to move up to a parent directory. When you reach the root directory of a volume, you see a list of other volumes or other servers that you can choose.

- Select any listed directory to switch to that directory. If that directory contains subdirectories, they appear in the list so you can move into a subdirectory. The directory path in the Current Directory Path dialog box changes to show the name of each directory you select. When you are done, press ESC to close the Network Directories list, and then press ENTER to accept the path in the Current Directory Path dialog box.

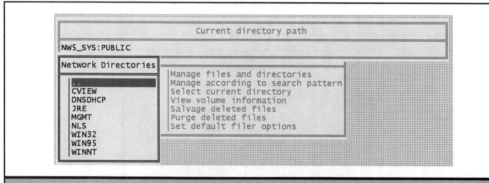

Figure 22-3.   *Choose a different directory or context*

Manage According to Search Patterns

The option on the FILER main menu called Manage According to Search Pattern lets you specify a search pattern so that only certain directory names and filenames are listed. After you set the pattern, you can begin managing files. When you choose the option, the dialog box shown here appears:

```
                    Set the search pattern and filter

    Pattern: *.*

    Exclude directory patterns: ↓  <empty>
    Include directory patterns: ↓  *

    Exclude file patterns: ↓  <empty>
    Include file patterns: ↓  *

    File search attributes: ↓  <empty>
    Directory search attributes: ↓  <empty>
```

Use the fields in this dialog box as described in the following list. Use the arrow keys to move among fields, and press ENTER to edit fields. In the Exclude File Patterns and Include File Patterns fields, press ENTER to add new patterns, and then press INS. All the patterns make up a list of directories or files that will be excluded or included. To remove a pattern, highlight it in the list and press DEL.

- **Pattern**   Use wildcard characters to specify the types of files you want to list. For example, to list all document files, type ***.DOC** or ***.TXT**.
- **Exclude Directory Patterns**   Type a wildcard pattern that specifies directories you don't want to see in listings.
- **Include Directory Patterns**   Type a wildcard pattern that specifies directory names you want to see in listings.
- **Exclude File Patterns**   Specify a pattern for files you want to exclude from listings.
- **Include File Patterns**   Specify a pattern for files you want to include in listings.
- **File Search Attributes**   Specify whether files that have the Hidden or System attribute should be included in listings. Press ENTER, and then press INS to choose attributes from a list.
- **Directory Search Attributes**   Specify whether directories that have the Hidden or System attribute should be included in listings. Press ENTER, and then press INS to choose attributes from a list.

Once you've set a search pattern, don't press ESC to jump back to the main menu. Press F10 to begin managing files by using the search pattern you have selected.

The NetWare File System

Working with Volumes

This section discusses techniques you can use to view and work with volumes using the FILER utility. If you want to work with directories, refer to the next section, "Working with Directories and Files."

Viewing Volume Information

Choose View Volume Information on FILER's main menu. A menu appears with the following options:

- **Statistics**   Choose the Statistics option to view available space and file settings. The space on the volume used by compressed and decompressed files is listed, along with information about how much space is saved by compressing files.

- **Features**   Choose the Features option to view the volume settings that were made during the volume's installation, such as its block size, name spaces, and whether compression and block suballocation are in use.

- **Dates and Times**   Choose the Dates and Times option to view the creation date and time of the volume, the last time it was modified, and the last time it was archived.

Working with Directories and Files

This section shows you how to manage directories and files using the FILER utility. Techniques for browsing, copying, moving, and deleting directories or files are similar, so both directories and files are covered together here.

Browsing in FILER

To browse the directory structure in FILER, choose the Manage Files and Directories option on the main menu. You then see a menu similar to the following.

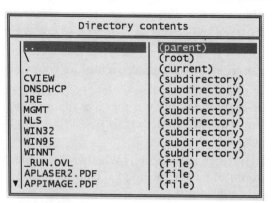

Highlight the parent line and press ENTER to move up the directory tree, or highlight a subdirectory and press ENTER to move down through the tree structure. If you move to the root directory of the volume, you see the following menu, where you can choose to look at other volumes, other servers, or other volumes on the same server.

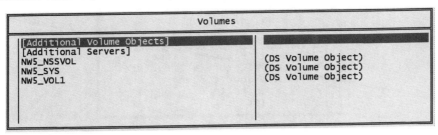

Moving, Copying, Renaming, and Deleting

You can move, copy, and delete folders and files using the commands discussed here, and you can perform these operations on multiple folders and files at the same time. You can rename only one folder or file at a time.

Choose Manage Files and Directories from the main menu, and then browse through the list to locate files and folders. Do the following:

1. Select a folder or file and press F3 to change its name.

2. To select multiple folders or files, highlight a folder or file and press F5. Repeat for each folder or file.

3. Press F10 to perform an operation on the selected files. The following menus appear, depending on whether you selected single or multiple files and folders.

This menu appears if you selected multiple files:

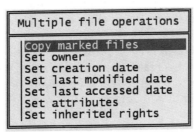

This menu appears if you selected a single file:

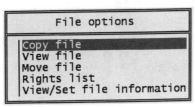

This menu appears if you selected a single folder:

```
╔════════════════════════════════════════╗
║          Subdirectory options          ║
╠════════════════════════════════════════╣
║ Copy subdirectory's files              ║
║ Copy subdirectory's structure          ║
║ Move subdirectory's structure          ║
║ Make this your current directory       ║
║ View/Set directory information         ║
║ Rights list                            ║
╚════════════════════════════════════════╝
```

This menu appears if you selected multiple folders:

```
╔════════════════════════════════════════╗
║     Multiple subdirectory operations   ║
╠════════════════════════════════════════╣
║ Copy subdirectories' files             ║
║ Copy subdirectories' structure         ║
║ Set owner                              ║
║ Set creation date                      ║
║ Set inherited rights                   ║
╚════════════════════════════════════════╝
```

As you can see, the operations you can perform depend on the selections you've made. Note that you can't move multiple files in FILER, and you can only move multiple folders if they are part of the same parent subtree.

Creating New Directories

You create new directories in FILER by first going to the volume and folder in which you want to put the new directory. If you choose to create a directory at a volume, it is created at the root level.

Creating directories in FILER is easy. Browse the directory list until you locate the directory in which you want to create a new subdirectory, and then press INS. Type a name for the subdirectory and press ENTER. If you want the new directory to branch from the root, scan the list until you get to the root, highlight the "single-dot" current option and press the INS key.

Getting Details

To view and change information about folders and files in FILER, choose Manage Files and Directories in the main menu, scan through the list, and select single folders and files or multiple files by pressing the F5 (Mark) key. Press F10 to view a menu with options for viewing and changing the selected objects. Which of the various menus you saw pictured in the previous section, "Moving, Copying, Renaming, and Deleting," depends on whether you selected single or multiple folders and files.

Managing Directory and File Attributes

Managing the attributes of directories and files in FILER is a little complicated:

1. Highlight a folder or file and press F10.
2. An information box for the folder or file appears. Click the arrow keys to move to the Attributes field and press ENTER. A box with the current settings appears. You can do one of the following:

   ■ To add new attributes, press the INS key, choose attributes in the list by marking them with the F5 key, and then press ENTER to add them to the list.

   ■ To remove existing attributes, mark them with the F5 key and press the DEL key.

Assigning Trustee Rights in the Filing System

Assigning network users rights to the file system is one of the most important tasks of a network administrator. Recall from Chapter 17 that you can grant file system rights to the following objects:

■ Group object

■ Organization object

■ Organizational Unit object

■ Organizational Role object

■ Profile object

■ User object

This section describes how to assign directory and file rights to users while you're working with a folder or file. It also shows you how to set Inherited Rights Filters in the file system.

About Inheritance

Rights that are granted in parent directories of the file system flow down the directory structure and are inherited by subdirectories and files within subdirectories. You use an Inherited Rights Filter (IRF) or remove the check from the Inheritable box to block these rights if they are not appropriate in a directory or for a file.

Note, however, that any user or object can be granted explicit rights to a directory or file, rights that override any rights that might be inherited or that you try to block with an IRF. This is a useful feature because it means you can put up an IRF in a directory to block the rights that a large group of people might inherit to it, and then assign explicit rights to just the people you want to access the directory.

Basically, the Inherited Rights Filter cannot *grant* rights to anyone; it can only *revoke* rights from a user or group that has more rights to an object than you want it to have. Note the following:

The Supervisor right cannot be blocked by the Inherited Rights Filter for directories and files. Even a reassignment downstream from a Supervisor assignment will not change the effective rights. The only way to assign lesser rights is to remove the Supervisor right upstream, assign a lesser set of rights, and then make appropriate rights assignments or use IRFs downstream.

For objects, the Supervisor right can be blocked by the Inherited Rights Filter. This difference in the handling of the Supervisor right results from the difference between file system rights and NDS rights.

Managing File System Trustees in FILER

The steps for managing trustees in FILER are relatively simple as long as you work with one directory or file at a time. If you choose multiple directories and files, you see menus with a confusing selection of options. However, you might want to try that method, especially if you are faced with setting rights for a number of objects.

1. Choose Manage Files and Directories from the FILER main menu.

2. When the Directory Contents menu appears, browse for the directory or file to which you want to assign trustee rights.

3. Press F10 to display the options menu for working with the directory or file.

4. Choose View/Set Directory Information or View/Set File Information, depending on whether you are working with directories or files.

5. On the Information menu that appears, select the Trustees option and press ENTER.

6. A trustee name list appears, which will look similar to the one shown here (but may not have any trustees). Press the INS key to add trustees.

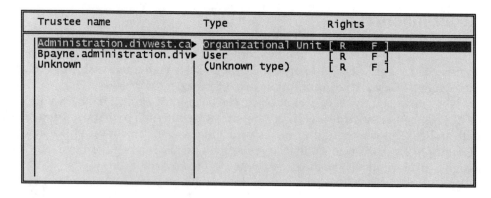

7. In the Object, Class menu that appears, scan through the directory tree to locate users or other objects that you want to make a trustee of the directory or file. Select the user or object and press ENTER.

The new user or object now appears in the trustee list, similar to the one shown in the preceding illustration. Now you need to assign trustee rights to the new user or object. Press ENTER on the new trustee to display the Trustee Rights menu, and then do one of the following:

■ To add new rights, press the INS key, choose rights in the list by marking them with the F5 key, and press ENTER to add them to the Trustee rights menu.

■ To revoke existing rights, mark them with the F5 key and press the DEL key.

MANAGING INHERITED RIGHTS FILTERS IN FILER   An Inherited Rights Filter lets you block the rights inherited from parent directories. You can block these rights at both the directory level and the file level.

■ If you select a single directory or file, choose the View/Set Directory Information option or the View/Set File Information option from the Subdirectory Options menu or the File Options menu. Scroll down to the Current Effective Rights field, and press ENTER.

■ If you select multiple directories or files, choose the Set Inherited Rights option from the Multiple Subdirectory Operations menu or the Multiple File Operations menu, and press ENTER.

The Inherited Rights menu appears. The rights displayed in this menu are rights that can be inherited.

■ To block rights from being inherited, remove them from the list. Highlight each right or mark multiple rights by using the F5 key, and then press the DEL key.

■ To add rights that are currently unavailable, press the INS key, and then mark rights on the list by using the F5 key. Press ENTER to add the rights.

When you are done changing the Inherited Rights Filter for the directories or files, press ESC to back out to the main menu. You are asked to confirm your changes.

Salvaging and Purging Files

When you delete a file, NetWare keeps a copy of the file around for a while in case you need to recover it. The file does not appear in directory listings and is not available for use, but the file is kept in a salvageable state until you restore or purge it. Deleted files are kept in the directory where they were deleted. If a directory is deleted, its files are saved in a file called DELETED.SAV, which is located in the root directory of the volume.

The NetWare File System

FILER lets you both view a list of deleted files and recover files from that list. You can also permanently remove deleted files to save disk space by purging them from the volume. Keep in mind that when the volume becomes full, NetWare purges recoverable files from it on a first-deleted, first-purged basis. Also, if you assigned the Purge attribute to a file or directory, the file or the directory's files will be purged immediately when deleted, and these files are not recoverable by using FILER.

To salvage deleted files by using the FILER utility, choose the Salvage Deleted Files option from its main menu. The following Salvage menu appears:

- ■ Choose the View/Recover Deleted Files option to list the salvageable files on the current volume and salvage the files.

- ■ Choose the Salvage from Deleted Directories option if the files are in a DELETED.SAV file in the root directory.

- ■ Choose the Set Salvage Options option to pick from a list of sort order options.

When you choose the View/Recover deleted files option, you are asked to specify a search pattern for the listing. If you press ENTER, all salvageable files are listed. Use wildcard characters to list specific files. Note the following:

- ■ Highlight the files you want to recover, and use the F5 key to mark them.

- ■ To change the sort order, press F3.

- ■ Press F6 to specify a wildcard pattern for marking files.

- ■ Press F8 to unmark files.

- ■ Press ENTER to recover a selected file or group of files.

- ■ If you select only a single file for salvaging, statistics for the file appear when you are asked if you want to recover it.

- ■ You can purge files from this list by pressing the DEL key after selecting the files you want to delete.

The NDIR Command

Use the NDIR command to view information about files, such as the size, creation date, owner (user who created the file), and attributes. You can also view information about directories, such as the Inherited Rights Filter and your effective rights in the directory. Sorting options are available, as well as extraction options, so you can view only those files that relate to a specific query. For example, you could list all files created by a user before a certain date that have not been backed up.

NDIR is a powerful command with many options, but the number of options it offers makes it difficult to use. You can display Help screens, but it is recommended that you create batch files for those commands you use often. You can also use DOS redirection options to save NDIR listings in files or send the listings directly to printers. For example, you could type **NDIR > LPT1** to send a listing to a printer.

The NDIR command has the following general syntax:

NDIR *path* /*options*

where *path* is the volume, directory, and (optionally) file you want to get information about, and *options* is one of the options described in the following sections.

HELP INFORMATION OPTIONS   To view Help information for the NDIR command, type it in the form shown as follows, replacing *option* with one of the options in the following table. The ALL option displays all the Help information in a paged format.

NDIR /? *option*

Option	Description
ALL	Display all Help information
AT	Display attribute filters
FOR	Display format options
OPT	Display miscellaneous options
RES	Display search filters
SORT	Display sorting options
SYN	Display syntax help

SPECIFIC INFORMATION OPTIONS   To display a specific type of information, type the command in the form shown as follows, replacing *path* with volume, directory, and file information, and *option* with one of the options that follow.

NDIR *path* /*option*

Option	Description
COMP	Compressed file information
D	Detailed file information
DA	File date information

Option	Description
MAC	Apple Macintosh files
L	Long filename
R	Filters and rights, file attributes

For example, to display a listing of files in the current directory and the rights you have to them, type this command:

```
NDIR *.* /R
```

To list document (DOC) files in a directory along with date information, you would type this:

```
NDIR *.DOC /DA
```

To list detailed information about a file called BUDGET.XLS, type this:

```
NDIR BUDGET.XLS /D
```

LISTING FILES BY ATTRIBUTES   The file attribute options let you list files according to the attributes they have. Use the /NOT option to display files according to attributes they don't have. The syntax is

NDIR *path* /*attributes*

or

NDIR *path* /NOT *attributes*

Here, *path* is the path to the directory where the files reside and/or a wildcard specifier, and *attributes* is one of the following:

Attribute	Description
A	Archive needed
Cc	Can't compress (status only, can't be assigned)
Ci	Copy-inhibit
Co	File compressed (status only, can't be assigned)
Dc	Don't compress

Attribute	Description
Di	Delete-inhibit
Dm	Don't migrate
Ds	Don't suballocate
H	Hidden
I	Indexed
Ic	Immediate compress
M	File migrated (status only, can't be assigned)
P	Purge
Ri	Rename-inhibit
Ro	Read-only
Rw	Read/write
Sh	Shareable
Sy	System
T	Transactional
X	Execute only

Note
The Execute Only attribute protects executable files from virus attack in some cases. Once a file is flagged X, you can't remove the flag unless you copy over the file. Some programs will not run if their executable files are flagged X.

For example, to list all files in a directory that are flagged read-only, type the following command:

```
NDIR *.* /RO
```

You can combine an option with the /NOT option. For example, to see which files are not marked indexed, type this:

```
NDIR *.* /NOT I
```

You can also combine options. In the following example, file attributes are listed (/R) for DOC files, and files with the delete-inhibit (DI) attribute are excluded:

```
NDIR *.DOC /R /NOT DI
```

SORTING NDIR LISTINGS The sorting options provide a way to list files according to date, owner, and size. You can use the /REV option to reverse the sort order in the listing. The syntax of the command is

NDIR *path* /SORT *option*

or

NDIR *path* /REV SORT *option*

Here, *path* is the path to the directory where the files reside and/or a wildcard specifier, and *option* is one of the following:

Option	Description
AC	Last accessed date
AR	Last archived date
CR	Date last created or copied
OW	Owner
SI	Size
UP	Last updated date
UN	Unsorted (no specific sort order)

For example, to sort files according to the creator of the files, type the following:

```
NDIR *.* /SORT OW
```

To reverse the listing, specify the /REV option as follows:

```
NDIR *.* /REV SORT OW
```

SPECIAL RESTRICTIONS The options listed here are used to restrict the type of file that is displayed in listings, either by date, owner, or size. Date formats must be *mm-dd-yy* or *mm/dd/yy*. The command takes these forms:

NDIR *path* /*option operator value*
NDIR *path* /*option* NOT *operator value*

Here, *path* is the path to the directory where the files reside and/or a wildcard specifier, and *option* is one of the following:

Option	Description
AC	Last accessed date
AR	Last archived date
CR	Date last created or copied
NAM	Name space
OW	Owner
SI	Size
UP	Last updated date

The *operator* variable is one of the following, and *value* is a value you supply, such as a date or owner name.

Value	Description
AFT	After
BEF	Before
EQ	Equal to
GR	Greater than
LE	Less than

The NOT option can also be used to list files not matching the specification. For example, you can execute commands that list file date information by replacing *option* in the following commands with AC, AR, CR, or UP and specifying a date:

NDIR *path* /*option* NOT *mm-dd-yy*
NDIR *path* /*option* BEF *mm-dd-yy*
NDIR *path* /*option* NOT BEF *mm-dd-yy*
NDIR *path* /*option* AFT *mm-dd-yy*
NDIR *path* /*option* NOT AFT *mm-dd-yy*

Following are formats for specifying owner names:

NDIR *path* /OW EQ *name*
NDIR *path* /OW NOT EQ *name*

And here are formats for using the size option to list files according to their size:

NDIR *path* /SI EQ *size*
NDIR *path* /SI NOT EQ *size*
NDIR *path* /SI LE *size*
NDIR *path* /SI NOT LE *size*
NDIR *path* /SI GR *size*
NDIR *path* /SI NOT GR *size*

You can also combine options. The next example shows how you might list files by size and creation date. All files greater than 1,000 bytes and created after December 25, 1998 will be listed.

NDIR *.* /SI GR 1000 /CR AFT 12/25/98

VIEW OPTIONS   The remaining options are useful for listing a particular type of file that belongs to a set not covered by the previous options. The command takes the following form:

NDIR *path* /*option*

Here, *path* is the path to the directory where the files reside and/or a wildcard specifier, and *option* is one of the following:

C	Scroll continuously through a screen of information
DO	View directories only
FI	View search drives where a file is found
FO	View files only
SUB	List information in all subdirectories
SPA	View directory space information
VER	View version information about files
VOL	View volume information

NDIR Directory Listing Examples

This section offers some examples of how you would list directory information using the NDIR command. To list directories on other servers, specify the server name and volume name in the command:

```
NDIR GATEWAY\COMTOOLS:APPS
```

To view directory information for all subdirectories branching from the SYS root directory, type this command:

```
NDIR SYS: /S /DO
```

To list directories on the SYS volume owned by a user (REWelch, in this example), type a command similar to this one:

```
NDIR SYS: /OW EQ REWELCH /S /DO
```

The /S option searches all subdirectories.

To list all directories on the SYS volume created after December 25, 1998, type this command:

```
NDIR SYS: /CR AFT 12/25/98 /S /DO
```

NDIR File Listing Examples

You can combine NDIR options to list specific types of files. A sampling is provided here. If you use long commands like those listed here on a regular basis, place them in a batch file. You can also direct the file listing to a file with a command similar to the following:

NDIR *.* > *file name*

The listing is sent to the file represented by *file name*. You can then save the file for later use or print it.

The following example lists files on drive K that include *.DOC in their filenames and are owned by John:

```
NDIR K:*.DOC /OW EQ JOHN
```

The next example lists files on drive K that include *.DOC in their filenames and have a size greater than 3,000 bytes:

```
NDIR K:*.DOC /SI GR 3000
```

The following command lists files on drive K that include *.DOC in their filenames and are owned by John. The list is then sorted by size.

```
NDIR K:*.DOC /OW EQ JOHN /SORT SIZE
```

The next example lists files on drive K that include *.DOC in their filenames, are owned by John, and were created after December 25, 1998:

```
NDIR K:*.DOC /OW EQ JOHN /CR AFT 12-25-98
```

The following command lists all files in the SYS volume owned by John (along with all subdirectory files):

```
NDIR SYS: /OW EQ JOHN /S
```

The next command lists all files in the SYS volume owned by John, in all subdirectories with a size greater than 3,000 bytes:

```
NDIR SYS: /OW EQ JOHN /S /SI GR 3000
```

The next command lists all files owned by John, in all subdirectories of SYS that have a size greater than 3,000. The /FO option produces a list of files only.

```
NDIR SYS: /OW EQ JOHN /S /SI GR 3000 /FO
```

The last command lists all files on the SYS volume that have the shareable and read-only attributes and that were accessed after December 25, 1998:

```
NDIR SYS: S RO /AC AFT 12-25-98
```

The NCOPY Command

NCOPY is the NetWare COPY command. Its use is similar to the DOS COPY command. You specify a source directory and files and a destination directory and files. The command takes the following form:

NCOPY *source-files destination-files /options*

Replace *source-files* with the directory and/or files you want to copy, and replace *destination-files* with the location of the directory to which you want to copy files. To change the name of files during a copy, specify the new names as part of *destination-files*. Use wildcard characters when working with multiple files. Replace *options* with an option from the following table.

Option	Description
?	Display Help information.
A	Copy files that have their archive bit set. When an archive bit is set, it indicates that the file has changed or is new and needs to be backed up. In this way, you can use NCOPY for backup purposes, if necessary. This does not copy hidden and system files, which can be a potential problem for some program and database files.
C	Copy only DOS information. Extended attributes and name space information are not saved.
F	Copy sparse files.
I	Specify this option when you want to be informed if any files copied have lost non-DOS information, such as extended attributes or name space information.
M	Copy files with archive bit set, and then clear the bit to indicate that the file has been backed up.
R	Specify this option to retain compression, but only if you are copying to a device that supports compression.
R/U	Specify this option to retain compression, even if you are copying to a device that doesn't support it. You can only decompress the information if it resides on a NetWare volume.
S	Specify this option to include subdirectories when copying.
S/E	Specify this option to include subdirectories in the NCOPY command, even if they are empty.
V	Verify the file for accuracy after writing it (DOS only).
VER	Display version information for the command.

The NCOPY command supports wildcard characters, so you can specify groups of files. For example, to copy all the DOC files on mapped drive H to mapped drive J, type this command:

```
NCOPY H:*.DOC J:
```

To copy an entire directory branch called APPS to the root of the VOL1 volume and include subdirectories and any empty subdirectories, use a command similar to the following:

```
NCOPY SYS:APPS VOL1: /S/E
```

The NetWare File System

If the directories might contain non-DOS attributes or name spaces, type a command similar to the following in order to be warned of any problems:

```
NCOPY SYS:APPS /S/E /I
```

The FLAG Command

Use the FLAG command to view and change the attributes of files and directories. Recall that attributes determine what users can do with files or how they are handled during backups, migrations, and file listings. In its simplest form, FLAG shows the attributes of all directories. Simply type **FLAG** at the command prompt to view attributes of files or specific files. You can use wildcard characters. For example, type the following to see the current attributes of all DOC files in the current directory:

```
FLAG *.DOC
```

To view help information for the FLAG command, type the command in the following form, replacing *option* with one of those in the following table:

FLAG /? *option*

Option	Description
ALL	View all Help information
DO	View Help on the directory attributes that you can assign to directories using the FLAG command
FO	View Help on the file attributes that you can assign to files using the FLAG command
MODES	View Help on assigning search modes
SYNTAX	View Help on FLAG's syntax
OPTIONS	View a list of miscellaneous options

Directory Attribute Options

Directory attribute options let you assign attributes to directories. The syntax is

FLAG *path attributes*

to create a new set of attributes, or

FLAG *path* + *attributes*

to add attributes to the current set, or

FLAG *path – attributes*

to remove attributes from the current set. In these syntax statements, *path* is the path to the directory, and *attributes* is one of the following:

Attribute	Description
Dc	Don't compress
Di	Delete-inhibit
Dm	Don't migrate
H	Hidden
Ic	Immediate compress
N	Normal
P	Purge
Ri	Rename-inhibit
Sy	System

For example, to flag a directory for immediate purging of deleted files, type the following command:

```
FLAG SYS:APPS\TEMPDOCS P
```

To add the Don't Compress attribute to the current set of attributes for the file MYFILE in the APPS directory, type this command:

```
FLAG SYS:APPS\MYFILE + Dc
```

File Attribute Options

File attribute options let you assign attributes to files. The syntax is

FLAG *path attributes*

to create a new set of attributes, or

FLAG *path + attributes*

to add attributes to the current set, or

FLAG *path – attributes*

to remove attributes from the current set. In these syntax statements, *path* is the path to the directory where the files reside and/or a wildcard specifier, and *attributes* is one of the following:

Attribute	Description
A	Archive needed
Ci	Copy-inhibit
Dc	Don't compress
Di	Delete-inhibit
Dm	Don't migrate
H	Hidden
Ic	Immediate compress
P	Purge
Ri	Rename-inhibit
Ro	Read-only
Rw	Read-write
Sh	Shareable
Sy	System
T	Transactional
ALL	All attributes
DS	Do not suballocate
N	Normal
X	Execute only

Note

The Execute only attribute protects executable files from virus attack in some cases. Once a file is flagged X, you can't remove the flag unless you copy over the file. Some programs will not run when their executable files are flagged X.

For example, to flag all files in a directory as read-only, type the following command:

```
FLAG *.* RO
```

Search Mode Options

The search mode options let you specify search modes for executable files. The command takes the form

FLAG *path* /M=*mode*

where *path* is a directory location and *mode* is a number, defined as follows:

Mode	Description
0	This is the default search mode in which executable files look for instructions in the shell default search path.
1	Search the path in the file and if unavailable, search the default directory, and then the search drive.
2	Search the path in the file first, and then only the default directory.
3	Search the path in the file first, then the default directory; and finally, search drives, but only if the request is read-only.
4	Reserved.
5	Search a specified path first, and then search drives; or, if there is no specified path, search the default directory, and then the search drives.
6	Reserved.
7	Search a specified path first, if the open request is read-only.

The following command sets the search mode to 1 for all executable files in the current directory:

```
FLAG *.EXE /M=1
```

Other Options

Following are some other options you can use with the FLAG command:

Option	Description
ALL	Set all attributes for the specified files or directories.
/C	Use this option to scroll the listing continuously.

Option	Description
/S	Include subdirectories.
/D	List detailed information.
/N	Set all attributes to defaults.
/OWNER=*name*	View all files and directories a user owns.
/NAME=*name*	Change who owns the file or directory by replacing *name* with the new owner's name.

The RIGHTS Command

Use the RIGHTS command at the command prompt to view or change the rights that users and groups have to files, directories, and volumes. The basic command takes the following form:

```
RIGHTS
```

You can type this in any directory to see what your current rights are. You'll see a list and description of the rights. To get Help information for the RIGHTS command, type the command in the following form, replacing *option* with one of the following:

RIGHTS /? *option*

Option	Description
ALL	View all Help information.
S	List the syntax of the RIGHTS command.
T	List the options you can use to view and change trustee rights.
F	List the options for setting Inherited Rights Filters.
I	List the options for viewing inherited rights.
O	View miscellaneous options.

Assigning Rights

To assign rights with the RIGHTS command, use one of the following forms:

RIGHTS *path rightslist* /NAME= *user,user...*
RIGHTS *path + rightslist* /NAME= *user,user...*
RIGHTS *path – rightslist* /NAME= *user,user...*

Here, *path* is the path to a directory or file, and *rightslist* is one or more of the rights listed next. Use the plus sign to assign additional rights to those already available, and the minus sign to take away specific existing rights. If you don't use + or –, the rights you specify override any existing rights. Replace user with one or more users, separated by a comma, to whom you want to assign the rights.

Option	Description
ALL	All rights except Supervisor rights
A	Access control
C	Create
E	Erase
F	File scan
M	Modify
N	No rights
R	Read
S	Supervisor
W	Write

For example, to give users Hank and Frank the rights to read, file scan, create, and write in the current directory, type the following:

```
RIGHTS . RFCW /NAME=HANK,FRANK
```

To add the Erase right to the rights that Hank and Frank now have, type this:

```
RIGHTS . + E /NAME=HANK,FRANK
```

To remove all rights that Frank has, type this:

```
RIGHTS . N /NAME=FRANK
```

The NetWare File System

To give Sally all rights in the SYS:APPS directory (except the Supervisor right), type this command:

```
RIGHTS SYS:APPS ALL /NAME=SALLY
```

Derived Rights

Use the following options to view a specific trustee's rights, to remove a trustee, or to view where the rights were assigned and inherited. The last option provides an important way to find out how a user inherited rights in a directory. The general syntax of the command is

RIGHTS *path* /*option*

Here, *path* is a directory and/or filename, and *option* is one of the following:

Option	Description
T	View trustees
I	View where the rights were assigned and inherited

To scroll continuously, search subdirectories, and view version information when executing RIGHTS commands, add the following:

Option	Description
C	Scroll continuously
S	Search subdirectories
VER	Display version information

For example, to view trustees of the current directory, type

```
RIGHTS /T
```

To list how the user DBoone obtained rights in the current directory, type

```
RIGHTS . /NAME=DBOONE /I
```

The REM option removes a trustee from the directory or file specified in *path*. In the following command, replace *user* with a user's name:

RIGHTS *path* REM /NAME=*user* option

To remove trustee JJones from the SYS:APPS directory, type the following:

```
RIGHTS SYS:APPS REM /NAME=JJONES
```

Inherited Rights Filter

Use the /F option to specify the rights in the Inherited Rights Filter for a directory. The command takes the following forms:

RIGHTS *path rightslist* /F
RIGHTS *path + rightslist* /F
RIGHTS *path – rightslist* /F

Here, *path* is the directory in which you want to control inherited rights, and *rightslist* is one or more of the rights listed next. Use the plus sign to add rights (rights are not blocked), and the minus sign to block rights. If you don't use + or –, the rights you specify become the new Inherited Rights Filter.

Option	Description
ALL	All rights filter through
A	Access control
C	Create
E	Erase
F	File scan
M	Modify
N	No rights
R	Read
S	Supervisor
W	Write

For example, to view the inherited rights filter of the current directory, type the following:

```
RIGHTS . /F
```

To set the inheritance filter so users do not have rights to create, erase, and write in the current directory, you would type this command:

```
RIGHTS . -CEW /F
```

The PURGE Command

You use the purge command to permanently delete previously erased files. It takes the following form:

PURGE *path* */options*

where *path* is the directory location of the file and *options* is one of the following:

Option	Description
?	Display Help for the command
A	Purge files in subdirectories
V	Display version information

For example, to purge all files in the current directory, type

```
PURGE *.*
```

or type

```
PURGE *.* /A
```

to purge all the files in the current directory and all its subdirectories.

The Complete Reference

NetWare 5

Part VI

Managing the NetWare Environment

The Complete Reference

NetWare 5

Chapter 23

Novell Printing Services

NetWare 5 printing services provide a way for you to share printing resources throughout your organization. Both the legacy printing services and Novell Distributed Print Services (NDPS) work with Novell Directory Services. This makes managing print services easier and allows users to quickly locate printers they want to use by type, location, or other features. Shared printers can be attached to special print servers; attached directly to the LAN; or attached to users' workstations, which can be shared so other network users can access them.

With NetWare 5, you can perform all necessary print management tasks from within the Windows environment. Printing services have been integrated with NetWare Administrator to make day-to-day management easier and more convenient. Windows clients can access network printers via the Windows-based NetWare Print Manager utility.

This chapter presents the legacy queue-based printing services first. After a thorough discussion of this older technology, we will present the new NDPS technology. Both of these technologies can coexist in the NetWare 5 environment. This allows users to implement NetWare 5 and to gradually migrate their older NetWare 4.x printing services into the NDPS environment.

How NetWare Legacy Printing Services Work

Figure 23-1 shows four different configurations available in the legacy printing environment. In the first configuration, a Novell client sends print jobs to a print queue. The print queue is directly accessed by a LAN-attached printer such as a Hewlett-Packard printer with an internal JetDirect card. The second configuration is the more traditional configuration in which the printer is directly connected to the file server. The Novell client sends print jobs to the print queue. The print queue is serviced by the print server. The print server then sends the print job to the locally attached printer. The third configuration is very similar to the traditional print configuration. The difference is that the printer is no longer directly attached to the file server running the print server software. Instead, it is attached to another server located on the LAN or WAN. In the fourth configuration, the printer is attached to a user's workstation. The Novell client sends print jobs to the queue serviced by the print server. The print server sends the print job to a user's workstation running a special printing program that allows LAN access to the locally attached printer.

As shown in Figure 23-1, NetWare legacy printing services centralize printing control with a loadable module that runs in a NetWare server. The print server manages shared printers throughout the network, including printers attached to the print server itself, printers attached to other NetWare file servers, and printers attached to workstations on the network.

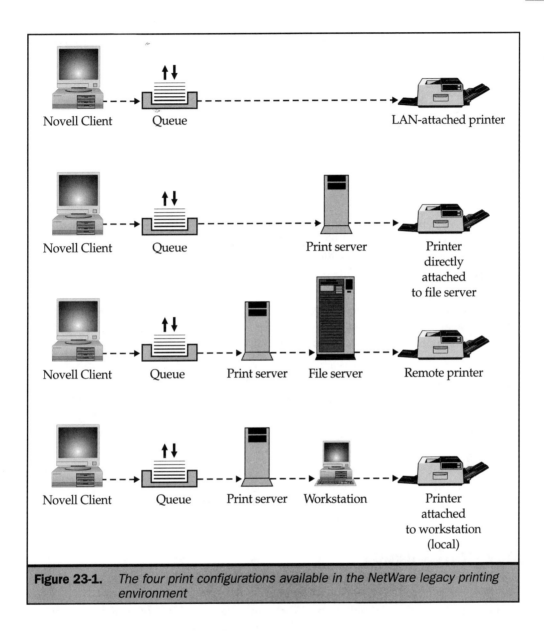

Figure 23-1. *The four print configurations available in the NetWare legacy printing environment*

There are three primary Printer objects in Novell Directory Services: the print server, printers, and print queues. The print server controls printing on printers through queues, which hold user print jobs until they are ready to print. Print servers, printers, and print queues appear in NetWare Administrator as pictured here:

Following is a list of the tools and programs you can use to configure and use NetWare legacy printing services:

- **PSERVER.NLM**   This is the all-important module that loads the print services management software at the designated file server. You load the module after configuring queues, printers, and the print server.

- **NPRINTER.NLM**   This Novell Loadable Module lets you attach network printers to the back of file servers. You must load the module for each printer attached.

- **NPRINTER.EXE**   You run NPRINTER on a workstation to share printers attached to that workstation with other network users. NPRINTER cannot be used to dedicate a workstation as a print server.

- **CAPTURE.EXE**   This is a command-line utility used at workstations or in login scripts. It dedicates one or more of the parallel or serial ports on a workstation for network printing. CAPTURE basically redirects print jobs sent to a local printer port to a network printer instead.

- **NPRINT.EXE**   This is a command-line utility used at workstations to print ASCII text files to network printers.

- **NetWare Administrator**   By now you're familiar with NWADMIN32.EXE, the NetWare Administrator utility. In this chapter, you'll see how to use it to control all types of network objects, such as Printer objects, Print Queue objects, and User objects. You can assign rights to printers and print queues.

Legacy Print Queues

A print queue is a holding place where print jobs from many different users are stored and then sent to a network printer. Print queues are located by default on the NetWare SYS volume in the QUEUES directory. You must select a volume other than the default when the Print Queue object is created. Otherwise, the SYS volume will store the queue when the Print Queue object is created. Remember, NetWare runs out of space on a volume basis. If the queues are placed on the SYS volume, they expand and contract based on the size and number of print jobs. This could lock out your SYS volume if a large number of print jobs with graphics are printed at the same time.

Let's look at how queues work. Assume a user wants to print a document from the current application to a network printer. Here are the steps:

1. The user specifies the printer port on his or her computer that correlates to a network print queue. For example, LPT1 might correspond to a directly attached printer, but LPT2 might be a "captured" port, in which print jobs sent to it are redirected to NetWare print queues.

2. The text formatting for the print job is done in the user's computer by the print drivers loaded there. It is then sent out over the network and stored in the queue on a volume of a NetWare server.

3. Print jobs from other users may already be in the queue waiting for the printer to complete the job it is currently printing. When the current print job completes, the next job in the queue is sent to the printer. A one-page *banner* can be printed to identify each print job in case the printer's output tray fills with many completed print jobs.

Novell recommends one print queue per printer for ease of management. Each print queue can contain up to 1,000 print jobs at a time; however, only the first 255 print jobs are seen by the queue administrator. When the first job is finished, it disappears from the screen and another print job scrolls onto the screen at the end of the list. Queues have the following features and advantages:

- Once the job is sent to the queue, the user can continue working. The user doesn't need to wait while the printer completes the job.

- Users can send jobs to printers at different locations. For example, rather than send a document overnight via express courier, a user could just send the print job to a printer at the destination location.

- Several queues can exist for the same printer. For example, one queue might hold print jobs for printing during evening hours, while other queues might be assigned immediate printing priority. Administrators can assign users rights to various queues. For example, company executives can get rights to priority queues, while users who produce jobs such as mailing labels and accounting reports get rights to the queue that only prints during evening hours.

- Several printers can exist for the same queue. This is the opposite of the previous point. It allows you to supplement a busy queue with a second or third printer to handle the workload and provide redundancy in case one printer jams or becomes inoperable.

Using a separate queue for each printer might seem like overkill, but it provides flexibility when configuring printers on the network. NetWare users can now identify network printers by name, no matter where they are geographically in the organization. If a printer is configured correctly, users who have the appropriate rights can print to a printer simply by choosing the printer's name. They do not have to know where the printer is located or which printer queue stores its print jobs.

Novell Directory Services makes it easy for users to identify a queue or a printer solely by its name. They can browse the directory tree until they find an appropriate printer or queue, and then send print jobs to it. Note that in order for the user to be able to browse the directory tree from within an application, that application must be compatible with NDS. Users can also use search commands to locate printers in the portions of the directory that they can view. If users send a print job to a printer instead of a queue, NetWare sends the job to a queue appropriate for that printer.

When you create a print queue, NetWare generates a directory for it, and this directory is assigned the same name as the queue. NetWare attaches the extension .QDR to every named queue. Within each new print queue directory, NetWare places two hidden system files whose names begin with Q_ and contain a derivation of the directory name. The two files have the extensions .SYS and .SRV, and only users with supervisor-level access rights can view them.

Legacy Network Printers

You must define a Printer object for each printer you want to share on the network. You use the NetWare Administrator utility to define these objects. As usual, you should make sure you are in the appropriate NDS tree context before creating the objects.

Note	*You must load the NPRINTER.NLM at a server for each network printer you want to attach to it. However, this module is loaded automatically for each attached printer at the server where you load PSERVER.NLM.*

You can attach printers to the print server itself and to individual workstations on the network. A print server manages the flow of print jobs through print queues and to printers. Several queues might send their print jobs to a single printer, or several printers might service a single queue. First you create a Printer object for each printer you want to share on the network, and then you assign it to a print server and assign queues to it.

Direct-connect printers manufactured by Compaq, Hewlett-Packard, and other companies have their own network interface cards so that they can become a node on the network without being attached to a workstation or server. By taking advantage of the new APIs available for developers, third-party printer manufacturers can load NPRINTER.EXE into the printer's memory to service print jobs directly, bypassing a print server. After you define the Printer object in the directory, the printer can begin servicing print jobs directly from an assigned queue. Consult the printer manufacturer's instructions for connecting a printer directly to a NetWare network.

Legacy Print Servers

The PSERVER.NLM module links queues and printers to print servers. It runs as a continuous process in the server; if you unload it, printer sharing is unavailable. A single print server can handle up to 255 network printers, including five local printers (three parallel and two serial).

In most organizations, printing is a mission-critical operation. Although NetWare's legacy printing services can theoretically handle many print jobs and a large number of printers, a heavily loaded printing environment might require more than one print server running PSERVER.NLM. If you have heavy database or imaging applications running on the file server, migrate the printing system to NDPS.

Configuring Legacy Printing Services

You can create and configure Print Queue objects, Printer objects, and Print Server objects using the NetWare Administrator utility. After you create objects, you can load (or reload) the PSERVER.NLM module at the server controlling your print services.

Creating Legacy Print Queue Objects

To create a print queue using the NetWare Administrator utility, first change your context in the directory tree, if necessary, and highlight the container you want to hold the Print Queue object. Then choose Create from the Object menu. When the list of objects appears, double-click the Print Queue (non-NDPS) object to display the Create Print Queue dialog box, where you can do the following:

1. Choose either Directory Services Queue or Reference a Bindery Queue. Choose the latter option to reference a NetWare 3.*x* queue.

2. Type a name for the queue in the Print Queue Name field.

3. In the Print Queue Volume field, type the name of a Volume object that will hold the queue, or click the Browse button to search the directory tree for a volume.

4. Check the Define Additional Properties box if you want to fill out the details dialog box for the new queue (recommended), or click Create Another Print Queue to create additional print queues.

5. Click Create to create the new queue.

If you choose to define additional properties in step 4, a details dialog box similar to that shown in Figure 23-2 appears. From this dialog box, you can change fields on the following pages:

■ **Identification**   This page shows the logical description and physical location of the department in which the print queue resides. You can change these fields as appropriate; they are mostly informational.

- **Assignments** This page shows the printer and print server attachments for the queue. You view these assignments in the details dialog box for the print queue, but you actually make the assignments in the details dialog box for the printer.

- **Operator** This page lists the objects that have a right to manage the queue and print jobs in the queue.

- **Users** This is the all-important page in which you grant users access to printers (through print queues). Click the Add button to add a User, Group, or other object. The container where the queue was created and the user who created the queue are the default users.

- **Security Equal To Me** This page lists other objects that are security-equivalent to this object.

- **Job List** This page lists the current print jobs in the queue. You can get details about the job, hold it, resume it, or delete it by pressing buttons under the list. You can also rearrange jobs in the list by clicking and dragging them to another location.

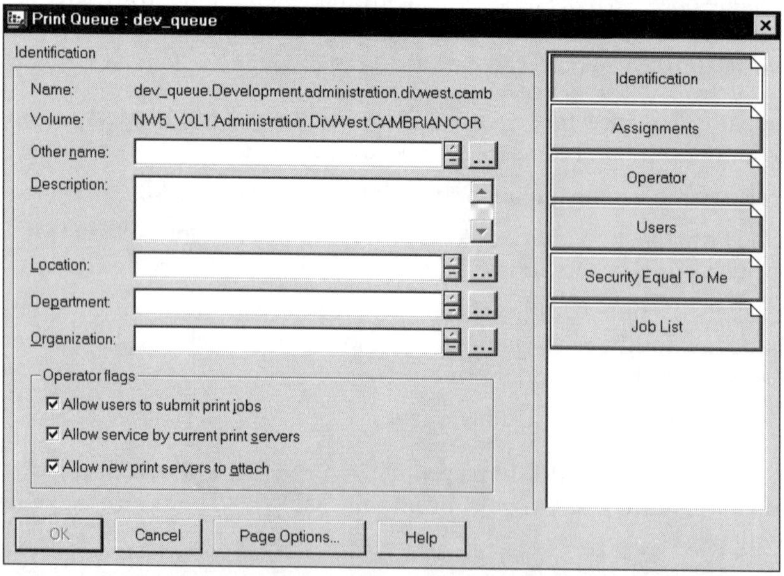

Figure 23-2. The details dialog box for a non-NDPS Print Queue object

Defining Legacy Printers

To define a printer using the NetWare Administrator utility, NWADMIN32, do the following:

1. Change your context in the directory tree, if necessary, and highlight the container you want to hold the Printer object.

2. Choose Create from the Object menu. When the list of objects appears, double-click the Printer (non-NDPS) object.

3. When the Create Printer dialog box appears, type a name for the printer in the Printer Name field, check the Define Additional Properties box, and click the Create button. A details dialog box similar to that shown in Figure 23-3 appears.

At the right side of the dialog box are buttons you can click to define additional properties, as described here:

- **Identification**   This page provides a description of the Printer object for informational purposes only, such as description, location, and other identification properties.

- **Assignments**   This page displays or lets you control the Print Queue objects assigned to this Printer object. See the next section, "Assignments Page," for details.

- **Configuration**   This page stores information about the hardware configuration and its use on the network. Choose the type of printer attached to the network (either other/unknown, parallel, serial, XNP, AIO, UNIX, or AppleTalk), the banner type (text or PostScript), the service interval (timeout delay between jobs), the buffer size, and the container printing form. In order to specify a remote printer (a printer that isn't attached to the print server) or to change communications parameters, click the Communication button. A dialog box similar to that shown in Figure 23-4 appears. Click the Help button for information on changing these options.

> **Note**   *Enable the Manual Load (Remote from Print Server) button on the Communication dialog box if the printer is not directly connected to the print server.*

- **Notification**   Use this page to identify users on the network who are notified when the printer requires servicing, such as when the paper trays need refilling or when a form needs changing.

- **Features**   Use this page to enter specific printer configuration options.

- **Security Equal To Me**   This page lists other objects that are security-equivalent to this object.

- **See Also**   Use this page to list the names of objects related to this object.

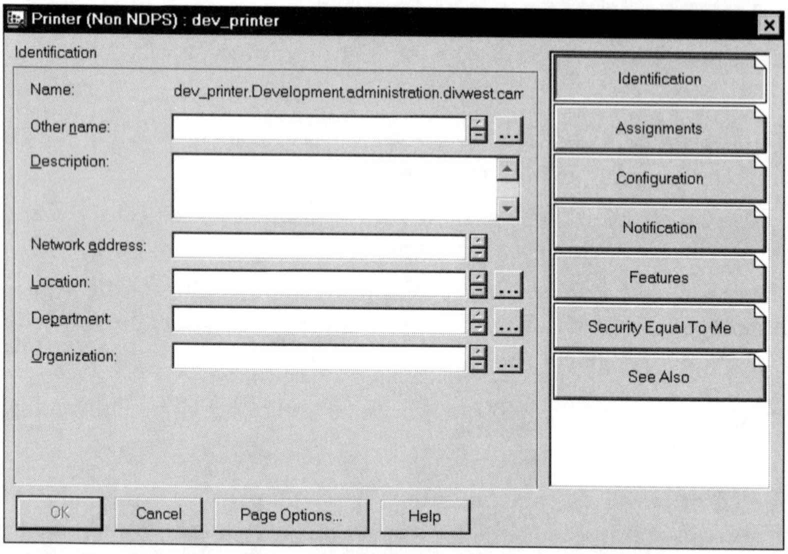

Figure 23-3. Defining non-NDPS printers in the NWADMIN32 utility

Assignments Page

The Assignments page, which is shown in Figure 23-5, lists the active print server, the network print queues serviced by the printer, and the default print queue. You can

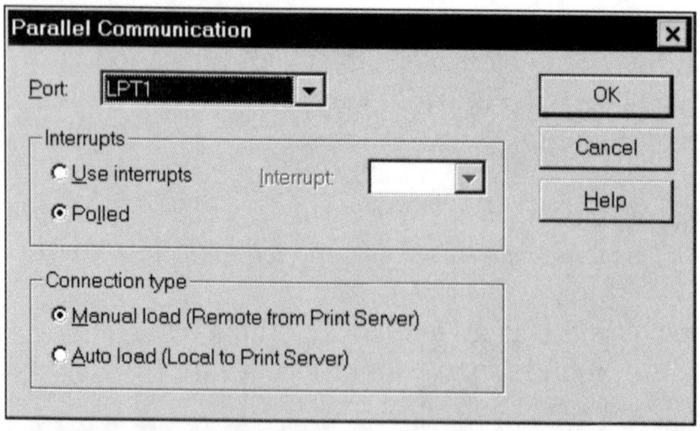

Figure 23-4. Changing printer communication parameters

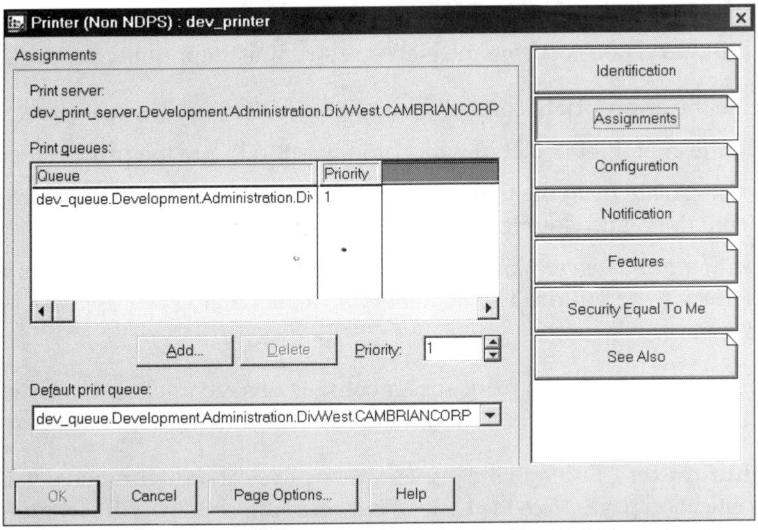

Figure 23-5. *The Assignments page of the Printer details dialog box*

click the Add button to assign additional queues to this printer. As you add queues to the lists, they appear in the Print Queues list.

- The print server that manages this printer is listed in the Print Server field. You must create a print server and assign printers to it, as discussed shortly, before you will see a name in this field.
- The Print Queues field shows the queues that have been assigned to the printer. The priority of a queue is important when more than one queue is assigned to a single printer. Queues with high priority are serviced before queues with lower priority; so, for example, you might want to create a Managers queue that has a priority of 1, and a Clerks queue that has a priority of 2. To change the priority of a queue, highlight the queue and change the Priority field value.
- The Default Print Queue field displays the name of the queue used by default if users choose to print to this Printer object, rather than to a Print Queue object.

Remember *When you switch default queues, make sure users have access rights to the new queue.*

Creating a Legacy Print Server Object

To create a Print Server object using the NetWare Administrator utility, follow these steps:

1. Locate the appropriate context in the Novell Directory Services tree.

2. Click the container object in which you want to locate the print server.

3. Choose Create from the Object menu to see the list of objects you can create in the container, and double-click the Print Server option.

4. Type in a print server name, check the Define Additional Properties box, and click the Create button. The Print Server details dialog box appears, as shown in Figure 23-6.

The details dialog box for a print server consists of seven pages, which are discussed next.

■ **Identification** Enter all the print server's physical configuration details on the Identification page. Note the Unload button at the bottom of the window, which lets you unload PSERVER.NLM from the system console remotely. (You cannot load the software remotely.) After you define the print server by using NetWare Administrator, you must load PSERVER.NLM at the server's system console. If that server is at a remote location, you will need a local operator to perform the steps.

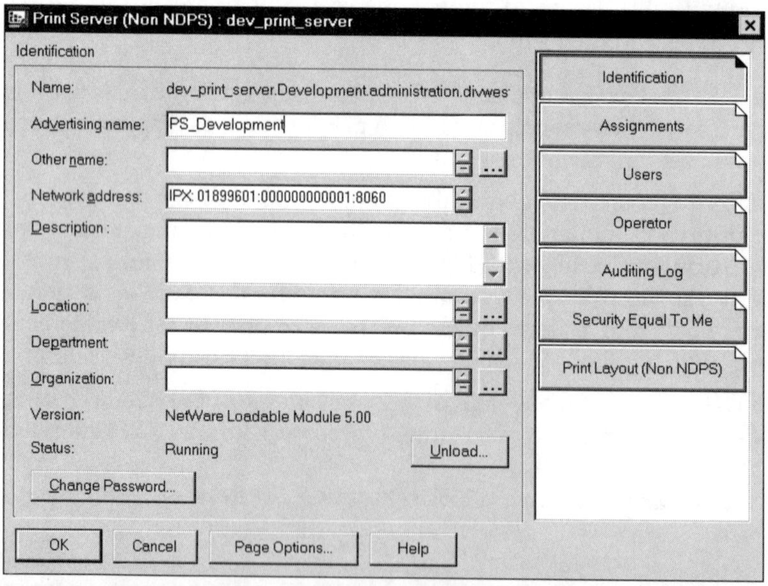

Figure 23-6. *The details dialog box for non-NDPS print servers*

- **Assignments** On the Assignments page, you can view, add, or delete printers assigned to the print server. Assigning printers is an important step, because the print server will not load properly unless one or more printers have been assigned to it. Click the Add button to assign new printers to the print server. You can then browse the directory tree to locate Printer objects you created previously and assign them to the print server. After printers are added, the printer will receive print jobs in its queue.

Note *If the printer is attached to a DOS or Windows 3.x workstation, be sure to load NPRINTER.EXE at the workstation. If it's a 95 or 98 workstation, load NPTWIN95.EXE.*

- **Users** On the Users page, you define users or groups with access to the print server.
- **Operator** You define the users responsible for the print server on the Operator page. Operators are responsible for downing the print server, viewing its status, and controlling the printers it services.
- **Auditing Log** On the Auditing Log page, you can enable print job logging and specify how you want to track print jobs in a log file. The log stores information such as the printer used for a job, its size, and the time it took to print. After enabling logging, you must unload and reload the print server. Auditing logs are retained as ASCII files so you can review them with an editor.

  - Choose Enable Auditing to enable auditing; or Disable Auditing to disable it.
  - Location of Auditing Log indicates where log files are stored. You can also limit the size of the file so it doesn't get too large by specifying a size in the Limit Size field.
  - The Maximum Print Jobs field allows you to limit the number of print jobs recorded in the auditing log.

- **Security Equal To Me** The Security Equal To Me page lists other objects that are security-equivalent to this object.
- **Print Layout (Non NDPS)** The Print Layout page displays a map of your printing services setup. You can see the relationships among Printer objects and determine the status of those objects. Double-click an object to expand or to collapse the tree.

  - A trouble icon indicates printing problems; you must expand the tree to see the troubled object.
  - A dashed line between objects means the connection is temporary and is not used every time the print server is loaded.
  - Click Update to refresh the print layout tree so it shows recent changes.
  - Right-click an object to view its status, or click it and choose the Status button.

Loading the Legacy Print Server (PSERVER.NLM)

After you define a print server and assign queues and printers to it by using the NetWare Administrator utility, you can load PSERVER.NLM at a file server's system console by typing the following command:

    [LOAD] PSERVER

The Enter print server name box appears with your current context in the Novell Directory Services tree listed. To change the context, press ENTER. The Contents of Current Context box appears, in which you can browse the directory tree until you find the context that holds the Print Server object you created previously. Highlight the object and press ENTER. In a moment, the PSERVER main menu appears. From the main menu, you can select Printer Status or Print Server Information.

After creating the printer and defining its options, you can add the command to load the print server to the server's AUTOEXEC.NCF file so it loads every time you start the server. The command should look like the following, where *context* is the fully qualified name of the print server:

    [LOAD] PSERVER *context*

When PSERVER is loaded on the server, a "picture" of the print services currently defined is loaded in memory. If a change is made to a Print Queue, Printer, or Print Server object, those changes are not effective until PSERVER is unloaded and then reloaded to take a new "picture." Sometimes the print services files in memory can become corrupted due to power hits or various other problems. Before doing anything else, unload and then reload PSERVER to take a new "picture."

Printer Status

Highlight the Printer Status option and press ENTER to see a list of network printers that have been assigned to the current print server. You will not be able to see printers that have been assigned to another print server. Select a printer and press ENTER to view printer status information, as shown in Figure 23-7. The fields on this screen are as follows:

- **Printer**   This field shows the full Novell Directory Services name of the printer.
- **Type**   This field displays the type of connection: either locally attached to the print server, or attached to a workstation (Remote) or another file server (OTHER).

Managing the NetWare
Environment

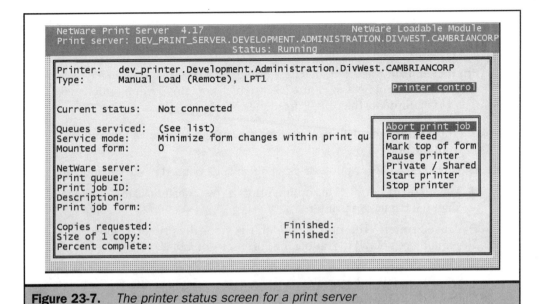

```
NetWare Print Server  4.17                         NetWare Loadable Module
Print server: DEV_PRINT_SERVER.DEVELOPMENT.ADMINISTRATION.DIVWEST.CAMBRIANCORP
                             Status: Running

 Printer:    dev_printer.Development.Administration.DivWest.CAMBRIANCORP
 Type:       Manual Load (Remote), LPT1
                                                     Printer control

 Current status:    Not connected

 Queues serviced:   (See list)              Abort print job
 Service mode:      Minimize form changes within print qu  Form feed
 Mounted form:      0                        Mark top of form
                                             Pause printer
 NetWare server:                             Private / Shared
 Print queue:                                Start printer
 Print job ID:                               Stop printer
 Description:
 Print job form:

 Copies requested:                  Finished:
 Size of 1 copy:                    Finished:
 Percent complete:
```

Figure 23-7.   *The printer status screen for a print server*

- **Current Status**   This field tells whether the printer is connected to the network. If the printer is remote (attached to a workstation on the network), this field will say "Not connected" until you load the NPRINTER.EXE file on the workstation (or the NPRINTER.NLM file on the file server).

- **Queues Serviced**   Select this field and press ENTER to see a list of queues. Press ENTER again to change the priority of a queue. As mentioned previously, queue priority provides a way to make sure some print jobs are printed before others.

- **Service Mode**   Press ENTER on this field to set how often you change print forms on the printer. The following options are available:

    - **Change Forms as Needed**   This option might require that you change forms often because it sends job to the printer based on their priority in the queue.

    - **Minimize Form Changes Within Print Queues**   The print server requires you to mount a new form for a print job before servicing print jobs with the currently mounted form in a print queue with a lower priority.

    - **Minimize Form Changes Across Print Queues**   This option requires that you change forms less often. It services all jobs in the print queue that use the currently mounted form, even if other jobs have higher priority.

    - **Service Only Currently Mounted Form**   The print server never requests a form change. If no print job requiring the current form is available, nothing is printed.

■ **Mounted Form** This field refers to a custom form created for the container by using the NetWare Administrator utility. This field can be left at 0 if no special form is used.

■ **Printer Control** Selecting this field brings up a secondary menu (shown under the Printer control field in Figure 23-7), which contains several options you can select to manipulate the printer from the console:

  ■ **Abort Print Job** This option stops the current print job and removes it from the print queue.

  ■ **Form Feed** This option ejects a page from a paused or stopped printer.

  ■ **Mark Top of Form** This option prints a row of asterisks (8) to help you align the paper in a printer.

  ■ **Pause Printer** This option temporarily stops the printer. Choose Start printer (see below) to resume the current print job.

  ■ **Private/Shared** You will see this option if the printer is attached to a workstation. It indicates whether other network users can use the printer (Shared), or only the local user can use the printer (Private).

  ■ **Start Printer** This option resumes a stopped or paused printer.

  ■ **Stop Printer** This option stops the printer and returns the current print job to the queue.

All of the remaining fields are blank until a print job is sent to a queue and printer. These options are described here:

■ **NetWare Server** This field indicates the name of the server holding the current queue.

■ **Print Queue** This field indicates the current print queue submitting jobs.

■ **Print Job ID** This field indicates the number of the current print job.

■ **Description** This field indicates the name of the banner used with the print job.

■ **Print Job Form** This field indicates the printer form used by the current print job.

■ **Copies Requested** This field indicates the number of copies that the submitting user requested.

■ **Size of 1 Copy** This field indicates the number of bytes printed.

■ **Percent Complete** This field indicates what percentage of the print job has been completed.

Legacy Print Server Information

When you choose the Print Server Information option from the PSERVER main menu, a Print Server Information and Status dialog box appears:

```
                    Print Server Information and Status
         ┌────────────────────────────────────────────────────┐
         │ Version:              5.00.0                         │
         │ Type:                 Netware Loadable Module        │
         │ Advertising name:     PS_TEST1                       │
         │ Number of printers:   1                              │
         │ Queue service modes:  4                              │
         │ Current status:       Running                        │
         └────────────────────────────────────────────────────┘
```

This dialog box lists the general characteristics of the print server, including its software version number, its program type, the official name by which it is known to the network, the number of printers it supports, the number of queue service modes, and its current status. Select Current Status to see a menu that allows you to unload the print server.

Setting Up Legacy Server-Attached Printers

You load NPRINTER.NLM to configure printers that are attached directly to the NetWare server where PSERVER.NLM is running (and controlling printing services) or to another NetWare file server that has directly attached printers. NPRINTER.NLM must be loaded on a NetWare server multiple times to support each of the printers attached to the server that you want to share on the network.

Note that the default mode for NPRINTER.NLM at the server that is running PSERVER.NLM is Auto Load, which means that NPRINTER.NLM is automatically loaded when you load PSERVER.NLM. You can choose to load NPRINTER.NLM manually in the NetWare Administrator utility. The Manual Load option lets you load the print driver when you want to load it, which can be useful if server or network resources must be limited.

To load NPRINTER.NLM, at the NetWare server console, type

[LOAD] NPRINTER *printername*

However, if you are in another context, you will need to specify the full context of the full name, including the directory where the Printer object is located. Here's an example:

NPRINTER .Dev_Printer.Development.Administration.DivWest.CambrianCorp

You can place these commands in the AUTOEXEC.NCF file of the server where you are loading NPRINTER so they load whenever the server is started. You do not need to do this on the server running PSERVER.NLM if the Auto Load option is set because PSERVER will automatically load NPRINTER at the server for any configured printers.

Setting Up Legacy Workstation-Attached Printers

The following steps describe how to share printers that are attached to network workstations by running NPRINTER.EXE at the workstation. NPRINTER.EXE is a terminate-and-stay-resident (TSR) program that runs on DOS computers.

1. Attach the printer to an LPT port or COM port on a workstation.

2. Use NetWare Administrator at an administrator's workstation to create one or more Print Queue objects for the printer, or to determine which existing queue will service the printer.

3. Use NetWare Administrator at an administrator's workstation to create a Printer object for the printer. Be sure to specify that the printer is remote from the print server:

   ■ Choose Manual Load in the Location field.

   ■ Choose Remote, OTHER in the Printer type field of the Printer Configuration menu.

   ■ Click the Communication button on the Configuration page when setting up a printer, and then enable the Remote from Print Server option on the dialog box that appears (see Figure 23-4).

4. Use NetWare Administrator to follow the steps described earlier in this chapter under "Configuring Legacy Printing Services" for assigning queues to the new Printer object.

5. Use NetWare Administrator to assign the new printer to a Print Server object. These steps are also described earlier in this chapter.

6. If PSERVER.NLM is already running at a file server, type **UNLOAD PSERVER** at the server's console and then bring the server back up. It should recognize the name of the new printer you entered in the directory.

   After installing PSERVER, remote printers are still not available until you load NPRINTER.EXE at the workstation or a server. Make sure you are logged into the network and have a search drive mapped to the SYS:PUBLIC directory.

7. Type the following to load the NPRINTER.EXE program:

   NPRINTER

8. A list of current print servers appears. Choose a print server, and then choose a printer and specify whether it is attached to a local parallel or serial port.

9. When everything is set, press F10 to complete the installation.

   After NPRINTER loads support for the printer attached to the workstation or file server, other users can access the printer from network-aware applications or with NetWare printing commands such as those discussed in the remainder of this chapter.

   Note that you can move the NPRINTER.EXE file and all its associated files to the local workstation so the driver can be loaded before the user logs onto the network. The files required for this utility are listed here. Unless otherwise noted, they are located in the SYS:PUBLIC\NLS\ENGLISH directory.

NPRINTER.MSG
NPRINTER.HEP
SCHEMA.XLT
NWDSBRWS.MSG
TEXTUTIL.MSG
TEXTUTIL.HEP
TEXTUTIL.IDX (located in the SYS:PUBLIC directory)
xxx_RUN.OVL (e.g., IBM_RUN.OVL, located in the SYS:PUBLIC directory)

   Note that you will also need the Unicode files appropriate for your country and keyboard. These files are located in the SYS:PUBLIC\NLS directory. The default U.S. Unicode files are listed here:

UNI_437.001
437_UNI.001
UNI_MON.001
UNI_COL.001

A similar utility must be loaded on Windows 95/98 workstations for remote printer operation. This is the NPTWIN95.EXE program. It performs the same functions on a Windows 95/98 workstation as NPRINTER does on a DOS-based machine.

Other Legacy Printing Utilities

Three container property pages and two text-based utilities (CAPTURE and NPRINT) are associated with legacy printing. The container property pages are used to define special printing options when you're using applications that are not network-aware, or you need special settings beyond what you can define in the applications you print from. Many applications are network-aware and let you print directly to shared network printers and queues. Others require the special settings discussed here.

It is important to understand the difference between *print forms* and *print job configurations*. A print form basically defines a paper size and gives it a name and number to which you can refer when specifying print jobs. When a user sends a print job with a form that is different than the current form, the printer operator will get a message to change the form.

You create a print job configuration using the container Print Job Configuration (non-NDPS) property page to define the parameters for a printing job. Users can choose from many different *print job configurations* when sending jobs to a printer. Keep in mind, however, that these options are not important with most modern applications that define the parameters internally.

Each of these container property pages and two utilities is briefly described in the following sections. Refer to each utility's Help options for more information, or type a command similar to the following to display a description of the utility:

    CAPTURE /?

Print Devices (non-NDPS) Property Page

You use the Print Devices property page for a container to define printer definition files (PDFs). Select the Print Devices property page from the details view of the selected container object. A screen similar to the one shown in Figure 23-8 will appear. Choose Create to generate a new PDF file, or Import to import an existing PDF file.

Printer Definition Format (PDF) Files

A PDF file defines the settings and parameters of a printing device, such as a Hewlett-Packard laser printer or an IBM line printer. NetWare has a large set of preconfigured PDFs in the SYS:PUBLIC directory for the most popular printers. You can list these files, which have the filename extension .PDF. You can create a print device that you can refer to when printing from applications on the network or from NetWare printing utilities. The definitions you create can use existing PDF files, or you can specify your own parameters if a PDF is not available for your printer. Creating your own PDFs can be tedious, so you might want to contact the printer manufacturer for a PDF. Keep in mind that most applications don't need NetWare's PDF because they have their own printer definition files.

The Print Devices property page menu consists of a Create option and an Import option. The remaining options are grayed out until you define at least one device. You use Create to create your own print device, and you use the Import option to call up one of the existing PDFs in the SYS:PUBLIC directory. Either way, you create a device that has a name and number you can refer to when running applications or using NetWare printing utilities. For example, you can create a default print form used by network queues. This print form can specify a particular PDF, such as the file for a Hewlett-Packard LaserJet printer.

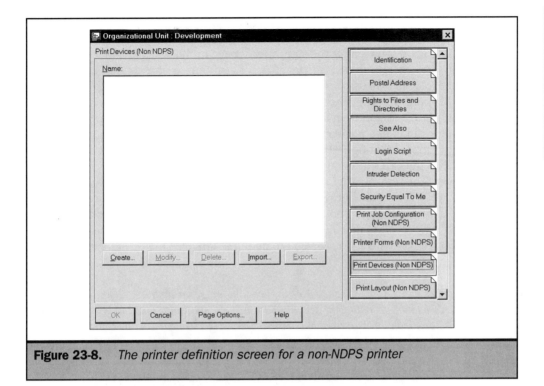

Figure 23-8.   *The printer definition screen for a non-NDPS printer*

Print Forms

Defining new print forms is easy. Select the Printer Forms property page from the
selected container object. Choose Create to display the following menu.

Type the name for the form, a number (which must be a unique number between 0
and 255), and the form length and width.

Print Job Configuration (non-NDPS) Property Page

You can use the Print Job Configuration property page of the selected container object to create print job configurations. A print job configuration defines a set of parameters used to print a job, such as the printer definition file, the printer or print queue to use, the number of copies to print, and banner information. You can define any number of print job configurations and then let users choose the one they want to use when they are sending a print job to a printer.

Select the Print Job Configuration property page for the container and click New. A screen similar to the one shown in Figure 23-9 will appear.

At the top of the screen, you can specify the number of copies for the job and whether it should have a banner. You can also specify the Print Job name and the Form name. At the bottom, you can specify the print device to use and the mode, which defines a special font. Note that jobs you define are sent to the printer specified in the Device field. This provides a way for you to define in advance the printers users will use when printing.

You can set a given Print Job name as the default for a given container. If a user does not list another Print Job name, the default will print automatically. This can be handy when there is a common job used most of the time. This can be set container by container.

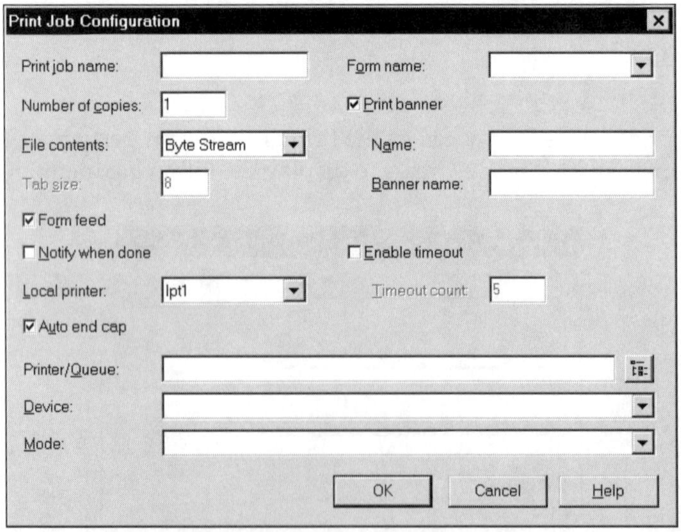

Figure 23-9.   *The Print Job Configuration screen*

CAPTURE

Applications that are network-aware, such as Microsoft Word and WordPerfect, let you specify and print directly to printers on the network. These applications display the printer names within their user interface. When printing from applications that are not network-aware, you need a way to divert printing from local DOS printers to NetWare printers. You can use the CAPTURE utility to do this. It lets you divert print jobs sent to a local device name such as LPT1 or LPT2 to a network printer. Then, in your applications, you can simply send print jobs to the diverted port when you want to print to network devices.

For example, you could use the CAPTURE command in the following form to divert all print jobs sent to LPT2 to the print queue called Managers:

```
CAPTURE L=2 Q=MANAGERS
```

This next command diverts print jobs sent to LPT2 to a printer called HP-LASER:

```
CAPTURE L=2 P=HP-LASER
```

To end the capturing of LPT2 as set up by one of the two previous examples, you would type the EC (End Capture) option as follows:

```
CAPTURE L=2 EC
```

The list of CAPTURE options and parameters is quite extensive. You can print them by typing the following command, which assumes that a local printer is attached to LPT1:

```
CAPTURE /? ALL > LPT1
```

Note the following with regard to the CAPTURE command:

- By default, only the device names LPT1, LPT2, and LPT3 are available on DOS workstations.
- To include the CAPTURE command in login scripts, precede it with a pound sign (#). See the definition for # under "# (DOS Only)" in Chapter 24.

NPRINT

You can use the NPRINT utility to send a specific print job to a network printer without actually having to divert a printer port by using the CAPTURE utility. You add options to the NPRINT command to specify which network queue or printer you want to print to. This command takes the form

> NPRINT *filename options*

where *filename* is the path and name of the file you want to print, and *options* is an option that specifies various parameters, such as the queue, printer, and print server to use. You can also specify a banner to separate the print job from others, and you can specify a specific form or print job configuration. You can type the following command to print a complete description of the NPRINT command:

```
NPRINT /? ALL > LPT1
```

Legacy Printing Utility Reference

Table 23-1 lists the majority of printing tasks you need to perform on your network. It indicates the various utilities you use to perform the associated task. See the preceding sections for further descriptions of each utility.

Task	Utility
Assign Print Queue objects to printers	NetWare Administrator (Printer object)
Assign Printer objects to print servers	NetWare Administrator (Print Server object)
Control printer and print server	NetWare Administrator, PSERVER.NLM
Create, assign, modify, or delete Print Queue, Print Server, and Printer objects	NetWare Administrator
Create print jobs	Capture, Nprint
Customize print job characteristics with print job configurations	NetWare Administrator (User, Organization, and Organizational Unit objects)
Customize printer characteristics with printer forms and print devices (PDF files)	NetWare Administrator (Organization and Organizational Unit objects)

Table 23-1. *Network Printing Tasks and Their Associated Utilities*

Task	Utility
Delete, modify, or reorder print jobs	NetWare Administrator
Display print configuration layout and status of printing	NetWare Administrator
Monitor printer and print server	NetWare Administrator, PSERVER.NLM
Monitor print jobs	NetWare Administrator, PSERVER.NLM
Print files	Capture, Nprint
Run Print Server on the NetWare server	PSERVER.NLM
Run network printer(s) on the NetWare server	NPRINTER.NLM
Run network printer(s) on DOS workstations	NPRINTER.EXE
Run network printer(s) on a Windows 95/98 workstation	NPTWIN95.EXE

Table 23-1. *Network Printing Tasks and Their Associated Utilities* (continued)

Novell Distributed Print Services (NDPS)

Using print services has often been a complex task. Initial setup required the creation of Print Queue, Printer, and Print Server objects. After these were created, it was necessary to link them together properly. A user had to redirect the print job from the workstation printer port using either the CAPTURE or NPRINT utility to send a print job to the print queue. With Novell Distributed Print Services (NDPS), users can now manage printers and printing resources through one NDS object and one management utility.

NDPS was developed to simplify the management of, and reduce the expenses related to maintaining, the legacy printing system. It replaces the legacy queue-based printing with improvements in printer configuration and administration. NDPS combines the legacy printer, legacy print queue, and legacy print server into one NDS object referred to as a *Printer Agent*. Printer Agents eliminate the need to create print queues and allow users to send print jobs directly to printers. In addition, NDPS stores printer drivers within the NDS database, instead of as files stored at the workstation.

NDPS supports the legacy-based printing system by allowing users to send print jobs through legacy print queues. This compatibility allows you to implement NDPS without disrupting your current printing environment. It gives you the flexibility to implement the full features and security of NDPS at your own pace. It improves overall network performance by eliminating SAP traffic and reduces network printing problems by downloading the print drivers upon demand. This reduces administrative costs and management time by simplifying the printing environment.

NDPS provides the following features:

- **Automatic detection of new print devices (plug and print)** Once NDPS is installed and configured, any printers that are plugged into the network are immediately available to all network users.

- **Automatic print driver download and installation** The print drivers you have selected at the client workstation are automatically downloaded and installed from the server.

- **Bidirectional control of printers and print jobs** Both clients and administrators can obtain real-time information regarding printer status and job status.

- **Tight integration with NDS** NDS provides security and a single point of administration for all your printing resources. Printers can be grouped by department, workgroup, or location. Clients can search for printers with specific capabilities through the NDS properties associated with the NDPS Printer object.

- **Configurable event notification** You can specify which users, operators, and administrators receive which types of notification. Administrators can specify the events or problems they want notification messages sent for.

- **Multiple printer configurations** You can set up a printer with multiple configurations. For example, you might allow all users in a department to use a color laser printer using only the black and white capabilities, but allow certain managers to access the color capabilities.

- **Print job scheduling options** You can schedule print jobs based on time of day or size.

- **Fault tolerance** The NDPS Manager can be loaded on multiple servers, thereby providing fault tolerance. If the main NDPS Manager is shut down or aborts, another server will automatically load the NDPS Manager to manage the print environment.

- **LPR/LPD on IP** NDPS supports LPR/LPD printing on IP networks through a gateway.

NDPS Components

There are four major components of NDPS: the Printer Agent, Print Gateway, NDPS Broker, and NDPS Manager. Each of these components is shown in Figure 23-10 and discussed in the following sections.

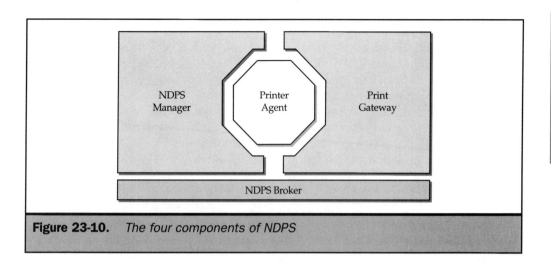

Figure 23-10.   *The four components of NDPS*

Printer Agent

The Printer Agent combines the functions of the legacy printer, print queue, and print
server into one simplified entity. All printers within NDPS must be represented by a
Printer Agent. It can be a software program running on a server that represents a
network-attached printer, a server-attached printer, a remote printer, or a workstation-
attached printer. It can also be an entity that is embedded internally in a network-
attached printer. A Printer Agent provides the following services:

- It manages print job processing and many operations performed by the printer
  itself.

- It answers network client queries about a print job, a document, or the
  attributes of the printer.

- It generates event notifications about print job completion, errors, or changes in
  the status of a print job, document, or printer.

- It allows you to print in LAN, WAN, and enterprise environments to a wide
  range of devices.

PUBLIC ACCESS PRINTERS   A public access printer is a printer that is not
registered as an NDS object in the directory tree. It is available to all users on the
network and does not take advantage of NDS security services or event notification. It
does, however, provide true plug-and-print capabilities.

CONTROLLED ACCESS PRINTERS   A controlled access printer is a printer that is
registered as an NDS object in the directory tree. It takes full advantage of NDS
security services and provides event notification. It provides tighter administrative
control for the printer than a public access printer.

Print Gateways

Printers that are not NDPS-aware must communicate with NDPS via *print gateways*. These gateways allow non-NDPS clients to send print jobs to NDPS printers, and NDPS users to send print jobs to older, non-NDPS-aware printing systems, such as UNIX, Macintosh, queue-based, and mainframe systems.

Gateways are configured to identify the specific make, model, and configuration of a printer. The gateway uses this information to translate NDPS queries and commands into printer-specific language that the printer can understand.

NetWare 5 ships with the three following NDPS gateways:

- **Hewlett-Packard Gateway**   This gateway provides access to HP printers that are non-NDPS-aware.

- **Xerox Gateway**   This gateway provides access to Xerox printers that are non-NDPS-aware.

- **Novell Gateway**   This gateway provides access to non-NDPS-aware printers that do not have a gateway written by the manufacturer. It supports local and remote printers, including those using NPRINTER or legacy queue-based technologies.

NDPS Broker

The NDPS Broker provides three network support services. It logs into NDS and authenticates to the server for each of these services. An NDPS Broker is created automatically when you install the first NetWare 5 server into an NDS tree. An additional broker is created only if you install NDPS on a server that is three hops away from the nearest existing NDPS Broker. Each of the three network support services is discussed next.

SERVICE REGISTRY SERVICES (SRS)   This service maintains information about the print device type, the device name, the device address, and device-specific information such as manufacturer and model number. It also allows public access printers to advertise themselves to the network and be discovered by administrators and users.

EVENT NOTIFICATION SERVICES (ENS)   This service allows printers to send notifications to users and operators about printer events and status. It supports a variety of notification delivery methods, including pop-up windows, log files, e-mail, and programs developed by third parties.

RESOURCE MANAGEMENT SERVICES (RMS)   This service allows resources to be installed in a central location and downloaded to either clients, printers, or any other entity on the network needing that resource. It supports adding, listing, replacing, and deleting resources, including printer drivers, printer definition files, printer fonts, and banners.

NDPS Manager

The NDPS Manager is responsible for managing Printer Agents. It is the logical entity used to create, start up, shut down, and delete Printer Agents. It is created as an object in the NDS tree. Only one NDPS Manager is allowed per network node. A single NDPS Manager can control an unlimited number of Printer Agents, as shown in Figure 23-11.

The NDPS Manager runs as an NLM on a NetWare 5 server (NDPSM.NLM). You should create an NDPS Manager for each server to which you want to assign NDPS Printer Agents. Each server can have only one NDPS Manager loaded. If a printer is directly attached to the server, you must load the NDPS Manager.

Configuring NDPS

You must have Supervisor rights to the first server in the directory tree that will have NDPS installed. For all other servers, you must have all rights except Supervisor for the container of the server on which you are installing NDPS. The server must also meet the following minimum system requirements:

- 80MB of available disk space on the SYS volume
- 4MB of RAM above the requirement for NetWare 5

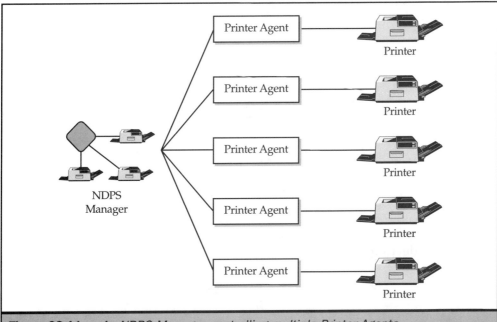

Figure 23-11. *An NDPS Manager controlling multiple Printer Agents*

An NDPS Broker is automatically installed by default during the NetWare 5 installation. A new Broker should be created only if the existing Broker cannot be found within three hops of the new server being installed.

Creating the NDPS Environment Using NetWare Administrator

You must create three objects using the NetWare Administrator utility in the NDS tree before NDPS becomes available to the network clients. Each of these objects is discussed in the following sections.

Creating and Loading an NDPS Manager

The first object to create is the NDPS Manager. This will allow you to create and manage the Printer Agents. Perform the following steps to create the NDPS Manager object:

1. Start the NetWare Administrator utility and select the container in which you want to create the NDPS Manager object.

2. Right-click the container object and select Create | NDPS Manager. The screen shown in Figure 23-12 will appear.

3. Type the desired name for the NDPS Manager in the Name dialog box. We have named ours NDPS_Manager for this example.

4. Click the Browse button to locate and select a Resident Server for the NDPS Manager.

5. Click the Browse button to locate and select the location for the database volume.

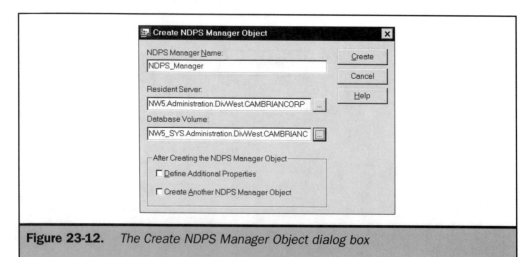

Figure 23-12. *The Create NDPS Manager Object dialog box*

6. Click the Select button to create the new NDS object.

7. Type **NDPSM NDPS_MANAGER** at the server console to start the manager. You should also include this command in the AUTOEXEC.NCF file.

Creating NDPS Printer Agents with the NDPS Manager

After you have created the NDPS Manager, your next step is to create the Printer Agents. Printer Agents represent printers that can be either public access printers or controlled access printers. Both of these printer types were discussed earlier in this chapter.

PUBLIC ACCESS PRINTERS   To create a public access printer, perform the following steps:

Note   *Remember that a public access printer does not show up in the NDS tree.*

1. Start the NetWare Administrator utility.

2. Select the NDPS Manager object you want to manage this printer and double-click the object. The screen shown in Figure 23-13 will appear.

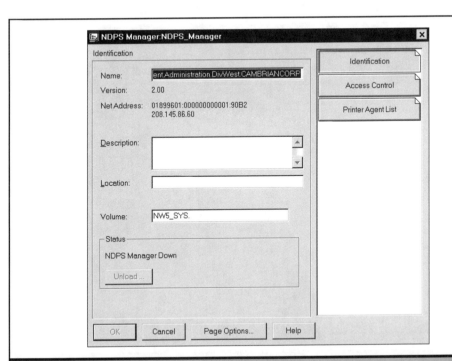

Figure 23-13.   *The Identification property page for the NDPS Manager object*

3. Click the Printer Agent List button on the Identification property page for the NDPS Manager object.

4. Click the New button from the screen shown in Figure 23-14. The screen shown in Figure 23-15 will be displayed.

5. Type the name for this Printer Agent in the top text box.

6. Select and configure the gateway type from the following list:

NOVELL PRINTER GATEWAY   This gateway provides generic functionality to all printer types. When this gateway is selected, the screen shown in Figure 23-16 will be displayed.

Perform the following steps to configure this gateway:

1. Select the connection type from the available list shown in Figure 23-17.

2. If you select Local or Remote connection type, the dialog box shown in Figure 23-18 will be displayed. Select the controller type and the appropriate interrupt.

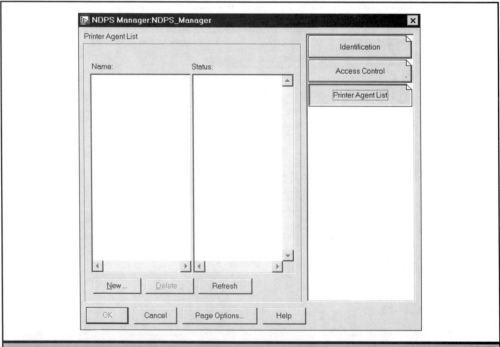

Figure 23-14.   *The known Printer Agents and their status is shown in this property page*

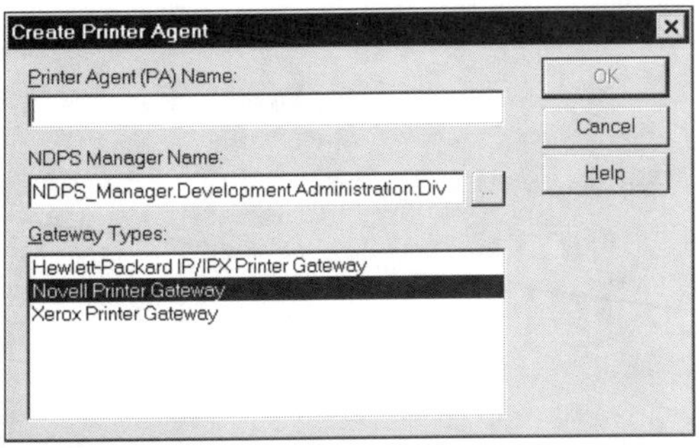

Figure 23-15. *The Create Printer Agent dialog box*

3. If you select the Remote (LPR on IP) connection type, the dialog box shown in Figure 23-19 will be displayed. Type the IP address of the printer and the Host name in the dialog box.

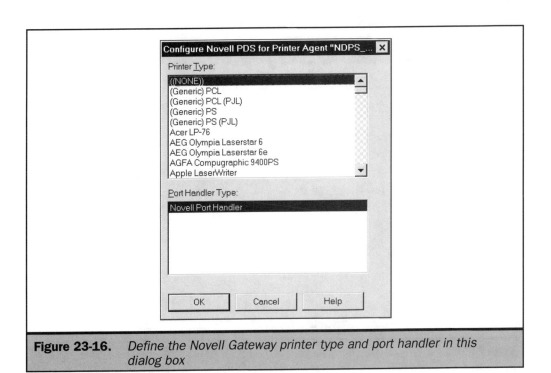

Figure 23-16. *Define the Novell Gateway printer type and port handler in this dialog box*

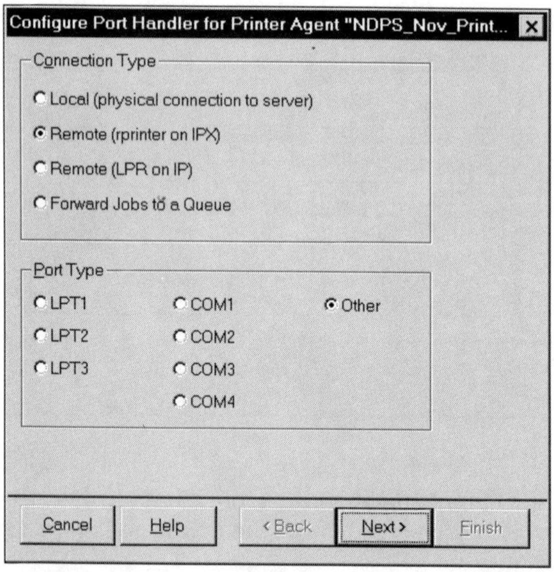

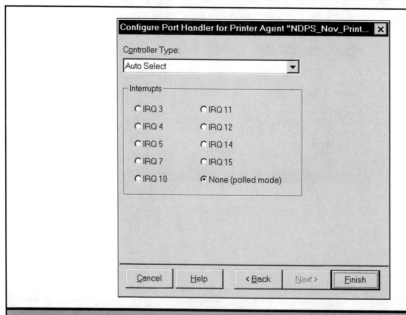

Figure 23-17. This dialog box lets you define the Novell Gateway printer connection to the network

Figure 23-18. The Novell Gateway port handler configuration screen allows you to set the controller type and interrupt

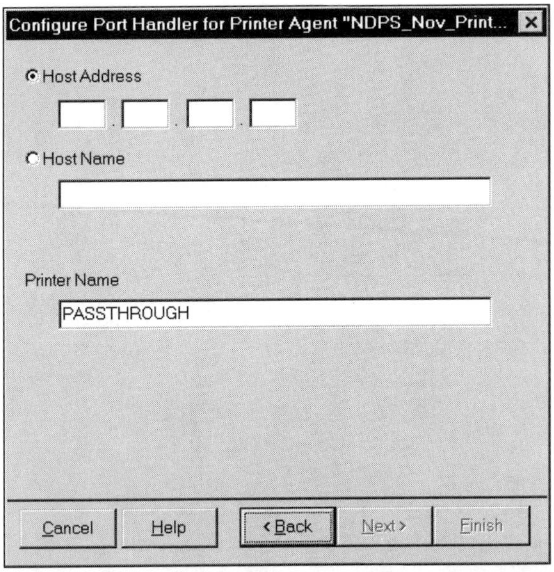

Managing the NetWare
Environment

Figure 23-19.   *The Novell Gateway Remote IP printer configuration dialog box*

4. If you select the Forward Jobs to a Queue connection type, the dialog box
   shown in Figure 23-20 will be displayed. Type the SAP Name and the IPX
   network address information in the dialog box. This configuration allows you
   to support the legacy print queue based printing environment.

HEWLETT-PACKARD GATEWAY   This gateway provides support for all Hewlett-
Packard printers and those connected to the network with a JetDirect card. When this
gateway is selected, the screen shown in Figure 23-21 will be displayed.

*This same screen will be displayed when using a HP network printer that is NDPS
aware. Software in some of the newer HP network printers can be upgraded to be NDPS
aware thereby treating a legacy printer as an NDPS printer.*

Perform the following steps to configure this gateway:

1. Select the printer type from the list displayed in Figure 23-21.

2. Select either IP or IPX as the communications protocol and enter the
   appropriate address information.

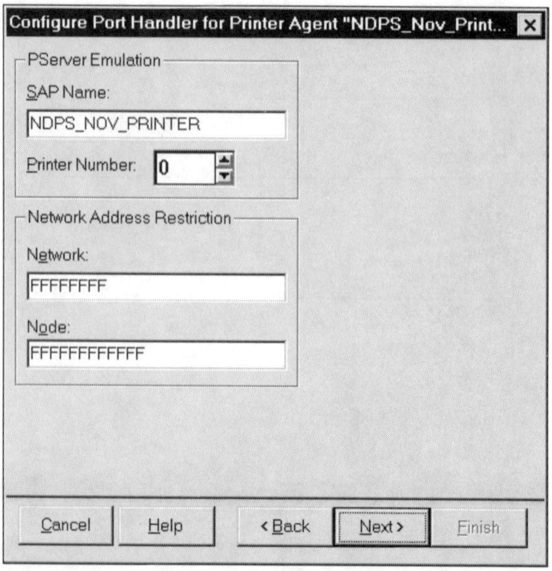

Figure 23-20. *The Novell Gateway legacy print queue configuration dialog box*

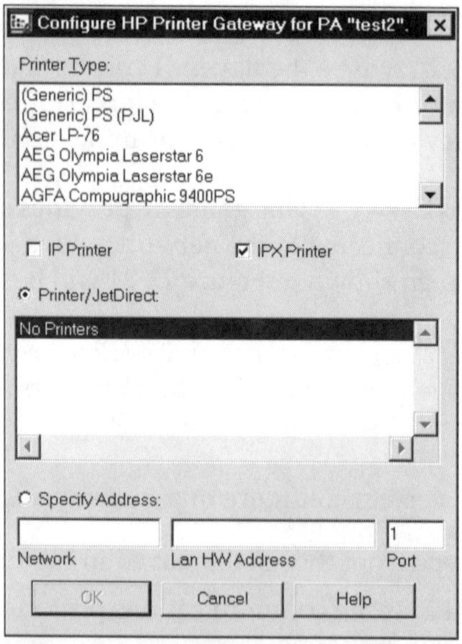

Figure 23-21. *The Hewlett-Packard Gateway configuration screen*

XEROX GATEWAY This gateway provides support for Xerox printers. When you select this gateway, the Xerox Setup Wizard is started, as shown in Figure 23-22.

CONTROLLED ACCESS PRINTERS A controlled access printer is a printer that is registered as an NDS object in the directory tree. It takes full advantage of NDS security services and provides event notification. It provides tighter administrative control for the printer than a public access printer. To create a controlled access printer perform the following steps:

1. Start the NetWare Administrator utility.

2. Select the desired container for the NDPS Printer object.

3. Right-click the container object and select Create | NDPS Printer. The dialog box shown in Figure 23-23 will be displayed.

4. Type a name for the printer in the text box.

5. Click the Create button and configure the associated gateway and NDPS Manager for the new printer. The screen shown in Figure 23-24 will be displayed showing all of the printer controls.

6. Add users by selecting the role they will have with the associated printer, as shown in Figure 23-25.

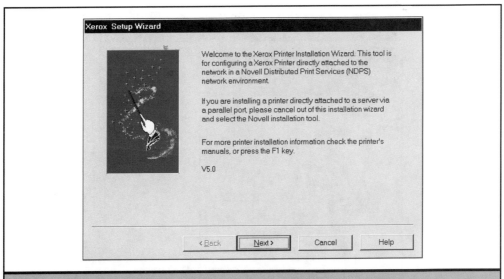

Figure 23-22. *The Xerox Setup Wizard Gateway configuration screen*

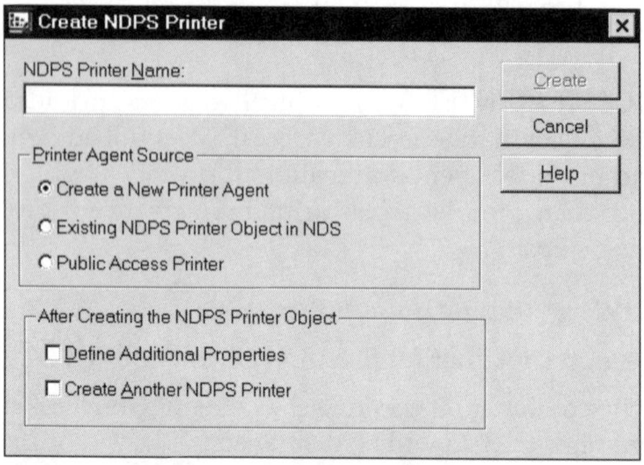

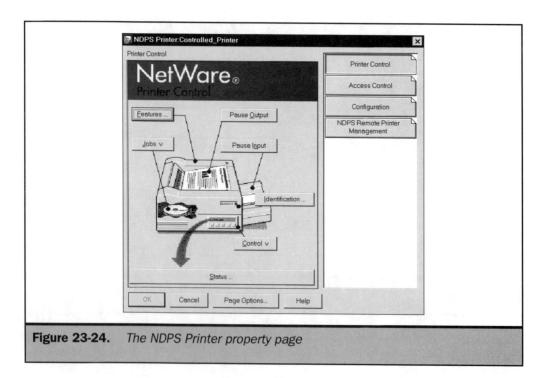

Figure 23-23. The create NDPS Printer dialog box

Configuring Workstations to use NDPS Printers

NDPS provides a printer driver database that includes drivers from most of the printer manufacturers. If the driver for your printer is not displayed in the list, you can add it to the database when it becomes available from the manufacturer.

Figure 23-24. The NDPS Printer property page

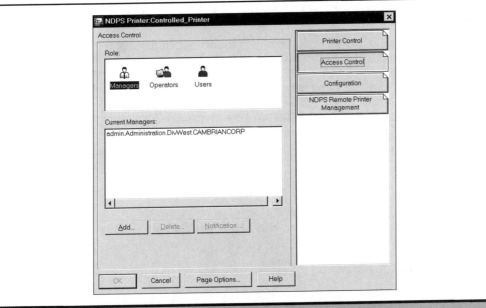

Figure 23-25. *The users associated with each role are displayed in the Access Control property page for the selected NDPS Printer*

NDPS allows you to choose the printer drivers you want to be downloaded and automatically installed on Windows 3.1, 95, 98, and NT workstations. You can configure each NDPS Printer that you create for automatic installation on each workstation within a container. With this option, the user never needs to install, configure, or designate a printer as the default on the workstation. You can configure the workstation to print to a NDPS printer in either of the following two ways:

- Configure NDS to download the printer drivers and configuration to the workstation automatically.
- Manually configure the workstation using the Novell Print Manager utility.

Note   *Workstations must have Client32 version 2.2 or higher installed to use NDPS.*

Perform the following steps to enable the automatic download of the associated printer drivers to the workstations in a specific container:

1. Start the NetWare Administrator utility.

2. Select the desired container.

3. Right-click the container object and select Details.

4. Select the NDPS Remote Printer Management property page. The screen shown in Figure 23-26 will be displayed.

5. Click the Add button to add printers to the installation list for workstations in the container.

Perform the following steps to manually install a printer on a workstation:

1. Run NWPM32 at the workstation. This program is located in the PUBLIC/WIN32 directory on the file server.

2. Click the New button on the Printer menu. A list of installed printers will be displayed in the dialog box.

3. Click the Add button. A list of available printers will be displayed in the dialog box.

4. Select the desired printer and click the Install button.

5. Click the OK button.

6. Click the Close button.

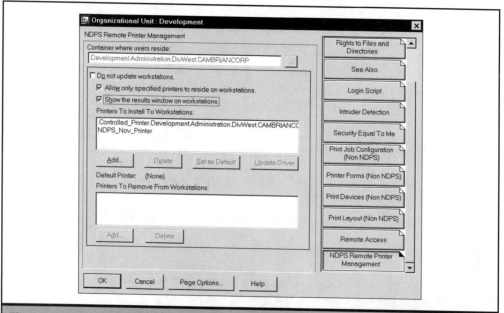

Figure 23-26. *The NDPS Remote Printer Management page displays the printer drivers that are to be downloaded to the workstations in the selected container*

> **Tip**
>
> *Only the printers defined in the NDPS database will be displayed. If you want to add new printers to the database, do this via the Add New Printers button on the Resources property page of the NDPS broker.*

Testing the NDPS Configuration

You can validate the NDPS configuration without physically connecting printers to the network. This trick comes from the developer side of the house. NetWare 5 has the ability to redirect printer output to the console screen instead of a physical printing device. This allows you to send print jobs to NDPS and watch the job print to the screen. Perform the following steps to enable printer output to the console screen:

1. At the server console, type **[LOAD] PH SHOW**. This command will show the current configuration for all of the loaded print handlers for each printer agent.

2. Type **UNLOAD PH**. This command will prompt you with a list of loaded print handlers. Select the one you want to unload and redirect to the console screen.

3. Type **[LOAD] PH PRINTERAGENT=***name_of_printer_agent* **PORT=SCREEN**. Type the name of the printer agent in the *name_of_printer_agent* field. You do not have to type the complete path to the agent.

4. Switch to the NDPS Manager screen on the server console.

5. Select the printer from the Printer Agent List display screen.

6. Select the Configuration option from displayed printer.

7. Select the proper gateway and printer type for the simulated print device.

8. Send output from a workstation to the selected NDPS printer. The output will appear on the server screen associated with that printer.

> **Tip**
>
> *When entering new printers via the Resources property page in the NDPS Broker object be aware that NDPS will not search multiple directories for printer driver files. If the driver files for the new printer are located in more than one directory or subdirectory, copy all of the driver files into the one directory for that device, then NDPS will see all the driver files.*

Chapter 24

Login Scripts

L ogin scripts are critical for setting up the environments of network users. A login script is a series of commands that executes when a user logs in. The commands placed in login scripts set up the general working environment for users and can map network drives, switch to specific drives, display messages and menus, and start applications. You can use IF...THEN statements in login scripts to execute commands that are based on the day of the week, the user's membership in a group, the type of workstation the user has, or other variables.

Types of Login Scripts

When any user logs into the network, a *default login script* executes, which sets a few essential environment settings for users. However, administrators (and users) can override the default login script by creating a *user login script* or by using the NO_DEFAULT command.

Two other login scripts are the *container login script* and the *profile login script*. A description of each type of login script follows:

- **Default login script** This login script executes as part of the LOGIN command and cannot be changed, but it can be overridden by creating a user login script. This login script sets up the basic environment, which includes mapping the SYS:PUBLIC directory so users can execute network commands.

- **Container login script** Each container object can have one login script that executes for each user that logs into the container. This login script is where you place commands that you want to execute for all users who belong to a container object.

- **Profile login script** This login script will execute for users anywhere on the network, not just in one container. Users can be assigned only one profile login script, but they can execute other profile login scripts at the command line. You might create a profile login script for department managers that displays special messages or drive mappings.

- **User login script** User login scripts execute after any container or profile login scripts. Users can edit their own user login scripts by default, although you can change this right. Because users can change their own user login script, they can create mappings for their own personal directories (home directories) and set other environment variables as necessary.

The most important thing to keep in mind is that you'll want to create container or profile login scripts that are as generic as possible and avoid creating user login scripts, which can be tedious. By default, users can change their own user login scripts, so unless you change this right, users might change the work you do on user login scripts. Remember that container login scripts execute for every user in a container, so you should first have users with similar network requirements grouped into the same container, and then set as many environment variables as you can in the container login script for the container. Login scripts work the same way for DOS, Windows 95/98, and Windows NT, although some of the login script commands may work differently on NT workstations.

The default login script runs if a user login script has not been created. This is true even when container and profile login scripts execute. However, if the NO_DEFAULT command is executed in the container or profile script, the Default script will not be executed.

How and When Login Scripts Execute

When a user logs in, the container login script executes first, followed by any profile login script, and then the user login script. The order is important. You want to set general environment settings for all users that belong to a container in the container login script, and then execute specific commands for users who fit a specific profile (managers, network administrators, temporary help, and so on) in a profile login script. Finally, user login scripts contain commands that are specific to a single user. To avoid creating a lot of login scripts, concentrate on putting as many commands in container login scripts as possible.

Be careful not to overwrite drive mappings or change environment settings that might have been set in other login scripts. Be aware of which letters are mapped to which drives. If you map drive G for all users in a container to a document directory, don't overwrite that drive mapping in a profile or user login script unless you really want to.

Options for Logging In

When users log in, they are presented with the screen shown in Figure 24-1. They can choose whether they want their login scripts to run or not, or whether they want to run a different login script or a different profile script.

SELECTING NOT TO RUN SCRIPTS   Uncheck this option to bypass all login scripts. Administrators can do this when troubleshooting to bypass existing login scripts or set up new environments. No search drives are mapped, and your default directory is the LOGIN directory. You'll need to switch to the PUBLIC directory and manually execute MAP commands to set up search drives so you can work in other directories with NetWare commands.

USING ANOTHER LOGIN SCRIPT   A better way to bypass your login script is to specify an alternative login script. Create a text file with a login script command such as MAP on a DOS drive and then select the login script in the Login Script text box. Include a command to map a search drive to the PUBLIC directory in the text file. For example, to log in as the ADMIN user to the CambrianCorp organization and run the commands in a text file called LOGIN.TXT on local drive C, type **C:\LOGIN.TXT** in the Login Script text box.

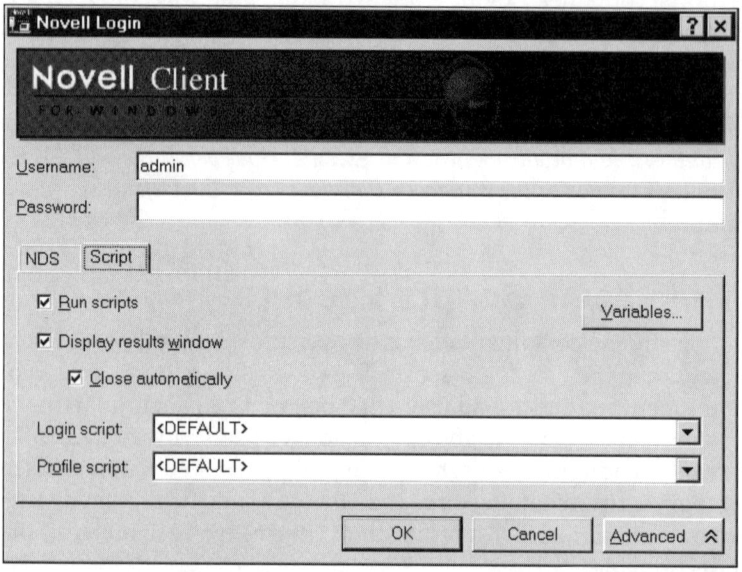

Figure 24-1.   *The Novell Client login script dialog box*

USING A PROFILE SCRIPT   You can direct LOGIN to run a login script that belongs to a profile object or a container object. Enter the name of the object in the Profile Script text box. It can be a DOS path, a UNC path, or an object in the NDS tree. The login script within that object executes when you log in. Note the following regarding the use of the Profile Script option:

- You must specify the complete directory services path (context) of the object unless you are already in the same context as the object. If the context is a long name and you log in this way often, create a batch file.

- You can only specify the Profile Script option once per login. In other words, you can't run one profile login script and then another immediately after it.

The Importance of the INCLUDE Command

In NetWare 5, users log into a specific context of the directory tree unless they are using the contextless login capability. Even with this, you must build an LDAP catalog that maps the user to a specific context within the NDS tree. The login script in the container of that context then runs. In addition, you can assign a user a profile login script, and then include specific commands in a user login script. Besides all of these options, you still have one more way to customize the login script: using the INCLUDE command.

INCLUDE is a login script command that can "call" a separate text file or another object that contains its own login script commands. By using INCLUDE statements in login scripts, you can set up external general login script files that can be called from many different login scripts. For example, you might have a set of commands that sets up an environment for word processing users (that is, maps a program and document directory) or another set of commands that sets special commands for managers. You don't need to type the commands in every login script. Instead, you would insert an INCLUDE statement that calls an external file containing the commands. Then, if the commands need to change, you can change them in the external text file, and all the login scripts that call it are automatically updated.

There is another useful way to use the INCLUDE statement. It involves creating and managing commands that must execute for all the login scripts in all the containers of your network. A simple analogy will help here.

Assume you are the administrator of the entire network and you have assigned subadministrators to manage branches of your directory tree. The subadministrators create the container login scripts for their departments or divisions. However, you want to display a company-wide message when any user logs on. This message might include company-wide announcements for the day or notices about copyrights, licensing, or other legal information. The information changes constantly, so you want to control its content from a single location.

First, you instruct all the department managers to insert a command similar to the following in their container login scripts:

```
INCLUDE SYS:MESSAGES\LOGIN.TXT
```

This example assumes that the file is stored on a SYS volume that is local to users. If you centrally locate the file on a single volume, you'll need to include the full context of the volume in the command. You can include WRITE commands that display lines of text, DISPLAY commands that list the contents of external text files, or other login script commands within the message file.

Users must have the Read right to the external files that are called by the INCLUDE command. If you store all of these files in one directory, you can globally grant all users on the network Read rights to it by granting the [Public] entity those rights. Recall that all users have the same rights as [Public], which is located in the [Root]. You can grant [Public] rights to a directory on a file server by selecting the directory in NetWare Administrator, and then making [Public] (in the [Root]) a trustee with Read rights.

Keep in mind that this analogy works best for small local networks in which the text files called by login scripts are on a local server. In a global environment, you would need to copy your external login script files to volumes on servers in the local environment so that users are not calling them from across a WAN link.

The Default Login Script

The default login script runs by default for every user that logs in unless the user has created a user login script, unchecked the Run Scripts check box in the client login screen, or has executed the NO_DEFAULT command in a prior script.

If users create user login scripts or use the NO_DEFAULT command, you must make sure that they retain a mapping to the SYS:PUBLIC directory on their local server so they can execute NetWare public commands. You can put this command in the container login script if necessary or just make sure users put it in their user login script.

Here's the default login script. You should become familiar with its structure and use similar commands in your own login script. Each command is discussed individually in later sections of this chapter. A brief explanation of each line is provided following the example.

```
1.  MAP DISPLAY OFF
2.  MAP ERRORS OFF
3.  MAP *1:SYS:
4.  MAP *1:=SYS:%LOGIN_NAME
5.  IF "%1"="ADMIN" THEN MAP *1:=SYS:SYSTEM
6.  MAP INS S1:=SYS:PUBLIC
7.  MAP DISPLAY ON
8.  MAP
```

The parameters with percent signs are login script identifiers that represent variables in the user's environment, such as the name supplied when logging in or the version of Windows running on the system. These are described later in this chapter, under "Login Script Identifier Variables" and listed in Table 24-1.

- **Line 1** This prevents MAP commands from displaying messages. It is used for aesthetic reasons.

- **Line 2** This prevents errors from displaying.

- **Line 3** This maps the first drive to the SYS volume. This mapping is used

- only if the user does not have a home directory; otherwise, the next command overrides it.

- **Line 4** This maps the first drive to the user's home directory. If it doesn't exist, the mapping in line 3 is preserved.

- **Line 5** If the user logging in is ADMIN, the MAP command following the THEN statement executes in this line, mapping the SYSTEM directory to the first network drive.

- **Line 6** This maps a search drive to the SYS:PUBLIC directory.

- **Line 7**   This restores the display of mapping information.
- **Line 8**   This displays a list of mapped drives.

After the last command executes, the user sees a command prompt, along with the list of mapped drives. These commands are discussed in more detail, with examples, under "Login Script Commands," later in this chapter.

Creating and Changing Login Scripts

To create new login scripts or change login scripts, first determine which type of login script you want to work with—container, profile, or user. Then use NetWare Administrator to edit the login scripts. The steps for accessing the editing screens of each type of login script in NetWare Administrator are described here:

- **Container login script**   Double-click the container where you want to create or edit the login script to open its details dialog box, and then click the Login Script button.
- **Profile login script**   Create a Profile object if it doesn't yet exist in a container that is appropriate for the users who will get the profile. When the Profile object appears, double-click it to open its details dialog box, and then click the Login Script button.
- **User login script**   In NetWare Administrator, double-click a User object, and then click the Login Script button.

More About Profile Login Scripts

To create a profile login script, you first create the Profile object; then (in NetWare Administrator), open the details dialog box for the Profile object and click the Login Script button to edit the login script.

After creating the Profile object and editing the login script, you assign users to the profile. In NetWare Administrator, double-click the User object, and then click the Login Script button. At the bottom of the Login Script page, you see the following Profile field:

Type the name of the profile login script in the field, or click the Browse button on the right to browse through the directory tree for the Profile object.

   At a minimum, you will have to assign the Read right to the login script property of the Profile object in order for the user to use it. This can be done using a container, group, or User object as the trustee.

Editing Login Scripts

When you click the Login Script button on the container, Profile, or User object details dialog box, you see a screen similar to the one shown in Figure 24-2. It contains an editing window, and you can use the HOME, END, DEL, and arrow keys to move around in the window.

In NetWare Administrator, you can highlight blocks of text and use the Cut (CTRL-X), Copy (CTRL-C), and Paste (CTRL-V) commands to move them about. Text removed with the DEL key is held in a buffer and can be inserted elsewhere by pressing the INS key.

Note the following rules for editing login scripts:

- Only users with the Supervisor right can edit the container login script. Users can edit their own user login scripts unless that right has been revoked. Supervisors can grant any user the rights to change a profile login script.

- To run a DOS program from the login script on a DOS machine, precede the executable program name with a pound sign (#). To run a DOS command in the login script, use the following form, replacing *filename* with the command to run:

    # COMMAND *filename* /C

- To run a program from the login script on a Windows machine, precede the executable program name with a percent sign (%). Use the following form, replacing *filename* with the executable name:

    %filename

- Text in a command line cannot exceed 150 characters. For clarity, try to use only 78 characters, which is the width of the edit window.

- Only one type of command per line is allowed, but you can place multiple drive maps on the same line. Just separate them with a semicolon. It is OK for the line to wrap to another line.

Login Script Identifier Variables

Login script identifier variables are your key to creating login scripts that run in a specific way for each user. You can have commands in the login scripts execute based on the value of variables in the user's environment. The most common usage is to assign a name to a computer when it boots, and then run commands in the login script based on the type of machine the user is using. For example, if you name a computer IBMDOS2, you can set NetWare search paths to directories that contain IBM DOS or IBM utilities. Each variable is described briefly in Table 24-1.

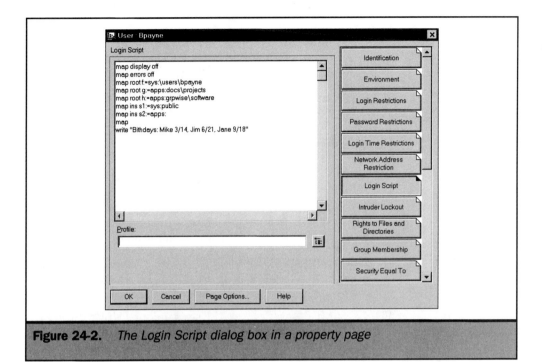

Figure 24-2.   *The Login Script dialog box in a property page*

Category	Variable Name	Function
Date	DAY	Day number (01 through 31)
	DAY_OF_WEEK	Day of week (Monday, etc.)
	MONTH	Month number (01 through 12)
	MONTH_NAME	Month name (January, etc.)
	NDAY_OF_WEEK	Day of week number (1 through 7; 1 = Sunday)
	SHORT_YEAR	Last two digits of the year (98, 99, etc.)
	YEAR	All four digits of the year (1999, 2000, etc.)

Table 24-1.   *Login Script Identifier Variables*

Category	Variable Name	Function
Time	AM_PM	Day or night (A.M. or P.M.)
	GREETING_TIME	Time of day (morning, afternoon, or evening)
	HOUR	Hour (12-hour scale)
	HOUR24	Hour (24-hour scale)
	MINUTE	Minute (00 through 59)
	SECOND	Second (00 through 59)
User	%CN	User's full login name if it exists in the NDS tree
	LOGIN_ALIAS_CONTEXT	"Y" if REQUESTER_CONTEXT is an alias
	FULL_NAME	User's unique FULL_NAME property from NDS (with underscores replacing spaces)
	LAST_NAME	User's last name (surname) in NDS or full login name in bindery-based NetWare
	LOGIN_CONTEXT	Context in which user exists
	LOGIN_NAME	User's unique login name (long names are truncated to eight characters)
	MEMBER OF *"group"*	Group object to which the user is assigned
	NOT MEMBER OF *"group"*	Group object to which the user is not assigned
	PASSWORD_EXPIRES	Number of days before the password expires
	REQUESTER_CONTEXT	Context in which login process started

Table 24-1.   *Login Script Identifier Variables* (continued)

Category	Variable Name	Function
	USER_ID	Unique number assigned to each user
Network	FILE_SERVER	NetWare server name
	NETWORK_ADDRESS	IPX external network number of the cabling system (8-digit hexadecimal)
Workstation	MACHINE	Type of computer (IBM_PC, etc.)
	NETWARE_REQUESTER	Version of the VLM-based NetWare requester
	OS	Type of operating system on the workstation (MS-DOS, OS/2, etc.)
	OS_VERSION	Operating system version on the workstation (6.0, etc.)
	P_STATION	Workstation's node number (12-digit hexadecimal)
	PLATFORM	Workstation's operating system platform (DOS, OS/2, WIN, WIN95, WIN98, WNT)
	SHELL_TYPE	Version of the workstation's DOS shell
	SMACHINE	Short machine name (IBM, etc.)
	STATION	Workstation's connection number
	WINVER	Version of the workstation's Windows operating system
NetWare Mobile	DIALUP	Client dialup profile (0 = not using dialup; 1 = using NetWare mobile)
	OFFLINE	0 = not offline; 1 = disconnected login

Table 24-1. *Login Script Identifier Variables* (continued)

Category	Variable Name	Function
DOS Environment	*variable*	Any DOS environment variable Comments: To use a DOS environment variable in MAP, COMSPEC, and FIRE PHASERS commands, add a percent sign (%) in front of the variable.
Misc.	ACCESS_SERVER	Shows whether the access server is functional (TRUE = functional, FALSE = not functional)
	ERROR_LEVEL	An error number (0 = no errors)
	%n	Replaced by parameters the user enters at the command line with the LOGIN utility
Object Properties	*%property name*	Property values of NDS objects used as variables Comments: If the property value includes a space, enclose the name in quotation marks. To use a property name with a space within a WRITE command, you must place it at the end of the quoted string.

Table 24-1. *Login Script Identifier Variables* (continued)

Another method is to identify variables in the user environment after they are authenticated. For example, after a user logs in, you can identify any property of their User object, such as LAST NAME, FULL NAME, LOGIN CONTEXT, LOGIN NAME, CN, and LOGIN ALIAS CONTEXT. Just look at the property names on the details

Managing the NetWare Environment

dialog box for any User object to get an idea of the values you can work with. Typically, you use them in IF...THEN statements such as the following:

```
IF %TITLE="Vice President" THEN DISPLAY VP.TXT
```

where the property called TITLE is compared to "Vice President." If they match, the text file VP.TXT (which might contain important messages or updated news for vice presidents) is displayed. Not all property values can be used in this way, or some may not work as expected. You can create a login script that lists the value of fields when users log in for informational purposes, as explained at the end of this chapter.

 You can also use the variables with the NLIST command, either at the command line or in login scripts.

 This section might be a little confusing if you're just learning about login scripts. You might want to browse through this section to see what variables are available, and then refer back here later after reading through the rest of the chapter.

Some variables are automatically set by NetWare, such as the date and time. For example, the following WRITE command displays the message "Good Morning," "Good Afternoon," or "Good Evening." The variable %GREETING_TIME inserts "Morning," "Afternoon," or "Evening" based on the current time of day.

The *%property* variable is most useful. You can reference any field in a User object's details dialog box. For example, if someone has the nickname "Mr. Know-it-all" in the Other Name field, you could display that name during login with the following command:

```
WRITE "Good %GREETING_TIME %OTHER_NAME"
```

This would display the following if the user logs in during morning hours:

```
Good Morning Mr. Know-it-all
```

Most of the variables are used with the WRITE command. WRITE displays any text between quotation marks as messages. When used in this way, variables must be typed in uppercase and preceded with a percent sign, as shown in the previous example.

You use variables in login scripts to provide every user with a unique login script, based on the values the user's environment supplies. For example, the login script can execute a set of commands if a user belongs to a group, such as Managers or Clerks. The names of groups a user belongs to are pulled from the user's object during the login process.

> **Note** *To include a variable in a WRITE command text string, type it in uppercase. For clarity, and to make your login script easier to examine at a later time, type all variables in uppercase. You may want to set All Caps on when creating login scripts to avoid the problem of not using uppercase for variables within the quotes for the WRITE command.*

Some information comes from the environment of the user's workstation, such as the DOS type and version number. By default, all machines have the name IBM_PC, but you can specify other names such as COMPAQ or IBMPS2.

Login Script Commands

The following sections explain each of the login script commands and options. They are broken down into five specific groups that relate to their functionality. Some command-specific examples are given. See "Login Script Examples," at the end of this chapter, for examples of how you can use the commands in the context of a complete login script.

Network Connection and Access to Resources

ATTACH

Use the ATTACH command to attach to a bindery-based file server that is running NetWare 2 or NetWare 3. This command is not necessary with NetWare servers running NDS. The command takes the following form:

ATTACH *servername/username; password*

where *servername* is the name of the server to attach to, *username* is the login name of the current user on the server, and *password* is the password required to gain access to the system.

ATTACH can be used in container login scripts to attach all users in the context to a bindery-based server, but do not include the password variable in the command. In this way, each user is prompted for a password and security is not compromised. Users who need to attach to other servers on a regular basis should place the command in their user login scripts.

EXAMPLE   The following command is placed in an AColgan user login script to attach her to the server ACCTG:

```
ATTACH ACCTG/AColgan
```

CONTEXT

The CONTEXT command displays the current context and can be used to change the user's context in the Directory Services tree. You can use this command to change the context for the specific user logging in. The command takes the following form:

> CONTEXT *context*

where *context* is the location in the directory tree where the user should be placed. Once a user is set in a particular context, he or she will see objects and containers at that level of the tree when using commands such as NLIST and NetWare Administrator.

You can use IF...THEN statements to specify the context, based on the groups a user belongs to or a variable pulled from the client login dialog box (see %*n* in Table 24-1).

EXAMPLE   The following command demonstrates how you would switch a user to the DivWest department in the CambrianCorp organization:

```
CONTEXT DivWest.CambrianCorp
```

DRIVE

Use the DRIVE command in a login script to switch users to a mapped drive. The first drive mapped normally becomes the default drive for the user after the login script completes. Typically, this is drive F and it is mapped to the user's home directory (although this is not mandatory). To switch to another mapped drive, use the DRIVE command. It is sometimes necessary to do this when you are running commands that execute only if users are in the directory where the commands are located. After executing such commands, include another DRIVE command to place users back in their personal directories. The DRIVE command takes the following form:

> DRIVE *n*:

where *n* is a drive letter, or

> DRIVE **n*:

where *n* is a drive number. In the first form, the command switches to a drive that was mapped earlier in the login script. In the second form, the user is switched to the *n*th drive, a drive that may have been reordered due to the deletion of a previously mapped drive.

EXAMPLE   The following command switches a user to drive R, which was mapped by a previous command in the login script:

```
DRIVE R:
```

MAP

The MAP command is used extensively in login scripts to establish the mappings for all users and selected users. The command takes the following form:

MAP *option drive*:=*path*

where *drive* is the drive letter you want to map and *path* is the directory to map. You might need to specify the NDS directory tree context in *path*. Replace *option* with one of the following:

- **DISPLAY ON/OFF**   As drives are mapped in a login script, they are displayed on the screen. Use this option to turn this display off to avoid screen clutter. If you want to display a user's drive mappings, include the MAP command on the last line of the login script.

- **ERRORS ON/OFF**   When errors are encountered during a login script, the error messages are not displayed if this command is used. In some cases you might use the IF...THEN...ELSE command in a way that produces errors for some users even though the errors are not serious, because processing would continue with the next statement. You can use the MAP ERRORS OFF command to suppress the error messages. It is recommended that you not use this command until the login script has been completely tested and debugged.

- **INS**   Inserts the drive mapping between existing search mappings.

- **DEL**   Deletes a drive mapping and makes the drive letter available so it can be used for other drive mappings.

- **ROOT**   Maps the directory as a fake root. To the user, the mapping appears as the root of the drive and the user cannot move up the directory tree or see higher directories, even though they may exist.

> **Tip**   *It is good practice to use root mappings. With them, the user cannot move closer toward the root of the volume than the directory level of the root mapping. Also, this provides for consistency since drive mappings in Explorer are root mappings.*

- **C (Change)**   Changes a search drive mapping to a regular mapping, and a regular mapping to a search drive mapping.

- **P (Physical)**   Maps a drive to the physical volume of a server, rather than to the Volume object's name.

- **N (Next)**   Maps the next available drive if you don't specify a drive letter or number.

MAPPING THE "NEXT" DRIVE   It's not always a good idea to map a specific letter in the alphabet to a directory. For example, mapping drive F to a user's personal directory may work if the user logs in at a machine that has a last drive of D or E. But if the workstation has local drives called F, there will be a drive letter conflict. Use the *n*th drive option when you're not sure of the drive lettering where a user is logging in. An *n*th drive mapping takes the following form:

MAP *n:=path*

where *n* is a number that specifies network drive 1, 2, and so on. In other words, the command MAP *1:=SYS:APPS is like saying "Map the first network drive, whatever it may be, to the SYS:APPS directory." On some systems, that drive letter may be F, while on others it might be G or H. Remember that local drives can include hard disks, optical disks, and RAM disks, so the number of letters for local drives can be great.

MAPPING DIRECTORY MAP OBJECTS   Recall that one of the objects available in Novell Directory Services is the Directory Map object. The Directory Map object contains a drive mapping that you can change at any time. If you include the Directory Map object in login scripts, you can easily change the mappings for all login scripts at the same time by changing the Directory Map object. It is usually necessary to change directory maps if you decide to move programs or files in directories that are mapped by many different login scripts. In the following example, the Directory Map object LOTUS in the Administration Organizational Unit object is mapped to search drive S3:

```
MAP S3:=.LOTUS.Administration.DivWest.CambrianCorp
```

MAPPING TO ANOTHER CONTEXT   Directories on volumes within a user's current context can be mapped by simply specifying the volume name and directory path. If you need to map a directory on another volume that is not in the same context as the user, you must specify that context. For example, the following command maps a directory called CUSTDATA on a volume and server in the Sales department to a user in the Administration department, assuming the Administration container is the user's current context:

```
MAP R:= SYS.Sales.DivEast.CambrianCorp:CUSTDATA
```

TREE
The TREE command can only be used with clients that support multiple NDS tree attachments. You use it to attach to another NDS tree within your network and access its resources. The TREE command changes the "focus" of your login script so that all NDS object references in subsequent script commands apply to the NDS tree specified in the TREE command. You can include multiple TREE commands within the login scripts. The command takes the following form:

TREE *tree_name* [/*complete_name*[;*password*]]

where *tree_name* is the name of the NDS tree that you want to attach to, *complete_name* is the user's distinguished NDS name for the NDS tree you are attaching to, and *password* is the correct password for that user and tree.

EXAMPLE To attach to another NDS tree named CORP as the user .bpayne.corp with the password testpswd, add the following to the bpayne user login script:

```
TREE CORP/.bpayne.corp;testpswd
```

Login Script Execution

BREAK

When the BREAK ON command is included in a login script, users logging in can stop the script by pressing CTRL-BREAK or CTRL-C. The BREAK OFF command is used to prevent a break in the login script.

This command is typically included when testing login scripts, or to provide a way to stop the execution of certain commands when you don't want to execute them for the current session. Place PAUSE and WAIT commands before the point at which you want to break so the script pauses. Then you can press CTRL-BREAK or CTRL-C to stop the login script, or any other key to continue with commands. All commands after the break do not execute. The command takes the following forms:

BREAK ON
BREAK OFF

When BREAK ON is specified, type-ahead keyboard input is not saved in the buffer.

Note that BREAK can be turned on for small segments of a login script, and then turned off again to prevent breakout.

FIRE PHASERS

Use the FIRE PHASERS command to generate sounds that alert users to messages on the screen. The command takes the following form:

FIRE PHASERS *n* TIMES

where *n* is the number of times you want to fire the phasers.

EXAMPLES The phasers are fired five times in the following example:

```
FIRE PHASERS 5 TIMES
```

Fire phasers only under certain conditions by using the IF...THEN BEGIN command. In the following example, a WRITE command displays a message, phasers are fired, and the PAUSE command pauses execution of the login script so the user can read the message:

```
IF DAY_OF_WEEK = "Monday" THEN BEGIN
    WRITE "Meetings are every Monday at 3:00"
    FIRE PHASERS 2 TIMES
    PAUSE
END
```

Note *Use phasers sparingly. Many users find the sound irritating.*

GOTO

The GOTO command lets you branch to a different part of the login script, usually when a condition evaluated by the IF...THEN command is met. For example, you could include the following command to branch to a label called MANAGERS: if the user belongs to a group called Managers:

```
IF MEMBER OF "MANAGERS" THEN GOTO MANAGERS
```

The label that the command branches to must include a colon, as shown here:

```
MANAGERS:
```

Note *Do not use GOTO within multiline IF...THEN commands.*

IF...THEN

The IF...THEN command is one of the most useful commands for login scripts. You can use it to execute commands only when a specific condition is met. An IF...THEN command evaluates the truth or equality of a condition, and then executes commands if true. For example, in the FIRE PHASERS example, a WRITE command and FIRE PHASERS are executed if the day of the week is Monday. The IF...THEN command takes the following form:

IF *conditional(s)* [AND;OR;NOR] THEN *command*

THE ELSE OPTION In the following example, the optional ELSE is used on a separate line, followed by an END command to close the IF...THEN:

IF *conditional(s)* [AND;OR;NOR] THEN
    (*commands to execute*)
    ELSE
    (*commands to execute*)
END

The *conditional* argument is evaluated, and if true, the commands following the THEN statement are executed. If false, the commands following the optional ELSE statement are executed. You can include another IF statement after ELSE to evaluate a true condition for executing commands under ELSE. If the condition is not true, the entire IF...THEN...ELSE command sequence is bypassed. You must place an END statement at the end of the sequence for each IF...THEN command.

THE BEGIN OPTION   In the following example, if the condition is true, a series of commands is executed on one or more lines following a BEGIN statement until the END statement is encountered. If the condition is false, the commands are skipped, and processing of the login script continues with commands following the END statement.

```
IF conditional(s) THEN BEGIN
    (commands to execute if true go here)
END
```

EXAMPLES   The IF...THEN command typically evaluates the condition of identifier variables. Here are three examples:

```
IF DAY_OF_WEEK="Monday" THEN ...

IF MEMBER OF "TEMPS" THEN ...

IF NOT MEMBER OF "TEMPS" THEN ...
```

The first example is similar to the statements previously described under the FIRE PHASERS command. The commands following THEN are executed if the day of the week is Monday. In the second example, commands are executed if the user is a member of the group Temps. The last example is just the opposite—commands are executed only if the user is *not* a member of the group Temps. Note the following:

- Values of conditionals must be enclosed in quotation marks.
- A WRITE command must be on a separate line.
- You can nest up to ten IF...THEN statements.
- END must be included when the IF...THEN statements have a BEGIN and use more than one line.

You can place the IF...THEN command anywhere in a login script, and you can use it more than once. As mentioned, the command takes two forms. In the first form, the entire statement takes up one line, as shown here:

```
IF DAY_OF_WEEK = "Monday" THEN WRITE "Wake up, you!"
```

The second form of the command encompasses two or more lines between BEGIN and END statements. All commands between BEGIN and END are executed if the condition is true. Each command must be typed on a separate line. In the following example, MAP commands are executed if a user is a member of the group Managers. Note that indenting sets off the commands between IF and END for clarity.

```
IF MEMBER OF "MANAGERS" THEN BEGIN
    MAP H:=SYS:MGR-DATA
    MAP I:=SYS:ACCTDATA
    MAP INS S3:=SYS:MGR-PROG
END
```

Because the mapped drives and search drives are only meant for managers, users who belong to the group Managers will get the drive mappings. You can write similar statements for other groups.

CONDITIONAL RELATIONSHIPS   Six relationships can be evaluated with the IF...THEN command. These are listed in Table 24-2. In addition, you can use AND, OR, and NOR to form compound conditionals in which commands execute only if all the conditions are true together. In the following example, the manager's news file is displayed if the user belongs to the Managers group and if the day is Monday.

```
IF MEMBER OF "MANAGERS" AND DAY_OF_WEEK = "Monday"
THEN DISPLAY SYS:NEWS\MGRNEWS
```

Note   *The preceding command should be typed on one line.*

Symbol	Relationship
=	Equal to
<>	Not equal to
>	Greater than
<	Less than
>=	Greater than or equal to
<=	Less than or equal to

Table 24-2.   *Relationships Evaluated by IF...THEN*

EVALUATING COMMAND-LINE PARAMETERS Parameters from the command line, such as the server name and user login name, are variables you can capture and use in login scripts. Each parameter has a parameter number. The command itself (LOGIN) is parameter %0. The second parameter is parameter %1, and so on. For example, in the following command, the server name EMAIL is parameter %1 and JJONES is parameter %2:

```
LOGIN EMAIL/JJONES
```

To use a parameter in a login script, simply insert its identifier variable in a command. For example, if JJONES types the following to log in:

```
LOGIN STARSHIP/JJONES ACCTG
```

then parameter %3 (ACCTG) can be used in the login script with a command like the following to attach the user to the server:

```
IF %3="ACCTG" ATTACH ACCTG
```

This command would be interpreted as "If parameter %3 is equal to ACCTG, attach to the ACCTG server." You can simplify this to "ATTACH %3."

EVALUATING GROUP MEMBERSHIP CONDITIONS You can evaluate whether a user is or is not a member of a group using the MEMBER OF or NOT MEMBER OF option with your IF...THEN commands. The commands take the following forms:

IF MEMBER OF *"groupname"* THEN *command*
IF NOT MEMBER OF *"groupname"* THEN *command*

Here, *groupname* is the name of the group the user belongs to, and *command* is the command to execute if the user is a member (or is not a member). The following two examples demonstrate how to use these commands on a single command line. They can also be used with block commands that use BEGIN and END.

```
IF MEMBER OF "SALES" THEN MAP T:=SYS:SALES

IF NOT MEMBER OF "TEMPS" THEN MAP J:=SYS:USERNEWS
```

INCLUDE

The INCLUDE command causes the login script to execute a set of commands in an external login script file. You can create this file with any text editor. For example, if you have a long set of commands to execute for a group of managers, you could place those commands in a text file called MANAGERS.LOG, and then call that file from within a container login script. The command takes the form

INCLUDE *path\filename*

where *path* is the path to the directory where the text file exists, and *filename* is the name of the file. This path must include the context name and Directory Services tree path if the file is stored on a volume outside of the current user's context. You can also run the login script of another object by using INCLUDE in the following form:

INCLUDE *objectname*

Replace *objectname* with the name of the User object or container object that contains the login script you want to run. If that object is outside the current context, include the path to the context and make sure any users who run the login script have Read rights to it.

Some tips and techniques for using INCLUDE are listed here:

■ If your login scripts are small, you probably won't need INCLUDE. But if they grow in size, you might want to break up the login script for clarity.

■ Use INCLUDE to specify group login commands. For example, you could include the following command to run an external file for members of the Sales department. If you need to change the login commands for members of Sales, you edit SALES.LOG, not the main login script.

```
IF MEMBER OF "SALES" THEN INCLUDE SALES.LOG
```

■ Because files called by INCLUDE are external text files, you can designate a user to make changes to the file. For instance, in the preceding example, the file might include WRITE commands that display messages about upcoming meetings or events. You can designate an administrative assistant to make those changes with a text editor, so that he or she won't need to start NetWare Administrator or ConsoleOne to make changes.

■ If you are testing login scripts, you might want to place untested commands in an external file to simplify editing. It's often easier to change the external login files with a text editor than it is to load NetWare Administrator for editing.

■ Under Novell Directory Services, potentially every container object can have its own login script. Chances are good that many of these scripts will have some commands in common, so you can add those common commands to a text file that you call from a container login script.

■ You can nest INCLUDE statements up to ten levels deep.

■ Users must have File Scan and Read rights to the file called by the INCLUDE command.

EXAMPLES   In the following example, the file MANAGERS.LOG in the SYS:PUBLIC directory is included in the login script:

```
INCLUDE SYS:PUBLIC\MANAGERS.DAT
```

The next example calls a set of commands in a file called COMMON.LOG. This is similar to the example discussed earlier in this chapter, under "The Importance of the INCLUDE Command." Assume for this example that the file is created by the network administrator, and that it contains commands the administrator wants departmental supervisors to include in their container login scripts. The file is located in a directory in which other users only have Read rights. Therefore, only the administrator can alter the file, thus providing a network-wide set of commands that only the administrator controls. Of course, the administrator must make sure that departmental supervisors add the appropriate INCLUDE command to their departmental login scripts.

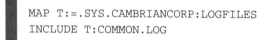

```
MAP T:=.SYS.CAMBRIANCORP:LOGFILES
INCLUDE T:COMMON.LOG
```

To include a login script in another container, add an INCLUDE command similar to the following. In this example, the login script commands are in a file called MANAGERS.TXT in a directory called SCRIPTS.

```
INCLUDE SYS.SALES.DIVWEST.CAMBRIANCORP:SCRIPTS\MANAGERS.TXT
```

NO_DEFAULT

Include this command in a container login script or a profile login script to prevent the default user login script from executing. A user login script will still execute. Insert the command shown here:

NO_DEFAULT

You must include a search drive mapping to the public directory in the container or profile script or the user will not be able to execute any NetWare public utilities.

PAUSE

You can use the PAUSE command to temporarily stop the login script from running, usually after displaying a message on the screen. Simply type **PAUSE** on a separate line. Processing continues when a key is pressed or, if the BREAK ON command was executed before PAUSE, users can break out of the login script by pressing CTRL-BREAK or CTRL-C.

EXAMPLE   In the following example, the PAUSE command is placed after the WRITE command, which displays an extended message on the screen:

```
WRITE "Software licensing rules are enforced by the company."
PAUSE
```

PROFILE

You use the PROFILE command only in container scripts to override a user's normal profile login script. The command takes the following form:

   PROFILE *profile_object_name*

where *profile_object_name* is the name of the profile object (and its context if necessary) in the NDS directory tree.

SCRIPT_SERVER

This command is for NetWare 2 and 3 users who need to set the location at which their bindery login script can be read. This command is not necessary for NetWare 4 users. The command takes the following form:

   SCRIPT_SERVER *server_name*

SHIFT

Use this command to change the order in which the %*n* identifier variables are interpreted in the login script. It allows users to enter LOGIN parameters in any order. The command takes the following form:

   SHIFT [*n*]

where *n* is the number of places you want the variable to shift. The default is 1, and you can shift up to ten login script variables (command-line arguments). Both positive and negative displacements are acceptable.

SWAP (DOS Only)

Include this command to move LOGIN to high memory and free conventional memory so # commands can execute. If you specify a path, LOGIN is moved to disk.

Workstation Environment

COMSPEC (DOS Only)

Use the COMSPEC command to specify the directory where the DOS COMMAND.COM file exists. When you enter an application, some of the DOS code in memory is discarded to create room for the application. When you exit the application, this DOS code must be replaced by executing COMMAND.COM again. COMSPEC specifies the location of COMMAND.COM. COMMAND.COM can be on a local DOS drive or on the server's hard drives. The COMSPEC command takes the following form:

COMSPEC=*drive*:COMMAND.COM

Here, *drive* is a local drive or the letter of a mapped directory where COMMAND.COM exists. You also can enter the command in the following form:

COMSPEC=*Sn*:COMMAND.COM

Here, *Sn* is the number of a previously mapped search drive. Here is another form of the command:

COMSPEC=**n*:COMMAND.COM

Here, *n* is the directory to which the *n*th network drive maps. Refer to the MAP command description in the section "Network Connection and Access to Resources," earlier in this chapter.

EXAMPLES   The following example shows how you can use the MAP command to map a search drive before you execute the COMSPEC command. In this way, the COMSPEC command can include the letter of the search drive. Note that the %MACHINE variable holds the name specified in the workstation's SHELL.CFG file with the LONG MACHINE TYPE command. This name relates the type of computer to a directory name on the server where DOS files for that computer are stored.

```
MAP S3:=SYS:PUBLIC\%MACHINE\%OS\%OS_VERSION
COMSPEC=S3:COMMAND.COM
```

DOS BREAK

Use the DOS BREAK command to specify that you can interrupt DOS commands with CTRL-BREAK or CTRL-C. This command is not the same as the BREAK ON command, which is used to interrupt a login script. The command takes these forms:

```
DOS BREAK ON
DOS BREAK OFF
```

The default is DOS BREAK OFF. See your DOS manual for more information.

DOS SET

The DOS SET command creates variables that can be used in batch files after the login script has completed. You can use these variables in many of the same ways that you use identifier variables. The command takes the following forms:

SET *name* = *"value"*
TEMP SET *name* = *"value"*

Here, *name* is the name of the variable, and *value* is the string that the variable is equal to. The value must be enclosed in quotation marks. Use the TEMP version of the command if you only want the variable to apply while the login script runs.

While NetWare has an extensive set of its own identifier variables, DOS SET is often used to configure individual workstations for different programs. You can assign the NetWare identifier variable to DOS SET variables and use them later in batch files. In the following example, the NetWare identifier variable LOGIN_NAME is made equal to the DOS variable USER. The USER variable can then be used in batch files.

```
DOS SET USER=%LOGIN_NAME
```

MACHINE

Use the MACHINE command to specify the name of the machine where the user is logging in. The name may contain up to 15 characters. The command takes the form

MACHINE = *name*

where *name* is the name you want to assign to the machine. The MACHINE command is often necessary for some programs written to run under PC DOS. The name can include identifier variables, as described earlier under "Login Script Identifier Variables."

NOSWAP (DOS Only)

Include the NOSWAP command to prevent LOGIN from being moved from conventional memory to high memory or onto disk when a workstation is low on memory. This causes a # command to fail, but the login script continues to execute.

PCCOMPATIBLE

Use the PCCOMPATIBLE command if the EXIT command does not work properly. This command designates non-IBM systems as compatible machines. If your machine is an IBM PC-compatible but you have changed the long machine type in the NET.CFG file to another name in order to access a different version of DOS, you will need to use PCCOMPATIBLE in the login script. Type the command in the login script before any EXIT commands.

SET

The SET command creates variables that can be used in batch files after the login script has completed. You can use these variables in many of the same ways that you use identifier variables. The command takes the following form:

SET *name* = *"value"*

Here, *name* is the name of the variable, and *value* is the string that the variable is equal to. The value must be enclosed in quotation marks.

While NetWare has an extensive set of its own identifier variables, SET is often used to configure individual workstations for different programs. You can assign the NetWare identifier variable to SET variables and use them later in batch files. In the following example, the NetWare identifier variable LOGIN_NAME is made equal to the variable USER. The USER variable can then be used in batch files.

```
SET USER=%LOGIN_NAME
```

SET_TIME

Include the SET_TIME command to set the time on the workstation to the same time as the server to which the user logged into. The command takes the following form, with the default setting of ON so that the workstation's time is always reset to the server's time:

```
SET_TIME ON/OFF
```

TEMP SET

The TEMP SET command creates variables that can be used in batch files after the login script has completed. You can use these variables in many of the same ways that you use identifier variables. The command takes the following form:

TEMP SET *name* = *"value"*

Here, *name* is the name of the variable, and *value* is the string that the variable is equal to. The value must be enclosed in quotation marks. Use the TEMP version of the command if you want the variable to apply only while the login script runs.

Text File Usage

@ (Microsoft Windows Only)

You use this command to execute a program that is external to the login script on a workstation running Microsoft Windows. You cannot use this command with a DOS login. This command will run the external program and then continue with the login script. It is similar to the Startup group programs in Windows. The command takes the following form:

@[*path*] FILENAME [*parameter(s)*]

where *path* is replaced with the drive letter, FILENAME is the executable file (.EXE, .COM, or .BAT), and *parameter(s)* are any parameters that must accompany the executable file.

EXAMPLE   If you want to start the GroupWise program from within the login script, you must either have a search drive mapped to where the executable is stored or enter the complete path. The command can be entered in the following forms in the login script:

```
@grpwise5

@sys:apps\grpwise5
```

(DOS Only)

You can execute external DOS commands from a login script if you place the pound sign (#) in front of the command. If you use this command in a Windows program, the login script will stay open until the called program terminates. If it happens to be a program that stays open all day, the login script will not finish until it is closed. The command takes the following form:

\# *path*/*filename parameters*

where *path* is the mapped drive letter or full path name where the command file is located. Replace *filename* with the name of the executable file, and replace *parameters* with any parameters required to execute the program. Map all necessary search drives before executing external program execution commands.

Note   *Starting major programs like word processors or spreadsheets from the login script can cause "Out of Memory" errors. Use the EXIT command before starting this type of DOS application.*

External command execution is different from command execution performed by the EXIT command. The login script is held in memory while the external program is running, and the remainder of the script resumes execution when the external program ends or is exited. The EXIT command ends the login script.

EXAMPLE   In the following example, a DOS program called INSET is executed during a user's login script. Note that a search drive is first mapped to the directory where the program is located.

```
MAP S16:=SYS:INSET
# INSET
```

CLS (DOS Only)

CLS is the clear screen command for login scripts. Use this command to clear any screen information for displaying messages. The cursor jumps to the top left of the screen. Simply include CLS as a line in the login script.

DISPLAY and FDISPLAY

The DISPLAY and FDISPLAY commands display the contents of text files. These text files can hold important login information, messages from managers, or messages from the network supervisor. For example, a message could inform users when a network server is down for maintenance. Use a text editor or word processor to create the text files displayed by DISPLAY or FDISPLAY. Note the following:

- DISPLAY shows the entire contents of a file, including the codes used for formatting. Only use DISPLAY with "pure" ASCII text files. FDISPLAY filters out formatting codes present in some word-processed files.

- For best results, save all messages you intend to display with DISPLAY or FDISPLAY as text-only, unformatted files.

- Use the DISPLAY and FDISPLAY commands when you need to display large blocks of text. The WRITE command, covered later, is best for one or two lines of text. The commands take the following forms:

    DISPLAY *path/filename*
    FDISPLAY *path/filename*

Here, *path* is the full path to the file (or a mapped drive letter), and *filename* is the name of the text file created by an editor or word processing program.

EXAMPLES   In the following example, a text file called DAILY.DOC that contains important daily messages is displayed for users:

```
DISPLAY DAILY.DOC
```

Use IF...THEN...ELSE to display messages only under certain conditions—for example, if the user is the member of a group or if the day is Friday. The next example assumes a text file exists in a directory called SYS:NEWS for each day of the week. The

%DAY_OF_WEEK identifier variable is replaced with the name of the current day, which then matches a text file of the same name, such as MONDAY.DOC or TUESDAY.DOC. Of course, you can update the daily files as necessary. Note the use of the percent sign to specify the identifier variable in the command.

```
DISPLAY SYS:NEWS\%DAY_OF_WEEK.DOC
```

The following example uses the IF...THEN...ELSE statement in another form to display a message if the day is Monday:

```
IF DAY_OF_WEEK = "MONDAY"
THEN DISPLAY SYS:NEWS\MEETINGS.DOC
```

The next example displays the message file COMPAQ.DOC in the SYS:NEWS directory if the workstations logging in have the machine name COMPAQ:

```
IF MACHINE = "COMPAQ"
THEN DISPLAY SYS:NEWS\COMPAQ.DOC
```

DOS VERIFY (DOS and Windows 3.x Only)

The DOS VERIFY command is used to verify that data written to a local drive is not written to a bad disk sector and can be read without an error. The command takes the following form:

DOS VERIFY [*on* | *off*]

EXIT

The EXIT command stops the execution of the remaining commands in a login script. Usually you use the command with an IF...THEN...ELSE statement after a condition is evaluated as true or false. For example, an EXIT command may stop the login script for a user if that user is a member of a group, such as a group called Temporary that includes the temporary personnel for a company. Any commands that follow the EXIT command are not executed. You would typically use it in this way in container and profile login scripts that execute for a number of users.

Note *If you have changed the long machine name to a name other than the default, which is IBM_PC, include the PCCOMPATIBLE command before the EXIT command.*

The EXIT command can take these forms:

EXIT
EXIT *"filename"*

where *filename* in the second form is the name of an executable file with the extension COM, EXE, or BAT.

Note the following rules for using EXIT:

- The PCCOMPATIBLE command must be placed before the EXIT command for non-IBM DOS systems.
- The command specified with EXIT must be located in the current directory or in a mapped search drive.
- The path to a command can be specified with EXIT, but the complete path and command cannot exceed 14 characters. The next rule also applies in this case.
- If backslashes are used with commands, they must be typed twice to differentiate them from backslashes used in other NetWare commands. A double backslash counts as a single character.

EXAMPLES   Use EXIT by itself while writing and testing login scripts to exit the script and prevent subsequent commands from actually executing. In the following example, a batch file called GRPWISE.BAT is executed when exiting the login script:

```
EXIT "GRPWISE.BAT"
```

The most common way to use the EXIT command is after evaluating a certain condition with the IF...THEN...ELSE command. In the following example, if a user belongs to the group Temporary, the login script stops and executes a batch file called TEMPS.BAT. This batch file might switch temporary personnel to a special data directory and start the application program that they are assigned to work with, such as a database entry program.

```
IF MEMBER OF "TEMPORARY" THEN EXIT "TEMPS"
```

TERM

The TERM command is normally used only for Novell Application Launcher (NAL) scripts. It causes the login script to stop and return an error code. If you add TERM to a container login script, it prevents other profile or user scripts from running. If you put it in a profile login script, it prevents the user login script from running. The command takes the following form:

TERM [*xxx*]

where *xxx* is a value you add for the return code.

WRITE

The WRITE command displays messages and other text. It can also be used with the identifier variables in a number of ways. The command takes the following forms:

WRITE *"text"; variable*
WRITE *"text %variable"*

In the first form, the text to display is in quotation marks. An identifier variable can then be added to display one of the system variables. A semicolon separates text and variable. In the second form, the same results are achieved, but all options are included within the quotation marks. Use semicolons to join several WRITE commands so they appear as a continuous block of text.

Note *When an identifier variable is used within quotation marks, it must be capitalized and preceded by a percent sign.*

You can use the following strings in WRITE commands:

```
\r   Carriage return
\n   New line
\"   An embedded quotation mark
\7   A beep
```

The identifier variables that can be used with the WRITE command are listed in Table 24-1, earlier in this chapter. Enter each variable as shown, including the underscore characters if listed. WRITE replaces the identifier variable with the text or value identified by the variable.

EXAMPLES   The following example creates four blank lines, displays a greeting message for a user, and then creates four more blank lines:

```
WRITE "\n\n\n\nGood %GREETING_TIME, %LOGIN_NAME\n\n\n\n"
```

In the next command, identifier variables are used to display month, day, and year. Note that percent signs and uppercase letters are used because the identifier variable is within quotes. Also notice the use of the comma, which appears when the text is displayed.

```
WRITE "Today is %MONTH_NAME %DAY, %YEAR"
```

Other Commands

LASTLOGINTIME

Include the LASTLOGINTIME command in a login script to display the last time the user logged into the system.

REMARK

You can use the REMARK command in a login script to include comments for your own use or for other users who may need to edit the scripts later. The command takes the following forms:

> REMARK *text*
> REM *text*
> * *text*
> ; *text*

Here, *text* is the text to include in the remark. The REMARK command must be on its own line.

EXAMPLE In the following example, REM is used to document the purpose of a series of MAP commands:

```
REM The following MAP commands are for managers only
```

Login Script Examples

This section provides examples of login scripts that you can refer to when creating your own login scripts. The first script is the most basic. You might want to include it in a container object so it runs for all users that log into the container. You can then let users customize their user login scripts to fit their own needs. The lines are numbered only for convenient reference; they are not part of the commands.

```
1.   MAP DISPLAY OFF
2.   SET PROMPT = "$P$G"
3.   MAP *1:=SYS:USERS\%LOGIN_NAME
4.   IF OS="DOS" THEN
5.       MAP P:=SYS:PUBLIC\DOS
6.       ELSE MAP INS S1:=SYS:PUBLIC
7.       MAP INS S2:=SYS:PUBLIC\%MACHINE\%OS\%OS_VERSION
8.   END
9.   COMSPEC=S2:COMMAND.COM
10.  MAP DISPLAY ON
11.  MAP
```

As mentioned, this is a basic login script, but you can build on it depending on your own needs. Each command is outlined here:

■ **Line 1**   MAP DISPLAY OFF disables messages displayed by commands as they execute.

■ **Line 2**   The SET PROMPT command sets the command prompt to display the current directory path.

■ **Line 3**   This first command maps the user's personal directory to the first network drive letter. The *1 designates the first drive letter.

■ **Line 4**   This command starts the IF...THEN...ELSE command for lines 4 through 8. If the user is logging in from a DOS workstation, line 5 executes; otherwise, lines 6 and 7 execute.

■ **Line 5**   This command maps the second network drive to the \PUBLIC\DOS directory for DOS users. Lines 6 and 7 are not executed for OS/2 users.

■ **Line 6**   This command executes if the workstation is not a DOS workstation. It maps the PUBLIC directory to the first search drive (Z).

■ **Line 7**   This command maps the second search drive to a directory that holds the DOS version matching the DOS running on the user's workstation. For example, if the user logged in from an IBM PC workstation running DOS version 6, this command would map the second search drive to \PUBLIC\IBM_PC\MSDOS\6.0.

■ **Line 8**   This command ends the IF...THEN...ELSE command in line 4.

■ **Line 9**   This command sets the path to the COMMAND.COM file for DOS workstations. The search drive specified in line 7 is used.

■ **Line 10**   This command turns the display of messages back on.

■ **Line 11**   This command displays the current maps for the user.

The next example is more elaborate. It includes commands to display greeting messages as well as maps and search drives according to the groups users belong to. This login script is designed for container or profile objects.

```
1.  MAP DISPLAY OFF
2.  SET PROMPT = "$P$G"
3.  MAP *1:=SYS:USERS\%LOGIN_NAME
4.  IF OS="DOS" THEN
5.       MAP P:=SYS:PUBLIC\DOS
6.       ELSE MAP INS S1:=SYS:PUBLIC
7.       MAP INS S2:=SYS:PUBLIC\%MACHINE\%OS\%OS_VERSION
8.  END
```

```
 9.  COMSPEC=S2:COMMAND.COM
10.  PCCOMPATIBLE
11.  MAP *3:=SYS:PUB-DATA
12.  MAP INS S16:=SYS:APPS\LOTUS
13.  MAP INS S16:=SYS:APPS\WORD
14.  IF MEMBER OF "TEMPS" THEN BEGIN
15.       MAP F:=VOL1:ACCTDATA
16.       MAP INS S1:=VOL1:ACCTPROG
17.       DRIVE F:
18.       EXIT "START"
19.  END
20.  IF MEMBER OF "MANAGERS" THEN BEGIN
21.       MAP *4:=SYS:MGR-DATA
22.       MAP INS S6:=SYS:MGR-PROG
23.  END
24.  WRITE "\n\n\n\nGood %GREETING_TIME, %LOGIN_NAME\n\n\n\n"
25.  DISPLAY SYS:NEWS\%DAY_OF_WEEK.DOC
26.  PAUSE
27.  IF DAY_OF_WEEK="MONDAY" THEN DISPLAY SYS:NEWS\MEETINGS.DOC
28.  PAUSE
29.  MAP DISPLAY ON
30.  EXIT "GRPWISE.BAT"
```

This login script makes effective use of group names to assign drive and search mappings to users according to the groups they belong to. The lines are described here:

- **Lines 1 through 9**   These are the same commands used in the previous example to set up a typical environment.

- **Line 10**   The PCCOMPATIBLE command enables the EXIT command in line 30 to execute on workstations that don't have the name IBM_PC.

- **Lines 11 through 13**   These commands map data directories and program directories accessed by all User objects in the container.

- **Lines 14 through 19**   These commands map an accounting data directory and its program directory for a group of temporary clerks (called Temps) with limited rights. Line 17 switches the Temps user to drive F; then line 18 exits the login script and runs START.BAT, which starts the accounting program.

- **Lines 20 through 23**   These commands execute special drive mappings for users who belong to the Managers group.

Note   *You could use an INCLUDE statement to call an external file that has a set of commands for managers or other groups.*

- **Line 24**   A greeting message is displayed with the user's name included.
- **Lines 25 through 28**   A greeting message is displayed that matches the day of the week, with a pause after each message.
- **Line 29**   This command sets map display back on.
- **Line 30**   This command exits the login script and starts the menu program called Main.

Displaying Login and Station Information

You can place the following commands in the container login script to display information about a system and the user who logs in. This information may be useful to the supervisor or technician who is attempting to resolve problems or assist a user. Insert the commands at the end of the login script so the information they display is not overwritten by other commands, and include a PAUSE if necessary so you can read the screen.

```
WRITE "Login name = %LOGIN_NAME"
WRITE "User ID = %USER_ID"
WRITE "Your User object context = %LOGIN_CONTEXT"
WRITE "Your current context = %REQUESTER_CONTEXT"
WRITE "Workstation = %STATION"
WRITE "Workstation address = %P_STATION"
WRITE "Machine name = %MACHINE"
WRITE "Network address = %NETWORK_ADDRESS"
WRITE "File server name = %FILE_SERVER"
WRITE "OS Type = %OS"
WRITE "OS version = %OS_VERSION"
```

Displaying NDS Property Information

The following login script pulls information from the environment and from the User's object property fields and displays the information on the user's screen when they log in. This information is also useful if you are troubleshooting a workstation or user login and want to view specific user login information. Note that the left side of the WRITE commands simply displays a label explaining the information displayed by the identifier variable on the right (which is preceded by a percent sign).

```
WRITE "Login script begin"
MAP DISPLAY ON
WRITE ""
WRITE "Access Server          : %ACCESS_SERVER"
WRITE "Account Balance        : %ACCOUNT BALANCE"
WRITE "Allow Unlimited Credit : %ALLOW UNLIMITED CREDIT"
WRITE "CN (Common Name)       : %CN"
```

```
WRITE "Description                : %DESCRIPTION"
WRITE "Fax                        : %FACSIMILE_TELEPHONE_NUMBER"
WRITE "File Server                : %FILE_SERVER"
WRITE "Full Name                  : %FULL_NAME"
WRITE "Group Membership           : %GROUP MEMBERSHIP"
WRITE "Home directory             : %HOME DIRECTORY"
WRITE "Language                   : %LANGUAGE"
WRITE "L (Locality)               : %L"
WRITE "Login Context              : %LOGIN_CONTEXT"
WRITE "Login Name                 : %LOGIN_NAME"
WRITE "Machine                    : %MACHINE"
WRITE "Minimum Account Balance    : %MINIMUM ACCOUNT BALANCE"
WRITE "Network Address            : %NETWORK"
WRITE "OS                         : %OS"
WRITE "OS Version                 : %OS_VERSION"
WRITE "Password Allow Change      : %PASSWORD ALLOW CHANGE"
WRITE "Password Expires           : %PASSWORD_EXPIRES"
WRITE "Password Minimum Length    : %PASSWORD MINIMUM LENGTH"
WRITE "Password Required          : %PASSWORD REQUIRED"
WRITE "Password Unique required   : %PASSWORD UNIQUE REQUIRED"
WRITE "Physical Station           : %P_STATION"
WRITE "Postal Office Box          : %POSTAL OFFICE BOX"
WRITE "Postal Code                : %POSTAL CODE"
WRITE "Profile                    : %PROFILE"
WRITE "Requester Context          : %REQUESTER_CONTEXT"
WRITE "Requester Version          : %REQUESTER_VERSION"
WRITE "S (State)                  : %S"
WRITE "SA (Street Address)        : %SA"
WRITE "Security Equals            : %SECURITY EQUALS"
WRITE "See Also                   : %SEE ALSO"
WRITE "Shell Version              : %SHELL_VERSION"
WRITE "Station                    : %STATION"
WRITE "Surname                    : %SURNAME"
WRITE "Telephone number           : %TELEPHONE NUMBER"
WRITE "Title                      : %TITLE"
WRITE "User ID                    : %USER_ID"
WRITE "COMSPEC                    : %<COMSPEC>"
MAP H:=%HOME_DIRECTORY
DRIVE H:
WRITE ""
WRITE "Login script end"
```

The Complete Reference

NetWare 5

Chapter 25

DNS/DHCP
Internet Services

etWare 5 integrates the standards-based Domain Name System (DNS) and Dynamic Host Configuration Protocol (DHCP) into Novell Directory Services (NDS). The DNS server maps and resolves network device IP addresses to human-intelligible host names. DHCP is a client-server protocol that automatically assigns and tracks IP host addresses and other configuration data throughout the network. DNS/DHCP Services support the Dynamic Domain Name System (DDNS), which dynamically updates the host name database with new IP addresses. These services work by extending the NDS schema to include new NDS objects related to DNS and DHCP. DHCP enables you to centrally administer and manage IP addresses and host names from the NetWare Administrator utility. In addition, by including this information in the NDS database, it is replicated and distributed throughout the network, eliminating a single point of failure. Also included in NetWare 5 is a Java-based DNS/DHCP Management Console that runs on any machine with a Java Virtual Machine (JVM) installed.

Some of the major features of DNS/DHCP Services are as follows:

- When the IP address of a host is changed, the information in the DNS database is dynamically updated to associate the existing host name with the new IP address using DDNS.

- You can customize your IP addressing procedures at the enterprise, subnet, or client level using DHCP.

- The NDS-based DNS server can interoperate with traditional DNS servers as either a primary or secondary server when used with non-NDS DNS servers.

- NetWare 5 DNS/DHCP Services include a Java Management Console that allows you to configure, monitor, and manage the DNS and DHCP services in NDS.

- DNS/DHCP Services enable you view an audit trail generated by the server that enables you to track address additions, deletions, rejections, and other information.

Installing DNS/DHCP

NetWare 5 integrates DNS and DHCP into NDS by extending the NDS database schema to support various objects specific to DNS and DHCP. When the NDS schema is extended, three new NDS objects are created, as shown in Figure 25-1.

DNSDHCP-GROUP OBJECT A DNSDHCP-GROUP object is automatically made a trustee of a DNS or DHCP object when it is created. Access to information contained in a DNS or DHCP object can be obtained by any object that is a member of the DNSDHCP-GROUP group object. NetWare DNS and DHCP servers are automatically made members of this group.

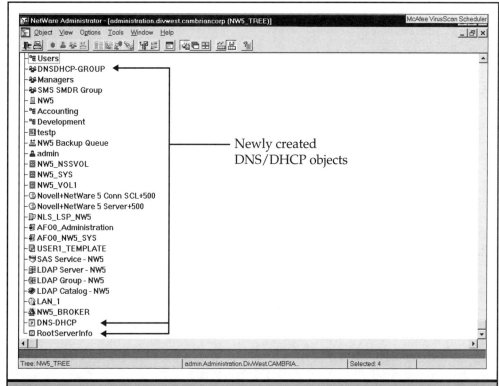

Figure 25-1.   *The DNSDHCP-GROUP, DNS-DHCP, and RootServerInfo objects are created in the NDS tree when you install DNS/DHCP Services*

DNS-DHCP LOCATOR OBJECT   The DNS-DHCP Locator object contains global defaults, DHCP options, and lists of all DHCP and DNS servers, subnets, and zones in the NDS tree. This object in not configurable by the administrator and is therefore not displayed in the DNS/DHCP management utility.

ROOTSERVERINFO ZONE OBJECT   The RootServerInfo Zone object points to root name servers on the Internet. These servers contain configuration information for the starting of a domain. This object allows you to resolve domain names that belong to domains not maintained in your NDS tree.

DHCP Objects

Five new DHCP objects are available after the NDS schema has been extended, each of which is discussed in detail later in the chapter:

- DHCP Server object
- Subnet object

- Subnet Address Range (SAR) object
- IP Address object
- Subnet Pool object

DNS Objects

Four new DNS objects are available after the NDS schema has been extended, each of which is discussed in detail later in the chapter:

- DNS Server object
- DNS Zone object
- Resource Record Set object
- Resource Record object

Installation Methods

There are three different ways to install DNS/DHCP Services on your NetWare 5 server. During the initial operating system install, the files necessary to run DNS/DHCP Services are copied to the SYS volume on the server. These files include various Novell Loadable Modules (NLMs), which are copied to the SYS:SYSTEM directory, and the DNS/DHCP Management Console setup files, which are copied to the SYS:SYSTEM\PUBLIC\DNSDHCP directory. You must complete the following tasks prior to the installation of DNS/DHCP Services:

- You must extend the NDS schema and create the default DNS/DHCP objects. You can install DNS/DHCP Services during the initial installation of the NetWare 5 operating system by running the NetWare 5 installation program from the Java-based GUI, or by running the DNIPINST.NLM.
- You must install the Novell Client on the machine that is going to run the DNS/DHCP Management Console.
- You must install the DNS/DHCP Management Console and NetWare Administrator snap-in files.

Extending the Schema Using the NetWare 5 Installation Program

Perform the following steps to extend the NDS schema and create the three default DNS/DHCP objects using the NetWare 5 installation program at the server console:

1. Select the NetWare GUI screen at the server console.
2. Click the Novell icon at the bottom left of the screen.

3. Click Install.

4. In the Installed Products window, click the New Product button.

5. Enter the path to the Install directory in the Source Path window. You can use the Browse button to find the NetWare 5 installation files. Click OK after entering the path.

6. Mark the Novell DNS/DHCP Services box in the Additional Products and Services window.

7. Authenticate yourself to NDS as a user with rights to extend the NDS schema. You must have Supervisor rights to the [Root] of the NDS tree.

8. Enter your fully distinguished name in the User Name field and enter your password in the Password field.

9. Click OK.

10. Enter the NDS context where you want to create the DNS-DHCP locator, DNSDHCP-GROUP group, and RootServerInfo Zone objects. When finished, click the Next button.

11. Click Finish in the Summary Window.

12. Click Yes to reboot the server.

Extending the Schema Using the DNIPINST.NLM Program

Perform the following steps to extend the NDS schema and create the three default DNS/DHCP objects using the DNIPINST.NLM program at the server console or using the RConsole utility:

1. Type **DNIPINST** at the server console prompt.

2. Authenticate yourself to NDS as a user with rights to extend the NDS schema. You must have Supervisor rights to the [Root] of the NDS tree to perform this operation.

3. Enter the NDS context where you want to create the DNS-DHCP locator, DNSDHCP-GROUP group, and RootServerInfo Zone objects. When finished, press ENTER to create objects in the NDS tree.

4. Press ENTER to terminate the program after the schema extensions have been added to the NDS tree.

Installing the DNS/DHCP Management Console

You must install the DNS/DHCP Management Console and NetWare Administrator snap-in files before you can see and manage the new NDS/DHCP objects in the NDS tree. Perform the steps listed next to install the management files.

1. Run the SYS:PUBLIC\DNSDHCP\SETUP.EXE program from a client workstation.

2. Install the DNS/DHCP Management Console on the local hard disk.

3. Install the NetWare Administrator snap-in files in the SYS:PUBLIC\WIN32 directory.

4. Restart the workstation.

Using the DNS/DHCP Management Console

You must assign a NetWare server as a DHCP server, configure the DHCP parameters, and start the DHCP service before you can use DHCP services on the network.

The first thing to do is to start the Management Console either from the NetWare Administrator utility or from the DNS/DHCP icon on the desktop. The screen shown here will be displayed, prompting you for the NDS tree name:

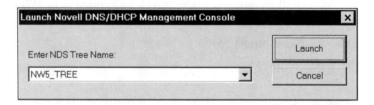

Enter the name of the NDS tree in which you want to configure the DHCP parameters. The screen shown in Figure 25-2 will be displayed, showing a DNS Service tab and a DHCP Service tab. Each tab page is divided into three frames. The left frame displays the managed objects, such as IP addresses and DNS zones. The right frame displays detailed information about the highlighted object in the left or bottom frame. The bottom frame lists the DHCP and DNS servers that exist in the NDS tree being managed.

You use the toolbar below the DNS and DHCP Service tabs to manage each highlighted item. Each button on the toolbar has an identification screen associated with it. This screen appears when you rest the mouse pointer on top of the button. The status bar at the bottom of the screen displays either the selected object, the current database access operation status, or the server interface status.

The Dynamic Host Configuration Protocol (DHCP)

A computer or another device must be configured with a number of parameters before it can operate on an IP network. Parameters such as the client's domain name and IP address, the DNS server's IP address for host name resolution, and the subnet mask must be configured. Without these configuration parameters, a computer or another device cannot interact with other devices on the IP network.

Managing the NetWare Environment

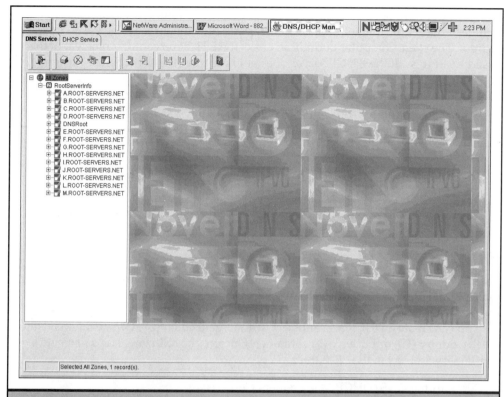

Figure 25-2. *The DNS/DHCP Management Console screen*

In the early days of IP networking, IP addresses were manually assigned through a service referred to as the Bootstrap Protocol (BOOTP). Today, most TCP/IP networks are using the Dynamic Host Configuration Protocol (DHCP) to automatically assign IP addresses and other parameters to clients.

DHCP is built on a client-server model. The DHCP server provides the initialization parameters for a client using the DHCP protocol. The client requests these parameters from the DHCP server. The DHCP protocol consists of the following two components:

■ A protocol to deliver host-specific configuration parameters from a DHCP server to a host

■ A protocol for assigning network addresses to a host

When a DHCP client starts up, it initiates a dialog with a DHCP server on the network. The DHCP server responds by sending an IP address that it has selected from a list or pool of available addresses, along with other configuration data. This data includes a lease time that tells the client computer how long it may use the assigned IP address. The client computer periodically asks the DHCP server for a renewal of the leased IP address. If the DHCP server does not hear from the client before the lease expires, it assumes the client is no longer connected and returns the IP address to the pool for reassignment. This enables much more efficient use of scarce IP addresses.

IP address assignments are supported in DHCP in one of the following three ways:

- **Automatic Allocation** The DHCP server assigns a permanent IP address to a host.

- **Dynamic Allocation** The IP address is assigned to a host for a limited time period, referred to as a *lease*.

- **Manual Allocation** The DHCP server delivers a manually configured address to a host.

Configuring the DHCP Server Object

The DHCP Server object represents the DHCP server in the NDS tree. It contains a listing of all subnet ranges the DHCP server is servicing. It also contains all server-specific policy and configuration information for the DHCP server.

You can create a DHCP Server object in an Organization (O), Organizational Unit (OU), Country (C), or Locality (L) container. Perform the following steps to create a DHCP Server object in the NDS tree:

1. Start the DNS/DHCP Management Console.

2. Click the DHCP Service tab, as shown in Figure 25-2.

3. Click the Create button (the cube-shaped object on the toolbar).

4. Highlight the DHCP Server selection and click OK , as shown in Figure 25-3.

5. Click the Browse button to navigate to the context that contains the NetWare file server, as shown here:

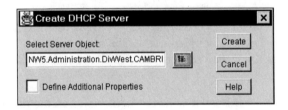

The DHCP server name will default to the name of the selected file server with a prefix of DHCP_.

6. Click the Create button.

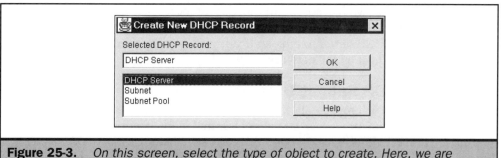

Figure 25-3. *On this screen, select the type of object to create. Here, we are creating a DHCP Server object*

7. Click the DHCP server icon in the bottom frame to bring up the details page, as shown in Figure 25-4. Notice that the DHCP Server object has a line drawn across it. This indicates that the service is not running.

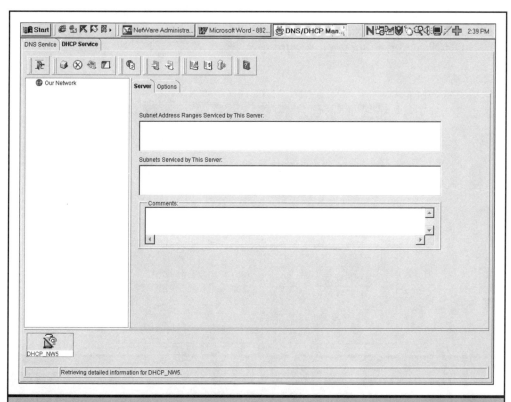

Figure 25-4. *The details page for the DHCP server shows current configurations and allows you to modify the DHCP parameters*

You can configure SMNP traps, audit trails, audit logs, audit alerts, mobile user options, and synchronization wait times from the DHCP server details page. You can also configure the DHCP server to ping an IP address to verify that it is not in use before leasing it to a host on the network.

Creating a DHCP Subnet Object

The DHCP Subnet object represents an IP network address that is assigned to a physical network segment. It is a container object that holds IP address configuration information that can be assigned to hosts that reside on that logical network segment. The configuration information is represented in NDS as the IP Address object and IP Address Range object. You can create a DHCP Subnet object in an Organization (O), Organizational Unit (OU), Country (C), or Locality (L) container. Perform the following steps to create a DHCP Subnet object:

1. Click the Create icon (the cube-shaped object) on the toolbar.

2. Select the Subnet entry on the Create New DHCP Record selection box shown in Figure 25-3.

3. Enter the subnet name, NDS context, subnet address, subnet mask, and default DHCP server, as shown in Figure 25-5.

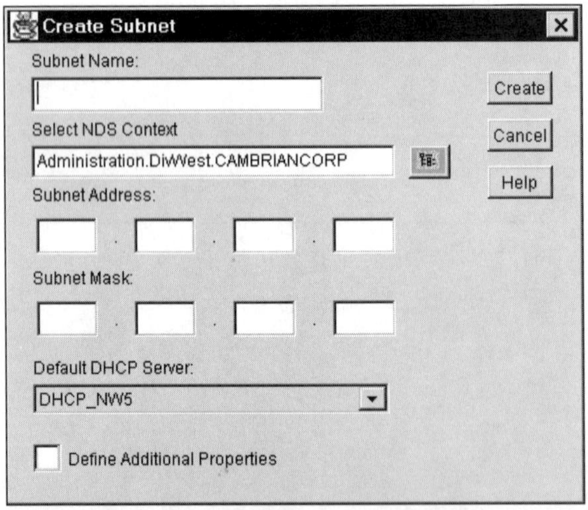

Figure 25-5. *The Create Subnet dialog box*

4. Click the Create button.

5. Select the DHCP Server object displayed in the bottom frame of the Management Console utility and click it. This brings up the details screen shown in Figure 25-6.

6. Select the Options tab shown in Figure 25-7 to configure SNMP traps, audit trail and alert options, mobile user options, and the Ping Enabled option.

Creating a Subnet Address Range Object

The Subnet Address Range (SAR) object specifies a range of IP addresses available for dynamic address assignment to hosts on the network. It can also be configured to exclude a range of IP addresses from the dynamic address assignment process. You can

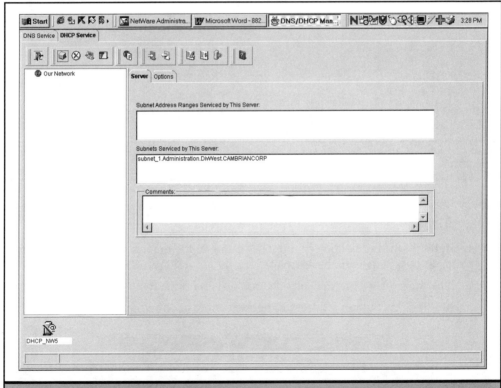

Figure 25-6. *The details page for the DHCP server, showing the subnets serviced by this server*

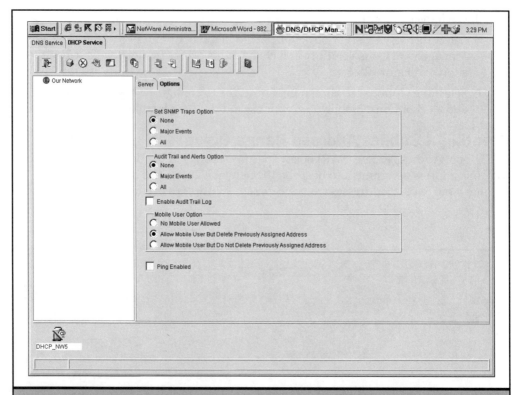

Figure 25-7.   *The Options tab allows you to configure SNMP traps, auditing, mobile user options, and ping capabilities*

create multiple SAR objects under a single Subnet object. Perform the following steps to create a Subnet Address Range (SAR) object:

1. Highlight the Subnet object in the left frame of the management utility in which the address range will be associated, as shown in Figure 25-8.

2. Click the Create icon (the cube-shaped object) on the toolbar.

3. Highlight the Subnet Address Range selection, as shown here, and click OK:

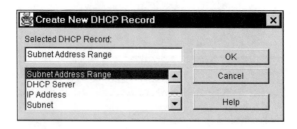

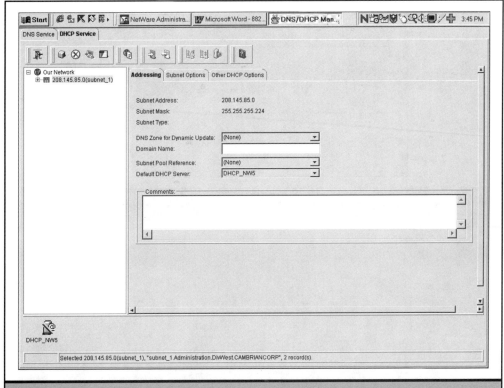

Figure 25-8.   *The left frame displays the available Subnet objects*

4. Enter the required configuration information for the subnet as shown in Figure 25-9.

5. Click the Create button.

6. A new SAR object will appear in the left frame of the management utility. When you select the SAR object, a details window will be displayed, as shown in Figure 25-10.

Creating an IP Address Object

You can manually assign an IP address to a specific machine on your network using an IP Address object. You can also use this object to restrict the assignment of an IP address to a specific machine on your network. You can create multiple IP Address objects in each subnet container, but they can represent only a single IP address.

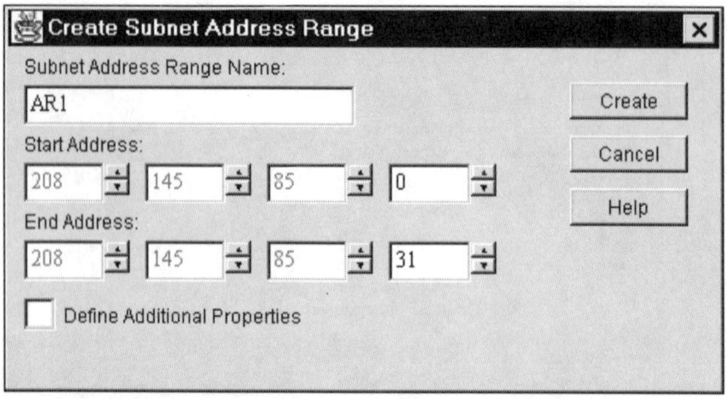

Figure 25-9.   Enter the name, starting address, and ending address for the SAR object on this screen

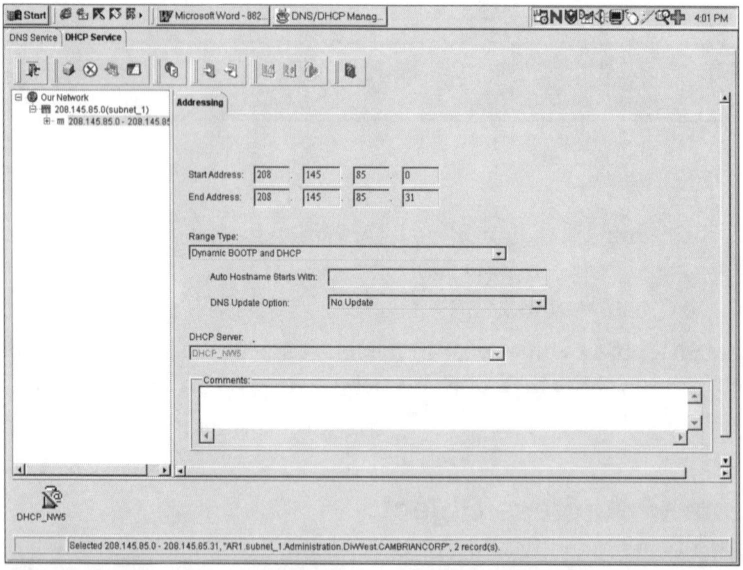

Figure 25-10.   The SAR details screen

Perform the following steps to create an IP Address object:

1. Highlight the Subnet object in which you want the IP Address object placed.

2. Click the Create button.

3. Select the IP Address and click OK.

4. The screen shown in Figure 25-11 will be displayed if you choose to exclude the IP address. The screen shown in Figure 25-12 will be displayed if you choose to manually assign a specific IP address to a specific MAC address.

5. Click the Create button. A new IP Address object will be displayed in the left frame of the management utility, as shown in Figure 25-13.

Creating a Subnet Pool Object

The Subnet Pool object allows you to assign multiple Subnet objects to service DHCP client requests for a network segment that has more than one IP subnet address configured on it. Many protocol stacks, including Novell's, support multiple IP subnet addresses on the same physical network segment. You may encounter older systems that allow only one IP subnet address per physical network segment. Subnet Pool objects can be created at the Organization (O), Organizational Unit (OU), Country (C), and Locality (L) container levels. Perform the following steps to create a Subnet Pool object:

1. Highlight the Our Network icon in the management utility.

2. Click the Create icon (the cube-shaped object) on the toolbar.

3. Select the Subnet Pool entry and click OK.

4. Enter the name for the new subnet in the text box.

5. Enter the context where you want the Subnet Pool object placed in the NDS tree. You can click the Browse button to navigate the NDS tree.

6. Click the Create button.

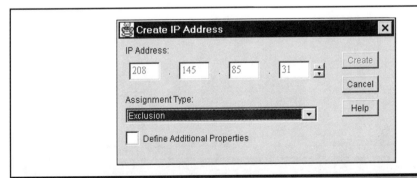

Figure 25-11.   *This screen allows you to exclude a specific IP address from an IP address range*

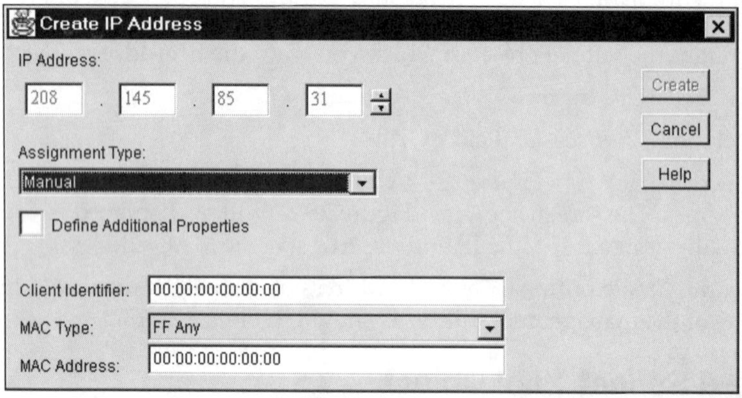

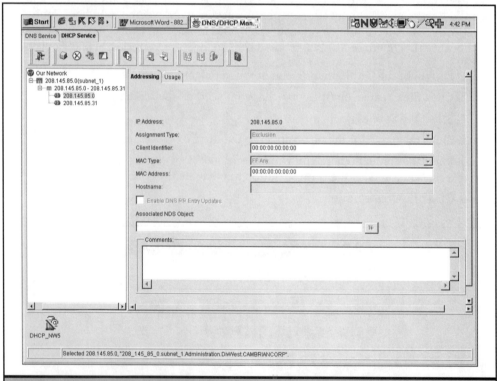

Figure 25-12. This screen allows you to set a specific IP address for a specific machine, based on the MAC address of the machine

Figure 25-13. The new IP Address object is displayed in the left frame of the DNS/DHCP management utility

7. Click the new Subnet Pool object that appears in the left frame of the management utility.

8. Click the Add button in the subnet pool details window.

9. Select the Subnet objects that you want to assign to the Subnet Pool object.

10. When you are finished with the assignments, click the Save Data to NDS button.

11. Click Yes to verify the save operation.

Starting the DHCP Server

The DHCP service can be started on the server after you have created a DHCP Server object and assigned it IP addresses to service. Enter the following command at the server console prompt to start the service:

```
[LOAD]  DHCPSRVR
```

This command will load the DHCPSRVR.NLM at the server. It will read IP address configuration information from NDS and load the information into the DHCP server's cache.

Setting DHCP Options

You can configure both DHCP administrative options and the information delivered to a client in the DNS/DHCP Management Console utility. The administrative options are configurable as part of the DHCP Server and DHCP Subnet objects. The delivery options allow you to select the information other than IP addresses that will be delivered to clients. This may include DNS servers, routers (gateways), preferred NDS server, NDS context information, and even custom parameters. Options delivered to clients can be configured so that they apply globally or to only a specific subnet. If the same option is set at both levels, the value set at the lower level will be the value assigned to the client.

SETTING GLOBAL DHCP OPTIONS   You can set global options by selecting the Global Preferences button on the toolbar. All options set here will apply to all DHCP configurations in your NDS tree. There are three tabs on the Global Preferences screen, as shown in Figure 25-14.

The Global DHCP Options tab displays the configuration parameters that are to be delivered to all clients when they receive their IP address. These options apply to all DHCP servers in your NDS tree. You select the parameters by clicking the Modify button on the dialog box. The screen shown in Figure 25-15 will be displayed, which allows you to select and configure the available options.

The Global DHCP Defaults tab, shown in Figure 25-16, displays the hardware addresses that are excluded from the DHCP server. You can select from any of the

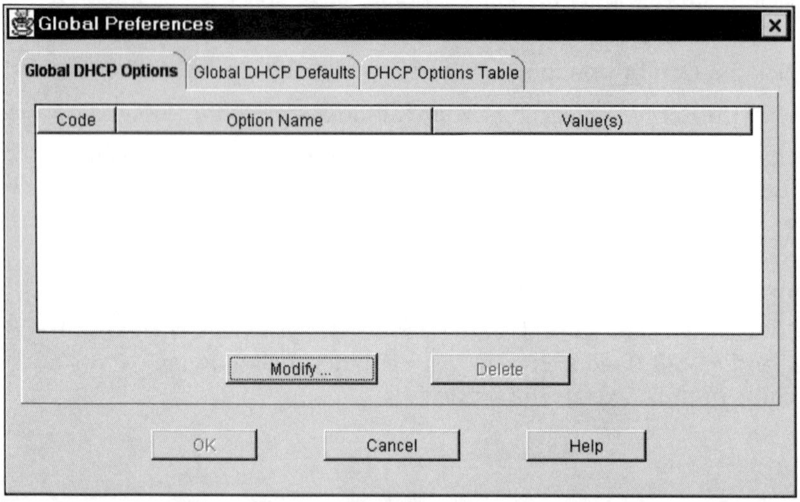

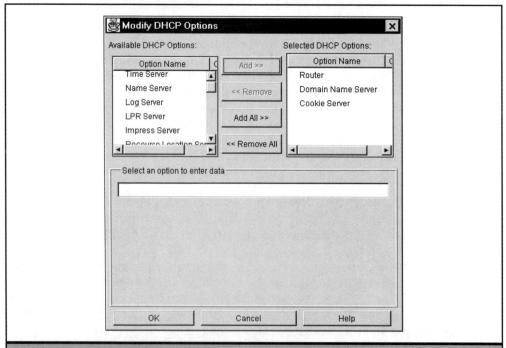

Figure 25-14. *The Global Preferences display and configuration window*

Figure 25-15. *This screen displays the DHCP options that are available to be configured globally*

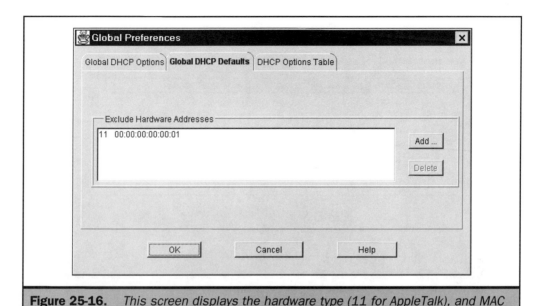

Figure 25-16. *This screen displays the hardware type (11 for AppleTalk), and MAC address (00:00:00:00:00:01), which have been excluded from the DHCP servers*

known network types, such as AppleTalk, ARCNET, and so on. Click the Add button to display the hardware address selection list.

The DHCP Options Table tab, shown in Figure 25-17, displays the options that have been defined globally. You can click the Add button to add your own DHCP option types. You can also make any existing DHCP type unavailable by removing it from this list.

Importing and Exporting DHCP Databases

You can import and export the DHCP databases. This allows you to import an older DHCP Services 2.0 database into your new DHCP server. You can also export your existing DHCP Services 3.0 database to a file. These operations are performed by clicking the appropriate icon on the toolbar. You will be led through the simple process by a series of prompts.

The Domain Name System (DNS)

Host names have been a part of the Internet and TCP/IP networks since the beginning. In prior implementations, computers located one another by looking up the host names in a database that had to be downloaded on a regular basis from the Network Information Center. These flat-file host name databases became difficult to manage, and replicating them across the network became very time-intensive. The solution to

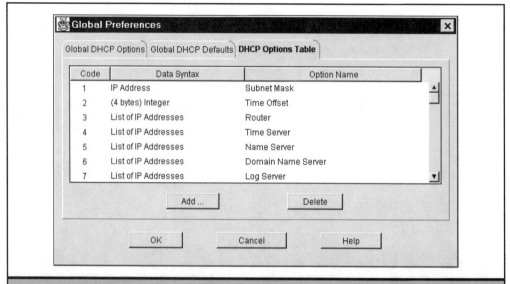

Figure 25-17. *This screen displays the options that have been defined globally. You can add your own types and remove existing types from this screen*

these problems was the hierarchical naming scheme that was developed, called the *Domain Name System (DNS)*.

DNS is nothing more than a database that matches the human-readable names of computers or other network devices to their IP addresses and other data. DNS is composed of two parts: the hierarchy and the name service. The DNS *hierarchy* is referred to as the *domain name space*. It specifies a host's relationship to the other hosts on the network. The hierarchy is best visualized as an inverted tree structure. There is a single domain at the root referred to as the *root domain*. Below the root domain are top-level domains. This is where the com, edu, gov, mil, org, net, and int domains reside. Each of these subdomains is further divided into sub-subdomains representing individual organizations. A host's domain name is simply a list of all the domains in the path from the host back to the root domain. For example, www.kramerkent.com is a host named *kramerkent* under the *com* domain.

The DNS *name service* is the part that maps the human-readable host name to the IP address so that computers can locate one another on a network. It uses a client-server setup in which client programs (resolvers) query one or more name servers for host address information. If the name server does not have the information about a requested domain, the query is forwarded to other name servers within the domain hierarchy until it receives an authoritative answer to the client's query.

A *zone* is a group of domains or subdomains for which an organization has authority. In a traditional DNS implementation, the one name server that maintains the authoritative database for the entire zone is called the *primary name server. Secondary name servers* are used to provide redundancy and load balancing for the zone. These secondary name servers contain read-only copies of the primary server's DNS database. They periodically receive updates from the primary name server in a process referred to as a *zone transfer*.

The DNS database contains numerous blocks of information referred to as *resource records (RRs)*. The most important of these RRs in a standard DNS implementation are as follows:

- **Address records (A)**   These records provide the IP addresses for the zone.
- **Name Server (NS)**   These records bind a domain name to a specific host name for a specific name server.
- **Start of Authority (SOA)**   These records specify the name server's zone of authority.
- **Canonical Name (CNAME)**   These records specify the primary name for the owner.
- **Pointer (PTR)**   These records point to other records and are used for the reverse lookup process when finding the domain name of a host when the IP address is known.

Dynamic Domain Name System (DDNS)

If your network is using DHCP to dynamically assign IP addresses, then you need some mechanism to dynamically update the host tables in the DNS database. This is what Dynamic DNS (DDNS) does. It is a means whereby the DNS database is instantly notified and updated with address assignments made by DHCP servers. By having the DNS and DHCP servers integrated into the NDS database, the DNS server can modify, add, or delete the appropriate RR, A, and PTR records in the DNS database. This allows the DNS server to always know which IP address belongs to which host.

DNS Zones in NDS

All DNS information is stored in the NDS schema in NetWare 5. This allows the DNS database to be replicated throughout the network. DNS information is updated and retrieved by NetWare 5 servers designated as domain name servers. The DNS information is defined in NDS as a zone. A zone contains all of the domain names and data for a particular domain. The DNS Zone object can represent three different types of zones: a standard zone, an IN-ADDR.ARPA zone, or an IP6.INT zone. It must also be configured as either a primary DNS zone or a secondary DNS zone.

Designated Servers

A *designated server* is a NetWare 5 server assigned to service a DNS Zone object. It obtains and updates the DNS data in the NDS tree. It can be either a primary Zone object or a secondary Zone object. If it is a primary Zone object, it performs the task of a master name server. If it is a secondary Zone object, it performs the task of a replica name server.

If the DNS server is designated as a secondary Zone object, it receives zone transfers from a traditional DNS master name server. The secondary server then places the received DNS information into the NDS tree. NDS distributes and replicates the information throughout the network.

Creating a DNS Server Object

The DNS Server object allows you designate a server that can respond to name queries about the DNS zone. Perform the following steps to create a DNS Server object:

1. Click the DNS Service tab in the DNS/DHCP Management Console, which displays the screen shown in Figure 25-18.

2. Click the Create button, which displays the screen shown in Figure 25-19.

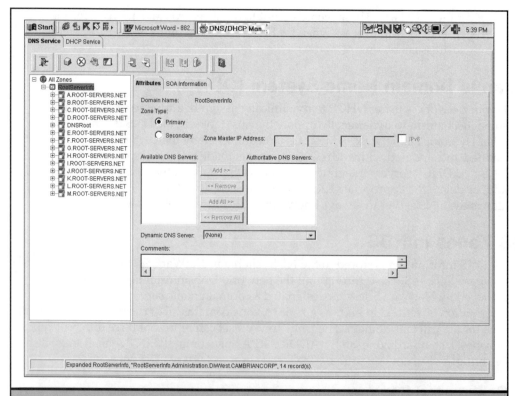

Figure 25-18. *The DNS Service tab displays details about the selected zone*

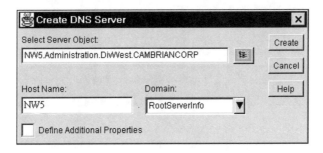

Figure 25-19. *The Create New DNS Record dialog box*

3. Select DNS Server from the list box shown in Figure 25-19.

4. Browse to the context where the Server object that you want to designate as a DNS Server object exists. Enter a name for the DNS server in the Host Name field. Then, in the Domain field, enter the domain in which the DNS server will be located, as shown here:

5. Click the Create button.

Click the DNS Server object that appears in the bottom frame of the management utility to view and configure the zones for the server, the forwarding list, the no-forwarding list, and to enable event logging for the server. The DNS Server object has a slash across it until it is running on the server. The basic information screen is shown in Figure 25-20.

Creating a DNS Zone Object

A DNS Zone object is a container object that holds all of the data for a single DNS zone. This includes Resource Record Set objects and Resource Record objects. You can have multiple DNS domains on a single NetWare 5 server by using separate Zone objects for each domain. The DNS Zone object correlates to a standard DNS Start of Authority

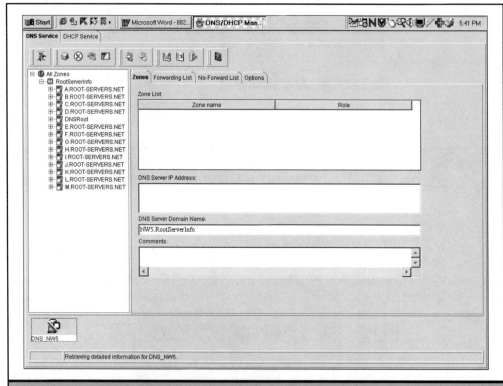

Figure 25-20. *The details display for a DNS Server object named DNS_NW5*

(SOA) resource record. It includes a member list of all NDS-based DNS servers that support the zone. Be aware that the DNS name space hierarchy is not represented within the NDS tree. A DNS domain and its subdomains can appear as peers within the NDS hierarchy even though they actually have a parent/child relationship within the DNS hierarchy. Perform the following steps to create a DNS Zone object:

1. Click the DNS Service tab in the DNS/DHCP Management Console, which displays the screen shown in Figure 25-20.

2. Highlight the All Zones virtual object in the left frame.

3. Click the Create button, which displays the screen shown in Figure 25-19.

4. Select the Zone entry from the text box shown in Figure 25-19.

5. Click OK, which displays the screen shown in Figure 25-21.

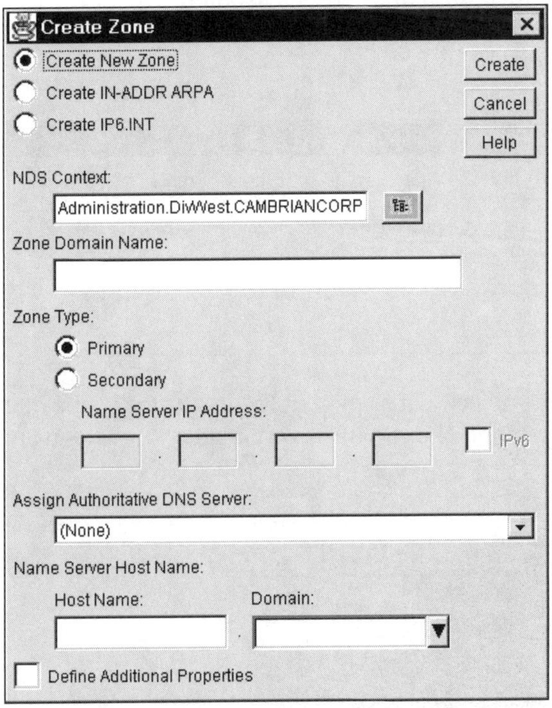

Figure 25-21.   *The DNS Create Zone dialog box*

6. Specify the type of DNS zone you want to create:

   ■ Standard DNS zone

   ■ IN-ADDR ARPA zone

   ■ IP6.INT zone (only one Zone object of this type is allowed in the NDS tree)

7. Enter the NDS context. You can click the Browse button to navigate the NDS tree.

8. Enter the zone domain name.

9. Specify the zone type, either primary or secondary. If you select Secondary, the domain name must match the name of the domain being replicated from the master name server. You must also enter the IP address of the master name server.

10. Assign a DNS server.

11. Click the Create button after you have entered all of the information. The message box shown here will be displayed, indicating that the zone has been successfully created:

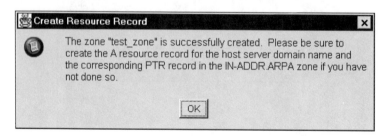

12. The new Zone object will appear in the left frame of the management utility. Click the new Zone object, which will display the screen shown in Figure 25-22.

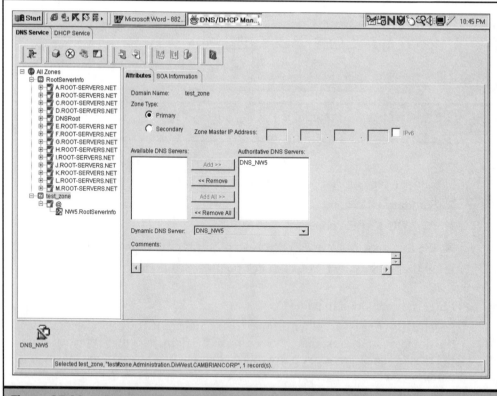

Figure 25-22. *The details are displayed for the selected zone*

Managing the NetWare
Environment

13. Select the SOA Information tab, shown in Figure 25-23, to configure the Start of
Authority zone information.

Creating a Resource Record Object

The Resource Record object is an NDS leaf object that contains the type and data of a
single resource record. Resource Record Set objects are collections of resource records.
They are created automatically when the Resource Record object is created. These are
the most commonly used resource records:

- **A record**   This record type maps a machine name to an IP address.
- **CNAME record**   This record type maps canonical names (alias names)
  to DNS names.
- **MX record**   This record type maps SMTP mail addresses to domain names.
- **NS record**   This record type maps domain names to host names.

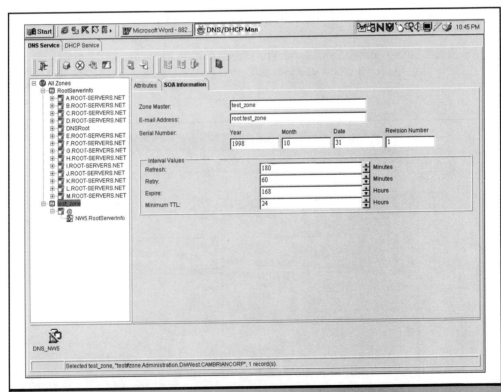

Figure 25-23.   *The SOA Information tab displays the other configurable options
for the zone*

■ **PTR record** This record type maps IP addresses to machine names within the IN-ADDR.ARPA zone.

Perform the following steps to create a Resource Record object:

1. Highlight a DNS Zone object in the left frame of the management utility.

2. Click the Create button, which displays the screen shown here:

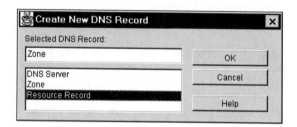

3. Select the Resource Record entry in the list box and click OK.

4. Enter a name for the Resource Record object in the Domain field shown in Figure 25-24.

5. Select the resource record type. The screen shown in Figure 25-24 shows the selection list for the Others radio button.

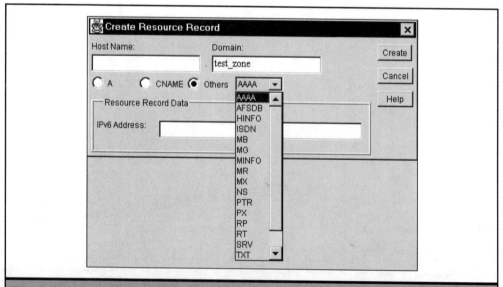

Figure 25-24. The Create Resource Record dialog box showing the list of available record types

6. Click the Create button after you have entered all of the information. You cannot modify a resource record after you have created it. If you need to, you must delete the resource record and create a new one.

Starting the DNS Server

You can start the DNS server after you have created and configured a DNS Server object and a DNS Zone object. Starting the DNS server allows it to respond to queries about hosts contained within the zone. Enter the NAMED command at the server console prompt to start the DNS Server.

At this time, the line through the DNS Server object in the bottom screen of the management utility should disappear, indicating that the DNS server is operational.

The Complete Reference

NetWare 5

Chapter 26

Data Protection and Backup

acking up the data on your server's hard drives is essential. You can perform backups in a number of ways, including copying data to magnetic tape, optical disks, or to other hard disk drives. In the event of a disk failure or loss, you can restore the data you have on other media. You can also use System Fault Tolerance features such as mirroring and duplexing, as discussed in Chapter 13, or you can use Novell StandbyServer or Novell SnapShot Server software, which is briefly described here as well.

This chapter covers NetWare 5's built-in Storage Management Services (SMS) and the NWBACK32 utility. This is a major improvement over the older SMS that shipped with the NetWare 4.x products. The enhanced SBCON console utility and the new NWBACK32 GUI-based workstation utility rival many earlier third-party storage management systems. SMS enables you to perform backups over a network. With it, you can back up Windows 95/98 and NT file systems, NetWare file systems, NetWare DOS partitions, Novell Directory Services (NDS), and GroupWise databases.

Backup Methods

Although NetWare provides a number of built-in data protection mechanisms, such as duplicate file directories and bad-block redirection, you must ensure that the data on a hard drive is backed up so that it is available even if the hard drive crashes. Keep the following points in mind:

- Back up the entire system on a regular basis or whenever you make major changes to its software, directory structure, or configuration.

- Store a duplicate backup set at an off-site location to protect the backups from local disasters such as fires.

- Schedule all of your backups during off-hours when network traffic is low.

- Run a test restoration on a regular basis, especially when an update to the backup application is installed.

- Remember that NetWare 5 consists of two major components: the file system and NDS. Because NDS is distributed, it requires special consideration and configuration.

- Plan to keep older backup software application levels and hardware that will play with the older archive tapes.

You must also ensure that the operating system configuration and environment, including user accounts and passwords, are backed up. In the NetWare 5 environment, this is done by replicating the NDS database onto at least two other servers. However, you should also back up the NDS database to tape or some other backup media in case the NDS database suffers a catastrophic disaster that corrupts all the replicas. Then you restore the NDS database and rebuild your replicas from it.

Backup Strategies

Three backup strategies can be implemented on your network:

- **Full** This type of backup copies all data regardless of when or if it has been previously backed up. It also clears the archive bit for each file and directory backed up.

- **Incremental** This type of backup copies only files and directories that have been created or modified since the last full or incremental backup. It also clears the archive bit for each file and directory backed up.

- **Differential** This type of backup copies all files that have been modified since the last full backup. It does not clear the archive bit for any files or directories.

 Do not combine the differential and incremental backup strategies. If you do, the differential backup will not contain all the changes that have been made since the last full backup.

Rotation Methods

The number of backups you perform depends on the backup strategy, the number of copies you want to keep, whether you want to keep on-site and off-site copies, and the age of the last backup (hours, days, or weeks). You should consider a backup rotation method that keeps copies of backup data available.

A backup rotation method stores current and older data on a set of media that you can store in other locations, thus reducing the risk of losing your only backup set. The *grandfather* method is popular with tape backup systems.

You need 20 tapes that are labeled as described next, but keep in mind that this method assumes you have a five-day work week. Increase the number of tapes and labeling if you have six- or seven-day work weeks.

- Four tapes are labeled Monday, Tuesday, Wednesday, and Thursday.

- Four tapes are labeled Week-1, Week-2, Week-3, and Week-4. You back up to these tapes on Friday.

- Twelve tapes are labeled for each month of the year, and you back up to these tapes at the end of each month.

- To create a duplicate backup set that you can carry to an off-site location, double the number of tapes.

With any backup system, you need to run a restoration test to ensure that your backup and restore procedures work. You might want to set aside a spare server and then run restoration tests using this server on a regular basis. Having spare servers is not a far-fetched idea. Remember, a downed network could cost your company thousands or millions of dollars, depending on how long it takes you to get the system back up and running.

Storage Management Services (SMS)

Novell's Storage Management Services (SMS) is a set of related services that allow data to be stored and retrieved on a network. Novell had hoped to create an industry standard from the specification and, indeed, many vendors use it, but primarily in the NetWare environment. Its most important feature is support for multiple operating systems.

Novell's goals in the development of SMS are listed here and will help you understand how the services work:

- SMS was designed to centralize and simplify the backup of data, no matter where it is on the network.

- It was designed to support the backup of many different file types, including those created in other operating systems.

- The goal was to make it easy for vendors to integrate their hardware or applications into SMS, even as NetWare versions change.

- Another goal was to continue to support old hardware devices as SMS changes, and provide access to old backups far into the future. For example, you could access a ten-year-old backup even if the SMS software has changed over time.

Backup on networks is much more complex than backups on a single computer using one operating system. Networks consist of a diversity of operating systems and file types. In addition, files have special attributes (compression, migration, and so on) and rights information. Novell's SMS is designed to handle this diversity.

The volume of information to back up on a network is also an issue. SMS works with a wide range of archiving devices, from single-tape backup systems to optical jukeboxes that hold terabytes of data. In this way, users can back up without worrying about backup device limitations. Because SMS is modular, hardware vendors simply write drivers and modules so their equipment fits into the system.

Other features of SMS are listed here:

- You can perform full, incremental, differential, or custom backups.

- You can schedule backups for any time.

- You can backup files on servers and workstations even when users are working at them. Open files are bypassed but remain marked for later backup.

- You can backup and restore multiple name space formats defined on a volume, including DOS, FTAM, Long, Macintosh, NFS, and OS/2 files, retaining file attributes associated with each format.

- You can restore all or part of your data either to its original location or to an alternate location in the directory structure.

| Caution | *The Novell Directory Services (NDS) database should be protected using partition and replication techniques discussed in Chapter 18. While SMS provides the tools you need to back up NDS, you should restore NDS from SMS backup only in the case of catastrophic data loss in which all replicas have been corrupted.* |

SMS Components

SMS is a collection of software programs that provide backup and restore services. These services are performed by various components that are independent of operating systems and hardware. To understand SMS, you need to know some terminology, which is used in the following discussions of the system and the backup procedures. Figure 26-1 shows the SMS architecture.

- **Backup engine** The enhanced SBACKUP.NLM is the Storage Management Engine (SME) for NetWare 5 that performs backup and restore operations.

- **Data Requester** The Storage Management Data Requester (SMDR) provides communications between the backup engine software and the Target Service Agent (TSA) software.

- **Storage Device Driver** This driver provides an interface between the SME and the storage device and allows the SME to control the storage device.

- **Data set** This is a data set that can be manipulated by SBCON.

- **Parent** This is a data set that can have subordinate data sets.

- **Child** This is a data set that has no subordinates.

- **Host** This is a NetWare server with an attached storage device that runs SBACKUP and that backs up data on "target" devices. If you are backing up the host's own data, it is both a host and a target.

- **Target** This is a device that has its data backed up or restored by a host. Any server or workstation on the network can potentially be a target.

- **Target Service Agent (TSA)** This is a program that helps handle data transfers between the host and the target. Different TSAs are required for different target operating systems or services. NetWare 5 comes with TSAs to back up the following servers, workstations, and services:

  - NetWare 5, 4.*x*, and 3.*x* servers
  - DOS partition on a NetWare server
  - Windows 95/98 workstations
  - Windows NT workstations and servers

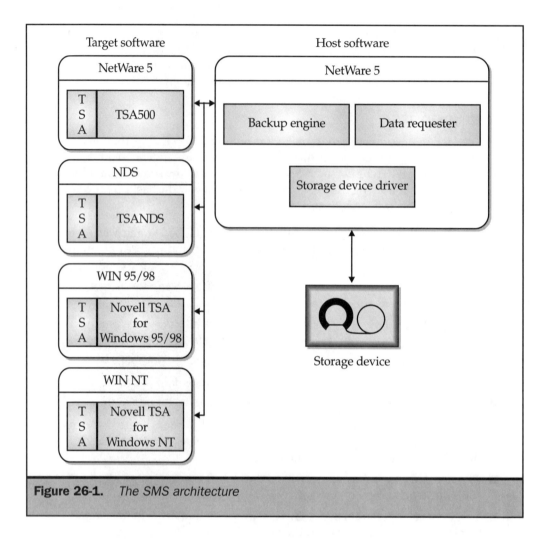

Figure 26-1.   *The SMS architecture*

- Macintosh, UNIX, and OS/2 workstations
- Novell Directory Services (NDS) database
- GroupWise databases

How SMS Works

A basic SMS configuration consists of an archive server that provides backup services, and one or more Target Service Agents (TSAs) that provide backup services for specific operating systems.

Backup device vendors can create modules that allow their devices to work with SMS. The SMS itself doesn't really care about the type of hardware attached. That is all handled by the vendor's interface module.

All data in the SMS is stored using a special System-Independent Data Format (SIDF). Workstations running TSA software provide the data in this format. Because SIDF is standardized, it's possible to restore data to other devices and operating systems, as long as they accept SIDF data. The TSA software is responsible for providing the SIDF data. In this way, each TSA is designed to work with the idiosyncrasies of the specific operating system it runs on. Because TSAs simply provide SIDF data to SMS backup devices, they can change over time as the operating systems or platforms they run on change. TSAs function as translators from the target platform to SMS (for the backup) and from SMS to the same or a different platform (for a restore).

Hardware Support

The SBCON utility in NetWare 5 supports industry-standard 0.25-inch, 4mm, and 8mm storage devices, but you should check with manufacturers before buying. If you are using 4mm tape, use only DDS-certified, computer-grade tapes.

The following driver files are included with NetWare 5, but you may need to contact the backup device vendor in order to obtain a driver appropriate for the device you have.

- **DLTTAPE.HAM**   This driver supports the Quantum DLT tape devices.
- **EXATAPE.HAM**   This driver supports the Exabyte SCSI tape devices.
- **BKSTROSM.HAM**   This driver supports all I2O generic bus and block storage devices.
- **NWTAPE.CDM**   This driver is compliant with the NetWare Peripheral Architecture (NWPA) and supports both SCSI-2 and ATAPI tape devices. You must load either the SCSI or ATAPI HAM in order to use this driver.

Loading and Running SMS

Use the following steps to load the appropriate SMS modules and run the SBCON utility at the server console. It is assumed that the server in these steps has an archiving device attached.

1. Load the device drivers for the backup device. For example, at the server, type **[LOAD] DLTTAPE.HAM** to install support for a Quantum tape backup device, or type **[LOAD] NWTAPE.CDM** and either **SCSI.HAM** or **ATAPI.HAM** to load Novell's generic driver.

2. Register the storage device with the system by typing the following at the server console prompt:

SCAN FOR NEW DEVICES

3. Verify that the new device is seen by the system by typing the following at the server console prompt:

LIST DEVICE

The screen shown here will be displayed, showing all devices known to the system:

```
NW5:list devices
0x0001: [V025-A0-D1:0] Conner Peripherals 1620MB - CFS1621A
0x0002: [V025-A0-D1:1] QUANTUM FIREBALL540A
0x0004: [V025-A1-D2:0] ATAPI CD-ROM DRIVE rev:242H
0x000D: [V040-A2-D0:0] EMULATOR_TAPE  1
NW5:
```

We have loaded a special emulator, EMULATOR_TAPE, that allows the server to store backup data to a file instead of a tape device. This is a utility provided by Novell to instructors for teaching this part of the NetWare 5 class.

4. Load the NetWare Storage Management Queue Manager by typing the following at the server prompt:

[LOAD] QMAN

5. This will automatically load the SMSDI and SMDR NLMs.

6. Load the SBACKUP command module by typing the following at the server prompt:

[LOAD] SBSC

7. Load the TSA modules appropriate for the type of backup you want to perform, as listed here. Note that you can load more than one module and you can include these load commands in the AUTOEXEC.NCF file to have them load every time you start the server.

- **[LOAD] TSA500**   Backs up the NetWare 5 host server
- **[LOAD] TSA500**   Backs up a NetWare 5 server
- **[LOAD] TSA400**   Backs up a NetWare 4.*x* server
- **[LOAD] TSA312**   Backs up a NetWare 3.12 server
- **[LOAD] TSA311**   Backs up a NetWare 3.11 server

- **[LOAD] TSADOSP**   Backs up the DOS partition on a server
- **[LOAD] TSAPROXY**   Backs up OS/2, UNIX, and Macintosh workstations
- **[LOAD] TSANDS**   Backs up any NetWare 5 or NetWare 4.*x* NDS database

8. After loading the appropriate TSA module, load the SBCON utility by typing **[LOAD] SBCON**. The SBCON utility is discussed in the next section.

If you intend to back up a workstation, enter the following commands at the server console prompt:

```
[LOAD]  TSAPROXY
[LOAD]  SMSDI
[LOAD]  SME
```

If you intend to back up Windows 95/98 workstations, go to those stations and type **W95TSA.EXE** at the command-line prompt.

In you intend to back up Windows NT systems, go to those stations and type **TSAPREFS.EXE, TSAMAIN.EXE,** and **NT TSA** at the command-line prompt.

If you intend to back up OS/2, UNIX, or Macintosh workstations, go to those stations and type **TSAPROXY** *parameters*, replacing *parameters* with a list of startup parameters you can view by first typing **TSAPROXY /?.**

Using the SBCON Console Utility

When you type **LOAD SBCON** at the host server, the screen shown in Figure 26-2 will be displayed. Each of its options are discussed here:

- **Job Administration**   Choose this option to submit a job (backup, restore, or verify) to the SMS queue manager and administer it.

- **Storage Device Administration**   Select this option to choose a storage device to back up to or restore from. This option also lets you check the status of a device or its media.

- **Log File Administration**   Backup sessions create log files that you can view to see if any errors occurred or to get a list of backup sessions and their names.

- **Change Target to Backup From or Restore To**   This option lets you view and change the target to which you are attached.

Note   *If you are backing up a server, you can load multiple TSAs for different operating systems and then back up files in any of those environments. Include the TSA for NDS and TSANDS to back up NDS. In SMS, NDS is treated as a special file set because it is a distributed file set.*

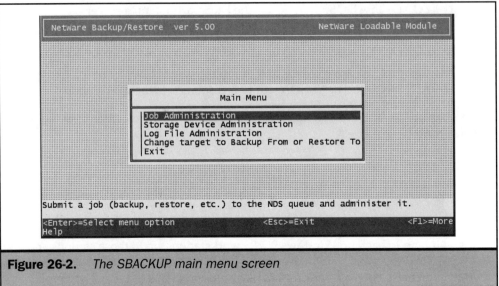

Figure 26-2.   *The SBACKUP main menu screen*

More About Log Files

If you choose Log File Administration from the SBCON main menu, you can choose to view a session log file or an error file. The contents of these files are covered next.

Session Log File Contents

A session log file contains information about the backup of a specific group of files. It holds the following information:

- Date and time of the backup
- Any descriptions specified for the backup
- Target from which the data was backed up
- Identification information for the media set
- Volume name, directory structure, and filenames that were backed up
- Index of data on the backup media

Error Log File Contents

The error log holds information you may need to consult about a particular backup session. The error log contains the same date, time, description, identification, and file information as the session log file, and it also includes the following:

- Total number of parents and children that were successfully backed up
- Names of files that were not backed up and any errors that were generated

A Typical Backup Session Using SBCON

The following exercise presents a typical backup session of files on the host server. The steps are outlined here for your reference:

1. Load the required modules at the host server, as described under "Loading and Running SMS," earlier in this chapter, and then start the SBCON utility as discussed previously under "Using the SBCON Console Utility."

2. Select Job Administration from the main menu, as shown in Figure 26-2.

3. Select Backup from the Select Job menu, as shown in Figure 26-3. The screen shown in Figure 26-4 will displayed, allowing you to configure the backup options.

4. Select Target Service and choose a target from the list. The screen shown in Figure 26-5 will be displayed. If the target is quite a distance from your location, you may not see it at first. Press ESC and then repeat this step.

5. You will be prompted for a user login name and the password to the target server you have selected. You must have a minimum of Read and File Scan rights to perform the file system backup operation. You will also need Browse and Read rights for NDS if you are including NDS in the backup.

6. Select What to Back Up? A screen showing the available resources will be displayed, as shown in Figure 26-6. If no resources are shown, press the INS key to view the resources on the selected target.

7. Select Description to enter a name for the backup job.

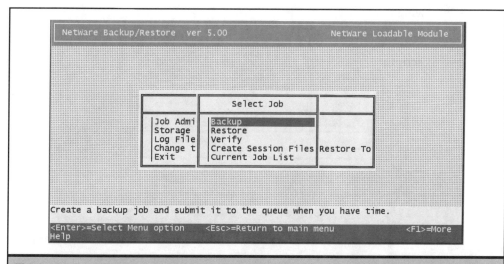

Figure 26-3.   *This menu allows you to select the type of operation you want to perform*

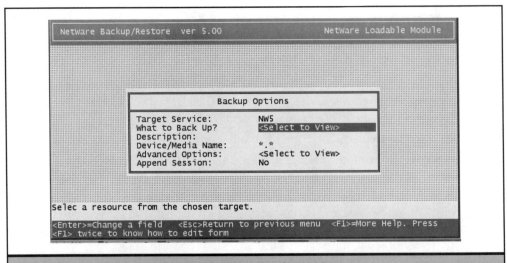

Figure 26-4. Configure the backup operation from this screen

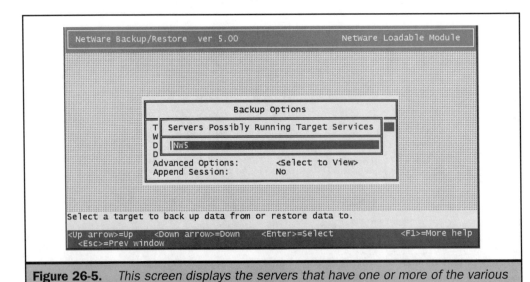

Figure 26-5. This screen displays the servers that have one or more of the various
TSAs loaded

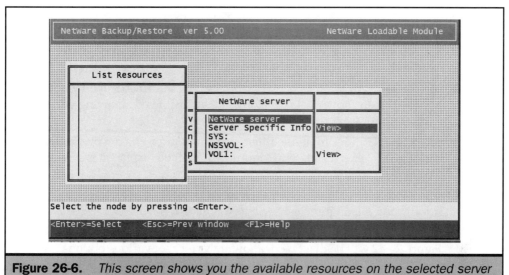

Figure 26-6. *This screen shows you the available resources on the selected server that can be backed up*

8. Select Device/Media Name to select the backup device, as shown in Figure 26-7. If your archive system has more than one backup device, choose a device to back up to.

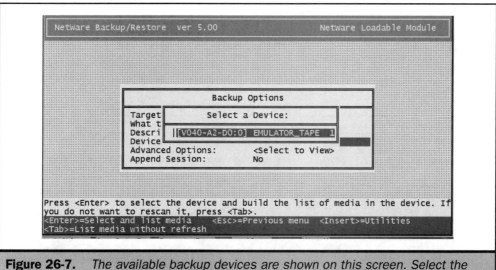

Figure 26-7. *The available backup devices are shown on this screen. Select the appropriate backup device that you want to use here*

9. Select Advanced Options to display the screen shown in Figure 26-8. This set of options enables you to configure the backup operation.

   ■ Select Backup Type to choose the type of backup you want to perform— either full, incremental, or differential.

   ■ Select Subsets of What to Back Up to select the information you want to back up. The screen shown in Figure 26-9 will be displayed, allowing you set various options.

   ■ Select Scan Options to define filters on the resource you are preparing to back up. The screen shown in Figure 26-10 will be displayed, showing the various filter options.

   ■ Select Execution Time to enter the time and date of the backup job. The screen shown in Figure 26-11 will be displayed.

   ■ Select Scheduling to rerun the job at another time. The screen shown in Figure 26-12 will be displayed, allowing you to set various options.

You can schedule the backup for after-hours or weekends, if necessary, to avoid excess network traffic and conflicts with files that are in use. Don't mount or dismount volumes or drivers during a backup session and don't attempt to compress files.

Consider changing the compression window from 0 to 6 (midnight to 6 A.M.) to 0 to 2, and then schedule the backup to start at 2:15 A.M. Use the Monitor utility and select Server Parameters to make these changes and incorporate them in the AUTOEXEC.NCF file. You trade off the amount of compression time, but there is never a conflict between compression and backup.

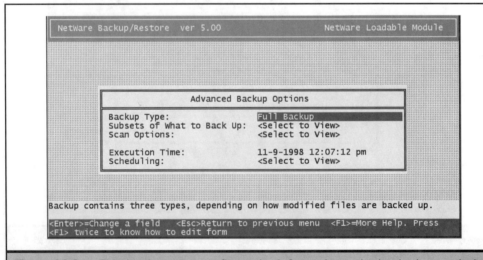

Figure 26-8.   *This is where you configure the information to be backed up and when the operation is to be run*

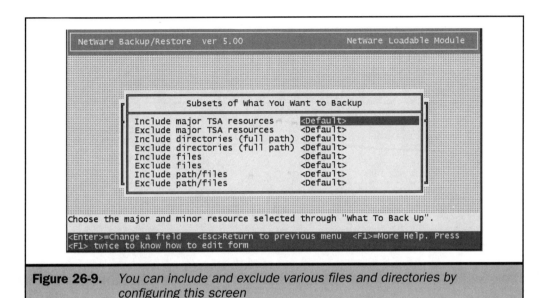

Figure 26-9. *You can include and exclude various files and directories by configuring this screen*

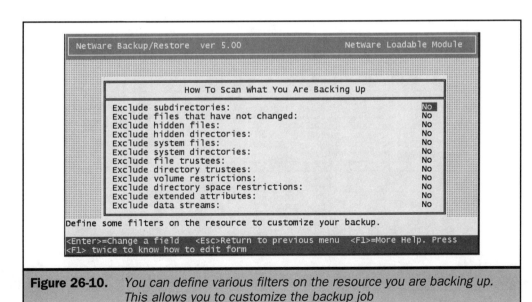

Figure 26-10. *You can define various filters on the resource you are backing up. This allows you to customize the backup job*

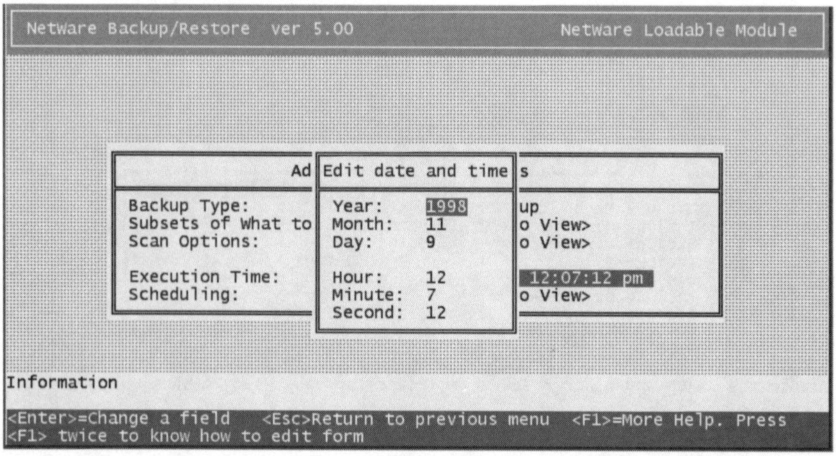

Figure 26-11. *Set the date and time that you want the backup job to start in this screen*

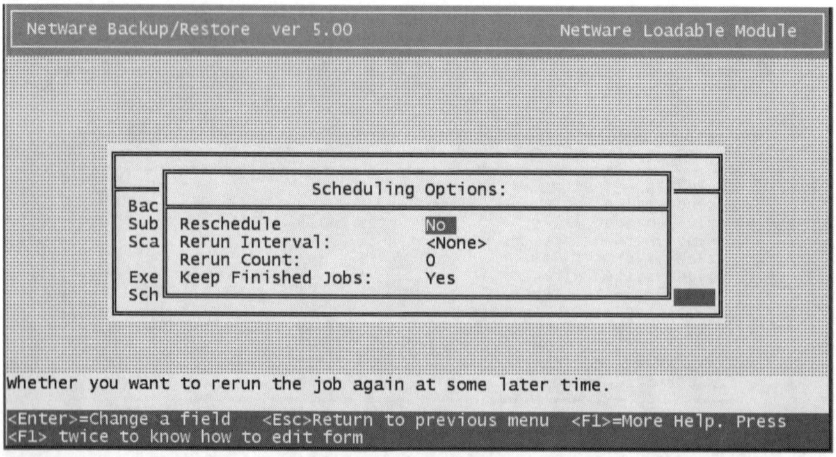

Figure 26-12. *You can schedule the job to be rerun at various intervals*

A Typical Restore Session Using SBCON

The following exercise presents a typical restore session. The steps are briefly outlined here for reference only. You should run the utility yourself and refer to the NetWare 5 manuals for more information. It's always a good idea to test a restore session with real backup data so you know how it works in case of emergency.

1. Load the required modules at the host server, as described under "Loading and Running SMS," earlier in this chapter, and then start the SBCON utility as discussed previously under the "Using the SBCON Console Utility."

2. Select Job Administration from the main menu, as shown in Figure 26-2.

3. Select Restore from the Select Job menu, as shown in Figure 26-3. The screen shown in Figure 26-13 will be displayed, allowing you to configure the restore options.

4. Select Target Service and choose a target from the list. If the target is quite a distance from your location, you may not see it at first. Press ESC, and then repeat this step.

5. You will be prompted for a user login name and the password to the target server you have selected. You must have a minimum of Read, Write, and File Scan rights to perform the file system restore operation. If you are restoring NDS also, you will need Browse, Read, and Write rights for NDS.

6. Select Description to enter a name for the restore job.

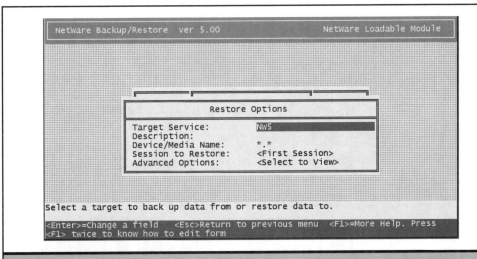

Figure 26-13.   *The Restore Options screen is very similar to the Backup Options screen*

7. Select Device/Media Name to select the backup device, as shown in Figure 26-7. If your archive system has more than one backup device, choose a device to restore from.

8. Select Session to Restore to restore using the session log files, or to restore without using the session log files.

   ■ If you choose to restore with session files, you select the session to restore.

   ■ If you choose to restore without session files, you must use the Advanced Options menu to specify the device where the backup media resides.

9. Select Advanced Options to modify configuration parameters used in the restore operation. The screen shown in Figure 26-14 will be displayed, allowing you to configure various options.

10. Select Rename Data Sets to restore data to a location other than the backup location.

11. Select Subsets of What to Restore to include or exclude subsets of the backup resources, as shown in Figure 26-15.

12. Select Open Mode Options to set the restore parameters for the type of data contained in the backup session. The screen shown in Figure 26-16 will be displayed, allowing you make your selections.

13. Select Overwrite Parent to overwrite a container that has subordinates.

14. Select Overwrite Child to overwrite individual subordinates such as files.

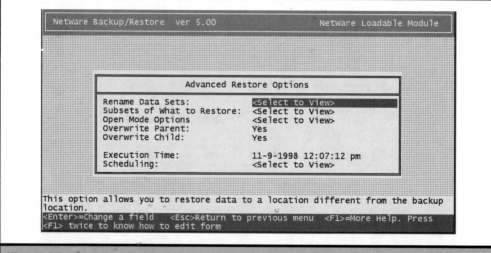

Figure 26-14.   *This screen allows you to configure the various parameters associated with the restore operation*

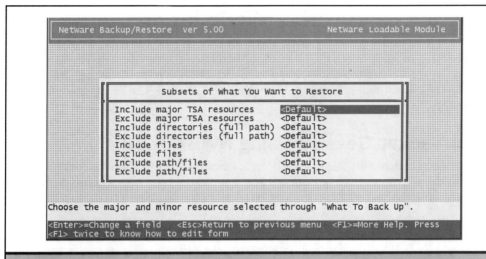

Figure 26-15. *You can include and exclude various resources from the backup resource to be restored*

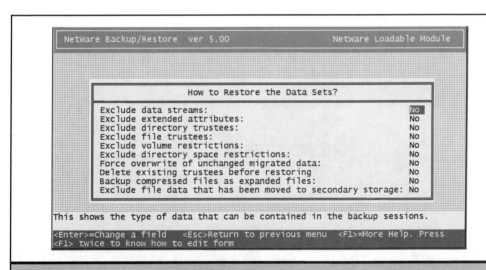

Figure 26-16. *You can configure various options on the data to be restored, such as allowing extended attributes to be written, or forcing the overwrite of existing files*

Using the NWBACK32 Workstation Utility

The NWBACK32 utility runs at a workstation and allows you to configure and run backup and restore jobs. It is a GUI-based utility that rivals most third-party tape backup software. To run the utility, go to the SYS:PUBLIC directory on the server where the backup software is running. Execute the NWBACK32.EXE program from this directory.

A Typical Backup Session Using NWBACK32

The steps necessary to run these operations are briefly outlined here for reference only. You should run the utility yourself and refer to the NetWare 5 manuals for more information.

1. Verify that the backup queue was created correctly in the NDS tree. It should appear as shown in Figure 26-17.

2. Load the Queue Manager by typing **[LOAD] QMAN** at the server console.

3. Load the SBACKUP Communications module by typing **[LOAD] SBSC** at the server console.

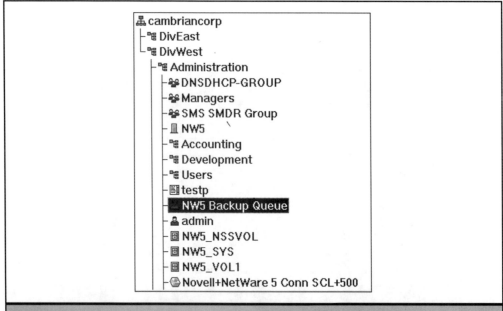

Figure 26-17.   *The backup queue is created in the container specified in the NDS tree*

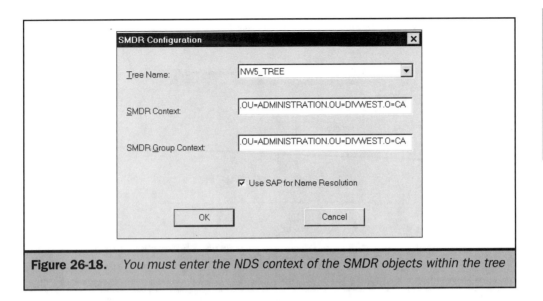

Figure 26-18. *You must enter the NDS context of the SMDR objects within the tree*

4. Load the Storage Management Console by typing **[LOAD] SBCON** at the server console.

5. Load the appropriate TSAs at the server console for your backup device.

6. Start the NWBACK32 utility at your workstation.

7. Enter the NDS tree name, SMDR context, and SMDR Group Context in the SMDR Configuration window, as shown in Figure 26-18.

8. Configure your tape device. It will initially be displayed as Unidentifiable Media, as shown here:

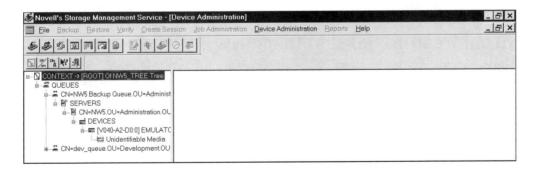

9. Right-click Unidentifiable Media and click New Label. The screen shown here will be displayed:

10. Enter the new name for the media.

11. Choose File | New Session | Backup. The screen shown here will be displayed:

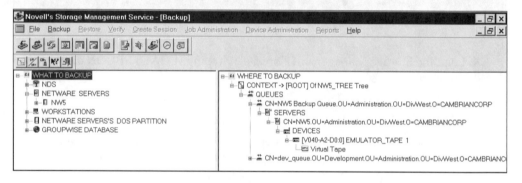

12. Select the items to be backed up and the destination for the items.

13. Click Submit the Job.

A Typical Restore Session Using NWBACK32

The steps necessary to run a restore operation are briefly outlined here for reference only. You should run the utility yourself and refer to the NetWare 5 manuals for more information.

1. Verify that the backup queue was created correctly in the NDS tree. It should appear as shown in Figure 26-17.

2. Load the Queue Manager by typing **[LOAD] QMAN** at the server console.

3. Load the SBACKUP Communications module by typing **[LOAD] SBSC** at the server console.

4. Load the Storage Management Console by typing **[LOAD] SBCON** at the server console.

5. Load the appropriate TSAs at the server console for your backup device.

6. Start the NWBACK32 utility at your workstation.

7. If prompted for SMDR information, enter the NDS tree name, SMDR context, and SMDR Group Context in the SMDR Configuration window, as shown in Figure 26-18. If not, the screen shown in Figure 26-19 will be displayed, allowing you to select the operation you desire.

8. Select a target to which you want the data restored.

9. Log in to the server as a user with the necessary rights to restore the data if required.

10. Insert the backup media into the backup device.

11. Select a restore device.

12. Select the session to be restored.

13. Select the data to restore from the backup.

14. Specify a schedule and rerun interval for the backup.

15. Submit the restore job.

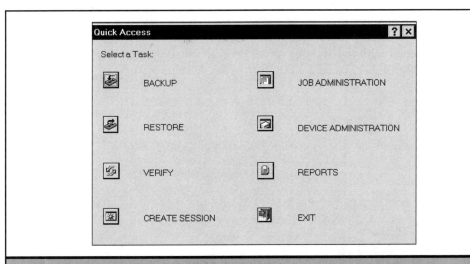

Figure 26-19.   *From this Quick Access window, you can select an operation with a simple mouse click*

Novell StandbyServer

Novell StandbyServer is a licensed product from Vinca. It provides high availability to the primary server with one or more standby servers. All data is mirrored between the servers to create a fully redundant system that protects users against both hardware and software failures. Users are automatically reconnected to another server within moments of a hardware or software failure, with their data files intact. It is a transaction-based solution, not a file-based copy. Complete images of all data on the primary server are kept on one or more standby servers.

StandbyServer does not require that the server hardware between the primary server and the standby servers be the same. Only the mirrored volumes on the primary server and the standby servers must match. In addition, you can connect the machines to a single RAID device if desired. This eliminates the need for redundancy in the number of disk drives attached to the primary server.

Novell SnapShotServer

Novell SnapShotServer is another licensed product from Vinca. It lets you back up open files and live databases at any time without affecting the performance of your primary server. SnapShotServer creates snapshot images of the primary server at designated intervals, which can be as often as every fifteen minutes. These images are mounted and manipulated on the standby server just like any other NetWare volumes.

SnapShotServer allows for 31 overlapping snapshots of the primary server at any time. If data loss or corruption occurs on the primary server, you can roll back the system to the snapshot before the problem occurred, rather than restore from the last backup tape.

When combined with the StandbyServer product, SnapShotServer allows multiple servers in the enterprise to be backed up from a single standby server.

Chapter 27

Netscape
FastTrack
Server

751

Netscape FastTrack Server for NetWare is the entry-level Web server that comes bundled with the NetWare 5 product. It is a software application that publishes documents as well as other types of files on an internal intranet or the World Wide Web. All Web servers operate in a client-server relationship in which the client, usually a Web browser such as Netscape Navigator or Microsoft Internet Explorer, requests information and the Web server application supplies it. The Web server application receives these requests and supplies the information to the client using the Hypertext Transfer Protocol (HTTP). The Web server must be physically attached to a TCP/IP network to function.

Overview of Netscape FastTrack Server

Netscape FastTrack Server is designed for small and medium-sized organizations that need a simple and low-cost solution for Web publishing. It is actually a subset of the Netscape Enterprise Server product. You should consider upgrading to Netscape Enterprise Server if you need to support multiple Web presences on the same Web server, have large amounts of data that need to be organized and maintained, or need advanced search capabilities and document management.

Netscape FastTrack Server is easily installed from a Windows 95/98/NT workstation running Novell's Client for network connectivity. Netscape FastTrack Server supports remote administration of the Web server through a browser-based interface. It provides support for server-side Java, JavaScript, PERL5, and NetBasic. It also provides centralized Lightweight Directory Access Protocol (LDAP) or NDS-based user and access management. It is based on open protocols and supports all existing Internet standards.

Web Basics

You need to consider a few basic things before you jump in and install a Web server. If you intend to connect your Web server to the World Wide Web, you must determine the best Internet service provider (ISP) and connection type for your Web server. Then, you must obtain a registered IP address and domain name. The following sections will cover these areas in enough detail to get you started.

What Is an Internet Service Provider (ISP)?

An Internet service provider (ISP) is a company that provides network bandwidth and resources to various Web sites. You either pay an ISP to host your Web site or to manage the routes from your Web server to the outside world. If you intend to use your Web server only for publishing Web pages internal to the company, you can skip this section.

Before you select an ISP, you need to evaluate several criteria. This includes the total subscribed bandwidth the ISP has to the Internet, what types of connections are offered by the ISP to you as a customer, and the complete breakdown of all associated costs such as line charges, technical support, and billing processes. Once you have this information in hand, you need to determine your bandwidth needs, the type of connection you intend to have to the ISP, and the cost of each service offered by the ISP.

Determining Needed Bandwidth

You have to estimate your bandwidth needs to determine your best connection type to your ISP. Recent research suggests that each simultaneous user needs 56 Kbit/sec bandwidth to your Web server. File size is the most important criterion for determining your bandwidth needs. The more bandwidth you have, the less time people accessing your Web server have to wait. Keep in mind that the longer you make visitors wait, the less likely it is they will stay at your site.

Calculate the approximate number of megabytes transmitted per day to estimate your bandwidth needs. Multiply the number of times the files are sent by your Web server by the average size of your Web files. Also be sure to add in all management and other services such as FTP and NNTP that your Web server performs. This will provide you with a general estimate of your bandwidth needs. However, you need to understand that a number of other variables can affect your bandwidth, such as line congestion, a higher than average number of user connections, and faulty equipment between connecting points on the network.

Let's look at an example for calculating the needed bandwidth for a Web server, as shown in Table 27-1.

Variable	Data
Number of hits per day	125
Size of Web site (total file size)	6MB
Average percentage of Web site viewed	35%
Number of forms that the Web server must download to the client	4
Average size of data per form sent back to the Web server	0.5K
Average percentage of forms filled out per site visit	45%
Average size of files sent to clients via FTP per day	3.8MB
DNS requests processed by the server	350
DNS datagram size in bytes per request	20 bytes

Table 27-1.   *Sample Web Server Bandwidth Needs*

Perform the following calculations to estimate your needed bandwidth:

- (Number of Web site hits) × (Size of Web site files) × (% of site viewed) = Total1
  125 × 6MB × 0.35 = 262.5MB

- (Number of forms) × (Size of form data) × (% of forms processed) = Total2
  4 × 0.5MB × 0.45 = 0.9MB

- (Size of FTP files) + (Management services) = Total3
  3.8MB + (350 × 20 bytes) = ~3.8MB

- Total1 + Total2 + Total3 = MB per day (bandwidth)
  262.5MB + 0.9MB + 3.8MB = ~267.2MB per day

Choosing the Connection Type

The next step in the process is to determine which type of connection to your ISP will meet your bandwidth requirements. Connection types are offered at different prices and require different hardware. Some hardware, such as routers, are on the high end, whereas modems are on the low end. The costs associated with the connection type may help you decide which connection to choose from your ISP. Each of the various connection types is discussed in the following sections.

Analog Line

Analog lines carry the smallest bandwidth and have a limit of either 28.8 Kbits/sec or 33.6 Kbits/sec. Newer modems advertise a speed of 56 Kbits/sec, which can be misleading. These modems are still limited in their transmit speed to a maximum of 33.6 Kbits/sec. Their download speeds are at 56 Kbits/sec up to 80 Kbits/sec with compression. Most of the newer 56 Kbit/sec modems are designed to the V.90 specifications. This specification replaced the older X2 and K56Flex standards that were incompatible with each other.

Be aware that only a limited number of analog lines are available at one time. This number may be as low as 10 percent in some areas. If you subscribe for a permanent analog connection, it may not be as permanent as you think.

56/64 Kbit/sec Dedicated Line

A 56 Kbit/sec dedicated line is a digital connection from your Web server to the local ISP. The European version of this is the 64 Kbit/sec dedicated line. When you select this type of connection, you are charged for full use of the line. Digital lines have significant advantages over analog lines. There is less signal degradation, they are less expensive, it is easier to regenerate and repeat the digital signals, and they provide higher bandwidth over telephone wires.

Integrated Services Digital Network (ISDN)

ISDN combines multiple digital lines for bandwidths from 64 Kbits/sec to 1.5 Mbits/sec. It is comprised of two channels. The first is the bearer, or B, channel used for voice and data transmission. The second is the data, or D, channel used for control of the B channels. When two channels are combined, it is called *bonding,* which stands for *b*andwidth *on d*emand *in*teroperability *g*roup. ISDN has two classifications:

- **Basic Rate Interface (BRI)** This consists of two 64 Kbit/sec B channels and one 16 Kbit/sec D channel. This provides up to 144 Kbit/sec bandwidth.

- **Primary Rate Interface (PRI)** This consists of twenty-three 64 Kbit/sec B channels and one 64 Kbit/sec D channel. This provides up to 1.544 Mbit/sec bandwidth.

Cable Modems

Cable Modems use the existing cable television wiring to connect you to the Internet. They provide up to 1.5 Mbits/sec of bandwidth for download and up to 500 Kbits/sec for uploading files to a client. They are limited in the amount of security they can provide because they rely on a broadband transmission scheme. This means that anybody attached to the cable can receive your transmissions.

Multiplexed Voice Channels

Multiplexed Voice Channels include the Tx digital lines in the United States and the Ex digital lines in Europe. They are dedicated full-time connections between your site and the ISP. The available Tx digital lines are as follows:

- **T1** This consists of 24 voice channels, each running at 64 Kbits/sec. The total bandwidth is 1.544 Mbits/sec.

- **T2** This consists of 4 T1 lines or 96 voice channels. The total bandwidth is 6.312 Mbits/sec.

- **T3** This consists of 7 T2s or 28 T1s. It contains 672 voice channels and has a total bandwidth of 44,736 Mbits/sec.

- **T4** This consists of 6 T3s, or 42 T2s, or 168 T1s. It contains 4,032 voice channels and has a total bandwidth of 274,176 Mbits/sec.

Registering Your IP Address and Domain Name

You must obtain a registered IP address and domain name for your Web site to enable users to access it via the World Wide Web. You can register either through your ISP, the InterNIC, the American Registry for Internet Numbers (ARIN), or any other international organization that manages IP addresses. You usually get a registered IP address from your ISP and then register your domain name with the InterNIC.

Installing Netscape FastTrack Server

Netscape FastTrack Server is installed from a Windows 95/98/NT workstation connected to the target server. The installation program installs two servers on the target server, an administration server used to manage and configure the Web server and the Web server used to deliver Web pages to the Internet or intranet.

There are a number of prerequisites for both hardware and software that must be met before proceeding with the installation:

- NetWare 5 must be installed on the server.
- The latest version of the Novell Client must be installed on the workstation (Windows 95/98/NT).
- You must have an Internet browser installed on the workstation (preferably Netscape Communicator 4.*x*).
- You must have long name support loaded on the target server (this is by default on a NetWare 5 server).

Your hardware for the target server must meet the following requirements:

- A minimum of 100MB of free disk space on the SYS volume of the target server.
- A minimum of 64MB of system RAM (preferably 128MB or more).

Your hardware requirements for the client workstation from which you are installing the product must be as follows:

- A 486 processor or better
- A minimum of 100MB of free disk space
- A minimum of 64MB system RAM

Novell cannot guarantee that the Netscape FastTrack Server will work with the following software:

- Microsoft Client for NetWare networks
- Microsoft file and printer sharing for NetWare networks
- Microsoft Service for Novell Directory Services
- Microsoft Internet Explorer

Installation Procedure

The installation procedure for the Netscape FastTrack Server is fairly painless. The steps are as follows:

1. Map a network drive at the installation workstation to the SYS volume on the target server.
2. Ensure that the TCP/IP protocol is installed and configured on both the workstation and the target server.

3. Insert the NetWare 5 Operating System CD in the workstation machine and navigate to the PRODUCTS\WEBSERV directory.

4. The setup program will present you with a welcome screen, as shown here, which lists the requirements necessary for a successful install of the product. Click the Finish button.

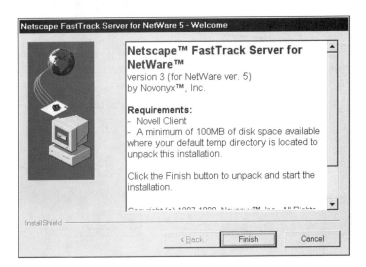

5. You must enter a destination folder for the installed product in the screen, as shown here. This is usually the drive mapped to the SYS volume on the target server.

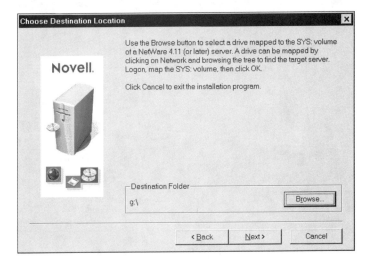

6. Enter the IP address and host name of the Web server, as shown here. If you do not have DNS set up with your host name entry, you need to enter the IP address of the target server in this field also. You can set up DNS and change the host name in the Administration Server console after the install.

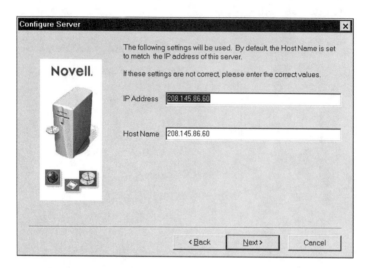

7. Enter the server port number, as shown here. The default port number for the HTTP listener is port 80.

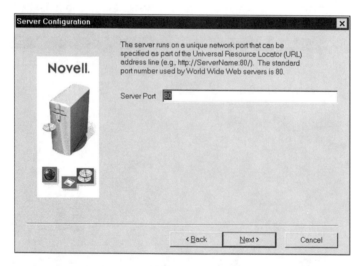

8. Enter the administration port number, as shown next. You can accept the default or enter another number of your choosing.

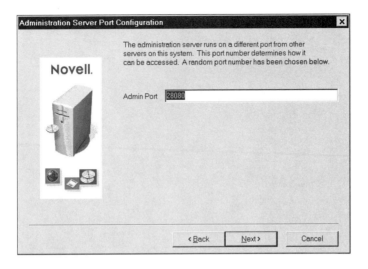

> **Note**   *You must remember the port number! Without it, you cannot manage and configure your Web server.*

9. Enter the username and password for the Web server administrator, as shown here. Remember, the administrator password is case-sensitive.

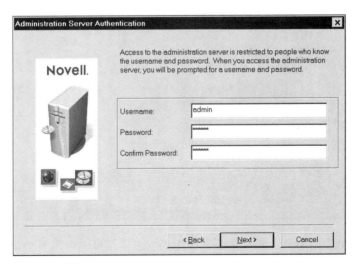

10. The screen shown next is an informational screen only. The Web server can be tied into both LDAP and NDS for maintaining user and group information.

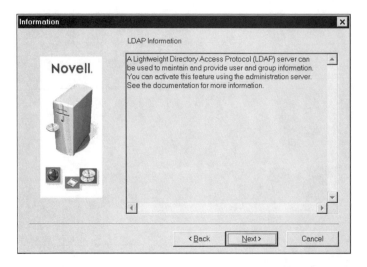

11. Select whether or not you want the AUTOEXEC.NCF startup file on the file server modified, as shown here. If you change the AUTOEXEC.NCF file, the Web server will start automatically whenever the file server is restarted.

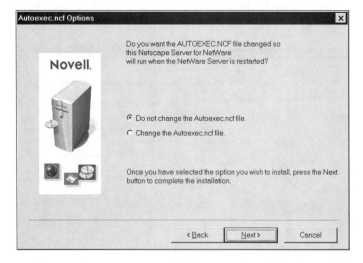

12. A summary screen is displayed, as shown next. This screen allows you to confirm your settings and go back and change any of the fields if necessary.

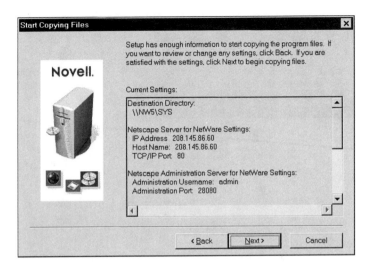

13. Congratulations! You have finished the installation of Netscape FastTrack Server. The Setup Complete screen, shown here, will be displayed, prompting you to click the Finish button to launch the Web server.

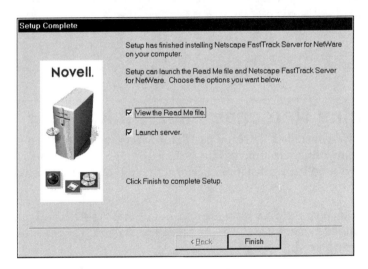

The information screen shown in Figure 27-1 will be displayed in your browser. Click the links for more information about the FastTrack Server product.

Figure 27-1. *The Welcome screen for the Web server is displayed in your browser at the installation workstation. Notice that the Netsite address entry is the IP address of the Web server. If you have configured DNS, the host name will be displayed here*

Configuring Netscape FastTrack Server

Now that you have installed Netscape FastTrack Server, you need to configure it to work properly in your environment. This is done through the Administration console via a Web browser on the workstation. Perform the following steps to start the configuration process:

1. Start your Web browser software and enter the IP address and port number you entered in steps 6 and 8 in the preceding section. The screen shown here will be displayed:

2. Enter your Web administrator user name and password in the dialog box. The screen shown in Figure 27-2 will be displayed if you entered the information correctly.

The screen in Figure 27-2 presents two options for administration, general or server-specific. The general options are used to configure common settings for all Web servers listed in the Netscape Server Administration page. The server-specific options allow you to select any of the listed Web servers and configure them individually.

General Administration

The five general administration options (refer to Figure 27-2) allow you to set specific configurations for all Web servers known to the administration console:

- Admin Preferences
- Global Settings
- Users & Groups
- Keys & Certificates
- Cluster Management

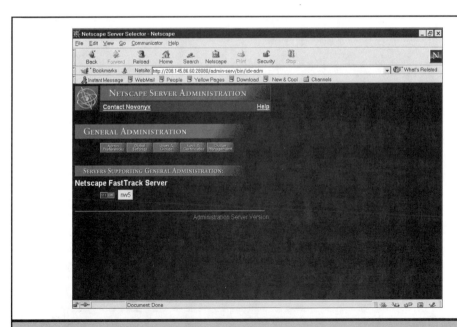

Figure 27-2.   *The Netscape Server Administration screen allows you to configure global and server-specific options for each Web server in your network*

Admin Preferences

The administrative preference screen shown in Figure 27-3 allows you configure the basic operating environment for the Web server. Each of these options is explained next.

SHUT DOWN   The Shut Down page allows you to shut down the administrative server software. It is a simple way to unload the ADMSERV.NLM on the Web server. This does not shut down the Web server, only the administrative server software. You can use this command to release the memory in the server that was allocated for the administrative software when it is not being used. The Shut Down page is shown in Figure 27-3. It is the first page that is displayed when you start the administrative server.

NETWORK SETTINGS   The Network Settings page, shown in Figure 27-4, allows you to change the administrative port number for all Web servers. If you decide to change this number, select a number greater than 2000. Port numbers less than 2000 are already reserved for industry-standard TCP/IP services.

SUPERUSER ACCESS CONTROL   The SuperUser Access Control page, shown in Figure 27-5, allows you to change the Web administrator user name and associated

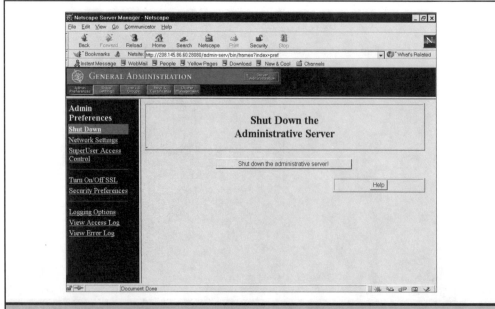

Figure 27-3.   *Shut down the administrative server after you have completed your administrative tasks*

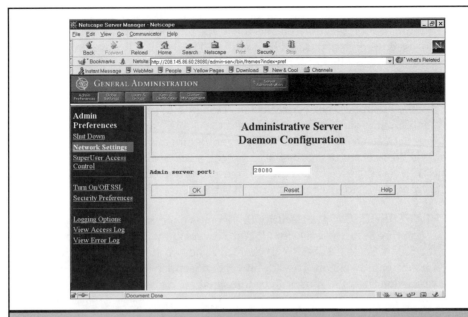

Figure 27-4. *Reconfigure the administrative server port address for all Web servers in your network*

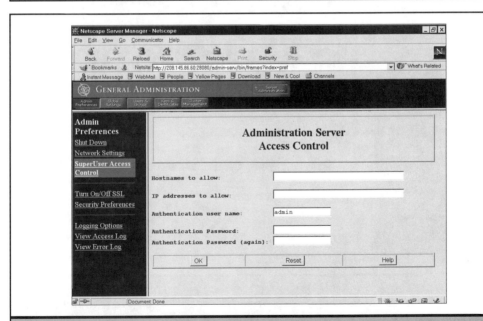

Figure 27-5. *Change the Web administrator name and password. You can also configure various restrictions as to which workstations can start the administrative server*

password. You can also configure multiple host names and IP addresses to restrict access to the administration server from specific workstations (hosts). Each host name or IP address entered is separated by commas. The use of wildcards such as *.cambriancorp.com or 208.145.86.* is permitted.

TURN ON/OFF SSL   The Turn On/Off SSL page, shown in Figure 27-6, allows you to enable or disable the use of the Secure Sockets Layer (SSL) protocol on the Web server. SSL is an industry-standard protocol used to establish and maintain secure communications between a client and a Web server. Before data is transferred between the client and the Web server using the SSL protocol, a *handshake* occurs in which the client and the Web server agree to use the strongest common cipher to encrypt data. After this, the cipher keys are exchanged and all message traffic is encrypted.

SECURITY PREFERENCES   The Security Preferences page, shown in Figure 27-7, allows you to configure security levels for all Web servers known to the Administration server using the Secure Sockets Layer (SSL) protocol. The two standards are either a 40-bit or 128-bit key length version. The 128-bit version is much stronger but is subject to some export restrictions because it uses algorithms that are considered part of United

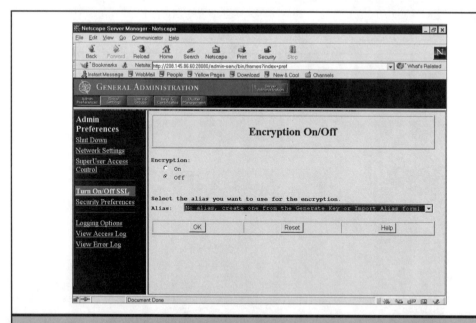

Figure 27-6.   *Enable or disable the use of the Secure Sockets Layer (SSL) protocol for encryption of message traffic between your clients and the Web servers*

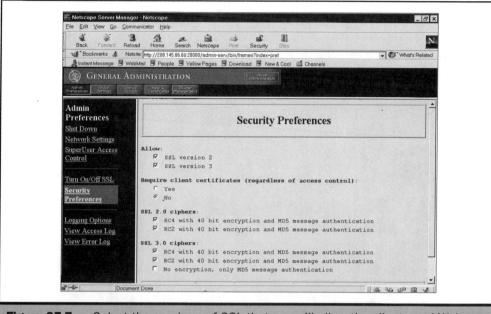

Figure 27-7. *Select the versions of SSL that you will allow the clients and Web server to use*

States national security. The 128-bit version is only available in the Netscape Enterprise Server product.

The version numbers relate to the SSL versions that the selected browser can handle. Some older browsers will only support SSL version 2. Both versions are supported by the Netscape Communicator 4.5 browser. The RC2 and RC4 encryption algorithms were developed by RSA Data Security, Inc.

LOGGING OPTIONS   The Logging Options page, shown in Figure 27-8, allows you to monitor your Web server's activity by establishing both an access log and an error log. The access log records information about all requests sent to the Web server and all responses returned by the Web server. The error log records all errors encountered on the Web server. The paths for the logs shown in Figure 27-8 are the defaults. You can change the locations for these files if you choose.

VIEW ACCESS LOG   The View Access Log page, shown in Figure 27-9, allows you to view the access logs for the Web server. Before any information is recorded, you must manually create an access log. You specified the file location when you defined the Logging Options path. Descriptions of the data logged in this file are shown in Tables 27-2 and 27-3.

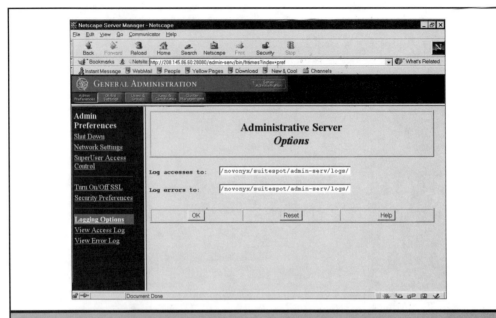

Figure 27-8. Set up the location where the access and error log files will be stored

Figure 27-9. View the access logs for the Web server on this page

Data Logged	Description
Host name	This is the IP address of the client if DNS is not enabled.
RFC 931 information	This is a character string used to identify the user based on the TCP connection to the Web server. It is not displayed unless you are running a proxy server that supports SOCKS connections.
Username	This is the user name of the client. A dash indicates that authentication was not provided by the user.
Date/time	This displays the date and time the client made a request to the Web server.
Request type	This specifies the type of request that was made by the client to the Web server.
Protocol and version	This is the protocol the client used to make the request to the Web server.
Status code	This is the HTTP 1.0 protocol status code for the client request. See Table 27-3 for a listing of the possible status codes.
Number of bytes transferred	This is the byte count for the client request.

Table 27-2.   *Format of Information Contained Within the Access Log*

VIEW ERROR LOG   The View Error Log page, shown in Figure 27-10 allows you to view the error log for the Web server. It records information such as the date and time the Web server starts and restarts, and lists Web server files that are missing, authentication errors from users, and bad URL links when the Web server could not send the requested file to the client.

Each entry in the error log has a header associated with it that identifies the type of message. The three types of messages are as follows:

- **Info**   This is an informational message. It does not indicate a problem.
- **Warning**   This is a noncritical message indicating that a Web server operation, such as Get or Post, had a problem.
- **Security**   This is a message indicating security-related problems with the Web server, such as a user authentication failure.

Status Code	Description
200	Request fulfilled
201	Success following a POST function
202	Request accepted, but not yet processed
203	Success following a GET function to an overlaid Web page
204	Web server received request, but is waiting for user input
301	Data requested by client has been assigned a new URL
302	Data requested by client has been assigned a temporary, different URL
304	Conditions of conditional GET issued by client have not been met
400	Bad request
401	Unauthorized request
402	Payment required
403	Forbidden request
404	Requested URL not found
500	Internal Web server error prevented Web server from fulfilling request
501	Request not supported by the Web server

Table 27-3.   *Status Codes Found in the Access Log*

Global Settings

The Global Settings page allows you to configure the directory service on the Web server. You select the method by which users are authenticated to the Web server. You can control access to all directories, certain files, or certain file types on the Web server with user authentication. The three methods available for authentication are discussed next.

LOCAL DATABASE   The Local Database option, shown in Figure 27-11, uses a database stored on the same machine as the Administration server for user authentication. The database cannot synchronize with other Web server databases dynamically and allows you to maintain a consistent database of users on each Web server.

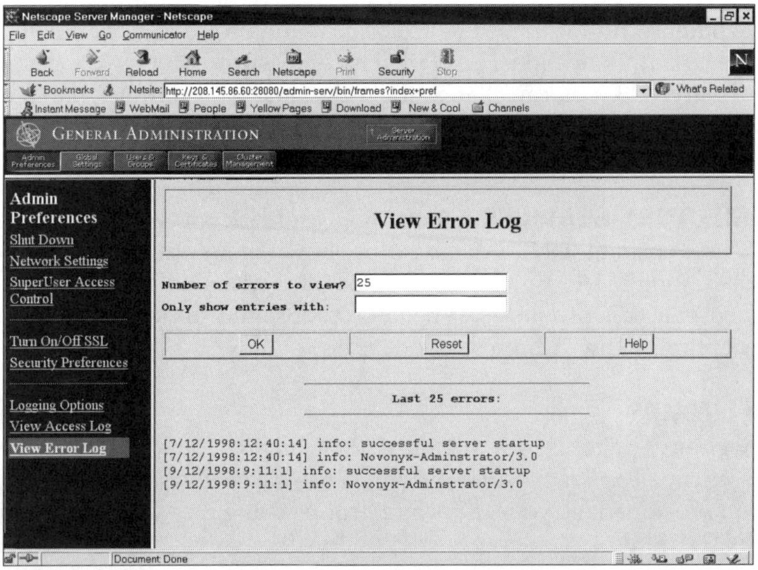

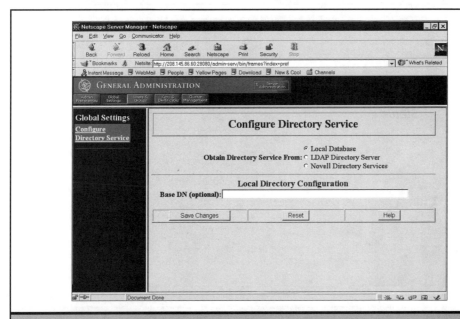

Figure 27-10.   *The error log displays status and security information for the specified Web server*

Figure 27-11.   *Users can be authenticated from a database local to the Web server when you select this option*

LDAP DIRECTORY SERVER The Lightweight Directory Access Protocol (LDAP) is an industry-standard protocol used to access user and group information in a directory database for user authentication. NetWare 5 natively supports LDAP services by integrating it into NDS. You can change the host name, port number, and base domain name from the screen shown in Figure 27-12. To use this option, your client must support LDAP as a means of authenticating users to the Web server.

NOVELL DIRECTORY SERVICES Netscape FastTrack Server allows you to authenticate users using the NDS database, as shown in Figure 27-13. This method bypasses the existing LDAP rights and uses the NDS-assigned rights and permissions to determine user access privileges. When you choose this option, it disables the Users and Groups options in the Administration server.

Users & Groups

The Users & Groups page, shown in Figure 27-14, allows you to manage users and groups on Netscape FastTrack Server using LDAP. If you configured Global Access to use NDS, you must manage your users and groups using the NetWare Administrator (NWADMIN32) utility.

The users, groups, and organizational units are configured in the same manner as with the NWADMIN32 utility. You create new users and assign them passwords. You

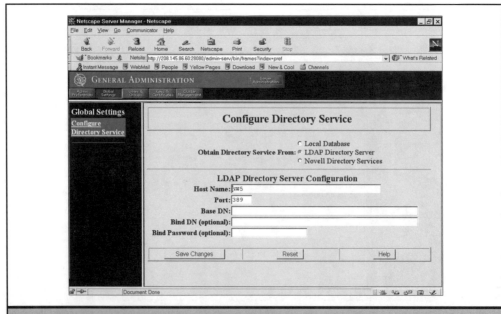

Figure 27-12. *This screen displays the location of the LDAP services on your network*

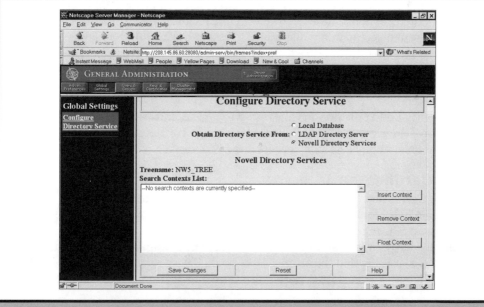

Figure 27-13. *If you decide to use NDS to authenticate users, you must specify the   context to be searched for the users when authenticating to the Web server*

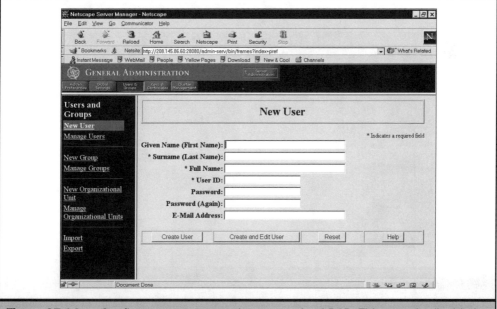

Figure 27-14. *Configure new users and groups using LDAP. This page is disabled if you configured Global Access to use NDS*

also can create new groups and assign LDAP users to these groups. Both LDAP and NWADMIN32 create new entities in the NDS tree for users and groups. Be aware that they use different object naming techniques to assign the new object names. This may cause some problems for duplicate names in your NDS tree.

The Manage options allow you to define search criteria for users and groups. All users or groups matching your search criteria can either be displayed on the screen or sent to a printer.

The Import and Export options allow you to import entries into or export entries out of the local directory using the LDAP Interchange Format (LDIF). These can be used on other Netscape FastTrack Servers.

Keys & Certificates

The Keys & Certificates page, shown in Figure 27-15, is used to administer the key-pair and certificate files required by the Secure Sockets Layer (SSL) protocol on your server. When using an SSL session between two hosts, certificates are used to authenticate the hosts; and the key pair is used to encrypt the data. The configuration and management of SSL on a server is beyond the scope of this book. Please refer to the documentation shipped with Netscape FastTrack Server for more information on this subject.

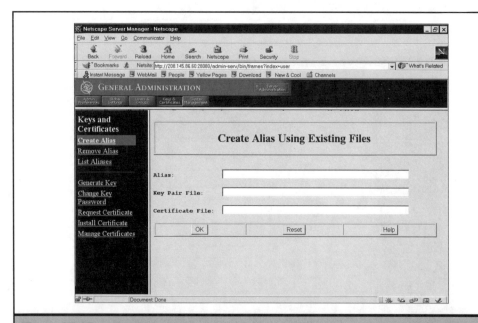

Figure 27-15.   *Configure the key pairs and certificates used when communicating with the Secure Sockets Layer (SSL) protocol*

Cluster Management

The Cluster Management page, shown in Figure 27-16, allows you to group Netscape servers that can be managed from the same Administration server. All of the servers in the cluster must be the same type. You cannot mix Messaging servers with Enterprise or FastTrack servers.

Server-Specific Options

The server-specific options are accessed by clicking on the specific server shown in the bottom half of Figure 27-2. These options are used to apply configuration changes to an individual server in a group or cluster. To access the Server Administration page for a specific server, click the button labeled with the server's name. The following sections describe the server-specific administration options, which are shown in Figure 27-17:

- Server Preferences
- Programs
- Server Status
- Configuration Styles
- Content Management

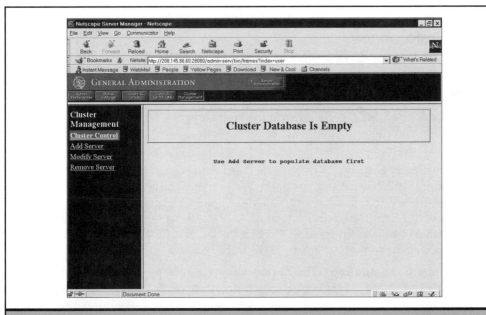

Figure 27-16.   *Configure multiple servers that can be controlled from the same Administration Server console*

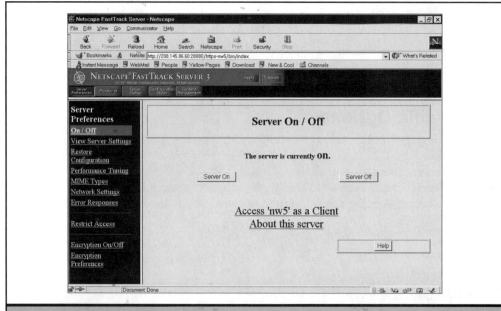

Figure 27-17.   *This page allows you to configure a specific server in a group or cluster*

Server Preferences

The Server Preferences screen, as shown in Figure 27-17, allows you configure the basic operating environment for the Web server. Each of these options is explained here:

- **On/Off**   This page displays the current state of the Web server. You can unload the NLMs associated with the Web server by clicking the Server Off button. You can also open another socket (connection) on the Web server as a client if desired.

- **View Server Settings**   The View Server Settings page displays both the technical and content settings of the Web server. The server's root, hostname, IP address, port, error log location, Mail Transport Agent (MTA) host name, Network News Transport Protocol (NNTP) host name, document directories, Common Gateway Interface (CGI) directories, and default MIME types are displayed, as shown in Figures 27-18 and 27-19.

- **Restore Configuration**   The Restore Configuration page allows you to revert back to an earlier server configuration if you encounter a problem with a new setting.

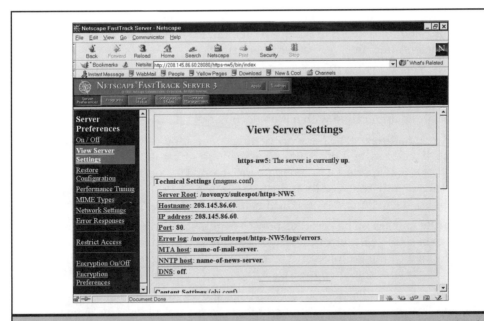

Figure 27-18. *The top part of the View Server Settings screen displays the basic configuration information for the Web server*

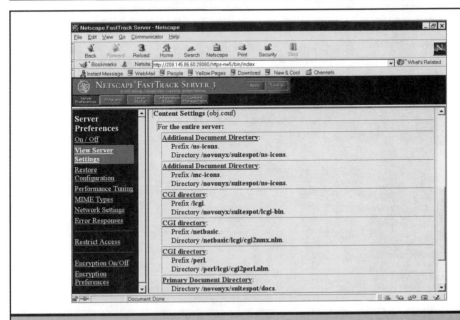

Figure 27-19. *The bottom part of the View Server Settings screen displays the location of various directories associated with Web documents and various scripting languages*

- **Performance Tuning**   The Performance Tuning page is used to enable DNS caching and to set the HTTP request time-out for the Web server. These parameters affect the Web server's performance.

- **MIME Types**   This MIME Types page displays the currently defined MIME types on the Web server, as shown in Figure 27-20. You can edit existing types, remove a type, or add a new type on this page. The MIME types are used to associate an application with a Web document.

- **Network Settings**   The Network Settings page allows you to change the server name, IP address, and port number of the Web server. If you decide to change the port number, select a number greater than 2000. Port numbers less than 2000 are already reserved for industry-standard TCP/IP services. You can also configure the MTA and NNTP host names for the server on this page.

- **Error Responses**   The Error Responses page, shown in Figure 27-21, allows you to customize the error messages a user sees when a request cannot be performed by the Web server. You can direct the server to a specific file or even a CGI script or program if desired.

- **Restrict Access**   The Restrict Access page allows you to implement access controls on existing resources or edit the Access Control List (ACL) on the Web server.

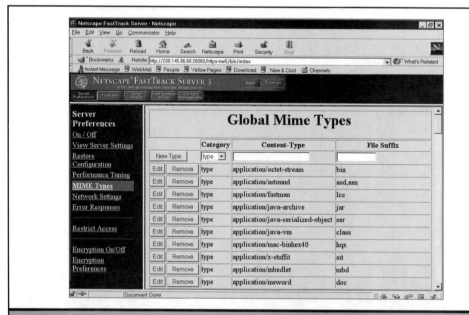

Figure 27-20.   *The MIME types are used to associate a file suffix with a particular application on the Web server*

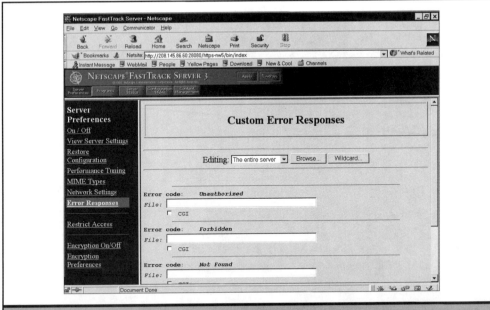

Figure 27-21.   *Configure customized responses here for requests that cannot be performed by the Web server*

- **Encryption On/Off**   The Encryption page allows you to turn Secure Sockets Layer (SSL) on or off for the server ports being used. You can also specify where the key pairs and certificates are located on the server.

- **Encryption Preferences**   The Encryption Preferences page allows you to specify the version of SSL that you want to implement and the level of encryption.

Programs

The Programs screen, shown in Figure 27-22, allows you to configure the Common Gateway Interface (CGI) and server-side includes (SSIs) operating environments for the Web server. Each of these options is explained here:

- **CGI Directory**   The CGI Directory page allows you to specify the location of CGI files on your Web server. You can edit the entries and change their prefixes and locations.

- **CGI File Type**   The CGI File Type page displays the association between file types and CGI files on your Web server.

- **Query Handler**   The Query Handler page specifies the default CGI script for processing queries posted to the Web server with the HTML tag ISINDEX.

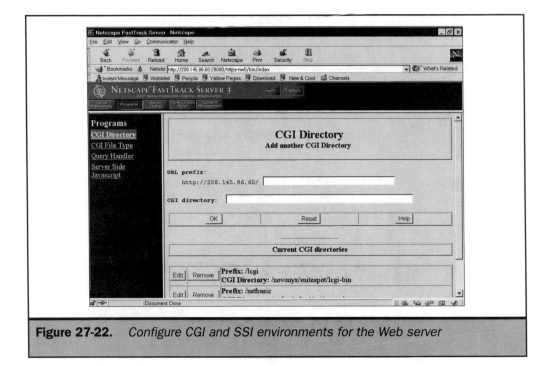

Figure 27-22.   *Configure CGI and SSI environments for the Web server*

- **Server Side JavaScript**   The Server Side JavaScript page is used to enable server-side JavaScripts. JavaScript can be used on both the server side and client side with Netscape FastTrack Server.

Server Status

The Server Status screen, as shown in Figure 27-23, allows you to monitor and track the operation of the Web server. Each of these options is explained here:

- **View Access Log**   The View Access Log page allows you to view current and archived entries from the access log. You can also specify the number of log entries to be viewed at one time.

- **View Error Log**   The View Error Log page allows you to view current and archived entries from the error log. You can also specify the number of log entries to be viewed at one time.

- **Monitor Current Activity**   The Monitor Current Activity page displays Web server performance in an HTML table. It summarizes all current Web server activity and can be used for performance tuning.

- **Archive Log**   The Archive Log page is used to configure the location of the archive logs and to set up a rotation time for the logs.

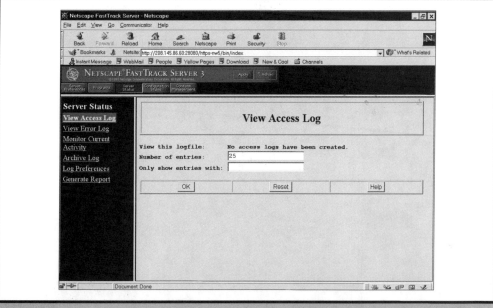

Figure 27-23.   *Access the server access and error logs on this page and monitor
the current activity on the Web server for performance tuning*

- ■ **Log Preferences**   The Log Preferences page allows you to specify what you
  want logged and in what format the logged data is to be saved. You can specify
  either the Common LogFile Format or define your own custom format.

- ■ **Generate Report**   The Generate Report page allows you to generate an
  HTML report document. You can select which information fields you want
  the report to contain.

Configuration Styles

The Configuration Styles screen, shown in Figure 27-24, allows you to create and use
profiles on each Web server in your network. Each of these options is explained here:

- ■ **New Style**   Use the New Style page to create a new style for the Web server.
  You are taken through a series of steps that allow you to set various
  configuration options for the server.

- ■ **Remove Style**   The Remove Style page is used to remove an existing style
  from the Web server.

- ■ **Edit Style**   Use the Edit Style page to edit the configuration options for the
  selected style.

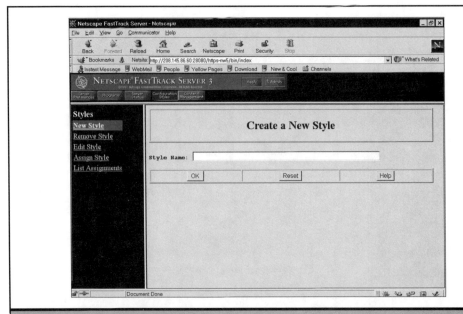

Figure 27-24. *Styles are analogous to profiles for workstations that can be applied to a Web server*

- **Assign Style**   The Assign Style page is used to associate a style with a Web server.

- **List Assignments**   The List Assignments page displays a list of Web servers and the style assignments for each server.

Content Management

The Content Management screen, shown in Figure 27-25, allows you to configure the location of your HTML documents, set up URL forwarding, and configure both hardware and virtual servers, as well as various other settings regarding documents stored on the Web server. Each of these options is explained here:

- **Primary Document Directory**   The Primary Document Directory page specifies the directory on the Web server designated for HTML document storage, such as your INDEX.HTM page.

- **Additional Document Directories**   The Additional Document Directories page is used to map any existing HTML document directories on the file server to the Web server's directory structure.

- **Document Preferences**   The Document Preferences page defines the HTML document defaults used by the Web server.

- **URL Forwarding**   The URL Forwarding page is used to redirect URLs to another location or Web server.
- **Hardware Virtual Servers**   The Hardware Virtual Servers page is used to configure hardware virtual servers. Use this when you want to load balance the Web server across multiple physical machines.
- **Software Virtual Servers**   The Software Virtual Servers page is used to configure software virtual servers. Use this when you want the Web server to host multiple Web sites on the same physical machine.
- **International Characters**   The International Characters page allows you to set individual character sets per Web server.
- **Document Footer**   Use the Document Footer page to assign a custom message or stamp to the bottom of all Web pages served by your Web server.
- **Parse HTML**   The Parse HTML page enables the Web server to parse HTML documents for server-side include (SSI) commands before delivering the Web page to the client.
- **Cache Control Directives**   The Cache Control Directives page enables the control of server caching instructions.

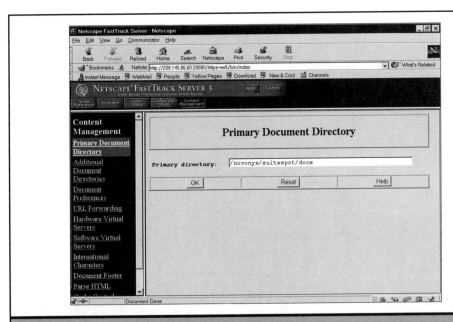

Figure 27-25.   *Configure settings associated with the Web pages you want your Web server to deliver to a client*

The Complete Reference

NetWare 5

Chapter 28

Z.E.N.works

Z ero Effort Networks (Z.E.N.works) is a group of products designed to simplify software management, software distribution, desktop maintenance, and desktop management. It uses the power of NDS to maintain and distribute a location-independent "digital persona" for each user on the network. This includes a unique configuration of desktop policies, profiles, printer assignments, and applications based on the login name of the user.

The complete Z.E.N.works product is an integrated set of technologies that includes the following applications and utilities:

- Desktop Management
- Novell Application Launcher (NAL)
- Remote Control
- Help Requestor
- Z.E.N. Client

NetWare 5 ships with the Z.E.N.works Starter Pack. It includes the Desktop Management, Novell Application Launcher, and Z.E.N. Client components. The Desktop Management component does not include the capability to inventory a network-attached workstation. You must purchase the complete Z.E.N.works product to get the full capabilities of Z.E.N.works.

The Desktop Management component allows all user account and desktop information for Windows clients to be stored in the NDS tree on the network. It also gives you the capability to create policies for each workstation, such as

- Creating a standard user interface on each Windows platform
- Creating a standard user interface for specific users
- Creating and distributing Windows user profiles
- Distributing and automatically updating print drivers on each user's desktop
- Updating client configurations without having to physically visit each workstation
- Scheduling software updates on user workstations during off-hours or when the user is not logged in to the network

The Novell Application Launcher component allows you to distribute network-based applications to your users and manage those applications as objects in the NDS tree. Users can only access those applications to which they have NDS access rights. The Novell Application Launcher component provides the following:

- Multilevel folder support in NDS to hierarchically order Application objects in the tree
- Automatic granting of file rights so users can access the applications assigned to them

- Automatic registration with the Windows NT Service Control Manager on a Windows NT server or workstation
- Scheduling of application access based on the time of day

Implementation Phases of Z.E.N.works

There are five phases to the successful implementation of the Z.E.N.works Starter Pack on your workstations and servers. You can configure the various components to suit your network management needs after you have completed the following phases.

Phase 1

This is the planning phase. You should first determine how many Workstation objects you will add to your NDS tree. You should then decide which containers will contain the Policy objects, and redesign you NDS tree if necessary.

Phase 2

In this phase, you install the Z.E.N.works Starter Pack on both the servers and the workstations. Each workstation you intend to manage must be updated with the Novell Client that ships with the Z.E.N.works Starter Pack. This is also the phase in which you set up a workstation import policy. The workstation import policy defines the location and naming of the Workstation object when the workstation is imported into the NDS tree.

Phase 3

In this phase, you register those workstations you have chosen to manage. When the user logs in to the network, the managed workstations will register information in the NDS tree. This registration information is used to update the Workstation Registration property of the selected containers in the NDS tree.

Phase 4

In this phase, you import the workstations as objects into the NDS tree using the NetWare Administrator (NWADMIN32) utility. They must exist as objects in the NDS tree before you can manage the workstations.

Phase 5

In this phase, you reregister the workstations in the NDS tree through users logging in to the network. This allows NDS to discover the physical objects represented by the Workstation objects in the NDS tree. Each workstation sends registration information to its own object in the NDS tree.

Installing the Z.E.N.works Starter Pack

The Z.E.N.works Starter Pack is installed from the NetWare 5 Client CD. The majority of the files are installed in the SYS:PUBLIC directory on the file server. You must use the NWADMIN32 utility installed in the SYS:PUBLIC\WIN32 directory to configure and manage the new NDS objects. The clients must have the Novell Client included on the CD installed on them and they must connect via NDS. Bindery connections are not supported. You will also need 70MB of available memory on the file server and 250MB of disk space.

Before you start the install, you must have the following NDS and file system rights:

- Supervisor object rights to the [Root] of the NDS tree.
- File system rights to the directory in which the Novell Application Launcher is installed and to the directories that contain the applications you intend to distribute.

Note   *Z.E.N.works automatically assigns the user Read and File Scan file system rights to an associated application. These rights are revoked when the user disassociates from the Application object.*

Perform the following steps to install the Z.E.N.works Starter Pack:

1. Log in to the server where Z.E.N.works will be installed. You must have Supervisor object rights to the [Root] of the NDS tree.

2. Insert the Novell Client CD into the workstation CD-ROM drive.

3. The following screen will be displayed, prompting you to select the language for the install.

4. Select the Install Z.E.N.works option to install the Z.E.N.works Starter Pack on the server, as shown here:

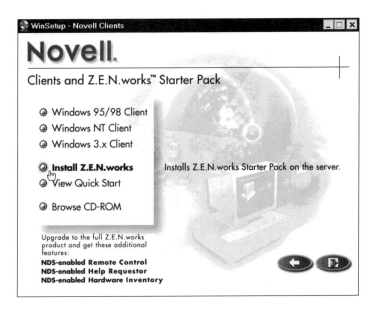

5. Select the type of installation you want from options shown here:

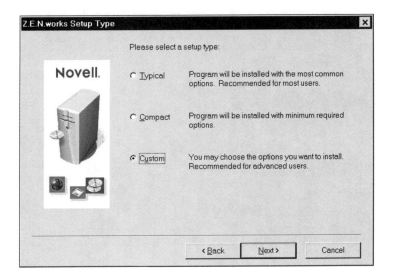

Use the Custom option if you want the client files on the server for downloading to the clients.

6. Select the products you want to install by checking the appropriate boxes, as shown here:

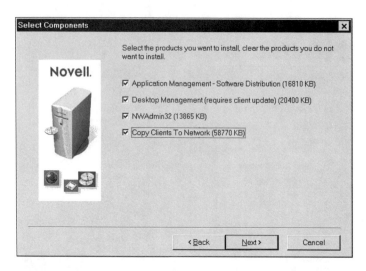

7. Select the NDS schema extensions you want displayed in your NDS tree, as shown next. These will be displayed when you select the Create option in the NetWare Administrator (NWADMIN32) utility.

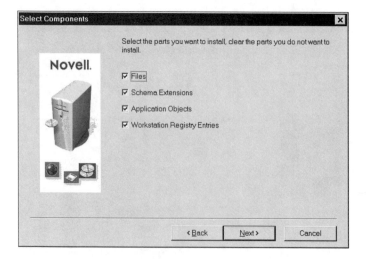

8. Select the NDS tree and server on which you want to perform the install, as shown here:

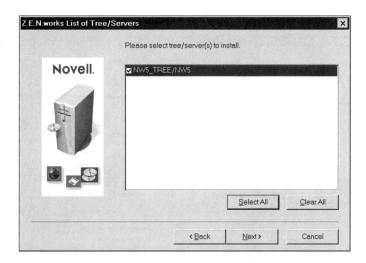

9. Select the languages you want the server to offer to administrators and users, as shown here:

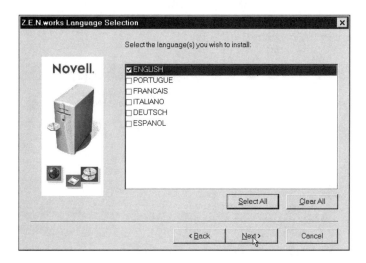

10. The summary screen shown next will be displayed for you to review your configuration settings. Click the Back button if you need to make changes to the installation configuration.

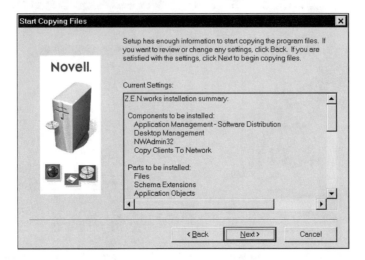

11. Enter the level in the NDS tree where rights should be granted for the workstation registration phase, as shown next. By entering the [Root] of the NDS tree, you can create and enter workstation registration information anywhere in the NDS tree.

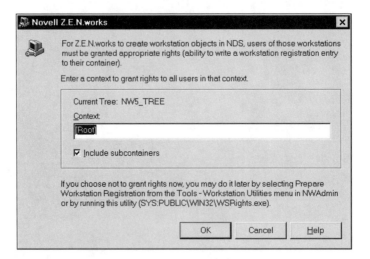

12. The message box shown next will be displayed after the workstation registration rights have been successfully configured for the NDS tree.

Managing the NetWare Environment

13. The screen shown next will be displayed when the setup is completed. Click the Finish button to return to the Z.E.N.works installation page and select the Exit option. If you leave the check boxes marked, you will have to exit WordPad to close this window.

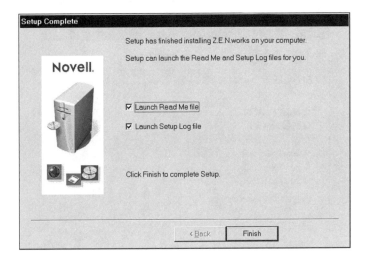

Installing the Z.E.N.works Client

You must install the Z.E.N.works Client on all Windows 3.*x*/95/98/NT workstations that you intend to manage. Each workstation must meet the following system requirements:

- Intel-based workstation running Windows 3.*x*/95/98/NT
- At minimum, a 486/33 processor
- 16MB of RAM for Windows 3.*x*/95/98 clients (at least 24MB of RAM for Windows NT)
- 24MB of hard disk space on the workstation

The client can be installed in one of the following three ways: local installation, network installation, or unattended installation with the Automatic Client Update (ACU). Each of these methods is discussed next.

Local Installation

Perform the following steps to complete a local installation of the NetWare Client:

1. Install the Novell Client CD on the workstation.

2. Start the WINSETUP.EXE program on the CD.

3. Select the language for the install.

4. Select the platform you are installing the client on from the options shown.

5. Select the Install Novell Client option from the screen, as shown here:

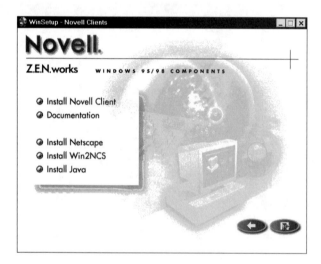

6. Select one of the following installation options:

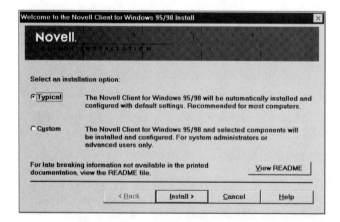

7. Select the protocol options for the client to use, as shown next.

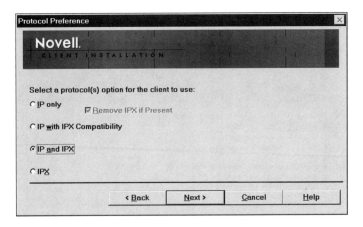

- **IP only**   This option installs support for the IP protocol only.

- **IP with IPX Compatibility**   This option allows IPX applications to run on an IP-only network by encapsulating IPX packets in IP packets. It also allows the client to communicate with services on an IPX-only network if the Migration Agent is installed on a NetWare 5 server. This mode is dependent on the Service Location Protocol (SLP) for locating network services. It does not use the older SAP protocol for this purpose.

- **IP and IPX**   This option installs both the IP and IPX protocol stacks on the client. The client will generate and respond to IPX/SPX traffic as needed.

- **IPX**   This option installs support for the IPX protocol only. It is used in older networks that do not support the IP protocol.

8. Select the type of network connection from the Login Authenticator screen shown next. Remember, to use Z.E.N.works, you must have an NDS connection. The Bindery option enables you to use the new client on workstations connected to older NetWare 3.*x* systems.

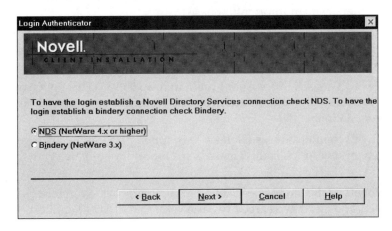

9. Select any optional components to install on the workstation, as shown here:

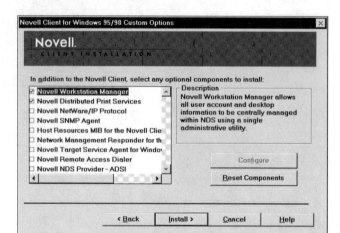

■ **Novell Workstation Manager** This option is the client component necessary for the management of workstation profiles using NDS.

■ **Novell Distributed Print Services** This option allows your workstation to communicate in real-time via a bidirectional interface to your network-attached printers.

■ **Novell NetWare/IP Protocol** This option provides IP requestor support for NetWare networks.

■ **Novell SNMP Agent** This option installs an extensible Simple Network Management Protocol (SNMP) agent on the client, which allows the client to be queried by an SNMP Management console.

■ **Host Resources MIB for the Novell Client** This option enables an SNMP Management console to poll the client for various information as defined in the Management Information Base (MIB).

■ **Network Management Responder for the Novell Client** This option allows the SNMP Management console to query the client concerning operating system, BIOS, and ODI information.

■ **Novell Target Service Agent for Windows 95/98** This option allows the Novell server to automatically back up selected hard drives from the workstation.

■ **Novell Remote Access Dialer** This option provides extended dial-up networking functionality, including support for both NetWare/IP and NWCAP.

■ **Novell NDS Provider - ADSI** This option provides an interface between NDS and an Active Directory Service Interface (ADSI) application.

10. The screen shown next is displayed when the installation program is finished. The new settings do not take effect until the workstation is restarted.

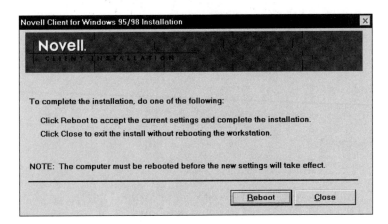

Network Installation

Perform the following steps to install the Novell Client over the network:

1. Authenticate to a NetWare server that contains the Novell Client installation files.

2. Run the appropriate installation program for the workstation, as follows:

   - **Windows 95/98**   Run the SETUP.EXE program from the SYS:PUBLIC\CLIENT\WIN95\IBM_ENU directory on the server.

   - **Windows NT**   Run the SETUPNW.EXE program from the SYS:PUBLIC\CLIENT\WINNT\i386 directory on the server.

   - **Windows 3.***x***   Run the INSTALL.EXE program from the SYS:PUBLIC\CLIENT\DOSWIN32 directory on the server.

3. Follow the installation prompts. These are discussed previously in the section "Local Installation."

Unattended Install Using the Automatic Client Update (ACU)

The unattended install using the Automatic Client Update (ACU) allows you to update the Novell Client automatically on multiple workstations from a single point of administration. The ACU works by checking the version level of the client and automatically updating it if it is not current. This process occurs when the user logs in to the network. The user can interrupt the update process if the unattended install parameter is not configured. You use the unattended install parameter to force an update on a client machine when the user logs in to the network.

Perform the following steps to enable the Automatic Client Update (ACU) process:

1. Grant users Read and File Scan rights to the appropriate installation program based on the workstation operating system:

   ■ **Windows 95/98**

   ```
   SYS:PUBLIC\CLIENT\WIN95\IBM_ENU
   ```

   ■ **Windows NT**

   ```
   SYS:PUBLIC\CLIENT\WINNT\i386
   ```

   ■ **Windows 3.*x***

   ```
   SYS:PUBLIC\CLIENT\DOSWIN32
   ```

2. Modify the login script for the container or profile login script to launch the ACU on the associated workstations, as follows:

   ■ **Windows 95/98**

   #*server_name*\SYS\PUBLIC\CLIENT\WIN95\IBM_ENU\SETUP.EXE /ACU

   ■ **Windows NT**

   #*server_name*\SYS\PUBLIC\CLIENT\i386\SETUPNW.EXE /ACU

   This will run properly only if you are a member of the Administrators or Power Users group.

   ■ **Windows 3.*x***

   #*server_name*\SYS\PUBLIC\CLIENT\DOSWIN32\INSTALL.EXE /ACU

The pound sign (#) suspends processing of the login script while the program executes. The at sign (@) allows the external program to execute concurrently with the login script processing.

Setting the unattended install parameter does not give the user a choice as to whether the workstation client is updated. Perform the following steps to set the unattended install parameter:

1. Grant users Read and File Scan rights to the appropriate installation program based on the workstation operating system:

   ■ **Windows 95/98**

   ```
   SYS:PUBLIC\CLIENT\WIN95\IBM_ENU
   ```

- **Windows NT**

    SYS:PUBLIC\CLIENT\WINNT\i386

- **Windows 3.*x***

    SYS:PUBLIC\CLIENT\DOSWIN32

2. Modify the login script for the container or profile login script to launch the ACU on the associated workstations, as follows:

    - **Windows 95/98**

        #*server_name*\SYS\PUBLIC\CLIENT\WIN95\IBM_ENU\SETUP.EXE /U

    - **Windows NT**

        #*server_name*\SYS\PUBLIC\CLIENT\i386\SETUPNW.EXE /U

    This will only run properly if you are a member of the Administrators or Power Users group.

    - **Windows 3.*x***

        #*server_name*\SYS\PUBLIC\CLIENT\DOSWIN32\INSTALL.EXE /U

Configuring the Novell Client

The Novell Client configuration consists of eight property pages with various options. Each property page and its associated options is detailed in the following sections.

Client

The Client property page contains basic information that is necessary for the user to authenticate to NDS and obtain a network connection. The screen shown in Figure 28-1 and the associated options are discussed.

Preferred Server

The preferred server is the server that NDS will attempt to authenticate the user to. It forces the client to attempt a connection to the specified server. In this example, it is the NW5 server.

Preferred Tree

The preferred tree is the NDS tree you attach to when you start the client program. The client will attempt to connect to any server in the NDS tree if only the preferred tree is

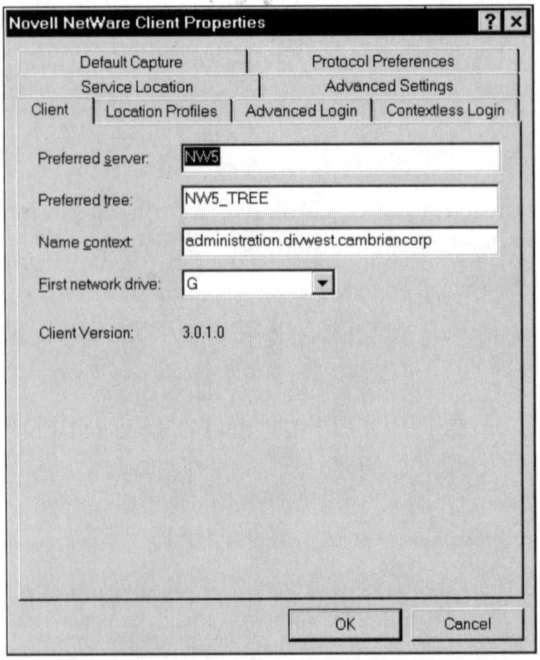

Figure 28-1. *The Client property page contains basic information necessary for a network connection*

set. If neither the preferred server nor the preferred tree is set, the client will connect to the server that responds to the Get Nearest Server request from the client. In this example, it is the NW5_TREE NDS tree.

Name Context

The name context sets your current position in the NDS tree. It is the path to the container that contains the User object in the NDS tree. It can be up to 256 characters long plus the NULL character. The NULL character represents the [Root] of the NDS tree. It is only applicable to NetWare 4 and 5 servers. In this example, the name context is administration.divwest.cambriancorp.

First Network Drive

The first network drive is the drive letter that will be used to map the first network drive to the workstation. In this example, it is the G drive.

Client Version

The client version is not configurable from this screen. It is informational only. The version level is obtained from the Windows registry settings related to the Novell Client. In this example, it is version 3.0.1.0.

Location Profiles

The Location Profiles property page, shown in Figure 28-2, is used to define multiple profiles for the user to use when logging in to the network. The profile automatically sets up the user's name, server, context, login script, and various other parameters. This frees the user from having to enter this information in the login screen. The login screen, shown in Figure 28-3, is displayed when the user selects the nondefault location profile. For example, you can create a profile that can be used when the user accesses the network from a remote location via a dial-up connection.

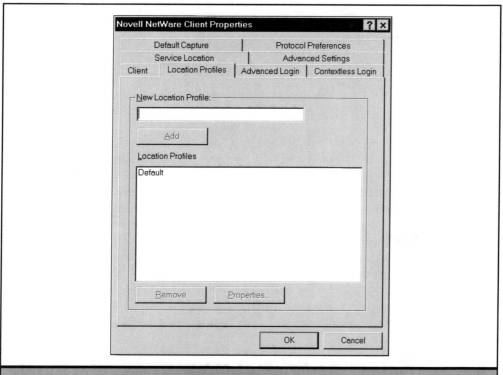

Figure 28-2.   *Define the new login profile for the user from this screen. Each user can have multiple location profiles defined*

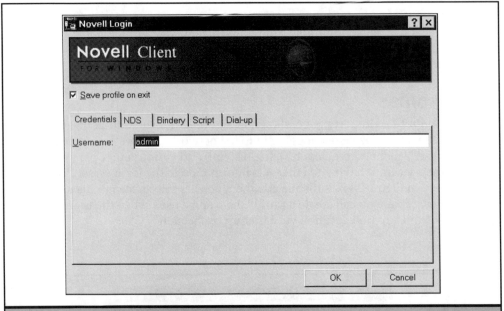

Figure 28-3. *The new location profile displays a login screen, which is defined in the location profiles settings*

Advanced Login

The Advanced Login property page, shown in Figure 28-4, is used to configure the options displayed to the user on the login screen and the workstation policy.

Default Policy Support

You can specify that the client will use a different user and workstation policy to configure the operating system if the default is unchecked. After the user authenticates to the network, the specified directory is searched for a policy file. If the file is found, the policy is downloaded and applied to the user and the workstation. The path to the policy must be a valid UNC path name.

Location List

The Location List check box allows you to display multiple location profiles to the user if they have been defined.

Advanced Button

The Advanced Button check box allows the user to display advanced information such as the NDS tree name and context, if desired, from the login screen.

Managing the NetWare Environment

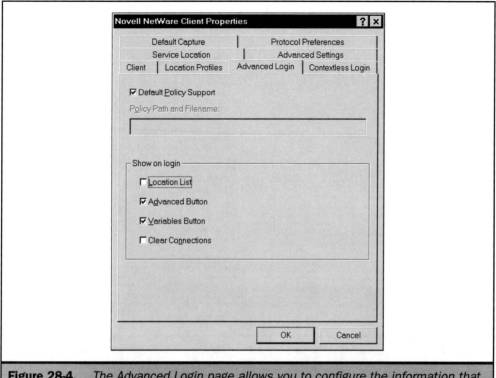

Figure 28-4. *The Advanced Login page allows you to configure the information that will be displayed to a user logging in to the network*

Variables Button
The Variables Button check box allows the user to display and configure up to four variables that may be used in login script processing.

Clear Connections
The Clear Connections check box will clear all existing network connections to the workstation before logging in.

Contextless Login

The Contextless Login property page, shown in Figure 28-5, allows the user to log in to the network without specifying a context location. This option uses NDS Catalog Services to retrieve context information for the user. All usable catalogs are automatically found. The user can specify an NDS tree name and the name of the

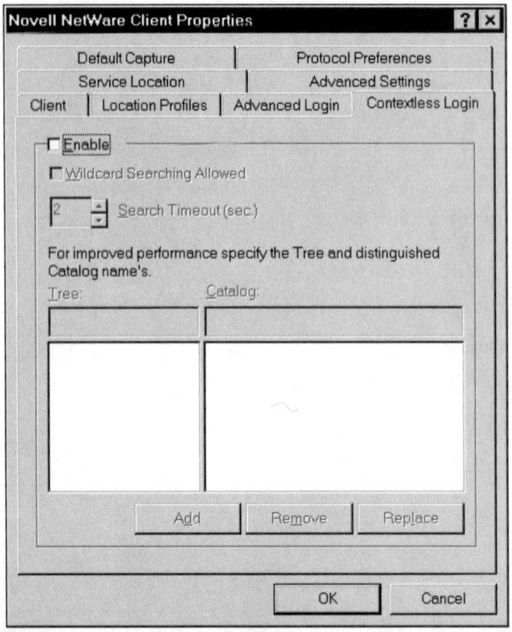

Figure 28-5. *The Contextless Login property page allows the user to log in to the network by supplying only the user name and the name of the associated Catalog object in the NDS tree*

Catalog pair to force the use of a specific catalog. If the user exists in multiple NDS trees and this option is configured to allow wildcards, the user will be prompted to select a user name and context from the displayed options.

Service Location

The Service Location property page, shown in Figure 28-6, displays the Scope List and the Directory Agent List, which are used by this workstation to resolve the names of service providers on the network using the Service Location Protocol (SLP). SLP uses entries in the NDS tree to resolve service provider names for the applications that request them. This function was performed by the Service Advertising Protocol (SAP) on NetWare 4 servers.

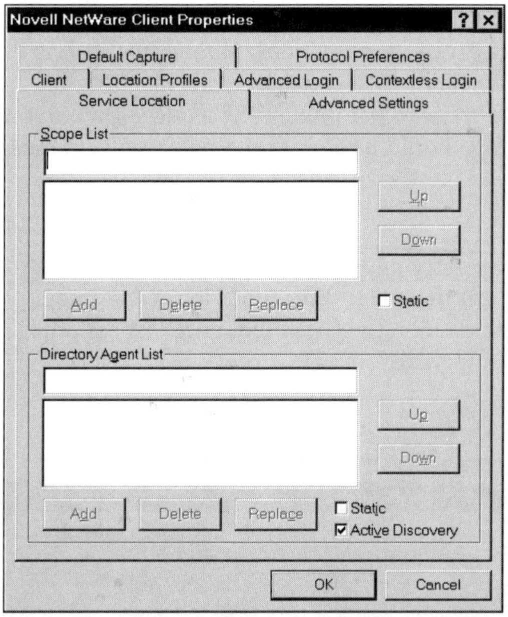

Figure 28-6. *The Service Location property page lists the names that the Service Location Protocol (SLP) uses to resolve client application requests for services on the network*

Scope List

The Scope List contains a list of scope names that will be reported to SLP applications on the workstation. The list order is the preference order. Scope names can also be configured using DHCP or discovered dynamically from the Directory Agents.

Directory Agent List

The Directory Agent List contains SLP Directory Agent addresses. These addresses can be either fully qualified domain names or dotted decimal IP addresses. The fully qualified domain names must be defined in your DNS lookup tables. Directory Agent addresses can be configured using DHCP or discovered dynamically.

Advanced Settings

The Advanced Settings property page, shown in Figure 28-7, is used to configure the internal workings of the client. You can select various parameter groups, which makes it easier to find specific types of parameters. The one shown in the figure specifies whether an audible beep should be sounded when a pop-up message is displayed.

Default Capture

The Default Capture property page, shown in Figure 28-8, allows the client to configure the printing environment. You can select the number of copies to be printed, the banner information to be printed, and various other settings.

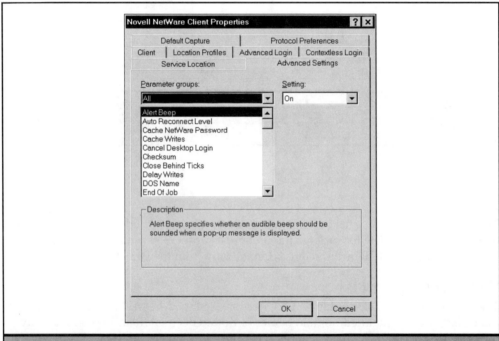

Figure 28-7. *The Advanced Settings property page allows you to fine-tune the operation of the client*

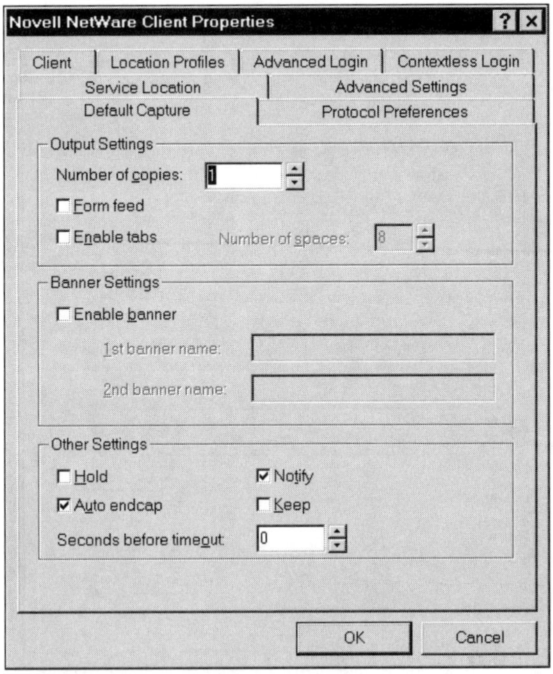

Figure 28-8. *The Default Capture property page sets up the client print job parameters*

Protocol Preferences

The Protocol Preferences property page, shown in Figure 28-9, allows the user to specify the protocols and name resolution methods to be used by the client.

Protocol Order

The Protocol Order list specifies the sequence of protocols the client uses when attempting to connect to a server. If the first protocol in the list fails to make a connection, the next one is tried, and so on, until a connection to a server can be established.

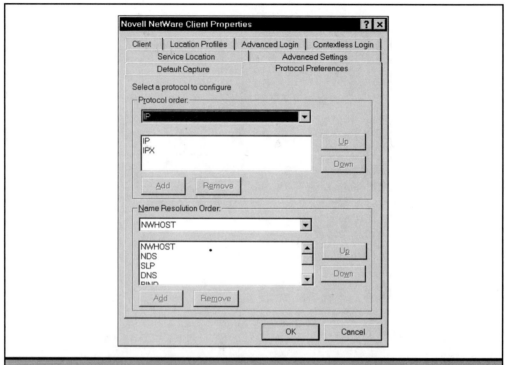

Figure 28-9.   *The Protocol Preferences property page allows you to specify the protocols and name resolution method for the client*

Name Resolution Order

The Name Resolution Order list specifies the order in which protocols are used to attempt to resolve names. The various protocols are defined as follows:

- **NWHOST**   Name resolution is attempted by scanning the contents of the NWHOST file in the C:\NOVELL\CLIENT32 directory. The file must contain the name of the server and the IP address. The name can be an alias.

- **NDS**   Name resolution is attempted by querying NDS. Both the IP and IPX protocols can use this name resolution method.

- **SLP**   Name resolution is attempted by using the Service Location Protocol (SLP).

- **DNS**   Name resolution is attempted by querying a DNS server for the associated IP address. The client will attempt to use this resolution method when the name provided by the user contains at least one period.

- **BIND**   Name resolution is attempted when there are no NDS server connections. The bindery of an NCP server (NetWare 2.*x*, 3.*x*) is scanned for the IPX address of the name.

- **SAP**   Name resolution is attempted using the Service Advertising Protocol (SAP) on IPX networks. The client makes an initial connection and resolves names as needed. This naming service is placed at the end of the list by default.

- **DHCP**   Name resolution is assisted by DHCP, establishing the initial connection and setting the preferred tree and server for the client.

Desktop Management

Desktop Management in the Z.E.N.works Starter Pack allows you to configure desktop and printing policies, register and import workstations, and schedule management tasks using the Z.E.N.works Scheduler. This allows all user and account information for Windows clients to be centrally managed within NDS.

Policy Packages

Policy packages are NDS objects created in the tree. Each policy package contains a collection of policies. These policies allow you to configure specific parameters for managing workstations, users, groups, and containers. Fault tolerance is provided through the replication of these objects throughout the NDS tree. They are included in any replicas stored on other servers in the network. Each policy package can be associated with other NDS objects in the tree. You must create a policy package before you can enable and configure individual policies. There are three different policy packages:

- **Container**   Applies only to containers
- **User, Group, or Container**
  - Windows 3.*x* User Package
  - Windows 95 User Package
  - Windows NT User Package
- **Workstations, Workstation Groups, or Containers**
  - Windows 3.*x* Workstation Package
  - Windows 95 Workstation Package
  - Windows NT Workstation Package

Container Policy Package

The Container policy package, shown in Figure 28-10, determines which policy packages are in effect for a specified container. The Windows 3.*x* platform does not accommodate the complete Z.E.N.works features because of the limited registry in the Windows 3.*x* product. The Windows 95 and NT platforms do accommodate the complete Z.E.N.works features, as they have a fully functional registry.

Policies

The Policies property page is used to enable or view details about any activated policies for the policy package. By clicking the Details button on a highlighted policy, you can establish a rule designating how many levels the system will search in the NDS tree for associated policy packages. You can also limit the search level. The default is 0, which means the system will search for policies up to the level you established in your rule. A setting of 1 limits the search to one level above the currently set level, and a setting of –1 limits the search up to, but not including, the currently set level. In addition, you can

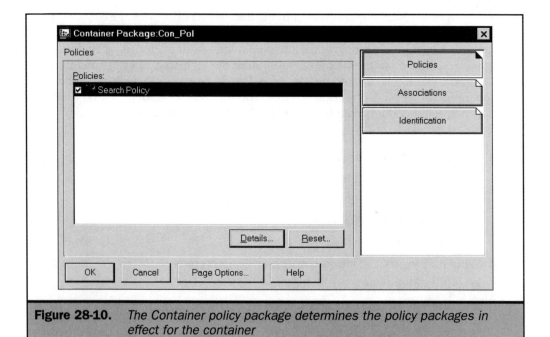

Figure 28-10. *The Container policy package determines the policy packages in effect for the container*

also set the search order. This list can contain a maximum of three items: object, group, and container.

Associations

The Associations property page is used to view all NDS objects associated with the policy package. You can add and remove NDS objects associated with the policy on this property page.

 Remember that if no associations are made between the policy and other NDS objects, the policy will not be effective.

Identification

The Identification property page is used to view the general naming information about this policy package. You can enter an optional alias name for the policy in the Other Name field. You can also enter descriptive information in the Description field.

User Policy Package

The User policy packages, shown in Figure 28-11, allow you to set up controls that apply to users logging in to the network from Windows 3.*x*/95/NT workstations. The controls you define apply only to the user who logs in from a Windows platform identified and associated with the policy package. Only one platform type can be associated with a user. In other words, you cannot have two Windows 95 policies defined for the same user in the same container. The following policies can be configured for each client:

- **95 Desktop Preferences**   These preferences set the default desktop configuration for the user.
- **95 User System Policies**   These policies define restrictions to desktop applications for the user.
- **Dynamic Local User**   This policy manages user access to Windows NT workstations using NDS.
- **NT Desktop Preferences**   These preferences set the default Windows NT workstation desktop configuration for the user.
- **NT User Printer**   This policy assigns printers and printer drivers to the Windows NT workstation for the user.
- **Workstation Import Policy**   This policy sets rules relating to workstation naming and object placement in the NDS tree.

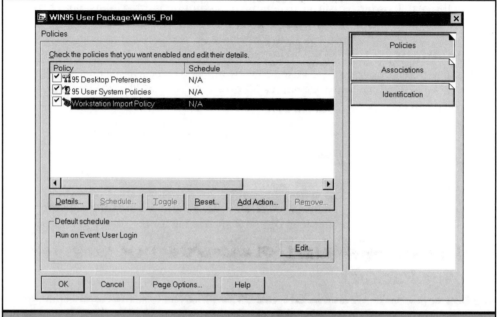

Figure 28-11.   *The User policy packages allow you to establish workstation controls that apply to users logging in to the network. This is the policy page for Windows 95 users*

Workstation Policy Package

The Workstation policy package, shown in Figure 28-12, allows you to establish controls that apply to the Windows workstations on your network. The controls apply only to the Windows platforms identified and associated with the policy package. The controls apply to the workstation regardless of which user is logging in to the network. The following policies can be configured for each workstation:

■ **3.*x* Computer System**   This policy specifies the files to download to the Windows 3.*x* workstation. You can manage ASCII files such as .BAT, .INI, and .CFG files, and binary files such as .EXE, .COM, and .DLL files.

■ **95 Computer Printer**   This policy is used to assign printers and printer drivers to Windows 95 workstations. The printer driver will be automatically installed on the workstation and the Printer object will appear in the user's printer control panel.

■ **95 Computer System Policies**   This policy specifies the applications that are delivered to a Windows 95 workstation regardless of the user authenticating to the network.

- **95 RAS Configuration** This policy is used to configure the dial-up networking settings for a Windows 95 workstation.

- **NT Computer Printer** This policy is used to assign printers and printer drivers to Windows NT workstations. The printer driver will be automatically installed on the workstation and the Printer object will appear in the user's printer control panel.

- **NT Computer System** This policy specifies the applications delivered to a Windows NT workstation regardless of the user authenticating to the network.

- **Novell Client Configuration** This policy is used to configure the Novell Client for both Windows 95 and NT workstations. You can configure the client, user name, default capture settings, protocols, and services.

- **Restrict Login** This policy is used to set rules regarding the login times for both Windows 95 and NT workstations.

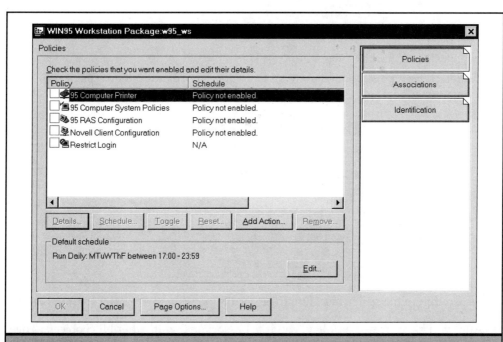

Figure 28-12.   *The workstation policy package applies to the workstation the user is logging in from. This is the workstation policy for a Windows 95 workstation*

Creating Policies

Now that you have an understanding of how the basic policies work, you can start creating them for your workstations. Perform the following steps to create a policy:

1. Start the NetWare Administrator utility (NWADMIN32).

2. Select the container in which you want to create the new policy.

3. Right-click the container object to pop-up the New Object menu, as shown here:

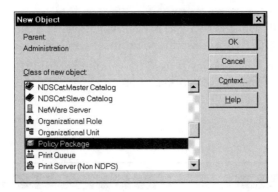

4. Select the Policy Package option and click the OK button.

5. Select the type of policy you want to create. The default policy type is a container package. Click the drop-down arrow to display the list shown here:

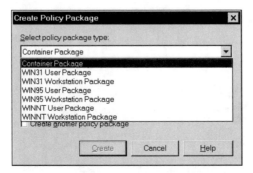

6. Configure the policy based on the information presented earlier in this chapter.

After you have created a policy, you must associate it with other NDS objects. This is done through the Associations property page in the given policy. User policies that configure the desktop, printer availability, and application privileges are effective immediately. Workstation policies will not take effect until the workstation is imported into NDS and reregistered in NDS.

| Note |

Container policies apply to all Workstation and User objects in the container associated with the policy.

Policies are applied to leaf objects in the same manner that NDS rights are applied. Policies associated with a user or Workstation object take precedence over policies associated with the container. Keep in mind that each NDS partition can contain no more that 1,500 objects. This includes existing objects, Policy objects, and Workstation objects.

Registering and Importing Workstations

Workstations must be registered with NDS before they can be imported into the NDS tree. A Workstation Registration Agent automatically registers the workstation with NDS. The following conditions must be met for this to occur:

- The workstation must be running the Novell Client for Z.E.N.works.
- The workstation must be logged into the network.

The NDS database stores the workstation's registration time, network address, last server connection, and last user to log in to the network. This information is transferred to NDS by the Workstation Registration program. A list of workstations is built as workstations are registered. The workstations must appear on the list before they can be imported into the NDS database. The Workstation Registration program running on the user workstation is one of the following:

- **WSREG32.EXE**   This is for Windows 95 and NT workstations.
- **WSREG16.EXE**   This is for Windows 3.*x* and DOS workstations.
- **WSREG32.DLL**   This is for Windows workstations using Desktop Management.

You should configure a Workstation Import policy before importing the registered workstations into the NDS database. Perform the following steps:

1. Create a User Policy package for each workstation platform on your network.
2. Configure the User Policy package Import policy to create Workstation objects in the desired container and with the desired naming features.

After you have configured the policies, you must run the Workstation Agent on each workstation. You can configure the Workstation Registration to run automatically using one of the following:

- Novell Application Launcher
- Z.E.N.works Scheduler
- User login script

Registration Using the Novell Application Launcher

The Workstation Registration program can be launched upon login by defining it as an Application object and using the Novell Application Launcher to deliver it to the desktop. This allows the workstation to register its address with NDS. This is one of the ways in which the workstation can be registered with NDS if the Desktop Management component of Z.E.N.works is not installed on the client. The Novell Application Launcher is discussed later in this chapter.

Z.E.N.works Scheduler

The Z.E.N.works Scheduler runs on any Windows 95/98/NT workstation that has the Novell Client for Z.E.N.works installed. Workstation registration is performed automatically by a preconfigured scheduled action in the Scheduler. The Desktop Management component of Z.E.N.works must be installed for this to run properly. It runs the first time a user logs in to the network. The Z.E.N.works Scheduler is discussed later in this chapter.

User Login Script

The user login script can be used to register the workstation address with NDS if the Novell Application Launcher and Desktop Management components are not installed on the client. The following lines can be added to the login script of a User, Group, or container object:

```
IF "%PLATFORM" = "WIN" THEN BEGIN
WRITE "Registering Windows 3.x Workstation"
#WSREG16.EXE
END

IF "%PLATFORM" = "W95" THEN BEGIN
WRITE "Registering Windows 95 Workstation"
#WSREG32.EXE
END

IF "%PLATFORM" = "WNT" THEN BEGIN
WRITE "Registering Windows NT Workstation"
#WSREG32.EXE
END
```

Verifying Registration

A log file is created at the root of the workstation's hard drive that indicates the success or failure of the workstation's registration with NDS. The name of the file is dependent upon the platform the registration program is running on, as follows:

- **Windows 95/98/NT**   WSREG32.LOG
- **Windows 3.x**   WSREG16.LOG

You can also verify the workstation's registration using the NetWare Administrator (NWADMIN32) utility. Perform the following steps:

1. Start the NetWare Administrator utility (NWADMIN32).

2. Highlight the container in which you are registering the workstation.

3. Right-click the container object to bring up the details page.

4. Select the Workstation Registration property page as shown in Figure 28-13 and verify that the workstation has been registered with NDS.

Importing Workstations

A registered workstation does not become an object within the NDS tree until it is imported. No management tasks can be performed on the workstation until it is an NDS object. You should periodically re-import your workstations into NDS to keep the network addresses current. This can be done with the Scheduler utility discussed later in this chapter.

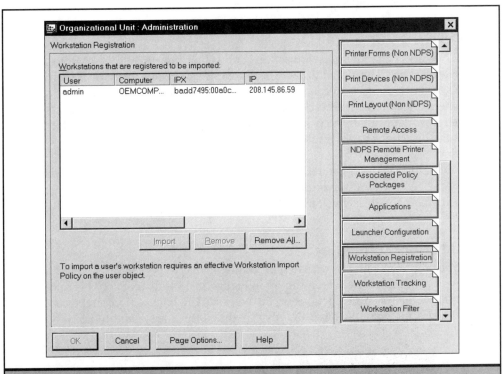

Figure 28-13. *The registered workstation appears in the Workstation Registration property page of the selected container*

Perform the following steps to manually import your workstations into the NDS tree:

1. Start the NetWare Administrator (NWADMIN32) utility.
2. Select the container that will hold the Workstation objects.
3. Create a User Policy package for the workstation platform being imported.
4. Enable and configure the Workstation Import policy with the location in the NDS tree where the object will be created, and the naming convention to be used for the import.
5. Associate the policy package with the container object.
6. Select Tools | Import Workstations from the NetWare Administrator main menu.
7. Enter the import location in the NDS tree in the Import Location field.
8. An information screen will be displayed indicating the number of workstations imported into the NDS tree and the number of new NDS objects created.
9. Collapse and expand the NDS container in which the objects were created to view the newly created Workstation objects.

Z.E.N.works Scheduler

The Z.E.N.works Scheduler lets you set up actions that can run on one or more workstations at predetermined times. These actions can be one or more .EXEs, .DLLs, ActiveXs, or JavaScripts. You can also specify the order in which these actions are to be run on the workstations. These scheduled actions will occur whether the user is logged in to the network or not. If the workstations are not powered on, the Scheduler will reschedule the actions based on the configuration of the startup block of time parameter.

The Scheduler features can be accessed from either a workstation-based Scheduler utility or the NetWare Administrator (NWADMIN32) utility. The interfaces of both utilities are basically the same, although each interface provides unique scheduling features.

Workstation Scheduler

The Workstation Scheduler is accessed by right-clicking the Calendar icon in the Windows system tray. The screen shown in Figure 28-14 is displayed. This folder contains all of the scheduled actions on the workstation. Each action can be configured to run at a specific time. We have already scheduled the virus scan program to run

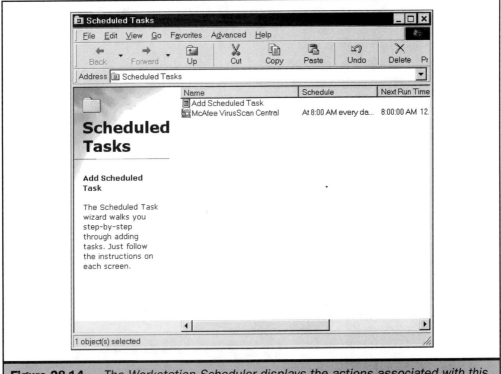

Figure 28-14.   *The Workstation Scheduler displays the actions associated with this workstation and allows you to schedule your own actions*

every day at 8:00 A.M. in this example. Only the Add Scheduled Task item will be displayed when you first start the Workstation Scheduler. Perform the following steps to schedule an action at the workstation:

1. Right-click the Calendar icon in the Windows system tray.

2. Double-click the Add Scheduled Task item in the Scheduled Task window. The Scheduled Task Wizard will start.

3. The screen shown next will be displayed, listing all of the programs known to the Windows operating system. Click the Browse button if you do not see the program you want to schedule.

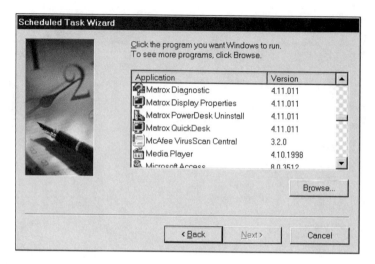

4. Enter the name for this action in the text box shown here and select when you want this action to run.

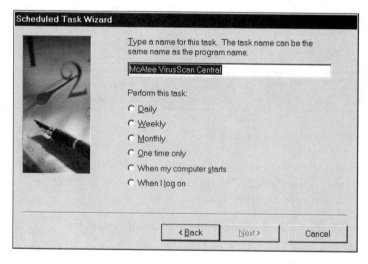

5. Enter the time and date when the action is to be run, as shown next.

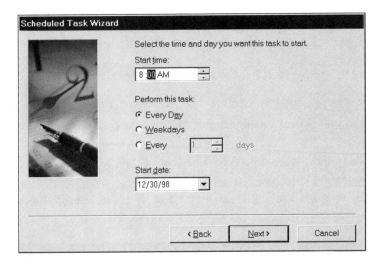

6. The screen shown here will be displayed, indicating that the action has been scheduled successfully:

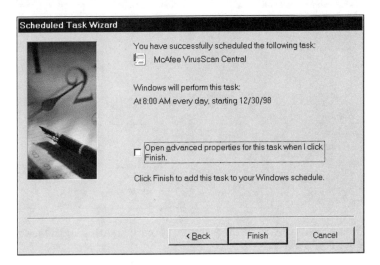

NetWare Administrator Scheduler

The NetWare Administrator (NWADMIN32) utility allows you to schedule an action through any Policy object created in the NDS tree. You can schedule actions to be run based on specific events or at specific times. These actions can apply to a single workstation policy or to all workstations in a container workstation policy.

Note   *You cannot use the NetWare Administrator Scheduler utility to view and edit the actions scheduled on the workstation with the Workstation Scheduler.*

Perform the following steps to schedule an action for a Policy object:

1. Start the NetWare Administrator (NWADMIN32) utility.

2. Select the Policy package object that contains the policy for which you want to schedule an action.

3. Select the policy you want add a scheduled action to.

4. Click the Toggle button to switch from the policy package's default schedule to the policy's default schedule as shown next. If it is not highlighted, click the Add Action button.

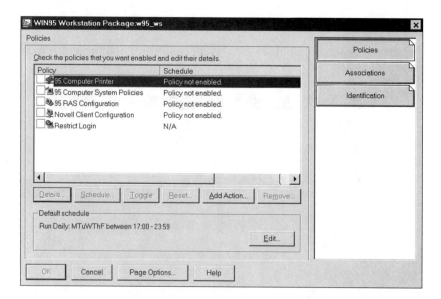

5. Enter the name of the scheduled action you are creating in the text box shown here:

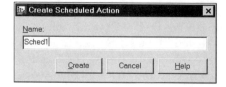

6. Click the Create button to add the action to the policy, as shown here:

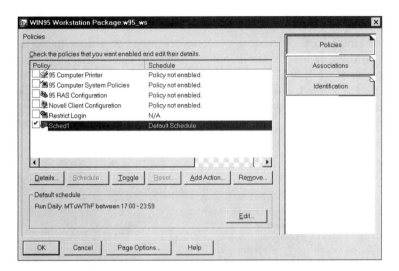

7. Click the Schedule button to display the screen shown next. The action item can assume the same priority as the object that contains it or you can override it by selecting Above Normal or Below Normal in the Priority box. The Impersonation box allows you to determine how the action is to run on the workstation.

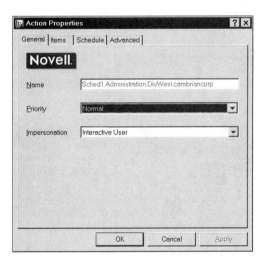

- The Interactive User option causes the action to run in the context of the user logged in on that workstation. The action is granted the same rights as the user.

■ The System option causes the action to run in the background as a local service on the workstation. The action is granted administrative rights to the workstation.

■ The Unsecure System option allows actions to run in the background on Windows NT workstations. This option allows address mappings between the user and system space on the Windows NT workstation. Use this option when protected areas of the registry and file system need modification and require a user interface to execute.

8. Select the Items tab, shown next, to define the action. Click the Add button to select the filename from either the workstation file system or the server file system.

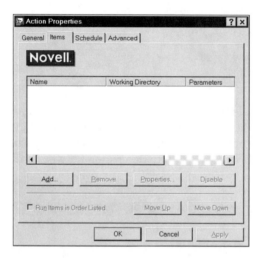

9. Select the Schedule tab, shown here, to configure when this action is to be performed:

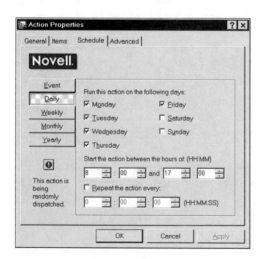

10. Select the Advanced tab, shown here, to define the actions to be taken when the action cannot be run on the workstation or what to do when the action completes:

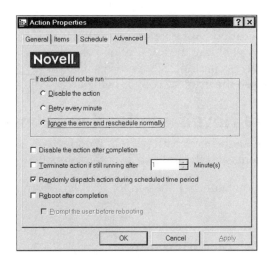

Novell Application Launcher

The Novell Application Launcher allows you to distribute and manage applications across the network. After you have defined the applications within NDS, you can install, launch, and even repair the applications using the Novell Application Launcher. Applications can be installed on each user's workstation or as shared applications on the network. You can manage each application by defining dates and times that the application will be available to network users. You can also use the power of NDS to limit access to each application. For example, users of the software development group can be defined as the only users who get access to the various compilers on the network. These applications can be delivered to users no matter where they log in to the network.

Each Application object defined in NDS represents a software application that can be delivered to a network user. You can configure each application's properties, such as

- Drive mapping or UNC path to the executable file
- Printer port captures necessary for the application
- Registry and INI entries required by the application
- Program files necessary to run the application
- Drive mappings and search drives necessary to run the application or access data

The Novell Application Launcher gives you centralized application maintenance and control by allowing you to control exactly what network users can see and do at their workstations. If a user accidentally deletes any program files associated with an application delivered to the workstation, they can simply right-click the application icon and select Verify to restore the deleted file and configuration settings.

You can enable application fault tolerance that allows users to access an application even if the primary server holding the application has gone down. You can also load-balance an application across multiple servers. This delivers an alternate copy of the application to a user when the primary copy is being accessed by other users.

Components of the Novell Application Launcher

The Novell Application Launcher consists of four components. There first two are administrative components and the last two are user components:

- Novell Application Launcher Snap-in for NetWare Administrator (NWADMIN32)
- snAppShot
- Novell Application Launcher Window
- Application Explorer

Novell Application Launcher Snap-in

The Novell Application Launcher Snap-in extends NDS with new Application objects. These extensions allow you to use the NetWare Administrator (NWADMIN32) utility to view Application objects, create and configure Application objects, distribute applications to users, and manage applications using NDS associations and rights. It also allows you to export Application objects, display all inherited applications, and migrate Application objects. This snap-in is automatically installed when you install the Z.E.N.works Starter Pack on the server.

snAppShot

The snAppShot utility is used to build the Application object that will be delivered to the user, and provides automatic correction/replacement capability for the associated application files if they become corrupted or are deleted. It works by leading you through a series of steps to create the object:

1. It takes a snapshot of the current configuration of the machine.

2. It prompts you to install the application you want to distribute.

3. It takes another snapshot of the machine to discover the changes made by the installation program.

4. It generates an Application Object Template (AOT) that contains the differences between the first snapshot and the last snapshot. All of the application dependencies, settings, and required files become part of the AOT.

Novell Application Launcher Window

The Novell Application Launcher Window displays the delivered applications in a window on the workstation. It can be used on Windows 3.x/95/98/NT workstations through the use of the NAL.EXE executable file. This file can be included in a login script to automatically launch the Novell Application Launcher Window when the user logs in to the network.

The NAL.EXE program works by determining the operating system on the client. It will launch the NALW31.EXE for Windows 3.x platforms or the NALWIN32.EXE for Windows 95/98/NT platforms. It updates the appropriate files on the workstation hard disk before activating the launcher. If it is being run from the local hard disk, it will update the files that belong in the WINDOWS\SYSTEM directory. It terminates itself when the proper executable is started on the workstation.

Application Explorer

The Application Explorer can only be run on Windows 95/98 or NT 4 workstations. It is an alternative to the Novell Application Launcher Window and can deliver applications to any of the following:

- Application Explorer Window
- Windows Explorer
- Start Menu
- System Tray
- Desktop

Application shortcuts delivered to the desktop will have a red arrow instead of the traditional black arrow. This helps the workstation user differentiate between network-delivered shortcuts and local shortcuts.

Using the Novell Application Launcher

You can distribute applications to network users after the Novell Application Launcher is installed. Once users have the proper file system rights to the application, distribution is accomplished by simply associating the application with other NDS objects such as users, groups, or containers. You follow a simple series of steps:

1. Create the Application object.
2. Associate the Application object with User, Group, or container objects.
3. Enable the Novell Application Launcher on the client by placing the NAL.EXE or NALWIN32.EXE file in the Startup folder on the client workstation or in a login script.

Creating Simple Application Objects

You create a simple Application object using the NetWare Administrator utility (NWADMIN32). Each Application object has multiple property pages associated with it. But the only information necessary to provide access to the simple Application object is the path to the application and a list of User objects allowed to access the application. The screen shown in Figure 28-15 displays the Simple Application objects that are created when you install the Z.E.N.works Starter Pack.

The following example creates an Application object for the NDS Manager (NDSMGR32) utility located in the SYS:PUBLIC\WIN32 directory. Perform the following steps:

1. Start the NetWare Administrator (NWADMIN32) utility.

2. Select the container in which the simple Application object will be created.

3. Right-click the container to display the Create menu.

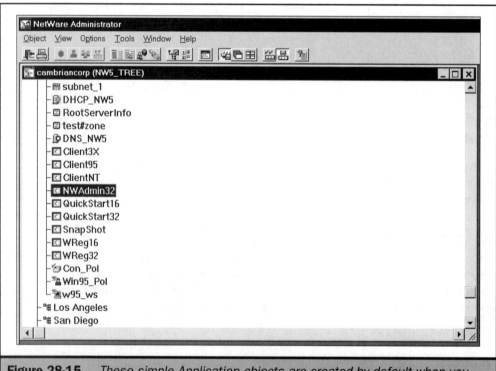

Figure 28-15. *These simple Application objects are created by default when you install the Z.E.N.works Starter Pack*

4. Select the Application object to display the screen shown here, and select the simple Application object option:

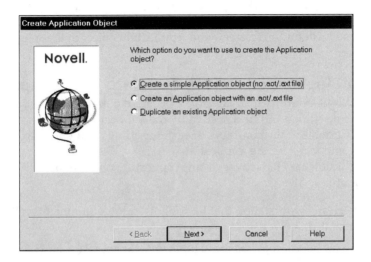

5. The screen shown next will be displayed, asking you to define the object name and the location of the executable file. Click the Browse button to graphically select the path to the application executable.

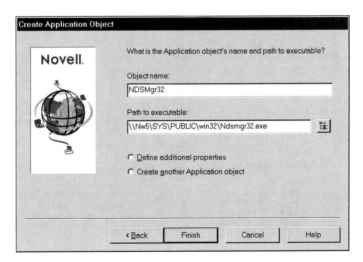

Tip	*Some applications may request a drive letter type path; others may want a UNC path; and some will work with either. This occurs here and also when building the path for mappings using the Drive/Ports property page.*

6. Click the Finish button to create the Application object in the selected NDS container.

Creating an Application Object Template with snAppShot

You use the snAppShot utility to create an Application object template that contains information about settings and files needed by the application. The distributed application will automatically configure or restore settings to the registry, INI files, drive mapping, and icons for the application.

Perform the following steps to create an Application object template (AOT) using the snAppShot utility:

1. Build a "clean" workstation that has only Windows and the Novell Client installed.

2. Log in to the server that has the Z.E.N.works Starter Pack NDS extensions installed.

3. Navigate to the SYS:PUBLIC\SNAPSHOT directory.

4. Run the SNAPSHOT.EXE program. The screen shown here will be displayed:

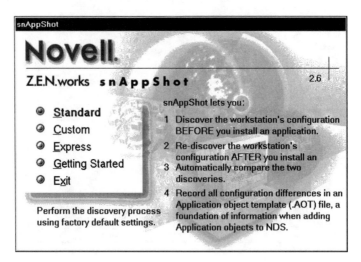

5. Select the discovery mode from the following:

- **Standard** Discovers the application installation changes using default settings.

■ **Custom** Allows you to specify the drives, files, folders, registry hives, and shortcuts that you want to include or exclude from the discovery process.

■ **Express** Allows you to use a preference file that you created in an earlier creation process.

6. Specify the name for the NDS Application object and the name for the icon that will appear on the user's desktop, as shown here:

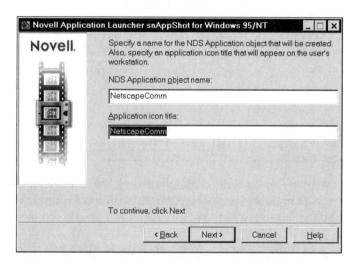

7. Enter the location where the AOT file will be saved, as shown next. This should be a drive on the server. You should also use UNC naming when defining the path.

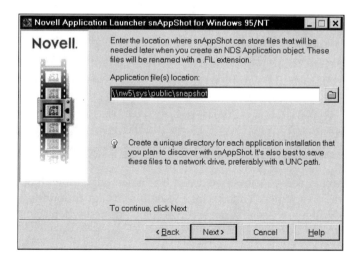

8. Enter the name of the AOT file and its location on the server, as shown here:

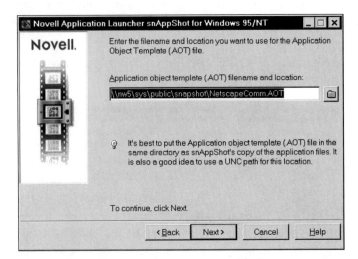

9. Specify the drives on the workstation that are to be scanned by the discovery process, as shown next. Simply click the Add button to add a drive to be scanned by the discovery process.

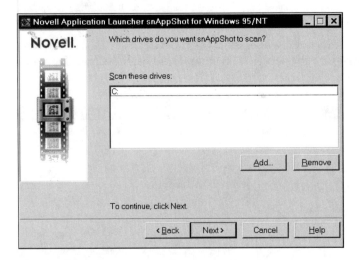

10. The summary screen shown next will be displayed, listing all of your configuration settings. You can also save this configuration file as a preference file. This will allow these same settings to be applied when selecting the Express mode from the startup window.

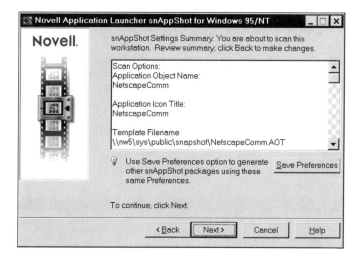

11. After you accept the configuration, the discovery process will begin, as shown next. This is the process that builds the first snapshot of the system before you install the application.

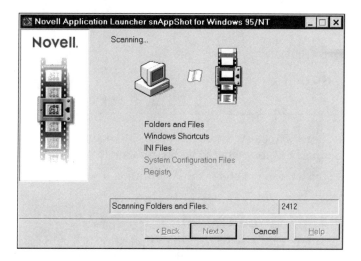

12. A Run Setup Program dialog box will be displayed after the discovery process completes.

13. Run the setup file for the application. If reboot is part of the installation process, snAppShot will pick up where it left off after the restart of the workstation.

Creating an Application Object from an AOT

You must create an Application object using the Application object template before it can be delivered to a user's workstation. Perform the following steps:

1. Start the NetWare Administrator (NWADMIN32) utility.

2. Select the container in which the simple Application object will be created.

3. Right-click the container to display the Create menu.

4. Select the Application object to display the screen shown here, and select the Create a simple Application Object (No .aot/.axt File) option:

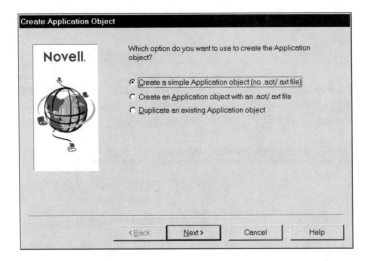

5. Enter the Target Directory where the workstation application will be installed and the Source Directory where the .FIL files are located.

6. Click the Finish button to create the Application object in the selected NDS container.

Associating Application Objects

You use the Associations property page of the Application object to associate other NDS objects with the Application object. If the Application object is associated with a container, all users created below the container will automatically receive the application.

Enabling Novell Application Launcher on the Workstation

You must add either the Novell Application Launcher Window or the Application Explorer command to the login script or the Startup folder to deliver the applications to the user's workstation. If you modify the login script, the Novell Application

Launcher will be started automatically when the user logs in to the network. Perform the following steps to modify the login script:

1. Start the NetWare Administrator (NWADMIN32) utility.

2. Access the details property page of a User, Group, Organization, or Organizational Unit object.

3. Add one of the following commands:

   @\\servername\SYS\PUBLIC\NAL.EXE
   @\\servername\SYS\PUBLIC\NALEXPLD.EXE

Managing the Application with the Novell Application Launcher

The Novell Application Launcher does not use separate icons to designate the platform on which the application is to be run. It uses various property pages associated with the Application object to manage the application. You can configure the following list of property pages to customize the application. Click the Help button to access additional information on each of the fields on the following property pages:

Identification
System Requirements
Environment
Distribution
Folders
Description
Drives/Ports
Scripts
Fault Tolerance
Contacts
Associations
Administrator Notes
Macros
Registry Settings
INI Settings
Application Files
Text Files
Schedule
Icons/Shortcuts
File Rights
Termination
Application Site List

Customizing the Desktop

A User System policy and a Computer System policy can be used to control the configuration of the desktop. The User System policy can be used to hide and control most of the options that can be configured using the Control Panel. This includes wallpaper, colors, company logo, sounds, and other restrictions. For example, a restriction could be applied to remove the Find command from the Start menu, or hide Network Neighborhood from the desktop. This policy would then apply to the associated users no matter what machine is being used to log in to the network.

The Computer System policy can be used in a similar manner to automatically launch various applications at each login or only once. It could be used to launch a utility that may be special to specific machines. For example, the Novell Application Launcher (NAL) NAL.EXE file could be added as a run option. Then, on the associated machines, no matter who the user is, the NAL window would be opened, displaying the icons that have been associated with a given container, group, or user.

If both the User System policy and Computer System policy are used, they will combine to create the desktop the user will see at login. As with all policies, you will need to create one for each platform you want to control. The restrictions and limitations of the combined policies can enable, disable, or change nothing on the user workstation. This corresponds to a marked box, a white box, or a gray box next to each item, respectively. Each item can be set independently. For example, a marked box next to Remove the Find Command from the Start Menu will remove the command at the next login. A white box will indicate not to remove the command, and a gray box implies that the command is to remain as it is.

Tip

It is a good practice to create policies for users and then create a policy for the administrator that neutralizes the effect of the user policy limitations when the administrator logs in using the same machine. For example, if the user policy removed the Find command, the administrator policy should have a white box so the Find command will never be removed. Otherwise, if the administrator policy left the box gray, then the Find command would be removed if the administrator logged in on a machine following the login of a regular user. By making the box white, it would not be removed from the administrator, no matter what the previous state of the machine was.

Chapter 29

Oracle8

NetWare 5 ships with a five-user version of Oracle8, a powerful application platform for developing and deploying network computing solutions. Oracle8 is a database system that can manage very large databases (VLDBs) containing hundreds of gigabytes or even terabytes of information. It can provide concurrent access to thousands of users and guarantee constant availability to mission-critical applications. Oracle8 is based on an open, standards-based computing model referred to as the Network Computing Architecture (NCA). The NCA model meets the needs of both network-centric computing and object-oriented development models. It is a true object-relational database management system (ORDBMS). Oracle8 is tightly integrated with Novell's NDS and provides single sign-on capabilities for database users. It provides support for symmetrical multiprocessing (SMP) and dynamic load balancing. It also supports the Net8, TCP/IP, and IPX/SPX communication protocols.

Oracle8 provides several management utilities to help you administer your databases:

- Oracle Database Assistant
- Oracle Web Publishing Assistant
- Oracle INTYPE File Assistant
- Oracle Net Assistant
- Database Backup/Recovery Manager

Oracle8 for NetWare ships with the following documentation on the CD-ROM:

- **Oracle8 Release Notes for NetWare**   This document contains last-minute installation and configuration information that was not included in the documentation on the CD-ROM.

- **Oracle User's Guide for NetWare**   This document contains post-installation, migration, and configuration information for the Oracle8 product.

- **Oracle Networking Products Getting Started for NetWare**   This document describes and defines the Oracle8 client-server networking environment, database networking concepts, network protocols, and the Oracle Protocol Adapters.

- **Oracle8 Server Concepts**   This document presents basic database concepts to the new user.

- **Oracle8 Server Administrator's Guide**   This document presents basic information needed to administer an Oracle8 database.

- **Oracle Enterprise Manager Concepts Guide**   This document presents basic information needed to use the Oracle Enterprise Manager utility.

Installing Oracle8

This section details the installation procedure to follow to install the Oracle8 product on a NetWare 5 server. Two requirements must be met prior to starting the Oracle8 installation. The first requirement deals with the file system type that Oracle8 is being installed on. The Starter Database installs with the NW_FSTYPE parameter set to CLIB. This allows the database to reside on a NetWare volume that has block suballocation turned on. This parameter can be found in the \NLM\CONFIG.ORA file in the directory where Oracle8 was installed. The second requirement is that file compression is to be turned off on the volume when the Oracle8 database is installed. Oracle8 uses its own compression and suballocation routines. To verify that the preceding two requirements have been met, type **VOLUMES** at the file server console. This command will display the mounted volumes on the NetWare 5 server and their settings.

You must install the Oracle8 product on a volume that does not have the Cp and Sa flags turned on. If the intended volume already has these settings, you must delete that volume and re-create it using the NWCONFIG utility.

> **Note**   *If you have problems with your CD-ROM drive, you probably need to update your drivers to ones that meet the Joilet specifications or you can copy the CD-ROM to a directory on the NetWare 5 server. If you have problems with your server not recognizing memory above 64MB, remove the HIMEM.SYS line from your CONFIG.SYS file. You may also need to upgrade the BIOS in the server.*

Perform the following steps to install the Oracle8 product on the server:

1. Insert the Oracle8 CD into the CD-ROM drive on the server.
2. Type **[LOAD] CDROM** at the server console prompt. This will automatically mount the CD-ROM as an NSS volume.
3. Start the installation utility by entering **[LOAD] NWCONFIG** at the server console.
4. Select Product Options, as shown here:

```
                    Configuration Options
 ┌──────────────────────────────────────────────────────────────┐
 │Driver Options            (load/unload disk and network drivers)│
 │Standard Disk Options     (configure NetWare partitions/volumes)│
 │NSS Disk Options          (configure NSS storage and volumes)   │
 │License Options           (install or remove licenses)          │
 │Copy Files Options        (install NetWare system files)        │
 │Directory Options         (install NDS)                         │
 │NCF files Options         (create/edit server startup files)    │
 │Multi CPU Options         (install/uninstall SMP)               │
 │Product Options           (other optional installation items)   │
 │Exit                                                            │
 └──────────────────────────────────────────────────────────────┘
```

5. Select Install a Product Not Listed, as shown here:

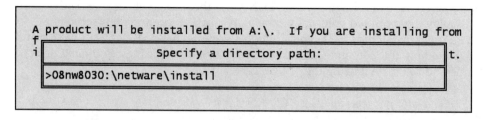

```
                Other Installation Actions
       Choose an item or product listed above
       Install a product not listed
       View/Configure/Remove installed products
       Return to the previous menu
```

6. Press F3 to specify the path to the installation executable, as shown in here:

```
A product will be installed from A:\.  If you are installing from
f
i              Specify a directory path:                    t.
   >08nw8030:\netware\install
```

7. The Oracle8 Installer will start.

8. Read through the export agreement and press ENTER while OK is highlighted to accept the terms.

9. Read through the license agreement and press ENTER while OK is highlighted to accept the terms.

10. Enter the name of the company to which this product has been licensed, as shown here:

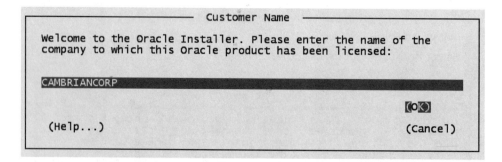

```
───────────────── Customer Name ─────────────────
Welcome to the Oracle Installer. Please enter the name of the
company to which this Oracle product has been licensed:

CAMBRIANCORP

                                                      [OK]
 (Help...)                                          (Cancel)
```

11. Select the language in which you would like to install the Oracle8 products, as shown in Figure 29-1.

12. Select the volume on which to install the Oracle8 products, as shown in Figure 29-2. If you select a volume that has file compression enabled, you will receive a warning screen.

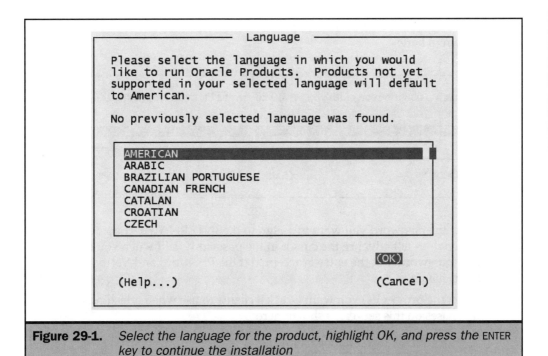

Figure 29-1.   Select the language for the product, highlight OK, and press the ENTER key to continue the installation

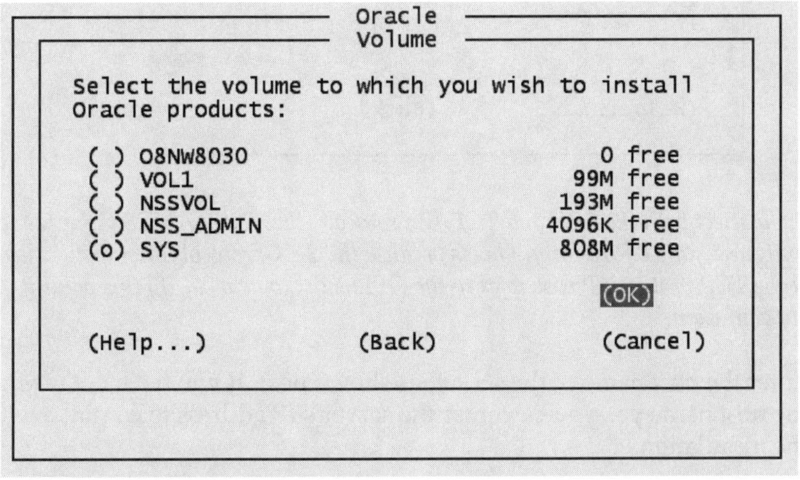

Figure 29-2.   All of the volumes known to the server are displayed in this screen. Select the desired location for the Oracle8 products and press ENTER

13. Specify the directory in which you want to install the Oracle8 products, as shown in here:

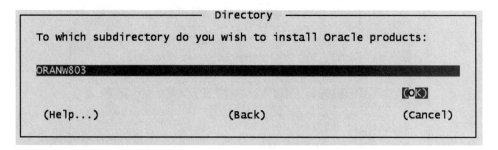

14. Enter the password you want to assign to the INTERNAL user account. This screen does not advance the cursor in the password field when you enter the new password, but the entry is accepted if the Password and Verify Password fields match.

15. Select the protocol(s) you want Oracle8 clients to use when attaching to the databases on this server, as shown here:

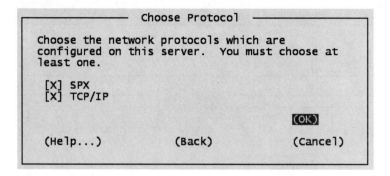

Note   *If you select both the SPX and TCP/IP protocols, the TNSNAMES.ORA file will be configured for TCP/IP only. This is because the SPX protocol functionality is replaced by the TCP protocol. Please refer to the OSI model to help clarify this point if you have any confusion.*

16. Enter the host name of the server, as shown next. If you have not configured the host name yet, you can enter the server's IP address to continue with the installation.

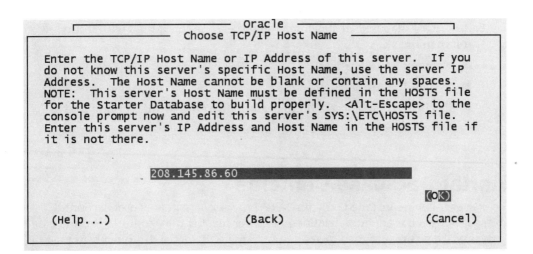

┌──────────────────── Oracle ────────────────────┐
│ ──────────── Choose TCP/IP Host Name ────────── │
│   │
│ Enter the TCP/IP Host Name or IP Address of this server. If you │
│ do not know this server's specific Host Name, use the server IP │
│ Address. The Host Name cannot be blank or contain any spaces. │
│ NOTE: This server's Host Name must be defined in the HOSTS file │
│ for the Starter Database to build properly. <Alt-Escape> to the │
│ console prompt now and edit this server's SYS:\ETC\HOSTS file. │
│ Enter this server's IP Address and Host Name in the HOSTS file if │
│ it is not there. │
│   │
│   208.145.86.60   │
│   [(OK)] │
│ (Help...)   (Back)   (Cancel) │
└───┘

Note   *You must enter the server name and IP address in the SYS:\ETC\HOSTS file in order for the database to operate. If not, the TNS listener will fail to load and you will not be able to access your database.*

17. Select the Java Database Connectivity (JDBC) drivers that you want to install on the server, as shown in Figure 29-3.

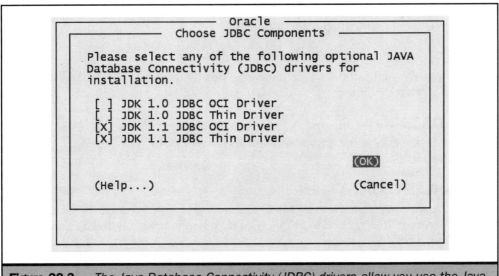

┌──────────────────── Oracle ────────────────────┐
│ ──────────── Choose JDBC Components ─────────── │
│   │
│ Please select any of the following optional JAVA │
│ Database Connectivity (JDBC) drivers for │
│ installation. │
│   │
│ [ ] JDK 1.0 JDBC OCI Driver │
│ [ ] JDK 1.0 JDBC Thin Driver │
│ [X] JDK 1.1 JDBC OCI Driver │
│ [X] JDK 1.1 JDBC Thin Driver │
│   [OK] │
│ (Help...)   (Cancel) │
└───┘

Figure 29-3.   *The Java Database Connectivity (JDBC) drivers allow you use the Java Software Developer's Kit (SDK) for client access*

18. A Starter Database is installed on the server. It is configured with the following information:

- **Name** Oracle
- **System Identifier (SID)** ORCL
- **INTERNAL database administrator (DBA) password** Configured as indicated above

Starter Database Contents

The Starter Database installed on your NetWare 5 server contains user accounts, tablespaces, data files, an initialization parameter file, log files, control files, and a data dictionary. These are designed to get you working with Oracle8 as quickly as possible.

User Accounts

The user accounts and passwords listed in Table 29-1 are created by default during the installation.

Tablespaces

An Oracle8 database is subdivided into smaller logical areas known as *tablespaces*. This is Oracle's method of implementing block suballocation and the reason why Novell's block suballocation must be disabled on the database volume. Each of these tablespaces corresponds to one or more physical files on the volume. Each tablespace contains a specific type of data, described in the following sections.

SYSTEM

This tablespace contains the data dictionary needed by the Oracle8 database. It is present in all Oracle8 databases.

USER_DATA

This tablespace contains the data you create and enter into tables from your database applications.

TEMPORARY_DATA

This tablespace contains temporary tables and indexes created during the processing of your SQL request. It may need to be enlarged if you are working with large databases and using sort-based functions.

ROLLBACK_DATA

This tablespace contains segments used for rolling back a group of transactions. It may be needed if you lose your communications link in the middle of a database update. The database can be rolled back to the start of the transaction without corrupting the data.

User	Password	Description
INTERNAL	Provided during the installation	This is an alias for the SYS user account and provides SYSDBA privileges such as starting and stopping the databases.
SYS	CHANGE_ON_INSTALL	This user account has access to everything. Be sure to change the password before using the product.
SYSTEM	MANAGER	This user is the Database Administrator (DBA) for the database. Change this password as soon as possible after the install.
SCOTT	TIGER	This is a user account with CONNECT and RESOURCE database access roles.
DEMO	DEMO	This user has the same access definitions as the SCOTT user. Delete this account as soon as possible.
DBSNMP	DBSNMP	This user is a DBA with SNMP access controls. If you are not using SNMP to manage your network, you can delete this user by running the program CATNSNMP.SQL.
CTXSYS	CTXSYS	This user is the ConText Administrator for the database and has the same access rights as the DEMO users, including the DBA role.

Table 29-1.   *Default Users Accounts Created When You Install the Oracle8 Product*

Data Files

Data files contain the contents of database structures, such as tables and indexes. A tablespace is created by forming a logical unit of storage from multiple data files. Each data file can only be associated with one tablespace. The Starter Database creates the following files in each tablespace:

- **SYSTEM** SYS1ORCL.ORA
- **USER_DATA** USR1ORCL.ORA
- **ROLLBACK_DATA** RBS1ORCL.ORA
- **TEMPORARY_DATA** TMP1ORCL.ORA

Initialization Parameter File

The INITORCL.ODA parameter file must exist in the DATABASE subdirectory under the installation directory. It is a text file that contains a list of instance configuration parameters for each database that you intend to start.

Redo Log Files

The DATABASE subdirectory contains the following two log files: LOG1ORCL.ORA and LOG2ORCL.ORA. These files record all of the changes made to data in a database buffer cache. This information can be used to back out of a series of transactions if an error occurs between the client application and the database.

Control File

A control file records the physical structure of the database on the server. It is required to start a database. It contains the database name and the locations and names of the database's files.

Data Dictionary

The data dictionary is a protected collection of tables and views that reference information contained within the database. All users and their associated privileges are also stored in the data dictionary.

Further Reading

Please refer to the online documentation provided on the Oracle8 CD for more specific information. The client setup information is included on this CD also. For additional information about Oracle8, please see the publications from Oracle Press at www.osborne.com.

The Complete Reference

NetWare 5

Appendix A

Upgrading to NetWare 5

N etWare 5 includes an upgrade option that is built in to the installation program for NetWare 3.1x and 4.1x servers. There are two methods associated with upgrading your Novell server to NetWare 5. You can upgrade an existing server, or you can migrate a server to NetWare 5. There are specific system and software requirements, as follows:

- Pentium or higher processor
- VGA or higher resolution display adapter (SVGA recommended)
- 64MB of system RAM (128MB to run Java applets on the server)
- 50MB of disk space on the DOS boot partition
- 550MB of disk space on the SYS volume
- ISO 9660–formated CD-ROM drive
- One or more network boards
- A PS/2 or serial mouse (recommended, but not required)
- An IP address if the server is attached to the Internet
- All NetWare 4.11 servers updated to NDS version 6 or later (If you have any NetWare 4.10 servers, they should be upgraded to NetWare 4.11. See the Novell site at www.novell.com for more current information.)
- All servers running Novell Licensing Services (NLS)

Same-Server Migration

The NetWare 5 installation program allows you to easily upgrade an existing Novell 3.1x or 4.1x server. All NetWare 3.1x bindery objects and the file system are upgraded automatically. Perform the following steps to upgrade an existing Novell 3.1x or 4.1x server:

1. Back up any mission-critical data to a storage device.
2. Boot the server with DOS 3.3 or higher.
3. Install the CD-ROM drivers on the DOS machine.
4. Install the Novell Client for DOS/Windows 3.1x if you are mapping to a drive on another server.
5. Check that CONFIG.SYS file settings are as follows:

   ```
   FILES=40 BUFFERS=30.
   ```

6. Insert the NetWare 5 Operating System CD into the CD-ROM drive.
7. Switch to the CD and type **INSTALL**.

8. Select Upgrade from a 3.1*x* or 4.1*x* Server on the Welcome screen.

9. Configure the platform support modules if applicable.

10. Configure the PCI Hot Plug module if applicable.

11. Configure the properties for the server disk drives.

12. Create additional volumes if desired.

13. Configure the properties for the network board.

14. Configure additional protocols if desired.

15. Set the server time zone parameters.

16. Configure NDS on the server if required.

17. Install the NetWare 5 server license.

18. Install any other networking products required on the server.

19. Customize the installation by selecting Customize on the Product Summary Screen.

20. Click Finish to reboot the server.

Across-the-Wire Migration

An across-the-wire migration involves copying and upgrading a NetWare 3.1*x* server's bindery and file system to an existing NDS tree via the network. The following prerequisites must be met before starting the migration:

- NetWare 5 must be installed on the destination server.

- The Novell Upgrade Wizard must be installed on a workstation. This self-extracting file is located on the NetWare 5 Operating System CD.

- Make sure you are using the latest version of the Novell Client software on the workstation.

- You should back up NDS and the NetWare 5 server volumes to which you are migrating the Novell 3.1*x* server.

- Verify that you have Supervisor rights to the source server and destination NDS tree.

- Ensure that SAP filtering is disabled on the destination server.

- Ensure that all NLMs on the NetWare 3.1*x* server are updated.

- Load TSA311.NLM or TSA312.NLM on the source NetWare 3.1*x* server.

- Load and add any necessary name spaces to the destination server volumes.

Once all of these prerequisites are met, proceed with the migration as follows:

1. Launch the Novell Upgrade Wizard on the client workstation.

2. Follow the instructions on each page in the Wizard until the Project Window is displayed.

3. Click and drag the NetWare 3.1x source server bindery and volume contents to the desired location in the NDS tree.

4. Click the Verify button to ensure that the bindery and file system of the source server can be migrated as specified.

5. Correct all errors that will impede the migration.

6. Click the Proceed button to migrate the bindery and file system to NDS.

7. Review the error and success log files.

8. Check the Novell Upgrade Wizard help system for any post-migration procedures that may need to be performed.

Index

Note: Page numbers in *italics* refer to illustrations or charts.

J

K

L

N